HERNDON'S LINCOLN

And now God bless you; and
all good union men.
Yours as ever
A. Lincoln

HERNDON'S LINCOLN

William H. Herndon
and Jesse W. Weik

Edited by
Douglas L. Wilson
and Rodney O. Davis

Published by the Knox College Lincoln Studies Center
and the University of Illinois Press Urbana and Chicago

Published in association with the
Abraham Lincoln Bicentennial Commission

The editors and publishers gratefully acknowledge that publication of this volume
has been assisted by a grant from the Abraham Lincoln Bicentennial Commission.

Portrait of Abraham Lincoln on p. iv from the photograph by Hesler, Chicago,
1860. Originally published as the frontispiece to the 1889 edition of *Herndon's Lincoln.*

♾ This book is printed on acid-free paper.

Library of Congress Cataloging-in-Publication Data
Herndon, William Henry, 1818–1891.
[Lincoln]
Herndon's Lincoln / William H. Herndon and Jesse W. Weik;
edited by Douglas L. Wilson and Rodney O. Davis.
p.   cm. — (The Knox College Lincoln Studies Center series)
"Published in association with the Abraham Lincoln Bicentennial
Commission."
Includes bibliographical references and index.
ISBN-13: 978-0-252-03072-7 (cloth : alk. paper)
ISBN-10: 0-252-03072-9 (cloth : alk. paper)
1. Lincoln, Abraham, 1809–1865. 2. Presidents—United States—Biography.
I. Weik, Jesse William, 1857–1930. II. Wilson, Douglas L. III. Davis,
Rodney O. IV. Knox College (Galesburg, Ill.). Lincoln Studies Center.
V. Abraham Lincoln Bicentennial Commission. VI. Title. VII. Series.
E457.H57   2006
973.7092—dc22   2006006964

The Abraham Lincoln Bicentennial Commission was established by Congress to plan the national celebration of the 200th anniversary of Lincoln's birth.

Supporting Lincoln scholarship through publications, documentaries, and exhibitions is central to our mission to share Lincoln's legacy with the world.

By celebrating Lincoln's bicentennial, we remind ourselves of Lincoln's historic contributions to freedom, democracy, and equal opportunity, and rededicate ourselves to the "unfinished work" that he called upon us all to advance.

The Abraham Lincoln Bicentennial Commission is grateful to the Union Station Foundation of Springfield, Illinois, and its directors, Michael J. Scully, Earl W. Henderson Jr., and John G. Hayes, for their support of this project.

Contents

Selected Original Illustrations

Editors' Preface

This volume is the first to appear in the Lincoln Studies Center Publication Series, which is aimed at making available, in a scholarly format, important sources for the study of Abraham Lincoln. In spite of the prevailing impression that Lincoln research has been well nigh exhausted, scholars working in the field are aware that there is much that needs to be done. Only very recently, for example, have the materials been assembled for the systematic study of Lincoln's law career, thanks to the completion of a comprehensive database by the Lincoln Legal Papers project. The forerunner of the present volume, *Herndon's Informants: Letters, Interviews, and Statements about Abraham Lincoln* (1998), made available for the first time in its entirety the voluminous archive compiled by Lincoln's law partner, William H. Herndon, the richest source of information about Lincoln's pre-presidential years. The same editors are preparing for publication in this series the first scholarly edition of Herndon's own letters, lectures, and interviews about Lincoln, many of which have never been published. This volume will, however, be preceded in the series by the first critical and fully annotated edition of the Lincoln-Douglas debates, which will be published in time for the observance of the 150th anniversary of the debates in 2008. Other titles that promise to shed new light on Lincoln are in the offing.

When the Lincoln Studies Center was established at Knox College, a board of advisors was created to counsel the co-directors. Recruited from the ranks of the leading scholars in Lincoln studies, the board has played an important role in evaluating the center's proposed activities and helping to establish priorities. One of the original board members, the late Prof. William E. Gienapp of Harvard University, first proposed the creation of a publication series in 2000. Observing that the major projects the center had under contemplation involved significant primary source material, he urged that these and comparable materials be published in a scholarly series under the sponsorship of the Lincoln Studies Center. He underlined his belief in the value of such a series by offering to contribute his own current project, a new edition of the diary of Lincoln's secretary of the Navy, Gideon Welles, one of the most notable sources for the study of Lincoln's presidency. His colleagues on the board and the co-directors of the center were all persuaded, and after considering several possible venues, a contractual agreement was reached with of the University of Illinois Press, and this series was born.

Professor Gienapp's untimely death in 2003 prevented him from seeing his proposal come to fruition, but in gratitude for his many contributions to the Lincoln Studies Center, and in recognition of his role in its creation, the co-directors and members of the board of advisors are pleased to dedicate this series to him.

Editors' Introduction

Herndon's Lincoln: The True Story of a Great Life is widely acknowledged to be the most important and, at the same time, most controversial book ever written about Abraham Lincoln. The result of a collaboration between William H. Herndon and Jesse W. Weik, *Herndon's Lincoln* created a stir from the moment of its first appearance in 1889. It was highly praised for its detailed and authoritative depiction of Lincoln's pre-presidential life, and it was roundly condemned for its indiscretions and lapses in taste. An attempt to balance these two perspectives is reflected in the verdict of the *Atlantic Monthly,* whose reviewer declared: "To any reader who wishes to know the truth about Lincoln, at whatever costs to illusions, this book is invaluable and suggestive."[1] To tell the truth about Lincoln was undoubtedly the biography's aim, but whether such a thing should even have been attempted was sharply debated by the first generation of readers, and whether, and to what extent, it succeeded has been at issue ever since. "Criticism of the work has often been severe," wrote distinguished Lincoln scholar Don E. Fehrenbacher in 1996, "but after more than a century it remains the most influential biography of Lincoln ever published."[2]

The book's second subtitle spelled out its special claim to attention and its point of view: *The History and Personal Recollections of Abraham Lincoln by William H. Herndon For Twenty Years his Friend and Law Partner.* In addition to his close personal association with his subject, Herndon had other advantages as a biographer. Soon after Lincoln's death, he launched an energetic campaign to collect information on his partner's early life. He corresponded with people who had known Lincoln at various stages of his life; he traveled extensively to interview, and sometimes to cross-examine, his informants; and he combed early newspapers for speeches and accounts of events involving the young Lincoln. But prompt as Herndon was to gather information and anecdotes about Lincoln, he was unable to get his biography written, so that by the time it was finally completed, it was the last, rather than the first, of the major nineteenth-century biographies of Lincoln to appear. The others—those by Josiah G. Holland (1866), Ward Hill Lamon (1872), Isaac N. Arnold (1885), and John G. Nicolay and John Hay (1886–90)[3]—all benefited to a considerable extent from Herndon's researches and his remarkably open-handed cooperation. Most of Lamon's information, in fact, was drawn from Herndon's archive of biographical materials. All of these authors except Holland had enjoyed some association with Lincoln; the others were personally familiar with certain aspects of his career, but only Herndon had the benefit of a long and close personal association with his subject. Nicolay and Hay, as Lincoln's secretaries, had a much better view of Lincoln as president than did other biographers of the time, including Herndon, but like Arnold, they largely avoided treatment of Lincoln's private life. For its colorful and detailed depiction of the private and personal Lincoln before he became president, *Herndon's Lincoln* was, and remains, unrivaled. "There can be little question," Paul M. Angle has written, "but that William H. Herndon contributed more than any other individual to our knowledge of Lincoln's life and character."[4]

But for all his contributions, Herndon and his book have continued to be the subject of controversy. From the beginning, Herndon held unorthodox views on what was appropriate for the biographies of great men. He began with the idea that Lincoln's life should be told in full, that the truth, whatever it might turn out to be, could do nothing to diminish Lincoln's stature or achievements. He believed that there were "necessary truths" that must be confronted, even if they touched on private matters that biographers would not ordinarily disclose.[5] But such a "warts-and-all" view was sharply contrary to the prevailing conventions of Victorian biography and to the elevated expectations of a worshipful American public. Herndon's insistence on presenting a realistic portrait of Lincoln as he appeared to those who knew him seems straightforward enough to modern readers, but it struck a great many observers at the time as irreverent and disrespectful. Nor could they be reconciled to the frank treatment of such unseemly subjects as the illegitimacy of Lincoln's mother or the difficulties of his home life.

While these objections have faded with the passage of time, others have emerged. In the twentieth century, scholars began to find fault with Herndon's informants and their testimony, which in almost every case was based on memories of what had happened years earlier. As the standards in the Lincoln field came to be set by professionally trained historians, the scarcity of strictly contemporary and documentary evidence in Lincoln's pre-presidential life became more apparent, and more of an issue. So did the standing and motives of Herndon's informants, whose stories and credibility came under sharper scrutiny. Some scholars were also troubled by Herndon's research methods. His selection and questioning of witnesses were seen as compromised by his own predispositions while at the same time lacking in objective safeguards against gullibility and fraud.[6] The doubts about Herndon and his evidence were sharply amplified by the major study published in 1948 by David Herbert Donald, for its well-researched findings and detailed analysis drew attention to Herndon's foibles and shortcomings and called into question the reliability of his informants and his own judgments.[7]

As a result of these developments, both Herndon and the testimony of his informants came to be regarded with greater and greater suspicion. This trend coincided with a growing disposition on the part of professional historians to regard the presidency as the principal focus of Lincoln studies, a development that further marginalized Herndon, who had little firsthand knowledge of Lincoln in Washington. Herndon himself became the object of considerable hostility with certain writers who viewed his reporting on Mary Todd Lincoln, and on some aspects of Lincoln himself, as malicious.[8] At the same time, Herndon's basic truthfulness was widely acknowledged, and his opinions and extensive compilations of evidence about the pre- presidential Lincoln could hardly be ignored. The resulting situation during the second half of the twentieth century was well characterized by Mary Todd Lincoln's biographer, Jean H. Baker, who remarked in 1983 that Herndon had become "every Lincoln scholar's reserve army—available to make a point when he agrees with whatever conclusion we wish to establish, but having been so often discredited, easily dismissed when we disagree."[9]

In the last decade of the twentieth century, the evidence about Lincoln supplied by Herndon and his informants began to be reevaluated. In a landmark reconsideration of Lincoln's love affair with Ann Rutledge, for example, a leading Civil War scholar, John Y. Simon, argued in 1990 that the critique of Herndon initiated by historians earlier in the century, while it had been a "commendable correction of the historical record," had been carried too far.[10] Other reconsiderations followed, and by the beginning of the twentieth-first century, it seems fair to say that many of the doubts and misgivings about the testimony of Herndon's informants have either been successfully addressed or put into better perspective. Especially in light of the importance that has come to be placed on oral history, it is generally conceded that whatever the perils and pitfalls of reminiscent evidence, the circumstances of Lincoln's early life were such that, where personal information is concerned, there is very little else for historians and biographers to work with.[11] Documentary evidence from this period being extremely scarce, Herndon's materials are acknowledged as indispensable. The most celebrated challenge to the reliability of Herndon's informants—a highly influential indictment of the historicity of Lincoln's love affair with Ann Rutledge—has itself been seriously challenged, with the result that the story of the tragic romance, at least in its essential outlines, has been found by Simon and others to be generally worthy of credence.[12]

Since 1998, Herndon's entire Lincoln archive of letters and interviews has been readily available in print, and its contents have been undergoing renewed scrutiny and reevaluation.[13] Just as it seems unlikely that controversy about Herndon will ever go away, it is just as unlikely that Lincoln studies can ever do without him. As Benjamin P. Thomas, himself a highly regarded Lincoln biographer, has declared, "Herndon is the most controversial figure in Lincoln literature, yet to him, more than to any other writer, we owe our knowledge of Lincoln the man—how he looked and walked, his love of fun, his melancholy, the way he thought, his personal habits and idiosyncrasies."[14]

William Henry Herndon was born in Kentucky in 1818 and was brought at the age of five to Sangamon County, Illinois, where he lived the rest of his life.[15] His father, Archer G. Herndon, was one of the earliest settlers in the Springfield area, where he steadily prospered as a businessman, stock farmer, and politician. His success enabled him to send his son William to Illinois College at nearby Jacksonville, an experience that reinforced the boy's bookishness and helped confirm him as a lifelong reader. But the young man's college career was terminated after one year by his father, who disapproved of the vocal abolitionism of the college's professors. Temporarily alienated from his father, the young Herndon secured a job clerking in the Springfield store of Joshua F. Speed and the privilege of sleeping in the large room above the store, which he shared with Speed and a young lawyer recently come to town, Abraham Lincoln. Lincoln and Speed had become intimate friends, and Speed's store became a gathering place where the young men of the town animatedly discussed literary, political, and other topics of the day.

From their first acquaintance, Herndon admired the affable lawyer and politician, whose star was so clearly on the rise. Herndon married and moved out of the store in 1840, but their relationship was renewed when he served an apprenticeship as a law clerk in the firm of Logan and Lincoln. When Lincoln and Stephen T. Logan dissolved their partnership in 1844, Lincoln, much to the surprise and gratification of the young student, invited him to become his partner. There were reportedly many observers who considered this a mismatch and a mistake, but Lincoln resisted all such criticism and remained steadfastly loyal to Herndon.

The Lincoln-Herndon partnership was a notable success from its beginning and remained active until Lincoln left Springfield for Washington in 1861. Herndon may have been the better legal scholar and more diligent researcher of the two, and Lincoln more adept as a courtroom litigator, although these may have been differences only of degree. Both were very able attorneys and increasingly in demand. Sharing an office as well as many political and intellectual interests, Lincoln and Herndon had many opportunities to discuss a wide range of topics. They both availed themselves of Herndon's substantial library, a portion of which was kept in the office. The partners occasionally rode the legal circuit together, were partners in Whig and Republican political causes, and shared a deep antipathy to slavery.

Financially, the partners shared equally, though Herndon once described himself as "the runt of the firm," whereas Lincoln was the "hoss."[16] Some scholars have taken this and other indications to mean that Herndon was much the lesser lawyer. A well-respected study of Lincoln's law career, for example, found it unthinkable that Lincoln would allow his "sometimes brilliant, but notoriously flighty and erratic partner" to argue so important a case as that of Joseph Dalby against the St. Louis, Chicago and Alton Railway Company, a key case involving the rights of railroad passengers.[17] But recent investigations of the firm of Lincoln and Herndon have shown beyond doubt that the precedent-setting verdict in this difficult case was gained by Herndon himself, without the aid of his partner, a clear indication that he was a very astute practitioner.[18] Between them, Lincoln and Herndon presided over one of the most successful law firms in Springfield.

Remembered by posterity as Lincoln's law partner and biographer, Herndon was, in the 1850s, a prominent and respected citizen of Springfield in his own right. A family man with a wife and six children, as well as a busy lawyer and a political activist, he still found time to devote to public causes. More radical than his partner and of a far more volatile temperament, Herndon entered into the reformist enthusiasm that swept America during the antebellum period, aiding in the promotion of such causes as the establishment of public schools in Springfield, local prohibition of the sale of alcoholic beverages (he himself had a drinking problem), and women's rights. He was an omnivorous reader and accumulated a large library, with which he kept current on a wide variety of social and scientific subjects. He was regularly in demand in Springfield and surrounding communities as a public speaker. In 1855, he was elected mayor of Springfield. The following year, he helped found the Republican party in Illinois, serving as one of the original members of the party's state central committee, and was seriously mentioned as a gubernatorial candidate. An articulate proponent of the

Republican position of opposition to the extension of slavery, he corresponded extensively with such prominent eastern antislavery figures as Theodore Parker, Wendell Phillips, and Horace Greeley.

Herndon does not seem to have had serious aspirations for political office, but he had long demonstrated a strong commitment to public service. When his former partner became a martyred president, Herndon felt an obligation to respond to the tremendous public interest that developed in Lincoln's background and personality. Looking back on his life following Lincoln's assassination from a perspective of twenty years, Herndon wrote to a correspondent:

> I commenced gathering up the facts of his life in 1865 quickly after he was assassinated. I felt that it was my duty as it was my pleasure to do so, and I have assisted all of his biographers with facts and opinions. I did so freely and without charge to any one and I shall continue to do so till I shall go hence. I have *given* yes *given* away hundreds of things—letters—speeches—&c. &c that I held dear and quite sacred to all persons who requested them—mere strangers and took no pay; and had I more of such articles I should do the same thing now.[19]

Within weeks of Lincoln's death on April 15, 1865, Herndon had made up his mind to write something about his former partner. He had been besieged by reporters, prospective biographers, and by a multitude of the curious, all seeking information about his former law partner, and he had been urged by others to share his unique perspective on a subject of paramount national interest. John L. Scripps, a principal editor for the *Chicago Tribune* and himself a campaign biographer of Lincoln, wrote: "Your long acquaintance and close association with him must have given you a clearer insight into his character than other men obtained."[20]

Having made the decision to write about Lincoln, Herndon's first impulse was to gather information. Not knowing much about Lincoln's life before he came to Springfield, the period of his childhood and youth, Herndon began sending off letters and establishing contacts in such places as Kentucky, where Lincoln had been born; Indiana, where he had lived between the ages of seven and twenty-one; and Menard County, Illinois, the location of the former village of New Salem, where Lincoln lived after he left home from 1831 to 1837. Within months of beginning his research in May 1865, Herndon had made several trips to seek out informants and take interviews, and he continued to carry on a very heavy correspondence in this line for the next two years.[21]

But his project was plagued by difficulties from the start. In a letter to Josiah G. Holland, who had embarked on the research for what was to become the first substantial full-length biography of Lincoln, Herndon explained his idea for a Lincoln memoir in his inimitable prose style:

> When you were in my office I casually informed you that it was my intention to write & publish the *subjective* Mr Lincoln—"the inner life" of Mr L. What I mean by that expression is this—I am writing Mr L's life—a short little thing—giving him in his passions—appetites—& affections—perceptions— memories—judgements—understanding—will, acting under & by motives, *just* as he lived, breathed—ate & laughed in this world, clothed in flesh & sinew—bone & nerve. He was not God—was man: he was not perfect—had some defects & a few positive faults: he was a good man—an honest man—a loving, true & noble man—such as the world scarcely, if ever saw. It is my intention to write out this *Life* of Mr L honestly fairly—impartially if I can, though mankind curse or bless me. It matters not to me.[22]

This passage reveals much about Herndon and the problems that would beleaguer the ambitious project he had in mind. He wants, he says, to write only "a short little thing" (not more than fifty or seventy-five pages, he says later), yet he intends to plumb the depths of the subjective Lincoln and capture all the complexity of his inner life, to render him realistically in all his common humanity, to show his imperfections and faults, to bring out his exceptional virtues and nobility, and to do all this impartially, letting the chips fall where they may. Herndon appears totally unaware of the impossibly tall order he has set for himself, but these difficulties would unavoidably emerge in due course. The passage also illustrates his characteristic way of expressing himself in writing, which, while lively and provocative, is inherently impulsive and thus poorly suited to the kind of orderly exposition and disciplined narration that such an ambitious effort would require.

But if Herndon was heedless of these potential difficulties at the outset, his researches would bring him startling new information that would further complicate his project. He knew at least one of Lincoln's secrets beforehand, for his partner had once confessed to him that his mother had been born out of wedlock and that he believed his maternal grandfather to be a Virginia planter.[23] When Herndon began to hear from the informants he had recruited in Kentucky, it became clear that many people there believed that Lincoln himself was illegitimate or at least was the offspring of someone other than his putative father, Thomas Lincoln. When questioning Lincoln's friends and neighbors from his New Salem days, Herndon discovered that Lincoln had been more than just the religious skeptic that he had known in Springfield but had reportedly ridiculed orthodox Christian beliefs. Also while living in New Salem, Lincoln had been involved in two serious love affairs, both of which led to proposals of marriage. Moreover, the first of these love affairs, Herndon was told, had ended with the tragic death in 1835 of Lincoln's fiancée, a beautiful young woman named Ann Rutledge, and as a result of this loss, Lincoln had become mentally deranged and had to be taken in hand by friends who feared he was suicidal. Mental derangement and fears of suicide were again mentioned in connection with Lincoln's courtship of Mary Todd, the Kentucky belle he would eventually marry, and this came from witnesses who were better placed at the time than Herndon himself. One of these witnesses, the older sister with whom Mary was living at the time, claimed that Lincoln failed to appear at their first wedding ceremony and left Mary standing at the altar.[24]

Herndon was well aware that these and other incidents he had uncovered were likely to be disturbing to the public, and that, even if true and undeniably important events in his partner's life, reporting them straightforwardly would not be considered appropriate by the prevailing standards of biography. But Herndon had come to the conclusion that such things were crucial elements in the shaping of Lincoln's character and behavior, and that, as such, they were "necessary truths" that should not be suppressed.

In November 1866, he got a taste of what kind of reception he might receive as a purveyor of such truths when, in a pre-printed public lecture, he created a national furor by describing Lincoln's tragic love affair with Ann Rutledge. Even more offensive than his indelicate revelation of deeply personal and private matters was his speculation that Lincoln had been so devastated by the death of Ann Rutledge that he never afterward loved another woman. The public at large was almost as mortified as Mary Todd Lincoln and her son Robert, who pleaded with Herndon not to persist in such revelations. As John Y. Simon has shown, Herndon had "grossly mishandled a major incident in the Lincoln story" and inflicted what would prove to be permanent damage to his own reputation.[25]

Though he professed not to be moved by the resulting outcry, it apparently made Herndon more anxious about the reliability of his reports, especially those from Kentucky that came from informants he did not know. "I am going to Ky myself," he wrote, "and look into the eyes of men & women—watch their features, investigate their motives—Enquire into their characters, opportunities—veracity &c &c"[26] The year 1867 was supposed to see the end of his investigations and the drafting of his biography, but doubts about the accuracy of his reports plagued Herndon, and he feared he needed more time. "I hope to write a correct Biog when it can be done," he wrote a confidant in June. "I shall make it truthful or not at all, and men shall intuitively feel that the Biog is true—correct & fair. The trouble is very *very* great, I assure you. Thousands of floating rumors—assertions & theories &c. &c have to be hunted down—dug out—inspected—Criticised &c. &c. before I can write. I can't Scribble on a sentence without knowing what I am doing."[27] He had had most of his informant materials copied in the fall of 1866 and placed in a bank vault against loss, and, unable to write, he consoled himself with having at least advanced the cause of Lincoln biography: "I sincerely wish I were a competent—a great man to write my friends Life—but I *can* gather *facts*—and give *truth* to mankind."[28] His planned Kentucky trip never came off, and when he took possession of his father's farm North of Springfield that same year, he retreated from the vexations of biography and the law and turned his attention more and more to the enticing prospects of rural life.

In 1869, Herndon's biography project was hopelessly stalled, and he was in need of money. Approached by Ward Hill Lamon, an old friend and aspiring biographer of Lincoln, he arranged to sell the transcribed copies of his informant materials to Lamon for four thousand dollars. Lamon turned these over to his partner and ghostwriter, Chauncey Black, who drew on them heavily in producing *The Life of Abraham Lincoln,* a substantial volume on Lincoln's pre-presidential life published under Lamon's name in 1872.[29] The scion of a prominent Democratic family, Black was no worshiper of Abraham Lincoln, and he used Herndon's most sensational informant material for all it was worth, undeterred by considerations of delicacy or privacy. This frank treatment of sensitive matters was largely in accord with Herndon's theory of "necessary truth," and although Herndon regretted some of its disclosures, the biography generally met with his approval. But the combination of Herndon's informant material and Black's critical perspective made for a vastly unpopular book, which even its publisher virtually repudiated.[30]

In the years that followed, Herndon often found himself under attack for his role in having gathered the "slanderous" materials employed in Lamon's biography. While he continued to answer questions about Lincoln, to assist biographers such as Isaac N. Arnold, and to give occasional lectures on his former partner, he no longer pursued new informants or information as he had in the past. His discouragement is reflected in a letter he wrote to a young correspondent in 1881: "Soon after Mr Lincoln's assassination I determined to gather up all the facts of his life—truly—honestly & impartially whatever it might cost in money or infamy, and to give the facts to the world as I understood them. I did so, and probably you know the result. I find that this age is not ready to meet its own great truths."[31] The following year, this same correspondent would come to work in Springfield, and his association with Lincoln's former law partner would eventually put Herndon's biographical project back on track.

Jesse W. Weik was the son of a German immigrant who had established a successful grocery business in Greencastle, Indiana. Born there in 1857, Weik grew up in a time and place that witnessed the virtual deification of Abraham Lincoln. As a student at Indiana Asbury University (later DePauw University) and an ardent admirer of Lincoln, Weik had written to Herndon in 1875 for an autograph of his hero. Six years later he wrote Herndon to remind him of his request, and Herndon responded generously by sending him a page from a notebook Lincoln had kept in his own hand in the 1820s.[32] After graduation, Weik had studied and practiced law and had tried other occupations before receiving, in 1882 through his Republican political connections, an appointment as a U.S. government pension agent with headquarters in Springfield, Illinois. Thus landing in the hometown of his idol, Weik embraced this opportunity to cultivate his interest in Lincoln and to write newspaper and magazine articles about him. For this, he took inspiration and encouragement from Herndon, though their close association and collaboration began only after he left Springfield in March 1885 to return to Greencastle.[33]

Back in his hometown where he now labored in his father's store, Weik continued to correspond with Herndon, who encouraged his aspirations to write about Lincoln. But he also warned him, "Persecution follows on the heels of truth, & worship is an element of man; and whoever dares to disturb that worship feels the weight of social scorn. This is my experience."[34] Before the year was out, Weik had suggested the idea of a collaboration on an article about Lincoln for *Harper's Weekly*. Herndon evaded the proposal of collaboration: "I have no objection to such a proceeding; & yet it will have a tendency to do you much injustice. You will be the real writer and yet the credit divided or taken away from you."[35] But he promised, "If I can help you in any way I will do so at all times willingly."[36] As good as his word, he began sending Weik a steady stream of informative letters, sometimes more than one in the same day, sometimes as many as four or five a week. These letters, as Donald has observed, are "chock-full of information and anecdote about Lincoln"[37] and remarkable for their range of topics and their detail.

By January 15, 1886, Herndon announced: "It seems to me that I have written to you enough matter [to] make a respectable life of Lincoln. . . . Had you not better change your plans and issue a little life of Lincoln yourself?"[38] Weik responded positively by return mail, and from this time forward the project would be understood as a joint venture. It was not, Herndon insisted, to be an ordinary biography. "The thing which we should publish should be something like this— 'Reminescences of Lincoln at home' or something like that: it should not be a life of Lincoln,"[39] he told Weik, though he allowed that biographical data would appear in the volume incidentally.

Both Weik and Herndon were motivated in part by the opportunity to make money. Herndon was desperately poor and, at age sixty-seven, still grubbing out a hand-to-mouth existence on his farm seven miles north of Springfield. Weik, who had not yet settled on a vocation, was ambitious to establish himself as a professional writer. Suggesting that their book take the form of magazine articles, Herndon laid out the division of labor: "You must write the articles & Ill give the facts. After this is done we can publish the things in a book form reserving the right, if we see proper to do so."[40] But Weik's first effort at incorporating Herndon's material into an article proved a harbinger of things to come, for when it appeared in a Cincinnati newspaper in July 1886, Weik reported to Herndon he had not been paid for it.[41]

Timing was also a problem, for another joint venture, the long-awaited biography by Lincoln's secretaries, John G. Nicolay and John Hay, began serial publication in the *Century* magazine in the autumn of 1886, just as Herndon and Weik began sounding out prospective publishers for their book. Predictably, it appeared to publishers, as one of them said, that Nicolay and Hay's book "will give the public all that they wish to know of Lincoln, just at present."[42] Herndon took a characteristically hopeful view. "Hay's & Nicolay's work I suppose it will be a grand affair," he wrote his discouraged partner. "However your & my ideas do not at all touch the same point of the circle: they are different— ours is *individual—domestic—social—forensic* ie Lincoln's law practice &c. &c breezy—funny—sad—gloomy &c. &c—Lincoln at home—Lincoln inside & outside, and in this field we will have no equals."[43]

After a meeting in Springfield in late October 1886, at which the two partners drew up a contract, Herndon packed up and sent to Weik what he called his "Lincoln Record"—the extensive archive of letters, interviews, and research materials that he had assembled over the years.[44] The contract has been lost, but from the characterizations of the project cited above and subsequent references, Weik's role was presumably defined as the compiler and editor of Herndon's "memoirs" of Lincoln, a combination of his recollections, ruminations, and anecdotes. A document in Herndon's hand appears to be a chapter outline of the book as it was envisioned at this time:

1st Lincolns parentage & birth
2d   Individually
3d   Domestically
4th Socially
5th As Lawyer
6th As politician
7th As Statesman & Presdt, including incidents &c &c during Each of
these periods[45]

But taking possession of Herndon's massive collection, which contained the testimony of some 250 informants, seems to have given Weik the glimmerings of a larger vista. Herndon refers several weeks later to Weik's having suggested that they "write the life of L, honestly—fairly—squarely, telling the whole truth and suppressing nothing, up to 1860 and there leaving him a grand figure standing up against the clear deep blue sky of the future." In other words, a full account of Lincoln's entire pre-presidential life. Eager to get their book into print and always susceptible to suggestion, Herndon readily agreed: "This is a good idea and I approve it in toto. Would it not be a good idea to have a *short* concluding chapter on him—not going into the details of his administration—the war—the reconstruction measures &c. &c.? We would thus give a full life of the man & yet leaving him standing up against the deep blue of the future. I am simply suggesting—not dictating."[46]

The practical effect of this new turn was not just an expanded scope for their book but a much-expanded role for the aspiring writer, Jesse Weik. As Weik read his way through the riches of Herndon's archive and pondered its uses, Herndon was taking note of Nicolay and Hay's evasions regarding Lincoln's early life then coming before the public in the *Century.* Their work suggested to Herndon that there was a place for a different kind of biography, one that would boldly tell the truth about Lincoln's early life, whereas, by contrast, Nicolay and Hay "handle things with silken gloves & 'a cammel hair pencil.'" In commenting on Nicolay and Hays's shortcomings, Herndon repeatedly endorsed the idea of presenting in their book a detailed picture of Lincoln's early years: "It does appear that the reading world wants to know every and all events—facts—incidents—thoughts, feelings and adventures of Lincoln, including the books he read and the girls he 'hugged,' and the like, upon the fact of human experience that the man grows out of the boy and the boy out of the child."[47]

Thus Herndon himself was here laying the basis for a different kind of book from the one he had signed on for a year earlier, a book that would now feature not only his own personal views and intimate glimpses of Lincoln but also all the important facts of Lincoln's pre-presidential life. Yet when Herndon arrived in Greencastle for their long-delayed joint drafting session in August 1887, his understanding of the character of the book does not seem to have changed, for he wrote Truman Bartlett: "I am hard at work on my inner—subjective life of Lincoln—his nature—characteristics &c. &c."[48] Nonetheless, it is clear that the book was now to have two tracks, a circumstance that was plainly reflected in the partners' activities. They sat side by side for the month of August, often sweltering in a small room over Weik's father's store in Greencastle, each working on his own task. An entry in Weik's diary for a day late in the month captures the scene: "Spent the bulk of the day at work in the office. Herndon at work on the philosophy of Lincoln and I, on the narrative of his life."[49]

By the end of the month, Herndon had written more than a dozen substantial pieces with titles reflecting the original conception, such as "Lincoln Individually," "Lincolns Domestic life," and "Lincoln as Lawyer—Politician & Statesman," as well as a number of others that took aim at particular aspects of Lincoln's character, such as his ambition, his superstition, and his power over others. Still other sketches addressed important relationships, such as those with Ann Rutledge, Mary Owens, and Mary Todd.[50] How these monographs were to be combined with the biographical material Weik was composing is indicated in the original preface Herndon drafted at the time: "The chapters are so arranged that those who wish to look immediately into Mr Lincoln's attributes—qualities and characteristics—not caring much to know his further history, because so well and thoroughly known to the reading world, may turn to Chapter __ and read every other one and including Chapter __ where he will find what he wants and in these chapters he will find all that I know of this great mans nature and its manifestations."[51] In spite of his earlier endorsements of the idea of a full and detailed account of Lincoln's pre-presidential life, Herndon's preface characterized the biographical narrative in minimal terms: "A mere thread of Lincoln's history will run through the book, except chapters [blank space] which will give a full—a very full and complete history of the youth and young manhood of Lincoln, fuller than ever before published."[52]

After a month's labor, Herndon left Greencastle in early September thinking the book was nearly finished, and Weik, indeed, completed a draft by month's end. But he immediately began a revision, and the form of the work continued to evolve.[53] For one thing, Weik had to recast Herndon's hastily written pieces, which Herndon later referred to as "notes [that] were simply intended as footlights for your guidance."[54] At some point, Weik seems to have determined that the scheme for alternating chapters was unworkable and that Herndon's contributions would have to be selectively integrated into the largely chronological narrative of Lincoln's life. There is no indication in Herndon's surviving letters that he was consulted in this process or that he was aware of the changes being made in the book's design. From this point on, the organization and character of the text were solely in the hands of Jesse Weik.[55]

◦◦◦

"The junior partner's share in this literary collaboration," as David Herbert Donald aptly observed, "has not received sufficient recognition."[56] When noticed at all, Weik is usually regarded as Herndon's amanuensis, but he played a much larger and far more significant role in the making of the biography. As we have seen, Herndon long had in view the writing of a brief, unconventional biography that would bring all his own special knowledge to bear and would feature, rather than a narrative history, a presentation of Lincoln's special qualities. In his original preface, Herndon was still affirming this concept. In refashioning the book's organization and revising the text over the course of several months between September 1887 and May 1888, Weik all but discarded these aims and opted instead for a narrative format very close to the conventional cradle-to-grave biography. While he retained the first-person narrative in which Herndon tells the story, the first seven of the book's twenty chapters mainly deal with Lincoln's life before Herndon knew him. This is made plausible by the fact that Herndon, having conducted extensive research in this period of his subject's life, could be made to quote from what his own informants had told him. That it seems to the reader natural that Herndon should tell the story in this way is testimony to Weik's literary ingenuity and skill.

To render Herndon's eccentric, nonlinear prose into a fluent narrative was initially one of Weik's most difficult problems. A surviving portion of what was probably Weik's original draft affords a glimpse of his initial struggle to remain true to one of Herndon's idiosyncratic descriptions, but in the end he simply abandoned most of Herndon's original and substituted his own succinct summary.[57] Another telling example of Weik's decisive role appears toward the end of the process, when Herndon sent him a wordy and none-too-coherent passage on Lincoln's view of law and order that referred, in passing, to Lincoln's "sleepless restless and untiring ambition."[58] Weik steadfastly ignored Herndon's repeated pleas to insert the passage, but it doubtless contained the basis for one of the book's most quoted lines: "His ambition was a little engine that knew no rest." What happened in these cases is what eventually happened in the book at large:

Weik simply gave up the attempt to represent Herndon in his own distinctive idiom. Instead, he presented what he understood to be Herndon's views, but in language and in a voice of his own creation.

This was only one of the ways in which Weik transformed the book. Another was his abandonment of Herndon's unpromising plan of alternating chapters, and with it, much of the Herndonian emphasis on special qualities and characteristics. As Donald has pointed out, "Herndon's rough drafts were extensively followed in only five of the twenty chapters in the completed Lincoln biography."[59] In Herndon's scheme, anecdotes were to appear as illustrations of qualities or characteristics, but in Weik's approach, biographical anecdotes might have an interest of their own. For example, although Herndon preferred not to make much of Lincoln's near-duel with James Shields in 1842—"Jesse, if I were you I wouldn't say much about the Shield's duel"[60]—Weik related this episode in great detail, making it, at thirty pages, one of the longest in the book.

Herndon seems always to have feared that his book would suffer a fate similar to that of Lamon. "My poor book will I guess suit no one," he wrote a correspondent, "but that I cannot help. The life is mostly an analysis of Lincoln—an attempt to let people peep into the inner man, a thread of his history running through the book at the same time."[61] In anticipating this negative reception, Herndon had in mind—perhaps even more than unwelcome disclosures about Lincoln's private life—revelations about such unheroic personal traits as Lincoln's habitual concealment of his true aims and purposes, his manipulation and use of his friends, his perceived coldness and lack of gratitude, his love of principles above persons, his gloomy fatalism, his extreme rationalism, and, paradoxically, his indelible streak of superstition. Although Herndon had always admired and looked up to his partner and after his death came to revere him as one of the world's great men, he conscientiously sought, in his lectures and other writings on Lincoln, to depict the distinctive traits that biographers and hagiographers were either ignorant of or had glossed over. Because these were the kinds of insights that only someone with his unique perspective on Lincoln could provide, they are prominently on display in the draft chapters, or monographs, he sketched out for Weik's use, but they are much less in evidence in Weik's narrative. Weik surely realized that such an emphasis would detract from the book's popularity, but he also seems to have had a considerably less complicated and more consistently upbeat view of Lincoln than Herndon. Weik also resisted Herndon's tendency to speculate about such things as Lincoln's psychological and physiological makeup, causing Herndon to complain at one point with unaccustomed bitterness: "I know that this [speculation] does not suit you—you dislike such stuff terribly."[62] Acting as a filter on Herndon's views was thus another important way that Weik affected the biography.

Just as Weik understood his role as recasting Herndon's statements into a more fluent and acceptable form, he treated the testimony of Herndon's informants in the same way. As a result, virtually all the letters and interviews cited in *Herndon's Lincoln* have been altered or rewritten. For example, in recording an interview with Henry Dummer, a lawyer in the firm from which Lincoln had borrowed books when studying law, Herndon's elliptical interview notes read:

> Lincoln used to come to our office in Spfgd and borrow books—don't Know whether he walked or rode: he was an uncouth looking lad—did not say much—what he did say he said it strongly—Sharply.

When this appeared as a footnote in *Herndon's Lincoln,* it had been considerably expanded by Weik:

> Lincoln used to come to our office—Stuart's and mine—in Springfield from New Salem and borrow law-books. Sometimes he walked but generally rode. He was the most uncouth looking young man I ever saw. He seemed to have but little to say; seemed to feel timid, with a tinge of sadness visible in the countenance, but when he did talk all this disappeared for the time and he demonstrated that he was both strong and acute. He surprised us more and more at every visit.—Henry E. Dummer, Statement, Sept. 16th, 1865.[63]

Though no great harm is done here by Weik's creative editing, some of the views expressed are not strictly Dummer's, and the potential for inadvertent error in such a practice is always present. That it occasionally takes its toll can be seen from Weik's treatment of the testimony of David Turnham, a boyhood friend of Lincoln's who had responded to a question from Herndon: "So far as his being accustomed to deep thoughtfulness and lost in reflection. He never was but on the Contrary was always quick-witted and ready for an answer."[64] In Weik's redaction, Turnham's view of Lincoln's "deep thoughtfulness" is reversed: "Although quick-witted and ready with an answer, he began to exhibit deep thoughtfulness, and was so often lost in studied reflection we could not help noticing the strange turn in his actions."[65] In this same way, a number of factual mistakes creep into the book that Herndon himself would not have made but that he either failed to catch or have corrected. An example is the rewritten version of the testimony of Mary Todd Lincoln's sister, which refers to the death in the Lincoln family of "an infant who died a few days after its birth in Springfield," an error which is not in the original interview. Because the documents in Herndon's informant archive are often difficult to read, it is not surprising that Weik frequently quotes, not from the original letters and interviews, but rather from the regularized versions of them that appeared in Lamon's biography. (In the present edition, quoted testimony that diverges significantly from its source or is obviously copied from Lamon has been reported in the annotations.)

In the end, the composition of *Herndon's Lincoln* was almost exclusively Weik's.[66] The fact that his role had been gradually but effectively elevated from editor to author was not without consequences. In negotiating with their prospective publisher, Weik seems to have had trouble explaining his somewhat anomalous role in the enterprise. At one point he went so far as to furnish them samples of Herndon's draft chapters, presumably to make the point that he, not Herndon, was the composer of the narrative text.[67] There are indications in his diary that his former professor and literary advisor, John Clark Ridpath, counseled him to take a more possessive stance,[68] and after the book was accepted for publication, Weik began referring to it in his diary as "my" book.[69] Things came to a head in November 1888, when Weik submitted a new preface for Herndon's approval. Earlier he had revised Herndon's original preface to conclude: "I am especially [obligated] to my associate in this undertaking, Mr. Jesse W. Weik, of Greencastle, Indiana, whose industry in investigation of facts, and whose literary assistance and zeal deserve the commendation of every reader of this book."[70] But now, with the book being set in type, and apparently egged on by Professor Ridpath, Weik proposed to modify the preface so as to bring himself forward as not merely Herndon's editor but as the actual composer of the biography.[71]

Since being notified of the manuscript's acceptance in September, Herndon had been increasingly frustrated by his partner's lack of responsiveness to his queries and suggestions and by the peremptory editorial actions of the publishers, who were in a hurry to get the book into print. He replied in dismay: "I received your note, dated the 3rd inst inclosed with *your* preface of our book and I would be astonished at it if I had not ceased to be astonished at anything."[72] Weik's proposed new language, which described Herndon as "unfamiliar with literary details" and "ill-adapted to carry out the undertaking," was regarded by Herndon as "insulting," but he had an even more potent objection. It was that Weik's preface "would ruin our book."[73] The authority of Herndon's name and its claim to be an intimate account from a unique and privileged vantage point constituted the major appeal of the biography. If this were undermined, Herndon argued, disaster would follow. "It would be said by critics and by the reading world that I had nothing to do with the book—that it was a fraud and a cheat—a fiction got up for money making &c. &c."[74]

Herndon was firm, but he characteristically held no grudge, and the brief storm over the preface was weathered amicably. In the final version, Weik was given ample credit for his "assistance in the preparation of the book," whose long-postponed composition Herndon had been "unable" to complete. When the book was published several months later, Jesse W. Weik was listed on the title page as coauthor, while the reamended preface ended on a strong Herndonian note:

> The vital matter of this narrative has been deduced directly from the consciousness, reminiscences, and collected data of
> WILLIAM H. HERNDON.[75]

The compromise did justice to both. Weik had taken the lead and had worked extremely hard on the book, as his diary makes clear, and his contributions were crucial. The narrative structure that he devised and his fluent, readable prose style were clearly beyond Herndon's abilities, and they were essential to the biography's broad appeal and eventual status as a classic. But the point of view and the distinctive authority of the book were unmistakably Herndon's, and some of his most incisive observations about Lincoln appear here and nowhere else in his writings. While he complained in his letters about some of the things Weik had not included and about some uncorrected minor errors, Herndon embraced the finished work enthusiastically and stoutly defended its representations and judgments. "I drew the picture of Mr. Lincoln as I saw and knew him," he told a correspondent after the book was published. "I told the naked God's truth, and I'll stand by it, let the consequences be what they may be."[76]

Review copies and advertisements of *Herndon's Lincoln* finally began to circulate in June 1889, and reviews followed for several months thereafter. The overall reception was favorable, with some commentators quick to discern its unique virtues. Gen. Jacob D. Cox, writing in the *Nation*, predicted that the biography would "doubtless remain the most authentic and trustworthy source of information concerning the great man in the period prior to his election to the Presidency."[77] But some reviews were also quite critical. The *Chicago Journal's* reviewer viewed the biography's vaunted candor with contempt: "It vilely distorts the image of an ideal statesman, patriot and martyr. It clothes him in vulgarity and grossness. Its indecencies are spread like a curtain to hide the collossal proportions and the splendid purity of his character. . . . It brings out all that should have been hidden."[78] So much for trying to tell the truth.

Herndon, however, was undaunted by such scathing critiques, for not only were they a predictable result of the book's philosophy and treatment of its subject, but, as he told his collaborator, they stimulated potential readers to want to buy the book and read it for themselves.[79] In fact, the biography's attempts to go beyond the smiling aspects of its subject were a regular source of comment and criticism. The *New York Times* accused Herndon of dusting off all the skeletons in Lincoln's closet and complained—as did a great many reviews—that the book "tells what a man of good taste would leave unsaid."[80] But the genie was out of the bottle, and the *Atlantic Monthly* reviewer spoke prophetically in saying that *Herndon's Lincoln* "will play a large part . . . in the future construction of Lincoln in the minds of men."[81]

Herndon was particularly gratified by the private assessment sent him by Horace White, editor of the *New York Post* and a longtime observer of Lincoln. "It is not only the best of all the biographies of Lincoln that have been written," he wrote expansively, "but in my judgment it is the best American biography that has ever been written." White, who had known Lincoln in the 1850s when he covered the Lincoln-Douglas debates, was emphatic in his approval of Herndon and Weik's realistic approach. "It is because you have put in all his warts that I consider yours the best biography."[82]

Unfortunately, the interest in the book generated by reviewers and commentators was not to translate into sales and profits. The book's marginal publisher, Belford, Clarke and Company, was in a shaky financial condition and had only printed fifteen hundred copies, the precise number the contract with their unwary authors permitted them to sell without payment of royalties, and many of these copies were sent gratis to reviewers. In late September 1889, when demand for the book was probably at its peak, the publishers went into bankruptcy. After reorganization and a new contract negotiated with Weik, the publishers managed to get a second printing of the same size into production, but by the time it came off the presses in the spring of 1890, with few corrections, the failing firm's inability to market and distribute its products was all too apparent and sales languished.

Despite his enthusiasm for the biography, Horace White had early pronounced the choice of Belford, Clarke and Company to be a mistake, and he now offered to connect Herndon and Weik with a "first-rate publishing house" in the East, even volunteering to contribute a chapter of his own on the Lincoln-Douglas debates to such an edition. After several months of bargaining, he was able to bring the authors together with Charles Scribner's Sons of New York in early 1891. Shortly after a contract was arranged, on March 18, 1891, William Henry Herndon died. Having counted heavily on realizing some desperately needed cash from the sales of his biography, Herndon had taken the failure of the first edition to earn its authors any royalty whatsoever particularly hard, and he was eagerly looking forward to the new and revised edition. He would never know that Scribner's, after learning that the biography was objectionable to Robert Todd Lincoln, the president's son, reneged on its promise to publish, or that White would find yet another eastern publisher, D. Appleton and Company, to bring out the new edition in 1892.[83] Nor would he know that the second edition, with material that White deemed objectionable excluded[84] and with White's introduction and new chapter on the Lincoln-Douglas debates added, would carry a new title: *Abraham Lincoln: The True Story of a Great Life.*

Jesse Weik continued to conduct interviews and seek out information about Lincoln, adding to the Herndon archive, which was now his property and which he guarded assiduously from other researchers. Before finally making these materials available to his friend and benefactor, Albert J. Beveridge, he published *The Real Lincoln* (1922), which drew on a broad assortment of previously unused Herndon materials as well as many letters and interviews he had collected subsequently on his own.[85]

When the copyright of the Appleton edition finally expired, it was succeeded by a one-volume edition edited by Paul M. Angle, first published in 1930 and reprinted many times. Angle's edition, prepared by a professionally trained Lincoln scholar, has proved very serviceable and has been the edition most often read and cited from that time forward. Its "Editor's Preface," though somewhat dated, is still authoritative and still a superb introduction to Herndon and his Lincoln biography. Restoring the material that the 1892 Appleton edition had deleted and correcting obvious errors, Angle further attempted to enhance the biography's readability by moving longer footnotes into the narrative text and even inserting, within brackets, his own supplementary material where he deemed it appropriate. Not having access to Herndon's original informant materials, Angle had no practical way of tracking or assessing the use made of them. Nor did he have access to Herndon's letters to Weik or other means of sizing up Weik's role in the project. But since the publication of Angle's edition, considerable light has been shed on *Herndon's Lincoln.*

In 1938, Emanuel Hertz published *The Hidden Lincoln,* a selection of Herndon's letters to Weik and others as well as a sampling of the letters and interviews from his Lincoln informants.[86] These were very poorly edited, and in fact a number of the documents turn out to have been badly garbled, but the collection afforded students of Lincoln a first glimpse of some revealing documents. Copies of some of this material had been sold to Ward Hill Lamon in 1869 and eventually made up part of the Lamon Papers acquired by the Huntington Library. In 1941, the Library of Congress acquired most of the originals that had been retained by Jesse W. Weik as well as most of Herndon's letters to Weik.[87] The availability of this material opened the way for the remarkably detailed and probing study of Herndon's career as a Lincoln biographer by David Herbert Donald in 1948, cited frequently here. Herndon's archive of informant letters and interviews, though available on microfilm, still remained difficult to access, but it was finally transcribed and published in its entirety in 1998 as *Herndon's Informants*.[88] Together with a wide range of important advancements in Lincoln studies since Angle's day, these developments have laid the basis for the present edition of *Herndon's Lincoln*.

In the more than one hundred years that have passed since the publication of *Herndon's Lincoln*, biographies of Abraham Lincoln have appeared that have surpassed it in terms of accuracy and completeness, but none can be said to have replaced it. Indeed, during this period it has been elevated to the status of a classic, so that we now read *Herndon's Lincoln* for the same reason that we read Boswell's *Life of Johnson*—because the author had a privileged position and point of view that cannot be rendered obsolete by subsequent scholarship and research and because, more than any other book, it shaped the picture and the impression Americans were to have of the early life and character of their greatest president. It is true that readers now have access to more faithful accounts of the observations and opinions of others that are reported in his book, but Herndon's own opinions and observations of the life and times of his great law partner are irreplaceable. One of the most apt characterizations of *Herndon's Lincoln* appeared in the perceptive review, referred to earlier, that appeared in the *Nation:* "The reader of these memoirs must not look for an adequate estimate of Lincoln's place in history, or for an authoritative judgment of his conduct of national affairs during the great civil war. He must expect, rather, to be helped to understand how Abraham Lincoln became the man he was, and what manner of man he was when the election of 1860 threw upon him a burden of responsibilities hardly paralleled in history."[89]

A Note on the Text and Annotations

This edition presents the text of the original 1889 edition of *Herndon's Lincoln*, complete and in the format in which it appeared. Only typographical and proofing errors have been corrected, and a list of these is given in the Corrigenda. The selection of original illustrations included here represents about one-third of those appearing in the 1889 edition. Two chapters that were added in the second edition, published by Appleton in 1892, are included as additional appendices, following those that were part of the 1889 edition.

The reader should note that the policy of faithfully presenting the text of the 1889 edition followed here entails the printing of variant spellings. For example, a word usually spelled "practice" appears a number of times in the text spelled "practise." Thus the appearance of both "sceptical" and "skeptical," "meagre" and "meager," and "trousers" and "trowsers." The spelling of proper names in this book, which was almost exclusively the work of Jesse Weik, is occasionally idiosyncratic, but where consistent, these have not been corrected.

The footnotes displayed at the bottom of the page are those of the original edition. Though they frequently make for awkward page layout and are lacking in consistency, they are nonetheless an essential feature of *Herndon's Lincoln* in its original form.

Editorial annotations are indicated in the text by superscript numerals; the annotations themselves appear in the back of the book. They typically report on the sources employed in the biography, so far as these can be identified. Significant differences between the source and the text have been noted, though all differences have not. Readers of the annotations must bear in mind that *Herndon's Lincoln* was composed not by Herndon himself but by his collaborator, Jesse W. Weik, using Herndon's source material and his many letters as his guide. Weik also made substantial use of Ward Hill Lamon's 1872 biography of Lincoln, which had been ghostwritten by Chauncey Black largely from copies of Herndon's source materials. Some, but by no means all, of the factual errors in the text are noted in the annotations. Where misstatements or errors are pointed out, the editors have sought, whenever possible, to shed light on where responsibility for the error lies— whether with Herndon himself, with his collaborator, or with an informant.

The square brackets that appear are part of the original text and do not, in this edition, indicate insertions by the editors. The few instances of such editorial insertions are indicated by round brackets.

HERNDON'S LINCOLN

HERNDON'S LINCOLN

The True Story Of A Great Life

Etiam in minimis major.

THE HISTORY AND PERSONAL RECOLLECTIONS

OF

ABRAHAM LINCOLN

BY

WILLIAM H. HERNDON

FOR TWENTY YEARS HIS FRIEND AND LAW
PARTNER

AND

JESSE WILLIAM WEIK, A. M.

TO

THE MEN AND WOMEN OF AMERICA

WHO HAVE GROWN UP SINCE HIS TRAGIC DEATH, AND
WHO HAVE YET TO LEARN THE STORY OF
HIS LIFE, THIS RECORD OF

ABRAHAM LINCOLN'S CAREER

IS FAITHFULLY INSCRIBED.

Preface

A quarter of a century has well-nigh rolled by since the tragic death of Abraham Lincoln.[1] The prejudice and bitterness with which he was assailed have disappeared from the minds of men, and the world is now beginning to view him as a great historical character. Those who knew and walked with him are gradually passing away, and ere long the last man who ever heard his voice or grasped his hand will have gone from earth. With a view to throwing a light on some attributes of Lincoln's character heretofore obscure, and thus contributing to the great fund of history which goes down to posterity, these volumes are given to the world.

If Mr. Lincoln is destined to fill that exalted station in history or attain that high rank in the estimation of the coming generations which has been predicted of him, it is alike just to his memory and the proper legacy of mankind that the whole truth concerning him should be known. If the story of his life is truthfully and courageously told—nothing colored or suppressed; nothing false either written or suggested—the reader will see and feel the presence of the living man. He will, in fact, live with him and be moved to think and act with him. If, on the other hand, the story is colored or the facts in any degree suppressed, the reader will be not only misled, but imposed upon as well. At last the truth will come, and no man need hope to evade it.

"There is but one true history in the world," said one of Lincoln's closest friends to whom I confided the project of writing a history of his life several years ago, "and that is the Bible. It is often said of the old characters portrayed there that they were bad men. They are contrasted with other characters in history, and much to the detriment of the old worthies. The reason is, that the Biblical historian told the whole truth—the inner life. The heart and secret acts are brought to light and faithfully photographed. In other histories virtues are perpetuated and vices concealed. If the life of King David had been written by an ordinary historian the affair of Uriah would at most have been a quashed indictment with a denial of all the substantial facts. You should not forget there is a skeleton in every house. The finest character dug out thoroughly, photographed honestly, and judged by that standard of morality or excellence which we exact for other men is never perfect. Some men are cold, some lewd, some dishonest, some cruel, and many a combination of all. The trail of the serpent is over them all! Excellence consists, not in the absence of these attributes, but in the degree in which they are redeemed by the virtues and graces of life. Lincoln's character will, I am certain, bear close scrutiny. I am not afraid of you in this direction. Don't let anything deter you from digging to the bottom; yet don't forget that if Lincoln had some faults, Washington had more—few men have less. In drawing the portrait tell the world what the skeleton was with Lincoln. What gave him that peculiar melancholy? What cancer had he inside?"[2]

Some persons will doubtless object to the narration of certain facts which appear here for the first time, and which they contend should have been consigned to the tomb. Their pretense is that no good can come from such ghastly exposures. To such over-sensitive souls, if any such exist, my answer is that these facts are indispensable to a full knowledge of Mr. Lincoln in all the walks of life. In order properly to comprehend him and the stirring, bloody times in which he lived, and in which he played such an important part, we must have all the facts—we must be prepared to take him as he was.

In determining Lincoln's title to greatness we must not only keep in mind the times in which he lived, but we must, to a certain extent, measure him with other men. Many of our great men and our statesmen, it is true, have been self-made, rising gradually through struggles to the topmost round of the ladder; but Lincoln rose from a lower depth than any of them—from a stagnant, putrid pool, like the gas which, set on fire by its own energy and self-combustible nature, rises in jets, blazing, clear, and bright. I should be remiss in my duty if I did not throw the light on this part of the picture, so that the world may realize what marvellous contrast one phase of his life presents to another.

The purpose of these volumes is to narrate facts, avoiding as much as possible any expression of opinion, and leaving the reader to form his own conclusions. Use has been made of the views and recollections of other persons, but only those known to be truthful and trustworthy. A thread of the narrative of Lincoln's life runs through the work, but an especial feature is an analysis of the man and a portrayal of his attributes and characteristics. The attempt to delineate his qualities, his nature and its manifestations, may occasion frequent repetitions of fact, but if truthfully done this can only augment the store of matter from which posterity is to learn what manner of man he was.

The object of this work is to deal with Mr. Lincoln individually and domestically; as lawyer, as citizen, as statesman. Especial attention is given to the history of his youth and early manhood; and while dwelling on this portion of his life the liberty is taken to insert many things that would be omitted or suppressed in other places, where the cast-iron rules that govern magazine writing are allowed to prevail. Thus much is stated in advance, so that no one need be disappointed in the scope and extent of the work. The endeavor is to keep Lincoln in sight all the time; to cling close to his side all the way through—leaving to others the more comprehensive task of writing a history of his times. I have no theory of his life to establish or destroy. Mr. Lincoln was my warm, devoted friend. I always loved him, and I revere his name to this day. My purpose to tell the truth about him need occasion no apprehension; for I know that "God's naked truth," as Carlyle puts it, can never injure the fame of Abraham Lincoln. It will stand that or any other test, and at last untarnished will reach the loftiest niche in American history.

My long personal association with Mr. Lincoln gave me special facilities in the direction of obtaining materials for these volumes. Such were our relations during all that portion of his life when he was rising to distinction, that I had only to exercise a moderate vigilance in order to gather and preserve the real data of his personal career. Being strongly drawn to the man, and believing in his destiny, I was not unobservant or careless in this respect. It thus happened that I became the personal depositary of the larger part of the most valuable *Lincolniana* in existence. Out of this store the major portion of the materials of the following volumes has been drawn. I take this, my first general opportunity, to return thanks to the scores of friends in Kentucky, Indiana, Illinois, and elsewhere for the information they have so generously furnished and the favors they have so kindly extended me. Their names are too numerous for separate mention, but the recompense of each one will be the consciousness of having contributed a share towards a true history of the "first American."

Over twenty years ago I began this book; but an active life at the bar has caused me to postpone the work of composition, until, now, being somewhat advanced in years, I find myself unable to carry out the undertaking. Within the past three years I have been assisted in the preparation of the book by Mr. Jesse W. Weik, of Greencastle, Ind., whose industry, patience, and literary zeal have not only lessened my labors, but have secured for him the approbation of Lincoln's friends and admirers. Mr. Weik has by his personal investigation greatly enlarged our common treasure of facts and information. He has for several years been indefatigable in exploring the course of Lincoln's life. In no particular has he been satisfied with anything taken at second hand. He has visited—as I also did in 1865[3]—Lincoln's birthplace in Kentucky, his early homes in Indiana and Illinois, and together, so to speak, he and I have followed our hero continuously and attentively till he left Springfield in 1861 to be inaugurated President. We have retained the original MSS. in all cases, and they have never been out of our hands. In relating facts therefore, we refer to them in most cases, rather than to the statements of other biographers.

This brief preliminary statement is made so that posterity, in so far as posterity may be interested in the subject, may know that the vital matter of this narrative has been deduced directly from the consciousness, reminiscences, and collected data of

WILLIAM H. HERNDON.
SPRINGFIELD, ILL.,
November 1, 1888.

Contents.

CHAPTER IV.

The settlement in Illinois.—Splitting rails with John Hanks.—Building the boat for Offut.—The return to Illinois.—New Salem described.—Clerking on the election board.—The lizard story.—Salesman in Offut's store.—The wrestle with Jack Armstrong.—Studying in the store.—Disappearance of Offut.—The *Talisman*.—Oliphant's poetry.—The reception at Springfield.—The Captain's wife.—Return trip of the *Talisman*.—Rowan Herndon and Lincoln pilot her through.—The navigability of the Sangamon fully demonstrated.—The vessel reaches Beardstown.

CHAPTER V.

The Black Hawk war.—Lincoln elected captain.—Under arrest.—Protecting the Indian.—Recollections of a comrade.—Lincoln re-enlists as a private.—Return to New Salem.—Candidate for the Legislature.—The handbill.—First political speech.—The canvass.—Defeat.—Partnership in the store with Berry.—The trade with William Greene.—Failure of the business.—Law studies.—Pettifogging.—Stories and poetry.—Referee in rural sports.—Deputy surveyor under John Calhoun.—Studying with Mentor Graham.—Postmaster at New Salem.—The incident with Chandler.—Feats of Strength.—Second race for the Legislature.—Election.

CHAPTER VI.

Lincoln falls in love with Anne Rutledge.—The old story.—Description of the girl.—The affair with John McNeil.—Departure of McNeil for New York.—Anne learns of the change of name.—Her faith under fire.—Lincoln appears on the scene.—Courting in dead earnest.—Lincoln's proposal accepted.—The ghost of another love.—Death of Anne.—Effect on Lincoln's mind.—His suffering.—Kindness of Bowlin Greene.—"Oh, why should the spirit of mortal be proud?"—Letter to Dr. Drake.—Return of McNamar.

CHAPTER VII.

An amusing courtship.—Lincoln meets Mary S. Owens.—Her nature, education, and mind.—Lincoln's boast.—He pays his addresses.—The lady's letters to Herndon.—Lincoln's letters.—His avowals of affection.—The letter to Mrs. Browning.—Miss Owens' estimate of Lincoln.

CHAPTER VIII.

Lincoln a member of the Legislature at Vandalia.—First meeting with Douglas.—The society of Vandalia.—Pioneer legislation.—Deputy surveyor under Thomas M. Neal.—Candidate for the Legislature again.—Another handbill.—Favors "Woman's Rights."—The letter to Col. Robert Allen.—The canvass.—The answer to George Forquer.—The election, Lincoln leading the ticket.—The "Long Nine."—Reckless legislation.—The "DeWitt Clinton" of Illinois.—Internal improvements.—The removal of the capital to Springfield.—The Committee on Finance.—The New England importation.—The Lincoln-Stone protest.—Return of the "Long Nine" to Springfield.—Lincoln removes to Springfield.—Licensed to practise law.—In partnership with John T. Stuart.—Early practice.—Generosity of Joshua F. Speed.—The bar of Springfield.—Speed's store.—Political discussions.—More poetry.—Lincoln addresses the "Young Men's Lyceum."—The debate in the Presbyterian Church.—Elected to the Legislature again.—Answering Col. Dick Taylor on the stump.—Rescue of Baker.—Last canvass for the Legislature.—The Thomas "skinning."—The Presidential canvass of 1840.

CHAPTER IX.

Lincoln still unmarried.—The Todd family.—Mary Todd.—Introduced to Lincoln.—The courtship.—The flirtation with Douglas.—The advice of Speed.—How Lincoln broke the engagement.—Preparations for marriage.—A disappointed bride.—A crazy groom.—Speed takes Lincoln to Kentucky.—Restored spirits.—Return of Lincoln to Illinois.—Letters to Speed.—The party at Simeon Francis's house.—The reconciliation.—The marriage.—The duel with James Shields.—The "Rebecca" letters.—"Cathleen" invokes the muse.—Whiteside's account of the duel.—Merryman's account.—Lincoln's address before the Washingtonian Society.—Meeting with Martin Van Buren.—Partnership with Stephen T. Logan.—Partnership with William H. Herndon.—Congressional aspirations.—Nomination and election of John J. Hardin.—The Presidential campaign of 1844.—Lincoln takes the stump in Southern Indiana.—Lincoln nominated for Congress.—The canvass against Peter Cartwright.—Lincoln elected.—In Congress.—The "Spot Resolutions."—Opposes the Mexican war.—Letters to Herndon.—Speeches in Congress.—Stumping through New England.—A Congressman's troubles.—A characteristic letter.—End of Congressional term.

CHAPTER X.

Early married life.—Boarding at the "Globe Tavern."—A plucky little wife.—Niagara Falls.—The patent for lifting vessels over shoals.—Candidate for Commissioner of the Land Office.—The appointment of Butterfield.—The offer of Territorial posts by President Taylor.—A journey to Washington and incidents.—Return to Illinois.—Settling down to practice law.—Life on the circuit.—Story-telling.—Habits as lawyer and methods of study.—Law-office of Lincoln and Herndon.—Recollections of Littlefield.—Studying Euclid.—Taste for literature.—Lincoln's first appearance in the Supreme Court of Illinois.—Professional honor and personal honesty.—The juror in the divorce case.

CHAPTER XI.

A glimpse into the law-office.—How Lincoln kept accounts and divided fees with his partner.—Lincoln in the argument of a case.—The tribute of David Davis.—Characteristics as a lawyer.—One of Lincoln's briefs.—The Wright case.—Defending the ladies.—Reminiscences of the circuit.—The suit against the Illinois Central railroad.—The Manny case. First meeting with Edwin M. Stanton.—Defense of William Armstrong.—Last law-suit in Illinois.—The dinner at Arnold's in Chicago.

CHAPTER XII.

Speech before the Scott Club.—A talk with John T. Stuart.—Newspapers and political literature.—Passage of the Kansas-Nebraska bill.—The signs of discontent.—The arrival of Douglas in Chicago.—Speech at the State Fair.—The answer of Lincoln.—The article in the *Conservative*.—Lincoln's escape from the Abolitionists.—Following up Douglas.—Breach of agreement by Douglas.—The contest in the Legislature for Senator.—Lincoln's magnanimity.—Election of Trumbull.—Interview with the Governor of Illinois.—The outrages in the Territories.—Lincoln's judicious counsel.—A letter to Speed.—The call for the Bloomington Convention.—Lincoln's telegram.—Speech at the Convention.—The ratification at Springfield.—The campaign of 1856.—Demands for Lincoln.—The letter to the Fillmore men.

CHAPTER XIII.

Growth of Lincoln's reputation.—His dejection.—Greeley's letters.—Herndon's mission to the Eastern states.—Interviews with Seward, Douglas, Greeley, Beecher, and others.—The letter from Boston.—The Springfield convention.—Lincoln nominated Senator.—The "house-divided-against-itself" speech.—Reading it to his friends.—Their comments and complaints.—Douglas's first speech in Chicago.—The joint canvass.—Lincoln and Douglas contrasted.—Lincoln on the stump.—Positions of Lincoln and Douglas.—Incidents of the debate.—The result.—More letters from Horace Greeley.—How Lincoln accepted his defeat.—A specimen of his oratory.

CHAPTER XIV.

A glimpse of Lincoln's home.—Sunday in the office with the boys.—Mrs. Lincoln's temper.—Troubles with the servants.—Letter to John E. Rosette.—What Lincoln did when the domestic sea was troubled.—A retrospect.—Lincoln's want of speculation.—His superstition.—Reading the life of Edmund Burke.—His scientific notions.—Writing the book against Christianity.—Recollections of Lincoln's views by old friends.—Statement of Mrs. Lincoln.

CHAPTER XV.

Effect of the canvass of 1858 on Lincoln's pocket-book.—Attempts to lecture.—On the stump with Douglas in Ohio.—Incidents of the Ohio canvass.—The dawn of 1860.—Presidential suggestions.—Meeting in the office of the Secretary of State.—The Cooper Institute speech.—Speaking in New England.—Looming up.—Preparing for Chicago.—Letters to a friend.— The Decatur convention.—John Hanks bringing in the rails.—The Chicago convention.—The canvass of 1860.—Lincoln casting his ballot.—Attitude of the clergy in Springfield.—The election and result.

CHAPTER XVI.

Arrival of the office-seekers in Springfield.—Recollections of a newspaper correspondent.—How Lincoln received the cabinet-makers.—Making up the cabinet.—A letter from Henry Wilson.—Visiting Chicago and meeting with Joshua F. Speed.—Preparing the Inaugural address.—Lincoln's self-confidence.—Separation from his step-mother.—Last days in Springfield.— Parting with old associates.—Departure of the Presidential party from Springfield.—The journey to Washington and efforts to interrupt the same.— The investigations of Allan Pinkerton.—The Inauguration.

CHAPTER XVII.

In the Presidential chair.—Looking after his friends.—Settling the claims of David Davis.—Swett's letter.—The visit of Herndon.—The testimony of Mrs. Edwards.—Letter from and interview with Mrs. Lincoln.—A glimpse into the White House.—A letter from John Hay.—Bancroft's eulogy.—Strictures of David Davis.—Dennis Hanks in Washington.

CHAPTER XVIII.

The recollections of Lincoln by Joshua F. Speed.—An interesting letter by Leonard Swett.

CHAPTER XIX.

Lincoln face to face with the realities of civil war.—Master of the situation.—The distrust of old politicians.—How the President viewed the battle of Bull Run.—An interesting reminiscence by Robert L. Wilson.—Lincoln's plan to suppress the Rebellion.—Dealing with McClellan and Grant.— Efforts to hasten the Emancipation Proclamation.—Lincoln withstands the pressure.—Calling the Cabinet together and reading the decree.—The letter to the "Unconditional-Union" men.—The campaign of 1864.—Lincoln and Andrew Johnson nominated and elected.—The sensational report of Judge Advocate General Holt.—Interesting statements by David Davis and Joseph E. McDonald.—How the President retained Indiana in the column of Republican

CHAPTER XX.

APPENDIX.

THE LIFE OF LINCOLN.

Your Friend
W. H. Herndon

CHAPTER I.

Beyond the fact that he was born on the 12th day of February, 1809, in Hardin county, Kentucky, Mr. Lincoln usually had but little to say of himself, the lives of his parents, or the history of the family before their removal to Indiana. If he mentioned the subject at all, it was with great reluctance and significant reserve. There was something about his origin he never cared to dwell upon. His nomination for the Presidency in 1860, however, made the publication of his life a necessity, and attracted to Springfield an army of campaign biographers and newspaper men. They met him in his office, stopped him in his walks, and followed him to his house. Artists came to paint his picture, and sculptors to make his bust. His autographs were in demand, and people came long distances to shake him by the hand. This sudden elevation to national prominence found Mr. Lincoln unprepared in a great measure for the unaccustomed demonstrations that awaited him. While he was easy of approach and equally courteous to all, yet, as he said to me one evening after a long day of hand-shaking, he could not understand why people should make so much over him.

Among the earliest newspaper men to arrive in Springfield after the Chicago convention was the late J. L. Scripps of the Chicago *Tribune*, who proposed to prepare a history of his life. Mr. Lincoln deprecated the idea of writing even a campaign biography. "Why, Scripps," said he, "it is a great piece of folly to attempt to make anything out of me or my early life. It can all be condensed into a single sentence, and that sentence you will find in Gray's Elegy,

'The short and simple annals of the poor.'

That's my life, and that's all you or anyone else can make out of it."[1]

He did, however, communicate some facts and meagre incidents of his early days, and, with the matter thus obtained, Mr. Scripps prepared his book. Soon after the death of Lincoln I received a letter from Scripps, in which, among other things, he recalled the meeting with Lincoln, and the view he took of the biography matter.

"Lincoln seemed to be painfully impressed," he wrote, "with the extreme poverty of his early surroundings, and the utter absence of all romantic and heroic elements. He communicated some facts to me concerning his ancestry, which he did not wish to have published then, and which I have never spoken of or alluded to before."

What the facts referred to by Mr. Scripps were we do not know; for he died several years ago without, so far as is known, revealing them to anyone.

On the subject of his ancestry and origin I only remember one time when Mr. Lincoln ever referred to it. It was about 1850, when he and I were driving in his one-horse buggy to the court in Menard county, Illinois. The suit we were going to try was one in which we were likely, either directly or collaterally, to touch upon the subject of hereditary traits. During the ride he spoke, for the first time in my hearing, of his mother,° dwelling on her characteristics, and mentioning or enumerating what qualities he inherited from her. He said, among other things, that she was the illegitimate daughter of Lucy Hanks and a well-bred Virginia farmer or planter; and he argued that from this last source came his power of analysis, his logic, his mental activity, his ambition, and all the qualities that distinguished him from the other members and descendants of the Hanks family.[3] His theory in discussing the matter of hereditary traits had been, that, for certain reasons, illegitimate children are oftentimes sturdier and brighter than those born in lawful wedlock; and in his case, he believed that his better nature and finer qualities came from this broad-minded, unknown Virginian. The revelation—painful as it was—called up the recollection of his mother, and, as the buggy jolted over the road, he added ruefully, "God bless my mother; all that I am or ever hope to be I owe to her,"† and immediately lapsed into silence. Our interchange of ideas ceased, and we rode on for some time without exchanging a word. He was sad and absorbed. Burying himself in thought, and musing no doubt over the disclosure he had just made, he drew round him a barrier which I

°Dennis and John Hanks have always insisted that Lincoln's mother was not a Hanks, but a Sparrow. Both of them wrote to me that such was the fact. Their object in insisting on this is apparent when it is shown that Nancy Hanks was the daughter of Lucy Hanks, who *afterward* married Henry Sparrow. It will be observed that Mr. Lincoln claimed that his mother was a Hanks.[2]

†If anyone will take the pains to read the Fell autobiography they will be struck with Lincoln's meagre reference to his mother. He even fails to give her maiden or Christian name, and devotes but three lines to her family. A history of the Lincolns occupies almost an entire page.[4]

feared to penetrate. His words and melancholy tone made a deep impression on me. It was an experience I can never forget. As we neared the town of Petersburg we were overtaken by an old man who rode beside us for awhile, and entertained us with reminiscences of days on the frontier. Lincoln was reminded of several Indiana stories, and by the time we had reached the unpretentious court-house at our destination, his sadness had passed away.

In only two instances did Mr. Lincoln over his own hand leave any record of his history or family descent. One of these was the modest bit of autobiography furnished to Jesse W. Fell, in 1859, in which, after stating that his parents were born in Virginia of "undistinguished or second families," he makes the brief mention of his mother, saying that she came "of a family of the name of Hanks." The other record was the register of marriages, births, and deaths which he made in his father's Bible.[5] The latter now lies before me. That portion of the page which probably contained the record of the marriage of his parents, Thomas Lincoln and Nancy Hanks, has been lost; but fortunately the records of Washington county, Kentucky, and the certificate of the minister who performed the marriage ceremony—the Rev. Jesse Head—fix the fact and date of the latter on the 12th day of June, 1806.

On the 10th day of February in the following year a daughter Sarah° was born, and two years later, on the 12th of February, the subject of these memoirs came into the world. After him came the last child, a boy—named Thomas after his father—who lived but a few days. No mention of his existence is found in the Bible record.

After Mr. Lincoln† had attained some prominence in the world, persons who

---

° Most biographers of Lincoln, in speaking of Mr. Lincoln's sister, call her Nancy, some—notably Nicolay and Hay—insisting that she was known by that name among her family and friends. In this they are in error. I have interviewed the different members of the Hanks and Lincoln families who survived the President, and her name was invariably given as Sarah. The mistake, I think, arises from the fact that, in the Bible record referred to, all that portion relating to the birth of "Sarah, daughter of Thomas and Nancy Lincoln," down to the word Nancy has been torn away, and the latter name has therefore been erroneously taken for that of the daughter. Reading the entry of Abraham's birth below satisfies one that it must refer to the mother.

† Regarding the paternity of Lincoln a great many surmises and a still larger amount of unwritten or, at least, unpublished history have drifted into the currents of western lore and journalism. A number of such traditions are extant in Kentucky and other localities. Mr. Weik has spent considerable time investigating the truth of a report current in Bourbon county, Kentucky, that Thomas Lincoln, for a consideration from one Abraham Inlow, a miller there, assumed the paternity of the infant child of a poor girl named Nancy Hanks; and, after marriage, removed with her to Washington or Hardin county, where the son, who was named "Abraham, after his real, and Lincoln after his putative, father," was born. A prominent citizen of the town of Mount Sterling in that state, who was at one time judge of the court and subsequently editor of a newspaper, and who was descended from the Abraham Inlow mentioned, has written a long argument in support of his alleged kinship through this source to Mr. Lincoln. He emphasizes the striking similarity in stature, facial features, and length of arms, notwithstanding the well established fact that the first-born child of the real Nancy Hanks was not a boy but a girl; and that the marriage did not take place in Bourbon, but in Washington county.[6]

knew both himself and his father were constantly pointing to the want of resemblance between the two.[7] The old gentleman was not only devoid of energy, and shiftless, but dull, and these persons were unable to account for the source of his son's ambition and his intellectual superiority over other men. Hence the charge so often made in Kentucky that Mr. Lincoln was in reality the offspring of a Hardin or a Marshall, or that he had in his veins the blood of some of the noted families who held social and intellectual sway in the western part of the State. These serious hints were the outgrowth of the campaign of 1860, which was conducted with such unrelenting prejudice in Kentucky that in the county where Lincoln was born only six persons could be found who had the courage to vote for him.[*] I remember that after his nomination for the Presidency Mr. Lincoln received from Kentucky many inquiries about his family and origin. This curiosity on the part of the people in one who had attained such prominence was perfectly natural, but it never pleased him in the least; in fact, to one man who was endeavoring to establish a relationship through the Hanks family he simply answered, "You are mistaken about my mother,"[9] without explaining the mistake or making further mention of the matter. Samuel Haycraft, the clerk of the Court in Hardin county, invited him to visit the scenes of his birth and boyhood, which led him to say this in a letter, June 4, 1860:[†] "You suggest that a visit to the place of my nativity might be pleasant to me. Indeed it would, but would it be safe? Would not the people lynch me?"[11] That reports reflecting on his origin and descent should arise in a community in which he felt that his life was unsafe is by no means surprising. Abraham Lincoln,[‡] the grandfather of the President, emigrated to Jefferson county, Kentucky, from Virginia about 1780, and from that time forward the former State became an important one in the history of the family, for in it was destined to be born its most illustrious member. About five years before this, a handful of Virginians had started across the mountains for Kentucky, and in the company, besides their historian, William Calk,—whose diary recently came to light,—was one Abraham Hanks.[12] They were evidently a crowd of jolly young men bent on adventure and fun, but their sport was attended with frequent disasters. Their journey began at "Mr. Priges' tavern on the Rapidan." When only a few days out "Hanks' Dog's leg got broke." Later in the course of the journey, Hanks and another companion became separated from the rest of the party and were lost in the mountains for two days; in crossing a stream "Abraham's saddle turned over and his load all fell in Indian creek;" finally they meet their brethren from whom they have been separated and then pursue their way without further interruption. Returning emigrants whom they meet, according to the journal of Calk, "tell such News of the indians" that certain members of the company are "afrade to go aney further." The following day more or less demoralization takes place among the members of this pioneer party when the announcement is made, as their chronicler so faithfully records it, that "Philip Drake Bakes bread without washing his hands." This was an unpardonable sin, and at it they revolted. A day later the record shows that "Abram turns Back." Beyond this we shall never know what became of Abraham Hanks, for no further mention of him is made in this or any other history. He may have returned to Virginia and become, for aught we know, one of the President's ancestors on the maternal side of the house; but if so his illustrious descendant was never able to establish the fact or trace his lineage satisfactorily beyond the first generation which preceded him. He never mentioned who his maternal grandfather was, if indeed he knew.

His paternal grandfather, Abraham Lincoln,° the pioneer from Virginia, met his death within two years after his settlement in Kentucky at the hands of the Indians; "not in battle," as his distinguished grandson tells us, "but by stealth, when he was laboring to open a farm in the forest."[14] The story of his death in sight of his youngest son Thomas, then only six years old, is by no means a new one to the world. In fact I have often heard the President describe the tragedy as he had inherited the story from his father. The dead pioneer had three sons, Mordecai, Josiah, and Thomas, in the order named. When the father fell, Mordecai, having hastily sent Josiah to the neighboring fort after assistance, ran into the cabin, and pointing his rifle through a crack between the logs, prepared for defense. Presently an Indian came stealing up to the dead father's body. Beside the latter sat the little boy Thomas. Mordecai took deliberate aim at a silver crescent which hung suspended from the Indian's breast, and brought him to the ground. Josiah returned from the fort with the desired relief, and the savages were easily dispersed, leaving behind one dead and one wounded.

The tragic death of his father filled Mordecai with an intense hatred of the Indians—a feeling from which he never recovered. It was ever with him like an avenging spirit. From Jefferson county he removed to Grayson, where he spent

---

°"They [the Lincolns] were also called Linkhorns. The old settlers had a way of pronouncing names not as they were spelled, but rather, it seemed, as they pleased. Thus they called Medcalf 'Medcap,' and Kaster they pronounced 'Custard.'"—MS. letter, Charles Friend, March 19, 1866.[13]

the remainder of his days.[15] A correspondent* from there wrote me in 1865: "Old Mordecai was easily stirred up by the sight of an Indian. One time, hearing of a few Indians passing through the county, he mounted his horse, and taking his rifle on his shoulder, followed on after them and was gone two days. When he returned he said he left one lying in a sink hole. The Indians, he said, had killed his father, and he was determined before he died to have satisfaction."[16] The youngest boy, Thomas, retained a vivid recollection of his father's death, which, together with other reminiscences of his boyhood, he was fond of relating later in life to his children to relieve the tedium of long winter evenings. Mordecai and Josiah,† both remaining in Kentucky, became the heads of good-sized families, and although never known or heard of outside the limits of the neighborhoods in which they lived, were intelligent, well-to-do men. In Thomas, roving and shiftless, to whom was "reserved the honor of an illustrious paternity," are we alone interested.[18] He was, we are told, five feet ten inches high, weighed one hundred and ninety-five pounds, had a well-rounded face, dark hazel eyes, coarse black hair, and was slightly stoop-shouldered. His build was so compact that Dennis Hanks used to say he could not find the point of separation between his ribs. He was proverbially slow of movement, mentally and physically; was careless, inert, and dull; was sinewy, and gifted with great strength; was inoffensively quiet and peaceable, but when roused to resistance a dangerous antagonist. He had a liking for jokes and stories, which was one of the few traits he transmitted to his illustrious son; was fond of the chase, and had no marked aversion for the bottle, though in the latter case he indulged no more freely than the average Kentuckian of his day. At the time of his marriage to Nancy Hanks he could neither read nor write; but his wife, who was gifted with more education, and was otherwise his mental superior, taught him, it is said, to write his name and to read—at least, he was able in later years to spell his way slowly through the Bible. In his religious belief he first affiliated with the Free-Will Baptists. After his removal to Indiana he changed his adherence to the Presbyterians—or Predestinarians, as they were then called—and later united with the Christian—vulgarly called Campbellite—Church, in which latter faith he is supposed to have died. He was a carpenter by trade, and essayed farming too; but in this, as in almost every other undertaking, he was singularly unsuccessful.

---

*W. T. Claggett, unpublished MS.

†"I knew Mordecai and Josiah Lincoln intimately. They were excellent men, plain, moderately educated, candid in their manners and intercourse, and looked upon as honorable as any men I have ever heard of. Mordecai was the oldest son, and his father having been killed by the Indians before the law of primogeniture was repealed, he inherited a very competent estate. The others were poor. Mordecai was celebrated for his bravery, and had been in the early campaigns of the West."—Henry Pirtle, letter, June 17, 1865, MS.[17]

He was placed in possession of several tracts of land at different times in his life, but was never able to pay for a single one of them. The farm on which he died was one his son purchased, providing a life estate therein for him and his wife. He never fell in with the routine of labor; was what some people would call unfortunate or unlucky in all his business ventures—if in reality he ever made one—and died near the village of Farmington in Coles county, Illinois, on the 17th day of January, 1851. His son, on account of sickness in his own family, was unable to be present at his father's bedside, or witness his death. To those who notified him of his probable demise he wrote: "I sincerely hope that father may yet recover his health; but at all events tell him to remember to call upon and confide in our great and good and merciful Maker, who will not turn away from him in any extremity. He notes the fall of a sparrow, and numbers the hairs of our heads; and He will not forget the dying man who puts his trust in him. Say to him that if we could meet now it is doubtful whether it would not be more painful than pleasant; but that if it be his lot to go now he will soon have a joyous meeting with the many loved ones gone before, and where the rest of us, through the help of God, hope ere long to join them."°

Nancy Hanks, the mother of the President, at a very early age was taken

House in Which Thomas Lincoln Died, Near Farmington, Coles County, Ill. (after recent photograph)

°MS. letter to John Johnston, Jan. 12, 1851.[19]

from her mother Lucy—afterwards married to Henry Sparrow—and sent to live with her aunt and uncle, Thomas and Betsy Sparrow.[20] Under this same roof the irrepressible and cheerful waif, Dennis Hanks*—whose name will be frequently seen in these pages—also found a shelter. At the time of her marriage to Thomas Lincoln, Nancy was in her twenty-third year. She was above the ordinary height in stature, weighed about 130 pounds, was slenderly built, and had much the appearance of one inclined to consumption. Her skin was dark, hair dark brown; eyes gray and small; forehead prominent; face sharp and angular, with a marked expression of melancholy which fixed itself in the memory of everyone who ever saw or knew her. Though her life was seemingly beclouded by a spirit of sadness, she was in disposition amiable and generally cheerful. Mr. Lincoln himself said to me in 1851, on receiving the news of his father's death, that whatever might be said of his parents, and however unpromising the early surroundings of his mother may have been, she was highly intellectual by nature, had a strong memory, acute judgment, and was cool and heroic. From a mental standpoint she no doubt rose above her surroundings, and had she lived, the stimulus of her nature would have accelerated her son's success, and she would have been a much more ambitious prompter than his father ever was.

As a family the Hankses were peculiar to the civilization of early Kentucky. Illiterate and superstitious, they corresponded to that nomadic class still to be met with throughout the South, and known as "poor whites." They are happily and vividly depicted in the description of a camp-meeting held at Elizabethtown, Kentucky, in 1806, which was furnished me in August, 1865, by an eye-witness.† "The Hanks girls," narrates the latter, "were great at camp-meetings. I remember one in 1806. I will give you a scene, and if you will then read the books written on the subject you may find some apology for the superstition that was said to be in Abe Lincoln's character. It was at a camp-meeting, as before said, when a general shout was about to commence. Preparations were being made; a young lady invited me to stand on a bench by her side where we could see all over the altar. To the right a strong, athletic young man, about twenty-five years old, was being put in trim for the occasion, which was done by divesting him of all apparel except shirt and pants. On the left a young lady was being put in trim in much the same manner, so that her clothes would not be in the way, and so that, when her combs flew out, her hair would go into graceful braids. She, too, was young—not

---

*Dennis Hanks, still living at the age of ninety years in Illinois, was the son of another Nancy Hanks—the aunt of the President's mother. I have his written statement that he came into the world through nature's back-door. He never stated, if he knew it, who his father was.[21]

†J. B. Helm, MS.

more than twenty perhaps. The performance commenced about the same time by the young man on the right and the young lady on the left. Slowly and gracefully they worked their way towards the centre, singing, shouting, hugging and kissing, generally their own sex, until at last nearer and nearer they came. The centre of the altar was reached, and the two closed, with their arms around each other, the man singing and shouting at the top of his voice,

"'I have my Jesus in my arms
Sweet as honey, strong as bacon ham.'

"Just at this moment the young lady holding to my arm whispered, 'They are to be married next week; her name is Hanks.' There were very few who did not believe this true religion, inspired by the Holy Spirit, and the man who could not believe it, did well to keep it to himself. The Hankses were the finest singers and shouters in our country."[22]

Here my informant stops, and on account of his death several years ago I failed to learn whether the young lady shouter who figured in the foregoing scene was the President's mother or not. The fact that Nancy Hanks did marry that year gives color to the belief that it was she. As to the probability of the young man being Thomas Lincoln it is difficult to say; such a performance as the one described must have required a little more emotion and enthusiasm than the tardy and inert carpenter was in the habit of manifesting.

CHAPTER II.

Sarah, the sister of Abraham Lincoln, though in some respects like her brother, lacked his stature.[1] She was thick-set, had dark-brown hair, deep-gray eyes, and an even disposition. In contact with others she was kind and considerate. Her nature was one of amiability, and God had endowed her with that invincible combination—modesty and good sense. Strange to say, Mr. Lincoln never said much about his sister in after years, and we are really indebted to the Hankses—Dennis and John—for the little we have learned about this rather unfortunate young woman. She was married to Aaron Grigsby, in Spencer county, Indiana, in the month of August, 1826, and died January 20, 1828. Her brother accompanied her to school while they lived in Kentucky, but as he was only seven, and as she had not yet finished her ninth year when their father removed with them to Indiana, it is to be presumed that neither made much progress in the matter of school education. Still it is authoritatively stated that they attended two schools during their short period.[2] One of these was kept by Zachariah Riney, the other by Caleb Hazel. It is difficult at this late day to learn much of the boy Abraham's life during those seven years of residence in Kentucky. One man,[*] who was a clerk in the principal store in the village where the Lincolns purchased their family supplies, remembers him as a "small boy who came sometimes to the store with his mother. He would take his seat on a keg of nails, and I would give him a lump of sugar. He would sit there and eat it like any other boy; but these little acts of kindness," observes my informant, in an enthusiastic statement made in 1865, "so impressed his mind that I made a steadfast friend in a man whose power and influence have since been felt

[*]John B. Helm, June 20, 1865.

throughout the world."[3] A school-mate° of Lincoln's at Hazel's school, speaking of the master, says: "He perhaps could teach spelling and reading and indifferent writing, and possibly could cipher to the rule of three; but he had no other qualification of a teacher, unless we accept large size and bodily strength. Abe was a mere spindle of a boy, had his due proportion of harmless mischief, but as we lived in a country abounding in hazel switches, in the virtue of which the master had great faith, Abe of course received his due allowance."[4]

This part of the boy's history is painfully vague and dim, and even after arriving at man's estate Mr. Lincoln was significantly reserved when reference was made to it. It is barely mentioned in the autobiography furnished to Fell in 1859. John Duncan,† afterwards a preacher of some prominence in Kentucky, relates how he and Abe on one occasion ran a ground-hog into a crevice between two rocks, and after working vainly almost two hours to get him out, "Abe ran off about a quarter of a mile to a blacksmith shop, and returned with an iron hook fastened to the end of a pole," and with this rude contrivance they virtually "hooked" the animal out of his retreat.[5] Austin Gollaher of Hodgensville, claims to have saved Lincoln from drowning one day as they were trying to "coon it" across Knob creek on a log. The boys were in pursuit of birds, when young Lincoln fell into the water, and his vigilant companion, who still survives to narrate the thrilling story, fished him out with a sycamore branch.[6]

Meanwhile Thomas Lincoln was becoming daily more dissatisfied with his situation and surroundings. He had purchased, since his marriage, on the easy terms then prevalent, two farms or tracts of land in succession; but none was easy enough for him, and the land, when the time for the payment of the purchase-money rolled around, reverted to its former owner. Kentucky, at that day, afforded few if any privileges, and possessed fewer advantages to allure the poor man; and no doubt so it seemed to Thomas Lincoln. The land he occupied was sterile and broken. A mere barren glade, and destitute of timber, it required a persistent effort to coax a living out of it; and to one of his easy-going disposition, life there was a never-ending struggle. Stories of vast stretches of rich and unoccupied lands in Indiana reaching his ears, and despairing of the prospect of any betterment in his condition so long as he remained in Kentucky, he resolved, at last, to leave the State and seek a more inviting lodgment beyond the Ohio. The assertion made by some of Mr. Lincoln's biographers, and so often repeated by sentimental writers, that his father left Kentucky to avoid the sight of or contact

°Samuel Haycraft, December 6, 1866.
†Letter, February 21, 1867.

with slavery, lacks confirmation.[7] In all Hardin county—at that time a large area of territory—there were not over fifty slaves; and it is doubtful if he saw enough of slavery to fill him with the righteous opposition to the institution with which he has so frequently been credited. Moreover, he never in later years manifested any especial aversion to it.

Having determined on emigrating to Indiana, he began preparations for removal in the fall of 1816 by building for his use a flat-boat. Loading it with his tools and other personal effects, including in the invoice, as we are told, four hundred gallons of whiskey, he launched his "crazy craft" on a tributary of Salt creek known as the Rolling Fork.[8] Along with the current he floated down to the Ohio river, but his rudely-made vessel, either from the want of experience in its navigator, or because of its ill adaptation to withstand the force and caprices of the currents in the great river, capsized one day, and boat and cargo went to the bottom. The luckless boatman set to work however, and by dint of great patience and labor succeeded in recovering the tools and the bulk of the whiskey. Righting his boat, he continued down the river, landing at a point called Thompson's Ferry, in Perry county, on the Indiana side. Here he disposed of his vessel, and placing his goods in the care of a settler named Posey, he struck out through the interior in search of a location for his new home. Sixteen miles back from the river he found one that pleased his fancy, and he marked it off for himself. His next move in the order of business was a journey to Vincennes to purchase the tract at the Land Office—under the "two-dollar-an-acre law," as Dennis Hanks puts it—and a return to the land to identify it by blazing the trees and piling up brush on the corners to establish the proper boundary lines. Having secured a place for his home he trudged back to Kentucky—walking all the way—for his family. Two horses brought them and all their household effects to the Indiana shore. Posey kindly gave or hired them the use of a wagon, into which they packed not only their furniture and carpenter tools, but the liquor, which it is presumed had lain undisturbed in the former's cellar. Slowly and carefully picking their way through the dense woods, they at last reached their destination on the banks of Little Pigeon creek. There were some detentions on the way, but no serious mishaps.[9]

The head of the household now set resolutely to work to build a shelter for his family.

The structure, when completed, was fourteen feet square, and was built of small unhewn logs. In the language of the day, it was called a "half-faced camp," being enclosed on all sides but one. It had neither floor, door, nor windows. In this forbidding hovel these doughty emigrants braved the exposure of the varying seasons for an entire year. At the end of that time Thomas and Betsy Sparrow followed, bringing with them Dennis Hanks; and to them Thomas Lincoln surrendered the "half-faced camp," while he moved into a more pretentious structure—a cabin enclosed on all sides. The country was thickly covered with forests of walnut, beech, oak, elm, maple, and an undergrowth of dog-wood, sumac, and wild grape-vine. In places where the growth was not so thick grass came up abundantly, and hogs found plenty of food in the unlimited quantity of mast the woods afforded. The country abounded in bear, deer, turkey, and other wild game, which not only satisfied the pioneer's love for sport, but furnished his table with its supply of meat.[10]

Thomas Lincoln, with the aid of the Hankses and Sparrows, was for a time an attentive farmer. The implements of agriculture then in use were as rude as they were rare, and yet there is nothing to show that in spite of the slow methods then in vogue he did not make commendable speed. "We raised corn mostly"—relates Dennis—"and some wheat—enough for a cake Sunday morning. Hog and venison hams were a legal tender, and coon skins also. We raised sheep and cattle, but they did not bring much. Cows and calves were only worth

Dennis Hanks

six to eight dollars; corn ten cents, and wheat twenty-five cents, a bushel."[11] So with all his application and frugality the head of this ill-assorted household made but little headway in the accumulation of the world's goods. We are told that he was indeed a poor man, and that during his entire stay in Indiana his land barely yielded him sufficient return to keep his larder supplied with the most common necessities of life. His skill as a hunter—though never brought into play unless at the angered demand of a stomach hungry for meat—in no slight degree made up for the lack of good management in the cultivation of his land. His son Abraham* never evinced the same fondness for hunting, although his cousin Dennis with much pride tells us how he could kill a wild turkey on the wing.[12] "At that time,"[13] relates one of the latter's playmates,† descanting on the abundance of wild game, "there were a great many deer-licks; and Abe and myself would go to these licks sometimes and watch of nights to kill deer, though Abe was not so fond of a gun or the sport as I was."‡

The cabin to which the Lincoln family removed after leaving the little half-faced camp to the Sparrows was in some respects a pretentious structure. It was of hewed logs, and was eighteen feet square. It was high enough to admit of a loft, where Abe slept, and to which he ascended each night by means of pegs driven in the wall. The rude furniture was in keeping with the surroundings. Three-legged stools answered for chairs. The bedstead, made of poles fastened in the cracks of the logs on one side, and supported by a crotched stick driven in the ground floor on the other, was covered with skins, leaves, and old clothes. A table of the same finish as the stools, a few pewter dishes, a Dutch oven, and a

---

*Abe was a good boy—an affectionate one—a boy who loved his parents well and was obedient to their every wish. Although anything but an impudent or rude boy he was sometimes uncomfortably inquisitive. When strangers would ride along or pass by his father's fence he always—either through boyish pride or to tease his father—would be sure to ask the first question. His father would sometimes knock him over. When thus punished he never bellowed, but dropped a kind of silent, unwelcome tear as evidence of his sensitiveness or other feelings."—Dennis Hanks, MS., June 13, 1865.

†David Turnham, MS. letter, June 10, 1866.

‡Mr. Lincoln used to relate the following "coon" story: His father had at home a little yellow house-dog, which invariably gave the alarm if the boys undertook to slip away unobserved after night had set in—as they oftentimes did—to go coon hunting. One evening Abe and his step-brother, John Johnston, with the usual complement of boys required in a successful coon hunt, took the insignificant little cur with them. They located the coveted coon, killed him, and then in a sportive vein sewed the hide on the diminutive yellow dog. The latter struggled vigorously during the operation of sewing on, and being released from the hands of his captors made a bee-line for home. Other large and more important canines, on the way, scenting coon, tracked the little animal home, and possibly mistaking him for real coon, speedily demolished him. The next morning old Thomas Lincoln discovered lying in his yard the lifeless remains of yellow "Joe," with strong proof of coon-skin accompaniment. "Father was much incensed at his death," observed Mr. Lincoln, in relating the story, "but as John and I, scantily protected from the morning wind, stood shivering in the doorway, we felt assured little yellow Joe would never be able again to sound the call for another coon hunt."[14]

skillet completed the household outfit.[15] In this uninviting frontier structure the future President was destined to pass the greater part of his boyhood. Withal his spirits were light, and it cannot be denied that he must have enjoyed unrestrained pleasure in his surroundings. It is related that one day the only thing that graced the dinner-table was a dish of roasted potatoes. The elder Lincoln, true to the custom of the day, returned thanks for the blessing. The boy, realizing the scant proportions of the meal, looked up into his father's face and irreverently observed, "Dad, I call these"—meaning the potatoes—"mighty poor blessings."[16] Among other children of a similar age he seemed unconsciously to take the lead, and it is no stretch of the truth to say that they, in turn, looked up to him. He may have been a little precocious—children sometimes are—but in view of the summary treatment received at the hands of his father it cannot truthfully be said he was a "spoiled child." One morning when his mother was at work he ran into the cabin from the outside to enquire, with a quizzical grin, "Who was the father of Zebedee's children?"[17] As many another mother before and since has done, she brushed the mischievous young inquirer aside to attend to some more important detail of household concern.*

The dull routine of chores and household errands in the boy's every-day life was brightened now and then by a visit to the mill. I often in later years heard Mr. Lincoln say that going to mill gave him the greatest pleasure of his boyhood days.

"We had to go seven miles to mill," relates David Turnham, the friend of his youth, "and then it was a hand-mill that would only grind from fifteen to twenty bushels of corn in a day. There was but little wheat grown at that time, and when we did have wheat we had to grind it in the mill described and use it without bolting, as there were no bolts in the country. Abe and I had to do the milling, frequently going twice to get one grist."[18]

In his eleventh year he began that marvellous and rapid growth in stature for which he was so widely noted in the Pigeon creek settlement. "As he shot up,"[19] says Turnham, "he seemed to change in appearance and action. Although quick-witted and ready with an answer, he began to exhibit deep thoughtfulness, and was so often lost in studied reflection we could not help noticing the strange turn in his actions. He disclosed rare timidity and sensitiveness, especially in the presence of men and women, and although cheerful enough in the presence of the boys, he did not appear to seek our company as earnestly as before."† It was only the development we find in the history of every boy. Nature was a little

*Harriet Chapman, MS. letter.
†D. Turnham, MS. letter.

abrupt in the case of Abraham Lincoln; she tossed him from the nimbleness of boyhood to the gravity of manhood in a single night.

In the fall of 1818, the scantily settled region in the vicinity of Pigeon creek— where the Lincolns were then living—suffered a visitation of that dread disease common in the West in early days, and known in the vernacular of the frontier as "the milk-sick." It hovered like a spectre over the Pigeon creek settlement for over ten years, and its fatal visitation and inroads among the Lincolns, Hankses, and Sparrows finally drove that contingent into Illinois. To this day the medical profession has never agreed upon any definite cause for the malady, nor have they in all their scientific wrangling determined exactly what the disease itself is. A physician, who has in his practice met a number of cases, describes the symptoms to be "a whitish coat on the tongue, burning sensation of the stomach, severe vomiting, obstinate constipation of the bowels, coolness of the extremities, great restlessness and jactitation, pulse rather small, somewhat more frequent than natural, and slightly chorded. In the course of the disease the coat on the tongue becomes brownish and dark, the countenance dejected, and the prostration of the patient is great. A fatal termination may take place in sixty hours, or life may be prolonged for a period of fourteen days. These are the symptoms of the disease in an acute form. Sometimes it runs into the chronic form, or it may assume that form from the commencement, and after months or years the patient may finally die or recover only a partial degree of health."[20]

When the disease broke out in the Pigeon creek region it not only took off the people, but it made sad havoc among the cattle. One man testifies that he "lost four milch cows and eleven calves in one week." This, in addition to the risk of losing his own life, was enough, he declared, to ruin him, and prompted him to leave for "points further west."[21]

Early in October of the year 1818, Thomas and Betsy Sparrow fell ill of the disease and died within a few days of each other. Thomas Lincoln performed the services of undertaker. With his whipsaw he cut out the lumber, and with commendable promptness he nailed together the rude coffins to enclose the forms of the dead. The bodies were borne to a scantily cleared knoll in the midst of the forest, and there, without ceremony, quietly let down into the grave. Meanwhile Abe's mother had also fallen a victim to the insidious disease. Her sufferings, however, were destined to be of brief duration. Within a week she too rested from her labors. "She struggled on, day by day," says one of the household, "a good Christian woman, and died on the seventh day after she was taken sick. Abe and his sister Sarah waited on their mother, and did the little jobs and errands required of them. There was no physician nearer than thirty-five miles. The mother knew she was going to die, and called the children to her bedside. She was very weak, and the children leaned over while she gave her last message. Placing her feeble hand on little Abe's head she told him to be kind and good to his father and sister; to both she said, 'Be good to one another,' expressing a hope that they might live, as they had been taught by her, to love their kindred and worship God."[22] Amid the miserable surroundings of a home in the wilderness Nancy Hanks passed across the dark river. Though of lowly birth, the victim of poverty and hard usage, she takes a place in history as the mother of a son who liberated a race of men. At her side stands another Mother whose son performed a similar service for all mankind eighteen hundred years before.

After the death of their mother little Abe and his sister Sarah began a dreary life—indeed, one more cheerless and less inviting seldom falls to the lot of any child. In a log-cabin without a floor, scantily protected from the severities of the weather, deprived of the comfort of a mother's love, they passed through a winter the most dismal either one ever experienced. Within a few months, and before the close of the winter, David Elkin, an itinerant preacher whom Mrs. Lincoln had known in Kentucky, happened into the settlement, and in response to the invitation from the family and friends, delivered a funeral sermon over her grave. No one is able now to remember the language of Parson Elkin's discourse, but it is recalled that he commemorated the virtues and good phases of character, and passed in silence the few shortcomings and frailties of the poor woman sleeping under the winter's snow. She had done her work in this world. Stoop-shouldered, thin-breasted, sad,—at times miserable,—groping through the perplexities of life, without prospect of any betterment in her condition, she passed from earth, little dreaming of the grand future that lay in store for the ragged, hapless little boy who stood at her bed-side in the last days of her life.[23]

Thomas Lincoln's widowerhood was brief. He had scarcely mourned the death of his first wife a year until he reäppeared in Kentucky at Elizabethtown in search of another. His admiration had centred for a second time on Sally Bush, the widow of Daniel Johnston, the jailer of Hardin county, who had died several years before of a disease known as the "cold plague." The tradition still kept alive in the Kentucky neighborhood is that Lincoln had been a suitor for the hand of the lady before his marriage to Nancy Hanks, but that she had rejected him for the hand of the more fortunate Johnston. However that may have been, it is certain that he began his campaign in earnest this time, and after a brief siege won her heart. "He made a very short courtship," wrote Samuel Haycraft° to me in

---

°Clerk of the Court.

Sarah Bush Lincoln (after
photograph in author's
possession)

a letter, December 7, 1866. "He came to see her on the first day of December,
1819, and in a straightforward manner told her that they had known each other
from childhood. '*Miss* Johnston,' said he, 'I have no wife and you no husband.
I came a-purpose to marry you. I knowed you from a gal and you knowed me
from a boy. I've no time to lose; and if you're willin' let it be done straight off.'
She replied that she could not marry him right off, as she had some little debts
which she wanted to pay first. He replied, 'Give me a list of them.' He got the
list and paid them that evening. Next morning I issued the license, and they were
married within sixty yards of my house."[24]

Lincoln's brother-in-law, Ralph Krume, and his four horses and spacious
wagon were again brought into requisition. With commendable generosity he
transported the newly married pair and their household effects to their home in
Indiana. The new Mrs. Lincoln was accompanied by her three children, John,
Sarah, and Matilda. Her social status is fixed by the comparison of a neighbor,
who observed that "life among the Hankses, the Lincolns, and the Enlows was
a long ways below life among the Bushes."[25]

In the eyes of her spouse she could not be regarded as a poor widow. She
was the owner of a goodly stock of furniture and household goods; bringing
with her among other things a walnut bureau valued at fifty dollars. What effect
the new family, their collection of furniture, cooking utensils, and comfort-

able bedding must have had on the astonished and motherless pair who from the door of Thomas Lincoln's forlorn cabin watched the well-filled wagon as it came creaking through the woods can better be imagined than described. Surely Sarah and Abe, as the stores of supplies were rolled in through the doorless doorways, must have believed that a golden future awaited them. The presence and smile of a motherly face in the cheerless cabin radiated sunshine into every neglected corner. If the Lincoln mansion did not in every respect correspond to the representations made by its owner to the new Mrs. Lincoln before marriage, the latter gave no expression of disappointment or even surprise. With true womanly courage and zeal she set resolutely to work to make right that which seemed wrong. Her husband was made to put a floor in the cabin, as well as to supply doors and windows. The cracks between the logs were plastered up. A clothes-press filled the space between the chimney jamb and the wall, and the mat of corn husks and leaves on which the children had slept in the corner gave way to the comfortable luxuriance of a feather bed. She washed the two orphans, and fitted them out in clothes taken from the stores of her own. The work of renovation in and around the cabin continued until even Thomas Lincoln himself, under the general stimulus of the new wife's presence, caught the inspiration, and developed signs of intense activity. The advent of Sarah Bush was certainly a red-letter day for the Lincolns. She was not only industrious and thrifty, but gentle and affectionate; and her newly adopted children for the first time, perhaps, realized the benign influence of a mother's love. Of young Abe she was especially fond, and we have her testimony that her kindness and care for him were warmly and bountifully returned.[26] Her granddaughter furnished me* in after years with this description of her:

"My grandmother is a very tall woman, straight as an Indian, of fair complexion, and was, when I first remember her, very handsome, sprightly, talkative, and proud. She wore her hair curled till gray; is kind-hearted and very charitable, and also very industrious."[27] In September, 1865, I visited the old lady† and spent an entire day with her. She was then living on the farm her stepson had purchased

---

*Harriet Chapman.

†During my interview with this old lady I was much and deeply impressed with the sincerity of her affection for her illustrious step-son. She declined to say much in answer to my questions about Nancy Hanks, her predecessor in the Lincoln household, but spoke feelingly of the latter's daughter and son. Describing Mr. Lincoln's last visit to her in February, 1861, she broke into tears and wept bitterly. "I did not want Abe to run for President," she sobbed, "and did not want to see him elected. I was afraid that something would happen to him, and when he came down to see me, after he was elected President, I still felt, and my heart told me, that something would befall Abe, and that I should never see him again. Abe and his father are in heaven now, I am sure, and I expect soon to go there and meet them."[28]

and given her, eight miles south of the town of Charleston, in Illinois. She died on the 10th of April, 1869.

The two sets of children in the Lincoln household—to their credit be it said—lived together in perfect accord. Abe was in his tenth year, and his stepmother, awake to the importance of an education, made a way for him to attend school. To her he seemed full of promise; and although not so quick of comprehension as other boys, yet she believed in encouraging his every effort. He had had a few weeks of schooling under Riney and Hazel in Kentucky, but it is hardly probable that he could read; he certainly could not write. As illustrating his moral make-up, I diverge from the chronological order of the narrative long enough to relate an incident which occurred some years later. In the Lincoln family, Matilda Johnston, or 'Tilda, as her mother called her, was the youngest child. After Abe had reached the estate of manhood, she was still in her 'teens. It was Abe's habit each morning one fall, to leave the house early, his axe on his shoulder, to clear a piece of forest which lay some distance from home. He frequently carried his dinner with him, and remained all day. Several times the young and frolicsome 'Tilda sought to accompany him, but was each time restrained by her mother, who firmly forbade a repetition of the attempt. One morning the girl escaped maternal vigilance, and slyly followed after the young woodman, who had gone some distance from the house, and was already hidden from view behind the dense growth of trees and underbrush. Following a deerpath, he went singing along, little dreaming of the girl in close pursuit. The latter gained on him, and when within a few feet, darted forward and with a cat-like leap landed squarely on his back. With one hand on each shoulder, she planted her knee in the middle of his back, and dexterously brought the powerful frame of the rail-splitter to the ground. It was a trick familiar to every schoolboy. Abe, taken by surprise, was unable at first to turn around or learn who his assailant was. In the fall to the ground, the sharp edge of the axe imbedded itself in the young lady's ankle, inflicting a wound from which there came a generous effusion of blood. With sundry pieces of cloth torn from Abe's shirt and the young lady's dress, the flow of blood was stanched, and the wound rudely bound up. The girl's cries having lessened somewhat, her tall companion, looking at her in blank astonishment, knowing what an infraction the whole thing was of her mother's oft-repeated instructions, asked; "'Tilda, what are you going to tell mother about getting hurt?"

"Tell her I did it with the axe," she sobbed. "That will be the truth, won't it?" To which last inquiry Abe manfully responded,

"Yes, that's the truth, but it's not all the truth. Tell the whole truth, 'Tilda, and trust your good mother for the rest."[29]

This incident was, many years afterward related to me by 'Tilda, who was then the mother of a devoted and interesting family herself.

Hazel Dorsey was Abe's first teacher in Indiana.[30] He held forth a mile and a half from the Lincoln farm. The school-house was built of round logs, and was just high enough for a man to stand erect under the loft. The floor was of split logs, or what were called puncheons. The chimney was made of poles and clay; and the windows were made by cutting out parts of two logs, placing pieces of split boards a proper distance apart, and over the aperture thus formed pasting pieces of greased paper to admit light. At school Abe evinced ability enough to gain him a prominent place in the respect of the teacher and the affections of his fellow-scholars.° Elements of leadership in him seem to have manifested themselves already. Nathaniel Grigsby—whose brother, Aaron, afterwards married Abe's sister, Sarah—attended the same school. He certifies to Abe's proficiency and worth in glowing terms.

"He was always at school early," writes Grigsby, "and attended to his studies. He was always at the head of his class, and passed us rapidly in his studies. He lost no time at home, and when he was not at work was at his books. He kept up his studies on Sunday, and carried his books with him to work, so that he might read when he rested from labor."[32] Now and then, the family exchequer running low, it would be found necessary for the young rail-splitter to stop school, and either work with his father on the farm, or render like service for the neighbors. These periods of work occurred so often and continued so long, that all his school days added together would not make a year in the aggregate. When he attended school, his sister Sarah usually accompanied him. "Sally was a quick-minded young woman," is the testimony of a school-mate. "She was more industrious than Abe, in my opinion. I can hear her good-humored laugh now. Like her brother, she could greet you kindly and put you at ease. She was really an intelligent woman."†

Abe's love for books, and his determined effort to obtain an education in spite of so many obstacles, induced the belief in his father's mind, that book-learning was absorbing a greater proportion of his energy and industry than the demands of the farm. The old gentleman had but little faith in the value of books or papers,‡ and

---

°"He always appeared to be very quiet during playtime; never was rude; seemed to have a liking for solitude; was the one chosen in almost every case to adjust difficulties between boys of his age and size, and when appealed to, his decision was an end of the trouble. He was also rather noted for keeping his clothes clean longer than any of the others, and although considered a boy of courage, had few, if any, difficulties."—E. R. Burba, letter, March 31, 1866.[31]

†Nat Grigsby, Sept. 12, 1865, MS.[33]

‡"I induced my husband to permit Abe to read and study at home as well as at school. At first he was not easily reconciled to it, but finally he too seemed willing to encourage him to a certain extent. Abe was a dutiful son to me always, and we took particular care when he was reading not to disturb him—would let him read on and on till he quit of his own accord."—Mrs. Thomas Lincoln, Sept. 8, 1865.[34]

hence the frequent drafts he made on the son to aid in the drudgery of daily toil. He undertook to teach him his own trade°—he was a carpenter and joiner—but Abe manifested such a striking want of interest that the effort to make a carpenter of him was soon abandoned.

At Dorsey's school Abe was ten years old; at the next one, Andrew Crawford's, he was about fourteen; and at Swaney's he was in his seventeenth year. The last school required a walk of over four miles, and on account of the distance his attendance was not only irregular but brief. Schoolmaster Crawford introduced a new feature in his school, and we can imagine its effect on his pupils, whose training had been limited to the social requirements of the backwoods settlement. It was instruction in manners. One scholar was required to go outside, and re-enter the room as a lady or gentleman would enter a drawing-room or parlor. Another scholar would receive the first party at the door, and escort him or her about the room, making polite introductions to each person in the room.[35] How the gaunt and clumsy Abe went through this performance we shall probably never know. If his awkward movements gave rise to any amusement, his school-mates never revealed it.

The books used at school were Webster's Spelling Book and the American Speller. All the scholars learned to cipher, and afterwards used Pike's Arithmetic. Mr. Lincoln told me in later years that Murray's English Reader was the best school-book ever put into the hands of an American youth. I conclude, therefore, he must have used that also. At Crawford's school Abe was credited with the authorship of several literary efforts—short dissertations in which he strove to correct some time-honored and wanton sport of the schoolboy. While in Indiana I met several persons who recalled a commendable and somewhat pretentious protest he wrote against cruelty to animals. The wholesome effects of a temperate life and the horrors of war were also subjects which claimed the services of his pen then, as they in later years demanded the devoted attention of his mind and heart.[36]

He was now over six feet high and was growing at a tremendous rate, for he added two inches more before the close of his seventeenth year, thus reaching the limit of his stature. He weighed in the region of a hundred and sixty pounds; was wiry, vigorous, and strong. His feet and hands were large, arms and legs long and in striking contrast with his slender trunk and small head. "His skin was shrivelled and yellow," declares one of the girls† who attended Crawford's school.[37] "His

---

°A little walnut cabinet, two feet high, and containing two rows of neat drawers, now in the possession of Captain J. W. Wartmann, clerk of the United States Court in Evansville, Ind., is carefully preserved as a specimen of the joint work of Lincoln and his father at this time.—J. W. W.
†Kate Gentry.

shoes, when he had any, were low. He wore buckskin breeches, linsey-woolsey shirt, and a cap made of the skin of a squirrel or coon. His breeches were baggy and lacked by several inches meeting the tops of his shoes, thereby exposing his shinbone, "sharp, blue, and narrow."[38] In one branch of school learning he was a great success; that was spelling. We are indebted to Kate Roby, a pretty miss of fifteen, for an incident which illustrates alike his proficiency in orthography and his natural inclination to help another out of the mire. The word "defied" had been given out by Schoolmaster Crawford, but had been misspelled several times when it came Miss Roby's turn. "Abe stood on the opposite side of the room" (related Miss Roby° to me in 1865) "and was watching me. I began d-e-f—and then I stopped, hesitating whether to proceed with an 'i' or a 'y.' Looking up I beheld Abe, a grin covering his face, and pointing with his index finger to his eye. I took the hint, spelled the word with an 'i,' and it went through all right."[39] There was more or less of an attachment between Miss Roby and Abe, although the lady took pains to assure me that they were never in love. She described with self-evident pleasure, however, the delightful experience of an evening's stroll down to the river with him, where they were wont to sit on the bank and watch the moon as it slowly rose over the neighboring hills. Dangling their youthful feet in the water, they gazed on the pale orb of night, as many a fond pair before them had done and will continue to do until the end of the world. One evening, when thus engaged, their conversation and thoughts turned on the movement of the planets. "I did not suppose that Abe, who had seen so little of the world, would know anything about it, but he proved to my satisfaction that the moon did not go down at all; that it only seemed to; that the earth, revolving from west to east, carried us under, as it were. 'We do the sinking,' he explained; 'while to us the moon is comparatively still. The moon's sinking is only an illusion.' I at once dubbed him a fool, but later developments convinced me that I was the fool, not he. He was well acquainted with the general laws of astronomy and the movements of the heavenly bodies, and where he could have learned so much, or how to put it so plainly, I never could understand."[40]

Absalom Roby is authority for the statement that even at that early day Abe was a patient reader of a Louisville newspaper, which some one at Gentryville kindly furnished him.[41] Among the books he read were the Bible, "Æsop's Fables," "Robinson Crusoe," Bunyan's "Pilgrim's Progress," a "History of the United States," and Weems' "Life of Washington."[42] A little circumstance attended the reading of the last-named book, which only within recent years found its way

---

°Miss Roby afterward married Allen Gentry.

into public print. The book was borrowed from a close-fisted neighbor, Josiah Crawford, and one night, while lying on a little shelf near a crack between two logs in the Lincoln cabin during a storm, the covers were damaged by rain. Crawford—not the schoolmaster, but old Blue Nose, as Abe and others called him—assessed the damage to his book at seventy-five cents, and the unfortunate borrower was required to pull fodder for three days at twenty-five cents a day in settlement of the account.[43] While at school it is doubtful if he was able to own an arithmetic. His stepmother was unable to remember his ever having owned one. She gave me, however, a few leaves from a book made and bound by Abe, in which he had entered, in a large, bold hand, the tables of weights and measures, and the "sums" to be worked out in illustration of each table. Where the arithmetic was obtained I could not learn. On one of the pages which the old lady gave me, and just underneath the table which tells how many pints there are in a bushel, the facetious young student had scrawled these four lines of schoolboy doggerel:

"Abraham Lincoln,
His hand and pen,
He will be good,
But God knows when."[44]

On another page were found, in his own hand, a few lines which it is also said he composed. Nothing indicates that they were borrowed, and I have always, therefore, believed that they were original with him. Although a little irregular in metre, the sentiment would, I think, do credit to an older head.

"Time, what an empty vapor 'tis,
And days how swift they are:
Swift as an Indian arrow—
Fly on like a shooting star.
The present moment just is here,
Then slides away in haste,
That we can never say they're ours,
But only say they're past."[45]

His penmanship, after some practice, became so regular in form that it excited the admiration of other and younger boys. One of the latter, Joseph C. Richardson, said that "Abe Lincoln was the best penman in the neighborhood." At Richardson's request he made some copies for practice. During my visit to Indiana I met Richardson, who showed these two lines, which Abe had prepared for him:

"Good boys who to their books apply
Will all be great men by and by."[46]

To comprehend Mr. Lincoln fully we must know in substance not only the facts of his origin, but also the manner of his development. It will always be a matter of wonder to the American people, I have no doubt—as it has been to me—that from such restricted and unpromising opportunities in early life, Mr. Lincoln grew into the great man he was. The foundation for his education was laid in Indiana and in the little town of New Salem in Illinois, and in both places he gave evidence of a nature and characteristics that distinguished him from every associate and surrounding he had. He was not peculiar or eccentric, and

A Leaf from Lincoln's Copy-book (original in possession of J. W. Weik)

yet a shrewd observer would have seen that he was decidedly unique and original. Although imbued with a marked dislike for manual labor, it cannot be truthfully said of him that he was indolent. From a mental standpoint he was one of the most energetic young men of his day. He dwelt altogether in the land of thought. His deep meditation and abstraction easily induced the belief among his horny-handed companions that he was lazy. In fact, a neighbor, John Romine, makes that charge. "He worked for me," testifies the latter, "but was always reading and thinking. I used to get mad at him for it. I say he was awful lazy. He would laugh and talk—crack his jokes and tell stories all the time; didn't love work half as much as his pay. He said to me one day that his father taught him to work; but he never taught him to love it."[47] Verily there was but one Abraham Lincoln!

His chief delight during the day, if unmolested, was to lie down under the shade of some inviting tree to read and study. At night, lying on his stomach in front of the open fireplace, with a piece of charcoal he would cipher on a broad wooden shovel. When the latter was covered over on both sides he would take his father's drawing knife or plane and shave it off clean, ready for a fresh supply of inscriptions the next day. He often moved about the cabin with a piece of chalk, writing and ciphering on boards and the flat sides of hewn logs. When every bare wooden surface had been filled with his letters and ciphers he would erase them and begin anew.[48] Thus it was always; and the boy whom dull old Thomas Lincoln and rustic John Romine conceived to be lazy was in reality the most tireless worker in all the region around Gentryville. His stepmother told me he devoured everything in the book line within his reach. If in his reading he came across anything that pleased his fancy, he entered it down in a copy-book—a sort of repository, in which he was wont to store everything worthy of preservation. "Frequently," related his stepmother, "he had no paper to write his pieces down on. Then he would put them with chalk on a board or plank, sometimes only making a few signs of what he intended to write. When he got paper he would copy them, always bringing them to me and reading them. He would ask my opinion of what he had read, and often explained things to me in his plain and simple language."[49] How he contrived at the age of fourteen to absorb information is thus told by John Hanks: "When Abe and I returned to the house from work he would go to the cupboard, snatch a piece of corn bread, sit down, take a book, cock his legs up as high as his head, and read. We grubbed, plowed, mowed, and worked together barefooted in the field. Whenever Abe had a chance in the field while at work, or at the house, he would stop and read."[50] He kept the Bible and "Æsop's Fables" always within reach, and read them over and over again. These two volumes furnished him with the many figures of speech and parables which he used with such happy effect in his later and public utterances.

Amid such restricted and unromantic environments the boy developed into the man. The intellectual fire burned slowly, but with a steady and intense glow. Although denied the requisite training of the school-room, he was none the less competent to cope with those who had undergone that discipline. No one had a more retentive memory. If he read or heard a good thing it never escaped him. His powers of concentration were intense, and in the ability through analysis to strip bare a proposition he was unexcelled. His thoughtful and investigating mind dug down after ideas, and never stopped till bottom facts were reached. With such a mental equipment the day was destined to come when the world would need the services of his intellect and heart. That he was equal to the great task when the demand came is but another striking proof of the grandeur of his character.

CHAPTER III.

The first law book Lincoln ever read was "The Statutes of Indiana." He obtained the volume from his friend David Turnham, who testifies that he fairly devoured the book in his eager efforts to abstract the store of knowledge that lay between the lids. No doubt, as Turnham insists, the study of the statutes at this early day led Abe to think of the law as his calling in maturer years.[1] At any rate he now began to evince no little zeal in the matter of public speaking—in compliance with the old notion, no doubt, that a lawyer can never succeed unless he has the elements of the orator or advocate in his construction—and even when at work in the field he could not resist the temptation to mount the nearest stump and practise on his fellow laborers. The latter would flock around him, and active operations would cease whenever he began. A cluster of tall and stately trees often made him a most dignified and appreciative audience during the delivery of these maiden forensic efforts. He was old enough to attend musters, log-rollings, and horse-races, and was rapidly becoming a favored as well as favorite character. "The first time I ever remember of seeing Abe Lincoln," is the testimony of one of his neighbors,* "was when I was a small boy and had gone with my father to attend some kind of an election. One of our neighbors, James Larkins, was there. Larkins was a great hand to brag on anything he owned. This time it was his horse. He stepped up before Abe, who was in the crowd, and commenced talking to him, boasting all the while of his animal.

"'I have got the best horse in the country' he shouted to his young listener. 'I ran him three miles in exactly nine minutes, and he never fetched a long breath.'

---

*John W. Lamar, MS. letter, June 29, 1866.[2]

"'I presume,' said Abe, rather dryly, 'he fetched a good many short ones though.'"[3]

With all his peaceful propensities Abe was not averse to a contest of strength, either for sport or in settlement—as in one memorable case—of grievances. Personal encounters were of frequent occurrence in Gentryville in those days, and the prestige of having thrashed an opponent gave the victor marked social distinction. Green B. Taylor, with whom Abe worked the greater part of one winter on a farm, furnished me with an account of the noted fight between John Johnston, Abe's step-brother and William Grigsby, in which stirring drama Abe himself played an important rôle before the curtain was rung down. Taylor's father was the second for Johnston, and William Whitten officiated in a similar capacity for Grigsby. "They had a terrible fight," relates Taylor, "and it soon became apparent that Grigsby was too much for Lincoln's man, Johnston. After they had fought a long time without interference, it having been agreed not to break the ring, Abe burst through, caught Grigsby, threw him off and some feet away. There he stood, proud as Lucifer, and swinging a bottle of liquor over his head swore he was 'the big buck of the lick.' 'If any one doubts it,' he shouted, 'he has only to come on and whet his horns.'"[4] A general engagement followed this challenge, but at the end of hostilities the field was cleared and the wounded retired amid the exultant shouts of their victors.

Much of the latter end of Abe's boyhood would have been lost in the midst of tradition but for the store of information and recollections I was fortunate enough to secure from an interesting old lady whom I met in Indiana in 1865. She was the wife of Josiah Crawford*—"Blue Nose," as Abe had named him— and possessed rare accomplishments for a woman reared in the backwoods of Indiana. She was not only impressed with Abe's early efforts, but expressed great admiration for his sister Sarah, whom she often had with her at her own hospitable home and whom she described as a modest, industrious, and sensible sister of a humorous and equally sensible brother. From Mrs. Crawford I

---

*In one of her conversations with me Mrs. Crawford told me of the exhibitions with which at school they often entertained the few persons who attended the closing day. Sometimes, in warm weather, the scholars made a platform of clean boards covered overhead with green boughs. Generally, however, these exhibitions took place in the school-room. The exercises consisted of the varieties offered at this day at the average seminary or school—declamations and dialogues or debates. The declamations were obtained principally from a book called "The Kentucky Preceptor," which volume Mrs. Crawford gave me as a souvenir of my visit. Lincoln had often used it himself, she said. The questions for discussion were characteristic of the day and age. The relative merits of the "Bee and the Ant," the difference in strength between "Wind and Water," taxed their knowledge of physical phenomena; and the all-important question "Which has the most right to complain, the Indian or the Negro?" called out their conceptions of a great moral or national wrong. In the discussion of all these grave subjects Lincoln took a deep interest.[5]

obtained the few specimens of Abe's early literary efforts and much of the matter that follows in this chapter. The introduction here of the literary feature as affording us a glimpse of Lincoln's boyhood days may to a certain extent grate harshly on over-refined ears; but still no apology is necessary, for, as intimated at the outset, I intend to keep close to Lincoln all the way through. Some writers would probably omit these songs and backwoods recitals as savoring too strongly of the Bacchanalian nature, but that would be a narrow view to take of history. If we expect to know Lincoln thoroughly we must be prepared to take him as he really was.

In 1826 Abe's sister Sarah was married to Aaron Grigsby, and at the wedding the Lincoln family sang a song composed in honor of the event by Abe himself. It is a tiresome doggerel and full of painful rhymes. I reproduce it here from the manuscript furnished me by Mrs. Crawford. The author and composer called it "Adam and Eve's Wedding Song."

"When Adam was created
    He dwelt in Eden's shade,
As Moses has recorded,
    And soon a bride was made.

Ten thousand times ten thousand
    Of creatures swarmed around
Before a bride was formed,
    And yet no mate was found.

The Lord then was not willing
    That man should be alone,
But caused a sleep upon him,
    And from him took a bone.

And closed the flesh instead thereof,
    And then he took the same
And of it made a woman,
    And brought her to the man.

Then Adam he rejoiced
    To see his loving bride
A part of his own body,
    The product of his side.

The woman was not taken
    From Adam's feet we see,
So he must not abuse her,
    The meaning seems to be.

The woman was not taken
    From Adam's head, we know,
To show she must not rule him—
    'Tis evidently so.

The woman she was taken
    From under Adam's arm,
So she must be protected
    From injuries and harm."[6]

Poor Sarah, at whose wedding this song was sung, never lived to see the glory nor share in the honor that afterwards fell to the lot of her tall and angular brother. Within two years after her marriage she died in childbirth. Something in the conduct of the Grigsbys and their treatment of his sister gave Abe great offense, and for a long time the relations between him and them were much strained. The Grigsbys were the leading family in Gentryville, and consequently were of no little importance in a social way. Abe, on the contrary, had no reserve of family or social influence to draw upon. He was only awaiting an opportunity to "even up" the score between them. Neither his father nor any of the Hankses were of any avail, and he therefore for the first time resorted to the use of his pen for revenge. He wrote a number of pieces in which he took occasion to lampoon those who provoked in any way his especial displeasure. It was quite natural to conceive therefore that with the gift of satire at command he should not have permitted the Grigsbys to escape. These pieces were called "Chronicles," and although rude and coarse, they served the purpose designed by their author of bringing public ridicule down on the heads of his victims. They were written in an attempted scriptural vein, and on so many different subjects that one might consistently call them "social ventilators." Their grossness must have been warmly appreciated by the early denizens of Gentryville, for the descendants of the latter up to this day have taken care that they should not be buried from sight under the dust of long-continued forgetfulness. I reproduce here, exactly as I obtained it, the particular chapter of the "Chronicles" which reflected on the Grigsbys so severely, and which must serve as a sample of all the others.°

°The original chapter in Lincoln's handwriting came to light in a singular manner after having been hidden or lost for years. Shortly before my trip to Indiana in 1865 a carpenter in Gentryville was rebuilding a house belonging to one of the Grigsbys. While so engaged his son and assistant had climbed through the ceiling to the inner side of the roof to tear away some of the timbers, and there found, tucked away under the end of a rafter, a bundle of yellow and dust-covered papers. Carefully withdrawing them from their hiding-place he opened and was slowly deciphering them, when his father, struck by the boy's silence, and hearing no evidence of work, enquired of him what he was doing. "Reading a portion of the Scriptures that hav'n't been revealed yet," was the response. He had found the "Chronicles of Reuben."[7]

Reuben and Charles Grigsby on the same day married° Betsy Ray and Matilda Hawkins respectively. The day following they with their brides returned to the Grigsby mansion, where the father, Reuben Grigsby, senior, gave them a cordial welcome. Here an old-fashioned infare, with feasting and dancing, and the still older fashion of putting the bridal party to bed, took place. When the invitations to these festivities were issued Abe was left out, and the slight led him to furnish an appreciative circle in Gentryville with what he was pleased to term "The First Chronicles of Reuben."†

"Now there was a man,"[9] begins this memorable chapter of backwoods lore, "whose name was Reuben, and the same was very great in substance; in horses and cattle and swine, and a very great household. It came to pass when the sons of Reuben grew up that they were desirous of taking to themselves wives, and being too well known as to honor in their own country they took a journey into a far country and there procured for themselves wives. It came to pass also that when they were about to make the return home they sent a messenger before them to bear the tidings to their parents. These, enquiring of the messengers what time their sons and wives would come, made a great feast and called all their kinsmen and neighbors in and made great preparations. When the time drew nigh they sent out two men to meet the grooms and their brides with a trumpet to welcome them and to accompany them. When they came near unto the house of Reuben the father, the messenger came on before them and gave a shout, and the whole multitude ran out with shouts of joy and music, playing on all kinds of instruments. Some were playing on harps, some on viols, and some blowing on rams' horns. Some also were casting dust and ashes towards heaven, and chief among them all was Josiah, blowing his bugle and making sound so great the neighboring hills and valleys echoed with the resounding acclamation. When they had played and their harps had sounded till the grooms and brides approached the gates, Reuben the father met them and welcomed them to his house. The wedding feast being now ready they were all invited to sit down to eat, placing the bridegrooms and their wives at each end of the table. Waiters were then appointed to serve and wait on the guests. When all had eaten and were full and merry they went out again and played and sung till night, and when they had made an end of feasting and rejoicing the multitude dispersed, each going to his own home. The family then

---

°April 16, 1829. Records Spencer Co., Indiana.
†Lincoln had shrewdly persuaded some one who was on the inside at the infare to slip upstairs while the feasting was at its height and change the beds, which Mamma Grigsby had carefully arranged in advance. The transposition of beds produced a comedy of errors which gave Lincoln as much satisfaction and joy as the Grigsby household embarrassment and chagrin.[8]

took seats with their waiters to converse while preparations were being made in an upper chamber for the brides and grooms to be conveyed to their beds. This being done the waiters took the two brides upstairs, placing one in a bed at the right hand of the stairs and the other on the left. The waiters came down, and Nancy the mother then gave directions to the waiters of the bridegrooms, and they took them upstairs but placed them in the wrong beds. The waiters then all came downstairs. But the mother, being fearful of a mistake, made enquiry of the waiters, and learning the true facts took the light and sprang upstairs. It came to pass she ran to one of the beds and exclaimed, 'O Lord, Reuben, you are in bed with the wrong wife.' The young men, both alarmed at this, sprang up out of bed and ran with such violence against each other they came near knocking each other down. The tumult gave evidence to those below that the mistake was certain. At last they all came down and had a long conversation about who made the mistake, but it could not be decided. So endeth the chapter."°

As the reader will naturally conclude, the revelation of this additional chapter of the Scriptures stirred up the social lions of Gentryville to the fighting point. Nothing but the blood of the author, who was endeavoring to escape public attention under the anonymous cloak, would satisfy the vengeance of the Grigsbys and their friends. But while the latter were discussing the details of discovery and punishment, the versatile young satirist was at work finishing up William, the remaining member of the Grigsby family, who had so far escaped the sting of his pen. The lines of rhyme in which William's weaknesses are handed down to posterity, Mrs. Crawford had often afterwards heard Abe recite, but she was very reluctant from a feeling of modesty to furnish them to me. At last, through the influence of her son, I overcame her scruples and obtained the coveted verses. A glance at them will convince the reader that the people of a community who could tolerate these lines would certainly not be surprised or offended at anything that might be found in the "Chronicles."

"I will tell you a joke about Joel and Mary,
It is neither a joke nor a story,
For Reuben and Charles have married two girls,
But Billy has married a boy.
The girls he had tried on every side,

°The reader will readily discern that the waiters had been carefully drilled by Lincoln in advance for the parts they were to perform in this rather unique piece of backwoods comedy. He also improved the rare opportunity which presented itself of caricaturing "Blue Nose" Crawford, who had exacted of him such an extreme penalty for the damage done to his "Weems' Life of Washington." He is easily identified as "Josiah blowing his bugle." The latter was also the husband of my informant, Mrs. Elizabeth Crawford.

But none could he get to agree;
All was in vain, he went home again,
And since that he's married to Natty.

So Billy and Natty agreed very well,
And mamma's well pleased with the match.
The egg it is laid, but Natty's afraid
The shell is so soft it never will hatch,
But Betsy, she said, 'You cursed bald head,
My suitor you never can be,
Besides your ill shape proclaims you an ape,
And that never can answer for me.'"[10]

That these burlesques and the publicity they attained aroused all the ire in the Grigsby family, and eventually made Abe the object on which their fury was spent is not surprising in the least. It has even been contended, and with some show of truth too, that the fight between John Johnston and William Grigsby was the outgrowth of these caricatures, and that Abe forebore measuring strength with Grigsby, who was considered his physical inferior, and selected Johnston to represent him and fight in his stead.[11] These crude rhymes and awkward imitations of scriptural lore demonstrated that their author, if assailed, was merciless in satire. In after years Lincoln, when driven to do so, used this weapon of ridicule

Josiah Crawford—"Blue Nose" (after a photograph in possession of J. W. Wartmann)

with telling effect. He knew its power, and on one occasion, in the rejoinder of a debate, drove his opponent in tears from the platform.[12]

Although devoid of any natural ability as a singer Abe nevertheless made many efforts and had great appreciation of certain songs. In after years he told me he doubted if he really knew what the harmony of sound was. The songs in vogue then were principally of the sacred order. They were from Watts' and Dupuy's hymn-books. David Turnham furnished me with a list, marking as especial favorites the following: "Am I a Soldier of the Cross;" "How Tedious and Tasteless the Hours;" "There is a Fountain Filled with Blood," and, "Alas, and did my Saviour Bleed?" One song pleased Abe not a little. "I used to sing it for old Thomas Lincoln," relates Turnham, "at Abe's request. The old gentleman liked it and made me sing it often. I can only remember one couplet:

> "'There was a Romish lady
> She was brought up in Popery.'"[13]

Dennis Hanks insists that Abe used to try his hand and voice at "Poor old Ned," but never with any degree of success. "Rich, racy verses" were sung by the big boys in the country villages of that day with as keen a relish as they are to-day. There is no reason and less evidence for the belief that Abe did not partake of this forbidden fruit along with other boys of the same age and condition in life. Among what Dennis called "field songs" are a few lines from this one:

> "The turbaned Turk that scorns the world
> And struts about with his whiskers curled,
> For no other man but himself to see."

Of another ballad we have this couplet:

> "Hail Columbia, happy land,
> If you aint drunk I will be damned."[14]

We can imagine the merry Dennis, hilarious with the exhilaration of deep potations at the village grocery, singing this "field song" as he and Abe wended their way homeward. A stanza from a campaign song which Abe was in the habit of rendering, according to Mrs. Crawford, attests his earliest political predilections:

> "Let auld acquaintance be forgot
> And never brought to mind
> May Jackson be our president,
> And Adams left behind."

A mournful and distressing ballad, "John Anderson's Lamentation," as rendered by Abe, was written out for me by Mrs. Crawford, but the first lines,

"Oh, sinners, poor sinners, take warning by me,
The fruits of transgression behold now and see,"

will suffice to indicate how mournful the rest of it was.[15]

The centre of wit and wisdom in the village of Gentryville was at the store. This place was in charge of one Jones, who soon after embarking in business seemed to take quite a fancy to Abe. He took the only newspaper—sent from Louisville—and at his place of business gathered Abe, Dennis Hanks, Baldwin, the blacksmith, and other kindred spirits to discuss such topics as are the exclusive property of the store lounger. Abe's original and ridiculous stories not only amused the crowd, but the display of his unique faculties made him many friends. One who saw him at this time says:

"Lincoln would frequently make political speeches to the boys; he was always calm, logical, and clear. His jokes and stories were so odd, original, and witty all the people in town would gather around him. He would keep them till midnight. Abe was a good talker, a good reasoner, and a kind of newsboy."[16] He attended all the trials before the "squire," as that important functionary was called, and frequently wandered off to Boonville, a town on the river, distant fifteen miles, and the county seat of Warrick County, to hear and see how the courts were conducted there. On one occasion, at the latter place, he remained during the trial of a murderer and attentively absorbed the proceedings. A lawyer named Breckenridge represented the defense, and his speech so pleased and thrilled his young listener that the latter could not refrain from approaching the eloquent advocate at the close of his address and congratulating him on his signal success. How Breckenridge accepted the felicitations of the awkward, hapless youth we shall probably never know. The story is told that during Lincoln's term as President, he was favored one day at the White House with a visit by this same Breckenridge, then a resident of Texas, who had called to pay his respects. In a conversation about early days in Indiana, the President, recalling Breckenridge's argument in the murder trial, remarked, "If I could, as I then thought, have made as good a speech as that, my soul would have been satisfied; for it was up to that time the best speech I had ever heard."[17]

No feature of his backwoods life pleased Abe so well as going to mill. It released him from a day's work in the woods, besides affording him a much desired opportunity to watch the movement of the mill's primitive and cumbersome machinery. It was on many of these trips that David Turnham accompanied him. In later years Mr. Lincoln related the following reminiscence of his experience as a miller in Indiana: One day, taking a bag of corn, he mounted the old flea-bitten gray mare and rode leisurely to Gordon's mill. Arriving somewhat late, his turn did not come till almost sundown. In obedience to the custom requiring each man to furnish his own power he hitched the old mare to the arm, and as the animal moved round, the machinery responded with equal speed. Abe was mounted on the arm, and at frequent intervals made use of his whip to urge the animal on to better speed. With a careless "Get up, you old hussy," he applied the lash at each revolution of the arm. In the midst of the exclamation, or just as half of it had escaped through his teeth, the old jade, resenting the continued use of the goad, elevated her shoeless hoof and striking the young engineer in the forehead, sent him sprawling to the earth. Miller Gordon hurried in, picked up the bleeding, senseless boy, whom he took for dead, and at once sent for his father. Old Thomas Lincoln came—came as soon as embodied listlessness could move—loaded the lifeless boy in a wagon and drove home. Abe lay unconscious all night, but towards break of day the attendants noticed signs of returning consciousness. The blood beginning to flow normally, his tongue struggled to loosen itself, his frame jerked for an instant, and he awoke, blurting out the words "you old hussy," or the latter half of the sentence interrupted by the mare's heel at the mill.

Mr. Lincoln considered this one of the remarkable incidents of his life.[18] He often referred to it, and we had many discussions in our law office over the psychological phenomena involved in the operation. Without expressing my own views I may say that his idea was that the latter half of the expression, "Get up, you old hussy," was cut off by a suspension of the normal flow of his mental energy, and that as soon as life's forces returned he unconsciously ended the sentence; or, as he in a plainer figure put it: "Just before I struck the old mare my will through the mind had set the muscles of my tongue to utter the expression, and when her heels came in contact with my head the whole thing stopped half-cocked, as it were, and was only fired off when mental energy or force returned."

By the time he had reached his seventeenth year he had attained the physical proportions of a full-grown man. He was employed to assist James Taylor in the management of a ferry-boat across the Ohio river near the mouth of Anderson's creek, but was not allowed a man's wages for the work. He received thirty-seven cents a day for what he afterwards told me was the roughest work a young man could be made to do. In the midst of whatever work he was engaged on he still found time to utilize his pen. He prepared a composition on the American Government, calling attention to the necessity of preserving the Constitution and perpetuating the Union, which with characteristic modesty he turned over to his friend and patron, William Wood, for safe-keeping and perusal. Through the instrumentality of Wood it attracted the attention of many persons, among them one Pitcher,* a lawyer at Rockport, who with faintly concealed enthusiasm declared "the world couldn't beat it."[20] An article on Temperance was shown under similar circumstance to Aaron Farmer, a Baptist preacher of local renown, and by him furnished to an Ohio newspaper for publication. The thing, however, which gave him such prominence—a prominence too which could have been attained in no other way—was his remarkable physical strength, for he was becoming not only one of the longest, but one of the strongest men around Gentryville. He enjoyed the brief distinction his exhibitions of strength gave him more than the admiration of his friends for his literary or forensic efforts. Some of the feats attributed to him almost surpass belief. One witness declares he was equal to three men, having on a certain occasion carried a load of six hundred pounds. At another time he walked away with a pair of logs which three robust men were skeptical of their ability to carry.[21] "He could strike with a maul a heavier blow—could sink an axe deeper into wood than any man I ever saw," is the testimony of another witness.[22]

After he had passed his nineteenth year and was nearing his majority he began to chafe and grow restless under the restraints of home rule. Seeing no prospect of betterment in his condition, so long as his fortune was interwoven with that of his father, he at last endeavored to strike out into the broad world for himself. Having great faith in the judgment and influence of his fast friend Wood, he solicited from him a recommendation to the officers of some one of the boats plying up and down the river, hoping thereby to obtain employment more congenial than the dull, fatiguing work of the farm. To this project the judicious Wood was much opposed, and therefore suggested to the would-be boatman the moral duty that rested on him to remain with his father till the law released him from that obligation.[23] With deep regret he retraced his steps to the paternal mansion, seriously determined not to evade the claim from which in a few weary months he would be finally released. Meanwhile occurred his first opportunity to see the world. In March, 1828, James Gentry, for whom he had been at work, had fitted out a boat with a stock of grain and meat for a

---

*This gentleman, Judge John Pitcher, ninety-three years old, is still living in Mount Vernon, Indiana. He says that young Lincoln often called at his office and borrowed books to read at home during leisure hours. On one occasion he expressed a desire to study law with Pitcher, but explained that his parents were so poor that he could not be spared from the farm on which they lived. "He related to me in my office one day," says Pitcher, "an account of his payment to Crawford of the damage done to the latter's book—Weems' 'Life of Washington.' Lincoln said, 'You see, I am tall and long-armed, and I went to work in earnest. At the end of the two days there was not a corn-blade left on a stalk in the field. I wanted to pay full damage for all the wetting the book got, and I made a clean sweep.'"[19]

trading expedition to New Orleans, and placed his son Allen in charge of the cargo for the voyage. Abe's desire to make a river trip was at last satisfied, and he accompanied the proprietor's son, serving as "bow hand." His pay was eight dollars a month and board. In due course of time the navigators returned from their expedition with the evidence of profitable results to gladden the heart of the owner. The only occurrence of interest they could relate of the voyage was the encounter with a party of marauding negroes at the plantation of Madame Duchesne, a few miles below Baton Rouge. Abe and Gentry, having tied up for the night, were fast asleep on their boat when aroused by the arrival of a crowd of negroes bent on plunder. They set to work with clubs, and not only drove off the intruders, but pursued them inland, then hastily returning to their quarters they cut loose their craft and floated down-stream till daylight.[24]

Before passing on further it may not be amiss to glance for a moment at the social side of life as it existed in Gentryville in Abe's day. "We thought nothing," said an old lady whom I interviewed when in Indiana, "of going eight or ten miles to church. The ladies did not stop for the want of a shawl, cloak, or riding-dress in winter time, but would put on their husbands' old overcoats and wrap up their little ones and take one or two of them on their beasts. Their husbands would walk, and thus they would go to church, frequently remaining till the second day before they returned home."[25]

The old men starting from the fields and out of the woods would carry their guns on their shoulders and go also. They dressed in deer-skin pants, moccasins, and coarse hunting shirts—the latter usually fastened with a rope or leather strap. Arriving at the house where services were to be held they would recite to each other thrilling stories of their hunting exploits, and smoke their pipes with the old ladies. They were treated, and treated each other, with the utmost kindness. A bottle of liquor, a pitcher of water, sugar, and glasses were set out for them; also a basket of apples or turnips, with, now and then, a pie or cakes. Thus they regaled themselves till the preacher found himself in a condition to begin. The latter, having also partaken freely of the refreshments provided, would "take his stand, draw his coat, open his shirt collar, read his text, and preach and pound till the sweat, produced alike by his exertions and the exhilarating effects of the toddy, rolled from his face in great drops. Shaking hands and singing ended the service."[26]

The houses were scattered far apart, but the people travelled great distances to participate in the frolic and coarse fun of a log-rolling and sometimes a wedding. Unless in mid-winter the young ladies carried their shoes in their hands, and only put them on when the scene of the festivities was reached. The ladies of maturer years drank whiskey toddy, while the men took the whiskey straight.

They all danced merrily, many of them barefooted, to the tune of a cracked fiddle the night through. We can imagine the gleeful and more hilarious swaggering home at daybreak to the tune of Dennis Hanks' festive lines:

"Hail Columbia, happy land,
If you ain't drunk I will be damned."[27]

Although gay, prosperous, and light-hearted, these people were brimming over with superstition. It was at once their food and drink. They believed in the baneful influence of witches, pinned their faith to the curative power of wizards in dealing with sick animals, and shot the image of a witch with a silver ball to break the spell she was supposed to have over human beings. They followed with religious minuteness the directions of the water-wizard, with his magic divining rod, and the faith doctor who wrought miraculous cures by strange sounds and signals to some mysterious agency. The flight of a bird in at the window, the breath of a horse on a child's head, the crossing by a dog of a hunter's path, all betokened evil luck in store for some one. The moon exercised greater influence on the actions of the people and the growth of vegetation than the sun and all the planetary system combined. Fence rails could only be cut in the light of the moon, and potatoes planted in the dark of the moon. Trees and plants which bore their fruit above ground could be planted when the moon shone full. Soap could only be made in the light of the moon, and it must only be stirred in one way and by one person. They had the horror of Friday which with many exists to this day. Nothing was to be begun on that unlucky day, for if the rule were violated an endless train of disasters was sure to follow.[28]

Surrounded by people who believed in these things, Lincoln grew to manhood. With them he walked, talked, and labored, and from them he also absorbed whatever of superstition showed itself in him thereafter. His early Baptist training made him a fatalist up to the day of his death, and, listening in boyish wonder to the legends of some toothless old dame led him to believe in the significance of dreams and visions. His surroundings helped to create that unique character which in the eyes of a great portion of the American people was only less curious and amusing than it was August and noble.

The winter of 1829 was marked by another visitation of that dreaded disease, "the milk-sick." It was making the usual ravages among the cattle. Human victims were falling before it every day, and it caused the usual stampede in southern Indiana. Dennis Hanks, discouraged by the prospect and grieving over the loss of his stock, proposed a move further westward. Returning emigrants had brought encouraging news of the newly developed state of Illinois. Vast stretches of rich alluvial lands were to be had there on the easiest of terms.

Besides this, Indiana no longer afforded any inducements to the poor man. The proposition of Dennis met with the general assent of the Lincoln family, and especially suited the roving and migratory spirit of Thomas Lincoln. He had been induced to leave Kentucky for the hills of Indiana by the same rosy and alluring reports. He had moved four times since his marriage and in point of worldly goods was no better off than when he started in life. His land groaned under the weight of a long neglected incumbrance and, like many of his neighbors, he was ready for another change. Having disposed of his land to James Gentry, and his grain and stock to young David Turnham, he loaded his household effects into a wagon drawn by two yoke of oxen, and in March, 1830, started for Illinois. The two daughters of Mrs. Lincoln had meanwhile married Dennis Hanks and Levi Hall, and with these additions the party numbered thirteen in all. Abe had just passed his twenty-first birthday.[29]

The journey was a long and tedious one; the streams were swollen and the roads were muddy almost to the point of impassability. The rude, heavy wagon, with its primitive wheels, creaked and groaned as it crawled through the woods and now and then stalled in the mud. Many were the delays, but none ever disturbed the equanimity of its passengers. They were cheerful in the face of all adversity, hopeful, and some of them determined; but none of them more so than the tall, ungainly youth in buckskin breeches and coon-skin cap who wielded the gad and urged the patient oxen forward. As these humble emigrants entered the new State little did the curious people in the towns through which they passed dream that the obscure and penniless driver who yelled his commands to the oxen would yet become Chief Magistrate of the greatest nation of modern times.*

---

*Mr. Lincoln once described this journey to me. He said the ground had not yet yielded up the frosts of winter; that during the day the roads would thaw out on the surface and at night freeze over again, thus making travelling, especially with oxen, painfully slow and tiresome. There were, of course, no bridges, and the party were consequently driven to ford the streams, unless by a circuitous route they could avoid them. In the early part of the day the latter were also frozen slightly, and the oxen would break through a square yard of thin ice at every step. Among other things which the party brought with them was a pet dog, which trotted along after the wagon. One day the little fellow fell behind and failed to catch up till after they had crossed the stream. Missing him they looked back, and there, on the opposite bank, he stood, whining and jumping about in great distress. The water was running over the broken edges of the ice, and the poor animal was afraid to cross. It would not pay to turn the oxen and wagon back and ford the stream again in order to recover a dog, and so the majority, in their anxiety to move forward, decided to go on without him. "But I could not endure the idea of abandoning even a dog," related Lincoln. "Pulling off shoes and socks I waded across the stream and triumphantly returned with the shivering animal under my arm. His frantic leaps of joy and other evidences of a dog's gratitude amply repaid me for all the exposure I had undergone."[30]

CHAPTER IV.

After a fortnight of rough and fatiguing travel the colony of Indiana emigrants reached a point in Illinois five miles north-west of the town of Decatur in Macon county. John Hanks, son of that Joseph Hanks in whose shop at Elizabethtown Thomas Lincoln had learned what he knew of the carpenter's art, met and sheltered them until they were safely housed on a piece of land which he had selected for them five miles further westward. He had preceded them over a year, and had in the meantime hewed out a few timbers to be used in the construction of their cabin. The place he had selected was on a bluff overlooking the Sangamon river,—for these early settlers must always be in sight of a running stream,—well supplied with timber. It was a charming and picturesque site, and all hands set resolutely to work to prepare the new abode. One felled the trees; one hewed the timbers for the cabin; while another cleared the ground of its accumulated growth of underbrush. All was bustle and activity. Even old Thomas Lincoln, infused with the spirit of the hour, was spurred to unwonted exertion. What part of the work fell to his lot our only chronicler, John Hanks, fails to note; but it is conjectured from the old gentleman's experience in the art of building that his services corresponded to those of the more modern supervising architect. With the aid of the oxen and a plow John and Abe broke up fifteen acres of sod, and "Abe and myself," observes Hanks in a matter-of-fact way, "split rails enough to fence the place in."[1] As they swung their axes, or with wedge and maul split out the rails, how strange to them the thought would have seemed that those self-same rails were destined to make one of them immortal. If such a vision flashed before the mind of either he made no sign of it, but each kept steadily on in his simple, unromantic task.

Abe had now attained his majority and began to throw from his shoulders the vexations of parental restraint. He had done his duty to his father, and felt able to begin life on his own account. As he steps out into the broad and inviting world we take him up for consideration as a man. At the same time we dispense with further notice of his father, Thomas Lincoln. In the son are we alone interested. The remaining years of his life marked no change in the old gentleman's nature. He still listened to the glowing descriptions of prosperity in the adjoining counties, and before his death moved three times in search of better times and a healthy location. In 1851 we find him living on forty acres of land on Goose Nest prairie, in Coles county, Illinois. The land bore the usual incumbrance—a mortgage for two hundred dollars, which his son afterwards paid. On the 17th of January, after suffering for many weeks from a disorder of the kidneys, he passed away at the ripe old age—as his son tells us—of "seventy-three years and eleven days."[2]

For a long time after beginning life on his own account Abe remained in sight of the parental abode. He worked at odd jobs in the neighborhood, or wherever the demand for his services called him. As late as 1831 he was still in the same parts, and John Hanks is authority for the statement that he "made three thousand rails for Major Warnick" walking daily three miles to his work.[3] During the intervals of leisure he read the few books obtainable, and continued the practice of extemporaneous speaking to the usual audience of undemonstrative stumps and voiceless trees. His first attempt at public speaking after landing in Illinois is thus described to me by John Hanks, whose language I incorporate: "After Abe got to Decatur, or rather to Macon county, a man by the name of Posey came into our neighborhood and made a speech. It was a bad one, and I said Abe could beat it. I turned down a box and Abe made his speech. The other man was a candidate—Abe wasn't. Abe beat him to death, his subject being the navigation of the Sangamon river. The man, after Abe's speech was through, took him aside and asked him where he had learned so much and how he could do so well. Abe replied, stating his manner and method of reading, and what he had read. The man encouraged him to persevere."[4]

For the first time we are now favored with the appearance on the scene of a very important personage—one destined to exert no little influence in shaping Lincoln's fortunes. It is Denton Offut,[5] a brisk and venturesome business man, whose operations extended up and down the Sangamon river for many miles. Having heard glowing reports of John Hanks' successful experience as a boatman in Kentucky he had come down the river to engage the latter's services to take a boat-load of stock and provisions to New Orleans. "He wanted me to go badly," observes Hanks, "but I waited awhile before answering. I hunted up Abe, and I introduced him and John Johnston, his step-brother, to Offut. After some

John Hanks

talk we at last made an engagement with Offut at fifty cents a day and sixty dollars to make the trip to New Orleans. Abe and I came down the Sangamon river
in a canoe in March, 1831; landed at what is now called Jamestown, five miles
east of Springfield, then known as Judy's Ferry."[6] Here Johnston joined them,
and, leaving their canoe in charge of one Uriah Mann, they walked to Springfield, where after some inquiry they found the genial and enterprising Offut
regaling himself with the good cheer dispensed at "The Buckhorn" inn.[7] This
hostelry, kept by Andrew Elliott, was the leading place of its kind in the then
unpretentious village of Springfield. The figure of a buck's head painted on a
sign swinging in front of the house gave rise to its name. Offut had agreed with
Hanks to have a boat ready for him and his two companions at the mouth of
Spring creek on their arrival, but too many deep potations with the new-comers
who daily thronged about the "Buckhorn" had interfered with the execution of
his plans, and the boat still remained in the womb of the future. Offut met the
three expectant navigators on their arrival, and deep were his regrets over his
failure to provide the boat. The interview resulted in the trio engaging to make
the boat themselves. From what was known as "Congress land" they obtained an

abundance of timber, and by the aid of the machinery at Kirkpatrick's mill they soon had the requisite material for their vessel. While the work of construction was going on a shanty was built in which they were lodged. Lincoln was elected cook, a distinction he never underestimated for a moment. Within four weeks the boat was ready to launch. Offut was sent for, and was present when she slid into the water. It was the occasion of much political chat and buncombe, in which the Whig party and Jackson alike were, strangely enough, lauded to the skies. It is difficult to account for the unanimous approval of such strikingly antagonistic ideas, unless it be admitted that Offut must have brought with him some substantial reminder of the hospitality on draught at the "Buckhorn" inn. Many disputes arose, we are told, in which Lincoln took part and found a good field for practice and debate.

A travelling juggler halted long enough in Sangamontown, where the boat was launched, to give an exhibition of his art and dexterity in the loft of Jacob Carman's house. In Lincoln's low-crowned, broad-brimmed hat the magician cooked eggs. As explanatory of the delay in passing up his hat Lincoln drolly observed, "It was out of respect for the eggs, not care for my hat."[8]

Having loaded the vessel with pork in barrels, corn, and hogs, these sturdy boatmen swung out into the stream. On April 19 they reached the town of New Salem, a place destined to be an important spot in the career of Lincoln. There they met with their first serious delay. The boat stranded on Rutledge's mill-dam and hung helplessly over it a day and a night. "We unloaded the boat," narrated one of the crew to explain how they obtained relief from their embarrassing situation; "that is, we transferred the goods from our boat to a borrowed one. We then rolled the barrels forward; Lincoln bored a hole in the end [projecting] over the dam; the water which had leaked in ran out and we slid over."[9] Offut was profoundly impressed with this exhibition of Lincoln's ingenuity. In his enthusiasm he declared to the crowd who covered the hill and who had been watching Lincoln's operation that he would build a steamboat to plow up and down the Sangamon, and that Lincoln should be her Captain. She would have rollers for shoals and dams, runners for ice, and with Lincoln in charge, "By thunder, she'd have to go!"[10]

After release from their embarrassing, not to say perilous, position the boat and her crew floated away from New Salem and passed on to a point known as Blue Banks, where as the historian of the voyage says: "We had to load some hogs bought of Squire Godbey. We tried to drive them aboard, but could not. They would run back past us. Lincoln then suggested that we sew their eyes shut. Thinking to try it, we caught them, Abe holding their heads and I their tails while Offut sewed up their eyes. Still they wouldn't drive. At last, becoming tired, we carried them to the boat. Abe received them and cut open their eyes, Johnston and I handing them to him."[11] After thus disposing of the hog problem they again swung loose and floated down-stream. From the Sangamon they passed to the Illinois. At Beardstown their unique craft, with its "sails made of planks and cloth," excited the amusement and laughter of those who saw them from the shore.[12] Once on the bosom of the broad Mississippi they glided past Alton, St. Louis, and Cairo in rapid succession, tied up for a day at Memphis, and made brief stops at Vicksburg and Natchez. Early in May they reached New Orleans, where they lingered a month, disposing of their cargo and viewing the sights which the Crescent City afforded.

In New Orleans, for the first time Lincoln beheld the true horrors of human slavery. He saw "negroes in chains—whipped and scourged." Against this inhumanity his sense of right and justice rebelled, and his mind and conscience were awakened to a realization of what he had often heard and read. No doubt, as one of his companions has said, "Slavery ran the iron into him then and there."[13] One morning in their rambles over the city the trio passed a slave auction. A vigorous and comely mulatto girl was being sold. She underwent a thorough examination at the hands of the bidders; they pinched her flesh and made her trot up and down the room like a horse, to show how she moved, and in order, as the auctioneer said, that "bidders might satisfy themselves" whether the article they were offering to buy was sound or not. The whole thing was so revolting that Lincoln moved away from the scene with a deep feeling of "unconquerable hate." Bidding his companions follow him he said, "By God, boys, let's get away from this. If ever I get a chance to hit that thing [meaning slavery], I'll hit it hard." This incident was furnished me in 1865, by John Hanks.[14] I have also heard Mr. Lincoln refer to it himself.

In June the entire party, including Offut, boarded a steamboat going up the river. At St. Louis they disembarked, Offut remaining behind while Lincoln, Hanks, and Johnston started across Illinois on foot. At Edwardsville they separated, Hanks going to Springfield, while Lincoln and his step-brother followed the road to Coles county, to which point old Thomas Lincoln had meanwhile removed. Here Abe did not tarry long, probably not over a month, but long enough to dispose most effectually of one Daniel Needham, a famous wrestler who had challenged the returned boatman to a test of strength. The contest took place at a locality known as "Wabash Point." Abe threw his antagonist twice with comparative ease, and thereby demonstrated such marked strength and agility as to render him forever popular with the boys of that neighborhood.[15]

In August the waters of the Sangamon river washed Lincoln in to New Salem. This once sprightly and thriving village is no longer in existence. Not a building, scarcely a stone, is left to mark the place where it once stood. To reach it now the traveller must ascend a bluff a hundred feet above the general level of the surrounding country. The brow of the ridge, two hundred and fifty feet broad where it overlooks the river, widens gradually as it extends westwardly to the forest and ultimately to broad pastures. Skirting the base of the bluff is the Sangamon river, which, coming around a sudden bend from the south-east, strikes the rocky hill and is turned abruptly north. Here is an old mill, driven by water-power, and reaching across the river is the mill-dam on which Offut's vessel hung stranded in April, 1831. As the river rolled her turbid waters over the dam, plunging them into the whirl and eddy beneath, the roar of waters, like low, continuous, distant thunder, could be distinctly heard through the village day and night.[16]

The country in almost every direction is diversified by alternate stretches of hills and level lands, with streams between each struggling to reach the river. The hills are bearded with timber—oak, hickory, walnut, ash, and elm. Below them are stretches of rich alluvial bottom land, and the eye ranges over a vast expanse of foliage, the monotony of which is relieved by the alternating swells and depressions of the landscape. Between peak and peak, through its bed of limestone, sand, and clay, sometimes kissing the feet of one bluff and then hugging the other, rolls the Sangamon river. The village of New Salem, which once stood on the ridge, was laid out in 1828; it became a trading place, and in 1836 contained twenty houses and a hundred inhabitants. In the days of land offices and stage-coaches it was a sprightly village with a busy market. Its people were progressive and industrious. Propitious winds filled the sails of its commerce, prosperity smiled graciously on its every enterprise, and the outside world encouraged its social pretensions. It had its day of glory, but, singularly enough, cotemporaneous with the departure of Lincoln from its midst it went into a rapid decline. A few crumbling stones here and there are all that attest its former existence. "How it vanished," observes one writer, "like a mist in the morning, to what distant places its inhabitants dispersed, and what became of the abodes they left behind, shall be questions for the local historian."[17]

Lincoln's return to New Salem in August, 1831, was, within a few days, contemporaneous with the reappearance of Offut, who made the gratifying announcement that he had purchased a stock of goods which were to follow him from Beardstown. He had again retained the services of Lincoln to assist him when his merchandise should come to hand. The tall stranger—destined to be a stranger in New Salem no longer—pending the arrival of his employer's goods, lounged about the village with nothing to do. Leisure never sat heavily on him. To him there was nothing uncongenial in it, and he might very properly have been dubbed at the time a "loafer." He assured those with whom he came in contact that he was a piece of floating driftwood; that after the winter of deep snow, he had come down the river with the freshet; borne along by the swelling waters, and aimlessly floating about, he had accidentally lodged at New Salem.[18] Looking back over his history we are forced to conclude that Providence or chance, or whatever power is responsible for it, could not have assigned him to a more favorable refuge.

His introduction to the citizens of New Salem, as Mentor Graham* the schoolteacher tells us, was in the capacity of clerk of an election board.[19] Graham furnishes ample testimony of the facility, fairness, and honesty which characterized the new clerk's work, and both teacher and clerk were soon bound together by the warmest of ties. During the day, when votes were coming in slowly, Lincoln began to entertain the crowd at the polls with a few attempts at story-telling. My cousin, J. R. Herndon, was present and enjoyed this feature of the election with the keenest relish. He never forgot some of Lincoln's yarns, and was fond of repeating them in after years. The recital of a few stories by Lincoln easily established him in the good graces of all New Salem. Perhaps he did not know it at the time, but he had used the weapon nearest at hand and had won.†

A few days after the election Lincoln found employment with one Dr. Nelson, who after the style of dignitaries of later days started with his family and effects in his "private" conveyance—which in this instance was a flat-boat—for

---

*Nicolay and Hay in the *Century* make the mistake of spelling this man's name "Menton" Graham. In all the letters and papers from him he signs himself "Mentor" in every case.—J. W. W.

†"In the afternoon, as things were dragging a little, Lincoln the new man, began to spin out a stock of Indiana yarns. One that amused me more than any other he called the lizard story. 'The meeting-house,' he said, 'was in the woods and quite a distance from any other house. It was only used once a month. The preacher—an old line Baptist—was dressed in coarse linen pantaloons, and shirt of the same material. The pants, manufactured after the old fashion, with baggy legs and a flap in front, were made to attach to his frame without the aid of suspenders. A single button held his shirt in position, and that was at the collar. He rose up in the pulpit and with a loud voice announced his text thus: "I am the Christ, whom I shall represent to-day." About this time a little blue lizard ran up underneath his roomy pantaloons. The old preacher, not wishing to interrupt the steady flow of his sermon, slapped away on his legs, expecting to arrest the intruder; but his efforts were unavailing, and the little fellow kept on ascending higher and higher. Continuing the sermon, the preacher slyly loosened the central button which graced the waist-band of his pantaloons and with a kick off came that easy-fitting garment. But meanwhile Mr. Lizard had passed the equatorial line of waist-band and was calmly exploring that part of the preacher's anatomy which lay underneath the back of his shirt. Things were now growing interesting, but the sermon was still grinding on. The next movement on the preacher's part was for the collar button, and with one sweep of his arm off came the tow linen shirt. The congregation sat for an instant as if dazed; at length one old lady in the rear of the room rose up and glancing at the excited object in the pulpit, shouted at the top of her voice; "If you represent Christ then I'm done with the Bible.""'—J. R. Herndon, MS., July 2, 1865.[20]

Texas. Lincoln was hired to pilot the vessel through to the Illinois river. Arriving at Beardstown the pilot was discharged, and returned on foot across the sand and hills to New Salem.[21] In the meantime Offut's long expected goods had arrived, and Lincoln was placed in charge. Offut relied in no slight degree on the business capacity of his clerk. In his effusive way he praised him beyond reason. He boasted of his skill as a business man and his wonderful intellectual acquirements. As for physical strength and fearlessness of danger, he challenged New Salem and the entire world to produce his equal. In keeping with his widely known spirit of enterprise Offut rented the Rutledge and Cameron mill, which stood at the foot of the hill, and thus added another iron to keep company with the half-dozen already in the fire. As a further test of his business ability Lincoln was placed in charge of this also. William G. Greene was hired to assist him, and between the two a life-long friendship sprang up. They slept in the store, and so strong was the intimacy between them that "when one turned over the other had to do likewise."[22] At the head of these varied enterprises was Offut, the most progressive man by all odds in the village. He was certainly an odd character, if we accept the judgment of his cotemporaries. By some he is given the character of a clear-headed, brisk man of affairs. By others he is variously described as "wild, noisy, and reckless," or "windy, rattle-brained, unsteady, and improvident."[23] Despite the unenviable traits ascribed to him he was good at heart and a generous friend of Lincoln. His boast that the latter could outrun, whip, or throw down any man in Sangamon county was soon tested, as we shall presently see, for, as another has truthfully expressed it, "honors such as Offut accorded to Abe were to be won before they were worn at New Salem."[24] In the neighborhood of the village, or rather a few miles to the south-west, lay a strip of timber called Clary's Grove. The boys who lived there were a terror to the entire region—seemingly a necessary product of frontier civilization. They were friendly and good-natured; they could trench a pond, dig a bog, build a house; they could pray and fight, make a village or create a state. They would do almost anything for sport or fun, love or necessity. Though rude and rough, though life's forces ran over the edge of the bowl, foaming and sparkling in pure deviltry for deviltry's sake, yet place before them a poor man who needed their aid, a lame or sick man, a defenceless woman, a widow, or an orphaned child, they melted into sympathy and charity at once. They gave all they had, and willingly toiled or played cards for more. Though there never was under the sun a more generous parcel of rowdies,[25] a stranger's introduction was likely to be the most unpleasant part of his acquaintance with them. They conceded leadership to one Jack Armstrong, a hardy, strong, and well-developed specimen of physical manhood, and under him they were in the habit of "cleaning out" New Salem whenever his order went forth to do so. Offut and "Bill" Clary—the latter skeptical of Lincoln's strength and agility—ended a heated discussion in the store one day over the new clerk's ability to meet the tactics of Clary's Grove, by a bet of ten dollars that Jack Armstrong was, in the language of the day, "a better man than Lincoln." The new clerk strongly opposed this sort of an introduction, but after much entreaty from Offut, at last consented to make his bow to the social lions of the town in this unusual way. He was now six feet four inches high, and weighed, as his friend and confidant, William Greene, tells us with impressive precision, "two hundred and fourteen pounds."[26] The contest was to be a friendly one and fairly conducted. All New Salem adjourned to the scene of the wrestle. Money, whiskey, knives, and all manner of property were staked on the result. It is unnecessary to go into the details of the encounter. Everyone knows how it ended; how at last the tall and angular rail-splitter, enraged at the suspicion of foul tactics, and profiting by his height and the length of his arms, fairly lifted the great bully by the throat and shook him like a rag; how by this act he established himself solidly in the esteem of all New Salem, and secured the respectful admiration and friendship of the very man whom he had so thoroughly vanquished.[*] From this time forward Jack Armstrong, his wife Hannah, and all the other Armstrongs became his warm and trusted friends. None stood readier than they to rally to his support, none more willing to lend a helping hand. Lincoln appreciated their friendship and support, and in after years proved his gratitude by saving one member of the family from the gallows.[28]

The business done over Offut's counter gave his clerk frequent intervals of rest, so that, if so inclined, an abundance of time for study was always at his disposal. Lincoln had long before realized the deficiencies of his education, and resolved, now that the conditions were favorable, to atone for early neglect by a course of study. Nothing was more apparent to him than his limited knowledge of language, and the proper way of expressing his ideas. Moreover, it may be said that he appreciated his inefficiency in a rhetorical sense, and therefore determined to overcome all these obstacles by mastering the intricacies of grammatical construction. Acting on the advice of Mentor Graham he hunted up one Vaner,[29]

---

[*]Mr. Lincoln's remarkable strength resulted not so much from muscular power as from the toughness of his sinews. He could not only lift from the ground enormous weight, but could throw a cannon-ball or a maul farther than anyone else in New Salem. I heard him explain once how he was enabled thus to excel others. He did not attribute it to a greater proportion of physical strength, but contended that because of the unusual length of his arms the ball or projectile had a greater swing and therefore acquired more force and momentum than in the hands of an average man.[27]

who was the reputed owner of Kirkham's Grammar, and after a walk of several miles returned to the store with the coveted volume under his arm. With zealous perseverance he at once applied himself to the book. Sometimes he would stretch out at full length on the counter, his head propped up on a stack of calico prints, studying it; or he would steal away to the shade of some inviting tree, and there spend hours at a time in a determined effort to fix in his mind the arbitrary rule that "adverbs qualify verbs, adjectives, and other adverbs." From the vapidity of grammar it was now and then a great relaxation to turn to the more agreeable subject of mathematics; and he might often have been seen lying face downwards, stretched out over six feet of grass, figuring out on scraps of paper some problem given for solution by a quizzical store lounger, or endeavoring to prove that, "multiplying the denominator of a fraction divides it, while dividing the denominator multiplies it." Rather a poor prospect one is forced to admit for a successful man of business.

At this point in my narrative I am pained to drop from further notice our buoyant and effusive friend Offut. His business ventures failing to yield the extensive returns he predicted, and too many of his obligations maturing at the same time, he was forced to pay the penalty of commercial delinquency and went to the wall. He soon disappeared from the village, and the inhabitants thereof never knew whither he went. In the significant language of Lincoln he "petered out." As late as 1873 I received a letter from Dr. James Hall, a physician living at St. Dennis, near Baltimore, Maryland, who, referring to the disappearance of Offut, relates the following reminiscence: "Of what consequence to know or learn more of Offut I cannot imagine; but be assured he turned up after leaving New Salem. On meeting the name it seemed familiar, but I could not locate him. Finally I fished up from memory that some twenty-five years ago one 'Denton Offut' appeared in Baltimore, hailing from Kentucky, advertising himself in the city papers as a veterinary surgeon and horse tamer, professing to have a secret to whisper in the horse's ear, or a secret manner of whispering in his ear, which he could communicate to others, and by which the most refractory and vicious horse could be quieted and controlled. For this secret he charged five dollars, binding the recipient by oath not to divulge it. I know several persons, young fancy horsemen, who paid for the trick. Offut advertised himself not only through the press, but by his strange attire. He appeared in the streets on horseback and on foot, in plain citizens' dress of black, but with a broad sash across his right shoulder, of various colored ribbons, crossed on his left hip under a large rosette of the same material, the whole rendering his appearance most ludicrously conspicuous. Having occasion to purchase a horse I encountered him at several of our stables and was strongly urged to avail myself of his secret. So much for Offut; but were he living in '61, I doubt not Mr. Lincoln would have heard of him."[30]

The early spring of 1832 brought to Springfield and New Salem a most joyful announcement. It was the news of the coming of a steamboat down the Sangamon river—proof incontestable that the stream was navigable. The enterprise was undertaken and carried through by Captain Vincent Bogue, of Springfield, who had gone to Cincinnati to procure a vessel and thus settle the much-mooted question of the river's navigability. When, therefore, he notified the people of his town that the steamboat *Talisman* would put out from Cincinnati for Springfield, we can well imagine what great excitement and unbounded enthusiasm followed the announcement. Springfield, New Salem, and all the other towns along the now interesting Sangamon° were to be connected by water with the outside world. Public meetings, with the accompaniment of long subscription lists, were held; the merchants of Springfield advertised the arrival of goods "direct from the East per steamer *Talisman;*"[31] the mails were promised as often as once a week from the same direction; all the land adjoining each enterprising and aspiring village along the river was subdivided into town lots—in fact, the whole region began to feel the stimulating effects of what, in later days, would have been called a "boom." I remember the occasion well, for two reasons. It was my first sight of a steamboat, and also the first time I ever saw Mr. Lincoln[32]—although I never became acquainted with him till his second race for the Legislature in 1834. In response to the suggestion of Captain Bogue, made from Cincinnati, a number of citizens—among the number Lincoln—had gone down the river to Beardstown to meet the vessel as she emerged from the Illinois. These were armed with axes having long handles, to cut away, as Bogue had recommended, "branches of trees hanging over from the banks."[33] After having passed New Salem, I and other boys on horseback followed the boat, riding along the river's bank as far as Bogue's mill, where she tied up. There we went aboard, and lost in boyish wonder, feasted our eyes on the splendor of her interior decorations. The *Sangamon Journal* of that period contains numerous poetical efforts celebrating the *Talisman's* arrival. A few lines under date of April 5, 1832, unsigned, but supposed to have been the product of a local poet—one Oliphant†—were sung to the tune of

---

°The final syllable of this name was then pronounced to rhyme with "raw." In later days the letter "n" was added—probably for euphony's sake.

†E. P. Oliphant, a lawyer.

"Clar de Kitchen." I cannot refrain from inflicting a stanza or two of this ode on the reader:

"O, Captain Bogue he gave the load,
And Captain Bogue he showed the road;
And we came up with a right good will,
And tied our boat up to his mill.

Now we are up the Sangamo,
And here we'll have a grand hurra,
So fill your glasses to the brim,
Of whiskey, brandy, wine, and gin.

Illinois suckers, young and raw,
Were strung along the Sangamo,
To see a boat come up by steam
They surely thought it was a dream."

On its arrival at Springfield, or as near Springfield as the river ran, the crew of the boat were given a reception and dance in the court-house.[34] The cream of the town's society attended to pay their respects to the newly arrived guests. The captain in charge of the boat—not Captain Bogue, but a vainly dressed fellow from the East—was accompanied by a woman, more gaudily attired than himself, whom he introduced as his wife. Of course the most considerate attention was shown them both, until later in the evening, when it became apparent that the gallant officer and his fair partner had imbibed too freely—for in those days we had plenty of good cheer—and were becoming unpleasantly demonstrative in their actions. This breach of good manners openly offended the high-toned nature of Springfield's fair ladies; but not more than the lamentable fact, which they learned on the following day, that the captain's partner was not his wife after all, but a woman of doubtful reputation whom he had brought with him from some place further east. But to return to the *Talisman.* That now interesting vessel lay for a week longer at Bogue's mill, when the receding waters admonished her officers that unless they purposed spending the remainder of the year there they must head her down-stream. In this emergency recourse was had to my cousin Rowan Herndon, who had had no little experience as a boatman, and who recommended the employment of Lincoln as a skilful assistant. These two inland navigators undertook therefore the contract of piloting the vessel—which had now become elephantine in proportions—through the uncertain channel of the Sangamon to the Illinois river. The average speed was four miles a day. At New Salem safe passage over the mill-dam was deemed impossible unless the same could be lowered or a portion removed.* To this, Cameron and Rutledge, owners of the mill, entered their most strenuous protest. The boat's officers responded that under the Federal Constitution and laws no one had the right to dam up or in any way obstruct a navigable stream, and they argued that, as they had just demonstrated that the Sangamon was navigable (?), they proposed to remove enough of the obstruction to let the boat through. Rowan Herndon, describing it to me in 1865, said: "When we struck the dam she hung. We then backed off and threw the anchor over. We tore away part of the dam and raising steam ran her over on the first trial."[36] The entire proceeding stirred up no little feeling, in which mill owners, boat officers, and passengers took part. The effect the return trip of the *Talisman* had on those who believed in the successful navigation of the Sangamon is shrewdly indicated by the pilot, who with laconic complacency adds: "As soon as she was over, the company that chartered her was done with her."[37] Lincoln and Herndon, in charge of the vessel, piloted her through to Beardstown. There they were paid forty dollars each, according to contract, and bidding adieu to the *Talisman's* officers and crew, set out on foot for New Salem again. A few months later the *Talisman* caught fire at the wharf in St. Louis and went up in flames. The experiment of establishing a steamboat line to Springfield proved an unfortunate venture for its projector, Captain Bogue. Finding himself unable to meet his rapidly maturing obligations, incurred in aid of the enterprise, it is presumed that he left the country, for the *Journal* of that period is filled with notices of attachment proceedings brought by vigilant creditors who had levied on his goods.

---

*The affair at New Salem is thus described by Oliphant in the poem before referred to:

"And when we came to Salem dam,
Up we went against it jam:
We tried to cross with all our might,
But found we couldn't and staid all night."[35]

CHAPTER V.

The departure of the *Talisman* for deeper waters, the downfall of Denton Offut's varied enterprises and his disappearance from New Salem, followed in rapid succession, and before the spring of 1832 had merged into summer Lincoln found himself a piece of "floating driftwood" again. Where he might have lodged had not the Black Hawk war intervened can only be a matter of conjecture. A glance at this novel period in his life may not be out of keeping with the purpose of this book. The great Indian chief, Black Hawk, who on the 30th of June, 1831, had entered into an agreement, having all the solemnity of a treaty, with Governor Reynolds and General Gaines that none of his tribe should ever cross the Mississippi "to their usual place of residence, nor any part of their old hunting grounds east of the Mississippi, without permission of the President of the United States or the governor of the State of Illinois," had openly broken the compact.[1] On the 6th of April, 1832, he recrossed the Mississippi and marched up Rock River Valley, accompanied by about five hundred warriors on horseback; while his women and children went up the river in canoes. The great chief was now sixty-seven years old, and believed that his plots were all ripe and his allies fast and true. Although warned by General Atkinson, then in command of Fort Armstrong, against this aggression, and ordered to return, he proudly refused, claiming that he had "come to plant corn."[2] On being informed of the movement of Black Hawk Governor Reynolds called for a thousand mounted volunteers to co-operate with the United States forces under command of General Atkinson, and drive the wily Indian back across the Mississippi. The response to the governor's call was prompt and energetic. In the company from Sangamon county Lincoln enlisted, and now for the first time entered on the vicissitudinous and dangerous life of a soldier. That he in fact regarded the campaign after the Indians as a sort of holiday affair and chicken-stealing expedition is clearly shown in a speech he afterwards made in Congress in exposure of the military pretensions of General Cass.[3] However, in grim, soldierly severity he marched with the Sangamon county contingent to Rushville,° in Schuyler county, where, much to his surprise, he was elected captain of the company over William Kirkpatrick. A recital of the campaign that followed, in the effort to drive the treacherous Indians back, or a description of the few engagements—none of which reached the dignity of a battle—which took place, have in no wise been overlooked by the historians of Illinois and of the Black Hawk war. With the exception of those things which relate to Lincoln alone I presume it would be needless to attempt to add anything to what has so thoroughly and truthfully been told.

On being elected captain, Lincoln replied in a brief response of modest and thankful acceptance. It was the first official trust ever turned over to his keeping, and he prized it and the distinction it gave him more than any which in after years fell to his lot.[5] His company savored strongly of the Clary's Grove order, and though daring enough in the presence of danger, were difficult to bring down to the inflexibilities of military discipline. Each one seemed perfectly able and willing to care for himself, and while the captain's authority was respectfully observed, yet, as some have said, they were none the less a crowd of "generous ruffians." I heard Mr. Lincoln say once on the subject of his career as captain in this company and the discipline he exercised over his men, that to the first order given one of them he received the response, "Go to the devil, sir!" Notwithstanding the interchange of many such unsoldierlike civilities between the officer and his men, a strong bond of affection united them together, and if a contest had arisen over the conflict of orders between the United States authorities and those emanating from Captain Lincoln or some other Illinois officer—as at one time was threatened—we need not be told to which side the Sangamon county company to a man would have gone.[6] A general order forbidding the discharge of firearms within fifty yards of the camp was disobeyed by Captain Lincoln himself. For this violation of rule he was placed under arrest and deprived of his sword for a day.[7] But this and other punishments in no way humiliated him in the esteem of his

---

°While at the rendezvous at Rushville and on the march to the front Lincoln of course drilled his men, and gave them such meager instruction in military tactics as he could impart. Some of the most grotesque things he ever related were descriptions of these drills. In marching one morning at the head of the company, who were following in lines of twenty abreast, it became necessary to pass through a gate much narrower than the lines. The captain could not remember the proper command to turn the company *endwise,* and the situation was becoming decidedly embarrassing, when one of those thoughts born of the depths of despair came to his rescue. Facing the lines, he shouted: "Halt! This company will break ranks for two minutes and form again on the other side of the gate." The manœuvre was successfully executed.[4]

men; if anything, they only clung the closer, and when Clary's Grove friendship asserted itself, it meant that firm and generous attachment found alone on the frontier—that bond, closer than the affinity of blood, which becomes stronger as danger approaches death.

A soldier of the Sangamon county company broke into the officers' quarters one night, and with the aid of a tomahawk and four buckets, obtained by stealth a good supply of wines and liquors, which he generously distributed to his appreciative comrades. The next morning at daybreak, when the army began to move, the Sangamon county company, much to their captain's astonishment, were unfit for the march. Their nocturnal expedition had been too much for them, and one by one they fell by the wayside, until but a mere handful remained to keep step with their gallant and astounded captain. Those who fell behind gradually overcame the effects of their carousal, but were hard pressed to overtake the command, and it was far into the night when the last one straggled into camp. The investigation which followed resulted only in the captain suffering the punishment for the more guilty men. For this infraction of military law he was put under arrest and made to carry a wooden sword for two days, "and this too," as one of his company has since assured me, "although he was entirely blameless in the matter."[8]

Among the few incidents of Lincoln's career in the Black Hawk war that have found a place in history was his manly interference to protect an old Indian who strayed, hungry and helpless, into camp one day, and whom the soldiers were conspiring to kill on the ground that he was a spy. A letter from General Cass, recommending him for his past kind and faithful services to the whites, which the trembling old savage drew from beneath the folds of his blanket failed in any degree to appease the wrath of the men who confronted him. They had come out to fight the treacherous Indians, and here was one who had the temerity even to steal into their camp. "Make an example of him," they exclaimed. "The letter is a forgery and he is a spy." They might have put their threats into execution had not the tall form of their captain, his face "swarthy with resolution and rage," interposed itself between them and their defenseless victim. Lincoln's determined look and demand that "it must not be done" were enough.[9] They sullenly desisted, and the Indian, unmolested, continued on his way.

Lincoln's famous wrestling match with the redoubtable Thompson, a soldier from Union county, who managed to throw him twice in succession, caused no diminution in the admiration and pride his men felt in their captain's muscle and prowess. They declared that unfair advantage had been taken of their champion, that Thompson had been guilty of foul tactics, and that, in the language of the sporting arena, it was a "dog-fall."[10] Lincoln's magnanimous action, however, in according his opponent credit for fair dealing in the face of the wide-spread and adverse criticism that prevailed, only strengthened him in the esteem of all.°

At times the soldiers were hard pressed for food, but by a combination of ingenuity and labor in proportions known only to a volunteer soldier, they managed to avoid the unpleasant results of long-continued and unsatisfied hunger. "At an old Winnebago town called Turtle Village," narrates a member of the company, "after stretching our rations over nearly four days, one of our mess, an old acquaintance of Lincoln, G. B. Fanchier, shot a dove, and having a gill of flour left we made a gallon and a half of delicious soup in an old tin bucket that had been lost by Indians. This soup we divided among several messes that were hungrier than we were and our own mess, by pouring in each man's cup a portion of the esculent. Once more, at another time, in the extreme northern part of Illinois, we had been very hungry for two days, but suddenly came upon a new cabin at the edge of the prairie that the pioneer sovereign squatter family had vacated and 'skedaddled' from for fear of losing their scalps. There were plenty of chickens about the cabin, much hungrier than we ourselves were, if poverty is to test the matter, and the boys heard a voice saying 'Slay and eat.' They at once went to running, clubbing, and shooting them as long as they could be found. Whilst the killing was going on I climbed to the ridge-pole of the smoke-house to see distinctly what I saw obscurely from the ground, and behold! the cleanest, sweetest jole[12] I ever saw—alone, half hid by boards and ridge-pole, stuck up no doubt for future use. By this time many of the chickens were on the fire, broiling, for want of grease or gravy to fry them in. Some practical fellow proposed to throw in with the fowls enough bacon to convert broiling into frying; the proposition was adopted, and they were soon fried. We began to eat the tough, dry chickens with alternating mouthfuls of the jole, when Lincoln came to the repast with the query, 'Eating chicken, boys?' 'Not much, sir,' I responded, for we had operated principally on the jole, it being sweeter and more palatable than the chickens. 'It is much like eating saddle-bags,' he responded; 'but I think the stomach can accomplish much to-day; but what have you got there with the skeletons, George?' 'We did have a sweet jole of a hog, sir,' I answered, 'but you are nearly too late for your share,'

°William L. Wilson, a survivor of the war, in a letter under date of February 3, 1882, after detailing reminiscences of Stillman's defeat, says: "I have during that time had much fun with the afterwards President of the United States, Abraham Lincoln. I remember one time of wrestling with him, two best in three, and ditched him. He was not satisfied, and we tried it in a foot-race for a five-dollar bill. I won the money, and 'tis spent long ago. And many more reminiscences could I give, but am of the Quaker persuasion, and not much given to writing."[11]

at the same time making room for him to approach the elm-bark dish. He ate the bacon a moment, then commenced dividing by mouthfuls to the boys from other messes, who came to 'see what Abe was at,' and saying many quaint and funny things suited to the time and the jole."[13] The captain, it will be seen, by his "freedom without familiarity" and his "courtesy without condescension," was fast making inroads on the respect of his rude but appreciative men. He was doubtless looking a long way ahead, when both their friendship and respect would be of avail, for as the chronicler last quoted from continues: "He was acquainted with everybody, and he had determined, as he told me, to become a candidate for the next Legislature. The mess immediately pitched on him as our standard-bearer, and he accepted."[14]

The term for which the volunteers had enlisted had now expired, and the majority, tiring of the service, the novelty of which had worn off, and longing for the comforts and good cheer of their homes, refused either to re-enlist or render further service. They turned their faces homeward, each with his appetite for military glory well satiated. But the war was not over, and the mighty Black Hawk was still east of the Mississippi. A few remained and re-enlisted. Among them was Lincoln. This time, eschewing the responsibility of a captaincy, and to avoid the possible embarrassment of dragging about camp a wooden sword, he entered the company of Elijah Iles as a dignified private.[15] It has pleased some of Mr. Lincoln's biographers to attribute this re-enlistment to pure patriotism on his part and a conscientious desire to serve his country. From the standpoint of sentiment that is a comfortable view to take of it; but I have strong reason to believe that Mr. Lincoln never entertained such serious notions of the campaign. In fact, I may say that my information comes from the best authority to be had in the matter—the soldier himself. Mr. Lincoln had no home; he had cut loose from his parents, from the Hankses and the Johnstons; he left behind him no anxious wife and children; and no chair before a warm fireside remained vacant for him. "I was out of work," he said to me once, "and there being no danger of more fighting, I could do nothing better than enlist again."

After his discharge from this last and brief period of service, along with the remainder of the Sangamon county soldiers, he departed from the scenes of recent hostilities for New Salem again. His soldier days had ended, and he returned now to enter upon a far different career. However much in later years he may have pretended to ridicule the disasters of the Black Hawk war, or the part he took in it, yet I believe he was rather proud of it after all. When Congress, along in the fifties, granted him a land warrant he was greatly pleased. He located it on some land in Iowa, and declared to me one day that he would die seized of that land, and although the tract never yielded him anything he never, so far as my knowledge extends parted with its ownership.°

The return of the Black Hawk warriors to New Salem occurred in the month of August, but a short time before the general election. A new Legislature was to be chosen, and as Lincoln had declared to his comrades in the army he would, and in obedience to the effusive declaration of principles which he had issued over his signature in March, before he went to the war, he presented himself to the people of his newly adopted county as a candidate for the Legislature.[17] It is not necessary to enter into an account of the political conditions in Illinois at that time, or the effect had on the same by those who had in charge the governmental machinery. Lincoln's course is all that interests us. Though he may not have distinctly avowed himself a Whig, yet, as one of his friends asserted, "he stood openly on Whig principles."[18] He favored a national bank, a liberal system of internal improvements, and a high protective tariff. The handbill or circular alluded to announcing his candidacy was a sort of literary fulmination, but on account of its length I deem it unnecessary to insert the whole of it here. I have been told that it was prepared by Lincoln, but purged of its most glaring grammatical errors by James McNamar, who afterwards became Lincoln's rival in an important love affair.†

The circular is dated March 9, 1832, and addressed to the "People of Sangamon County." In it he takes up all the leading questions of the day: railroads, river navigation, internal improvements, and usury. He dwells particularly on the matter of public education, alluding to it as the most important subject before the people. Realizing his own defects arising from a lack of school instruction he contends that every man and his children, however poor, should be permit-

---

°"In regard to the Bounty Land Warrants issued to Abraham Lincoln for military services during the Black Hawk war as Captain of 4th Illinois Volunteers, the first warrant, No. 52,076, for forty acres (Act of 1850), was issued to Abraham Lincoln, Captain, etc. on the 16th of April, 1852, and was located in his name by his duly appointed attorney, John P. Davis, at Dubuque, Iowa, July 21, 1854, on the north-west quarter of the south-west quarter of section 20, in Township 84, north of Range 39, west, Iowa. A patent as recorded in volume 280, page 21, was issued for this tract to Abraham Lincoln on the 1st of June, 1855, and transmitted the 26th October, 1855, to the Register of delivery.

"Under the Act of 1855, another Land Warrant, No. 68,465, for 120 acres, was issued to Abraham Lincoln, Captain Illinois Militia, Black Hawk war, on the 22d April, 1856, and was located by himself at Springfield, Illinois, December 27, 1859, on the east half of the north-east quarter and the north-west quarter of the north-east quarter of section 18, in Township 84, north of Range 39, west; for which a patent, as recorded in volume 468, page 53, was issued September 10, 1860, and sent October 30, 1860, to the Register for delivery."—Letter Jos. S. Wilson Acting Commissioner Land Office, June 27, 1865.[16]

†In a letter dated May 5, 1866, McNamar says: "I corrected at his request some of the grammatical errors in his first address to the voters of Sangamon county, his principal hobby being the navigation of the Sangamon river."[19]

ted to obtain at least a moderate education, and thereby be enabled "to read the Scriptures and other works both of a moral and religious nature for themselves." The closing paragraph was so constructed as to appeal to the chivalrous sentiments of Clary's Grove. "I was born and have ever remained," he declares, "in the most humble walks of life. I have no wealthy or popular relatives or friends to recommend me. My case is thrown exclusively upon the independent voters of the county; and if elected they will have conferred a favor upon me for which I shall be unremitting in my labors to compensate. But if," he dryly concludes, "the good people in their wisdom shall see fit to keep me in the background, I have been too familiar with disappointments to be very much chagrined."[20]

The election being near at hand only a few days remained for his canvass. One° who was with him at the time describing his appearance, says: "He wore a mixed jeans coat, clawhammer style, short in the sleeves and bobtail—in fact it was so short in the tail he could not sit on it; flax and tow-linen pantaloons, and a straw hat. I think he wore a vest, but do not remember how it looked. He wore pot-metal boots."[21] His maiden effort on the stump was a speech on the occasion of a public sale at Pappsville, a village eleven miles west of Springfield. After the sale was over and speechmaking had begun, a fight—a "general fight," as one of the bystanders relates—ensued, and Lincoln, noticing one of his friends about to succumb to the energetic attack of an infuriated ruffian, interposed to prevent it. He did so most effectually. Hastily descending from the rude platform he edged his way through the crowd, and seizing the bully by the neck and seat of his trowsers, threw him by means of his strength and long arms, as one witness stoutly insists, "twelve feet away."[22] Returning to the stand and throwing aside his hat he inaugurated his campaign with the following brief but juicy declaration:

"Fellow Citizens, I presume you all know who I am. I am humble Abraham Lincoln. I have been solicited by many friends to become a candidate for the Legislature. My politics are short and sweet, like the old woman's dance. I am in favor of a national bank. I am in favor of the internal improvement system and a high protective tariff. These are my sentiments and political principles. If elected I shall be thankful; if not it will be all the same."[23]

I obtained this speech from A. Y. Ellis, who in 1865 wrote it out.[24] Ellis was his friend and supporter, and took no little interest in his canvass. "I accompanied him," he relates, "on one of his electioneering trips to Island Grove, and he made a speech which pleased his party friends very well indeed, though some of the Jackson men tried to make sport of it. He told several anecdotes, and

---

°A. Y. Ellis, letter, June 5, 1866, MS.

applied them, as I thought, very well. He also told the boys several stories which drew them after him. I remember them, but modesty and my veneration for his memory forbid me to relate them."[25] His story-telling propensity, and the striking fitness of his yarns—many of them being of the bar-room order—in illustrating public questions, as we shall see further along in these chapters, was really one of the secrets of his popularity and strength. The election, as he had predicted, resulted in his defeat—the only defeat, as he himself afterward stated, that he ever suffered at the hands of the people. But there was little defeat in it after all. Out of the eight unsuccessful candidates he stood third from the head of the list, receiving 657 votes. Five others received less. The most gratifying feature of it all was the hearty support of his neighbors at New Salem. Of the entire 208 votes in the precinct he received every one save three.[26]

It may not be amiss to explain the cause of this remarkable endorsement of Lincoln by the voters in New Salem. It arose chiefly from his advocacy of the improvement of the Sangamon river. He proposed the digging of a canal a few miles east of the point where the Sangamon enters the Illinois river, thereby giving the former two mouths. This, he explained to the farmers, would prevent the accumulation of back-water and consequent overflow of their rich alluvial bottom lands in the spring. It would also avert the sickness and evil results of stagnant pools, which formed in low places after the high waters receded. His scheme—that is the name by which it would be known to-day—commended itself to the judgment of his neighbors, and the flattering vote he received shows how they endorsed it.

The unsuccessful result of the election did not dampen his hopes nor sour his ambition. The extensive acquaintance, the practice in public speaking, the confidence gained with the people, together with what was augmented in himself, made a surplus of capital on which he was free to draw and of which he afterwards frequently availed himself. The election being over, however, he found himself without money, though with a goodly supply of experience, drifting again. His political experience had forever weaned him from the dull routine of common labor. Labor afforded him no time for study and no incentive to profitable reflection. What he seemed to want was some lighter work, employment in a store or tavern where he could meet the village celebrities, exchange views with strangers, discuss politics, horse-races, cock-fights, and narrate to listening loafers his striking and significant stories. In the communities where he had lived, the village store-keeper held undisturbed sway. He took the only newspapers, owned the only collection of books and half the property in the village; and in general was the social, and oftentimes the political head of the community. Naturally, therefore the prominence the store gave the merchant attracted Lincoln. But there seemed no favorable opening for him—clerks in New Salem were not in demand just then.

My cousins, Rowan and James Herndon, were at that time operating a store, and tiring of their investment and the confinement it necessitated, James sold his interest to an idle, shiftless fellow named William Berry. Soon after Rowan disposed of his to Lincoln. That the latter, who was without means and in search of work, could succeed to the ownership of even a half interest in a concern where but a few days before he would in all probability gladly have exchanged his services for his board, doubtless seems strange to the average young business man of to-day. I once asked Rowan Herndon what induced him to make such liberal terms in dealing with Lincoln, whom he had known for so short a time.

"I believed he was thoroughly honest," was the reply, "and that impression was so strong in me I accepted his note in payment of the whole. He had no money, but I would have advanced him still more had he asked for it."

Lincoln and Berry had been installed in business but a short time until one Reuben Radford, the proprietor of another New Salem grocery, who, happening to incur the displeasure of the Clary's Grove boys, decided suddenly one morning, in the commercial language of later days, to "retire from business." A visit by night of the Clary's Grove contingent always hastened any man's retirement from business. The windows were driven in, and possession taken of the stock without either ceremony or inventory. If, by break of day, the unfortunate proprietor found any portion of his establishment standing where he left it the night before, he might count himself lucky. In Radford's case, fearing "his bones might share the fate of his windows," he disposed of his stock and good-will to William Greene for a consideration of four hundred dollars. The latter employed Lincoln to make an inventory of the goods, and when completed, the new merchant, seeing in it something of a speculation, offered Greene an advance of two hundred and fifty dollars on his investment. The offer was accepted, and the stock and fixtures passed into the ownership and control of the now enterprising firm of Lincoln & Berry. They subsequently absorbed the remnant of a store belonging to one Rutledge, which last transaction cleared the field of all competitors and left them in possession of the only mercantile concern in New Salem.[27]

To effect these sales not a cent of money was required—the buyer giving the seller his note and the latter assigning it to someone else in another trade. Berry gave his note to James Herndon, Lincoln his to Rowan Herndon, while Lincoln & Berry as a firm, executed their obligation to Greene, Radford, and Rutledge in succession. Surely Wall Street at no time in its history has furnished a brace of speculators who in so brief a period accomplished so much and with so little money. A few weeks only were sufficient to render apparent Lincoln's ill adaptation to the requirements of a successful business career. Once installed behind the counter he gave himself up to reading and study, depending for the practical management of the business on his partner. A more unfortunate selection than Berry could not have been found; for, while Lincoln at one end of the store was dispensing political information, Berry at the other was disposing of the firm's liquors, being the best customer for that article of merchandise himself. To put it more plainly, Lincoln's application to Shakespeare and Burns was only equalled by Berry's attention to spigot and barrel. That the latter in the end succeeded in squandering a good portion of their joint assets, besides wrecking his own health, is not to be wondered at. By the spring of 1833 they, like their predecessors, were ready to retire. Two brothers named Trent coming along, they sold to them on the liberal terms then prevalent the business and good-will; but before the latter's notes fell due they in turn had failed and fled. The death of Berry following soon after, released him from the payment of any notes or debts, and thus Lincoln was left to meet the unhonored obligations of the ill-fated partnership, or avoid their payment by dividing the responsibility and pleading the failure of the business. That he assumed all the liability and set resolutely to work to pay everything, was strictly in keeping with his fine sense of honor and justice. He was a long time meeting these claims, even as late as 1848 sending to me from Washington portions of his salary as Congressman to be applied on the unpaid remnant of the Berry & Lincoln indebtedness—but in time he extinguished it all, even to the last penny.[28]

Conscious of his many shortcomings as a merchant, and undaunted by the unfortunate complications from which he had just been released, Lincoln returned to his books. Rowan Herndon, with whom he had been living, having removed to the country, he became for the first time a sojourner at the tavern, as it was then called—a public-house kept by Rutledge, Onstatt, and Alley in succession.[29] "It was a small log house," he explained to me in later years, "covered with clapboards, and contained four rooms." It was second only in importance to the store, for there he had the opportunity of meeting passing strangers—lawyers and others from the county seat, whom he frequently impressed with his knowledge as well as wit. He had, doubtless, long before determined to prepare himself for the law; in fact, had begun to read Blackstone while in the store, and now went at it with renewed zeal. He borrowed law-books of his former comrade in the Black Hawk war, John T. Stuart, who was practicing law in Springfield, frequently walking there to return one and borrow another. His determination to master any subject he undertook and his application to study were of the most intense order. On the road to and from Springfield he would read and recite from the book he carried open in his hand, and claimed to have mastered forty pages of Blackstone during the first day after his return from Stuart's office. At New Salem he frequently sat barefooted under the shade of a tree near the store, poring over a volume of Chitty or Blackstone, sometimes lying on his back, putting his feet up the tree, which provokes one of his biographers to denote the latter posture as one which might have been "unfavorable to mental application, in the case of a man with shorter extremities."[30]

That Lincoln's attempt to make a lawyer of himself under such adverse and unpromising circumstances excited comment is not to be wondered at. Russell Godby, an old man who still survives, told me in 1865, that he had often employed Lincoln to do farm work for him, and was surprised to find him one day sitting barefoot on the summit of a woodpile and attentively reading a book. "This being an unusual thing for farm hands in that early day to do, I asked him," relates Godby, "what he was reading. 'I'm not reading,' he answered. 'I'm studying.' 'Studying what?' I enquired. 'Law, sir,' was the emphatic response. It was really too much for me, as I looked at him sitting there proud as Cicero. 'Great God Almighty!' I exclaimed, and passed on."[31]

But Lincoln kept on at his studies. Wherever he was and whenever he could do so the book was brought into use. He carried it with him in his rambles through the woods and his walks to the river. When night came he read it by the aid of any friendly light he could find. Frequently he went down to the cooper's shop and kindled a fire out of the waste material lying about, and by the light it afforded read until far into the night.[32]

One of his companions at this time relates that, "while clerking in the store or serving as postmaster he would apply himself as opportunity offered to his studies, if it was but five minutes time—would open his book which he always kept at hand, study it, reciting to himself; then entertain the company present or wait on a customer without apparent annoyance from the interruption. Have frequently seen him reading while walking along the streets. Occasionally he would become absorbed with his book; would stop and stand for a few moments, then walk on, or pass from one house to another or from one crowd or squad of men to another. He was apparently seeking amusement, and with his thoughtful face and ill-fitting clothes was the last man one would have singled out for a student. If the company he was in was unappreciative, or their conversation at all irksome, he would open his book and commune with it for a time, until a happy thought suggested itself and then the book would again return to its wonted resting-place under his arm.

He never appeared to be a hard student, as he seemed to master his studies with little effort, until he commenced the study of the law. In that he became wholly engrossed, and began for the first time to avoid the society of men, in order that he might have more time for study. He was not what is usually termed a quick-minded man, although he would usually arrive at his conclusions very readily. He seemed invariably to reflect and deliberate, and never acted from impulse so far as to force a wrong conclusion on a subject of any moment."°

It was not long until he was able to draw up deeds, contracts, mortgages, and other legal papers for his neighbors. He figured conspicuously as a pettifogger before the justice of the peace, but regarding it merely as a kind of preliminary practice, seldom made any charge for his services. Meanwhile he was reading not only law books but natural philosophy and other scientific subjects. He was a careful and patient reader of newspapers, the *Sangamon Journal*—published at Springfield—*Louisville Journal, St. Louis Republican,* and *Cincinnati Gazette* being usually within his reach.[34] He paid a less degree of attention to historical works, although he read Rollin and Gibbon while in business with Berry.[35] He had a more pronounced fondness for fictitious literature, and read with evident relish Mrs. Lee Hentz's novels, which were very popular books in that day, and which were kindly loaned him by his friend A. Y. Ellis.[36] The latter was a prosperous and shrewd young merchant who had come up from Springfield and taken quite a fancy to Lincoln. The two slept together and Lincoln frequently assisted him in the store. He says that Lincoln was fond of short, spicy stories one and two columns long, and cites as specimens, "Cousin Sally Dillard," "Becky William's Courtship," "The Down-Easter and the Bull," and others, the very titles suggesting the character of the productions. He remembered everything he read, and could afterwards without apparent difficulty relate it. In fact, Mr. Lincoln's fame as a story-teller spread far and wide. Men quoted his sayings, repeated his jokes, and in remote places he was known as a story-teller before he was heard of either as lawyer or politician.

It has been denied as often as charged that Lincoln narrated vulgar stories; but the truth is he loved a story however extravagant or vulgar, if it had a good point. If it was merely a ribald recital and had no sting in the end, that is, if it exposed no weakness or pointed no moral, he had no use for it either in conversation or public speech; but if it had the necessary ingredients of mirth and moral no one could use it with more telling effect. As a mimic he was unequalled, and with his characteristic gestures, he built up a reputation

---

°R. B. Rutledge, letter, Nov. 30. 1866, MS.[33]

for story-telling—although fully as many of his narratives were borrowed as original—which followed him through life. One who listened to his early stories in New Salem says: "His laugh was striking. Such awkward gestures belonged to no other man. They attracted universal attention, from the old sedate down to the schoolboy. Then in a few moments he was as calm and thoughtful as a judge on the bench, and as ready to give advice on the most important matters; fun and gravity grew on him alike."[37]

Lincoln's lack of musical adaptation has deprived us of many a song. For a ballad or doggerel he sometimes had quite a liking. He could memorize or recite the lines but some one else had to do the singing. Listen to one in which he shows "*How St. Patrick Came to be Born on the 17th of March.*" Who composed it or where Lincoln obtained it I have never been able to learn. Ellis says he often inflicted it on the crowds who collected in his store of winter evenings. Here it is:

"The first factional fight in old Ireland, they say,
Was all on account of Saint Patrick's birthday,
It was somewhere about midnight without any doubt,
And certain it is, it made a great rout.

On the eighth day of March, as some people say,
St. Patrick at midnight he first saw the day;
While others assert 'twas the ninth he was born—
'Twas all a mistake—between midnight and morn.

Some blamed the baby, some blamed the clock;
Some blamed the doctor, some the crowing cock.
With all these close questions sure no one could know,
Whether the babe was too fast or the clock was too slow.

Some fought for the eighth, for the ninth some would die;
He who wouldn't see right would have a black eye.
At length these two factions so positive grew,
They each had a birthday, and Pat he had two.

Till Father Mulcahay who showed them their sins,
He said none could have two birthdays but as twins.
'Now Boys, don't be fighting for the eight or the nine
Don't quarrel so always, now why not combine.'

Combine eight with nine. It is the mark;
Let that be the birthday. Amen! said the clerk.
So all got blind drunk, which completed their bliss,
And they've kept up the practice from that day to this."°

_____

°From MS., furnished by Ellis in August, 1866.[38]

As a salesman, Lincoln was lamentably deficient. He was too prone to lead off into a discussion of politics or morality, leaving someone else to finish the trade which he had undertaken. One of his employers says: "He always disliked to wait on the ladies, preferring, he said, to wait on the men and boys. I also remember he used to sleep on the store counter when they had too much company at the tavern. He wore flax and tow linen pantaloons—I thought about five inches too short in the legs—and frequently had but one suspender, no vest or coat. He wore a calico shirt, such as he had in the Black Hawk war; coarse brogans, tan color; blue yarn socks and straw hat, old style, and without a band."[39] His friend Ellis attributed his shyness in the presence of the ladies to the consciousness of his awkward appearance and the unpretentious condition of his wearing apparel. It was more than likely due to pure bashfulness. "On one occasion," continues Ellis, "while we boarded at the tavern, there came a family consisting of an old lady, her son, and three stylish daughters, from the State of Virginia, who stopped there for two or three weeks, and during their stay I do not remember of Mr. Lincoln's ever appearing at the same table with them."[40]

As a society man, Lincoln was singularly deficient while he lived in New Salem, and even during the remainder of his life. He never indulged in gossip about the ladies, nor aided in the circulation of village scandal. For woman he had a high regard, and I can testify that during my long acquaintance with him his conversation was free from injurious comment in individual cases—freer from unpleasant allusions than that of most men. At one time Major Hill charged him with making defamatory remarks regarding his wife. Hill was insulting in his language to Lincoln who never lost his temper. When he saw a chance to edge a word in, Lincoln denied emphatically using the language or anything like that attributed to him. He entertained, he insisted, a high regard for Mrs. Hill, and the only thing he knew to her discredit was the fact that she was Major Hill's wife.[41]

At this time in its brief history New Salem was what in the parlance of large cities would be called a fast place; and it was difficult for a young man of ordinary moral courage to resist the temptations that beset him on every hand. It remains a matter of surprise that Lincoln was able to retain his popularity with the hosts of young men of his own age, and still not join them in their drinking bouts and carousals. "I am certain," contends one of his companions, "that he never drank any intoxicating liquors—he did not even in those days smoke or chew tobacco."[42] In sports requiring either muscle or skill he took no little interest. He indulged in all the games of the day, even to a horse-race or cock-fight. At one eventful chicken fight, where a fee of twenty-five cents for the entrance of each fowl was assessed, one Bap. McNabb brought a little red rooster, whose fighting qualities had been well advertised for days in advance by his owner. Much interest was naturally taken in the contest. As the outcome of these contests was generally a quarrel, in which each man, charging foul play, seized his victim, they chose Lincoln umpire, relying not only on his fairness but his ability to enforce his decisions. In relating what followed I cannot improve on the description furnished me in February, 1865, by one° who was present.

"They formed a ring, and the time having arrived, Lincoln, with one hand on each hip and in a squatting position, cried, 'Ready.' Into the ring they toss their fowls, Bap's red rooster along with the rest. But no sooner had the little beauty discovered what was to be done than he dropped his tail and ran. The crowd cheered, while Bap. in disappointment picked him up and started away, losing his quarter and carrying home his dishonored fowl. Once arrived at the latter place he threw his pet down with a feeling of indignation and chagrin. The little fellow, out of sight of all rivals, mounted a wood pile and proudly flirting out his feathers, crowed with all his might. Bap. looked on in disgust. 'Yes, you little cuss,' he exclaimed, irreverently, 'you're great on dress parade, but not worth a d——n in a fight.'"[43] It is said—how truthfully I do not know—that at some period during the late war Mr. Lincoln in conversation with a friend likened McClellan to Bap. McNabb's rooster. So much for New Salem sports.

While wooing that jealous-eyed mistress, the law, Lincoln was earning no money. As another has said, "he had a running board bill to pay, and nothing to pay it with."[44] By dint of sundry jobs here and there, helping Ellis in his store to-day, splitting rails for James Short to-morrow, he managed to keep his head above the waves. His friends were firm—no young man ever had truer or better ones—but he was of too independent a turn to appeal to them or complain of his condition. He never at any time abandoned the idea of becoming a lawyer. That was always a spirit which beckoned him on in the darkest hour of his adversity. Someone, probably a Democrat who voted for him in the preceding fall, recommended him to John Calhoun, then surveyor of the county, as suitable material for an assistant. This office, in view of the prevailing speculation in lands and town lots, was the most important and possibly the most profitable in the county. Calhoun, the incumbent, was a Yankee and a typical gentleman. He was brave, intellectual, self-possessed, and cultivated. He had been educated for the law, but never practiced much after coming to Illinois—taught school in preference. As an instructor he was the popular one of his day and age. I attended the school he taught when I was a boy, in Springfield, and was in later years clerk of the city under his admin-

---

° A. Y. Ellis, MS.

istration as Mayor. Lincoln, I know, respected and admired him. After Lincoln's removal to Springfield they frequently held joint debates on political questions. At one time I remember they discussed the tariff question in the court house, using up the better part of two evenings in the contest. Calhoun was polite, affable, and an honest debater, never dodging any question. This made him a formidable antagonist in argumentative controversy. I have heard Lincoln say that Calhoun gave him more trouble in his debates than Douglas ever did, because he was more captivating in his manner and a more learned man than Douglas.

But to resume. The recommendation of Lincoln's friends was sufficient to induce Calhoun to appoint him one of his deputies. At the time he received notice of his selection by Calhoun, Lincoln was out in the woods near New Salem splitting rails. A friend named Pollard Simmons, who still survives and has related the incident to me, walked out to the point where he was working with the cheering news. Lincoln, being a Whig and knowing Calhoun's pronounced Democratic tendencies, enquired if he had to sacrifice any principle in accepting the position. "If I can be perfectly free in my political action I will take the office," he remarked; "but if my sentiments or even expression of them is to be abridged in any way I would not have it or any other office."[45] A young man hampered by poverty as Lincoln was at this time, who had the courage to deal with public office as he did, was certainly made of unalloyed material. No wonder in after years when he was defeated by Douglas he could inspire his friends by the admonition not to "give up after one nor one hundred defeats."[46]

After taking service with Calhoun, Lincoln found he had but little if any practical knowledge of surveying—all that had to be learned. Calhoun furnished him with books, directing him to study them till he felt competent to begin work. He again invoked the assistance of Mentor Graham, the schoolmaster, who aided him in his efforts at calculating the results of surveys and measurements. Lincoln was not a mathematician by nature, and hence, with him, learning meant labor. Graham's daughter is authority for the statement that her father and Lincoln frequently sat up till midnight engrossed in calculations, and only ceased when her mother drove them out after a fresh supply of wood for the fire.[47] Meanwhile Lincoln was keeping up his law studies. "He studied to see the subject-matter clearly," says Graham, "and to express it truly and strongly. I have known him to study for hours the best way of three to express an idea."[48] He was so studious and absorbed in his application at one time, that his friends, according to a statement made by one° of them, "noticed that he was so emaciated we feared he might

---

°Henry McHenry, MS., Oct. 5, 1865.

bring on mental derangement."[49] It was not long, however, until he had mastered surveying as a study, and then he was sent out to work by his superior—Calhoun. It has never been denied that his surveys were exact and just, and he was so manifestly fair that he was often chosen to settle disputed questions of corners and measurements. It is worthy of note here that, with all his knowledge of lands and their value and the opportunities that lay open to him for profitable and safe investments, he never made use of the information thus obtained from official sources, nor made a single speculation on his own account. The high value he placed on public office was more fully emphasized when as President, in answer to a delegation of gentlemen who called to press the claims of one of his warm personal friends for an important office, he declined on the ground that "he did not regard it as just to the public to pay the debts of personal friendship with offices that belonged to the people."[50]

As surveyor under Calhoun he was sent for at one time to decide or locate a disputed corner for some persons in the northern part of the county. Among others interested was his friend and admirer Henry McHenry. "After a good deal of disputing we agreed," says the latter, "to send for Lincoln and to abide by his decision. He came with compass, flag-staff, and chain. He stopped with me three or four days and surveyed the whole section. When in the neighbor-hood of the disputed corner by actual survey he called for his staff and driving it in the ground at a certain spot said, 'Gentlemen, here is the corner.' We dug down into the ground at the point indicated and, lo! there we found about six or eight inches of the original stake sharpened at the end, and beneath which was the usual piece of charcoal placed there by Rector the surveyor who laid the ground off for the government many years before."[51] So fairly and well had the young surveyor done his duty that all parties went away completely satisfied. As late as 1865 the corner was preserved by a mark and pointed out to strangers as an evidence of the young surveyor's skill. Russell Godby, mentioned in the ear-lier pages of this chapter, presented to me a certificate of survey given to him by Lincoln. It was written January 14, 1834, and is signed "J. Calhoun, S. S. C., by A. Lincoln." "The survey was made by Lincoln," says Godby, "and I gave him as pay for his work two buckskins, which Hannah Armstrong 'foxed' on his pants so that the briers would not wear them out."[52]

Honors were now crowding thick and fast upon him. On May 7, 1833, he was commissioned postmaster at New Salem, the first office he ever held under the Federal Government. The salary was proportionate to the amount of business done. Whether Lincoln solicited the appointment himself, or whether it was given him without the asking, I do not know; but certain it is his "administration" gave general satisfaction. The mail arrived once a week, and we can imagine the extent of time and labor required to distribute it, when it is known that "he carried the office around in his hat." Mr. Lincoln used to tell me that when he had a call to go to the country to survey a piece of land, he placed inside his hat all the letters belonging to people in the neighborhood and distributed them along the way. He made head-quarters in Samuel Hill's store, and there the office may be said to have been located, as Hill himself had been postmaster before Lincoln. Between the revenue derived from the post-office and his income from land surveys Lincoln was, in the expressive language of the day, "getting along well enough." Suddenly, however, smooth sailing ceased and all his prospects of easy times ahead were again brought to naught. One Van Bergen brought suit against him and obtained judgment on one of the notes given in payment of the store debt—a relic of the unfortunate partnership with Berry. His personal effects were levied on and sold, his horse and surveying instruments going with the rest. But again a friend, one James Short, whose favor he had gained, interposed; bought in the property and restored it to the hopeless young surveyor.[53] It will be seen now what kind of friends Lincoln was gaining. The bonds he was thus making were destined to stand the severest of tests. His case never became so desperate but a friend came out of the darkness to relieve him.

There was always something about Lincoln in his earlier days to encourage his friends. He was not only grateful for whatever aid was given him, but he always longed to help some one else. He had an unfailing disposition to succor the weak and the unfortunate, and was always, in his sympathy, struggling with the under dog in the fight. He was once overtaken when about fourteen miles from Springfield by one Chandler, whom he knew slightly, and who, having already driven twenty miles, was hastening to reach the land office before a certain other man who had gone by a different road. Chandler explained to Lincoln that he was poor and wanted to enter a small tract of land which adjoined his, that another man of considerable wealth had also determined to have it, and had mounted his horse and started for Springfield. "Meanwhile, my neighbors," continued Chandler, "collected and advanced me the necessary one hundred dollars, and now, if I can reach the land office first, I can secure the land." Lincoln noticed that Chandler's horse was too much fatigued to stand fourteen miles more of a forced march, and he therefore dismounted from his own and turned him over to Chandler, saying, "Here's my horse—he is fresh and full of grit; there's no time to be lost; mount him and put him through. When you reach Springfield put him up at Herndon's tavern and I'll call and get him." Thus encouraged Chandler moved on, leaving Lincoln to follow on the jaded animal. He reached Springfield over an hour in advance of his rival and thus secured the coveted tract of land. By nightfall Lincoln rode leisurely into town and was met by the now radiant Chandler, jubilant over his success. Between the two a friendship sprang up which all the political discords of twenty-five years never shattered nor strained.[54]

About this time Lincoln began to extend somewhat his system—if he really ever had a system in anything—of reading. He now began to read the writings of Paine, Volney, and Voltaire. A good deal of religious skepticism existed at New Salem, and there were frequent discussions at the store and tavern, in which Lincoln took part. What views he entertained on religious questions will be more fully detailed in another place.[55]

No little of Lincoln's influence with the men of New Salem can be attributed to his extraordinary feats of strength. By an arrangement of ropes and straps, harnessed about his hips, he was enabled one day at the mill to astonish a crowd of village celebrities by lifting a box of stones weighing near a thousand pounds.[56] There is no fiction either, as suggested by some of his biographers, in the story that he lifted a barrel of whisky from the ground and drank from the bung; but in performing this latter almost incredible feat he did not stand erect and elevate the barrel, but squatted down and lifted it to his knees, rolling it over until his mouth came opposite the bung.[57] His strength, kindness of manner, love of fairness and justice, his original and unique sayings, his power of mimicry, his perseverance—all made a combination rarely met with on the frontier. Nature had burnt him in her holy fire, and stamped him with the seal of her greatness.

In the summer of 1834 Lincoln determined to make another race for the legislature; but this time he ran distinctly as a Whig. He made, it is presumed, the usual number of speeches, but as the art of newspaper reporting had not reached the perfection it has since attained, we are not favored with even the substance of his efforts on the stump. I have Lincoln's word for it that it was more of a hand-shaking campaign than anything else. Rowan Herndon relates that he came to his house during harvest, when there were a large number of men at work in the field. He was introduced to them, but they did not hesitate to apprize him of their esteem for a man who could labor; and their admiration for a candidate for office was gauged somewhat by the amount of work he could do. Learning these facts, Lincoln took hold of a cradle, and handling it with ease and remarkable speed, soon distanced those who undertook to follow him. The men were satisfied, and it is presumed he lost no votes in that crowd. One Dr. Barrett, seeing Lincoln, enquired of the latter's friends: "Can't the party raise any better material than that?" but after hearing his speech the doctor's opinion was considerably altered, for he declared that Lincoln filled him with amazement;

"that he knew more than all of the other candidates put together."[58] The election took place in August. Lincoln's friend, John T. Stuart, was also a candidate on the legislative ticket. He encouraged Lincoln's canvass in every way, even at the risk of sacrificing his own chances. But both were elected.[59] The four successful candidates were Dawson, who received 1390 votes,* Lincoln 1376, Carpenter 1170, and Stuart 1164.

At last Lincoln had been elected to the legislature, and by a very flattering majority. In order, as he himself said, "to make a decent appearance in the legislature," he had to borrow money to buy suitable clothing and to maintain his new dignity. Coleman Smoot, one of his friends, advanced him "two hundred dollars, which he returned," relates the generous Smoot, "according to promise."[60] Here we leave our rising young statesman, to take up a different but very interesting period of his history.

---

*In all former biographies of Lincoln, including the Nicolay and Hay history in the "Century Magazine," Dawson's vote is fixed at 1370, and Lincoln is thereby made to lead the ticket; but in the second issue of the *Sangamon Journal* after the election—August 16, 1834—the count is corrected, and Dawson's vote is increased to 1390. Dr. A. W. French, of Springfield, is the possessor of an official return of the votes cast at the New Salem precinct, made out in the handwriting of Lincoln, which also gives Dawson's vote at 1390.

CHAPTER VI.

Since the days when in Indiana Lincoln sat on the river's bank with little Kate Roby, dangling his bare feet in the water, there has been no hint in these pages of tender relations with any one of the opposite sex. Now we approach in timely order the "grand passion" of his life—a romance of much reality, the memory of which threw a melancholy shade over the remainder of his days. For the first time our hero falls in love. The courtship with Anne Rutledge and her untimely death form the saddest page in Mr. Lincoln's history.[1] I am aware that most of his biographers have taken issue with me on this phase of Mr. Lincoln's life. Arnold says: "The picture has been somewhat too highly colored, and the story made rather too tragic."[2] Dr. Holland and others omit the subject altogether, while the most recent biography—the admirable history by my friends Nicolay and Hay—devotes but five lines to it. I knew Miss Rutledge myself, as well as her father and other members of the family, and have been personally acquainted with every one of the score or more of witnesses whom I at one time or another interviewed on this delicate subject. From my own knowledge and the information thus obtained, I therefore repeat, that the memory of Anne Rutledge was the saddest chapter in Mr. Lincoln's life.°

James Rutledge, the father of this interesting girl, was one of the founders of New Salem, having come there from Kentucky in 1829. He was born in South Carolina and belonged to the noted Rutledge family of that State. I knew him as early as 1833, and have often shared the hospitality of his home. My father was a politician and an extensive stock dealer in that early day, and he and Mr.

° In a letter dated Dec. 4, 1866, one of Miss Rutledge's brothers writes: "When he first came to New Salem and up to the day of Anne's death Mr. Lincoln was all life and animation. He seemed to see the bright side of every picture."[3]

Rutledge were great friends. The latter was a man of no little force of character; those who knew him best loved him the most. Like other Southern people he was warm,—almost to impulsiveness,—social, and generous. His hospitality, an inherited quality that flashed with him before he was born, developed by contact with the brave and broadminded people whom he met in Illinois. Besides his business interests in the store and mill at New Salem, he kept the tavern where Lincoln came to board in 1833. His family, besides himself and wife, consisted of nine children, three of whom were born in Kentucky, the remaining six in Illinois. Anne, the subject of this chapter, was the third child. She was a beautiful girl, and by her winning ways attached people to her so firmly that she soon became the most popular young lady in the village. She was quick of apprehension, industrious, and an excellent housekeeper. She had a moderate education, but was not cultured except by contrast with those around her. One of her strong points was her womanly skill. She was dexterous in the use of the needle—an accomplishment of far more value in that day than all the acquirements of art in china painting and hammered brass are in this—and her needle-work was the wonder of the day. At every "quilting" Anne was a necessary adjunct, and her nimble fingers drove the needle more swiftly than anyone's else. Lincoln used to escort her to and from these quilting-bees, and on one occasion even went into the house—where men were considered out of place—and sat by her side as she worked on the quilt.

He whispered into her ear the old, old story. Her heart throbbed and her soul was thrilled with a joy as old as the world itself. Her fingers momentarily lost their skill. In her ecstasy she made such irregular and uneven stitches that the older and more sedate women noted it, and the owner of the quilt, until a few years ago still retaining it as a precious souvenir, pointed out the memorable stitches to such persons as visited her.[4]

L. M. Greene, who remembered Anne well, says, "She was amiable and of exquisite beauty, and her intellect was quick, deep, and philosophic as well as brilliant. She had a heart as gentle and kind as an angel, and full of love and sympathy. Her sweet and angelic nature was noted by every one who met her. She was a woman worthy of Lincoln's love."[5] This is a little overstated as to beauty— Greene writes as if he too had been in love with her—but is otherwise nearly correct.

"Miss Rutledge," says a lady° who knew her, "had auburn hair, blue eyes, fair complexion. She was pretty, slightly slender, but in everything a good hearted

---

°Mrs. Hardin Bale.

young woman. She was about five feet two inches high, and weighed in the neighborhood of a hundred and twenty pounds. She was beloved by all who knew her. She died as it were of grief. In speaking of her death and her grave Lincoln once said to me, 'My heart lies buried there.'"[6]

Before narrating the details of Lincoln's courtship with Miss Rutledge, it is proper to mention briefly a few facts that occurred before their attachment began.

About the same time that Lincoln drifted into New Salem there came in from the Eastern States John NcNeil, a young man of enterprise and great activity, seeking his fortune in the West.[7] He went to work at once, and within a short time had accumulated by commendable effort a comfortable amount of property. Within three years he owned a farm, and a half interest with Samuel Hill in the leading store. He had good capacity for business, and was a valuable addition to that already pretentious village—New Salem. It was while living at James Cameron's house that this plucky and industrious young business man first saw Anne Rutledge. At that time she was attending the school of Mentor Graham, a pedagogue of local renown whose name is frequently met with in these pages, and who flourished in and around New Salem from 1829 to 1860. McNeil fell deeply in love with the school-girl—she was then only seventeen— and paid her the usual unremitting attentions young lovers of that age had done before him and are still doing to-day. His partner in the store, Samuel Hill, a young man of equal force of character, who afterwards amassed a comfortable fortune, and also wielded no little influence as a local politician, laid siege to the heart of this same attractive maiden, but he yielded up the contest early. Anne rejected him, and he dropped from the race. McNeil had clear sailing from this time forward. He was acquiring property and money day by day. As one of the pioneers puts it, "Men were honest then, and paid their debts at least once a year.[8] The merchant surrounded by a rich country suffered little from competition. As he placed his goods on the shelf he added an advance of from seventy-five to one hundred and fifty per cent over cost price, and thus managed to get along." After "managing" thus for several years, McNeil, having disposed of his interest in the store to Hill, determined to return to New York, his native State, for a visit. He had accumulated up to this time, as near as we can learn, ten or possibly twelve thousand dollars. Before leaving he made to Anne a singular revelation. He told her the name NcNeil was an assumed one; that his real name was McNamar.

"I left behind me in New York," he said, "my parents and brothers and sisters. They are poor, and were in more or less need when I left them in 1829. I vowed that I would come West, make a fortune, and go back to help them. I am going to start now and intend, if I can, to bring them with me on my return to Illinois and place them on my farm."[9] He expressed a sense of deep satisfaction in being able to clear up all mysteries which might have formed in the mind of her to whom he confided his love. He would keep nothing, he said, from her. They were engaged to be married, and she should know it all. The change of his name was occasioned by the fear that if the family in New York had known where he was they would have settled down on him, and before he could have accumulated any property would have sunk him beyond recovery. Now, however, he was in a condition to help them, and he felt overjoyed at the thought. As soon as the journey to New York could be made he would return. Once again in New Salem he and his fair one could consummate the great event to which they looked forward with undisguised joy and unbounded hope. Thus he explained to Anne the purpose of his journey—a story with some remarkable features, all of which she fully believed.

"She would have believed it all the same if it had been ten times as incredible. A wise man would have rejected it with scorn, but the girl's instinct was a better guide, and McNamar proved to be all that he said he was, although poor Anne never saw the proof which others got of it."[*]

At last McNamar, mounting an old horse that had participated in the Black Hawk war, began his journey. In passing through Ohio he became ill with a fever. For almost a month he was confined to his room, and a portion of the time was unconscious. As he approached a return to good health he grew nervous over the delay in his trip. He told no one around him his real name, destination, or business. He knew how his failure to write to New Salem would be construed, and the resulting irritation gave way to a feeling of desperation. In plainer language, he concluded it was "all up with him now."[10] Meanwhile a different view of the matter was taken by Miss Rutledge. Her friends encouraged the idea of cruel desertion. The change of McNeil to McNamar had wrought in their minds a change of sentiment.[11] Some contended that he had undoubtedly committed a crime in his earlier days, and for years had rested secure from apprehension under the shadow of an assumed name; while others with equal assurance whispered in the unfortunate girl's ear the old story of a rival in her affections. Anne's lady friends, strange to relate, did more to bring about a discordant feeling than all others. Women are peculiar creatures. They love to nettle and mortify one another; and when one of their own sex has fallen, how little sympathy they seem

---

*Lamon, p. 161.

to have! But under all this fire, in the face of all these insidious criticisms, Anne remained firm. She had faith, and bided her time.

McNamar, after much vexatious delay, finally reached his birthplace in New York, finding his father in the decline of years and health. He provided for his immediate needs, and by his assiduous attentions undertook to atone for the years of his neglect; but all to no purpose. The old gentleman gradually faded from the world, and early one winter morning crossed the great river. McNamar was thus left to settle up the few unfinished details of his father's estate, and to provide for the pressing needs of the family. His detention necessitated a letter to Anne, explaining the nature and cause of the delay. Other letters followed; but each succeeding one growing less ardent in tone, and more formal in phraseology than its predecessor, Anne began to lose faith. Had his love gradually died away like the morning wind? was a question she often asked herself. She had stood firm under fire before, but now her heart grew sick with hope deferred. At last the correspondence ceased altogether.[12]

At this point we are favored with the introduction of the ungainly Lincoln, as a suitor for the hand of Miss Rutledge. Lincoln had learned of McNamar's strange conduct, and conjecturing that all the silken ties that bound the two together had been sundered, ventured to step in himself. He had seen the young lady when a mere girl at Mentor Graham's school, and he, no doubt, then had formed a high opinion of her qualities. But he was too bashful, as his friend Ellis declares, to tell her of it.[13] No doubt, when he began to pay her attentions she was the most attractive young lady whom up to that time he had ever met. She was not only modest and winning in her ways, and full of good, womanly common-sense, but withal refined, in contrast with the uncultured people who surrounded both herself and Lincoln. "She had a secret, too, and a sorrow,—the unexplained and painful absence of McNamar,—which, no doubt, made her all the more interesting to him whose spirit was often even more melancholy than her own."[14]

In after years, McNamar himself, describing her to me, said: "Miss Rutledge was a gentle, amiable maiden, without any of the airs of your city belles, but winsome and comely withal; a blonde in complexion, with golden hair, cherry-red lips, and a bonny blue eye. As to her literary attainments, she undoubtedly was as classic a scholar as Mr. Lincoln. She had at the time she met him, I believe, attended a literary institution at Jacksonville, in company with her brother."[15]

McNamar seems to have considered Lincoln's bashfulness as proof against the alluring charms of Miss Rutledge or anybody else, for he continues:

"Mr. Lincoln was not to my knowledge paying particular attention to any of the young ladies of my acquaintance when I left for my home in New York. There was no rivalry between us on that score; on the contrary, I had every reason to believe him my warm, personal friend. But by-and-by I was left so far behind in the race I did not deem my chances worthy of notice. From this time forward he made rapid strides to that imperishable fame which justly fills a world."[16]

Lincoln began to court Miss Rutledge in dead earnest. Like David Copperfield, he soon realized that he was in danger of becoming deeply in love, and as he approached the brink of the pit he trembled lest he should indeed fall in. As he pleaded and pressed his cause the Rutledges and all New Salem encouraged his suit. McNamar's unexplained absence and apparent neglect furnished outsiders with all the arguments needed to encourage Lincoln and convince Anne. Although the attachment was growing and daily becoming an intense and mutual passion, the young lady remained firm and almost inflexible. She was passing through another fire. A long struggle with her feelings followed; but at length the inevitable moment came. She consented to have Lincoln, provided he gave her time to write to McNamar and obtain his release from her pledge.[17] The slow-moving mails carried her tender letter to New York. Days and weeks—which to the ardent Lincoln must have seemed painfully long—passed, but the answer never came. In a half-hearted way she turned to Lincoln, and her looks told him that he had won. She accepted his proposal. Now that they were engaged he told her what she already knew, that he was poverty itself. She must grant him time to gather up funds to live on until he had completed his law studies. After this trifling delay "nothing on God's footstool," argued the emphatic lover, could keep them apart. To this the thoughtful Anne consented. To one of her brothers, she said: "As soon as his studies are completed we are to be married."[18] But the ghost of another love would often rise unbidden before her. Within her bosom raged the conflict which finally undermined her health. Late in the summer she took to her bed. A fever was burning in her head. Day by day she sank, until all hope was banished. During the latter days of her sickness, her physician had forbidden visitors to enter her room, prescribing absolute quiet. But her brother relates that she kept enquiring for Lincoln so continuously, at times demanding to see him, that the family at last sent for him. On his arrival at her bedside the door was closed and he was left alone with her. What was said, what vows and revelations were made during this sad interview, were known only to him and the dying girl.[19] A few days afterward she became unconscious and remained so until her death on the 25th day of August, 1835. She was buried in what is known as the Concord grave-yard, about seven miles north-west of the town of Petersburg.°

The most astonishing and sad sequel to this courtship was the disastrous effect of Miss Rutledge's death on Mr. Lincoln's mind. It operated strangely on one of his calm and stoical make-up. As he returned from the visit to the bed-side of Miss Rutledge, he stopped at the house of a friend, who relates that his face showed signs of no little mental agony. "He was very much distressed," is the language of this friend, "and I was not surprised when it was rumored sub-sequently that his reason was in danger."[21] One of Miss Rutledge's brothers† says: "The effect upon Mr. Lincoln's mind was terrible. He became plunged in despair, and many of his friends feared that reason would desert her throne. His extraordinary emotions were regarded as strong evidence of the existence of the tenderest relations between himself and the deceased."[22] The truth is Mr. Lincoln was strangely wrought up over the sad ending of the affair. He had fits of great mental depression, and wandered up and down the river and into the woods woefully abstracted—at times in the deepest distress. If, when we read what the many credible persons who knew him at the time tell us, we do not conclude that he was deranged, we must admit that he walked on that sharp and narrow line which divides sanity from insanity.[23] To one friend he complained that the thought "that the snows and rains fall upon her grave filled him with indescribable grief."‡ He was watched with especial vigilance during damp, stormy days, under the belief that dark and gloomy weather might produce such a depression of spirits as to induce him to take his own life. His condition finally became so alarming, his friends consulted together and sent him to the house of a kind friend, Bowlin Greene, who lived in a secluded spot hidden by the hills, a mile south of town. Here he remained for some weeks under the care and ever watchful eye of this noble friend, who gradually brought him back to reason, or at least a realization of his true condition. In the years that followed Mr. Lincoln never forgot the kindness of Greene through those weeks of suf-fering and peril. In 1842, when the latter died, and Lincoln was selected by the Masonic lodge to deliver the funeral oration, he broke down in the midst of his

---

°"I have heard mother say that Anne would frequently sing for Lincoln's benefit. She had a clear, ringing voice. Early in her illness he called, and she sang a hymn for which he always expressed a great prefer-ence. It begins:

'Vain man, thy fond pursuits forbear.'

You will find it in one of the standard hymn-books. It was likewise the last thing she ever sung."—Letter, John M.Rutledge, MS., Nov. 25, 1866.[20]
†R. B. Rutledge, MS., letter, Oct. 21, 1866.
‡Letter, Wm. Greene, MS., May 29, 1865.[24]

address. "His voice was choked with deep emotion; he stood a few moments while his lips quivered in the effort to form the words of fervent praise he sought to utter, and the tears ran down his yellow and shrivelled cheeks. Every heart was hushed at the spectacle. After repeated efforts he found it impossible to speak, and strode away, bitterly sobbing, to the widow's carriage and was driven from the scene."[25]

It was shortly after this that Dr. Jason Duncan placed in Lincoln's hands a poem called "Immortality." The piece starts out with the line, "Oh! why should the spirit of mortal be proud." Lincoln's love for this poem has certainly made it immortal. He committed these lines to memory, and any reference to or mention of Miss Rutledge would suggest them, as if "to celebrate a grief which lay with continual heaviness on his heart."[26] There is no question that from this time forward Mr. Lincoln's spells of melancholy became more intense than ever. In fact a tinge of this desperate feeling of sadness followed him to Springfield. He himself was somewhat superstitious about it, and in 1840–41 wrote to Dr. Drake, a celebrated physician in Cincinnati, describing his mental condition in a long letter. Dr. Drake responded, saying substantially, "I cannot prescribe in your case without a personal interview." Joshua F. Speed, to whom Lincoln showed the letter addressed to Dr. Drake, writing to me from Louisville, November 30, 1866, says: "I think he (Lincoln) must have informed Dr. Drake of his early love for Miss Rutledge, as there was a part of the letter which he would not read."[27] It is shown by the declaration of Mr. Lincoln himself made to a fellow member[*] of the Legislature within two years after Anne Rutledge's death that "although he seemed to others to enjoy life rapturously, yet when alone he was so overcome by mental depression he never dared to carry a pocket knife."[28]

It may not be amiss to suggest before I pass from mention of McNamar that, true to his promise, he drove into New Salem in the fall of 1835 with his mother and brothers and sisters. They had come through from New York in a wagon, with all their portable goods. Anne Rutledge had meanwhile died, and McNamar could only muse in silence over the fading visions of "what might have been." On his arrival he met Lincoln, who, with the memory of their mutual friend, now dead, constantly before him, "seemed desolate and sorely distressed."[29] The little acre of ground in Concord cemetery contained the form of his first love, rudely torn from him, and the great world, throbbing with life but cold and heartless, lay spread before him.

---

[*]Robert L. Wilson, MS., letter, Feb. 10, 1866.

CHAPTER VII.

Before taking up an account of Lincoln's entry into the Legislature, which, following strictly the order of time, properly belongs here, I beg to digress long enough to narrate what I have gathered relating to another courtship—an affair of the heart which culminated in a sequel as amusing as the one with Anne Rutledge was sad. I experienced much difficulty in obtaining the particulars of this courtship. After no little effort I finally located and corresponded with the lady participant herself, who in 1866 furnished me with Lincoln's letters and her own account of the affair, requesting the suppression of her name and residence. Since then, however, she has died, and her children have not only consented to a publication of the history, but have furnished me recently with more facts and an excellent portrait of their mother made shortly after her refusal of Lincoln's hand.[1]

Mary S. Owens—a native of Green county, Kentucky, born September 29, 1808—first became acquainted with Lincoln while on a visit to a sister, the wife of Bennet Able, an early settler in the country about New Salem. Lincoln was a frequent visitor at the house of Able, and a warm friend of the family. During the visit of Miss Owens in 1833, though only remaining a month, she lingered long enough to make an impression on Lincoln; but returned to Kentucky and did not reappear in New Salem till 1836. Meanwhile Anne Rutledge had died, and Lincoln's eyes began to wander after the dark-haired visitor from Kentucky. Miss Owens differed from Miss Rutledge in early education and the advantages of wealth. She had received an excellent education, her father being one of the wealthiest and most influential men of his time and locality.[2] A portion of her schooling was obtained in a Catholic convent, though in religious faith she was a Baptist. According to a description furnished me by herself she "had fair skin, deep blue eyes, and dark curling hair; height five feet, five inches; weight about a hundred and fifty pounds."[3] She was good-looking in girlhood; by many esteemed handsome, but became fleshier as she grew older. At the time of her second visit she reached New Salem on the day of the Presidential election, passing the polls where the men had congregated, on the way to her sister's house. One man in the crowd who saw her then was impressed with her beauty. Years afterwards, in relating the incident,* he wrote me:

"She was tall, portly, had large blue eyes and the finest trimmings I ever saw. She was jovial, social, loved wit and humor, had a liberal English education, and was considered wealthy. None of the poets or romance writers have ever given us a picture of a heroine so beautiful as a good description of Miss Owens in 1836 would be."[4]

A lady friend† says she was "handsome, truly handsome, matronly-looking, over ordinary size in height and weight."[5]

A gentleman‡ who saw her a few years before her death describes her as a "nervous, muscular woman, very intellectual, with a forehead massive and angular, square, prominent, and broad."[6]

At the time of her advent into the society of New Salem she was polished in her manners, pleasing in her address, and attractive in many ways. She had a little dash of coquetry in her intercourse with that class of young men who arrogated to themselves claims of superiority, but she never yielded to this disposition to an extent that would willingly lend encouragement to an honest suitor sincerely desirous of securing her hand, when she felt she could not in the end yield to a proposal of marriage if he should make the offer. She was a good conversationalist and a splendid reader, very few persons being found to equal her in this accomplishment. She was light-hearted and cheery in her disposition, kind and considerate for those with whom she was thrown in contact.

One of Miss Owens' descendants is authority for the statement that Lincoln had boasted that "if Mary Owens ever returned to Illinois a second time he would marry her;"[7] that a report of this came to her ears, whereupon she left her Kentucky home with a pre-determination to show him if she met him that she was not to be caught simply by the asking. On this second visit Lincoln paid her more marked attention than before, and his affections became more and more enlisted in her behalf. During the earlier part of their acquaintance, following the natural bent of her temperament she was pleasing and entertain-

---

*L. M. Greene.
†Mrs. Hardin Bale.
‡Johnson G. Greene.

Mary S. Owens (after
daguerreotype loaned by
B. R. Vineyard, Esq.)

ing to him. Later on he discovered himself seriously interested in the blue-eyed
Kentuckian, whom he had really under-estimated in his preconceived opinions
of her. In the meantime she too had become interested, having discovered the
sterling qualities of the young man who was paying her such devoted attention;
yet while she admired she did not love him. He was ungainly and angular in his
physical make-up, and to her seemed deficient in the nicer and more delicate
attentions which she felt to be due from the man whom she had pictured as an
ideal husband. He had given her to understand that she had greatly charmed
him; but he was not himself certain that he could make her the husband with
whom he thought she would be most happy. Later on by word and letter he told
her so. His honesty of purpose showed itself in all his efforts to win her hand.
He told her of his poverty, and while advising her that life with him meant to her
who had been reared in comfort and plenty, great privation and sacrifice, yet he
wished to secure her as a wife. She, however, felt that she did not entertain for
him the same feeling that he professed for her and that she ought to entertain
before accepting him, and so declined his offer. Judging from his letters alone
it has been supposed by some that she, remembering the rumor she had heard
of his determination to marry her, and not being fully certain of the sincerity of
his purposes, may have purposely left him in the earlier stages of his courtship

somewhat in uncertainty. Later on, however, when by his manner and repeated announcement to her that his hand and heart were at her disposal, he demonstrated the honesty and sincerity of his intentions, she declined his offer kindly but with no uncertain meaning.

The first letter I received from Mrs. Vineyard—for she was married to Jesse Vineyard, March 27, 1841—was written at Weston, Mo., May 1, 1866. Among other things she says: "After quite a struggle with my feelings I have at last decided to send you the letters in my possession written by Mr. Lincoln, believing as I do that you are a gentleman of honor and will faithfully abide by all you have said. My associations with your lamented friend were in Menard county whilst visiting a sister who then resided near Petersburg. I have learned that my maiden name is now in your possession; and you have ere this, no doubt, been informed that I am a native Kentuckian."[8]

The letters written by Lincoln not revealing enough details of the courtship, I prepared a list of questions for the lady to answer in order that the entire history of their relations might be clearly shown. I perhaps pressed her too closely in such a delicate matter, for she responded in a few days as follows:

"Weston, Mo., May 22, 1866.

"Mr. W. H. Herndon,

"My Dear Sir: Really, you catechize me in true lawyer style; but I feel you will have the goodness to excuse me if I decline answering all your questions in detail, being well assured that few women would have ceded as much as I have under all the circumstances.

"You say you have heard why our acquaintance terminated as it did. I too have heard the same bit of gossip; but I never used the remark which Madame Rumor says I did to Mr. Lincoln. I think I did on one occasion say to my sister, who was very anxious for us to be married, that I thought Mr. Lincoln was deficient in those little links which make up the chain of woman's happiness—at least it was so in my case. Not that I believed it proceeded from a lack of goodness of heart; but his training had been different from mine; hence there was not that congeniality which would otherwise have existed.

"From his own showing you perceive that his heart and hand were at my disposal; and I suppose that my feelings were not sufficiently enlisted to have the matter consummated. About the beginning of the year 1838 I left Illinois, at which time our acquaintance and correspondence ceased, without ever again being renewed.

"My father, who resided in Green county, Kentucky, was a gentleman of

considerable means; and I am persuaded that few persons placed a higher estimate on education than he did.

"Respectfully yours,

"Mary S. Vineyard."[9]

The reference to Lincoln's deficiency "in those little links which make up
the chain of woman's happiness" is of no little significance. It proved that his
training had indeed been different from hers. In a short time I again wrote Mrs.
Vineyard to enquire as to truth of a story current in New Salem, that one day as
she and Mrs. Bowlin Greene were climbing up the hill to Able's house they were
joined by Lincoln; that Mrs. Greene was obliged to carry her child, a fat baby
boy, to the summit; that Lincoln strolled carelessly along, offering no assistance
to the woman who bent under the load. Thereupon Miss Owens, censuring him
for his neglect, reminded him that in her estimation he would not make a good
husband. In due time came her answer:

"Weston, Mo., July 22, 1866.

"Mr. W. H. Herndon:

"Dear Sir: I do not think you are pertinacious in asking the question
relative to old Mrs. Bowlin Greene, because I wish to set you right on that
question. Your information, no doubt, came through my cousin, Mr. Gaines
Greene, who visited us last winter. Whilst here, he was laughing at me about
Mr. Lincoln, and among other things spoke about the circumstance in connection with Mrs. Greene and child. My impression is now that I tacitly admitted
it, for it was a season of trouble with me, and I gave but little heed to the matter. We never had any hard feelings towards each other that I know of. On no
occasion did I say to Mr. Lincoln that I did not believe he would make a kind
husband, because he did not tender his services to Mrs. Greene in helping of
her carry her babe. As I said to you in a former letter, I thought him lacking
in smaller attentions. One circumstance presents itself just now to my mind's
eye. There was a company of us going to Uncle Billy Greene's. Mr. Lincoln
was riding with me, and we had a very bad branch to cross. The other gentlemen were very officious in seeing that their partners got safely over. We were
behind, he riding in, never looking back to see how I got along. When I rode
up beside him, I remarked, 'You are a nice fellow! I suppose you did not care
whether my neck was broken or not.' He laughingly replied (I suppose by way
of compliment), that he knew I was plenty smart to take care of myself.

"In many things he was sensitive almost to a fault. He told me of an incident: that he was crossing a prairie one day and saw before him, 'a hog mired down,' to use his own language. He was rather 'fixed up,' and he resolved that he would pass on without looking at the shoat. After he had gone by, he said the feeling was irresistible; and he had to look back, and the poor thing seemed to say wistfully, 'There now, my last hope is gone;' that he deliberately got down and relieved it from its difficulty.

"In many things we were congenial spirits. In politics we saw eye to eye, though since then we differed as widely as the South is from the North. But methinks I hear you say, 'Save me from a political woman!' So say I.

"The last message I ever received from him was about a year after we parted in Illinois. Mrs. Able visited Kentucky, and he said to her in Springfield, 'Tell your sister that I think she was a great fool because she did not stay here and marry me.' Characteristic of the man!

"Respectfully yours,

"Mary S. Vineyard."[10]

We have thus been favored with the lady's side of this case, and it is but fair that we should hear the testimony of her honest but ungainly suitor. Fortunately for us and for history we have his view of the case in a series of letters which have been preserved with zealous care by the lady's family.* The first letter was written from Vandalia, December 13, 1836, where the Legislature to which he belonged was in session. After reciting the progress of legislation and the flattering prospect that then existed for the removal of the seat of government to Springfield, he gets down to personal matters by apprising her of his illness for a few days, coupled with the announcement that he is mortified by daily trips to the post-office in quest of her letter, which it seemed never would arrive. "You see," he complains, "I am mad about that old letter yet. I don't like to risk you again. I'll try you once more, anyhow." Further along in the course of the missive, he says: "You recollect, I mentioned at the outset of this letter, that I had been unwell. That is the fact, though I believe I am about well now; but that, with other things I cannot account for, have conspired, and have gotten my spirits so low that I feel that I would rather be in any place in the world than here. I really cannot endure the thought of staying here ten weeks. Write back as soon as you get this, and if possible, say something that will please me; for really, I have not been pleased since I left you. This letter is so dry and stupid," he mournfully

---

*The copies of these letters were carefully made by Mr. Weik from the originals, now in the possession of B. R. Vineyard, St. Joseph, Mo.

concludes, "that I am ashamed to send it, but with my present feelings I cannot do any better."[11]

After the adjournment of the Legislature he returned to Springfield, from which point it was a matter of easy driving to reach New Salem, where his lady-love was sojourning, and where he could pay his addresses in person. It should be borne in mind that he had by this time removed to Springfield, the county seat, and entered on the practice of the law. In the gloom resulting from lack of funds and the dim prospect for business, he found time to communicate with the friend whose case was constantly uppermost in his mind. Here is one characteristic letter:

"Springfield, May 7, 1837.

"Friend Mary:

"I have commenced two letters to send you before this, both of which displeased me before I got half done, and so I tore them up. The first I thought wasn't serious enough, and the second was on the other extreme. I shall send this, turn out as it may.

"This thing of living in Springfield is rather a dull business after all—at least it is so to me. I am quite as lonesome here as [I] ever was anywhere in my life. I have been spoken to by but one woman since I've been here, and should not have been by her if she could have avoided it. I've never been to church yet, and probably shall not be soon. I stay away because I am conscious I should not know how to behave myself. I am often thinking of what we said of your coming to live at Springfield. I am afraid you would not be satisfied. There is a great deal of flourishing about in carriages here, which it would be your doom to see without sharing in it. You would have to be poor without the means of hiding your poverty. Do you believe you could bear that patiently? Whatever woman may cast her lot with mine, should anyone ever do so, it is my intention to do all in my power to make her happy and contented, and there is nothing I can imagine that would make me more unhappy than to fail in the effort. I know I should be much happier with you than the way I am, provided I saw no signs of discontent in you.

"What you have said to me may have been in jest or I may have misunderstood it. If so, then let it be forgotten; if otherwise I much wish you would think seriously before you decide. For my part I have already decided. What I have said I will most positively abide by, provided you wish it. My opinion is you had better not do it. You have not been accustomed to hardship, and it may be more severe than you imagine. I know you are capable of thinking correctly on any subject; and if you deliberate maturely upon this before you decide, then I am willing to abide your decision.

"You must write me a good long letter after you get this. You have nothing else to do, and though it might not seem interesting to you after you have written it, it would be a good deal of company in this busy wilderness. Tell your sister I don't want to hear any more about selling out and moving. That gives me the hypo whenever I think of it.

"Yours, etc.

"Lincoln."[12]

Very few if any men can be found who in fond pursuit of their love would present their case voluntarily in such an unfavorable light. In one breath he avows his affection for the lady whose image is constantly before him, and in the next furnishes her reasons why she ought not to marry him! During the warm, dry summer months he kept up the siege without apparent diminution of zeal. He was as assiduous as ever, and in August was anxious to force a decision. On the 16th he had a meeting with her which terminated much like a drawn battle—at least it seems to have afforded him but little encouragement, for on his return to Springfield he immediately indulged in an epistolary effusion stranger than any that preceded it.

"Friend Mary:

"You will no doubt think it rather strange that I should write you a letter on the same day on which we parted; and I can only account for it by supposing that seeing you lately makes me think of you more than usual, while at our late meeting we had but few expressions of thoughts. You must know that I cannot see you or think of you with entire indifference; and yet it may be that you are mistaken in regard to what my real feelings towards you are. If I knew you were not, I should not trouble you with this letter. Perhaps any other man would know enough without further information, but I consider it my peculiar right to plead ignorance and your bounden duty to allow the plea.

"I want in all cases to do right; and most particularly so in all cases with women. I want, at this particular time, more than anything else, to do right with you, and if I knew it would be doing right, as I rather suspect it would, to let you alone, I would do it. And for the purpose of making the matter as plain as possible, I now say, that you can now drop the subject, dismiss your thoughts (if you ever had any) from me forever, and leave this letter unanswered, without calling forth one accusing murmur from me. And I will even go farther, and say, that if it will add anything to your comfort or peace of mind to do so, it is my sincere wish that you should. Do not understand by this that I wish to cut your acquaintance. I mean no such thing. What I do wish is that our further acquaintance shall depend upon yourself. If such further acquaintance would contribute nothing to your happiness, I am sure it would not to mine. If you feel yourself in any degree bound to me, I am now willing to release you, provided you wish it; while, on the other hand, I am willing and even anxious to bind you faster if I can be convinced that it will in any considerable degree add to your happiness. This, indeed, is the whole question with me. Nothing would make me more miserable, nothing more happy, than to know you were so.

"In what I have now said, I think I cannot be misunderstood; and to make myself understood is the sole object of this letter.

"If it suits you best to not answer this—farewell—a long life and a merry one attend you. But if you conclude to write back, speak as plainly as I do. There can be neither harm nor danger in saying to me anything you think, just in the manner you think it.

"My respects to your sister.

"Your friend,

"Lincoln."[13]

For an account of the final outcome of this *affaire du cœur* the reader is now referred to the most ludicrous letter Mr. Lincoln ever wrote. It has been said, but with how much truth I do not know, that during his term as President the lady to whom it was written—Mrs. O. H. Browning, wife of a fellow-member of the Legislature—before giving a copy of it to a biographer, wrote to Lincoln asking his consent to the publication, but that he answered warning her against it because it was too full of truth. The only biographer who ever did insert it apologized for its appearance in his book, regarding it for many reasons as an extremely painful duty. "If it could be withheld," he laments, "and the act decently reconciled to the conscience of a biographer* professing to be honest and candid, it should never see the light in these pages. Its grotesque humor, its coarse exaggerations in describing the person of a lady whom the writer was willing to marry; its imputation of toothless and weather-beaten old age to a woman really young and handsome; its utter lack of that delicacy of tone and sentiment which one naturally expects a gentleman to adopt when he thinks proper to discuss the

---

*Lamon, p. 181.

merits of his late mistress—all these, and its defective orthography, it would certainly be more agreeable to suppress than to publish. But if we begin by omitting or mutilating a document which sheds so broad a light upon one part of his life and one phase of his character, why may we not do the like as fast and as often as the temptation arises? and where shall the process cease?"

I prefer not to take such a serious view of the letter or its publication. My idea is, that Mr. Lincoln got into one of his irresistible moods of humor and fun—a state of feeling into which he frequently worked himself to avert the overwhelming effects of his constitutional melancholy—and in the inspiration of the moment penned this letter, which many regard as an unfortunate composition. The class who take such a gloomy view of the matter should bear in mind that the letter was written by Mr. Lincoln in the fervor of early manhood, just as he was emerging from a most embarrassing situation, and addressed to a friend whom he supposed would keep it sacredly sealed from the public eye. As a matter of fact Mr. Lincoln was not gifted with a ready perception of the propriety of things in all cases. Nothing with him was intuitive. To have profound judgment and just discrimination he required time to think; and if facts or events were forced before him in too rapid succession the machinery of his judgment failed to work. A knowledge of this fact will account for the letter, and also serve to rob the offence—if any was committed—of half its severity.

The letter was written in the same month Miss Owens made her final departure from Illinois.

"Springfield, April 1, 1838.
"Dear Madam:—

"Without apologizing for being egotistical, I shall make the history of so much of my life as has elapsed since I saw you the subject of this letter. And, by the way, I now discover that, in order to give a full and intelligible account of the things I have done and suffered since I saw you, I shall necessarily have to relate some that happened before.

"It was, then, in the autumn of 1836 that a married lady of my acquaintance and who was a great friend of mine, being about to pay a visit to her father and other relatives residing in Kentucky, proposed to me that on her return she would bring a sister of hers with her on condition that I would engage to become her brother-in-law with all convenient despatch. I, of course, accepted the proposal, for you know I could not have done otherwise, had I really been averse to it; but privately, between you and me I was most confoundedly well pleased with the project. I had seen the said sister some three years before, thought her intelligent and agreeable, and saw no good objection to plodding life through hand in hand with her. Time passed on, the lady took her journey, and in due time returned, sister in company sure enough. This astonished me a little; for it appeared to me that her coming so readily showed that she was a trifle too willing; but, on reflection, it occurred to me that she might have been prevailed on by her married sister to come, without anything concerning me ever having been mentioned to her; and so I concluded that, if no other objection presented itself, I would consent to waive this. All this occurred to me on hearing of her arrival in the neighborhood; for, be it remembered, I had not yet seen her, except about three years previous, as above mentioned. In a few days we had an interview; and, although I had seen her before, she did not look as my imagination had pictured her. I knew she was over-size, but she now appeared a fair match for Falstaff. I knew she was called an 'old maid,' and I felt no doubt of the truth of at least half of the appellation; but now, when I beheld her, I could not for my life avoid thinking of my mother; and this, not from withered features, for her skin was too full of fat to permit of its contracting into wrinkles, but from her want of teeth, weather-beaten appearance in general, and from a kind of notion that ran in my head that nothing could have commenced at the size of infancy and reached her present bulk in less than thirty-five or forty years; and, in short, I was not at all pleased with her. But what could I do? I had told her sister I would take her for better or for worse; and I made a point of honor and conscience in all things to stick to my word, especially if others had been induced to act on it, which in this case I had no doubt they had; for I was now fairly convinced that no other man on earth would have her, and hence the conclusion that they were bent on holding me to my bargain. 'Well,' thought I, 'I have said it, and be the consequences what they may, it shall not be my fault if I fail to do it.' At once I determined to consider her my wife; and, this done, all my powers of discovery were put to work in search of perfections in her which might be fairly set off against her defects. I tried to imagine her handsome, which, but for her unfortunate corpulency, was actually true. Exclusive of this, no woman that I have ever seen has a finer face. I also tried to convince myself that the mind was much more to be valued than the person; and in this she was not inferior, as I could discover, to any with whom I had been acquainted.

"Shortly after this, without coming to any positive understanding with her, I set out for Vandalia, when and where you first saw me. During my stay there I had letters from her which did not change my opinion of either her intellect or intention, but on the contrary confirmed it in both.

"All this while, although I was fixed, 'firm as the surge-repelling rock,'[14] in my resolution, I found I was continually repenting the rashness which had led me to make it. Through life, I have been in no bondage, either real or imaginary, from the thraldom of which I so much desired to be free. After my return home, I saw nothing to change my opinions of her in any particular. She was the same, and so was I. I now spent my time in planning how I might get along through life after my contemplated change of circumstances should have taken place, and how I might procrastinate the evil day for a time, which I really dreaded as much, perhaps more, than an Irishman does the halter.

"After all my suffering upon this deeply interesting subject, here I am, wholly, unexpectedly, completely, out of the 'scrape;' and now I want to know if you can guess how I got out of it—out, clear, in every sense of the term; no violation of word, honor, or conscience. I don't believe you can guess, and so I might as well tell you at once. As the lawyer says, it was done in the manner following, to-wit: After I had delayed the matter as long as I thought I could in honor do (which, by the way, had brought me round into the last fall), I concluded I might as well bring it to a consummation without further delay; and so I mustered my resolution, and made the proposal to her direct; but, shocking to relate, she answered, No. At first I supposed she did it through an affectation of modesty, which I thought but ill became her under the peculiar circumstances of her case; but on the renewal of the charge, I found she repelled it with greater firmness than before. I tried it again and again, but with the same success, or rather with the same want of success.

"I finally was forced to give it up; at which I very unexpectedly found myself mortified almost beyond endurance. I was mortified, it seemed to me, in a hundred different ways. My vanity was deeply wounded by the reflection that I had been too stupid to discover her intentions, and at the same time never doubting that I understood them perfectly; and also that she, whom I had taught myself to believe nobody else would have, had actually rejected me with all my fancied greatness. And, to cap the whole, I then for the first time began to suspect that I was really a little in love with her. But let it all go. I'll try and outlive it. Others have been made fools of by the girls; but this can never with truth be said of me. I most emphatically, in this instance, made a fool of myself. I have now come to the conclusion never again to think of marrying, and for this reason: I can never be satisfied with any one who would be blockhead enough to have me.

"When you receive this, write me a long yarn about something to amuse me. Give my respects to Mr. Browning.

"Your sincere friend,

"A. Lincoln."

Mrs. O. H. Browning.[15]

As before mentioned Miss Owens was afterwards married and became the mother of five children. Two of her sons served in the Confederate army. She died July 4, 1877. Speaking of Mr. Lincoln a short time before her death she referred to him as "a man with a heart full of human kindness and a head full of common-sense."[16]

CHAPTER VIII.

In December, 1834, Lincoln prepared himself for the Legislature to which he had been elected by such a complimentary majority. Through the generosity of his friend Smoot he purchased a new suit of clothes, and entering the stage at New Salem, rode through to Vandalia, the seat of government. He appreciated the dignity of his new position, and instead of walking to the capitol, as some of his biographers have contended, availed himself of the usual mode of travel. At this session of the Legislature he was anything but conspicuous. In reality he was very modest, but shrewd enough to impress the force of his character on those persons whose influence might some day be of advantage to him. He made but little stir, if we are to believe the record, during the whole of this first session. Made a member of the committee on Public Accounts and Expenditures, his name appears so seldom in the reports of the proceedings that we are prone to conclude that he must have contented himself with listening to the flashes of border oratory and absorbing his due proportion of parliamentary law. He was reserved in manner, but very observant; said little, but learned much; made the acquaintance of all the members and many influential persons on the outside. The lobby at that day contained the representative men of the state— men of acknowledged prominence and respectability, many of them able lawyers, drawn thither in advocacy of some pet bill.[1] Schemes of vast internal improvements attracted a retinue of log-rollers, who in later days seem to have been an indispensable necessity in the movement of complicated legislative machinery. Men of capital and brains were there. He early realized the importance of knowing all these, trusting to the inspiration of some future hour to impress them with his skill as an organizer or his power as an orator. Among the members of the outside or "third body" was Stephen A. Douglas, whom Lincoln then saw for the first time. Douglas had come from Vermont only the year before, but was already undertaking to supplant John J. Hardin in the office of States Attorney for the district in which both lived. What impression he made on Lincoln, what opinions each formed of the other, or what the extent of their acquaintance then was, we do not know. It is said that Lincoln afterwards in mentioning their first meeting observed of the newly-arrived Vermonter that he was the "least man he had ever seen."[2] The Legislature proper contained the youth and blood and fire of the frontier. Some of the men who participated in these early parliamentary battles were destined to carry the banners of great political parties, some to lead in war and some in the great council chamber of the nation. Some were to fill the Governor's office, others to wear the judicial ermine, and one was destined to be Chief Magistrate and die a martyr to the cause of human liberty.

The society of Vandalia and the people attracted thither by the Legislature made it, for that early day, a gay place indeed. Compared to Lincoln's former environments, it had no lack of refinement and polish. That he absorbed a good deal of this by contact with the men and women who surrounded him there can be no doubt. The "drift of sentiment and the sweep of civilization" at this time can best be measured by the character of the legislation. There were acts to incorporate banks, turnpikes, bridges, insurance companies, towns, railroads, and female academies. The vigor and enterprise of New England fusing with the illusory prestige of Kentucky and Virginia was fast forming a new civilization to spread over the prairies! At this session Lincoln remained quietly in the background, and contented himself with the introduction of a resolution in favor of securing to the State a part of the proceeds of sales of public lands within its limits. With this brief and modest record he returned to his constituents at New Salem.[3] With zealous perseverance, he renewed his application to the law and to surveying, continuing his studies in both departments until he became, as he thought, reliable and proficient. By reason of a change in the office of Surveyor for the county he became a deputy under Thomas M. Neale, who had been elected to succeed John Calhoun. The speculation in lands made a brisk business for the new surveyor, who even added Calhoun, his predecessor, to the list of deputies. Lincoln had now become somewhat established in the good-will and respect of his constituents. His bashfulness and timidity was gradually giving way to a feeling of self-confidence, and he began to exult over his ability to stand alone. The brief taste of public office which he had just enjoyed, and the distinction it gave him only whetted his appetite for further honors. Accordingly, in 1836 we find him a candidate for the Legislature again. I well remember this campaign and the election which followed, for my father, Archer G. Herndon, was also a candidate, aspiring to a seat in the State Senate. The Legislature at the session previous had in its apportionment bill increased the delegation from Sangamon county to seven Representatives and two Senators. Party conventions had not yet been invented, and there being no nominating machinery to interfere, the field was open for any and all to run. Lincoln again resorted, in opening his canvass, to the medium of the political handbill. Although it had not operated with the most satisfactory results in his first campaign, yet he felt willing to risk it again. Candidates of that day evinced far more willingness to announce their position than political aspirants do now. Without waiting for a convention to construct a platform, or some great political leader to "sound the key-note of the campaign," they stepped to the forefront and blew the bugle themselves. This custom will account for the boldness of Lincoln's utterances and the unequivocal tone of his declarations. His card—a sort of political fulmination—was as follows:

"New Salem, June 13, 1836.

"To the Editor of The Journal:

"In your paper of last Saturday I see a communication over the signature of 'Many Voters' in which the candidates who are announced in the *Journal* are called upon to 'show their hands.' Agreed. Here's mine:

"I go for all sharing the privileges of the government who assist in bearing its burdens. Consequently, I go for admitting all whites to the right of suffrage who pay taxes or bear arms (by no means excluding females).

"If elected I shall consider the whole people of Sangamon my constituents, as well those that oppose as those that support me.

"While acting as their Representative, I shall be governed by their will on all subjects upon which I have the means of knowing what their will is; and upon all others I shall do what my own judgment teaches me will best advance their interests. Whether elected or not, I go for distributing the proceeds of the sales of public lands to the several States to enable our State, in common with others, to dig canals and construct railroads without borrowing money and paying the interest on it.

"If alive on the first Monday in November, I shall vote for Hugh L. White, for President.

"Very respectfully,
"A. Lincoln."[4]

It is generally admitted that the bold and decided stand Lincoln took—though too audacious and emphatic for statesmen of a later day—suited the temper of the times. Leaving out of sight his expressed preference for White of Tennessee,—on whom all the anti-Jackson forces were disposed to concentrate, and which was but a mere question of men,—there is much food for thought in the second paragraph. His broad plan for universal suffrage certainly commends itself to the ladies, and we need no further evidence to satisfy our minds of his position on the subject of "Woman's Rights," had he lived. In fact, I cannot refrain from noting here what views he in after years held with reference to the great questions of moral and social reforms, under which he classed universal suffrage, temperance, and slavery. "All such questions," he observed one day, as we were discussing temperance in the office, "must first find lodgment with the most enlightened souls who stamp them with their approval. In God's own time they will be organized into law and thus woven into the fabric of our institutions."

The canvass which followed this public avowal of creed, was more exciting than any which had preceded it. There were joint discussions, and, at times, much feeling was exhibited. Each candidate had his friends freely distributed through the crowd, and it needed but a few angry interruptions or insinuating rejoinders from one speaker to another to bring on a conflict between their friends. Frequently the speakers led in the battle themselves, as in the case of Ninian W. Edwards—afterwards a brother-in-law of Lincoln—who, in debate, drew a pistol on his opponent Achilles Morris, a prominent Democrat.[5] An interesting relic of this canvass recently came to light, in a letter which Mr. Lincoln wrote a week after he had announced his candidacy. It is addressed to Colonel Robert Allen, a Democratic politician of local prominence, who had been circulating some charges intended to affect Lincoln's chances of election. The affair brought to the surface what little satire there was in Lincoln's nature, and he administers—by way of innuendo—such a flaying as the gallant colonel doubtless never wanted to have repeated. The strangest part of it all is that the letter was recently found and given to the public by Allen's own son.° It is as follows:

"New Salem, June 21, 1836.
"Dear Colonel:
"I am told that during my absence last week you passed through the place and stated publicly that you were in possession of a fact or facts, which if known to the public would entirely destroy the prospects of N. W. Edwards and myself at the ensuing election, but that through favor to us you would forbear to divulge them. No one has needed favors more than I, and gener-

---

°The MS. is now in possession of the Lincoln Monument Association of Springfield.

ally few have been less unwilling to accept them, but in this case favor to me would be injustice to the public, and therefore I must beg your pardon for declining it. That I once had the confidence of the people of Sangamon county is sufficiently evident; and if I have done anything, either by design or misadventure, which if known would subject me to a forfeiture of that confidence, he that knows of that thing, and conceals it, is a traitor to his country's interest.

"I find myself wholly unable to form any conjecture of what fact or facts, real or supposed, you spoke; but my opinion of your veracity will not permit me for a moment to doubt that you at least believed what you said. I am flattered with the personal regard you manifested for me; but I do hope that on mature reflection you will view the public interest as a paramount consideration and therefore let the worst come.

"I assure you that the candid statement of facts on your part, however low it may sink me, shall never break the ties of personal friendship between us.

"I wish an answer to this, and you are at liberty to publish both if you choose.

"Very respectfully,
"A. Lincoln."
Col. Robert Allen.[6]

Lincoln was sure the letter never would be published or answered, because Allen had no facts whatever upon which to base any such charges. He also knew that Allen, who was a hide-bound Democrat, was in politics the most unreliable man in Sangamon county. A vein of irony runs all through the letter, especially where in such a delicate way he pays tribute to the veracity of Allen, who, although a generous fellow in the ordinary sense of the term, was unlimited in exaggeration and a veritable bag of wind. The effort to smoke him out seems to have been of little effect, but enough appears in Lincoln's letter to show that he was thoroughly warmed up.

A joint debate in which all the candidates participated, took place on the Saturday preceding the election. "The speaking began in the forenoon," says one of the participants, "the candidates speaking alternately until everyone who could speak had had his turn, generally consuming the whole afternoon."[7] Dr. Early, a Democratic candidate, in his speech took issue with Ninian W. Edwards, stigmatizing some of the latter's statements as untrue. This brought Edwards to his feet with a similar retort. His angry tone and menacing manner, as he mounted a table and with clenched fist hurled defiance at his challenger, foreboded a tumultuous scene. "The excitement that followed," relates another one of the candidates,° "was intense—so much so that fighting men thought a duel must settle the difficulty. Mr. Lincoln by the programme followed Early. Taking up the subject in dispute, he handled it so fairly and with such ability, all were astonished and pleased."[8] The turbulent spirits were quieted and the difficulty was easily overcome.

Lincoln's friend Joshua F. Speed relates that during this campaign he made a speech in Springfield a few days before the election. "The crowd was large," says Speed, "and great numbers of his friends and admirers had come in from the country. I remember that his speech was a very able one, using with great power and originality all the arguments used to sustain the principles of the Whig party as against its great rival, the Democratic party of that day. The speech produced a profound impression—the crowd was with him. George Forquer, an old citizen, a man of recognized prominence and ability as a lawyer, was present. Forquer had been a Whig—one of the champions of the party—but had then recently joined the Democratic party, and almost simultaneous with the change had been appointed Register of the Land Office, which office he then held. Just about that time Mr. Forquer had completed a neat frame house—the best house then in Springfield—and over it had erected a lightning rod, the only one in the place and the first one Mr. Lincoln had ever seen. He afterwards told me that seeing Forquer's lightning rod had led him to the study of the properties of electricity and the utility of the rod as a conductor. At the conclusion of Lincoln's speech the crowd was about dispersing, when Forquer rose and asked to be heard. He commenced by saying that the young man would have to be taken down, and was sorry the task devolved on him. He then proceeded to answer Lincoln's speech in a style which, while it was able and fair, in his whole manner asserted and claimed superiority."[9] Lincoln stood a few steps away with arms folded, carefully watching the speaker and taking in everything he said. He was laboring under a good deal of suppressed excitement. Forquer's sting had roused the lion within him. At length Forquer concluded, and he mounted the stand to reply.

"I have heard him often since," continued Speed, "in the courts and before the people, but never saw him appear and acquit himself so well as upon that occasion. His reply to Forquer was characterized by great dignity and force. I shall never forget the conclusion of that speech: 'Mr. Forquer commenced his speech by announcing that the young man would have to be taken down. It is for you, fellow citizens, not for me to say whether I am up or down. The gentleman has seen fit to allude to my being a young man; but he forgets that I am older in

°R. L. Wilson, letter, Feb. 10, 1866, MS.

years than I am in the tricks and trades of politicians. I desire to live, and I desire place and distinction; but I would rather die now than, like the gentleman, live to see the day that I would change my politics for an office worth three thousand dollars a year, and then feel compelled to erect a lightning rod to protect a guilty conscience from an offended God.'"[10] The effect of this rejoinder was wonderful, and gave Forquer and his lightning rod a notoriety the extent of which no one envied him.

In the election which followed, Sangamon county in a political sense was entirely turned over. Hitherto the Democrats had always carried it, but now the Whigs gained control by an average majority of four hundred. This time Lincoln led his ticket. The nine elected were, Abraham Lincoln, Ninian W. Edwards, John Dawson, Andrew McCormick, Dan Stone, Wm. F. Elkin, Robert L. Wilson, Job Fletcher, and Archer G. Herndon. The last two were senators. On assembling at Vandalia they were at once, on account of their stature, dubbed the "Long Nine." In height they averaged over six feet, and in weight over two hundred pounds. "We were not only noted," says one° of them, "for our number and length, but for our combined influence. All the bad or objectional laws passed at that session of the Legislature and for many years afterwards were chargeable to the management and influence of the 'Long Nine.'"[11] It is not my purpose to enter into a detailed account of legislation at this period or to rehearse the history of the political conditions. Many and ingenious were the manœuvres, but it would fill page after page to narrate them. One thing which deserves mention in passing was "that Yankee contrivance," the convention system, which for the first time was brought into use. The Democrats, in obedience to the behests of Jackson, had adopted it, and, singularly enough, among the very first named for office under the operation of the new system was Stephen A. Douglas, who was elected to the Legislature from Morgan county. Its introduction was attributed to Ebenezer Peck, of Chicago, a Democrat who had once, it was said, served in the Canadian Parliament. This latter supposed connection with a monarchical institution was sufficient to bring down on his head the united hostility of the Whigs, a feeling in which even Lincoln joined. But after witnessing for a time the wonderful effects of its discipline in Democratic ranks, the Whigs too fell in, and resorted to the use of the improved machinery.

The Legislature of which Mr. Lincoln thus became a member was one that will never be forgotten in Illinois. Its legislation in aid of the so-called internal improvement system was significantly reckless and unwise. The gigantic and stu-

---

°R. L. Wilson, MS.

pendous operations of the scheme dazzled the eyes of nearly everybody, but in the end it rolled up a debt so enormous as to impede the otherwise marvelous progress of Illinois. The burdens imposed by this Legislature under the guise of improvements became so monumental in size it is little wonder that at intervals for years afterward the monster of repudiation often showed its hideous face above the waves of popular indignation. These attempts at a settlement of the debt brought about a condition of things which it is said led the Little Giant, in one of his efforts on the stump, to suggest that "Illinois ought to be honest if she never paid a cent."[12] However much we may regret that Lincoln took part and aided in this reckless legislation, we must not forget that his party and all his constituents gave him their united endorsement. They gave evidence of their approval of his course by two subsequent elections to the same office. It has never surprised me in the least that Lincoln fell so harmoniously in with the great system of improvement. He never had what some people call "money sense." By reason of his peculiar nature and construction he was endowed with none of the elements of a political economist. He was enthusiastic and theoretical to a certain degree; could take hold of, and wrap himself up in, a great moral question; but in dealing with the financial and commercial interests of a community or government he was equally as inadequate as he was ineffectual in managing the economy of his own household. In this respect alone I always regarded Mr. Lincoln as a weak man.

One of his biographers, describing his legislative career at this time, says of him: "He was big with prospects: his real public service was just now about to begin. In the previous Legislature he had been silent, observant, studious. He had improved the opportunity so well that of all men in this new body, of equal age in the service, he was the smartest parliamentarian and cunningest 'log roller.' He was fully determined to identify himself conspicuously with the liberal legislation in contemplation, and dreamed of a fame very different from that which he actually obtained as an anti-slavery leader. It was about this time he told his friend Speed that he aimed at the great distinction of being called the 'DeWitt Clinton of Illinois.'"[13]

The representatives in the Legislature from Sangamon county had been instructed by a mass convention of their constituents to vote "for a general system of internal improvements." Another convention of delegates from all the counties in the State met at Vandalia and made a similar recommendation to the members of the Legislature, specifying that it should be "commensurate with the wants of the people."[14] Provision was made for a gridiron of railroads. The extreme points of the State, east and west, north and south, were to be brought together by thirteen hundred miles of iron rails. Every river and stream of the least importance was to be widened, deepened, and made navigable. A canal to connect the Illinois River and Lake Michigan was to be dug, and thus the great system was to be made "commensurate with the wants of the people." To effect all these great ends, a loan of twelve million dollars was authorized before the session closed. Work on all these gigantic enterprises was to begin at the earliest practicable moment; cities were to spring up everywhere; capital from abroad was to come pouring in; attracted by the glowing reports of marvelous progress and great internal wealth, people were to come swarming in by colonies, until in the end Illinois was to outstrip all the others, and herself become the Empire State of the Union.

Lincoln served on the Committee on Finance, and zealously labored for the success of the great measures proposed, believing they would ultimately enrich the State, and redound to the glory of all who aided in their passage. In advocating these extensive and far-reaching plans he was not alone. Stephen A. Douglas, John A. McClernand, James Shields, and others prominent in the subsequent history of the State, were equally as earnest in espousing the cause of improvement, and sharing with him the glory that attended it. Next in importance came the bill to remove the seat of government from Vandalia. Springfield, of course, wanted it. So also did Alton, Decatur, Peoria, Jacksonville, and Illiopolis. But the Long Nine, by their adroitness and influence, were too much for their contestants. They made a bold fight for Springfield, intrusting the management of the bill to Lincoln. The friends of other cities fought Springfield bitterly, but under Lincoln's leadership the Long Nine contested with them every inch of the way. The struggle was warm and protracted. "Its enemies," relates one of Lincoln's colleagues,° "laid it on the table twice. In those darkest hours when our bill to all appearances was beyond resuscitation, and all our opponents were jubilant over our defeat, and when friends could see no hope, Mr. Lincoln never for one moment despaired; but collecting his colleagues to his room for consultation, his practical common-sense, his thorough knowledge of human nature, then made him an overmatch for his compeers and for any man that I have ever known."[15] The friends of the bill at last surmounted all obstacles, and only a day or two before the close of the session secured its passage by a joint vote of both houses.

Meanwhile the great agitation against human slavery, which like a rare plant had flourished amid the hills of New England in luxuriant growth, began to make

---

°R. L. Wilson, MS.

its appearance in the West. Missionaries in the great cause of human liberty were settling everywhere. Taunts, jeers, ridicule, persecution, assassination even, were destined to prove ineffectual in the effort to suppress or exterminate these pioneers of Abolitionism. These brave but derided apostles carried with them the seed of a great reform. Perhaps, as was then said of them, they were somewhat in advance of their season, and perhaps too, some of the seed might be sown in sterile ground and never come to life, but they comforted themselves with the assurance that it would not all die. A little here and there was destined to grow to life and beauty.

It is not surprising, I think, that Lincoln should have viewed this New England importation with mingled suspicion and alarm. Abstractly, and from the standpoint of conscience, he abhorred slavery. But born in Kentucky, and surrounded as he was by slave-holding influences, absorbing their prejudices and following in their line of thought, it is not strange, I repeat, that he should fail to estimate properly the righteous indignation and unrestrained zeal of a Yankee Abolitionist. On the last day but one of the session, he solicited his colleagues to sign with him a mild and carefully worded protest against certain resolutions on the subject of domestic slavery, which had been passed by both houses of the Legislature. They all declined, however, save one, Dan Stone,° who with his associate will probably be known long after mention of all other members of the Long Nine has dropped from history. The language and sentiment are clearly Lincolnian, and over twenty years afterward, when it was charged that Lincoln was an Abolitionist, and this protest was cited as proof, it was only necessary to call for a careful reading of the paper for an unqualified and overwhelming refutation of the charge. The records of the Legislature for March 3, 1837, contain this entry:

"Resolutions upon the subject of domestic slavery having passed both branches of the General Assembly at its present session, the undersigned hereby protest against the passage of the same.

"They believe that the institution of slavery is founded on both injustice and bad policy, but that the promulgation of abolition doctrines tends rather to increase than abate its evils.

"They believe that the Congress of the United States has no power

---

°Following are the resolutions against the passage of which Lincoln and Stone made their protest:

Resolved by the General Assembly of the State of Illinois: That we highly disapprove of the formation of Abolition societies and of the doctrines promulgated by them,

That the right of property in slaves is sacred to the slave-holding States by the Federal Constitution, and that they cannot be deprived of that right without their consent,

That the General Government cannot abolish slavery in the District of Columbia against the consent of the citizens of said District, without a manifest breach of good faith,

That the Governor be requested to transmit to the States of Virginia, Alabama, Mississippi, New York, and Connecticut, a copy of the foregoing report and resolutions.[16]

under the Constitution to interfere with the institution of slavery in the different States.

"They believe that the Congress of the United States has the power under the Constitution to abolish slavery in the District of Columbia, but that the power ought not to be exercised unless at the request of the people of the District.

"The difference between these opinions and those contained in the above resolutions is their reason for entering this protest.

"Dan Stone,

"A. Lincoln,

"Representatives from the county of Sangamon."[17]

This document so adroitly drawn and worded, this protest pruned of any offensive allusions, and cautiously framed so as to suit the temper of the times, stripped of its verbal foliage reveals in naked grandeur the solemn truth that "the institution of slavery is founded on both injustice and bad policy." A quarter of a century later finds one of these protesters righting the injustice and correcting the bad policy of the inhuman and diabolical institution.

The return of the "Long Nine" to Springfield was the occasion of much enthusiasm and joy. The manifestations of public delight had never been equalled before, save when the steamer *Talisman* made its famous trip down the Sangamon in 1831. The returning legislators were welcomed with public dinners and the effervescent buncombe of local orators. Amid the congratulations of warm friends and the approval of their enthusiastic constituents, in which Lincoln received the lion's share of praise, they separated, each departing to his own home.

After his return from the Legislature, Lincoln determined to remove to Springfield, the county seat, and begin the practice of the law. Having been so instrumental in securing the removal of the State Capital from Vandalia, and having received such encouraging assurances from Major John T. Stuart and other leading citizens, he felt confident of a good start.° He had little, if any, money, but hoped to find in Springfield, as he had in New Salem, good and influential friends, who, recognizing alike his honesty and his nobility of character, would aid him whenever a crisis came and their help was needed. In this hope he was by no means in error, for his subsequent history shows that he indeed united his friends to himself with hooks of steel. I had up to this time frequently seen

---

°"Lincoln used to come to our office—Stuart's and mine—in Springfield from New Salem and borrow law-books. Sometimes he walked but generally rode. He was the most uncouth looking young man I ever saw. He seemed to have but little to say; seemed to feel timid, with a tinge of sadness visible in the countenance, but when he did talk all this disappeared for the time and he demonstrated that he was both strong and acute. He surprised us more and more at every visit."—Henry E. Dummer, Statement, Sept. 16th, 1865.[18]

Mr. Lincoln—had often, while visiting my cousins, James and Rowan Herndon, at New Salem, met him at their house—but became warmly attached to him soon after his removal to Springfield. There was something in his tall and angular frame, his ill-fitting garments, honest face, and lively humor that imprinted his individuality on my affection and regard. What impression I made on him I had no means of knowing till many years afterward. He was my senior by nine years, and I looked up to him, naturally enough, as my superior in everything—a thing I continued to do till the end of his days.

Now that the State capital was to be located at Springfield, that place began, by way of asserting its social superiority, to put on a good many airs. Wealth made its gaudy display, and thus sought to attain a pre-eminence from which learning and refinement are frequently cut off. Already, people had settled there who could trace their descent down a long line of distinguished ancestry. The established families were mainly from Kentucky. They re-echoed the sentiments and reflected the arrogance and elegance of a slave-holding aristocracy. "The Todds, Stuarts, and Edwardses were there, with priests, dogs, and servants;"[19] there also were the Mathers, Lambs, Opdykes, Forquers, and Fords. Amid all "the flourishing about in carriages" and the pretentious elegance of that early day was Lincoln. Of origin, doubtful if not unknown; "poor, without the means of hiding his poverty," he represented yet another importation from Kentucky which is significantly comprehended by the term, "the poor whites." Springfield, containing between one and two thousand people, was near the northern line of settlement in Illinois. Still it was the center of a limited area of wealth and refinement. Its citizens were imbued with the spirit of push and enterprise. Lincoln therefore could not have been thrown into a better or more appreciative community.

In March, 1837, he was licensed to practice law. His name appears for the first time as attorney for the plaintiff in the case of Hawthorne *vs.* Woolridge. He entered the office and became the partner of his comrade in the Black Hawk war, John T. Stuart, who had gained rather an extensive practice, and who, by the loan of sundry textbooks several years before, had encouraged Lincoln to continue in the study of law. Stuart had emigrated from Kentucky in 1828, and on account of his nativity, if for no other reason, had great influence with the leading people in Springfield. He used to relate that on the next morning after his arrival in Springfield he was standing in front of the village store, leaning against a post in the sidewalk and wondering how to introduce himself to the community, when he was approached by a well-dressed old gentleman, who, interesting himself in the newcomer's welfare, enquired after his history and business. "I'm from Kentucky," answered Stuart, "and my profession is that of a lawyer,

A Page from Stuart & Lincoln's Fee Book. Entries Written By Abraham Lincoln (slightly reduced).

sir. What is the prospect here?" Throwing his head back and closing his left eye the old gentleman reflected a moment. "Young man, d——d slim chance for that kind of a combination here," was the response.[20]

At the time of Lincoln's entry into the office, Stuart was just recovering from the effects of a congressional race in which he had been the loser. He was still deeply absorbed in politics, and was preparing for the next canvass, in which he was finally successful—defeating the wily and ambitious Stephen A. Douglas. In consequence of the political allurements, Stuart did not give to the law his undivided time or the full force of his energy and intellect. Thus more or less responsibility in the management of business and the conduct of cases soon devolved on Lincoln. The entries in the account books of the firm are all in the handwriting of Lincoln. Most of the declarations and pleas were written by him also. This sort of exercise was never congenial to him, and it was the only time, save a brief period under Judge Logan, that he served as junior partner and performed the labor required of one who serves in that rather subordinate capacity. He had not yet learned to love work. The office of the firm was in the upper story of a building opposite the north-west corner of the present Court-house Square. In the room underneath, the county court was held. The furniture was in keeping with the pretensions of the firm—a small lounge or bed, a chair containing a buffalo robe, in which the junior member was wont to sit and study, a hard wooden bench, a feeble attempt at a book-case, and a table which answered for a desk. Lincoln's first attempt at settlement in Springfield, which preceded a few days his partnership with Stuart, has been graphically described by his friend, Joshua F. Speed, who generously offered to share his quarters with the young legal aspirant. Speed, who was a prosperous young merchant, reports that Lincoln's personal effects consisted of a pair of saddle-bags containing two or three law books and a few pieces of clothing. "He had ridden into town on a borrowed horse," relates Speed, "and engaged from the only cabinet-maker in the village a single bedstead. He came into my store, set his saddle-bags on the counter, and enquired what the furniture for a single bedstead would cost. I took slate and pencil, made a calculation, and found the sum for furniture complete would amount to seventeen dollars in all. Said he: 'It is probably cheap enough; but I want to say that, cheap as it is, I have not the money to pay. But if you will credit me until Christmas, and my experiment here as a lawyer is a success, I will pay you then. If I fail in that I will probably never pay you at all.' The tone of his voice was so melancholy that I felt for him. I looked up at him and I thought then, as I think now, that I never saw so gloomy and melancholy a face in my life. I said to him, 'So small a debt seems to affect you so deeply, I think I can suggest a plan by which you will be able to attain your end without incurring any debt. I have a very large room and a very large double bed in it, which you are perfectly welcome to share with me if you choose.' 'Where is your room?' he asked. 'Upstairs,' said I, pointing to the stairs leading from the store to my room. Without saying a word he took his saddle-bags on his arm, went upstairs, set them down on the floor, came down again, and with a face beaming with pleasure and smiles, exclaimed, 'Well, Speed, I'm moved.'"[21]

William Butler, who was prominent in the removal of the capital from Vandalia to Springfield, took no little interest in Lincoln, while a member of the Legislature. After his removal to Springfield, Lincoln boarded at Butler's house for several years. He became warmly attached to the family, and it is probable the matter of pay never entered Butler's mind. He was not only able but willing to befriend the young lawyer in this and many other ways.

Stephen T. Logan was judge of the Circuit court, and Stephen A. Douglas was prosecuting attorney. Among the attorneys we find many promising spirits. Edward D. Baker, John T. Stuart, Cyrus Walker, Samuel H. Treat, Jesse B. Thomas, George Forquer, Dan Stone, Ninian W. Edwards, John J. Hardin, Schuyler Strong, A. T.

Joshua F. Speed

Bledsoe, and Josiah Lamborn—a galaxy of names, each destined to shed more or less lustre on the history of the State. While I am inclined to believe that Lincoln did not, after entering Stuart's office, do as much deep and assiduous studying as people generally credit him with, yet I am confident he absorbed not a little learning by contact with the great minds who thronged about the courts and State Capitol. The books of Stuart and Lincoln, during 1837, show a practice more extensive than lucrative, for while they received a number of fees, only two or three of them reached fifty dollars; and one of these has a credit of: "Coat to Stuart, $15.00," showing that they were compelled, now and then, even to "trade out" their earnings. The litigation was as limited in importance as in extent. There were no great corporations, as in this progressive day, retaining for counsel the brains of the bar in every county seat, but the greatest as well as the least had to join the general scramble for practice. The courts consumed as much time deciding who had committed an assault or a trespass on a neighbor's ground, as it spent in the solution of questions arising on contracts, or unravelling similar legal complications. Lawyers depended for success, not on their knowledge of the law or their familiarity with its underlying principles, but placed their reliance rather on their frontier oratory and the influence of their personal bearing before the jury.

Lincoln made Speed's store headquarters. There politics, religion, and all other subjects were discussed. There also public sentiment was made. The store had a large fire-place in the rear, and around it the lights of the town collected every evening. As the sparks flew from the crackling logs, another and more brilliant fire flashed when these great minds came into collision. Here were wont to gather Lincoln, Douglas, Baker, Calhoun, Browning, Lamborn, Jesse B. Thomas and others. Only those who were present and listened to these embryonic statesmen and budding orators will ever be able to recall their brilliant thoughts and appreciate their youthful enthusiasm. In the fall and winter of 1837, while I was attending college at Jacksonville, the persecution and death of Elijah P. Lovejoy at Alton took place. This cruel and uncalled-for murder had aroused the anti-slavery sentiment everywhere. It penetrated the college, and both faculty and students were loud and unrestrained in their denunciation of the crime. My father, who was thoroughly pro-slavery in his ideas, believing that the college was too strongly permeated with the virus of Abolitionism, forced me to withdraw from the institution and return home. But it was too late. My soul had absorbed too much of what my father believed was rank poison. The murder of Lovejoy filled me with more desperation than the slave scene in New Orleans did Lincoln; for while he believed in non-interference with slavery, so long as the Constitution permitted and authorized its existence, I, although acting nominally with the Whig party up to 1853, struck out for Abolitionism pure and simple.

On my return to Springfield from college, I hired to Joshua F. Speed as clerk in his store. My salary, seven hundred dollars per annum, was considered good pay then. Speed, Lincoln, Charles R. Hurst, and I slept in the room upstairs over the store. I had worked for Speed before going to college, and after hiring to him this time again, continued in his employ for several years. The young men who congregated about the store formed a society for the encouragement of debate and literary efforts. Sometimes we would meet in a lawyer's office and often in Speed's room. Besides the debates, poems and other original productions were read. Unfortunately we ruled out the ladies. I am free to admit I would not encourage a similar thing nowadays; but in that early day the young men had not the comforts of books and newspapers which are within the reach of every boy now. Some allowance therefore should be made for us. I have forgotten the name of the society—if it had any—and can only recall a few of its leading spirits. Lincoln, James Matheney, Noah Rickard, Evan Butler, Milton Hay, and Newton Francis were members. I joined also. Matheney was secretary. We were favored with all sorts of literary productions. Lincoln himself entertained us with a few lines of rhyme intended to illustrate some weakness in woman—her frailty, perhaps. Matheney was able several years ago to repeat the one stanza which follows, and that was all he could recall—perhaps it was best he could remember no more:[22]

"Whatever spiteful fools may say,
Each jealous, ranting yelper,
No woman ever went astray
Without a man to help her."°

Besides this organization we had a society in Springfield, which contained and commanded all the culture and talent of the place. Unlike the other one its meetings were public, and reflected great credit on the community. We called it the "Young Men's Lyceum." Late in 1837, Lincoln delivered before the society a carefully prepared address on the "Perpetuation of Our Free Institutions."† The inspiration and burthen of it was law and order. It has been printed in full so often, and is always to be found in the list of Lincoln's public speeches, that I presume I need not reproduce it here. It was highly sophomoric in character and abounded in striking and lofty metaphor. In point of rhetorical effort it excels anything he ever afterward attempted. Probably it was the thing people expect from a young man of twenty-eight. The address was published in the *Sangamon Journal* and created for the young orator a reputation which soon extended beyond the limits of the locality in which he lived. As illustrative of his style of oratory, I beg to introduce the concluding paragraph of the address. Having characterized the surviving soldiers of the Revolution as "living histories," he closes with this thrilling flourish: "But these histories are gone. They can be read no more forever. They were a fortress of strength; but what invading foeman never could do, the silent artillery of time has—the levelling of its walls. They are gone. They were a forest of giant oaks; but the all-resistless hurricane has swept over them, and left only here and there a lonely trunk, despoiled of its verdure, shorn of its foliage, unshading and unshaded, to murmur in a few

---

°Near Hoffman's Row, where the courts were held in 1839–40, lived a shoemaker who frequently would get drunk and invariably whipped his wife. Lincoln, hearing of this, told the man if he ever repeated it he would thrash him soundly himself. Meanwhile he told Evan Butler, Noah Rickard, and myself of it, and we decided if the offense occurred again to join with Lincoln in suppressing it. In due course of time we heard of it. We dragged the offender up to the court-house, stripped him of his shirt, and tied him to a post or pump which stood over the well in the yard back of the building. Then we sent for his wife and arming her with a good limb bade her "light in." We sat on our haunches and watched the performance. The wife did her work lustily and well. When we thought the culprit had had enough Lincoln released him; we helped him on with his shirt and he crept sorrowfully homeward. Of course he threatened vengeance, but still we heard no further reports of wife-whipping from him.—James H. Matheney.[23]
†Mr. Lincoln's speech was brought out by the burning in St. Louis a few weeks before, by a mob, of a negro. Lincoln took this incident as a sort of text for his remarks. James Matheney was appointed by the Lyceum to request of Lincoln a copy of his speech and see to its publication.[24]

more gentle breezes, and to combat with its mutilated limbs a few more rude storms, then to sink and be no more. They were pillars of the temple of liberty, and now that they have crumbled away, that temple must fall, unless we, their descendants, supply their places with other pillars hewn from the same solid quarry of sober reason. Passion has helped us, but can do so no more. It will in future be our enemy. Reason—cold, calculating, unimpassioned reason—must furnish all the materials for our future support and defense. Let these materials be moulded into general intelligence, sound morality, and in particular, a reverence for the Constitution and the laws. ° ° ° Upon these let the proud fabric of freedom rest as the rock of its basis, and as truly as has been said of the only greater institution, 'The gates of hell shall not prevail against it.'"[25]

In time Lincoln's style changed: he became more eloquent but with less gaudy ornamentation. He grew in oratorical power, dropping gradually the alliteration and rosy metaphor of youth, until he was able at last to deliver that grandest of all orations—the Gettysburg address.

One evening, while the usual throng of loungers surrounded the inviting fireplace in Speed's store, the conversation turned on political matters. The disputants waxed warm and acrimonious as the discussion proceeded. Business being over for the day, I strolled back and seating myself on a keg listened with eager interest to the battle going on among these would-be statesmen. Douglas, I recollect, was leading on the Democratic side. He had already learned the art of dodging in debate, but still he was subtle, fiery, and impetuous. He charged the Whigs with every blunder and political crime he could imagine. No vulnerable spot seemed to have escaped him. At last, with great vehemence, he sprang up and abruptly made a challenge to those who differed with him to discuss the whole matter publicly, remarking that, "This store is no place to talk politics." In answer to Douglas's challenge the contest was entered into. It took place in the Presbyterian Church. Douglas, Calhoun, Lamborn, and Thomas represented the Democrats; and Logan, Baker, Browning, and Lincoln, in the order named, presented the Whig side of the question. One evening was given to each man, and it therefore required over a week to complete the tournament. Lincoln occupied the last evening, and although the people by that time had necessarily grown a little tired of the monotony and well-worn repetition; yet Lincoln's manner of presenting his thoughts and answering his Democratic opponents excited renewed interest. So deep was the impression he created that he was asked to furnish his speech to the *Sangamon Journal* for publication, and it afterwards appeared in the columns of that organ.[26]

Meanwhile Mr. Lincoln had attended one special session of the Legislature

in July, 1837. The session was called to take some action with regard to the financial condition of the State. The Bank of the United States and the New York and
Philadelphia Banks had suspended specie payments. This action had precipitated
general ruin among business men and interests over the entire country. The called
session of the Legislature was intended to save the Illinois banks from impending dissolution. Lincoln retained his position on the Committee on Finance, and
had lost none of his enthusiasm over the glorious prospects of internal improvements. The Legislature, instead of abridging, only extended the already colossal
proportions of the great system. In this they paid no heed to the governor, whose
head seems to have been significantly clear on the folly of the enterprise.

In 1838 Mr. Lincoln was again elected to the Legislature. At this session, as
the nominee of the Whig party, he received thirty-eight votes for Speaker. Wm.
L. D. Ewing, his successful competitor, the Democratic candidate, received
forty-three votes, and was elected. Besides retaining his place on the Finance
Committee, Lincoln was assigned to the Committee on Counties. The enthusiasm and zeal of the friends of internal improvements began to flag now in
view of the fact that the bonds issued were beginning to find their true level in
point of value. Lincoln, together with others of kindred views, tried to bolster
the "system" up; but soon the discouraging fact became apparent that no more
money could be obtained, and the Legislature began to descant on what part of
the debt was lawful and what unlawful. Repudiation seemed not far off. Mr. Lincoln despaired now of ever becoming the "DeWitt Clinton of Illinois." We find
him admitting "his share of the responsibility in the present crisis," and finally
concluding that he was "no financier" after all.[27] No sooner had the Legislature
adjourned than he decided—if he had not already so determined—to run for
the same place again. He probably wanted it for a vindication. He was pursued
now more fiercely than ever, and he was better able to endure the vilification
of a political campaign than when he first offered himself to the voters in New
Salem.

Among the Democratic orators who stumped the county at this time was
one Taylor—commonly known as Col. Dick Taylor. He was a showy, bombas-
tic man, with a weakness for fine clothes and other personal adornments. Frequently he was pitted against Lincoln, and indulged in many bitter flings at the
lordly ways and aristocratic pretensions of the Whigs. He had a way of appealing
to "his horny-handed neighbors," and resorted to many other artful tricks of a
demagogue. When he was one day expatiating in his accustomed style, Lincoln,
in a spirit of mischief and, as he expressed it, "to take the wind out of his sails,"
slipped up to the speaker's side, and catching his vest by the lower edge gave it a

sharp pull.[28] The latter instantly opened and revealed to his astonished hearers a ruffled shirt-front glittering with watch-chain, seals, and other golden jewels. The effect was startling. The speaker stood confused and dumbfounded, while the audience roared with laughter. When it came Lincoln's turn to answer he covered the gallant colonel over in this style: "While Colonel Taylor was making these charges against the Whigs over the country, riding in fine carriages, wearing ruffled shirts, kid gloves, massive gold watch-chains with large gold seals, and flourishing a heavy gold-headed cane, I was a poor boy, hired on a flat-boat at eight dollars a month, and had only one pair of breeches to my back, and they were buckskin. Now if you know the nature of buckskin when wet and dried by the sun, it will shrink; and my breeches kept shrinking until they left several inches of my legs bare between the tops of my socks and the lower part of my breeches; and whilst I was growing taller they were becoming shorter, and so much tighter that they left a blue streak around my legs that can be seen to this day. If you call this aristocracy I plead guilty to the charge."°

It was during this same canvass that Lincoln by his manly interference protected his friend E. D. Baker from the anger of an infuriated crowd. Baker was a brilliant and effective speaker, and quite as full too of courage as invective. He was addressing a crowd in the court room, which was immediately underneath Stuart and Lincoln's office. Just above the platform on which the speaker stood was a trap door in the floor, which opened into Lincoln's office. Lincoln at the time, as was often his habit, was lying on the floor looking down through the door at the speaker. I was in the body of the crowd. Baker was hot-headed and impulsive, but brave as a lion. Growing warm in his arraignment of the Democratic party, he charged that "wherever there was a land office there was a Democratic newspaper to defend its corruptions." This angered the brother of the editor of our town paper, who was present, and who cried out, "Pull him down," at the same time advancing from the crowd as if to perform the task himself. Baker, his face pale with excitement, squared himself for resistance. A shuffling of feet, a forward movement of the crowd, and great confusion followed. Just then a long pair of legs were seen dangling from the aperture above, and instantly the figure of Lincoln dropped on the platform. Motioning with his hands for silence and not succeeding, he seized a stone water-pitcher standing near by, threatening to break it over the head of the first man who laid hands on Baker. "Hold on, gentlemen," he shouted, "this is the land of free speech. Mr. Baker has a right to speak and ought to be heard. I am here to protect him, and no man shall take

---

°From MS. of Ninian W. Edwards.[29]

him from this stand if I can prevent it." His interference had the desired effect. Quiet was soon restored, and the valiant Baker was allowed to proceed.[30] I was in the back part of the crowd that night, and an enthusiastic Baker man myself. I knew he was a brave man, and even if Lincoln had not interposed, I felt sure he wouldn't have been pulled from the platform without a bitter struggle.

This canvass—1840—was Mr. Lincoln's last campaign for the Legislature. Feeling that he had had enough honor out of the office he probably aspired for a place of more distinction. Jesse B. Thomas, one of the men who had represented the Democratic side in the great debate in the Presbyterian Church, in a speech at the court-house during this campaign, indulged in some fun at the expense of the "Long Nine," reflecting somewhat more on Lincoln than the rest. The latter was not present, but being apprised by his friends of what had been said, hastened to the meeting, and soon after Thomas closed, stepped upon the platform and responded. The substance of his speech on this occasion was not so memorable as the manner of its delivery. He felt the sting of Thomas's allusions, and for the first time, on the stump or in public, resorted to mimicry for effect. In this, as will be seen later along, he was without a rival. He imitated Thomas in gesture and voice, at times caricaturing his walk and the very motion of his body. Thomas, like everybody else, had some peculiarities of expression and gesture, and these Lincoln succeeded in rendering more prominent than ever. The crowd yelled and cheered as he continued. Encouraged by these demonstrations, the ludicrous features of the speaker's performance gave way to intense and scathing ridicule. Thomas, who was obliged to sit near by and endure the pain of this unique ordeal, was ordinarily sensitive; but the exhibition goaded him to desperation. He was so thoroughly wrought up with suppressed emotion that he actually gave way to tears. I was not a witness of this scene, but the next day it was the talk of the town, and for years afterwards it was called the "skinning" of Thomas.[31] Speed was there, so were A. Y. Ellis, Ninian W. Edwards, and David Davis, who was just then coming into prominence. The whole thing was so unlike Lincoln, it was not soon forgotten either by his friends or enemies. I heard him afterwards say that the recollection of his conduct that evening filled him with the deepest chagrin. He felt that he had gone too far, and to rid his good-nature of a load, hunted up Thomas and made ample apology. The incident and its sequel proved that Lincoln could not only be vindictive but manly as well.

He was selected as an Elector on the Harrison ticket for President in 1840, and as such stumped over a good portion of the State. In debate he frequently met Douglas, who had already become the standard-bearer and exponent of Democratic principles. These joint meetings were spirited affairs sometimes;

but at no time did he find the Little Giant averse to a conflict. "He was very sensitive," relates one of his colleagues on the stump, "where he thought he had failed to meet the expectations of his friends. I remember a case. He was pitted by the Whigs in 1840 to debate with Mr. Douglas, the Democratic champion. Lincoln did not come up to the requirements of the occasion. He was conscious of his failure, and I never saw any man so much distressed. He begged to be permitted to try it again, and was reluctantly indulged; and in the next effort he transcended our highest expectations.° I never heard and never expect to hear such a triumphant vindication as he then gave of Whig measures or policy. He never after, to my knowledge, fell below himself."[32]

The campaign ended in his election to the Legislature. He was again the caucus nominee of the Whigs for Speaker, receiving thirty-six votes; but his former antagonist, William L. D. Ewing, was elected by a majority of ten votes over him. The proceedings of, and laws enacted by, this Legislature are so much a matter of history and so generally known that it seems a needless task on my part to enter into details. It is proper to note, however, in passing, that Mr. Lincoln was neither prompt nor constant in his attendance during the session. He had been to a certain extent "upset" by another love affair, the particulars of which must be assigned to a future chapter.

°Joseph Gillespie, MS. letter, June 5, '66.

CHAPTER IX.

The year 1840 finds Mr. Lincoln entering his thirty-second year and still unmarried. "I have come to the conclusion," he suggests in a facetious letter, two years before, "never again to think of marrying."[1] But meanwhile he had seen more of the world. The State Capital had been removed to Springfield, and he soon observed the power and influence one can exert with high family and social surroundings to draw upon. The sober truth is that Lincoln was inordinately ambitious. He had already succeeded in obtaining no inconsiderable political recognition, and numbered among his party friends men of wealth and reputation; but he himself was poor, besides lacking the graces and ease of bearing obtained through mingling in polite society—in fact, to use the expressive language of Mary Owens, he was "deficient in those little links which make up the chain of woman's happiness."[2] Conscious, therefore, of his humble rank in the social scale, how natural that he should seek by marriage in an influential family to establish strong connections and at the same time foster his political fortunes! This may seem an audacious thing to insinuate, but on no other basis can we reconcile the strange course of his courtship and the tempestuous chapters in his married life. It is a curious history, and the facts, long chained down, are gradually coming to the surface. When all is at last known, the world I believe will divide its censure between Lincoln and his wife.

Mary Todd, who afterwards became the wife of Mr. Lincoln, was born in Lexington, Kentucky, December 13, 1818. "My mother," related Mrs. Lincoln to me in 1865, "died when I was still young. I was educated by Madame Mantelli, a lady who lived opposite Mr. Clay's, and who was an accomplished French scholar. Our conversation at school was carried on entirely in French—in fact we were allowed to speak nothing else. I finished my education at Mrs. Ward's

Academy, an institution to which many people from the North sent their daughters. In 1837 I visited Springfield, Illinois, remaining three months. I returned to Kentucky, remaining till 1839, when I again set out for Illinois, which State finally became my home."[3]

The paternal grandfather of Mary Todd, General Levi Todd, was born in 1756, was educated in Virginia, and studied law in the office of General Lewis of that State.[4] He emigrated to Kentucky, was a lieutenant in the campaigns conducted by General George Rogers Clark against the Indians, and commanded a battalion in the battle of Blue Licks, August 18, 1782, where his brother, John Todd, was killed. He succeeded Daniel Boone in command of the militia, ranking as major-general, and was one of the first settlers in Lexington, Ky. February 25, 1779, he married Miss Jane Briggs. The seventh child of this union, born February 25, 1791, was Robert S. Todd, the father of Mrs. Lincoln. On her maternal side Mrs. Lincoln was highly connected. Her great-grandfather, General Andrew Porter, was in the war of the Revolution. He succeeded Peter Muhlenberg as major-general of the Pennsylvania militia. Her great uncles, George B. Porter, who was governor of Michigan, James Madison Porter, secretary of the navy under President Tyler, and David R. Porter, governor of Pennsylvania, were men of ability and distinction. Her mother, Anne Eliza Parker, was a cousin of her father, Robert S. Todd. The latter had served in both houses of the Kentucky Legislature, and for over twenty years was president of the Bank of Kentucky at Lexington. He died July 16, 1849.

To a young lady in whose veins coursed the blood that had come down from this long and distinguished ancestral line, who could even go back in the genealogical chart to the sixth century, Lincoln, the child of Nancy Hanks, whose descent was dimmed by the shadow of tradition, was finally united in marriage.

When Mary Todd came to her sister's house in Springfield in 1839, she was in her twenty-first year. She was a young woman of strong, passionate nature and quick temper, and had "left her home in Kentucky to avoid living under the same roof with a stepmother."° She came to live with her oldest sister, Elizabeth, who was the wife of Lincoln's colleague in the Legislature, Ninian W. Edwards. She had two other sisters, Frances, married to Dr. William Wallace, and Anne, who afterwards became the wife of C. M. Smith, a prominent and wealthy merchant. They all resided in Springfield. She was of the average height, weighing when I first saw her about a hundred and thirty pounds. She was rather compactly built, had a well rounded face, rich dark-brown hair, and bluish-gray eyes. In her bear-

---

°Mrs. Edwards, statement, Aug. 3, 1887.[5]

ing she was proud, but handsome and vivacious. Her education had been in no wise defective; she was a good conversationalist, using with equal fluency the French and English languages. When she used a pen, its point was sure to be sharp, and she wrote with wit and ability. She not only had a quick intellect but an intuitive judgment of men and their motives. Ordinarily she was affable and even charming in her manners; but when offended or antagonized, her agreeable qualities instantly disappeared beneath a wave of stinging satire or sarcastic bitterness, and her entire better nature was submerged. In her figure and physical proportions, in education, bearing, temperament, history—in everything she was the exact reverse of Lincoln.

On her return to Springfield she immediately entered society, and soon became one of the belles, leading the young men of the town a merry dance. She was a very shrewd observer, and discreetly and without apparent effort kept back all the unattractive elements in her unfortunate organization. Her trenchant wit, affability, and candor pleased the young men not less than her culture and varied accomplishments impressed the older ones with whom she came in contact. The first time I met her was at a dance at the residence of Col. Robert Allen, a gentleman mentioned in the preceding chapter. I engaged her for a waltz, and as we glided through it I fancied I never before had danced with a young lady who moved with such grace and ease. A few moments later, as we were promenading through the hall, I thought to compliment her graceful dancing by telling her that while I was conscious of my own awkward movements, she seemed to glide through the waltz with the ease of a serpent. The strange comparison was as unfortunate as it was hideous. I saw it in an instant, but too late to recall it. She halted for a moment, drew back, and her eyes flashed as she retorted: "Mr. Herndon, comparison to a serpent is rather severe irony, especially to a newcomer."

Through the influence of Joshua F. Speed, who was a warm friend of the Edwardses, Lincoln was led to call on Miss Todd. He was charmed with her wit and beauty, no less than by her excellent social qualities and profound knowledge of the strong and weak points in individual character. One visit succeeded another. It was the old story. Lincoln had again fallen in love. "I have often happened in the room where they were sitting," relates Mrs. Edwards, describing this courtship, "and Mary invariably led the conversation. Mr. Lincoln would sit at her side and listen. He scarcely said a word, but gazed on her as if irresistibly drawn towards her by some superior and unseen power. He could not maintain himself in a continued conversation with a lady reared as Mary was. He was not educated and equipped mentally to make himself either interesting or attractive to the ladies. He was a good, honest, and sincere young man whose rugged, manly qualities I admired; but to me he somehow seemed ill-constituted by nature and education to please such a woman as my sister. Mary was quick, gay, and in the social world somewhat brilliant. She loved show and power, and was the most ambitious woman I ever knew. She used to contend when a girl, to her friends in Kentucky, that she was destined to marry a President. I have heard her say that myself, and after mingling in society in Springfield she repeated the seemingly absurd and idle boast. Although Mr. Lincoln seemed to be attached to Mary, and fascinated by her wit and sagacity, yet I soon began to doubt whether they could always be so congenial. In a short time I told Mary my impression that they were not suited, or, as some persons who believe matches are made in heaven would say, not intended for each other."[6]

But Mrs. Edwards' advice was seed sown on rocky soil. The courtship ran on smoothly to the point of engagement, when a new and disturbing element loomed up ahead in their paths. It was no less than the dashing and handsome Stephen A. Douglas, who now appeared on the scene in the guise of a rival. As a society man Douglas was infinitely more accomplished, more attractive and influential than Lincoln, and that he should supplant the latter in the affections of the proud and aristocratic Miss Todd is not to be marveled at. He was unremitting in his attentions to the lady, promenaded the streets arm-in-arm with her—frequently passing Lincoln—and in every way made plain his intention to become the latter's rival. There are those who believe this warm reciprocation of young Douglas' affection was a mere flirtation on Mary Todd's part, intended to spur Lincoln up, to make him more demonstrative, and manifest his love more positively and with greater fervor. But a lady relative who lived with Lincoln and his wife for two years after their marriage is authority for the statement coming from Mrs. Lincoln herself that "she loved Douglas, and but for her promise to marry Lincoln would have accepted him." The unfortunate attitude she felt bound to maintain between these two young men ended in a spell of sickness. Douglas, still hopeful, was warm in the race, but the lady's physician,—her brother-in-law,—Dr. William Wallace, to whom she confided the real cause of her illness, saw Douglas and induced him to end his pursuit,° which he did with great reluctance.[7]

If Miss Todd intended by her flirtation with Douglas to test Lincoln's devotion, she committed a grievous error. If she believed, because he was ordinarily so undemonstrative, that he was without will-power and incapable of being aroused, she certainly did not comprehend the man. Lincoln began now to feel the sting. Miss Todd's spur had certainly operated and with awakening effect.

°Mrs. Harriett Chapman, statement, Nov. 8, 1887.

One evening Lincoln came into our store and called for his warm friend Speed. Together they walked back to the fireplace, where Lincoln, drawing from his pocket a letter, asked Speed to read it. "The letter," relates Speed, "was addressed to Mary Todd, and in it he made a plain statement of his feelings, telling her that he had thought the matter over calmly and with great deliberation, and now felt that he did not love her sufficiently to warrant her in marrying him. This letter he desired me to deliver. Upon my declining to do so he threatened to intrust it to some other person's hand. I reminded him that the moment he placed the letter in Miss Todd's hand, she would have the advantage over him. 'Words are forgotten,' I said, 'misunderstood, unnoticed in a private conversation, but once put your words in writing and they stand a living and eternal monument against you.' Thereupon I threw the unfortunate letter in the fire. 'Now,' I continued, 'if you have the courage of manhood, go see Mary yourself; tell her, if you do not love her, the facts, and that you will not marry her. Be careful not to say too much, and then leave at your earliest opportunity.' Thus admonished, he buttoned his coat, and with a rather determined look started out to perform the serious duty for which I had just given him explicit directions."[8]

That night Speed did not go upstairs to bed with us, but under pretense of wanting to read, remained in the store below. He was waiting for Lincoln's return. Ten o'clock passed, and still the interview with Miss Todd had not ended. At length, shortly after eleven, he came stalking in. Speed was satisfied, from the length of Lincoln's stay, that his directions had not been followed.

"Well, old fellow, did you do as I told you and as you promised?" were Speed's first words.

"Yes, I did," responded Lincoln, thoughtfully, "and when I told Mary I did not love her, she burst into tears and almost springing from her chair and wringing her hands as if in agony, said something about the deceiver being himself deceived." Then he stopped.

"What else did you say?" inquired Speed, drawing the facts from him.

"To tell you the truth, Speed, it was too much for me. I found the tears trickling down my own cheeks. I caught her in my arms and kissed her."

"And that's how you broke the engagement," sneered Speed. "You not only acted the fool, but your conduct was tantamount to a renewal of the engagement, and in decency you cannot back down now."

"Well," drawled Lincoln, "if I am in again, so be it. It's done, and I shall abide by it."*

---

*Statement, Joshua F. Speed, Sep. 17, 1866, MS.[9]

Convinced now that Miss Todd regarded the engagement ratified,—instead of broken, as her tall suitor had at first intended,—Lincoln continued his visits, and things moved on smoothly as before. Douglas had dropped out of the race, and everything pointed to an early marriage. It was probably at this time that Mr. and Mrs. Edwards began to doubt the wisdom of the marriage, and now and then to intimate the same to the lady; but they went no farther in their opposition and placed no obstacle in their paths.

The time fixed for the marriage was the first day in January, 1841.[10] Careful preparations for the happy occasion were made at the Edwards mansion. The house underwent the customary renovation; the furniture was properly arranged, the rooms neatly decorated, the supper prepared, and the guests invited. The latter assembled on the evening in question, and awaited in expectant pleasure the interesting ceremony of marriage. The bride, bedecked in veil and silken gown, and nervously toying with the flowers in her hair, sat in the adjoining room. Nothing was lacking but the groom. For some strange reason he had been delayed. An hour passed, and the guests as well as the bride were becoming restless. But they were all doomed to disappointment. Another hour passed; messengers were sent out over town, and each returning with the same report, it became apparent that Lincoln, the principal in this little drama, had purposely failed to appear![11] The bride, in grief, disappeared to her room; the wedding supper was left untouched; the guests quietly and wonderingly withdrew; the lights in the Edwards mansion were blown out, and darkness settled over all for the night. What the feelings of a lady as sensitive, passionate, and proud as Miss Todd were we can only imagine—no one can ever describe them. By daybreak, after persistent search, Lincoln's friends found him. Restless, gloomy, miserable, desperate, he seemed an object of pity. His friends, Speed among the number, fearing a tragic termination, watched him closely in their rooms day and night. "Knives and razors, and every instrument that could be used for self-destruction were removed from his reach."[*] Mrs. Edwards did not hesitate to regard him as insane, and of course her sister Mary shared in that view. But the case was hardly so desperate. His condition began to improve after a few weeks, and a letter written to his partner Stuart, on the 23d of January, 1841, three weeks after the scene at Edwards' house, reveals more perfectly how he felt. He says: "I am now the most miserable man living. If what I feel were equally distributed to the whole human family, there would not be one cheerful face on earth. Whether I shall ever be better, I cannot tell; I awfully forebode I

---

[*]J. F. Speed, MS. letter, January 6, 1866.[12]

shall not. To remain as I am is impossible. I must die or be better, as it appears to me . . . I fear I shall be unable to attend to any business here, and a change of scene might help me. If I could be myself I would rather remain at home with Judge Logan. I can write no more."[13]

During all this time the Legislature to which Lincoln belonged was in special session, but for a time he was unable to attend.* Towards the close of the session, however, he resumed his seat. He took little if any part in the proceedings, made no speeches, and contented himself with answers to the monotonous roll-call, and votes on a few of the principal measures. After the adjournment of the Legislature, his warm friend Speed, who had disposed of his interests in Springfield, induced Lincoln to accompany him to Kentucky.[15] Speed's parents lived in a magnificent place a few miles from Louisville. Their farm was well stocked, and they, in the current phrase, "lived well." Thither he was taken, and there amid the quiet surroundings he found the "change of scene" which he told Stuart might help him. He was living under the cloud of melancholia, and sent to the *Sangamon Journal* a few lines under the gloomy title of "Suicide." They were published in the paper, and a few years since I hunted over the files, and coming across the number containing them, was astonished to find that some one had cut them out. I have always supposed it was done by Lincoln or by some one at his instigation.[16]

Speed's mother was much impressed with the tall and swarthy stranger her son had brought with him. She was a God-fearing mother, and besides aiding to lighten his spirits, gave him a Bible, advising him to read it and by adopting its precepts obtain a release from his troubles which no other agency, in her judgment, could bring him. "He was much depressed. At first he almost contemplated suicide. In the deepest of his depression he said one day he had done nothing to make any human being remember that he had lived; and that to connect his name with the events transpiring in his day and generation, and so impress himself upon them as to link his name with something that would redound to the interest of his fellow-men, was what he desired to live for."† The congenial associations at the Speed farm,‡ the freedom from unpleasant reminders, the company of his

---

*His illness and consequent incapacity for duty in the Legislature, continued for almost three weeks. On the 19th of January, 1841, John J. Hardin announced his illness in the House. Four days afterward he wrote the letter to Stuart from which I have quoted a few lines.[14]

†Letter, J. F. Speed, February 9, 1866, MS.[17]

‡At the time of Lincoln's visit at the Speed mansion, James Speed, a brother of Joshua, and afterward Attorney-General in Lincoln's Cabinet, was practicing law in Louisville. Lincoln came into his office daily. "He read my books," related Mr. Speed in after years; "talked with me about his life, his reading, his studies, his aspirations." Mr. Speed discredits the thought that Lincoln was insane at the time, although he understood he was saddened and melancholy over an unfortunate love affair.[18]

staunch friend, and above all the motherly care and delicate attentions of Mrs. Speed exerted a marked influence over Lincoln. He improved gradually, day by day gaining strength and confidence in himself, until at last the great cloud lifted and passed away. In the fall he and Speed returned to Springfield. At this point, as affording us the most reliable account of Mr. Lincoln's condition and views, it is proper to insert a portion of his correspondence with Mr. Speed. For some time Mr. Speed was reluctant to give these letters to the world. After some argument, however, he at last shared my view that they were properly a matter of history, and sent them to me, accompanied by a letter, in which he says:

"I enclose you copies of all the letters of any interest from Mr. Lincoln to me. Some explanation may be needed that you may rightly understand their import. In the winter of 1840 and 1841, he was unhappy about his engagement to his wife—not being entirely satisfied that his heart was going with his hand. How much he suffered then on that account none knew so well as myself; he disclosed his whole heart to me.*

"In the summer of 1841 I became engaged to my wife. He was here on a visit when I courted her; and, strange to say, something of the same feeling which I regarded as so foolish in him took possession of me and kept me very unhappy from the time of my engagement until I was married. This will explain the deep interest he manifested in his letters on my account.

"One thing is plainly discernible; if I had not been married and happy—far more happy than I ever expected to be—he would not have married."[19]

The first of these letters is one which he gave Speed when the latter started on his journey from Illinois to Kentucky. It bears no date, but was handed him January 1, 1842, as Speed has testified, in another letter to me, that he left Springfield on that day. It is full of consolation and advice how best to conduct himself when the periods of gloom which he feels sure will follow come upon his friend. "I know," he says, "what the painful point with you is at all times when you are unhappy; it is an apprehension that you do not love her as you should. What nonsense! How came you to court her? . . . Did you court her for her wealth? Why, you say she had none. But you say you reasoned yourself into it. What do you mean by that? Was it not that you found yourself unable to reason yourself out of it? Did you not think, and partly form the purpose, of courting her the first

---

*"Lincoln wrote a letter—a long one which he read to me—to Dr. Drake of Cincinnati, descriptive of his case. Its date would be in December, 1840, or early in January, 1841. I think that he must have informed Dr. Drake of his early love for Miss Rutledge, as there was a part of the letter which he would not read . . . I remember Dr. Drake's reply, which was, that he would not undertake to prescribe for him without a personal interview."—Joshua F. Speed, MS. letter, November 30, 1866.

time you ever saw her or heard of her? What had reason to do with it at that early stage? There was nothing at that time for reason to work upon. Whether she was moral, amiable, sensible, or even of good character, you did not nor could then know, except perhaps you might infer the last from the company you found her in. . . . Say candidly, were not those heavenly black eyes the whole basis of all your reasoning on the subject? After you and I had once been at the residence, did you not go and take me all the way to Lexington and back for no other purpose but to get to see her again on our return on that evening to take a trip for that express object?"[20]

The next paragraph is significant as affording us an idea of how the writer perhaps viewed Miss Todd's flirtation with Douglas: "What earthly consideration," he asks, "would you take to find her scouting and despising you and giving herself up to another? But of this you need have no apprehension, and therefore you cannot bring it home to your feelings."[21]

February 3, he writes again, acknowledging receipt of a letter dated January 25. The object of Speed's affection had been ill, and her condition had greatly intensified his gloomy spirits. Lincoln proffers his sympathy. "I hope and believe," he continues, "that your present anxiety about her health and her life must and will forever banish those horrid doubts which I know you sometimes felt as to the truth of your affection for her. If they can once and forever be removed (and I almost feel a presentiment that the Almighty has sent your present affliction expressly for that object), surely nothing can come in their stead to fill their immeasurable measure of misery . . .

"It really appears to me that you yourself ought to rejoice and not sorrow at this indubitable evidence of your undying affection for her. Why, Speed, if you did not love her, although you might not wish her death, you would most certainly be resigned to it. Perhaps this point is no longer a question with you, and my pertinacious dwelling upon it is a rude intrusion upon your feelings. If so you must pardon me. You know the hell I have suffered on that point, and how tender I am upon it. You know I do not mean wrong. I have been quite clear of hypo since you left, even better than I was along in the fall."[22]

The next letter, February 13, was written on the eve of Speed's marriage. After assurances of his desire to befriend him in everything, he suggests: "But you will always hereafter be on ground that I have never occupied, and consequently, if advice were needed, I might advise wrong. I do fondly hope, however, that you will never again need any comfort from abroad . . . I incline to think it probable that your nerves will occasionally fail you for awhile; but once you get them firmly graded now, that trouble is over forever. If you went through the ceremony calmly or even with sufficient composure not to excite alarm in any present, you are safe beyond question, and in two or three months, to say the most, will be the happiest of men."[23]

Meanwhile Lincoln had been duly informed of Speed's marriage, and on the 25th he responds: "Yours of the 16th, announcing that Miss Fanny and you are 'no more twain, but one flesh,' reached me this morning. I have no way of telling how much happiness I wish you both, though I believe you both can conceive it. I feel somewhat jealous of both of you now. You will be so exclusively concerned for one another that I shall be forgotten entirely . . . I shall be very lonesome without you. How miserably things seem to be arranged in this world! If we have no friends we have no pleasure; and if we have them we are sure to lose them, and be doubly pained by the loss."[24]

In another letter, written the same day, he says, "I have no doubt it is the peculiar misfortune of both you and me to dream dreams of Elysium far exceeding all that anything earthly can realize. Far short of your dreams as you may be, no woman could do more to realize them than that same blackeyed Fanny. If you could but contemplate her through my imagination, it would appear ridiculous to you that any one should for a moment think of being unhappy with her. My old father used to have a saying, that, 'If you make a bad bargain hug it all the tighter,' and it occurs to me that if the bargain just closed can possibly be called a bad one it is certainly the most pleasant one for applying that maxim to which my fancy can by any effort picture."[25]

Speed having now safely married, Lincoln's mind began to turn on things nearer home. His relations with Mary Todd were still strained, but reminders of his period of gloom the year before began now to bring her again into view. In a letter to Speed, March 27, he says:

"It cannot be told how it thrills me with joy to hear you say you are 'far happier than you ever expected to be.' That much, I know, is enough. I know you too well to suppose your expectations were not at least sometimes extravagant, and if the reality exceeds them all, I say, 'Enough, dear Lord.' I am not going beyond the truth when I tell you that the short space it took me to read your last letter gave me more pleasure than the total sum of all I have enjoyed since that fatal first of January, 1841. Since then it seems to me I should have been entirely happy but for the never-absent idea that there is one still unhappy whom I have contributed to make so. That kills my soul. I cannot but reproach myself for even wishing to be happy while she is otherwise. She accompanied a large party on the railroad cars to Jacksonville last Monday, and on her return spoke, so that I heard of it, of having enjoyed the trip exceedingly. God be praised for that!"[26]

The last paragraph of this letter contains a bit of sentiment by Lincoln in acknowledgment of a violet. In the margin of the letter which he gave me, Speed made this note in pencil: "The violet was sent by my wife, who dropped it in the letter as I was in the act of sealing it. How beautiful the acknowledgment!" This is the paragraph: "The sweet violet you enclosed came safely to hand, but it was so dry, and mashed so flat, that it crumbled to dust at the first attempt to handle it. The juice that mashed out of it stained a place in the letter, which I mean to preserve and cherish for the sake of her who procured it to be sent. My renewed good wishes to her."[27]

Meanwhile the coldness that existed between Lincoln and his "Mary" was gradually passing away, and with it went all of Lincoln's resolution never to renew the engagement. In a letter, July 4, he says: "I must gain confidence in my own ability to keep my resolves when they are made. In that ability I once prided myself as the only chief gem of my character; that gem I lost, how and where you know too well. I have not regained it; and until I do I cannot trust myself in any matter of much importance. I believe now that had you understood my case at the time as well as I understood yours afterwards, by the aid you would have given me I should have sailed through clear; but that does not now afford me sufficient confidence to begin that or the like of that again. . . . I always was superstitious; I believe God made me one of the instruments of bringing Fanny and you together, which union I have no doubt he had foreordained. Whatever he designs he will do for me yet. 'Stand still and see the salvation of the Lord,' is my text just now. If, as you say, you have told Fanny all, I should have no objection to her seeing this letter, but for its reference to our friend here; let her seeing it depend upon whether she has ever known anything of my affairs; and if she has not, do not let her. I do not think I can come to Kentucky this season. I am so poor and make so little headway in the world that I drop back in a month of idleness as much as I gain in a year's sowing."[28]

The last letter, and the one which closes this series, was written October 5, 1842. In it he simply announces his "duel with Shields," and then goes on to "narrate the particulars of the duelling business, which still rages in this city."[29] This referred to a challenge from the belligerent Shields to William Butler, and another from General Whiteside to Dr. Merryman. In the latter, Lincoln acted as the "friend of Merryman," but in neither case was there any encounter, and both ended in smoke. The concluding paragraph of this letter is the most singular in the entire correspondence. I give it entire without further comment:

"But I began this letter not for what I have been writing, but to say something on that subject which you know to be of such infinite solicitude to me. The immense sufferings you endured from the first days of September till the middle of February you never tried to conceal from me, and I well understood. You have now been the husband of a lovely woman nearly eight months. That you are happier now than the day you married her, I well know, for without, you could not be living. But I have your word for it, too, and the returning elasticity of spirits which is manifested in your letters. But I want to ask a close question: 'Are you in *feeling* as well as *judgment* glad you are married as you are?' From anybody but me this would be an impudent question, not to be tolerated, but I know you will pardon it in me. Please answer it quickly, as I am impatient to know."[30]

Lincoln again applied himself to the law. He re-entered the practice, after the long hiatus of rest, with renewed vigor. He permitted the memory of his engagement with Mary Todd to trouble him no longer. Their paths had diverged, the pain of the separation was over, and the whole thing was a history of the past. And so it might ever have remained but for the intervention of a very shrewd and sagacious lady—one who was capable of achieving success anywhere in the ranks of diplomacy. This lady was the wife of Simeon Francis, the editor of the *Sangamon Journal.* She was a warm friend of Mary Todd and a leader in society. Her husband was warmly attached to Lincoln. He ran the Whig organ, and entertained great admiration for Lincoln's brains and noble qualities. The esteem was mutual, and it is no stretch of the truth to say that for years Lincoln exercised undisputed control of the columns of the *Journal* himself. Whatever he wrote or had written, went into the editorial page without question. Mrs. Francis, sharing her husband's views of Lincoln's glorious possibilities, and desiring to do Mary Todd a kindly act, determined to bring about a reconciliation. She knew that Miss Todd had by letter a few days after "that fatal first of January, 1841," as Lincoln styled it, released him from the engagement, and that since then their relations had been strained, if not entirely broken off. As she viewed it, a marriage between a man as promising in the political world as Lincoln, and a woman as accomplished and brilliant in society as Mary Todd, would certainly add to the attractions of Springfield and reflect great credit on those who brought the union about. She was a great social entertainer, and one day arranged a gathering at her house for the express purpose of bringing these two people together. Both were invited and both attended; but neither suspected the other's presence. Having arranged things so ingeniously and with so much discretion, it was no difficult task for the hostess to bring the couple together by a warm introduction and the encouraging admonition, "Be friends again." Much to the surprise of both they found the web woven around them. They entered into the spirit of the reconciliation, and found Mrs. Francis' roof an inviting place for many succeeding meetings. A wall reared itself between them and the past, and they started again under the auspicious omens of another engagement. The tact of a woman and the diplomacy of society had accomplished what love had long since despaired of ever doing or seeing done.

The meetings in the parlor of Mrs. Francis' house were conducted with no little privacy. At first even Mrs. Edwards knew nothing of it, but presently it came to her ears. "I asked Mary," said this lady, "why she was so secretive about it. She said evasively that after all that had occurred, it was best to keep the courtship from all eyes and ears. Men and women and the whole world were uncertain and slippery, and if misfortune befell the engagement all knowledge of it would be hidden from the world."*

It is unnecessary to prolong the account of this strange and checkered courtship. The intervention of the affair with Shields, which will be detailed in a subsequent chapter,[32] in no way impeded, if it did not hasten the marriage. One morning in November, Lincoln, hastening to the room of his friend James H. Matheney before the latter had arisen from bed, informed him that he was to be married that night, and requested him to attend as best man.† That same morning Miss Todd called on her friend Julia M. Jayne, who afterward married Lyman Trumbull, and made a similar request. The Edwardses were notified, and made such meager preparations as were possible on so short notice. License was obtained during the day, the minister, Charles N. Dresser,‡ was sent for, and in the evening of November 4, 1842, "as pale and trembling as if being driven to slaughter,"[35] Abraham Lincoln was at last married to Mary Todd.§

---

*Statement, January 10, 1866, MS.[31]

†"Marriages in Springfield up to that time had been rather commonplace affairs. Lincoln's was perhaps the first one ever performed with all the requirements of the Episcopal ceremony. A goodly number of friends had gathered, and while witnessing the ceremony one of the most amusing incidents imaginable occurred. No description on paper can do it justice. Among those present was Thomas C. Brown, one of the judges of the Supreme Court. He was in truth an 'old-timer,' and had the virtue of saying just what he thought, without regard to place or surroundings. He had been on the bench for many years and was not less rough than quaint and curious. There was, of course, a perfect hush in the room as the ceremony progressed. Brown was standing just behind Lincoln. Old Parson Dresser, in canonical robes, with much and impressive solemnity recited the Episcopal service. He handed Lincoln the ring, who, placing it on the bride's finger, repeated the Church formula, 'With this ring I thee endow with all my goods and chattels, lands and tenements.' Brown, who had never witnessed such a proceeding, was struck with its utter absurdity. 'God Almighty! Lincoln,' he ejaculated, loud enough to be heard by all, 'the statute fixes all that!' This unlooked-for interruption almost upset the old parson; he had a keen sense of the ridiculous, and for the moment it seemed as if he would break down; but presently recovering his gravity, he hastily pronounced them husband and wife."—Letter, James H. Matheney, MS., Aug. 21, 1888.[33]

‡"My father, Rev. Charles Dresser, was a graduate of Brown University, Providence, R. I., of the class of 1822."—Thomas W. Dresser, MS. letter, Sept. 17, 1888.[34]

§While dressing for the wedding in his room at Butler's house, the latter's little boy, Speed, seeing Lincoln so handsomely attired, in boyish innocence asked him where he was going? "To hell, I suppose," was Lincoln's reply.

One great trial of his life was now over, and another still greater one was yet to come. To me it has always seemed plain that Mr. Lincoln married Mary Todd to save his honor, and in doing that he sacrificed his domestic peace. He had searched himself subjectively, introspectively, thoroughly: he knew he did not love her, but he had promised to marry her! The hideous thought came up like a nightmare. As the "fatal first of January, 1841," neared, the clouds around him blackened the heavens and his life almost went out with the storm. But soon the skies cleared. Friends interposed their aid to avert a calamity, and at last he stood face to face with the great conflict between honor and domestic peace. He chose the former, and with it years of self-torture, sacrificial pangs, and the loss forever of a happy home.

With Miss Todd a different motive, but one equally as unfortunate, prompted her adherence to the union. To marry Lincoln meant not a life of luxury and ease, for Lincoln was not a man to accumulate wealth; but in him she saw position in society, prominence in the world, and the grandest social distinction. By that means her ambition would be satisfied. Until that fatal New Year's day in 1841 she may have loved him, but his action on that occasion forfeited her affection. He had crushed her proud, womanly spirit. She felt degraded in the eyes of the world. Love fled at the approach of revenge. Some writer—it is Junius, I believe—has said that, "Injuries may be forgiven and forgotten, but insults admit of no compensation: they degrade the mind in its own self-esteem and force it to recover its level by revenge."[36] Whether Mrs. Lincoln really was moved by the spirit of revenge or not she acted along the lines of human conduct. She led her husband a wild and merry dance. If, in time, she became soured at the world it was not without provocation, and if in later years she unchained the bitterness of a disappointed and outraged nature, it followed as logically as an effect does the cause.

I have told this sad story as I know and have learned it. In rehearsing the varied scenes of the drama,* I have unearthed a few facts that seem half-buried, perhaps, but they were not destined to lay buried deep or long. The world will have the truth as long as the name of Lincoln is remembered by mankind.

---

*For many years I had reason to believe that Sarah Rickard, who was a sister of Mrs. William Butler, had been the recipient of some attentions at the hand of Mr. Lincoln. The lady, long since married, is now living in a Western State. I applied to her for information recently, and after some entreaty received this answer in her own handwriting: "As an old friend I will answer the question propounded to me, though I can scarcely see what good it can do history. Mr. Lincoln did make a proposal of marriage to me in the summer, or perhaps later, in the year of 1840. He brought to my attention the accounts in the Bible of the patriarch Abraham's marriage to Sarah, and used that historical union as an argument in his own behalf. My reason for declining his proposal was the wide difference in our ages. I was then only sixteen, and had given the subject of matrimony but very little, if any, thought. I entertained the highest regard for Mr. Lincoln. He seemed almost like an older brother, being, as it were, one of my sister's family."[37]

Springfield Residence of Ninian W. Edwards. House in Which Lincoln and Mary Todd Were Married, and Which the Latter Died.

There were two things Mr. Lincoln always seemed willing to forget. One was his unparliamentary escape with Joseph Gillespie from the Legislature by jumping through the church window, in 1839,[38] and the other was the difficulty with James Shields, or, as he expressed it in a letter to Speed, the "duel with Shields."[39] Other incidents in his career he frequently called up in conversation with friends, but in after years he seldom if ever referred to the affair with Shields. People in Illinois did gradually forget or, at least, cease mention of it, but in more remote quarters where Mr. Lincoln was less extensively known, the thing, much to his regret, kept rising to the surface. During a visit which I made to the Eastern States in 1858, I was often asked for an account of the so-called duel; so often, in fact, that on my return home I told Mr. Lincoln of it. "If all the good things I have ever done," he said regretfully, "are remembered as long and well as my scrape with Shields, it is plain I shall not soon be forgotten."

James Shields, a "gallant, hot-headed bachelor from Tyrone county, Ireland," and a man of inordinate vanity, had been elected Auditor of State. Encouraged somewhat by the prominence the office gave him, he at once assumed a conspicuous position in the society of Springfield. He was extremely sensitive by nature, but exposed himself to merciless ridicule by attempting to establish his supremacy as a beau among the ladies. Blind to his own defects, and very pronounced in support of every act of the Democratic party, he made himself the target for all the bitterness and ridicule of the day. It happened that the financial resources of the State, owing to the collapse of the great internal improvement system, were exceedingly limited, and people were growing restless under what they deemed excessive taxation. The State officers were all Democrats, and during the summer they issued an order declining to receive any more State Banknotes or bills in payment of taxes. This made the tax-payer's burdens greater than ever, as much of this paper remained outstanding in the hands of the people. The order met with opposition from every quarter—the Whigs of course losing no opportunity to make it as odious as possible. It was perfectly natural, therefore, that such an ardent Whig as Lincoln should join in the popular denunciation. Through the columns of the *Springfield Journal,* of which he had the undisputed use, he determined to encourage the opposition by the use of his pen. No object seemed to merit more ridicule and caricature than the conspicuous figure of the Auditor of State. At this time Lincoln was enjoying stolen conferences under the hospitable roof of Mrs. Francis with Mary Todd and her friend Julia M. Jayne. These two young ladies, to whom he confided his purpose, encouraged it and offered to lend their aid. Here he caught the idea of puncturing Shields. The thing took shape in an article published in the *Journal,* purporting to have come from a poor widow, who with her pockets full of State Bank paper was still unable to obtain the coveted receipt for her taxes. It was written by Lincoln and was headed:

A Letter from the Lost Townships.

Lost Townships, August 27, 1842.

Dear Mr. Printer,

I see you printed that long letter I sent you a spell ago. I'm quite encouraged by it, and can't keep from writing again. I think the printing of my letters will be a good thing all round—it will give me the benefit of being known by the world, and give the world the advantage of knowing what's going on in the Lost Townships, and give your paper respectability besides. So here comes another. Yesterday afternoon I hurried through cleaning up the dinner dishes and stepped over to neighbor S—— to see if his wife Peggy was as well as mout be expected, and hear what they called the baby. Well, when I got there and just turned round the corner of his log cabin, there he was, setting on the doorstep reading a newspaper.

"How are you, Jeff?" says I. He sorter started when he heard me, for he hadn't seen me before.

"Why," says he, "I'm mad as the devil, Aunt 'Becca!" "What about?" says I;

"ain't its hair the right color? None of that nonsense, Jeff; there ain't an hon-ester woman in the Lost Townships than"—"Than who?" says he; "what the mischief are you about?" I began to see I was running the wrong trail, and so says I, "Oh! nothing: I guess I was mistaken a little, that's all. But what is it you're mad about?"

"Why," says he, "I've been tugging ever since harvest, getting out wheat and hauling it to the river to raise State Bank paper enough to pay my tax this year and a little school debt I owe; and now, just as I've got it, here I open this infernal *Extra Register*, expecting to find it full of 'Glorious Democratic Vic-tories' and 'High Comb'd Cocks,' when, lo and behold! I find a set of fellows, calling themselves officers of the State, have forbidden the tax collectors and school commissioners to receive State paper at all; and so here it is dead on my hands. I don't now believe all the plunder I've got will fetch ready cash enough to pay my taxes and that school debt."

I was a good deal thunderstruck myself; for that was the first I had heard of the proclamation, and my old man was pretty much in the same fix with Jeff. We both stood a moment staring at one another without knowing what to say. At last says I, "Mr. S——, let me look at that paper." He handed it to me, when I read the proclamation over.

"There now," says he, "did you ever see such a piece of impudence and imposition as that?" I saw Jeff was in a good tune for saying some ill-natured things, and so I tho't I would just argue a little on the contrary side, and make him rant a spell if I could. "Why," says I, looking as dignified and thoughtful as I could, "it seems pretty tough, to be sure, to have to raise silver where there's none to be raised; but then, you see, 'there will be danger of loss' if it ain't done."

"Loss! damnation!" says he. "I defy Daniel Webster, I defy King Solomon, I defy the world—I defy—I defy—yes, I defy even you, Aunt 'Becca, to show how the people can lose anything by paying their taxes in State paper."

"Well," says I, "you see what the officers of State say about it, and they are a desarnin' set of men. But," says I, "I guess you're mistaken about what the proclamation says. It don't say the people will lose anything by the paper money being taken for taxes. It only says 'there will be danger of loss;' and though it is tolerable plain that the people can't lose by paying their taxes in something they can get easier than silver, instead of having to pay silver; and though it's just as plain that the State can't lose by taking State Bank paper, however low it may be, while she owes the bank more than the whole revenue, and can pay that paper over on her debt, dollar for dollar;—still there is danger of loss to the 'officers of State;' and you know, Jeff, we can't get along without officers of State."

"Damn officers of State!" says he; "that's what Whigs are always hurrah-ing for."

"Now, don't swear so, Jeff," says I; "you know I belong to the meetin', and swearin' hurts my feelings."

"Beg pardon, Aunt 'Becca," says he; "but I do say it's enough to make Dr. Goddard[40] swear, to have tax to pay in silver, for nothing only that Ford may get his two thousand a year, and Shields his twenty-four hundred a year, and Carpenter his sixteen hundred a year, and all without 'danger of loss' by tak-ing it in State paper. Yes, yes: it's plain enough now what these officers of State mean by 'danger of loss.' Wash, I s'pose, actually lost fifteen hundred dollars out of the three thousand that two of these 'officers of State' let him steal from the treasury, by being compelled to take it in State paper. Wonder if we don't have a proclamation before long, commanding us to make up this loss to Wash in silver."[41]

And so he went on till his breath run out, and he had to stop. I couldn't think of anything to say just then, and so I begun to look over the paper again. "Ay! here's another proclamation, or something like it."

"Another?" says Jeff; "and whose egg is it, pray?"

I looked to the bottom of it, and read aloud, "Your obedient servant, James Shields, Auditor."

"Aha!" says Jeff, "one of them same three fellows again. Well, read it, and let's hear what of it."

I read on till I came to where it says, "The object of this measure is to sus-pend the collection of the revenue for the current year."

"Now stop, now stop!" says he; "that's a lie a'ready, and I don't want to hear of it."

"Oh! may be not," says I.

"I say it—is—a—lie. Suspend the collection, indeed! Will the collectors, that have taken their oaths to make the collection, dare to suspend it? Is there anything in law requiring them to perjure themselves at the bidding of James Shields?

"Will the greedy gullet of the penitentiary be satisfied with swallowing him instead of all of them, if they should venture to obey him? And would he not discover some 'danger of loss,' and be off about the time it came to taking their places?

"And suppose the people attempt to suspend, by refusing to pay; what then? The collectors would just jerk up their horses and cows, and the like, and sell them to the highest bidder for silver in hand, without valuation or redemption.

Why, Shields didn't believe that story himself: it was never meant for the truth. If it was true, why was it not writ till five days after the proclamation? Why didn't Carlin and Carpenter sign it as well as Shields? Answer me that, Aunt 'Becca. I say it's a lie, and not a well told one at that. It grins out like a copper dollar. Shields is a fool as well as a liar. With him truth is out of the question; and as for getting a good, bright, passable lie out of him, you might as well try to strike fire from a cake of tallow. I stick to it, it's all an infernal Whig lie!"

"A Whig lie! Highty tighty!"

"Yes, a Whig lie; and it's just like everything the cursed British Whigs do. First they'll do some divilment, and then they'll tell a lie to hide it. And they don't care how plain a lie it is: they think they can cram any sort of a one down the throats of the ignorant Locofocos, as they call the Democrats."

"Why, Jeff, you're crazy: you don't mean to say Shields is a Whig!"

"Yes, I do."

"Why, look here! the proclamation is in your own Democratic paper, as you call it."

"I know it; and what of that? They only printed it to let us Democrats see the deviltry the Whigs are at."

"Well, but Shields is the auditor of this Loco—I mean this Democratic State."

"So he is, and Tyler appointed him to office."

"Tyler appointed him?"

"Yes (if you must chaw it over), Tyler appointed him; or, if it wasn't him, it was old Granny Harrison, and that's all one. I tell you, Aunt 'Becca, there's no mistake about his being a Whig. Why, his very looks shows it; everything about him shows it: if I was deaf and blind, I could tell him by the smell. I seed him when I was down in Springfield last winter. They had a sort of a gatherin' there one night among the grandees, they called a fair. All the gals about town was there, and all the handsome widows and married women, finickin' about trying to look like gals, tied as tight in the middle, and puffed out at both ends, like bundles of fodder that hadn't been stacked yet, but wanted stackin' pretty bad. And then they had tables all around the house kivered over with [ ]⁴² caps and pincushions and ten thousand such little knic-knacks, tryin' to sell 'em to the fellows that were bowin' and scrapin' and kungeerin' about 'em. They wouldn't let no Democrats in, for fear they'd disgust the ladies, or scare the little gals, or dirty the floor. I looked in at the window, and there was this same fellow Shields floatin' about on the air, without heft or earthly substances, just like a lock of cat fur where cats had been fighting.

"He was paying his money to this one, and that one, and t'other one, and sufferin' great loss because it wasn't silver instead of State paper; and the sweet distress he seemed to be in,—his very features, in the ecstatic agony of his soul, spoke audibly and distinctly, 'Dear girls, it is distressing, but I cannot marry you all. Too well I know how much you suffer; but do, do remember, it is not my fault that I am so handsome and so interesting.'

"As this last was expressed by a most exquisite contortion of his face, he seized hold of one of their hands, and squeezed, and held on to it about a quarter of an hour. 'Oh, my good fellow!' says I to myself, 'if that was one of our Democratic gals in the Lost Townships, the way you'd get a brass pin let into you would be about up to the head.' He a Democrat! Fiddlesticks! I tell you, Aunt 'Becca, he's a Whig, and no mistake: nobody but a Whig could make such a conceity dunce of himself."

"Well," says I, "maybe he is; but, if he is, I'm mistaken the worst sort. Maybe so, maybe so; but, if I am, I'll suffer by it; I'll be a Democrat if it turns out that Shields is a Whig, considerin' you shall be a Whig if he turns out a Democrat."

"A bargain, by jingoes!" says he; "but how will we find out?"

"Why," says I, "we'll just write and ax the printer."

"Agreed again!" says he; "and by thunder! if it does turn out that Shields is a Democrat, I never will"—

"Jefferson! Jefferson!"

"What do you want, Peggy?"

"Do get through your everlasting clatter some time, and bring me a gourd of water; the child's been crying for a drink this livelong hour."

"Let it die, then; it may as well die for water as to be taxed to death to fatten officers of State."

Jeff run off to get the water, though, just like he hadn't been saying anything spiteful for he's a raal good-hearted fellow, after all, once you get at the foundation of him.

I walked into the house, and, "Why, Peggy," says I, "I declare we like to forgot you altogether."

"Oh, yes," says she, "when a body can't help themselves, everybody soon forgets 'em; but, thank God! by day after to-morrow I shall be well enough to milk the cows, and pen the calves, and wring the contrary ones' tails for 'em, and no thanks to nobody."

"Good evening, Peggy," says I, and so I sloped, for I seed she was mad at me for making Jeff neglect her so long.

And now, Mr. Printer, will you be sure to let us know in your next paper whether this Shields is a Whig or a Democrat? I don't care about it for my self, for I know well enough how it is already; but I want to convince Jeff. It may do some good to let him, and others like him, know who and what these officers of State are. It may help to send the present hypocritical set to where they belong, . and to fill the places they now disgrace, with men who will do more work for less pay, and take a fewer airs while they are doing it. It ain't sensible to think that the same men who get us into trouble will change their course; and yet it's pretty plain if some change for the better is not made, it's not long that either Peggy or I or any of us will have a cow left to milk, or a calf's tail to wring.

  Yours truly,

   Rebecca———.[43]

Within a week another epistle from Aunt Rebecca appeared, in which, among other things, she offered the gallant Shields her hand. This one was written by Miss Todd and Miss Jayne. I insert it without further comment:

         Lost Townships, September 8, 1842.

Dear Mr. Printer:

  I was a-standin' at the spring yesterday a-washin' out butter when I seed Jim Snooks a-ridin' up towards the house for very life, when, jist as I was a-wonderin' what on airth was the matter with him, he stops suddenly, and ses he, "Aunt 'Becca, here's somethin' for you;" and with that he hands out your letter. Well, you see, I steps out towards him, not thinkin' that I had both hands full of butter; and seein' I couldn't take the letter, you know, without greasin' it, I ses, "Jim, jist you open it, and read it for me." Well, Jim opens it and reads it; and would you believe it, Mr. Editor, I was so completely dum-founded and turned into stone that there I stood in the sun a-workin' the but-ter, and it a-running on the ground, while he read the letter, that I never thunk what I was about till the hull on't run melted on the ground and was lost. Now, sir, it's not for the butter, nor the price of the butter, but, the Lord have massy on us, I wouldn't have sich another fright for a whole firkin of it. Why, when I found out that it was the man what Jeff seed down to the fair that had demanded the author of my letters, threatnin' to take personal satisfaction of the writer, I was so skart that I tho't I should quill-wheel right where I was.

  You say that Mr. S—— is offended at being compared to cats' fur, and is as mad as a March hare (that ain't fur), because I told about the squeezin'. Now I want you to tell Mr. S—— that, rather than fight, I'll make any apology; and, if he wants personal satisfaction, let him only come here, and he may squeeze my hand as hard as I squeezed the butter, and, if that ain't personal satisfaction, I can only say that he is the fust man that was not satisfied with squeezin' my hand. If this should not answer, there is one thing more that I would rather do than get a lickin'. I have long expected to die a widow; but, as Mr. S——— is rather good-looking than otherwise, I must say I don't care if we compromise the matter by—really, Mr. Printer, I can't help blushin'—but I—it must come out—I—but widowed modesty—well, if I must, I must—wouldn't he—may be sorter let the old grudge drap if I was to consent to be—be—h-i-s w-i-f-e? I know he's a fightin' man, and would rather fight than eat; but isn't marryin' better than fightin', though it does sometimes run in to it? And I don't think, upon the whole, that I'd be sich a bad match neither: I'm not over sixty, and am jist four feet three in my bare feet, and not much more around the girth; and for color, I wouldn't turn my back to nary a gal in the Lost Townships. But, after all, maybe I'm countin' my chickins before they are hatched, and dreamin' of matrimonial bliss when the only alternative reserved for me may be a lickin'. Jeff tells me the way these fire-eaters do is to give the challenged party choice of weapons, etc., which bein' the case, I'll tell you in confidence that I never fights with anything but broomsticks or hot water or a shovelful of coals or some such thing; the former of which, being somewhat like a shillalah, may not be very objectional to him. I will give him choice, however, in one thing, and that is, whether, when we fight, I shall wear breeches or he petticoats, for, I presume that change is sufficient to place us on an equality.

     Yours, etc.

     Rebecca———.

P. S.—Jist say to your friend, if he concludes to marry rather than fight, I shall only inforce one condition, that is, if he should ever happen to gallant any young gals home of nights from our house, he must not squeeze their hands.[44]

Not content with their epistolary efforts, the ladies invoked the muse. "Rebecca" deftly transformed herself into "Cathleen," and in jingling rhyme sang the praises of Shields, and congratulated him over the prospect of an early marriage to the widow. Following are the verses, rhyme, metre, and all:

Ye Jew's-harps awake! The Auditor's won.
Rebecca the widow has gained Erin's son;

The pride of the north from Emerald Isle
Has been wooed and won by a woman's smile.
The combat's relinquished, old loves all forgot:
To the widow he's bound. Oh, bright be his lot!
In the smiles of the conquest so lately achieved.
Joyful be his bride, "widowed modesty" relieved,
The footsteps of time tread lightly on flowers,
May the cares of this world ne'er darken his hours!
But the pleasures of life are fickle and coy
As the smiles of a maiden sent off to destroy.
Happy groom! in sadness far distant from thee
The fair girls dream only of past times of glee
Enjoyed in thy presence; whilst the soft blarnied store
Will be fondly remembered as relics of yore,
And hands that in rapture you oft would have pressed.
In prayer will be clasped that your lot may be blest.
    Cathleen.[45]

The satire running through these various compositions, and the publicity their appearance in the *Journal* gave them, had a most wonderful effect on the vain and irascible Auditor of State. He could no longer endure the merriment and ridicule that met him from every side. A man of cooler head might have managed it differently, but in the case of a high-tempered man like Shields he felt that his integrity had been assailed and that nothing but an "affair of honor" would satisfy him. Through General John D. Whiteside he demanded of editor Francis the name of the author. The latter hunted up Lincoln, who directed him to give his name and say nothing about the ladies. The further proceedings in this grotesque drama were so graphically detailed by the friends of both parties in the columns of the *Journal* at that time, that I copy their letters as a better and more faithful narrative than can be obtained from any other source. The letter of Shields' second, General Whiteside, appearing first in the *Journal*, finds the same place in this chapter:

"Springfield, Oct. 3, 1842.
"To the Editor of the Sangamon Journal:
    "Sir: To prevent misrepresentation of the recent affair between Messrs. Shields and Lincoln, I think it proper to give a brief narrative of the facts of the case, as they came within my knowledge; for the truth of which I hold myself responsible, and request you to give the same publication. An offensive article in relation to Mr. Shields appeared in the *Sangamon Journal* of the

2d of September last; and, on demanding the author, Mr. Lincoln was given up by the editor. Mr. Shields, previous to this demand, made arrangements to go to Quincy on public business; and before his return Mr. Lincoln had left for Tremont to attend the court, with the intention, as we learned, of remaining on the circuit several weeks. Mr. Shields, on his return, requested me to accompany him to Tremont; and, on arriving there, we found that Dr. Merryman and Mr. Butler had passed us in the night, and got there before us. We arrived in Tremont on the 17th ult., and Mr. Shields addressed a note to Mr. Lincoln immediately, informing him that he was given up as the author of some articles that appeared in the *Sangamon Journal* (one more over the signature having made its appearance at this time), and requesting him to retract the offensive allusions contained in said articles in relation to his private character. Mr. Shields handed this note to me to deliver to Mr. Lincoln, and directed me, at the same time, not to enter into any verbal communication, or be the bearer of any verbal explanation, as such were always liable to misapprehension. This note was delivered by me to Mr. Lincoln, stating, at the same time, that I would call at his convenience for an answer. Mr. Lincoln, in the evening of the same day, handed me a letter addressed to Mr. Shields. In this he gave or offered no explanation, but stated therein that he could not submit to answer further, on the ground that Mr. Shields's note contained an assumption of facts and also a menace. Mr. Shields then addressed him another note, in which he disavowed all intention to menace, and requested to know whether he (Mr. Lincoln) was the author of either of the articles which appeared in the *Journal,* headed 'Lost Townships,' and signed 'Rebecca;' and, if so, he repeated his request of a retraction of the offensive matter in relation to his private character; if not, his denial would be held sufficient. This letter was returned to Mr. Shields unanswered, with a verbal statement 'that there could be no further negotiation between them until the first note was withdrawn.' Mr. Shields thereupon sent a note designating me as a friend, to which Mr. Lincoln replied by designating Dr. Merryman. These three last notes passed on Monday morning, the 19th. Dr. Merryman handed me Mr. Lincoln's last note when by ourselves. I remarked to Dr. Merryman that the matter was now submitted to us, and that I would propose that he and myself should pledge our words of honor to each other to try to agree upon terms of amicable arrangement, and compel our principals to accept of them. To this he readily assented, and we shook hands upon the pledge. It was then mutually agreed that we should adjourn to Springfield, and there procrastinate the matter, for the purpose of effecting the secret arrangement between him and myself. All this I kept concealed from Mr. Shields. Our horse had got a little lame in going to Tremont, and Dr. Merryman invited me to take a seat in his buggy. I accepted the invitation the more readily, as I thought that leaving Mr. Shields in Tremont until his horse would be in better condition to travel would facilitate the private agreement between Dr. Merryman and myself. I travelled to Springfield part of the way with him, and part with Mr. Lincoln; but nothing passed between us on the journey in relation to the matter in hand. We arrived in Springfield on Monday night. About noon on Tuesday, to my astonishment, a proposition was made to meet in Missouri, within three miles of Alton, on the next Thursday! The weapons, cavalry broadswords of the largest size; the parties to stand on each side of a barrier, and to be confined to a limited space. As I had not been consulted at all on the subject, and considering the private understanding between Dr. Merryman and myself, and it being known that Mr. Shields was left at Tremont, such a proposition took me by surprise. However, being determined not to violate the laws of the State, I declined agreeing upon the terms until we should meet in Missouri. Immediately after, I called upon Dr. Merryman and withdrew the pledge of honor between him and myself in relation to a secret arrangement. I started after this to meet Mr. Shields, and met him about twenty miles from Springfield. It was late on Tuesday night when we both reached the city and learned that Dr. Merryman had left for Missouri, Mr. Lincoln having left before the proposition was made, as Dr. Merryman had himself informed me. The time and place made it necessary to start at once. We left Springfield at eleven o'clock on Tuesday night, travelled all night, and arrived in Hillsborough on Wednesday morning, where we took in General Ewing. From there we went to Alton, where we arrived on Thursday; and, as the proposition required three friends on each side, I was joined by General Ewing and Dr. Hope, as the friends of Mr. Shields. We then crossed to Missouri, where a proposition was made by General Hardin and Dr. English (who had arrived there in the mean time as mutual friends) to refer the matter to, I think, four friends for a settlement. This I believed Mr. Shields would refuse, and declined seeing him; but Dr. Hope, who conferred with him upon the subject, returned and stated that Mr. Shields declined settling the matter through any other than the friends he had selected to stand by him on that occasion. The friends of both the parties finally agreed to withdraw the papers (temporarily) to give the friends of Mr. Lincoln an opportunity to explain. Whereupon the friends of Mr. Lincoln, to wit, Messrs. Merryman, Bledsoe, and Butler, made a full and satisfactory explanation in relation to the article which appeared in the *Sangamon Journal* of the 2d, the only one written by him. This was all done without the knowledge or consent of Mr. Shields, and he refused to accede to it, until Dr. Hope, General Ewing, and myself declared the apology sufficient, and that we could not sustain him in going further. I think it necessary to state further, that no explanation or apology had been previously offered on the part of Mr. Lincoln to Mr. Shields, and that none was ever communicated by me to him, nor was any even offered to me, unless a paper read to me by Dr. Merryman after he had handed me the broadsword proposition on Tuesday. I heard so little of the reading of the paper, that I do not know fully what it purported to be; and I was the less inclined to inquire, as Mr. Lincoln was then gone to Missouri, and Mr. Shields not yet arrived from Tremont. In fact, I could not entertain any offer of the kind, unless upon my own responsibility; and that I was not disposed to do after what had already transpired.

"I make this statement, as I am about to be absent for some time, and I think it due to all concerned to give a true version of the matter before I leave.

"Your obedient servant,

"John D. Whiteside."[46]

Springfield, October 8, 1842.

Editors of the Journal:

Gents;—By your paper of Friday, I discover that General Whiteside has published his version of the late affair between Messrs. Shields and Lincoln, I now bespeak a hearing of my version of the same affair, which shall be true and full as to all material facts.

On Friday evening, the 16th of September, I learned that Mr. Shields and General Whiteside had started in pursuit of Mr. Lincoln, who was at Tremont, attending court. I knew that Mr. Lincoln was wholly unpractised both as to the diplomacy and weapons commonly employed in similar affairs; and I felt it my duty, as a friend, to be with him, and, so far as in my power, to prevent any advantage being taken of him as to either his honor or his life. Accordingly, Mr. Butler and myself started, passed Shields and Whiteside in the night, and arrived at Tremont ahead of them on Saturday morning. I told Mr. Lincoln what was brewing, and asked him what course he proposed to himself. He stated that he was wholly opposed to duelling, and would do anything to avoid it that might not degrade him in the estimation of himself and friends; but, if such degradation or a fight were the only alternatives, he would fight.

In the afternoon Shields and Whiteside arrived, and very soon the former sent to Mr. Lincoln, by the latter, the following note or letter:—

Tremont, September 17, 1842.

A. Lincoln, Esq.:—I regret that my absence on public business compelled me to postpone a matter of private consideration a little longer than I could have desired. It will only be necessary, however, to account for it by informing you that I have been to Quincy on business that would not admit of delay. I will now state briefly the reasons of my troubling you with this communication, the disagreeable nature of which I regret, as I had hoped to avoid any difficulty with any one in Springfield while residing there, by endeavoring to conduct myself in such a way amongst both my political friends and opponents, as to escape the necessity of any. Whilst thus abstaining from giving provocation, I have become the object of slander, vituperation, and personal abuse which, were I capable of submitting to, I would prove myself worthy of the whole of it.

In two or three of the last numbers of the *Sangamon Journal,* articles of the most personal nature, and calculated to degrade me, have made their appearance. On inquiring, I was informed by the editor of that paper, through the medium of my friend, General Whiteside, that you are the author of those articles. This information satisfies me that I have become, by some means or other, the object of secret hostility. I will not take the trouble of inquiring into the reason of all this, but I will take the liberty of requiring a full, positive, and absolute retraction of all offensive allusions used by you in these communications, in relation to my private character and standing as a man, as an apology for the insults conveyed in them.

This may prevent consequences which no one will regret more than myself.

Your ob't serv't,
Jas. Shields.[47]

About sunset, General Whiteside called again, and secured from Mr. Lincoln the following answer to Mr. Shields's note:—

Tremont, September 17, 1842.

Jas. Shields, Esq.:—Your note of to-day was handed me by General Whiteside. In that note you say you have been informed, through the medium of the editor of the *Journal,* that I am the author of certain articles in that paper which you deem personally abusive of you; and, without stopping to inquire whether I really am the author, or to point out what is offensive in them, you demand an unqualified retraction of all that is offensive, and then proceed to hint at consequences.

Now, sir, there is in this so much assumption of facts, and so much of menace as to consequences, that I cannot submit to answer that note any further than I have, and to add, that the consequences to which I suppose you allude would be matter of as great regret to me as it possibly could to you.

Respectfully,
A. Lincoln.[48]

In about an hour, General Whiteside called again with another note from Mr. Shields; but after conferring with Mr. Butler for a long time, say two or three hours, returned without presenting the note to Mr. Lincoln. This was in consequence of an assurance from Mr. Butler that Mr. Lincoln could not receive any communication from Mr. Shields, unless it were a withdrawal of his first note, or a challenge. Mr. Butler further stated to General White-side, that, on the withdrawal of the first note, and a proper and gentlemanly request for an explanation, he had no doubt one would be given. General Whiteside admitted that that was the course Mr. Shields ought to pursue, but deplored that his furious and intractable temper prevented his having any influence with him to that end. General Whiteside then requested us to wait with him until Monday morning, that he might endeavor to bring Mr. Shields to reason.

On Monday morning he called and presented Mr. Lincoln the same note as Mr. Butler says he had brought on Saturday evening. It was as follows:—

> Tremont, September 17, 1842.
>
> A. Lincoln, Esq.:—In your reply to my note of this date, you intimate that I assume facts and menace consequences, and that you cannot sub-mit to answer it further. As now, sir, you desire it, I will be a little more particular. The editor of the *Sangamon Journal* gave me to understand that you are the author of an article which appeared, I think, in that paper of the 2d September inst., headed "The Lost Townships" and signed Rebecca or 'Becca. I would therefore take the liberty of asking whether you are the author of said article, or any other of the same signature which has appeared in any of the late numbers of that paper. If so, I repeat my request of an absolute retraction of all offensive allusions contained therein in relation to my private character and standing.
>
> If you are not the author of any of the articles, your denial will be suf-ficient. I will say further, it is not my intention to menace, but to do myself justice.
>
> > Your ob't serv't,
> > Jas. Shields.[49]

This Mr. Lincoln perused, and returned to General Whiteside, telling him verbally, that he did not think it consistent with his honor to negotiate for peace with Mr. Shields, unless Mr. Shields would withdraw his former offensive letter.

In a very short time General Whiteside called with a note from Mr. Shields, designating General Whiteside as his friend, to which Mr. Lincoln instantly replied designating me as his. On meeting General Whiteside, he proposed that we should pledge our honor to each other that we would endeavor to settle the matter amicably; to which I agreed, and stated to him the only conditions on which it could be settled; viz., the withdrawal of Mr. Shields's first note, which he appeared to think reasonable, and regretted that the note had been written, saying however, that he had endeavored to prevail on Mr. Shields to write a milder one, but had not succeeded. He added, too, that I must promise not to mention it, as he would not dare to let Mr. Shields know that he was negotiating peace; for, said he, "He would challenge me next, and as soon cut my throat as not." Not willing that he should suppose my principal less dangerous than his own, I promised not to mention our pacific intentions to Mr. Lincoln or any other person; and we started for Springfield forthwith.

We all, except Mr. Shields, arrived in Springfield late at night on Monday. We discovered that the affair had, somehow, got great publicity in Springfield, and that an arrest was probable. To prevent this, it was agreed by Mr. Lincoln and myself that he should leave early on Tuesday morning. Accordingly, he prepared the following instructions for my guide, on a suggestion from Mr. Butler that he had reason to believe that an attempt would be made by the opposite party to have the matter accommodated:

> In case Whiteside shall signify a wish to adjust this affair without further difficulty, let him know that, if the present papers be withdrawn, and a note from Mr. Shields asking to know if I am the author of the articles of which he complains, and asking that I shall make him gentlemanly satisfaction if I am the author, and this without menace or dictation as to what that satisfaction shall be, a pledge is made that the following answer shall be given:
>
> "I did write the 'Lost Township' letter which appeared in the *Journal* of the 2d inst., but had no participation in any form in any other article alluding to you. I wrote that wholly for political effect. I had no intention of injuring your personal or private character, or standing as a man or a gentleman; and I did not then think, and do not now think, that that article could produce, or has produced, that effect against you; and had I anticipated such an effect, I would have forborne to write it. And I will add, that your conduct towards me, so far as I knew, had always been gentlemanly, and that I had no personal pique against you, and no cause for any."
>
> If this should be done, I leave it with you to manage what shall and what shall not be published.
>
> If nothing like this is done, the preliminaries of the fight are to be:
>
> 1st. Weapons:—Cavalry broadswords of the largest size, precisely equal in all respects, and such as now used by the cavalry company at Jacksonville.
>
> 2d. Position:—A plank ten feet long, and from nine to twelve inches broad, to be firmly fixed on edge on the ground as the lines between us, which neither is to pass his foot over upon forfeit of his life. Next, a line drawn on the ground on either side of said plank and parallel with it, each at the distance

of the whole length of the sword and three feet additional from the plank; and the passing of his own such line by either party during the fight shall be deemed a surrender of the contest.

3d. Time:—On Thursday evening at five o'clock, if you can get it so; but in no case to be at a greater distance of time than Friday evening at 5 o'clock.

4th. Place:—Within three miles of Alton, on the opposite side of the river, the particular spot to be agreed on by you.

Any preliminary details coming within the above rules, you are at liberty to make at your discretion; but you are in no case to swerve from these rules, or to pass beyond their limits.[50]

In the course of the forenoon I met General Whiteside, and he again intimated a wish to adjust the matter amicably. I then read to him Mr. Lincoln's instructions to an adjustment, and the terms of the hostile meeting, if there must be one, both at the same time.

He replied that it was useless to talk of an adjustment, if it could only be effected by the withdrawal of Mr. Shields's paper, for such withdrawal Mr. Shields would never consent to; adding, that he would as soon think of asking Mr. Shields to "butt his brains out against a brick wall as to withdraw that paper." He proceeded: "I see but one course—that is a desperate remedy: 'tis to tell them, if they will not make the matter up, they must fight us." I replied, that, if he chose to fight Mr. Shields to compel him to do right, he might do so; but as for Mr. Lincoln, he was on the defensive, and, I believe, in the right, and I should do nothing to compel him to do wrong. Such withdrawal having been made indispensable by Mr. Lincoln, I cut the matter short as to an adjustment, and I proposed to General Whiteside to accept the terms of the fight, which he refused to do until Mr. Shields' arrival in town, but agreed, verbally, that Mr. Lincoln's friends should procure the broadswords, and take them to the ground. In the afternoon he came to me, saying that some persons were swearing out affidavits to have us arrested, and that he intended to meet Mr. Shields immediately, and proceed to the place designated, lamenting, however, that I would not delay the time, that he might procure the interference of Governor Ford and General Ewing to mollify Mr. Shields. I told him that an accommodation, except upon the terms I mentioned, was out of question; that to delay the meeting was to facilitate our arrest; and, as I was determined not to be arrested, I should leave the town in fifteen minutes. I then pressed his acceptance of the preliminaries, which he disclaimed upon the ground that it would interfere with his oath of office as Fund Commissioner. I then, with two other friends, went to Jacksonville, where we joined Mr. Lincoln about 11 o'clock on Tuesday night. Wednesday morning we procured the broadswords, and proceeded to Alton, where we arrived about 11 o'clock A. M. on Thursday. The other party were in town before us. We crossed the river, and they soon followed. Shortly after, General Hardin and Dr. English presented to General Whiteside and myself the following note:

Alton, September 22, 1842.

Messrs. Whiteside and Merryman: As the mutual personal friends of Messrs. Shields and Lincoln, but without authority from either, we earnestly desire to see a reconciliation of the misunderstanding which exists between them. Such difficulties should always be arranged amicably, if it is possible to do so with honor to both parties.

Believing, ourselves, that such an arrangement can possibly be effected, we respectfully but earnestly submit the following proposition for your consideration:

Let the whole difficulty be submitted to four or more gentlemen, to be selected by ourselves, who shall consider the affair, and report thereupon for your consideration.

John J. Hardin,
R. W. English.

To this proposition General Whiteside agreed: I declined doing so without consulting Mr. Lincoln. Mr. Lincoln remarked that, as they had accepted the proposition, he would do so, but directed that his friends should make no terms except those first proposed. Whether the adjustment was finally made upon these very terms and no other, let the following documents attest:

Missouri, September 22, 1842.

Gentlemen:—All papers in relation to the matter in controversy between Mr. Shields and Mr. Lincoln having been withdrawn by the friends of the parties concerned, the friends of Mr. Shields ask the friends of Mr. Lincoln to explain all offensive matter in the articles which appeared in the *Sangamon Journal,* of the 2d, 9th, and 16th of September, under the signature of "Rebecca," and headed "Lost Townships."

It is due General Hardin and Mr. English to state that their interference was of the most courteous and gentlemanly character.

John D. Whiteside.
Wm. Lee D. Ewing.
T. M. Hope.

Missouri, September 22, 1842.

Gentlemen:—All papers in relation to the matter in controversy between Mr. Lincoln and Mr. Shields having been withdrawn by the friends of the parties concerned, we, the undersigned, friends of Mr. Lincoln, in accordance with your request that explanation of Mr. Lincoln's publication in relation to Mr. Shields in the *Sangamon Journal* of the 2d, 9th, and 16th of September be made, take pleasure in saying, that, although Mr. Lincoln was the writer of the article signed "Rebecca" in the *Journal* of the 2d, and that only, yet he had no intention of injuring the personal or private character or standing of Mr. Shields as a gentleman or a man, and that Mr. Lincoln did not think, nor does he now think, that said article could produce such an effect; and, had Mr. Lincoln anticipated such an effect, he would have forborne to write it. We will state further, that said article was written solely for political effect, and not to gratify any personal pique against Mr. Shields, for he had none and knew of no cause for any. It is due to General Hardin and Mr. English to say that their interference was of the most courteous and gentlemanly character.

     E. H. Merryman.

     A. T. Bledsoe.

     Wm. Butler.

Let it be observed now, that Mr. Shields's friends, after agreeing to the arbitrament of four disinterested gentlemen, declined the contract, saying that Mr. Shields wished his own friends to act for him. They then proposed that we should explain without any withdrawal of papers. This was promptly and firmly refused, and General Whiteside himself pronounced the papers withdrawn. They then produced a note requesting us to "disavow" all offensive intentions in the publications, etc., etc. This we declined answering, and only responded to the above request for an explanation.

These are the material facts in relation to the matter, and I think present the case in a very different light from the garbled and curtailed statement of General Whiteside. Why he made that statement I know not, unless he wished to detract from the honor of Mr. Lincoln. This was ungenerous, more particularly as he on the ground requested us not to make in our explanation any quotations from the "Rebecca papers;" also, not to make public the terms of reconciliation, and to unite with them in defending the honorable character of the adjustment.

General Whiteside, in his publication, says: "The friends of both parties agreed to withdraw the papers (temporarily) to give the friends of Mr. Lincoln an opportunity to explain." This I deny. I say the papers were withdrawn to enable Mr. Shields's friends to ask an explanation; and I appeal to the documents for proof of my position.

By looking over these documents, it will be seen that Mr. Shields had not before asked for an explanation, but had all the time been dictatorially insisting on a retraction.

General Whiteside, in his communication, brings to light much of Mr. Shields's manifestations of bravery behind the scenes. I can do nothing of the kind for Mr. Lincoln. He took his stand when I first met him at Tremont, and maintained it calmly to the last, without difficulty or difference between himself and his friends.

I cannot close this article, lengthy as it is, without testifying to the honorable and gentlemanly conduct of General Ewing and Dr. Hope, nor indeed can I say that I saw anything objectionable in the course of General Whiteside up to the time of his communication. This is so replete with prevarication and misrepresentation, that I cannot accord to the General that candor which I once supposed him to possess. He complains that I did not procrastinate time according to agreement. He forgets that by his own act he cut me off from that chance in inducing me, by promise, not to communicate our secret contract to Mr. Lincoln. Moreover, I could see no consistency in wishing for an extension of time at that stage of the affair, when in the outset they were in so precipitate a hurry that they could not wait three days for Mr. Lincoln to return from Tremont, but must hasten there, apparently with the intention of bringing the matter to a speedy issue. He complains, too, that, after inviting him to take a seat in the buggy I never broached the subject to him on our route here. But was I, the defendant in the case, with a challenge hanging over me, to make advances, and beg a reconciliation?

Absurd! Moreover, the valorous General forgets that he beguiled the tedium of the journey by recounting to me his exploits in many a well-fought battle,—dangers by "flood and field," in which I don't believe he ever participated,—doubtless with a view to produce a salutary effect on my nerves, and impress me with a proper notion of his fire-eating propensities.

One more main point of his argument and I have done. The General seems to be troubled with a convenient shortness of memory on some occasions. He does not remember that any explanations were offered at any time, unless it were a paper read when the "broadsword proposition" was tendered, when his mind was so confused by the anticipated clatter of broadswords, or something else, that he did "not know fully what it purported to be." The truth is, that, by unwisely refraining from mentioning it to his principal, he placed himself in a dilemma which he is now endeavoring to shuffle out of. By his inefficiency and want of knowledge of those laws which govern gentlemen in matters of this kind, he has done great injustice to his principal, a gentleman who, I believe, is ready at all times to vindicate his honor manfully, but who has been unfortunate in the selection of his friends, and this fault he is now trying to wipe out by doing an act of still greater injustice to Mr. Lincoln.

   E. H. Merryman.[51,*]

 Dr. Merryman's elaborate and graphic account of the meeting at the duelling ground and all the preliminary proceedings is as full and complete a history of this serio-comic affair as any historian could give. Mr. Lincoln, as mentioned in the outset of this chapter, in the law office and elsewhere, as a rule, refrained from discussing it. I only remember of hearing him say this, in reference to the duel: "I did not intend to hurt Shields unless I did so clearly in self-defense. If it had been necessary I could have split him from the crown of his head to the end of his backbone;" and when one takes into consideration the conditions of weapons and position required in his instructions to Dr. Merryman the boast does not seem impossible.

 The marriage of Lincoln in no way diminished his love for politics; in fact, as we shall see later along, it served to stimulate his zeal in that direction. He embraced every opportunity that offered for a speech in public. Early in 1842 he entered into the Washingtonian movement organized to suppress the evils of

---

*The following letter from Lincoln to his friend Speed furnishes the final outcome of the "duelling business."

Springfield, October 5, 1842.

Dear Speed:—

 You have heard of my duel with Shields, and I have now to inform you that the duelling business still rages in this city. Day before yesterday Shields challenged Butler, who accepted, proposed fighting next morning at sunrising in Bob Allen's meadow, one hundred yards distance, with rifles. To this Whiteside, Shields's second, said 'no' because of the law. Thus ended duel No. 2. Yesterday Whiteside chose to consider himself insulted by Dr. Merryman, so sent him a kind of quasi-challenge inviting him to meet him at the Planter's House in St. Louis, on the next Friday, to settle their difficulty. Merryman made me his friend, and sent Whiteside a note, inquiring to know if he meant his note as a challenge, and if so, that he would, according to the law in such case made and provided, prescribe the terms of the meeting. Whiteside returned for answer that if Merryman would meet him at the Planter's House as desired, he would challenge him. Merryman replied in a note, that he denied Whiteside's right to dictate time and place, but that he (Merryman) would waive the question of time, and meet him at Louisiana, Mo. Upon my presenting this note to Whiteside, and stating verbally its contents, he declined receiving it, saying he had business in St. Louis, and it was as near as Louisiana. Merryman then directed me to notify Whiteside that he should publish the correspondence between them, with such comments as he saw fit. This I did. Thus it stood at bed-time last night. This morning Whiteside, by his friend Shields, is praying for a new trial, on the ground that he was mistaken in Merryman's proposition to meet him at Louisiana, Mo., thinking it was the State of Louisiana. This Merryman hoots at, and is preparing his publication; while the town is in a ferment, and a street-fight somewhat anticipated. ° ° °

 Yours forever,

  Lincoln."[52]

intemperance. At the request of the society he delivered an admirable address, on Washington's birthday, in the Presbyterian Church, which, in keeping with former efforts, has been so often published that I need not quote it in full. I was then an ardent temperance reformer myself, and remember well how one paragraph of Lincoln's speech offended the church members who were present. Speaking of certain Christians who objected to the association of drunkards, even with the chance of reforming them, he said: "If they (the Christians) believe, as they profess, that Omnipotence condescended to take on himself the form of sinful man, and as such die an ignominious death, surely they will not refuse submission to the infinitely lesser condescension, for the temporal and perhaps eternal salvation of a large, erring, and unfortunate class of their fellow-creatures. Nor is the condescension very great. In my judgment such of us as have never fallen victims have been spared more from the absence of appetite than from any mental or moral superiority over those who have. Indeed, I believe, if we take habitual drunkards as a class, their heads and their hearts will bear an advantageous comparison with those of any other class."[53] The avowal of these sentiments proved to be an unfortunate thing for Lincoln. The professing Christians regarded the suspicion suggested in the first sentence as a reflection on the sincerity of their belief, and the last one had no better effect in reconciling them to his views. I was at the door of the church as the people passed out, and heard them discussing the speech. Many of them were open in the expression of their displeasure. "It's a shame," I heard one man say, "that he should be permitted to abuse us so in the house of the Lord." The truth was the society was composed mainly of the roughs and drunkards of the town, who had evinced a desire to reform. Many of them were too fresh from the gutter to be taken at once into the society of such people as worshipped at the church where the speech was delivered. Neither was there that concert of effort so universal to-day between the churches and temperance societies to rescue the fallen. The whole thing, I repeat, was damaging to Lincoln, and gave rise to the opposition on the part of the churches which confronted him several years afterwards when he became a candidate against the noted Peter Cartwright for Congress. The charge, therefore, that in matters of religion he was a skeptic was not without its supporters, especially where his opponent was himself a preacher. But, nothing daunted, Lincoln kept on and labored zealously in the interest of the temperance movement. He spoke often again in Springfield, and also in other places over the country, displaying the same courage and adherence to principle that characterized his every undertaking.

Meanwhile, he had one eye open for politics as he moved along. He was growing more self-reliant in the practice of law every day, and felt amply able to take charge of and maintain himself in any case that happened to come into his hands. His propensity for the narration of an apt story was of immeasurable aid to him before a jury, and in cases where the law seemed to lean towards the other side won him many a case. In 1842, Martin Van Buren, who had just left the Presidential chair, made a journey through the West. He was accompanied by his former Secretary of the Navy, Mr. Paulding, and in June they reached the village of Rochester, distant from Springfield six miles. It was evening when they arrived, and on account of the muddy roads they decided to go no farther, but to rest there for the night. Word was sent into Springfield, and of course the leading Democrats of the capital hurried out to meet the distinguished visitor. Knowing the accommodations at Rochester were not intended for or suited to the entertainment of an ex-President, they took with them refreshments in quantity and variety, to make up for all deficiencies. Among others, they prevailed on Lincoln, although an ardent and pronounced Whig, to accompany them. They introduced him to the venerable statesman of Kinderhook as a representative lawyer, and a man whose wit was as ready as his store of anecdotes was exhaustless. How he succeeded in entertaining the visitor and the company, those who were present have often since testified. Van Buren himself entertained the crowd with reminiscences of politics in New York, going back to the days of Hamilton and Burr, and many of the crowd in turn interested him with graphic descriptions of early life on the western frontier. But they all yielded at last to the piquancy and force of Lincoln's queer stories. "Of these," relates one of the company,* "there was a constant supply, one following another in rapid succession, each more irresistible than its predecessor. The fun continued until after midnight, and until the distinguished traveller insisted that his sides were sore from laughing."[54] The yarns which Lincoln gravely spun out, Van Buren assured the crowd, he never would forget.

After April 14, 1841, when Lincoln retired from the partnership with Stuart, who had gone to Congress, he had been associated with Stephen T. Logan, a man who had, as he deserved, the reputation of being the best *nisi prius* lawyer in the State. Judge Logan was a very orderly but somewhat technical lawyer. He had some fondness for politics, and made one race for Congress, but he lacked the elements of a successful politician. He was defeated, and returned to the law. He was assiduous in study and tireless in search of legal principles. He was industrious and very thrifty, delighted to make and save money, and died a rich man. Lincoln had none of Logan's qualities. He was anything but studious, and

---

*Jos. Gillespie, MS. letter, September 6, 1866.

had no money sense. He was five years younger, and yet his mind and makeup so impressed Logan that he was invited into the partnership with him. Logan's example had a good effect on Lincoln, and it stimulated him to unusual endeavors. For the first time he realized the effectiveness of order and method in work, but his old habits eventually overcame him. He permitted his partner to do all the studying in the preparation of cases, while he himself trusted to his general knowledge of the law and the inspiration of the surroundings to overcome the judge or the jury. Logan was scrupulously exact, and used extraordinary care in the preparation of papers. His words were well chosen, and his style of composition was stately and formal. This extended even to his letters. This Lincoln lacked in every particular. I have before me a letter written by Lincoln at this time to the proprietors of a wholesale store in Louisville, for whom suit had been brought, in which, after notifying the latter of the sale of certain real estate in satisfaction of their judgment, he adds: "As to the real estate we cannot attend to it. We are not real estate agents, we are lawyers. We recommend that you give the charge of it to Mr. Isaac S. Britton, a trustworthy man, and one whom the Lord made on purpose for such business."[55] He gravely signs the firm name, Logan and Lincoln, to this unlawyerlike letter and sends it on its way. Logan never would have written such a letter. He had too much gravity and austere dignity to permit any such looseness of expression in letters to his clients or to anyone else.

In 1843, Logan and Lincoln both had their eyes set on the race for Congress. Logan's claim to the honor lay in his age and the services he had rendered the Whig party, while Lincoln, overflowing with ambition, lay great stress on his legislative achievements, and demanded it because he had been defeated in the nominating conventions by both Hardin and Baker in the order named. That two such aspiring politicians, each striving to obtain the same prize, should not dwell harmoniously together in the same office is not strange. Indeed, we may reasonably credit the story that they considered themselves rivals, and that numerous acrimonious passages took place between them. I was not surprised, therefore, one morning, to see Mr. Lincoln come rushing up into my quarters and with more or less agitation tell me he had determined to sever the partnership with Logan. I confess I was surprised when he invited me to become his partner. I was young in the practice and was painfully aware of my want of ability and experience; but when he remarked in his earnest, honest way, "Billy, I can trust you, if you can trust me," I felt relieved, and accepted the generous proposal. It has always been a matter of pride with me that during our long partnership, continuing on until it was dissolved by the bullet of the assassin Booth, we never had any personal controversy or disagreement. I never stood in his way for political honors or office, and I believe we understood each other perfectly. In after years, when he became more prominent, and our practice grew to respectable proportions, other ambitious practitioners undertook to supplant me in the partnership. One of the latter, more zealous than wise, charged that I was in a certain way weakening the influence of the firm. I am flattered to know that Lincoln turned on this last named individual with the retort, "I know my own business, I reckon. I know Billy Herndon better than anybody, and even if what you say of him is true I intend to stick by him."

Lincoln's effort to obtain the Congressional nomination in 1843 brought out several unique and amusing incidents. He and Edward D. Baker were the two aspirants from Sangamon county, but Baker's long residence, extensive acquaintance, and general popularity were obstacles Lincoln could not overcome; accordingly, at the last moment, Lincoln reluctantly withdrew from the field. In a letter to his friend Speed, dated March 24, 1843, he describes the situation as follows: "We had a meeting of the Whigs of the county here on last Monday, to appoint delegates to a district convention; and Baker beat me, and got the delegation instructed to go for him. The meeting, in spite of my attempt to decline it, appointed me one of the delegates; so that in getting Baker the nomination I shall be fixed a good deal like a fellow who is made groomsman to a man that has cut him out, and is marrying his own dear gal."[56] Only a few days before this he had written a friend anent the Congressional matter, "Now if you should hear any one say that Lincoln don't want to go to Congress, I wish you, as a personal friend of mine, would tell him you have reason to believe he is mistaken. The truth is I would like to go very much. Still, circumstances may happen which may prevent my being a candidate. If there are any who be my friends in such an enterprise, what I now want is that they shall not throw me away just yet."° To another friend in the adjoining county of Menard a few days after the meeting of the Whigs in Sangamon, he explains how Baker defeated him.

The entire absence of any feeling of bitterness, or what the politicians call revenge, is the most striking feature of the letter. "It is truly gratifying," he says, "to me to learn that while the people of Sangamon have cast me off, my old friends of Menard, who have known me longest and best, stick to me. It would astonish if not amuse the older citizens to learn that I (a strange, friendless, uneducated, penniless boy, working on a flat-boat at ten dollars per month) have been put down here as the candidate of pride, wealth, and aristocratic family distinction. Yet so, chiefly, it was. There was, too, the strangest combina-

---

°Letter to R. S. Thomas, Virginia, Ill., Feb. 14, '43, MS.[57]

tion of church influence against me. Baker is a Campbellite, and therefore as I suppose, with few exceptions, got all that church. My wife has some relations in the Presbyterian churches and some with the Episcopalian churches, and therefore, wherever it would tell, I was set down as either the one or the other, while it was everywhere contended that no Christian ought to go for me, because I belonged to no church, was suspected of being a deist, and had talked about fighting a duel. With all these things Baker, of course, had nothing to do; nor do I complain of them. As to his own church going for him I think that was right enough; and as to the influences I have spoken of in the other, though they were very strong, it would be grossly untrue and unjust to charge that they acted upon them in a body, or were very near so. I only mean that those influences levied a tax of considerable per cent, and throughout the religious controversy." To a proposition offering to instruct the Menard delegation for him he replies: "You say you shall instruct your delegates for me unless I object. I certainly shall not object. That would be too pleasant a compliment for me to tread in the dust. And besides, if anything should happen (which, however, is not probable) by which Baker should be thrown out of the fight, I would be at liberty to accept the nomination if I could get it. I do, however, feel myself bound not to hinder him in any way from getting the nomination. I should despise myself were I to attempt it."[58]

Baker's friends had used as an argument against Lincoln that he belonged to a proud and aristocratic family, referring doubtless to some of the distinguished relatives who were connected with him by marriage. The story reaching Lincoln's ears, he laughed heartily over it one day in a Springfield store and remarked:

"That sounds strange to me, for I do not remember of but one who ever came to see me, and while he was in town he was accused of stealing a jew's-harp."* In the convention which was held shortly after at the town of Pekin neither Baker nor Lincoln obtained the coveted honor; but John J. Hardin, of Morgan, destined to lose his life at the head of an Illinois regiment in the Mexican war, was nominated, and in the following August, elected by a good majority. Lincoln bore his defeat manfully. He was no doubt greatly disappointed, but by no means soured. He conceived the strange notion that the publicity given his so-called "aristocratic family distinction" would cost him the friendship of his humbler constituents—his Clary's Grove friends. He took his friend James Matheney out into the woods with him one day and, calling up the bitter features of the canvass, protested "vehemently and with great emphasis" that he was anything but

---

*Letter, A. Y. Ellis, July 16, '66, MS.[59]

aristocratic and proud. "Why, Jim," he said, "I am now and always shall be the same Abe Lincoln I was when you first saw me."[60]

In the campaign of 1844 Lincoln filled the honorable post of Presidential Elector, and he extended the limits of his acquaintance by stumping the State. This was the year the gallant and magnetic Clay went down in defeat. Lincoln, in the latter end of the canvass, crossed over into Indiana and made several speeches. He spoke at Rockport and also at Gentryville, where he met the Grigsbys, the Gentrys, and other friends of his boyhood. The result of the election was a severe disappointment to Mr. Lincoln as well as to all other Whigs. No election since the foundation of the Government created more widespread regret than the defeat of Clay by Polk. Men were never before so enlisted in any man's cause, and when the great Whig chieftain went down his followers fled from the field in utter demoralization. Some doubted the success of popular government, while others, more hopeful still in the face of the general disaster, vowed they would never shave their faces or cut their hair till Henry Clay became President. As late as 1880 I saw one man who had lived up to his insane resolution. One political society organized to aid Clay's election sent the defeated candidate an address, in which they assured him that, after the smoke of battle had cleared away, he would ever be remembered as one "whose name honored defeat and gave it a glory which victory could not have brought."[61] In Lincoln's case his disappointment was no greater than that of any other Whig. Many persons have yielded to the impression that Mr. Lincoln visited Clay at his home in Lexington and felt a personal loss in his defeat, but such is not the case. He took no more gloomy view of the situation than the rest of his party. He had been a leading figure himself in other campaigns, and was fully inured to the chilling blasts of defeat. They may have driven him in, but only for a short time, for he soon evinced a willingness to test the temper of the winds again.

No sooner had Baker been elected to Congress in August, 1844, than Lincoln began to manifest a longing for the tempting prize to be contended for in 1846. Hardin and Baker both having been required to content themselves with a single term each, the struggle among Whig aspirants narrowed down to Logan and Lincoln.* The latter's claim seemed to find such favorable lodgment with the party workers, and his popularity seemed so apparent, that Logan soon realized

---

*The Whig candidates for Congress in the Springfield district "rotated" in the following order: Baker succeeded Hardin in 1844, Lincoln was elected in 1846, and Logan was nominated but defeated in 1848. Lincoln publicly declined to contest the nomination with Baker in 1844; Hardin did the same for Lincoln in 1846— although both seem to have acted reluctantly; and Lincoln refused to run against Logan in 1848. Many persons insist that an agreement among these four conspicuous Whig leaders to content themselves with one term each actually existed. There is, however, no proof of any bargain, although there seems to have been a tacit understanding of the kind—maintained probably to keep other and less tractable candidates out of the field.[62]

his own want of strength and abandoned the field to his late law partner. The convention which nominated Lincoln met at Petersburg May 1, 1846. Hardin, who, in violation of what was then regarded as precedent, had been seeking the nomination, had courteously withdrawn. Logan, ambitious to secure the honor next time for himself, with apparent generosity presented Lincoln's name to the convention, and there being no other candidate he was chosen unanimously. The reader need not be told whom the Democrats placed in the field against him. It was Peter Cartwright, the famous Methodist divine and circuit rider. An energetic canvass of three months followed, during which Lincoln kept his forces well in hand. He was active and alert, speaking everywhere, and abandoning his share of business in the law office entirely. He had a formidable competitor in Cartwright, who not only had an extensive following by reason of his church influence, but rallied many more supporters around his standard by his pronounced Jacksonian attitude. He had come into Illinois with the early immigrants from Kentucky and Tennessee, and had at one time or another preached to almost every Methodist congregation between Springfield and Cairo. He had extensive family connections all over the district, was almost twenty-five years older than Lincoln, and in every respect a dangerous antagonist. Another thing which operated much to Lincoln's disadvantage was the report circulated by Cartwright's friends with respect to Lincoln's religious views. He was charged with the grave offence of infidelity, and sentiments which he was reported to have expressed with reference to the inspiration of the Bible were given the campaign varnish and passed from hand to hand. His slighting allusion expressed in the address at the Presbyterian Church before the Washington Temperance Society, February 2d, four years before, to the insincerity of the Christian people was not forgotten. It, too, played its part; but all these opposing circumstances were of no avail. Cartwright was personally very popular, but it was plain the people of the Springfield district wanted no preacher to represent them in Congress. They believed in an absolute separation of Church and State. The election, therefore, of such a man as Cartwright would not, to their way of thinking, tend to promote such a result. I was enthusiastic and active in Lincoln's interest myself. The very thought of my associate's becoming a member of Congress was a great stimulus to my self-importance. Many other friends in and around Springfield were equally as vigilant, and, in the language of another, "long before the contest closed we snuffed approaching victory in the air." Our laborious efforts met with a suitable reward. Lincoln was elected by a majority of 1511 in the district, a larger vote than Clay's two years before, which was only 914. In Sangamon county his majority was 690, and exceeded that of any of his predecessors on the Whig ticket, commencing with Stuart in 1834 and continuing on down to the days of Yates in 1852.

Before Lincoln's departure for Washington to enter on his duties as a member of Congress, the Mexican war had begun. The volunteers had gone forward, and at the head of the regiments from Illinois some of the bravest men and the best legal talent in Springfield had marched. Hardin, Baker, Bissell, and even the dramatic Shields had enlisted. The issues of the war and the manner of its prosecution were in every man's mouth. Naturally, therefore, a Congressman-elect would be expected to publish his views and define his position early in the day. Although, in common with the Whig party, opposing the declaration of war, Lincoln, now that hostilities had commenced, urged a vigorous prosecution. He admonished us all to permit our Government to suffer no dishonor, and to stand by the flag till peace came and came honorably to us. He declared these sentiments in a speech at a public meeting in Springfield, May 29, 1847.[63] In the following December he took his seat in Congress. He was the only Whig from Illinois. His colleagues in the Illinois delegation were John A. McClernand,

Rev. Peter Cartwright (after a photograph from life)

O. B. Ficklin, William A. Richardson, Thomas J. Turner, Robert Smith, and John Wentworth. In the Senate Douglas had made his appearance for the first time. The Little Giant is always in sight! Robert C. Winthrop, of Massachusetts, was chosen Speaker. John Quincy Adams, Horace Mann, Caleb Smith, Alexander H. Stephens, Robert Toombs, Howell Cobb, and Andrew Johnson were important members of the House. With many of these the newly elected member from Illinois was destined to sustain another and far different relation.

On the 5th of December, the day before the House organized, Lincoln wrote me a letter about our fee in a law-suit, and reported the result of the Whig caucus the night before. On the 13th, he wrote again: "Dear William:—Your letter, advising me of the receipt of our fee in the bank case, is just received, and I don't expect to hear another as good a piece of news from Springfield while I am away." He then directed me from the proceeds of this fee to pay a debt at the bank, and out of the balance left to settle sundry dry-goods and grocery bills. The modest tone of the last paragraph is its most striking feature. "As you are all so anxious for me to distinguish myself," he said, "I have concluded to do so before long."[64] January 8 he writes: "As to speech-making, by way of getting the hang of the House, I made a little speech two or three days ago on a post-office question of no general interest. I find speaking here and elsewhere about the same thing. I was about as badly scared, and no worse, as I am when I speak in court. I expect to make one within a week or two in which I hope to succeed well enough to wish you to see it." Meanwhile, in recognition of the assurances I had sent him from friends who desired to approve his course by a re-election, he says: "It is very pleasant to me to learn from you that there are some who desire that I should be re-elected. I most heartily thank them for the kind partiality, and I can say, as Mr. Clay said of the annexation of Texas, that, 'personally, I would not object' to a re-election, although I thought at the time, and still think, it would be quite as well for me to return to the law at the end of a single term. I made the declaration that I would not be a candidate again, more from a wish to deal fairly with others, to keep peace among our friends, and to keep the district from going to the enemy, than for any cause personal to myself, so that if it should happen that nobody else wishes to be elected I could not refuse the people the right of sending me again. But to enter myself as a competitor of others, or to authorize any one so to enter me, is what my word and honor forbid."[65]

His announcement of a willingness to accept a re-election if tendered him by the people was altogether unnecessary, for within a few days after this letter was written his constituents began to manifest symptoms of grave disapproval of his course on the Mexican war question. His position on this subject was evidenced by certain resolutions offered by him in the House three weeks before. These latter were called the "Spot Resolutions," and they and the speech which followed on the 12th of January in support of them not only sealed Lincoln's doom as a Congressman, but in my opinion, lost the district to the Whigs in 1848, when Judge Logan had succeeded at last in obtaining the nomination.

Although differing with the President as to the justice or even propriety of a war with Mexico, Lincoln was not unwilling to vote, and with the majority of his party did vote, the supplies necessary to carry it on. He did this, however, with great reluctance, protesting all the while that "the war was unnecessarily and unconstitutionally begun by the President."[66] The "Spot Resolutions," which served as a text for his speech on the 12th of January, and which caused such unwonted annoyance in the ranks of his constituents, were a series following a preamble loaded with quotations from the President's messages. These resolutions requested the President to inform the House: "*First.* Whether the *spot* on which the blood of our citizens was shed as in his messages declared was or was not within the territory of Spain, at least after the treaty of 1819, until the Mexican revolution. *Second.* Whether that spot is or is not within the territory which was wrested from Spain by the revolutionary government of Mexico. *Third.* Whether that spot is or is not within a settlement of people, which settlement has existed ever since long before the Texas revolution, and until its inhabitants fled before the approach of the United States army."[67] There were eight of these interrogatories, but it is only necessary to reproduce the three which foreshadow the position Lincoln was then intending to assume. On the 12th of January, as before stated, he followed them up with a carefully prepared and well-arranged speech, in which he made a severe arraignment of President Polk and justified the pertinence and propriety of the inquiries he had a few days before addressed to him. The speech is too long for insertion here. It was constructed much after the manner of a legal argument. Reviewing the evidence furnished by the President in his various messages, he undertook to "smoke him out" with this: "Let the President answer the interrogatories I proposed, as before mentioned, or other similar ones. Let him answer fully, fairly, candidly. Let him answer with facts, not with arguments. Let him remember, he sits where Washington sat; and so remembering, let him answer as Washington would answer. As a nation should not, and the Almighty will not, be evaded, so let him attempt no evasion, no equivocation. And if, so answering, he can show the soil was ours where the first blood of the war was shed; that it was not within an inhabited country, or if within such; that the inhabitants had submitted themselves to the civil authority of Texas or of the United States; and that the same is true of the site of Fort

Brown, then I am with him for his justification . . . But if he cannot or will not do this—if, on any pretence, or no pretence, he shall refuse or omit it—then I shall be fully convinced of what I more than suspect already—that he is deeply conscious of being in the wrong; that he feels the blood of this war, like the blood of Abel, is crying to Heaven against him; that he ordered General Taylor into the midst of a peaceful Mexican settlement purposely to bring on a war; that, originally having some strong motive—which I will not now stop to give my opinion concerning—to involve the countries in a war, and trusting to escape scrutiny by fixing the public gaze upon the exceeding brightness of military glory,—that attractive rainbow that rises in showers of blood, that serpent's eye that charms to destroy,—he plunged into it, and has swept on and on, till disappointed in his calculation of the ease with which Mexico might be subdued, he now finds himself he knows not where. He is a bewildered, confounded, and miserably perplexed man. God grant that he may be able to show that there is not something about his conscience more painful than all his mental perplexity."[68] This speech, however clear may have been its reasoning, however rich in illustration, in restrained and burning earnestness, yet was unsuccessful in "smoking out" the President. He remained within the official seclusion his position gave him, and declined to answer. In fact it is doubtless true that Lincoln anticipated no response, but simply took that means of defining clearly his own position.

On the 19th inst., having occasion to write me with reference to a note with which one of our clients, one Louis Candler, had been "annoying" him, "not the least of which annoyance," he complains, "is his cursed unreadable and ungodly handwriting," he adds a line, in which with noticeable modesty he informs me: "I have made a speech, a copy of which I send you by mail."[69] He doubtless felt he was taking rather advanced and perhaps questionable ground. And so he was, for very soon after, murmurs of dissatisfaction began to run through the Whig ranks. I did not, as some of Lincoln's biographers would have their readers believe, inaugurate this feeling of dissatisfaction. On the contrary, as the law partner of the Congressman, and as his ardent admirer, I discouraged the defection all I could. Still, when I listened to the comments of his friends everywhere after the delivery of his speech, I felt that he had made a mistake. I therefore wrote him to that effect, at the same time giving him my own views, which I knew were in full accord with the views of his Whig constituents. My argument in substance was: That the President of the United States is Commander-in-Chief of the Army and Navy; that as such commander it was his duty, in the absence of Congress, if the country was about to be invaded and armies were organized in Mexico for that purpose, to go—if necessary—into the very heart of Mexico and prevent the invasion. I argued further that it would be a crime in the Executive to let the country be invaded in the least degree. The action of the President was a necessity, and under a similar necessity years afterward Mr. Lincoln himself emancipated the slaves, although he had no special power under the Constitution to do so. In later days, in what is called the Hodges letter, concerning the freedom of the slaves, he used this language:

"I felt that measures otherwise unconstitutional might become lawful by becoming indispensable."[70]

Briefly stated, that was the strain of my argument. My judgment was formed on the law of nations and of war. If the facts were as I believed them, and my premises correct, then I assumed that the President's acts became lawful by becoming indispensable.

February 1 he wrote me, "Dear William: You fear that you and I disagree about the war. I regret this, not because of any fear we shall remain disagreed after you have read this letter, but because if you misunderstand I fear other good friends may also."[71]

Speaking of his vote in favor of the amendment to the supply bill proposed by George Ashmun, of Massachusetts, he continues:

"That vote affirms that the war was unnecessarily and unconstitutionally commenced by the President; and I will stake my life that if you had been in my place you would have voted just as I did. Would you have voted what you felt and knew to be a lie? I know you would not. Would you have gone out of the House,—skulked the vote? I expect not. If you had skulked one vote you would have had to skulk many more before the close of the session. Richardson's resolutions, introduced before I made any move or gave any vote upon the subject, make the direct question of the justice of the war; so that no man can be silent if he would. You are compelled to speak; and your only alternative is to tell the truth or tell a lie. I cannot doubt which you would do . . . I do not mean this letter for the public, but for you. Before it reaches you you will have seen and read my pamphlet speech and perhaps have been scared anew by it. After you get over your scare read it over again, sentence by sentence, and tell me honestly what you think of it. I condensed all I could for fear of being cut off by the hour rule; and when I got through I had spoken but forty-five minutes.

"Yours forever,
"A. Lincoln."[72]

I digress from the Mexican war subject long enough to insert, because in the order of time it belongs here, a characteristic letter which he wrote me regarding a man who was destined at a later day to play a far different role in the national drama. Here it is:

"Washington, Feb. 2, 1848.
"Dear William:
"I just take up my pen to say that Mr. Stephens, of Georgia, a little, slim, pale-faced, consumptive man, with a voice like Logan's, has just concluded the very best speech of an hour's length I ever heard. My old, withered, dry eyes are full of tears yet. If he writes it out anything like he delivered it our people shall see a good many copies of it.

"Yours truly,
"A. Lincoln."
To Wm. H. Herndon, Esq.[73]

February 15 he wrote me again in criticism of the President's invasion of foreign soil. He still believed the Executive had exceeded the limit of his authority. "The provision of the Constitution giving the war-making power to Congress," he insists, "was dictated, as I understand it, by the following reasons: Kings had always been involving and impoverishing their people in wars, pretending generally, if not always, that the good of the people was the object. This, our convention understood to be the most oppressive of all kingly oppressions; and they resolved to so frame the Constitution that no one man should hold the power of bringing this oppression upon us. But your view destroys the whole matter, and places our President where kings have always stood."[74]

In June the Whigs met in national convention at Philadelphia to nominate a candidate for President. Lincoln attended as a delegate. He advocated the nomination of Taylor because of his belief that he could be elected, and was correspondingly averse to Clay because of the latter's signal defeat in 1844. In a letter from Washington a few days after the convention he predicts the election of "Old Rough." He says: "In my opinion we shall have a most overwhelming glorious triumph. One unmistakable sign is that all the odds and ends are with us—Barn-burners, Native Americans, Tylermen, disappointed office-seeking Locofocos, and the Lord knows what not. . . . Taylor's nomination takes the Locos on the blind side. It turns the war thunder against them. The war is now to them the gallows of Haman, which they built for us and on which they are doomed to be hanged themselves."[75]

Meanwhile, in spite of the hopeful view Lincoln seemed to take of the prospect, things in his own district were in exceedingly bad repair. I could not refrain from apprising him of the extensive defections from the party ranks, and the injury his course was doing him. My object in thus writing to him was not to threaten him. Lincoln was not a man who could be successfully threatened; one had to approach him from a different direction. I warned him of public disappointment over his course, and I earnestly desired to prevent him from committing what I believed to be political suicide. June 22d he answered a letter I had written him on the 15th. He had just returned from a Whig caucus held in relation to the coming Presidential election. "The whole field of the nation was scanned; all is high hope and confidence," he said, exultingly. "Illinois is expected to better her condition in this race. Under these circumstances judge how heartrending it was to come to my room and find and read your discouraging letter of the 15th." But still he does not despair. "Now, as to the young men," he says, "you must not wait to be brought forward by the older men. For instance, do you suppose that I should ever have got into notice if I had waited to be hunted up and pushed forward by older men? You young men get together and form a Rough and Ready club, and have regular meetings and speeches. Take in everybody that you can get. . . . As you go along gather up all the shrewd, wild boys about town, whether just of age or a little under age. Let every one play the part he can play best—some speak, some sing, and all halloo. Your meetings will be of evenings; the older men and the women will go to hear you, so that it will not only contribute to the election of 'Old Zack,' but will be an interesting pastime and improving to the faculties of all engaged."[76] He was evidently endeavoring through me to rouse up all the enthusiasm among the youth of Springfield possible under the circumstances. But I was disposed to take a dispirited view of the situation, and therefore was not easily warmed up. I felt at this time, somewhat in advance of its occurrence, the death throes of the Whig party. I did not conceal my suspicions, and one of the Springfield papers gave my sentiments liberal quotation in its columns.[77] I felt gloomy over the prospect, and cut out these newspaper slips and sent them to Lincoln. Accompanying these I wrote him a letter equally melancholy in tone, in which among other things I reflected severely on the stubbornness and bad judgment of the old fossils in the party, who were constantly holding the young men back. This brought from him a letter, July 10, 1848, which is so clearly Lincolnian and so full of plain philosophy, that I copy it in full. Not the least singular of all is his allusion to himself as an old man, although he had scarcely passed his thirty-ninth year.

"Washington, July 10, 1848.

"Dear William:

"Your letter covering the newspaper slips was received last night. The subject of that letter is exceedingly painful to me, and I cannot but think there is some mistake in your impression of the motives of the old men. I suppose I am now one of the old men; and I declare on my veracity, which I think is good with you, that nothing could afford me more satisfaction than to learn that you and others of my young friends at home were doing battle in the contest and endearing themselves to the people and taking a stand far above any I have ever been able to reach in their admiration. I cannot conceive that other men feel differently. Of course I cannot demonstrate what I say; but I was young once, and I am sure I was never ungenerously thrust back. I hardly know what to say. The way for a young man to rise is to improve himself every way he can, never suspecting that anybody wishes to hinder him. Allow me to assure you that suspicion and jealousy never did help any man in any situation. There may sometimes be ungenerous attempts to keep a young man down; and they will succeed, too, if he allows his mind to be diverted from its true channel to brood over the attempted injury. Cast about and see if this feeling has not injured every person you have ever known to fall into it.

"Now, in what I have said I am sure you will suspect nothing but sincere friendship. I would save you from a fatal error. You have been a laborious, studious young man. You are far better informed on almost all subjects than I ever have been. You cannot fail in any laudable object unless you allow your mind to be improperly directed. I have some the advantage of you in the world's experience merely by being older; and it is this that induces me to advise.

"Your friend, as ever,

"A. Lincoln."[78]

Before the close of the Congressional session he made two more speeches. One of these, which he hastened to send home in pamphlet form, and which he supposes "nobody will read,"[79] was devoted to the familiar subject of internal improvements, and deserves only passing mention. The other, delivered on the 27th of July, was in its way a masterpiece; and it is no stretch of the truth to say that while intended simply as a campaign document and devoid of any effort at classic oratory, it was, perhaps, one of the best speeches of the session. It is too extended for insertion here without abridgment; but one who reads it will lay it down convinced that Lincoln's ascendency for a quarter of a century among the political spirits in Illinois was by no means an accident; neither will the reader wonder that Douglas, with all his forensic ability, averted, as long as he could, a contest with a man whose plain, analytical reasoning was not less potent than his mingled drollery and caricature were effective. The speech in the main is an arraignment of General Cass, the Democratic candidate for President, who had already achieved great renown in the political world, principally on account of his career as a soldier in the war of 1812, and is a triumphant vindication of his Whig opponent, General Taylor, who seemed to have had a less extensive knowledge of civil than of military affairs, and was discreetly silent about both. Lincoln caricatured the military pretensions of the Democratic candidate in picturesque style. This latter section of the speech has heretofore been omitted by most of Mr. Lincoln's biographers because of its glaring inappropriateness as a Congressional effort. I have always failed to see wherein its comparison with scores of others delivered in the halls of Congress since that time could in any way detract from the fame of Mr. Lincoln, and I therefore reproduce it here:

"But the gentleman from Georgia [Mr. Iverson] further says, we have deserted all our principles, and taken shelter under General Taylor's military coat-tail; and he seems to think this is exceedingly degrading. Well, as his faith is, so be it unto him. But can he remember no other military coat-tail, under which a certain other party have been sheltering for near a quarter of a century? Has he no acquaintance with the ample military coat-tail of General Jackson? Does he not know that his own party have run the last five Presidential races under that coat-tail? and that they are now running the sixth under the same cover? Yes, sir, that coat-tail was used not only for General Jackson himself, but has been clung to with the grip of death by every Democratic candidate since. You have never ventured, and dare not now venture from under it. Your campaign papers have constantly been 'Old Hickory's,' with rude likenesses of the old general upon them; hickory poles and hickory brooms your never-ending emblems. Mr. Polk himself was 'Young Hickory,' 'Little Hickory,' or something so; and even now your campaign paper here is proclaiming that Cass and Butler are of the 'Hickory stripe.' No, sir, you dare not give it up. Like a horde of hungry ticks, you have stuck to the tail of the Hermitage lion to the end of his life; and you are still sticking to it, and drawing a loathsome sustenance from it, after he is dead. A fellow once advertised that he had made a discovery by which he could make a new man out of an old one and have enough of the stuff left to make a little yellow dog. Just such a discovery has General Jackson's popularity been to you. You not only twice made Presidents of him out of it, but you have enough of the stuff left to make Presidents of several comparatively small men since; and it is your chief reliance now to make still another.

"Mr. Speaker, old horses and military coat-tails, or tails of any sort, are not figures of speech such as I would be the first to introduce into discussion here; but as the gentleman from Georgia has thought fit to introduce them, he and you are welcome to all you have made or can make by them. If you have any more old horses, trot them out; any more tails, just cock them and come at us. I repeat, I would not introduce this mode of discussion here; but I wish gentlemen on the other side to understand that the use of degrading figures is a game at which they may find themselves unable to take all the winnings. [A voice 'No, we give it up.'] Aye! you give it up, and well you may; but for a very different reason from that which you would have us understand. The point— the power to hurt—of all figures consists in the truthfulness of their application; and, understanding this, you may well give it up. They are weapons which hit you, but miss us.

"But in my hurry I was very near closing on this subject of military tails before I was done with it. There is one entire article of the sort I have not discussed yet; I mean the military tail you Democrats are now engaged in dovetailing on to the great Michigander. Yes, sir, all his biographers (and they are legion) have him in hand, tying him to a military tail, like so many mischievous boys tying a dog to a bladder of beans. True, the material is very limited, but they are at it might and main. He invaded Canada without resistance, and he outvaded it without pursuit. As he did both under orders, I suppose there was to him neither credit nor discredit; but they are made to constitute a large part of the tail. He was not at Hull's surrender, but he was close by; he was volunteer aid to General Harrison on the day of the battle of the Thames; and as you said in 1840 Harrison was picking whortleberries two miles off while the battle was fought, I suppose it is a just conclusion with you to say Cass was aiding Harrison to pick whortleberries. This is about all, except the mooted question of the broken sword. Some authors say he broke it: some say he threw it away; and some others, who ought to know, say nothing about it. Perhaps it would be a fair historical compromise to say if he did not break it, he did not do anything else with it.

"By the way, Mr. Speaker, did you know I am a military hero? Yes, sir, in the days of the Black Hawk war, I fought, bled, and came away. Speaking of General Cass's career, reminds me of my own. I was not at Stillman's defeat, but I was about as near it as Cass was to Hull's surrender; and, like him, I saw the place very soon afterward. It is quite certain I did not break my sword, for

I had none to break, but I bent my musket pretty badly on one occasion. If Cass broke his sword, the idea is, he broke it in desperation; I bent the musket by accident. If General Cass went in advance of me picking whortleberries, I guess I surpassed him in charges upon the wild onions. If he saw any live fighting Indians, it was more than I did, but I had a good many bloody struggles with the mosquitos; and, although I never fainted from loss of blood, I can truly say I was often very hungry. Mr. Speaker, if ever I should conclude to doff whatever our Democratic friends may suppose there is of black-cockade Federalism about me, and, thereupon they shall take me up as their candidate for the Presidency, I protest that they shall not make fun of me as they have of General Cass by attempting to write me into a military hero."[80]

After the adjournment of Congress on the 14th of August, Lincoln went through New York and some of the New England States making a number of speeches for Taylor, none of which, owing to the limited facilities attending newspaper reporting in that day, have been preserved. He returned to Illinois before the close of the canvass and continued his efforts on the stump till the election. At the second session of Congress, which began in December, he was less conspicuous than before. The few weeks spent with his constituents had perhaps taught him that in order to succeed as a Congressman it is not always the most politic thing to tell the truth because it is the truth, or do right because it is right. With the opening of Congress, by virtue of the election of Taylor, the Whigs obtained the ascendency in the control of governmental machinery. He attended to the duties of the Congressional office diligently and with becoming modesty. He answered the letters of his constituents, sent them their public documents, and looked after their pension claims. His only public act of any moment was a bill looking to the emancipation of the slaves in the District of Columbia. He interested Joshua R. Giddings and others of equally as pronounced anti-slavery views in the subject, but his bill eventually found a lodgment on "the table," where it was carefully but promptly laid by a vote of the House.[81]

Meanwhile, being chargeable with the distribution of official patronage, he began to flounder about in explanation of his action in a sea of seemingly endless perplexities. His recommendation of the appointment of T. R. King to be Register or Receiver of the Land Office had produced no little discord among the other aspirants for the place. He wrote to a friend who endorsed and urged the appointment, "either to admit it is wrong, or come forward and sustain him." He then transmits to this same friend a scrap of paper—probably a few lines approving the selection of King—which is to be copied in the friend's own

184 I HERNDON'S LINCOLN

handwriting. "Get everybody," he insists, "(not three or four, but three or four hundred) to sign it, and then send to me. Also have six, eight, or ten of our best known Whig friends to write me additional letters, stating the truth in this matter as they understood it. Don't neglect or delay in the matter. I understand," he continues, "information of an indictment having been found against him three years ago for gaming or keeping a gaming house has been sent to the Department." He then closes with the comforting assurance: "I shall try to take care of it at the Department till your action can be had and forwarded on."[82] And still people insist that Mr. Lincoln was such a guileless man and so free from the politician's sagacity!

In June I wrote him regarding the case of one Walter Davis, who was soured and disappointed because Lincoln had overlooked him in his recommendation for the Springfield post-office. "There must be some mistake," he responds on the 5th, "about Walter Davis saying I promised him the post-office. I did not so promise him. I did tell him that if the distribution of the offices should fall into my hands he should have something; and if I shall be convinced he has said any more than this I shall be disappointed. I said this much to him because, as I understand, he is of good character, is one of the young men, is of the mechanics, is always faithful and never troublesome, a Whig, and is poor, with the support of a widow-mother thrown almost exclusively on him by the death of his brother. If these are wrong reasons then I have been wrong; but I have certainly not been selfish in it, because in my greatest need of friends he was against me and for Baker."[83]

Judge Logan's defeat in 1848 left Lincoln still in a measure in charge of the patronage in his district. After his term in Congress expired the "wriggle and struggle" for office continued; and he was often appealed to for his influence in obtaining, as he termed it, "a way to live without work." Occasionally, when hard pressed, he retorted with bitter sarcasm. I append a letter written in this vein to a gentleman still living in central Illinois, who, I suppose, would prefer that his name[84] should be withheld:

"Springfield, Dec. 15, 1849.

"_____ Esq.

"Dear Sir:

"On my return from Kentucky I found your letter of the 7th of November, and have delayed answering it till now for the reason I now briefly state. From the beginning of our acquaintance I had felt the greatest kindness for you and had supposed it was reciprocated on your part. Last summer, under circumstances which I mentioned to you, I was painfully constrained to withhold a recommendation which you desired, and shortly afterwards I learned, in such a way as to believe it, that you were indulging in open abuse of me. Of course my feelings were wounded. On receiving your last letter the question occurred whether you were attempting to use me at the same time you would injure me, or whether you might not have been misrepresented to me. If the former, I ought not to answer you; if the latter, I ought, and so I have remained in suspense. I now enclose you the letter, which you may use if you see fit.

"Yours, etc.

"A. Lincoln."[85]

No doubt the man, when Lincoln declined at first to recommend him, did resort to more or less abuse. That would have been natural, especially with an unsuccessful and disappointed office-seeker. I am inclined to the opinion, and a careful reading of the letter will warrant it, that Lincoln believed him guilty. If the recommendation which Lincoln, after so much reluctance, gave was ever used to further the applicant's cause I do not know it.

With the close of Lincoln's congressional career he drops out of sight as a political factor, and for the next few years we take him up in another capacity. He did not solicit or contend for a renomination to Congress, and such was the unfortunate result of his position on public questions that it is doubtful if he could have suceeded had he done so.

CHAPTER X.

After the wedding of Lincoln and Miss Todd at the Edwards mansion we hear but little of them as a married couple till the spring of 1843, when the husband writes to his friend Speed, who had been joined to his "black-eyed Fanny" a little over a year, with regard to his life as a married man. "Are you possessing houses and lands," he writes, "and oxen and asses and men-servants and maid-servants, and begetting sons and daughters? We are not keeping house, but boarding at the Globe Tavern, which is very well kept now by a widow lady of the name of Beck. Our room (the same Dr. Wallace occupied there) and boarding only costs us four dollars a week."[1] Gaining a livelihood was slow and discouraging business with him, for we find him in another letter apologizing for his failure to visit Kentucky, "because," he says, "I am so poor and make so little headway in the world that I drop back in a month of idleness as much as I gain in a year's sowing."[2] But by dint of untiring efforts and the recognition of influential friends he managed through rare frugality to move along. In his struggles, both in the law and for political advancement, his wife shared in his sacrifices. She was a plucky little woman, and in fact endowed with a more restless ambition than he. She was gifted with a rare insight into the motives that actuate mankind, and there is no doubt that much of Lincoln's success was in a measure attributable to her acuteness and the stimulus of her influence. His election to Congress within four years after their marriage afforded her extreme gratification. She loved power and prominence, and when occasionally she came down to our office, it seemed to me then that she was inordinately proud of her tall and ungainly husband. She saw in him bright prospects ahead, and his every move was watched by her with the closest interest. If to other persons he seemed homely, to her he was the embodiment of noble manhood, and each succeeding day impressed upon her the wisdom of her choice of Lincoln over Douglas—if in reality she ever seriously accepted the latter's attentions. "Mr. Lincoln may not be as handsome a figure," she said one day in the office during her husband's absence, when the conversation turned on Douglas, "but the people are perhaps not aware that his heart is as large as his arms are long."

Mrs. Lincoln accompanied her husband to Washington and remained during one session of Congress. While there they boarded at the same house with Joshua R. Giddings, and when in 1856 the valiant old Abolitionist came to take part in the canvass in Illinois, he early sought out Lincoln, with whom he had been so favorably impressed several years before. On his way home from Congress Lincoln came by way of Niagara Falls and down Lake Erie to Toledo or Detroit. It happened that, some time after, I went to New York and also returned by way of Niagara Falls. In the office, a few days after my return, I was endeavoring to entertain my partner with an account of my trip, and among other things described the Falls. In the attempt I indulged in a good deal of imagery. As I warmed up with the subject my descriptive powers expanded accordingly. The mad rush of water, the roar, the rapids, and the rainbow furnished me with an abundance of material for a stirring and impressive picture. The recollection of the gigantic and awe-inspiring scene stimulated my exuberant powers to the highest pitch. After well-nigh exhausting myself in the effort I turned to Lincoln for his opinion. "What," I inquired, "made the deepest impression on you when you stood in the

Globe Tavern, Springfield (after photograph taken in 1887)

presence of the great natural wonder?" I shall never forget his answer, because it in a very characteristic way illustrates how he looked at everything. "The thing that struck me most forcibly when I saw the Falls," he responded, "was, where in the world did all that water come from?" He had no eye for the magnificence and grandeur of the scene, for the rapids, the mist, the angry waters, and the roar of the whirlpool, but his mind, working in its accustomed channel, heedless of beauty or awe, followed irresistibly back to the first cause. It was in this light he viewed every question. However great the verbal foliage that concealed the nakedness of a good idea Lincoln stripped it all down till he could see clear the way between cause and effect. If there was any secret in his power this surely was it.

After seeing Niagara Falls he continued his journey homeward. At some point on the way, the vessel on which he had taken passage stranded on a sand bar. The captain ordered the hands to collect all the loose planks, empty barrels and boxes and force them under the sides of the boat. These empty casks were used to buoy it up. After forcing enough of them under the vessel she lifted gradually and at last swung clear of the opposing sand bar. Lincoln had watched this operation very intently. It no doubt carried him back to the days of his navigation on the turbulent Sangamon, when he and John Hanks had rendered similar service at New Salem dam to their employer, the volatile Offut. Continual thinking on the subject of lifting vessels over sand bars and other obstructions in the water suggested to him the idea of inventing an apparatus for that purpose. Using the principle involved in the operation he had just witnessed, his plan was to attach a kind of bellows on each side of the hull of the craft just below the water line, and, by an odd system of ropes and pulleys, whenever the keel grated on the sand these bellows were to be filled with air, and thus buoyed up, the vessel was expected to float clear of the shoal. On reaching home he at once set to work to demonstrate the feasibility of his plan. Walter Davis, a mechanic having a shop near our office, granted him the use of his tools, and likewise assisted him in making the model of a miniature vessel with the arrangement as above described. Lincoln manifested ardent interest in it. Occasionally he would bring the model in the office, and while whittling on it would descant on its merits and the revolution it was destined to work in steamboat navigation. Although I regarded the thing as impracticable I said nothing, probably out of respect for Lincoln's well-known reputation as a boatman. The model was sent or taken by him to Washington, where a patent was issued, but the invention was never applied to any vessel, so far as I ever learned, and the threatened revolution in steamboat architecture and navigation never came to pass. The model still reposes in undisturbed slumber on the shelves in the Patent Office, and is the only evidence now existing of Lincoln's success as an inventor.°

Shortly before the close of his term in Congress he appears in a new rôle. Having failed of a re-election he became an applicant for the office of Commissioner of the General Land Office. He had been urged to this step by many of his Whig friends in Illinois, but he was so hedged about with other aspirants from his own State that he soon lost all heart in the contest. He was too scrupulous, and lacked too much the essentials of self-confidence and persistence, to be a successful suitor for office. In a letter to Joshua Speed, who had written him of a favorable reference to him by Mr. Crittenden, of Kentucky,† he says, February 20, 1849, "I am flattered to learn that Mr. Crittenden has any recollection of me which is not unfavorable; and for the manifestation of your kindness towards me I sincerely thank you. Still, there is nothing about me to authorize me to think of a first-class office, and a second-class one would not compensate me for being sneered at by others who want it for themselves. I believe that, so far as the Whigs in Congress are concerned, I could have the General Land Office almost by common consent; but then Sweet and Dav. Morrison and Browning and Cyrus Edwards all want it, and what is worse, while I think I could easily take it myself I fear I shall have trouble to get it for any other man in Illinois. The reason is that McGaughey, an Indiana ex-member of Congress, is here after it, and being personally known he will be hard to beat by any one who is not."[5] But, as the sequel proved, there was no need to fear the Hoosier statesman, for although he had the endorsement of General Scott and others of equal influence, yet he was left far behind in the race, and along with him Lincoln, Morrison, Browning, and Edwards. A dark horse in the person of Justin Butterfield, sprang into view, and with surprising facility captured the tempting prize. This latter and successful aspirant was a lawyer of rather extensive practice and reputation in

---

°Following is a copy of Lincoln's application for the patent on his "Improved Method of Lifting Vessels Over Shoals": "What I claim as my invention, and desire to secure by letters patent, is the combination of expansible buoyant chambers placed at the sides of a vessel with the main shaft or shafts by means of the sliding spars, which pass down through the buoyant chambers and are made fast to their bottoms and the series of ropes and pulleys or their equivalents in such a manner that by turning the main shaft or shafts in one direction the buoyant chambers will be forced downwards into the water, and at the same time expanded and filled with air for buoying up the vessel by the displacement of water, and by turning the shafts in an opposite direction the buoyant chambers will be contracted into a small space and secured against injury. "A. Lincoln."[3]

†Lincoln had asked Speed to see Crittenden (then Governor of Kentucky) and secure from the latter a recommendation for Baker, who wanted a first-class foreign mission. Crittenden did not approve of Baker, but suggested that he would favor Lincoln, whom he regarded as a rising man. Speed suggested to Lincoln to apply for the place himself. "I have pledged myself to Baker," he answered, "and cannot under any circumstances consent to the use of my name so long as he is urged for the same place."[4]

Chicago. He was shrewd, adroit, and gifted with a knowledge of what politicians would call good management—a quality or characteristic in which Lincoln was strikingly deficient. He had endorsed the Mexican war, but, strangely enough, had lost none of his prestige with the Whigs on that account.°

The close of Congress and the inauguration of Taylor were the signal for Lincoln's departure from Washington. He left with the comforting assurance that as an office-seeker he was by no means a success. Besides his lack of persistence, he had an unconscious feeling of superiority and pride that admitted of no such flexibility of opinion as the professional suitor for office must have, in order to succeed. He remained but a few days at his home in Illinois, however, before he again set out for Washington. The administration of President Taylor feeling that some reward was due Lincoln for his heroic efforts on the stump and elsewhere in behalf of the Whig party and its measures, had offered him the office of either Governor or Secretary of Oregon, and with the view of considering this and other offers he returned to Washington. Lincoln used to relate of this last-named journey an amusing incident illustrating Kentucky hospitality. He set out from Ransdell's tavern in Springfield, early in the morning. The only other passenger in the stage for a good portion of the distance was a Kentuckian, on his way home from Missouri. The latter, painfully impressed no doubt with Lincoln's gravity and melancholy, undertook to relieve the general monotony of the ride by offering him a chew of tobacco. With a plain "No, sir, thank you; I never chew," Lincoln declined, and a long period of silence followed. Later in the day the stranger, pulling from his pocket a leather-covered case, offered Lincoln a cigar, which he also politely declined on the ground that he never smoked. Finally, as they neared the station where horses were to be changed, the Kentuckian, pouring out a cup

---

°The following letter by Butterfield's daughter is not without interest:

"Chicago, Oct. 12th, 1888.
"Mr. Jesse W. Weik.
  "*Dear Sir:*
    "My father was born in Keene, N. H., in 1790, entered Williams College, 1807, and removed to Chicago in 1835. After the re-accession of the Whigs to power he was on the 21st of June in 1849 appointed Commissioner of the Land Office by President Taylor. A competitor for the position at that time was Abraham Lincoln, who was beaten, it was said, by 'the superior dispatch of Butterfield in reaching Washington by the Northern route,' but more correctly by the paramount influence of his friend Daniel Webster.
    "He held the position of Land Commissioner until disabled by paralysis in 1852. After lingering for three years in a disabled and enfeebled condition, he died at his home in Chicago, October 23d, 1855, in his sixty-third year.
      "Very respectfully,
        "Elizabeth Sawyer."[6]

of brandy from a flask which had lain concealed in his satchel, offered it to Lincoln with the remark, "Well, stranger, seeing you don't smoke or chew, perhaps you'll take a little of this French brandy. It's a prime article and a good appetizer besides." His tall and uncommunicative companion declined this last and best evidence of Kentucky hospitality on the same ground as the tobacco. When they separated that afternoon, the Kentuckian, transferring to another stage, bound for Louisville, shook Lincoln warmly by the hand. "See here, stranger," he said, good-humoredly, "you're a clever, but strange companion. I may never see you again, and I don't want to offend you, but I want to say this: my experience has taught me that a man who has no vices has d——d few virtues. Good-day."[7] Lincoln enjoyed this reminiscence of the journey, and took great pleasure in relating it. During this same journey occurred an incident for which Thomas H. Nelson, of Terre Haute, Indiana, who was appointed Minister to Chili by Lincoln, when he was President, is authority. "In the spring of 1849," relates Nelson, "Judge Abram Hammond, who was afterwards Governor of Indiana, and I arranged to go from Terre Haute to Indianapolis in the stage coach. An entire day was usually consumed in the journey. By daybreak the stage had arrived from the West, and as we stepped in we discovered that the entire back seat was occupied by a long, lank individual, whose head seemed to protrude from one end of the coach and his feet from the other. He was the sole occupant, and was sleeping soundly. Hammond slapped him familiarly on the shoulder, and asked him if he had chartered the stage for the day. The stranger, now wide awake, responded, 'Certainly not,' and at once took the front seat, politely surrendering to us the place of honor and comfort. We took in our travelling companion at a glance. A queer, odd-looking fellow he was, dressed in a well-worn and ill-fitting suit of bombazine, without vest or cravat, and a twenty-five-cent palm hat on the back of his head. His very prominent features in repose seemed dull and expressionless. Regarding him as a good subject for merriment we perpetrated several jokes. He took them all with the utmost innocence and good-nature, and joined in the laugh, although at his own expense. At noon we stopped at a wayside hostelry for dinner. We invited him to eat with us, and he approached the table as if he considered it a great honor. He sat with about half his person on a small chair, and held his hat under his arm during the meal. Resuming our journey after dinner, conversation drifted into a discussion of the comet, a subject that was then agitating the scientific world, in which the stranger took the deepest interest. He made many startling suggestions and asked many questions. We amazed him with words of learned length and thundering sound. After an astounding display of wordy pyrotechnics the dazed and bewildered stranger asked: 'What is going to be the upshot of this comet business?' I replied that I was not certain, in fact I differed from most scientists and philosophers, and was inclined to the opinion that the world would follow the darned thing off! Late in the evening we reached Indianapolis, and hurried to Browning's hotel, losing sight of the stranger altogether. We retired to our room to brush and wash away the dust of the journey. In a few minutes I descended to the portico, and there descried our long, gloomy fellow-traveller in the center of an admiring group of lawyers, among whom were Judges McLean and Huntington, Edward Hannigan, Albert S. White, and Richard W. Thompson, who seemed to be amused and interested in a story he was telling. I enquired of Browning, the landlord, who he was. "Abraham Lincoln, of Illinois, a member of Congress," was the response. I was thunderstruck at the announcement. I hastened upstairs and told Hammond the startling news, and together we emerged from the hotel by a back door and went down an alley to another house, thus avoiding further contact with our now distinguished fellow-traveller. Curiously enough, years after this, Hammond had vacated the office of Governor of Indiana a few days before Lincoln arrived in Indianapolis, on his way to Washington to be inaugurated President. I had many opportunities after the stage ride to cultivate Mr. Lincoln's acquaintance, and was a zealous advocate of his nomination and election to the Presidency. Before leaving his home for Washington, Mr. Lincoln caused John P. Usher and myself to be invited to accompany him. We agreed to join him in Indianapolis. On reaching that city the Presidential party had already arrived, and upon inquiry we were informed that the President-elect was in the dining-room of the hotel, at supper. Passing through, we saw that every seat at the numerous tables was occupied, but failed to find Mr. Lincoln. As we were nearing the door to the office of the hotel, a long arm reached to my shoulder and a shrill voice exclaimed, 'Hello, Nelson! do you think, after all, the world is going to follow the darned thing off?' It was Mr. Lincoln."[8]

The benefits and advantages of the territorial posts offered by President Taylor to Lincoln were freely discussed by the latter's friends. Some urged his acceptance on the usual ground that when Oregon was admitted as a State, he might be its first Senator.[9] Lincoln himself had some inclination to accept. He told me himself that he felt by his course in Congress he had committed political suicide, and wanted to try a change of locality—hence the temptation to go to Oregon. But when he brought the proposition home to his fireside, his wife put her foot squarely down on it with a firm and emphatic No. That always ended it with Lincoln. The result of the whole thing proved a fortunate deliverance for him, the propriety of which became more apparent as the years rolled by.°

While a member of Congress and otherwise immersed in politics Lincoln seemed to lose all interest in the law. Of course, what practice he himself controlled passed into other hands. I retained all the business I could, and worked steadily on until, when he returned, our practice was as extensive as that of any other firm at the bar. Lincoln realized that much of this was due to my efforts, and on his return he therefore suggested that he had no right to share in the business and profits which I had made. I responded that, as he had aided me and given me prominence when I was young and needed it, I could afford now to be grateful if not generous. I therefore recommended a continuation of the partnership, and we went on as before. I could notice a difference in Lincoln's movement as a lawyer from this time forward. He had begun to realize a certain lack of discipline—a want of mental training and method. Ten years had wrought some change in the law, and more in the lawyers, of Illinois. The conviction had settled in the minds of the people that the pyrotechnics of court room and stump oratory did not necessarily imply extensive or profound ability in the lawyer who resorted to it. The courts were becoming graver and more learned, and the lawyer was learning as a preliminary and indispensable condition to success that he must be a close reasoner, besides having at command a broad knowledge of the principles on which the statutory law is constructed. There was of course the same riding on circuit as before, but the courts had improved in tone and morals, and there was less laxity—at least it appeared so to Lincoln. Political defeat had wrought a marked effect on him. It went below the skin and made a changed man of him. He was not soured at his seeming political decline, but still he determined to eschew politics from that time forward and devote himself entirely to the law. And now he began to make up for time lost in politics by studying the law in earnest. No man had greater power of application than he. Once fixing his mind on any subject, nothing could interfere with or disturb him. Frequently I would go out on the circuit with him. We, usually, at the little country inns occupied the same bed. In most cases the beds were too short for him, and his feet would hang over the foot-board, thus exposing a limited expanse

---

°About this time Grant Goodrich, a lawyer in Chicago, proposed to take Lincoln into partnership with him. Goodrich had an extensive and paying practice there, but Lincoln refused the offer, giving as a reason that he tended to consumption, and, if he removed to a city like Chicago, he would have to sit down and study harder than ever. The close application required of him and the confinement in the office, he contended, would soon kill him. He preferred going around on the circuit, and even if he earned smaller fees he felt much happier.[10]

of shin bone. Placing a candle on a chair at the head of the bed, he would read and study for hours. I have known him to study in this position till two o'clock in the morning. Meanwhile, I and others who chanced to occupy the same room would be safely and soundly asleep. On the circuit in this way he studied Euclid until he could with ease demonstrate all the propositions in the six books. How he could maintain his mental equilibrium or concentrate his thoughts on an abstract mathematical proposition, while Davis, Logan, Swett, Edwards, and I so industriously and volubly filled the air with our interminable snoring was a problem none of us could ever solve. I was on the circuit with Lincoln probably one-fourth of the time. The remainder of my time was spent in Springfield looking after the business there, but I know that life on the circuit was a gay one. It was rich with incidents, and afforded the nomadic lawyers ample relaxation from all the irksome toil that fell to their lot. Lincoln loved it. I suppose it would be a fair estimate to state that he spent over half the year following Judges Treat and Davis around on the circuit. On Saturdays the court and attorneys, if within a reasonable distance, would usually start for their homes. Some went for a fresh supply of clothing, but the greater number went simply to spend a day of rest with their families. The only exception was Lincoln, who usually spent his Sundays with the loungers at the country tavern, and only went home at the end of the circuit or term of court. "At first,"* relates one of his colleagues on the circuit, "we wondered at it, but soon learned to account for his strange disinclination to go home. Lincoln himself never had much to say about home, and we never felt free to comment on it. Most of us had pleasant, inviting homes, and as we struck out for them I'm sure each one of us down in our hearts had a mingled feeling of pity and sympathy for him."[11] If the day was long and he was oppressed, the feeling was soon relieved by the narration of a story. The tavern loungers enjoyed it, and his melancholy, taking to itself wings, seemed to fly away. In the role of a story-teller I am prone to regard Mr. Lincoln as without an equal. I have seen him surrounded by a crowd numbering as many as two and in some cases three hundred persons, all deeply interested in the outcome of a story which, when he had finished it, speedily found repetition in every grocery and lounging place within reach. His power of mimicry, as I have before noted, and his manner of recital, were in many respects unique, if not remarkable. His countenance and all his features seemed to take part in the performance. As he neared the pith or point of the joke or story every vestige of seriousness disappeared from his face. His little gray eyes sparkled; a smile seemed to gather up, curtain like, the cor-

*David Davis, MS.

ners of his mouth; his frame quivered with suppressed excitement; and when the point—or "nub" of the story, as he called it—came, no one's laugh was heartier than his. These backwoods allegories are out of date now, and any lawyer, ambitious to gain prominence, would hardly dare thus to entertain a crowd, except at the risk of his reputation; but with Lincoln it gave him, in some mysterious way, a singularly firm hold on the people.

Lincoln was particularly strong in Menard county, and while on the circuit there he met with William Engle and James Murray, two men who were noted also for their story-telling proclivities.[12] I am not now asserting for the country and the period what would at a later day be considered a very high standard of taste. Art had not such patrons as to-day, but the people loved the beautiful as Nature furnished it, and the good as they found it, with as much devotion as the more refined classes now are joined to their idols. Newspapers were scarce, and the court-house, with its cluster of itinerant lawyers, disseminated much of the information that was afterwards broken up into smaller bits at the pioneer's fireside. A curious civilization indeed, but one through which every Western State distant from the great arterial river or seaboard has had to pass.

When Lincoln, Murray, and Engle met, there was sure to be a crowd. All were more or less masters in their art. I have seen the little country tavern where these three were wont to meet after an adjournment of court, crowded almost to suffocation with an audience of men who had gathered to witness the contest among the members of the strange triumvirate. The physician of the town, all the lawyers, and not unfrequently a preacher could be found in the crowd that filled the doors and windows. The yarns they spun and the stories they told would not bear repetition here, but many of them had morals which, while exposing the weaknesses of mankind, stung like a whip-lash. Some were no doubt a thousand years old, with just enough "verbal varnish" and alterations of names and dates to make them new and crisp. By virtue of the last-named application, Lincoln was enabled to draw from Balzac a "droll story," and locating it in "Egypt"* or in Indiana, pass it off for a purely original conception. Every recital was followed by its "storm of laughter and chorus of cheers." After this had all died down, some unfortunate creature, through whose thickened skull the point had just penetrated, would break out in a guffaw, starting another wave of laughter which, growing to the proportions of a billow, would come rolling in like a veritable breaker. I have known these story-

---

*The word Egypt, so frequently used in this book, refers to that portion of Illinois which lies south of the famous National Road.

telling jousts to continue long after midnight—in some cases till the very small hours of the morning. I have seen Judge Treat, who was the very imperson-ation of gravity itself, sit up till the last and laugh until, as he often expressed it, "he almost shook his ribs loose." The next day he would ascend the bench and listen to Lincoln in a murder trial, with all the seeming severity of an English judge in wig and gown. Amid such surroundings, a leading figure in such soci-ety, alternately reciting the latest effusion of the bar-room or mimicking the clownish antics of the negro minstrel, he who was destined to be an immortal emancipator, was steadily and unconsciously nearing the great trial of his life. We shall see further on how this rude civilization crystallized both his logic and his wit for use in another day.

Reverting again to Mr. Lincoln as a lawyer, it is proper to add that he detested the mechanical work of the office. He wrote few papers—less perhaps than any other man at the bar. Such work was usually left to me for the first few years we were together. Afterwards we made good use of students who came to learn the law in our office. A Chicago lawyer,° in a letter to me about Mr. Lincoln, in 1866, says: "Lincoln once told me that he had taken you in as a partner, supposing you had system and would keep things in order, but that he found out you had no more system than he had, but that you were in reality a good lawyer, so that he was doubly disappointed."[13] Lincoln knew no such thing as order or method in his law practice. He made no preparation in advance, but trusted to the hour for its inspiration and to Providence for his supplies. In the matter of letter-writing† he made no distinction between one of a business nature or any other kind. If a happy thought or expression struck him he was by no means reluctant to use it. As early as 1839 he wrote to a gentleman about a matter of business, observing crustily that "a d——d hawk-billed Yankee is here besetting me at every turn I take, saying that Robert Kenzie never received the $80 to which he was entitled."[15] In July, 1851, he wrote a facetious message to one of his clients,[16] saying: "I have news from Ottawa that we win our case. As the Dutch justice said when he mar-

---

°H. C. Whitney, MS.

†"I wish you would learn of Everett what he would take, over and above a discharge, for all trouble we have been at to take his business out of our hands and give it to somebody else. It is impossible to collect money on that or any other claim here, now, and although you know I am not a very petulant man, I declare that I am almost out of patience with Mr. Everett's endless importunities. It seems like he not only writes all the letters he can himself, but he gets everybody else in Louisville and vicinity to be constantly writing to us about his claim. I have always said that Mr. Everett is a very clever fellow, and I am very sorry he cannot be obliged; but it does seem to me he ought to know we are interested to collect his claim, and therefore would do it if we could. I am neither joking nor in a pet when I say we would thank him to transfer his business to some other, without any compensation for what we have done, provided he will see the court costs paid for which we are security."—MS. letter to Joshua F. Speed, March 27, 1842.[14]

ried folks, 'Now where ish my hundred tollars.'"° He was proverbially careless as to habits. In a letter to a fellow-lawyer in another town, apologizing for failure to answer sooner, he explains: "First, I have been very busy in the United States Court; second, when I received the letter I put it in my old hat and buying a new one the next day the old one was set aside, and so the letter was lost sight of for a time."[18] This hat of Lincoln's—a silk plug—was an extraordinary receptacle. It was his desk and his memorandum-book. In it he carried his bank-book and the bulk of his letters. Whenever in his reading or researches he wished to preserve an idea, he jotted it down on an envelope or stray piece of paper and placed it inside the lining. Afterwards when the memorandum was needed there was only one place to look for it.†

How Lincoln appeared and acted in the law office has been graphically and, I must confess, truthfully told by a gentleman now in New York, who was for several years a student in our office. I beg to quote a few lines from him: "My brother met Mr. Lincoln in Ottawa, Ill.,‡ one day, and said to him: 'I have a brother whom I would very much like to have enter your office as a student.' 'All right!' was his reply; 'send him down and we will take a look at him.' I was then studying law at Grand Rapids, Mich., and on hearing from my brother I immediately packed up and started for Springfield. I arrived there on Saturday night. On Sunday Mr. Lincoln was pointed out to me. I well remember this first sight of him. He was striding along, holding little Tad, then about six years old,

---

°The following unpublished letter in possession of C. F. Gunther, Esq., Chicago, Ills., shows how he proposed to fill a vacancy in the office of Clerk of the United States Court. It reads like the letter of a politician in the midst of a canvass for office:

"Springfield, Ill., December 6, 1854.

"Hon. Justice McLean.

"Sir: I understand it is in contemplation to displace the present Clerk and appoint a new one for the Circuit and District Courts of Illinois. I am very friendly to the present incumbent, and both for his own sake and that of his family, I wish him to be retained so long as it is possible for the Court to do so.

"In the contingency of his removal, however, I have recommended William Butler as his successor, and I do not wish what I write now to be taken as any abatement of that recommendation.

"William J. Black is also an applicant for the appointment, and I write this at the solicitation of his friends to say that he is every way worthy of the office, and that I doubt not the conferring it upon him will give great satisfaction.

"Your ob't servant,

"A. Lincoln."[17]

†Lincoln had always on the top of our desk a bundle of papers into which he slipped anything he wished to keep and afterwards refer to. It was a receptacle of general information. Some years ago, on removing the furniture from the office, I took down the bundle and blew from the top the liberal coat of dust that had accumulated thereon. Immediately underneath the string was a slip bearing this endorsement in his hand: "When you can't find it anywhere else, look in this."

‡John H. Littlefield, *Brooklyn Eagle*, October 16, 1887.

by the hand, who could with the greatest difficulty keep up with his father. In the morning I applied at the office of Lincoln and Herndon for admission as a student. The office was on the second floor of a brick building on the public square, opposite the court-house. You went up one flight of stairs and then passed along a hallway to the rear office, which was a medium-sized room. There was one long table in the center of the room, and a shorter one running in the opposite direction, forming a T, and both were covered with green baize. There were two windows which looked into the back yard. In one corner was an old-fashioned secretary with pigeon-holes and a drawer, and here Mr. Lincoln and his partner kept their law papers. There was also a book-case containing about 200 volumes of law as well as miscellaneous books. The morning I entered the office Mr. Lincoln and his partner, Mr. Herndon, were both present. Mr. Lincoln addressed his partner thus: 'Billy, this is the young man of whom I spoke to you. Whatever arrangement you make with him will be satisfactory to me.' Then, turning to me, he said, 'I hope you will not become so enthusiastic in your studies of Blackstone and Kent as did two young men whom we had here. Do you see that spot over there?' pointing to a large ink stain on the wall. 'Well, one of these young men got so enthusiastic in his pursuit of legal lore that he fired an inkstand at the other one's head, and that is the mark he made.' I immediately began to clean up about the office a little. Mr. Lincoln had been in Congress and had the usual amount of seeds to distribute to the farmers. These were sent out with Free Soil and Republican documents. In my efforts to clean up, I found that some of the seeds had sprouted in the dirt that had collected in the office. Judge Logan and Milton Hay occupied the front offices on the same floor with Lincoln and Herndon, and one day Mr. Hay came in and said with apparent astonishment: 'What's happened here?' 'Oh, nothing,' replied Lincoln, pointing to me, 'only this young man has been cleaning up a little.' One of Lincoln's striking characteristics was his simplicity, and nowhere was this trait more strikingly exhibited than in his willingness to receive instruction from anybody and everybody. One day he came into the office and addressing his partner, said: 'Billy, what's the meaning of antithesis?' Mr. Herndon gave him the definition of the word, and I said: 'Mr. Lincoln, if you will allow me, I will give you an example.' 'All right, John, go ahead,' said Mr. Lincoln in his hearty manner. 'Phillips says, in his essay on Napoleon, "A pretended patriot, he impoverished the country; a professed Catholic, he imprisoned the Pope,"' etc. Mr. Lincoln thanked me and seemed very much pleased. Returning from off the circuit once he said to Mr. Herndon: 'Billy, I heard a good story while I was up in the country. Judge D—— was complimenting the landlord on the excellence of his beef. "I am surprised," he said, "that you have such good beef. You must have to kill a whole critter when you want any." "Yes," said the landlord, "we never kill less than a whole critter.'"

"Lincoln's favorite position when unravelling some knotty law point was to stretch both of his legs at full length upon a chair in front of him. In this position, with books on the table near by and in his lap, he worked up his case. No matter how deeply interested in his work, if any one came in he had something humorous and pleasant to say, and usually wound up by telling a joke or an anecdote. I have heard him relate the same story three times within as many hours to persons who came in at different periods, and every time he laughed as heartily and enjoyed it as if it were a new story. His humor was infectious. I had to laugh because I thought it funny that Mr. Lincoln enjoyed a story so repeatedly told.

"There was no order in the office at all. The firm of Lincoln and Herndon kept no books. They divided their fees without taking any receipts or making any entries on books. One day Mr. Lincoln received $5000 as a fee in a railroad case. He came in and said: 'Well, Billy,' addressing his partner, Mr. Herndon, 'here is our fee; sit down and let me divide.' He counted out $2,500 to his partner, and gave it to him with as much nonchalance as he would have given a few cents for a paper. Cupidity had no abiding place in his nature.

"I took a good deal of pains in getting up a speech which I wanted to deliver during a political campaign. I told Mr. Lincoln that I would like to read it to him. He sat down in one chair, put his feet into another one, and said: 'John, you can fire away with that speech; I guess I can stand it.' I unrolled the manuscript, and proceeded with some trepidation. 'That's a good point, John,' he would say, at certain places, and at others: 'That's good—very good indeed,' until I felt very much elated over my effort. I delivered the speech over fifty times during the campaign. Elmer E. Ellsworth, afterwards colonel of the famous Zouaves, who was killed in Alexandria, early in the war, was nominally a student in Lincoln's office. His head was so full of military matters, however, that he thought little of law. Of Ellsworth, Lincoln said: 'That young man has a real genius for war!'"[19]

During the six years following his retirement from Congress, Lincoln, realizing in a marked degree his want of literary knowledge, extended somewhat his research in that direction. He was naturally indisposed to undertake anything that savored of exertion, but his brief public career had exposed the limited area of his literary attainments. Along with his Euclid therefore he carried a well-worn copy of Shakespeare, in which he read no little in his leisure moments.

"In travelling on the circuit," relates one of his associates at the bar,* "he was in the habit of rising earlier than his brothers of the bar. On such occasions he was wont to sit by the fire, having uncovered the coals, and muse, and ponder, and soliloquize, inspired, no doubt, by that strange psychological influence which is so poetically described by Poe in 'The Raven.' On one of these occasions, at the town of Lincoln, sitting in the position described, he quoted aloud and at length the poem called 'Immortality.' When he had finished he was questioned as to the authorship and where it could be found. He had forgotten the author, but said that to him it sounded as much like true poetry as anything he had ever heard. He was particularly pleased with the last two stanzas."[20]

Beyond a limited acquaintance with Shakespeare, Byron, and Burns, Mr. Lincoln, comparatively speaking, had no knowledge of literature. He was familiar with the Bible, and now and then evinced a fancy for some poem or short sketch to which his attention was called by some one else, or which he happened to run across in his cursory reading of books or newspapers. He never in his life sat down and read a book through, and yet he could readily quote any number of passages from the few volumes whose pages he had hastily scanned. In addition to his well-known love for the poem "Immortality" or "Why should the Spirit of Mortal be Proud," he always had a great fondness for Oliver Wendell Holmes' "Last Leaf," the fourth stanza of which, beginning with the verse, "The mossy marbles rest," I have often heard him repeat. He once told me of a song a young lady had sung in his hearing at a time when he was laboring under some dejection of spirits. The lines struck his fancy, and although he did not know the singer—having heard her from the sidewalk as he passed her house—he sent her a request to write the lines out for him. Within a day or two he came into the office, carrying in his hand a delicately perfumed envelope which bore the address, "Mr. Lincoln—Present," in an unmistakable female hand. In it, written on gilt-edged paper, were the lines of the song. The plaintive strain of the piece and its melancholy sentiment struck a responsive chord in a heart already filled with gloom and sorrow. Though ill-adapted to dissipate one's depression, something about it charmed Lincoln, and he read and re-read it with increasing relish. I had forgotten the circumstance until recently, when, in going over some old papers and letters turned over to me by Mr. Lincoln, I ran across the manuscript, and the incident was brought vividly to my mind. The envelope, still retaining a faint reminder of the perfumed scent given it thirty years before, bore the laconic endorsement, "Poem—I like this," in the handwriting of Mr.

---

*Lawrence Weldon, letter, Feb. 10, 1866, MS.

Lincoln. Unfortunately no name accompanied the manuscript, and unless the lady on seeing this chooses to make herself known, we shall probably not learn who the singer was. The composition is headed, "The Enquiry." I leave it to my musical friends to render it into song. Following are the lines:

"Tell me, ye winged winds
That round my pathway roar,
Do ye not know some spot
Where mortals weep no more?
Some lone and pleasant vale
Some valley in the West,
Where, free from toil and pain,
The weary soul may rest?
The loud wind dwindled to a whisper low,
And sighed for pity as it answered, No.

"Tell me, thou mighty deep,
Whose billows round me play,
Knows't thou some favored spot,
Some island far away,
Where weary man may find
The bliss for which he sighs;
Where sorrow never lives
And friendship never dies?
The loud waves rolling in perpetual flow
Stopped for awhile and sighed to answer, No.

"And thou, serenest moon,
That with such holy face
Dost look upon the Earth
Asleep in Night's embrace—
Tell me, in all thy round
Hast thou not seen some spot
Where miserable man
Might find a happier lot?
Behind a cloud the moon withdrew in woe,
And a voice sweet but sad responded, No.

"Tell me, my secret soul,
Oh, tell me, Hope and Faith,
Is there no resting-place
From sorrow, sin, and death?
Is there no happy spot
Where mortals may be blessed,
Where grief may find a balm

And weariness a rest?
Faith, Hope, and Love, best boon to mortals given,
Waved their bright wings and whispered, Yes, in Heaven."°, 21

Judge S. H. Treat, recently deceased, thus describes Lincoln's first appearance in the Supreme Court of Illinois. "A case being called for hearing, Mr. Lincoln stated that he appeared for the appellant and was ready to proceed with the argument. He then said: 'This is the first case I have ever had in this court, and I have therefore examined it with great care. As the Court will perceive by looking at the abstract of the record, the only question in the case is one of authority. I have not been able to find any authority to sustain my side of the case, but I have found several cases directly in point on the other side. I will now give these authorities to the court, and then submit the case.'"22

A lawyer in Beardstown relates this:† "Lincoln came into my office one day with the remark: 'I see you've been suing some of my clients, and I've come down to see about it.' He had reference to a suit I had brought to enforce the specific performance of a contract. I explained the case to him, and showed my proofs. He seemed surprised that I should deal so frankly with him, and said he would be as frank with me; that my client was justly entitled to a decree, and he should so represent it to the court; and that it was against his principles to contest a clear matter of right. So my client got a deed for a farm which, had another lawyer been in Mr. Lincoln's place, would have been consumed by the costs of litigation for years, with the result probably the same in the end."23 A young man once wrote to Lincoln, enquiring for the best mode of obtaining a thorough knowledge of the law. "The mode is very simple," he responded, "though laborious and tedious. It is only to get books and read and study them carefully. Begin with Blackstone's Commentaries, and after reading carefully through, say twice, take up Chitty's Pleadings, Greenleaf's Evidence, and Story's Equity in succession. Work, work, work, is the main thing."‡

Lincoln never believed in suing for a fee. If a client would not pay on request he never sought to enforce collection. I remember once a man who had been indicted for forgery or fraud employed us to defend him. The illness of the prosecuting attorney caused some delay in the case, and our client, becoming dissat-

---

°Persons familiar with literature will recognize this as a poem written by Charles Mackay, an English writer who represented a London newspaper in the United States during the Rebellion as its war correspondent. It was set to music as a chant, and as such was frequently rendered in public by the famous Hutchinson family of singers. I doubt if Mr. Lincoln ever knew who wrote it.
†J. Henry Shaw, letter, June 13, 1866, MS.
‡Letter to J. M. Brockman, Sep. 25, 1859, MS.24

isfied at our conduct of the case, hired some one else, who superseded us most effectually. The defendant declining to pay us the fee demanded, on the ground that we had not represented him at the trial of the cause, I brought suit against him in Lincoln's absence and obtained judgment for our fee. After Lincoln's return from the circuit the fellow hunted him up and by means of a carefully constructed tale prevailed on him to release the judgment without receiving a cent of pay. The man's unkind treatment of us deserved no such mark of generosity from Lincoln, and yet he could not resist the appeal of any one in poverty and want. He could never turn from a woman in tears.° It was no surprise to me or any of his intimate friends that so many designing women with the conventional widows' weeds and easy-flowing tears overcame him in Washington. It was difficult for him to detect an impostor, and hence it is not to be marvelled at that he cautioned his secretaries: "Keep them away—I cannot stand it."

On many questions I used to grow somewhat enthusiastic, adopting sometimes a lofty metaphor by way of embellishment. Lincoln once warned me: "Billy, don't shoot too high—aim lower and the common people will understand you. They are the ones you want to reach—at least they are the ones you ought to reach. The educated and refined people will understand you any way. If you aim too high your ideas will go over the heads of the masses, and only hit those who need no hitting."[25] While it is true that from his peculiar construction Lincoln dwelt entirely in the head and in the land of thought, and while he was physically a lazy man, yet he was intellectually energetic; he was not only energetic, but industrious; not only industrious, but tireless; not only tireless, but indefatigable. Therefore if in debate with him a man stood on a questionable foundation he might well watch whereon he stood. Lincoln could look a long distance ahead and calculate the triumph of right. With him justice and truth were paramount. If to him a thing seemed untrue he could not in his nature simulate truth. His retention by a man to defend a lawsuit did not prevent him from throwing it up in its most critical stage if he believed he was espousing an unjust cause. This extreme conscientiousness and disregard of the alleged sacredness of the professional cloak robbed him of much so-called success at the bar. He once wrote to one of our clients: "I do not think there is the least use of doing anything more with your lawsuit. I not only do not think you are sure to gain it, but I do think you are sure to lose it. Therefore the sooner it ends the better."† Messrs. Stuart and Edwards once brought a suit against a client of ours which involved the title

---

°I have heard Lincoln say he thanked God that he was not born a woman, because he could not refuse any request if it was not apparently dishonest.
†Letter to H. Keeling, Esq., March 3, 1858, MS.[26]

to considerable property. At that time we had only two or three terms of court, and the docket was somewhat crowded. The plaintiff's attorneys were pressing us for a trial, and we were equally as anxious to ward it off. What we wanted were time and a continuance to the next term. We dared not make an affidavit for continuance, founded on facts, because no such pertinent and material facts as the law contemplated existed. Our case for the time seemed hopeless. One morning, however, I accidentally overheard a remark from Stuart indicating his fear lest a certain fact should happen to come into our possession. I felt some relief, and at once drew up a fictitious plea, averring as best I could the substance of the doubts I knew existed in Stuart's mind. The plea was as skilfully drawn as I knew how, and was framed as if we had the evidence to sustain it. The whole thing was a sham, but so constructed as to work the desired continuance, because I knew that Stuart and Edwards believed the facts were as I pleaded them. This was done in the absence and without the knowledge of Lincoln. The plea could not be demurred to, and the opposing counsel dared not take the issue on it. It perplexed them sorely. At length, before further steps were taken, Lincoln came into court. He looked carefully over all the papers in the case, as was his custom, and seeing my ingenious subterfuge, asked, "Is this seventh plea a good one?" Proud of the exhibition of my skill, I answered that it was. "But," he inquired, incredulously, "is it founded on fact?" I was obliged to respond in the negative, at the same time following up my answer with an explanation of what I had overheard Stuart intimate, and of how these alleged facts could be called facts if a certain construction were put upon them. I insisted that our position was justifiable, and that our client must have time or be ruined. I could see at once it failed to strike Lincoln as just right. He scratched his head thoughtfully and asked, "Hadn't we better withdraw that plea? You know it's a sham, and a sham is very often but another name for a lie. Don't let it go on record. The cursed thing may come staring us in the face long after this suit has been forgotten." The plea was withdrawn. By some agency—not our own—the case was continued and our client's interests were saved.[27] I only relate this incident to illustrate Lincoln's far-seeing capacity; it serves to show how over-cautious he seemed to be with regard to how his record might look in the future. I venture the assertion that he was the only member of the bar in Springfield who would have taken such a conscientious view of the matter.

One phase of Lincoln's character, almost lost sight of in the commonly accepted belief in his humility and kindly feeling under all circumstances, was his righteous indignation when aroused. In such cases he was the most fearless man I ever knew. I remember a murder case in which we appeared for the defence, and during the trial of which the judge—a man of ability far inferior to Lincoln's—kept ruling against us. Finally, a very material question, in fact one around which the entire case seemed to revolve, came up, and again the Court ruled adversely. The prosecution was jubilant, and Lincoln, seeing defeat certain unless he recovered his ground, grew very despondent. The notion crept into his head that the Court's rulings, which were absurd and almost spiteful, were aimed at him, and this angered him beyond reason. He told me of his feelings at dinner, and said: "I have determined to crowd the Court to the wall and regain my position before night." From that time forward it was interesting to watch him. At the reassembling of court he arose to read a few authorities in support of his position. In his comments he kept within the bounds of propriety just far enough to avoid a reprimand for contempt of court. He characterized the continued rulings against him as not only unjust but foolish; and, figuratively speaking, he peeled the Court from head to foot. I shall never forget the scene. Lincoln had the crowd, a portion of the bar, and the jury with him. He knew that fact, and it, together with the belief that injustice had been done him, nerved him to a feeling of desperation. He was wrought up to the point of madness. When a man of large heart and head is wrought up and mad, as the old adage runs, "he's mad all over." Lincoln had studied up the points involved, but knowing full well the calibre of the judge, relied mostly on the moral effect of his personal bearing and influence. He was alternately furious and eloquent, pursuing the Court with broad facts and pointed inquiries in marked and rapid succession. I remember he made use of this homely incident in illustration of some point: "In early days a party of men went out hunting for a wild boar. But the game came upon them unawares, and scampering away they all climbed the trees save one, who, seizing the animal by the ears, undertook to hold him, but despairing of success cried out to his companions in the trees, 'For God's sake, boys, come down and help me let go.'" The prosecution endeavored to break him down or even "head him off," but all to no purpose. His masterly arraignment of law and facts had so effectually badgered the judge that, strange as it may seem, he pretended to see the error in his former position, and finally reversed his decision in Lincoln's favor. The latter saw his triumph, and surveyed a situation of which he was the master. His client was acquitted, and he had swept the field.[28]

In the case of Parker *vs.* Hoyt, tried in the United States Court in Chicago, Lincoln was one of the counsel for the defendant. The suit was on the merits of an infringement of a patent water wheel. The trial lasted several days and Lincoln manifested great interest in the case. In his earlier days he had run, or aided in running, a saw-mill, and explained in his argument the action of the water on the wheel in a manner so clear and intelligible that the jury were enabled to comprehend the points and line of defence without the least difficulty. It was evident he had carried the jury with him in a most masterly argument, the force of which could not be broken by the reply of the opposing counsel. After the jury retired he became very anxious and uneasy. The jury were in another building, the windows of which opened on the street, and had been out for some two hours. "In passing along the street, one of the jurors on whom we very much relied," relates Lincoln's associate in the case,° "he being a very intelligent man and firm in his convictions, held up to him one finger. Mr. Lincoln became very much excited, fearing it indicated that eleven of the jury were against him. He knew if this man was for him he would never yield his opinion. He added, if he was like a juryman he had in Tazewell county, the defendant was safe. He was there employed, he said, to prosecute a suit for divorce. His client was a pretty, refined, and interesting little woman, and in court. The defendant, her husband, was a gross, morose, querulous, fault-finding, and uncomfortable man, and entirely unfitted for the husband of such a woman; but although he was able to prove the use of very offensive and vulgar epithets applied by the husband to his wife, and all sorts of annoyances, yet there were no such acts of personal violence as were required by the statute to justify a divorce. Lincoln did the best he could, and appealed to the jury to have compassion on the woman, and not to bind her to such a man and such a life as awaited her if required to live longer with him. The jury took about the same view of it in their deliberations. They desired to find for his fair client, but could discover no evidence which would really justify a verdict for her. At last they drew up a verdict for the defendant, and all signed but one fellow, who on being approached with the verdict said, coolly: 'Gentlemen, I am going to lie down to sleep, and when you get ready to give a verdict for that little woman, then wake me and not until then; for before I will give a verdict against her I will lie here till I rot and the pismires carry me out through the key-hole.' 'Now,' observed Lincoln, 'if that juryman will stick like the man in Tazewell county we are safe.' Strange to relate, the jury did come in, and with a verdict for the defendant. Lincoln always regarded this as one of the gratifying triumphs of his professional life."[29]

°Grant Goodrich, letter, Nov. 9, 1866, MS.

CHAPTER XI.

A Law office is a dull, dry place so far as pleasurable or interesting incidents are concerned. If one is in search of stories of fraud, deceit, cruelty, broken promises, blasted homes, there is no better place to learn them than a law office. But to the majority of persons these painful recitals are anything but attractive, and it is well perhaps that it should be so. In the office, as in the court room, Lincoln, when discussing any point, was never arbitrary or insinuating. He was deferential, cool, patient, and respectful. When he reached the office, about nine o'clock in the morning, the first thing he did was to pick up a newspaper, spread himself out on an old sofa, one leg on a chair, and read aloud, much to my discomfort. Singularly enough Lincoln never read any other way but aloud. This habit used to annoy me almost beyond the point of endurance. I once asked him why he did so. This was his explanation: "When I read aloud two senses catch the idea: first, I see what I read; second, I hear it, and therefore I can remember it better." He never studied law books unless a case was on hand for consideration—never followed up the decisions of the supreme courts, as other lawyers did. It seemed as if he depended for his effectiveness in managing a lawsuit entirely on the stimulus and inspiration of the final hour. He paid but little attention to the fees and money matters of the firm—usually leaving all such to me. He never entered an item in the account book. If any one paid money to him which belonged to the firm, on arriving at the office he divided it with me. If I was not there, he would wrap up my share in a piece of paper and place it in my drawer—marking it with a pencil, "Case of Roe *vs.* Doe.—Herndon's half."

On many topics he was not a good conversationalist, because he felt that he was not learned enough. Neither was he a good listener. Putting it a little strongly, he was often not even polite. If present with others, or participating in a conversation, he was rather abrupt, and in his anxiety to say something apt or to illustrate the subject under discussion, would burst in with a story. In our office I have known him to consume the whole forenoon relating stories. If a man came to see him for the purpose of finding out something which he did not care to let him know and at the same time did not want to refuse him, he was very adroit. In such cases Lincoln would do most of the talking, swinging around what he suspected was the vital point, but never nearing it, interlarding his answers with a seemingly endless supply of stories and jokes. The interview being both interesting and pleasant, the man would depart in good humor, believing he had accomplished his mission. After he had walked away a few squares and had cooled off, the question would come up, "Well, what did I find out?" Blowing away the froth of Lincoln's humorous narratives he would find nothing substantial left.

"As he entered the trial," relates one of his colleagues at the bar,° "where most lawyers would object he would say he 'reckoned' it would be fair to let this in, or that; and sometimes, when his adversary could not quite prove what Lincoln knew to be the truth, he 'reckoned' it would be fair to admit the truth to be so-and-so. When he did object to the court, and when he heard his objections answered, he would often say, 'Well, I reckon I must be wrong.' Now, about the time he had practised this three-fourths through the case, if his adversary didn't understand him, he would wake up in a few minutes learning that he had feared the Greeks too late, and find himself beaten. He was wise as a serpent in the trial of a cause, but I have had too many scars from his blows to certify that he was harmless as a dove. When the whole thing was unravelled, the adversary would begin to see that what he was so blandly giving away was simply what he couldn't get and keep. By giving away six points and carrying the seventh he carried his case, and the whole case hanging on the seventh he traded away everything which would give him the least aid in carrying that. Any man who took Lincoln for a simple-minded man would very soon wake up with his back in a ditch."[1]

Lincoln's restless ambition found its gratification only in the field of politics. He used the law merely as a stepping-stone to what he considered a more attractive condition in the political world. In the allurements held out by the latter he seemed to be happy. Nothing in Lincoln's life has provoked more discussion than the question of his ability as a lawyer. I feel warranted in saying that he was at the same time a very great and a very insignificant lawyer. Judge David Davis, in his eulogy on Lincoln at Indianapolis,[2] delivered at the meeting of the bar there in May, 1865, said this: "In all the elements that constituted a lawyer he

---

°Leonard Swett.

had few equals. He was great at *nisi prius* and before an appellate tribunal. He seized the strong points of a cause and presented them with clearness and great compactness. His mind was logical and direct, and he did not indulge in extraneous discussion. Generalities and platitudes had no charm for him. An unfailing vein of humor never deserted him, and he was able to claim the attention of court and jury when the cause was most uninteresting by the appropriateness of his anecdotes. His power of comparison was large, and he rarely failed in a legal discussion to use that mode of reasoning. The framework of his mental and moral being was honesty, and a wrong case was poorly defended by him. The ability which some eminent lawyers possess of explaining away the bad points of a cause by ingenious sophistry was denied him. In order to bring into full activity his great powers it was necessary that he should be convinced of the right and justice of the matter which he advocated. When so convinced, whether the cause was great or small he was usually successful."*

This statement of Judge Davis in general is correct, but in some particulars is faulty. It was intended as a eulogy on Lincoln, and as such would not admit of as many limitations and modifications as if spoken under other circumstances. In 1866 Judge Davis said in a statement made to me in his home at Bloomington, which I still have, "Mr. Lincoln had no managing faculty nor organizing power; hence a child could conform to the simple and technical rules, the means and the modes of getting at justice, better than he. The law has its own rules, and a student could get at them or keep with them better than Lincoln. Sometimes he was forced to study these if he could not get the rubbish of a case removed. But all the way through his lack of method and organizing ability was clearly apparent."[4] The idea that Mr. Lincoln was a great lawyer in the higher courts and a good *nisi prius* lawyer and yet that a child or student could manage a case in court better than he, seems strangely inconsistent but the facts of his life as a lawyer will reconcile this and other apparent contradictions.

I was not only associated with Mr. Lincoln in Springfield, but was frequently on the circuit with him, but of course not so much as Judge Davis, who held the court, and whom Lincoln followed around on the circuit for at least six months out of the year.[5] I easily realized that Lincoln was strikingly deficient in the technical rules of the law. Although he was constantly reminding young legal aspirants to study and "work, work," yet I doubt if he ever read a single elementary law book through in his life. In fact, I may truthfully say, I never knew him to read through

---

*He never took advantage of a man's low character to prejudice the jury. Mr. Lincoln thought his duty to his client extended to what was honorable and high-minded, just and noble—nothing further. Hence the meanest man at the bar always paid great deference and respect to him.—David Davis, Sept. 10, 1866, MS.[3]

David Davis

a law book of any kind. Practically, he knew nothing of the rules of evidence, of pleading, or practice, as laid down in the text-books, and seemed to care nothing about them. He had a keen sense of justice, and struggled for it, throwing aside forms, methods, and rules, until it appeared pure as a ray of light flashing through a fog-bank. He was not a general reader in any field of knowledge, but when he had occasion to learn or investigate any subject he was thorough and indefatigable in his search. He not only went to the root of a question, but dug up the root, and separated and analyzed every fibre of it. He was in every respect a case lawyer, never cramming himself on any question till he had a case in which the question was involved. He thought slowly and acted slowly; he must needs have time to analyze all the facts in a case and wind them into a connected story. I have seen him lose cases of the plainest justice, which the most inexperienced member of the bar would have gained without effort. Two things were essential to his success in managing a case. One was time; the other a feeling of confidence in the justice of the cause he represented. He used to say, "If I can free this case from technicalities and get it properly swung to the jury, I'll win it." But if either of these essentials were lacking, he was the weakest man at the bar. He was greatest in my opinion as a lawyer in the Supreme Court of Illinois. There the cases were never hurried. The attorneys generally prepared their cases in the form of briefs, and the movements of the court and counsel were so slow that no one need be caught by surprise. I was with Lincoln once and listened to an oral argument by him in which he rehearsed an extended history of the law. It was a carefully prepared and masterly discourse, but, as I thought, entirely useless. After he was through and we were walking home I asked him why he went so far back in the history of the law. I presumed the court knew enough history. "That's where you're mistaken," was his instant rejoinder. "I dared not trust the case on the presumption that the court knows everything—in fact I argued it on the presumption that the court didn't know anything," a statement which, when one reviews the decision of our appellate courts, is not so extravagant as one would at first suppose.

I used to grow restless at Lincoln's slow movements and speeches in court. "Speak with more vim," I would frequently say, "and arouse the jury—talk faster and keep them awake." In answer to such a suggestion he one day made use of this illustration: "Give me your little pen-knife, with its short blade, and hand me that old jack-knife, lying on the table." Opening the blade of the pen-knife he said: "You see, this blade at the point travels rapidly, but only through a small portion of space till it stops; while the long blade of the jack-knife moves no faster but through a much greater space than the small one. Just so with the long, labored movements of my mind. I may not emit ideas as rapidly as others, because I am compelled by nature to speak slowly, but when I do throw off a thought it seems to me, though it comes with some effort, it has force enough to cut its own way and travel a greater distance." This was said to me when we were alone in our office simply for illustration. It was not said boastingly.

As a specimen of Lincoln's method of reasoning I insert here the brief or notes of an argument used by him in a lawsuit as late as 1858. I copy from the original:

"Legislation and adjudication must follow and conform to the progress of society.

"The progress of society now begins to produce cases of the transfer for debts of the entire property of railroad corporations; and to enable transferees to use and enjoy the transferred property *legislation* and *adjudication* begin to be necessary.

"Shall this class of legislation just now beginning with us be *general* or *special?*

"Section Ten of our Constitution requires that it should be general, if possible, (Read the Section.)

"Special legislation always trenches upon the judicial department; and in so far violates Section Two of the Constitution. (Read it.)

"Just reasoning—policy—is in favor of general legislation—else the legislature will be *loaded* down with the investigation of smaller cases—a work which the courts *ought* to perform, and can perform much more perfectly. How can the Legislature rightly decide the facts between P. & B. and S. C. & Co.

"It is said that under a general law, whenever a R. R. Co. gets tired of its debts, it may transfer *fraudulently* to get rid of them. So they may—so may individuals; and which—the *Legislature* or the *courts*—is best suited to try the question of fraud in either case?

"It is said, if a purchaser have acquired legal rights, let him not be robbed of them, but if he needs *legislation* let him submit to just terms to obtain it.

"Let him, say we, have general law in advance (guarded in every possible way against fraud), so that, when he acquires a legal right, he will have no occasion to wait for additional legislation; and if he has practiced fraud let the courts so decide."[6]

David Davis said this of Lincoln: "When in a lawsuit he believed his client was oppressed,—as in the Wright case,—he was hurtful in denunciation. When he attacked meanness, fraud, or vice, he was powerful, merciless in his castigation."[7] The Wright case referred to was a suit brought by Lincoln and myself to compel a pension agent to refund a portion of a fee which he had withheld from the widow of a revolutionary soldier. The entire pension was $400, of which sum the agent had retained one-half. The pensioner, an old woman crippled and bent with age, came hobbling into the office and told her story. It stirred Lincoln up, and he walked over to the agent's office and made a demand for a return of the money, but without success. Then suit was brought. The day before the trial I hunted up for Lincoln, at his request, a history of the Revolutionary War, of which he read a good portion. He told me to remain during the trial until I had heard his address to the jury. "For," said he, "I am going to skin Wright, and get that money back." The only witness we introduced was the old lady, who through her tears told her story. In his speech to the jury, Lincoln recounted the causes leading to the outbreak of the Revolutionary struggle, and then drew a vivid picture of the hardships of Valley Forge, describing with minuteness the men, barefooted and with bleeding feet, creeping over the ice. As he reached that point in his speech wherein he narrated the hardened action of the defendant in fleecing the old woman of her pension his eyes flashed, and throwing aside his handkerchief, which he held in his right hand, he fairly launched into him. His speech for the next five or ten minutes justified the declaration of Davis, that he was "hurtful in denunciation and merciless in castigation." There was no rule of court to restrain him in his argument, and I never, either on the stump or on other occasions in court, saw him so wrought up. Before he closed, he drew an ideal picture of the plaintiff's husband, the deceased soldier, parting with his wife at the threshold of their home, and kissing their little babe in the cradle, as he started for the war. "Time rolls by," he said, in conclusion; "the heroes of '76 have passed away and are encamped on the other shore. The soldier has gone to rest, and now, crippled, blinded, and broken, his widow comes to you and to me, gentlemen of the jury, to right her wrongs. She was not always thus. She was once a beautiful young woman. Her step was as elastic, her face as fair, and her voice as sweet as any that rang in the mountains of old Virginia. But now she is poor and defenceless. Out here on the prairies of Illinois, many hundreds of miles away from the scenes of her childhood, she appeals to us, who enjoy the privileges achieved for us by the patriots of the Revolution, for our sympathetic aid and manly protection. All I ask is, shall we befriend her?" The speech made the desired impression on the jury. Half of them were in tears, while the defendant sat in the court room, drawn up and writhing under the fire of Lincoln's fierce invective. The jury returned a verdict in our favor for every cent we demanded. Lincoln was so much interested in the old lady that he became her surety for costs, paid her way home, and her hotel bill while she was in Springfield. When the judgment was paid we remitted the proceeds to her and made no charge for our services. Lincoln's notes for the argument were unique: "No contract.—Not professional services.—Unreasonable charge.—Money retained by Def't not given by Pl'ff.— Revolutionary War.—Describe Valley Forge privations.—Ice—Soldier's bleeding feet.—Pl'ff's husband.—Soldier leaving home for army.—*Skin Def't.*—Close."

It must not be inferred from this that Lincoln was in the habit of slopping over. He never hunted up acts of injustice, but if they came to him he was easily enlisted. In 1855 he was attending court at the town of Clinton, Illinois. Fifteen ladies from a neighboring village in the county had been indicted for trespass. Their offence consisted in sweeping down on one Tanner, the keeper of a saloon in the village, and knocking in the heads of his barrels. Lincoln was not employed in the case, but sat watching the trial as it proceeded. In defending the ladies their attorney seemed to evince a little want of tact, and this prompted one of the former to invite Mr. Lincoln to add a few words to the jury, if he thought he could aid their cause. He was too gallant to refuse and, their attorney having consented, he made use of the following argument: "In this case I would change the order of indictment and have it read The State *vs.* Mr. Whiskey, instead of The State *vs.* The Ladies; and touching these there are three laws: The law of self-protection; the law of the land, or statute law; and the moral law, or law of God. First, the law of self-protection is a law of necessity, as evinced by our forefathers in casting the tea overboard and asserting their right to the pursuit of life, liberty, and happiness. In this case it is the only defense the ladies have, for Tanner neither feared God nor regarded man. Second, the law of the land, or statute law, and Tanner is recreant to both. Third, the moral law, or law of God, and this is probably a law for the violation of which the jury can fix no punishment." Lincoln gave some of his own observations on the ruinous effects of whiskey in society, and demanded its early suppression. After he had concluded, the Court, without awaiting the return of the jury, dismissed the ladies, saying: "Ladies, go home. I will require no bond of you, and if any fine is ever wanted of you, we will let you know."[8]

After Lincoln's death a fellow-lawyer paid this tribute to him:[o] "He was wonderfully kind, careful, and just. He had an immense stock of common-sense, and he had faith enough in it to trust it in every emergency. Mr. Lincoln's love of justice and fair-play was his predominating trait. I have often listened to him when I thought he would certainly state his case out of court. It was not in his nature to assume or attempt to bolster up a false position.[†] He would abandon his case first. He did so in the case of Buckmaster for the use of Dedham vs. Beems and Arthur, in our Supreme Court, in which I happened to be opposed to him. Another gentleman, less fastidious, took Mr. Lincoln's place and gained the case."[10]

A widow who owned a piece of valuable land employed Lincoln and myself to examine the title to the property, with the view of ascertaining whether certain alleged tax liens were just or not. In tracing back the title we were not satisfied with the description of the ground in one of the deeds of conveyance. Lincoln, to settle the matter, took his surveying instruments and surveyed the ground himself. The result proved that Charles Matheney, a former grantor, had sold the land at so much per acre, but that in describing it he had made an error and conveyed more land than he received pay for. This land descended to our client, and Lincoln after a careful survey and calculation, decided that she ought to pay

[o]Joseph Gillespie, MS., Letter, Oct. 8, 1866.
[†]"Early in 1858 at Danville, Ill., I met Lincoln, Swett, and others who had returned from court in an adjoining county, and were discussing the various features of a murder trial in which Lincoln had made a vigorous fight for the prosecution and Swett had defended. The plea of the defense was insanity. On inquiring the name of the defendant I was surprised to learn that it was my old friend Isaac Wyant, formerly of Indiana. I told them that I had been Wyant's counsel frequently and had defended him from almost every charge in the calendar of crimes; and that he was a weak brother and could be led into almost everything. At once Lincoln began to manifest great interest in Wyant's history, and had to be told all about him. The next day on the way to the court-house he told me he had been greatly troubled over what I related about Wyant; that his sleep had been disturbed by the fear that he had been too bitter and unrelenting in his prosecution of him. 'I acted,' he said, 'on the theory that he was "possuming" insanity, and now I fear I have been too severe and that the poor fellow may be insane after all. If he cannot realize the wrong of his crime, then I was wrong in aiding to punish him.'"—Hon. Joseph E. McDonald, August, 1888. Statement to J. W. W.[9]

to Matheney's heirs the sum which he had shown was due them by reason of the erroneous conveyance. To this she entered strenuous objections, but when assured that unless she consented to this act of plain justice we would drop the case, she finally, though with great reluctance, consented. She paid the required amount, and this we divided up into smaller sums proportioned to the number of heirs. Lincoln himself distributed these to the heirs, obtaining a receipt from each one.°

While Mr. Lincoln was no financier and had no propensity to acquire property,—no avarice of the get,—yet he had the capacity of retention, or the avarice of the keep. He never speculated in lands or anything else. In the days of land offices and "choice lots in a growing town" he had many opportunities to make safe ventures promising good returns, but he never availed himself of them. His brother lawyers were making good investments and lucky turns, some of them, Davis, for example, were rapidly becoming wealthy; but Lincoln cared nothing for speculation; in fact there was no venturesome spirit in him. His habits were very simple. He was not fastidious as to food or dress. His hat was brown, faded, and the nap usually worn or rubbed off.[12] He wore a short cloak and sometimes a shawl. His coat and vest hung loosely on his gaunt frame, and his trousers were invariably too short. On the circuit he carried in one hand a faded green umbrella, with "A. Lincoln" in large white cotton or muslin letters sewed on the inside. The knob was gone from the handle, and when closed a piece of cord was usually tied around it in the middle to keep it from flying open. In the other hand he carried a literal carpet-bag, in which were stored the few papers to be used in court, and underclothing enough to last till his return to Springfield. He slept in a long, coarse, yellow flannel shirt, which reached half-way between his knees and ankles. It probably was not made to fit his bony figure as completely

---

° "Dear Herndon:

"One morning, not long before Lincoln's nomination—a year perhaps—I was in your office and heard the following: Mr. Lincoln, seated at the baize-covered table in the center of the office, listened attentively to a man who talked earnestly and in a low tone. After being thus engaged for some time Lincoln at length broke in, and I shall never forget his reply. 'Yes,' he said, 'we can doubtless gain your case for you; we can set a whole neighborhood at loggerheads; we can distress a widowed mother and her six fatherless children and thereby get for you six hundred dollars to which you seem to have a legal claim, but which rightfully belongs, it appears to me, as much to the woman and her children as it does to you. You must remember that some things legally right are not morally right. We shall not take your case, but will give you a little advice for which we will charge you nothing. You seem to be a sprightly, energetic man; we would advise you to try your hand at making six hundred dollars in some other way.'

"Yours,

"Lord."

From undated MS., about 1866.[11]

as Beau Brummel's shirt, and hence we can somewhat appreciate the sensation of a young lawyer who, on seeing him thus arrayed for the first time, observed afterwards that, "He was the ungodliest figure I ever saw."[13]

"He never complained of the food, bed, or lodgings. If every other fellow grumbled at the bill-of-fare which greeted us at many of the dingy taverns," says David Davis, "Lincoln said nothing."[14] He was once presiding as judge in the absence of Davis, and the case before him was an action brought by a merchant against the father of a minor son for a suit of clothes sold to the son without parental authority. The real question was whether the clothes were necessary, and suited to the condition of the son's life. The father was a wealthy farmer; the bill for the clothing was twenty-eight dollars. I happened in court just as Lincoln was rendering his decision. He ruled against the plea of necessity. "I have rarely in my life," said he, "worn a suit of clothes costing twenty-eight dollars."[15]

"Several of us lawyers," remarked one of his colleagues,° "in the eastern end of the circuit annoyed Lincoln once while he was holding court for Davis by attempting to defend against a note to which there were many makers. We had no legal, but a good moral defense, but what we wanted most of all was to stave it off till the next term of court by one expedient or another. We bothered 'the court' about it till late on Saturday, the day of adjournment. He adjourned for supper with nothing left but this case to dispose of. After supper he heard our twaddle for nearly an hour, and then made this odd entry: 'L. D. Chaddon *vs.* J. D. Beasley *et al.* April Term, 1856. Champaign County Court. Plea in abatement by B. Z. Green, a defendant not served, filed Saturday at 11 o'clock A.M., April 24, 1856, stricken from the files by order of court. Demurrer to declaration, if there ever was one, overruled. Defendants who are served now, at 8 o'clock, P. M., of the last day of the term, ask to plead to the merits, which is denied by the court on the ground that the offer comes too late, and therefore, as by *nil dicet,* judgment is rendered for Pl'ff. Clerk assess damages. A. Lincoln, Judge *pro tem.*'."[16] The lawyer who reads this singular entry will appreciate its oddity if no one else does. After making it one of the lawyers,[17] on recovering his astonishment, ventured to enquire, "Well, Lincoln, how can we get this case up again?" Lincoln eyed him quizzically a moment, and then answered, "You have all been so 'mighty smart about this case you can find out how to take it up again yourselves."†

°H. C. Whitney, MS., letter, Nov. 13, 1865.

†"During my first attendance at court in Menard County," relates a lawyer who travelled the circuit with Lincoln, "some thirty young men had been indicted for playing cards, and Lincoln and I were employed in their defense. The prosecuting attorney, in framing the indictments, alternately charged the defendants with playing a certain game of cards called 'seven-up,' and in the next bill charged them with playing cards at a

The same gentleman who furnishes this last incident, and who was afterward a trusted friend of Mr. Lincoln, Henry C. Whitney, has described most happily the delights of a life on the circuit. A bit of it, referring to Lincoln, I apprehend, cannot be deemed out of place here. "In October, 1854, Abraham Lincoln," he relates, "drove into our town (Urbana) to attend court. He had the appearance of a rough, intelligent farmer, and his rude, home-made buggy and raw-boned horse enforced this belief. I had met him for the first time in June of the same year. David Davis and Leonard Swett had just preceded him. The next morning he started North, on the Illinois Central Railroad, and as he went in an old omnibus he played on a boy's harp all the way to the depot. I used to attend the Danville court, and while there, usually roomed with Lincoln and Davis. We stopped at McCormick's hotel, an old-fashioned frame country tavern. Jurors, counsel, prisoners, everybody ate at a long table. The judge, Lincoln, and I had the ladies' parlor fitted up with two beds. Lincoln, Swett, McWilliams, of Bloomington, Voorhees, of Covington, Ind., O. L. Davis, Drake, Ward Lamon, Lawrence, Beckwith, and O. F. Harmon, of Danville, Whiteman, of Iroquois County, and Chandler, of Williamsport, Ind., constituted the bar. Lincoln, Davis, Swett, I, and others who came from the western part of the state would drive from Urbana. The distance was thirty-six miles. We sang and exchanged stories all the way. We had no hesitation in stopping at a farm-house and ordering them to kill and cook a chicken for dinner. By dark we reached Danville. Lamon would have whiskey in his office for the drinking ones, and those who indulged in petty gambling would get by themselves and play till late in the night. Lincoln, Davis, and a few local wits would spend the evening in Davis's room, talking politics, wisdom, and fun. Lincoln and Swett were the great lawyers, and Lincoln always wanted Swett in jury cases. We who stopped at the hotel would all breakfast together and frequently go out into the woods and hold court. We were of more consequence than a court and bar is now. The feelings were those of great fraternity in the bar, and if we desired to restrict our circle it was no trouble for Davis to freeze out any disagreeable persons. Lincoln was fond of going all by himself to any little show or concert. I have known him to slip away and spend the entire evening at a little magic lantern show intended for children. A travelling concert

---

certain game called 'old sledge.' Four defendants were indicted in each bill. The prosecutor, being entirely unacquainted with games at cards, did not know the fact that both 'seven-up' and 'old sledge' were one and the same. Upon the trial on the bills describing the game as 'seven-up' our witnesses would swear that the game played was 'old sledge,' and vice versa on the bills alleging the latter. The result was an acquittal in every case under the instructions of the Court. The prosecutor never found out the dodge until the trials were over, and immense fun and rejoicing were indulged in at the result."[18]

company, calling themselves the 'Newhall Family,' were sure of drawing Lincoln. One of their number, Mrs. Hillis, a good singer, he used to tell us was the only woman who ever seemed to exhibit any liking for him. I attended a negro-minstrel show in Chicago, where we heard Dixie sung. It was entirely new, and pleased him greatly. In court he was irrepressible and apparently inexhaustible in his fund of stories. Where in the world a man who had travelled so little and struggled amid the restrictions of such limited surroundings could gather up such apt and unique yarns we never could guess. Davis appreciated Lincoln's talent in this direction, and was always ready to stop business to hear one of his stories. Lincoln was very bashful when in the presence of ladies. I remember once we were invited to take tea at a friend's house, and while in the parlor I was called to the front gate to see a client. When I returned, Lincoln, who had undertaken to entertain the ladies, was twisting and squirming in his chair, and as bashful as a schoolboy. Everywhere, though we met a hard crowd at every court, and though things were free and easy, we were treated with great respect."[19]

Probably the most important lawsuit Lincoln and I conducted was one in which we defended the Illinois Central Railroad in an action brought by McLean County, Illinois, in August, 1853, to recover taxes alleged to be due the county from the road. The Legislature had granted the road immunity from taxation, and this was a case intended to test the constitutionality of the law. The road sent a retainer fee of $250. In the lower court the case was decided in favor of the railroad. An appeal to the Supreme Court followed, and there it was argued twice, and finally decided in our favor. This last decision was rendered some time in 1855. Mr. Lincoln soon went to Chicago and presented our bill for legal services. We only asked for $2000 more. The official to whom he was referred,—supposed to have been the superintendent George B. McClellan who afterwards became the eminent general,—looking at the bill expressed great surprise.[20] "Why, sir," he exclaimed, "this is as much as Daniel Webster himself would have charged. We cannot allow such a claim." Stung by the rebuff, Lincoln withdrew the bill, and started for home. On the way he stopped at Bloomington. There he met Grant Goodrich, Archibald Williams, Norman B. Judd, O. H. Browning, and other attorneys, who, on learning of his modest charge for such valuable services rendered the railroad, induced him to increase the demand to $5000, and to bring suit for that sum. This was done at once. On the trial six lawyers certified that the bill was reasonable, and judgment for that sum went by default. The judgment was promptly paid. Lincoln gave me my half, and much as we deprecated the avarice of great corporations, we both thanked the Lord for letting the Illinois Central Railroad fall into our hands.

In the summer of 1857 Lincoln was employed by one Manny, of Chicago, to defend him in an action brought by McCormick,° who was the inventor of the reaping machine, for infringement of patent. Lincoln had been recommended to Manny by E. B. Washburne, then a member of Congress from northern Illinois. The case was to be tried before Judge McLean at Cincinnati, in the Circuit Court of the United States. The counsel for McCormick was Reverdy Johnson. Edwin M. Stanton and George Harding, of Philadelphia, were associated on the other side with Lincoln. The latter came to Cincinnati a few days before the argument took place, and stopped at the house of a friend. "The case was one of great importance pecuniarily," relates a lawyer† in Cincinnati, who was a member of the bar at the time, "and in the law questions involved. Reverdy Johnson represented the plaintiff. Mr. Lincoln had prepared himself with the greatest care; his ambition was up to speak in the case and to measure swords with the renowned lawyer from Baltimore. It was understood between his client and himself before his coming that Mr. Harding, of Philadelphia, was to be associated with him in the case, and was to make the 'mechanical argument.' After reaching Cincinnati, Mr. Lincoln was a little surprised and annoyed to learn that his client had also associated with him Mr. Edwin M. Stanton, of Pittsburg, and a lawyer of our own bar, the reason assigned being that the importance of the case required a man of the experience and power of Mr. Stanton to meet Mr. Johnson. The Cincinnati lawyer was appointed for his 'local influence.' These reasons did not remove the slight conveyed in the employment without consultation with him of this additional counsel. He keenly felt it, but acquiesced. The trial of the case came on; the counsel for defense met each morning for consultation. On one of these occasions one of the counsel moved that only two of them should speak in the case. This matter was also acquiesced in. It had always been understood that Mr. Harding was to speak to explain the mechanism of the reapers. So this motion excluded either Mr. Lincoln or Mr. Stanton,—which? By the custom of the bar, as between counsel of equal standing, and in the absence of any action of the client, the original counsel speaks. By this rule Mr. Lincoln had precedence. Mr. Stanton suggested to Mr. Lincoln to make the speech. Mr. Lincoln answered, 'No, you speak.' Mr. Stanton replied, 'I will,' and taking up his hat, said he would go and make preparation. Mr. Lincoln acquiesced in this, but was greatly grieved and mortified; he took but little more interest in the case, though remaining until the conclusion of the trial. He seemed to be greatly depressed,

---

°The case, McCormick *vs.* Manny, is reported in 6 McLean's Rep., p. 539.
†W. M. Dickson.

and gave evidence of that tendency to melancholy which so marked his character. His parting on leaving the city cannot be forgotten. Cordially shaking the hand of his hostess he said: 'You have made my stay here most agreeable, and I am a thousand times obliged to you; but in reply to your request for me to come again, I must say to you I never expect to be in Cincinnati again. I have nothing against the city, but things have so happened here as to make it undesirable for me ever to return.' Lincoln felt that Stanton had not only been very discourteous to him, but had purposely ignored him in the case, and that he had received rather rude, if not unkind, treatment from all hands. Stanton, in his brusque and abrupt way, it is said, described him as a 'long, lank creature from Illinois, wearing a dirty linen duster for a coat, on the back of which the perspiration had splotched wide stains that resembled a map of the continent.' Mr. Lincoln," adds Mr. Dickson, "remained in Cincinnati about a week, moving freely around, yet not twenty men knew him personally or knew he was here; not a hundred would have known who he was had his name been given to them. He came with the fond hope of making fame in a forensic contest with Reverdy Johnson. He was pushed aside, humiliated and mortified. He attached to the innocent city the displeasure that filled his bosom, and shook its dust from his feet."[21] On his return to Springfield he was somewhat reticent regarding the trial, and contrary to his custom, communicated to his associates at the bar but few of its incidents. He told me that he had been "roughly handled by that man Stanton;" that he overheard the latter from an adjoining room, while the door was slightly ajar, referring to Lincoln, inquire of another, "Where did that long-armed creature come from, and what can he expect to do in this case?" During the trial Lincoln formed a poor opinion of Judge McLean. He characterized him as an "old granny," with considerable vigor of mind, but no perception at all. "If you were to point your finger at him," he put it, "and a darning needle at the same time he never would know which was the sharpest."[22]

As Lincoln grew into public favor and achieved such marked success in the profession, half the bar of Springfield began to be envious of his growing popularity. I believe there is less jealousy and bitter feeling among lawyers than professional men of any other class; but it should be borne in mind that in that early day a portion of the bar in every county seat, if not a majority of the lawyers everywhere, were politicians. Stuart frequently differed from Lincoln on political questions, and was full of envy. Likewise those who coincided with Lincoln in his political views were disturbed in the same way. Even Logan was not wholly free from the degrading passion. But in this respect Lincoln suffered no more than other great characters who preceded him in the world's history.

That which Lincoln's adversaries in a lawsuit feared most of all was his apparent disregard of custom or professional propriety in managing a case before a jury. He brushed aside all rules, and very often resorted to some strange and strategic performance which invariably broke his opponent down or exercised some peculiar influence over the jury. Hence the other side in a case were in constant fear of one of his dramatic strokes, or trembled lest he should "ring in" some ingeniously planned interruption not on the programme. In a case where Judge Logan—always earnest and grave—opposed him, Lincoln created no little merriment by his reference to Logan's style of dress. He carried the surprise in store for the latter, till he reached his turn before the jury. Addressing them, he said: "Gentlemen, you must be careful and not permit yourselves to be overcome by the eloquence of counsel for the defense. Judge Logan, I know, is an effective lawyer. I have met him too often to doubt that; but shrewd and careful though he be, still he is sometimes wrong. Since this trial has begun I have discovered that, with all his caution and fastidiousness, he hasn't knowledge enough to put his shirt on right."[23] Logan turned red as crimson, but sure enough, Lincoln was correct, for the former had donned a new shirt, and by mistake had drawn it over his head with the pleated bosom behind. The general laugh which followed destroyed the effect of Logan's eloquence over the jury—the very point at which Lincoln aimed.

The trial of William Armstrong° for the murder of James P. Metzger, in May, 1858, at Beardstown, Illinois, in which Lincoln secured the acquittal of the defendant, was one of the gratifying triumphs in his career as a lawyer. Lincoln's defense, wherein he floored the principal prosecuting witness, who had testified positively to seeing the fatal blow struck in the moonlight, by showing from an almanac that the moon had set, was not more convincing than his eloquent and irresistible appeal in his client's favor. The latter's mother, old Hannah Armstrong, the friend of his youth, had solicited him to defend her son. "He told the jury," relates the prosecuting attorney, "of his once being a poor, friendless boy; that Armstrong's parents took him into their house, fed and clothed him, and gave him a home. There were tears in his eyes as he spoke. The sight of his tall, quivering frame, and the particulars of the story he so pathetically told, moved the jury to tears also, and they forgot the guilt of the defendant in their admiration of his advocate. It was the most touching scene I ever witnessed."† Before passing it may be well to listen to the humble tribute of old Hannah Armstrong, the defendant's mother:

°This incident in Lincoln's career has been most happily utilized by Dr. Edward Eggleston in his story "The Graysons," recently published in the *Century Magazine.*[24]

†J. Henry Shaw, letter, Aug. 22, 1866, MS.[25]

"Lincoln had said to me, 'Hannah, your son will be cleared before sundown.' I left the court-room, and they came and told me that my son was cleared and a free man. I went up to the court-house. The jury shook hands with me; so did the judge and Lincoln; tears streamed down Lincoln's eyes. . . . After the trial I asked him what his fee would be; told him I was poor. 'Why, Hannah,' he said, 'I sha'n't charge you a cent, and anything else I can do for you, will do it willingly and without charge.' He afterwards wrote to me about a piece of land which certain men were trying to get from me, and said: 'Hannah, they can't get your land. Let them try it in the Circuit Court, and then you appeal it; bring it to the Supreme Court and I and Herndon will attend to it for nothing.'"°

The last suit of any importance in which Lincoln was personally engaged, was known as the Johnson sand-bar case. It involved the title to certain lands, the accretion on the shores of Lake Michigan, in or near Chicago. It was tried in the United States Circuit Court at Chicago in April and May, 1860. During the trial, the Court—Judge Drummond—and all the counsel on both sides dined at the residence of Isaac N. Arnold, afterwards a member of Congress. "Douglas and Lincoln," relates Mr. Arnold, "were at the time both candidates for the nomination for President. There were active and ardent political friends of each at the table, and when the sentiment was proposed, 'May Illinois furnish the next President,' it was drank with enthusiasm by the friends of both Lincoln and Douglas."†

I could fill this volume with reminiscences of Lincoln's career as a lawyer, but lest the reader should tire of what must savor in many cases of monotony it is best to move on. I have made this portion of the book rather full; but as Lincoln's individuality and peculiarities were more marked in the law office and court-room than anywhere else it will play its part in making up the picture of the man. Enough has been told to show how, in the face of adverse fortune and the lack of early training, and by force of his indomitable will and self-confidence, he gained such ascendency among the lawyers of Illinois. The reader is enabled thereby to understand the philosophy of his growth.

But now another field is preparing to claim him. There will soon be great need for his clear reason, masterly mind and heroic devotion to principle. The distant mutterings of an approaching contest are driving scattered factions into a union of sentiment and action. As the phalanxes of warriors are preparing for action, amid the rattle of forensic musketry, Lincoln, their courageous leader, equipped for battle, springs into view.

°From statement, Nov. 24, 1865.[26]
†Arnold's "Lincoln," p. 90.[27]

CHAPTER XII.

While Lincoln in a certain sense was buried in the law from the time his career in Congress closed till, to use his own words, "the repeal of the Missouri Compromise aroused him again,"[1] yet he was a careful student of his times and kept abreast of the many and varied movements in politics. He was generally on the Whig electoral tickets, and made himself heard during each successive canvass,* but he seemed to have lost that zealous interest in politics which characterized his earlier days. He plodded on unaware of, and seemingly without ambition for, the great distinction that lay in store for him. John T. Stuart relates† that, as he and Lincoln were returning from the court in Tazewell county in 1850, and were nearing the little town of Dillon, they engaged in a discussion of the political situation. "As we were coming down the hill," are Stuart's words, "I said, 'Lincoln, the time is coming when we shall have to be all either

---

*In the campaign of 1852, when Pierce was the Democratic candidate for President, Douglas made speeches for him in almost every State in the Union. His "key-note" was sounded at Richmond, Va. Lincoln, whose reputation was limited by the boundaries of Illinois, was invited by the Scott Club of Springfield to answer it, but his soul and heart were not in the undertaking. He had not yet been awakened, and, considering it entire, the speech was a poor effort. Another has truthfully said of it, "If it was distinguished by one quality above another it was by its attempts at humor, and all those attempts were strained and affected, as well as very coarse. He displayed a jealous and petulant temper from the first to the last, wholly beneath the dignity of the occasion and the importance of the topic. Considered as a whole it may be said that none of his public performances was more unworthy of its really noble author than this one." The closing paragraph will serve as a fair sample of the entire speech: "Let us stand by our candidate [Gen. Scott] as faithfully as he has always stood by our country, and I much doubt if we do not perceive a slight abatement of Judge Douglas's confidence in Providence as well as the people. I suspect that confidence is not more firmly fixed with the Judge than it was with the old woman whose horse ran away with her in a buggy. She said she trusted in Providence till the 'britchen' broke, and then she didn't know what on 'airth' to do. The chance is the Judge will see the 'britchen' broke, and then he can at his leisure bewail the fate of Locofocoism as the victim of misplaced confidence."[2]

†Statement, J. T. S., MS., July 21, 1865.

Abolitionists or Democrats.' He thought a moment and then answered, ruefully and emphatically, 'When that time comes my mind is made up, for I believe the slavery question can never be successfully compromised.' I responded with equal emphasis, 'My mind is made up too.'"[3] Thus it was with Lincoln. But he was too slow to suit the impetuous demand of the few pronounced Abolitionists whom he met in his daily walks. The sentiment of the majority in Springfield tended in the other direction, and, thus environed, Lincoln lay down like the sleeping lion. The future would yet arouse him. At that time I was an ardent Abolitionist in sentiment. I used to warn Lincoln against his apparent conservatism when the needs of the hour were so great; but his only answer would be, "Billy, you're too rampant and spontaneous." I was in correspondence with Sumner, Greeley, Phillips, and Garrison, and was thus thoroughly imbued with all the rancor drawn from such strong anti-slavery sources. I adhered to Lincoln, relying on the final outcome of his sense of justice and right. Every time a good speech on the great issue was made I sent for it. Hence you could find on my table the latest utterances of Giddings, Phillips, Sumner, Seward, and one whom I considered grander than all the others—Theodore Parker.[4] Lincoln and I took such papers as the Chicago *Tribune*, New York *Tribune, Anti-Slavery Standard, Emancipator,* and *National Era.* On the other side of the question we took the Charleston *Mercury* and the Richmond *Enquirer.* I also bought a book called "Sociology," written by one Fitzhugh, which defended and justified slavery in every conceivable way. In addition I purchased all the leading histories of the slavery movement, and other works which treated on that subject. Lincoln himself never bought many books, but he and I both read those I have named. After reading them we would discuss the questions they touched upon and the ideas they suggested, from our different points of view. I was never conscious of having made much of an impression on Mr. Lincoln, nor do I believe I ever changed his views. I will go further and say, that, from the profound nature of his conclusions and the labored method by which he arrived at them, no man is entitled to the credit of having either changed or greatly modified them. I remember once, after having read one of Theodore Parker's sermons on slavery, saying to Mr. Lincoln substantially this: "I have always noticed that ill-gotten wealth does no man any good. This is as true of nations as individuals. I believe that all the ill-gotten gain wrenched by us from the negro through his enslavement will eventually be taken from us, and we will be set back where we began." Lincoln thought my prophecy rather direful. He doubted seriously if either of us would live to see the righting of so great a wrong; but years after, when writing his second Inaugural address, he endorsed the idea. Clothing it in the most beautiful language, he says: "Yet if God wills that it [the war] continue till all the wealth piled by the bondsman's two hundred and fifty years of unrequited toil shall be sunk, and until every drop of blood drawn by the lash shall be paid by another drawn by the sword, as was said three thousand years ago, so still it must be said, 'The judgments of the Lord are true and righteous altogether.'"[5]

The passage in May, 1854, of the Kansas-Nebraska bill swept out of sight the Missouri Compromise and the Compromise measures of 1850. This bill, designed and carried through by Douglas, was regarded by him as the masterpiece of all his varied achievements in legislation. It served to prove more clearly than anything he had ever before done his flexibility and want of political conscience. Although in years gone before he had invoked the vengeance of Heaven on the ruthless hand that should dare to disturb the sanctity of the compact of 1821, yet now he was the arrogant and audacious leader in the very work he had so heartily condemned. When we consider the bill and the unfortunate results which followed it in the border States we are irresistibly led to conclude that it was, all things considered, a great public wrong and a most lamentable piece of political jugglery. The stump speech which Thomas H. Benton charged that Douglas had "injected into the belly of the bill" contains all there was of Popular Sovereignty—"It being the true intent and meaning of this act not to legislate slavery into any Territory or State nor to exclude it therefrom, but to leave the people thereof perfectly free to form and regulate their domestic institutions in their own way, subject only to the Constitution of the United States,"[6] an argument which, using Lincoln's words, "amounts to this: That if any one man chooses to enslave another no third man shall be allowed to object."[7] The widespread feeling the passage of this law aroused everywhere over the Union is a matter of general history. It stirred up in New England the latent hostility to the aggression of slavery; it stimulated to extraordinary endeavors the derided Abolitionists, arming them with new weapons; it sounded the death-knell of the gallant old Whig party; it drove together strange, discordant elements in readiness to fight a common enemy; it brought to the forefront a leader in the person of Lincoln.

The revolt of Cook, Judd, and Palmer, all young and progressive, from the Democratic majority in the Legislature was the first sign of discontent in Illinois. The rude and partly hostile reception of Douglas, on his arrival in Chicago, did not in any degree tend to allay the feeling of disapproval so general in its manifestation. The warriors, young and old, removed their armor from the walls, and began preparations for the impending conflict. Lincoln had made a few speeches in aid of Scott during the campaign of 1852, but they were efforts entirely unworthy of the man. Now, however, a live issue was presented to him. No one realized

Stephen A. Douglas

this sooner than he. In the office discussions he grew bolder in his utterances. He insisted that the social and political difference between slavery and freedom was becoming more marked; that one must overcome the other; and that postponing the struggle between them would only make it the more deadly in the end. "The day of compromise," he still contended, "has passed. These two great ideas have been kept apart only by the most artful means. They are like two wild beasts in sight of each other, but chained and held apart. Some day these deadly antagonists will one or the other break their bonds, and then the question will be settled." In a conversation with a fellow-lawyer° he said of slavery: "It is the most glittering, ostentatious, and displaying property in the world, and now, if a young man goes courting, the only inquiry is how many negroes he or his lady-love owns. The love for slave property is swallowing up every other mercenary possession. Slavery is a great and crying injustice—an enormous national crime."[8] At another time he made the observation that it was "singular that the courts would hold that a man never lost his right to his property that had been stolen from him, but that he instantly

°Joseph Gillespie, MS. letter, June 9, '66.

lost his right to himself if he was stolen."[9] It is useless to add more evidence—for it could be piled mountain high—showing that at the very outset Mr. Lincoln was sound to the core on the injustice and crime of human slavery.

After a brief rest at his home in Chicago Mr. Douglas betook himself to the country, and in October, during the week of the State Fair, we find him in Springfield. On Tuesday he made a speech in the State House which, in view of the hostile attitude of some of his own party friends, was a labored defense of his position. It was full of ingenious sophistry and skilful argument. An unprecedented concourse of people had gathered from all parts of the State, and Douglas, fresh from the halls of Congress, was the lion of the hour. On the following day Mr. Lincoln, as the champion of the opponents of Popular Sovereignty, was selected to represent those who disagreed with the new legislation, and to answer Douglas. His speech encouraged his friends no less than it startled his enemies. At this time I was zealously interested in the new movement, and not less so in Lincoln. I frequently wrote the editorials in the Springfield *Journal*, the editor, Simeon Francis, giving to Lincoln and to me the utmost liberty in that direction. Occasionally Lincoln would write out matter for publication, but I believe I availed myself of the privilege oftener than he. The editorial in the issue containing the speeches of Lincoln and Douglas on this occasion was my own, and while in description it may seem rather strongly imbued with youthful enthusiasm, yet on reading it in maturer years I am still inclined to believe it reasonably faithful to the facts and the situation. "The anti-Nebraska speech of Mr. Lincoln," says the article, "was the profoundest in our opinion that he has made in his whole life. He felt upon his soul the truths burn which he uttered, and all present felt that he was true to his own soul. His feelings once or twice swelled within, and came near stifling utterance. He quivered with emotion. The whole house was as still as death. He attacked the Nebraska bill with unusual warmth and energy; and all felt that a man of strength was its enemy, and that he intended to blast it if he could by strong and manly efforts. He was most successful, and the house approved the glorious triumph of truth by loud and continued huzzas. Women waved their white handkerchiefs in token of woman's silent but heartfelt assent. Douglas felt the sting; the animal within him was roused because he frequently interrupted Mr. Lincoln. His friends felt that he was crushed by Lincoln's powerful argument, manly logic, and illustrations from nature around us. The Nebraska bill was shivered, and like a tree of the forest was torn and rent asunder by the hot bolts of truth. Mr. Lincoln exhibited Douglas in all the attitudes he could be placed, in a friendly debate. He exhibited the bill in all its aspects to show its humbuggery and falsehood, and, when thus torn to rags, cut into slips, held up to the gaze of the vast crowd, a kind of scorn and mockery was visible upon the face of the crowd and upon the lips of their most eloquent speaker. At the conclusion of this speech every man and child felt that it was unanswerable. He took the heart captive and broke like a sun over the understanding."[10]

Anent the subject of editorial writing it may not be inappropriate to relate that Lincoln and I both kept on furnishing political matter of many varieties for the Springfield *Journal* until 1860. Many of the editorials that I wrote were intended directly or indirectly to promote the interest of Lincoln. I wrote one on the advisability of annexing Cuba to the United States, taking the rather advanced ground that slavery would be abolished in Cuba before it would in this country—a position which aroused no little controversy with other papers. One little incident occurs to me in this connection which may not be without interest to newspaper men. A newspaper had been started in Springfield called the *Conservative,* which, it was believed, was being run in the interest of the Democratic party. While pretending to support Fillmore it was kept alive by Buchanan men and other kindred spirits, who were somewhat pro-slavery in their views. The thing was damaging Lincoln and the friends of freedom more than an avowed Democratic paper could. The editor,[11] an easy, good-natured fellow, simply placed in charge to execute the will of those who gave the paper its financial backing, was a good friend of mine, and by means of this friendship I was always well informed of matters in the *Conservative* editorial room. One day I read in the Richmond *Enquirer* an article endorsing slavery, and arguing that from principle the enslavement of either whites or blacks was justifiable and right. I showed it to Lincoln, who remarked that it was "rather rank doctrine for Northern Democrats to endorse. I should like to see," he said, with emphasis, "some of these Illinois newspapers champion that." I told him if he would only wait and keep his own counsel I would have a pro-slavery organ in Springfield publish that very article. He doubted it, but when I told him how it was to be done he laughed and said, "Go in." I cut the slip out and succeeded in getting it in the paper named. Of course it was a trick, but it acted admirably. Its appearance in the new organ, although without comment, almost ruined that valuable journal, and my good-natured friend the editor was nearly overcome by the denunciation of those who were responsible for the organ's existence. My connection, and Lincoln's too,—for he endorsed the trick,—with the publication of the condemned article was eventually discovered, and we were thereafter effectually prevented from getting another line in the paper. The anti-slavery people quoted the article as having been endorsed by a Democratic newspaper in Springfield, and Lincoln himself used it with telling effect. He joined in the popular denunciation, expressing great astonishment that such a sentiment could find lodgment in any paper in Illinois, although he knew full well how the whole thing had been carried through.[12]

During the remainder of the State-Fair week, speeches were made by Lyman Trumbull, Sidney Breese, E. D. Taylor, and John Calhoun, none of which unfortunately have been preserved. Among those who mingled in the crowd and listened to them was Owen Lovejoy, a radical, fiery, brave, fanatical man, it may be, but one full of the virus of Abolitionism. I had been thoroughly inoculated with the latter myself, and so had many others, who helped to swell the throng. The Nebraska movement had kindled anew the old zeal, and inspired us with renewed confidence to begin the crusade. As many of us as could, assembled together to organize for the campaign before us. As soon therefore as Lincoln finished his speech in the hall of the House of Representatives, Lovejoy, moving forward from the crowd, announced a meeting in the same place that evening of all the friends of Freedom. That of course meant the Abolitionists with whom I had been in conference all the day. Their plan had been to induce Mr. Lincoln to speak for them at their meeting. Strong as I was in the faith, yet I doubted the propriety of Lincoln's taking any stand yet. As I viewed it, he was ambitious to climb to the United States Senate, and on grounds of policy it would not do for him to occupy at that time such advanced ground as we were taking. On the other hand, it was equally as dangerous to refuse a speech for the Abolitionists. I did not know how he felt on the subject, but on learning that Lovejoy intended to approach him with an invitation, I hunted up Lincoln and urged him to avoid meeting the enthusiastic champion of Abolitionism. "Go home at once," I said. "Take Bob with you and drive somewhere into the country and stay till this thing is over."[13] Whether my admonition and reasoning moved him or not I do not know, but it only remains to state that under pretence of having business in Tazewell county he drove out of town in his buggy, and did not return till the apostles of Abolitionism had separated and gone to their homes.° I have always believed this little arrangement—it would dignify it too much to call it a plan—saved Lincoln. If he had endorsed the resolutions passed at the meeting, or spoken simply in favor of freedom that night, he would have been identified with all the rancor and extremes of Abolitionism. If, on the contrary, he had been invited to join them, and then had refused to take a position as advanced as theirs, he would have lost their support. In either event he was in great danger; and so he who was aspiring to succeed his old rival, James Shields, in the United States Senate was forced to avoid the issue by driving hastily in his one horse buggy to the

---

°See Lincoln's Speech, Joint Debate, Ottawa, Ills., Aug. 20, 1858.[14]

court in Tazewell county. A singular coincidence suggests itself in the fact that, twelve years before, James Shields and a friend drove hastily in the same direction, and destined for the same point, to force Lincoln to take issue in another and entirely different matter.

By request of party friends Lincoln was induced to follow after Douglas and, at the various places where the latter had appointments to speak, reply to him. On the 16th of October they met at Peoria, where Douglas enjoyed the advantages of an "open and close." Lincoln made an effective speech, which he wrote out and furnished to the Sangamon *Journal* for publication, and which can be found among his public utterances.[15] His party friends in Springfield and elsewhere, who had urged him to push after Douglas till he cried, "enough," were surprised a few days after the Peoria debate to find him at home, with the information that by an agreement with the latter they were both to return home and speak no more during the campaign. Judge of his astonishment a few days later to find that his rival, instead of going direct to his home in Chicago, had stopped at Princeton and violated his express agreement by making a speech there! Lincoln was much displeased at this action of Douglas, which tended to convince him that the latter was really a man devoid of fixed political morals. I remember his explanation in our office made to me, William Butler, William Jayne, Ben. F. Irwin, and other friends, to account for his early withdrawal from the stump. After the Peoria debate Douglas approached him and flattered him by saying that he was giving him more trouble on the territorial and slavery questions than all the United States Senate, and he therefore proposed to him that both should abandon the field and return to their homes. Now Lincoln could never refuse a polite request—one in which no principle was involved. I have heard him say, "It's a fortunate thing I wasn't born a woman, for I cannot refuse anything, it seems." He therefore consented to the cessation of debate proposed by Douglas, and the next day both went to the town of Lacon, where they had been billed for speeches. Their agreement was kept from their friends, and both declined to speak—Douglas, on the ground of hoarseness, and Lincoln gallantly refusing to take advantage of "Judge Douglas's indisposition." Here they separated, Lincoln going directly home, and Douglas, as before related, stopping at Princeton and colliding in debate with Owen Lovejoy. Upon being charged afterwards with his breach of agreement Douglas responded that Lovejoy "bantered and badgered" him so persistently he could not gracefully resist the encounter. The whole thing thoroughly displeased Lincoln.°

° In a letter from Princeton, Ill., March 15, 1866, John H. Bryant, brother of the poet William Cullen Bryant, writes: "I have succeeded in finding an old file of our Princeton papers, from which I learn that Mr. Douglas spoke here on Wednesday, Oct. 18, 1854. This fixes the date. I recollect that he staid at Tiskilwa,

During this campaign Lincoln was nominated and elected to the Legislature. This was done in the face of his unwillingness and over his protest. On the ticket with him was Judge Logan. Both were elected by a majority of about 600 votes. Lincoln, being ambitious to reach the United States Senate, and warmly encouraged in his aspirations by his wife, resigned his seat in the Legislature in order that he might the more easily be elected to succeed his old rival James Shields, who was then one of the senators from Illinois. His canvass for that exalted office was marked by his characteristic activity and vigilance. During the anxious moments that intervened between the general election and the assembling of the Legislature he slept, like Napoleon, with one eye open. While attending court at Clinton on the 11th of November, a few days after the election, he wrote to a party friend in the town of Paris: "I have a suspicion that a Whig has been elected to the Legislature from Edgar. If this is not so, why then, *'nix cum arous;'* but if it is so, then could you not make a mark with him for me for U. S. Senator? I really have some chance. Please write me at Springfield giving me the names, post-offices, and political positions of your Representative and Senator, whoever they may be. Let this be confidential."°

That man who thinks Lincoln calmly sat down and gathered his robes about him, waiting for the people to call him, has a very erroneous knowledge of Lincoln. He was always calculating, and always planning ahead. His ambition was a little engine that knew no rest. The vicissitudes of a political campaign brought into play all his tact and management and developed to its fullest extent his latent industry. In common with other politicians he never overlooked a newspaper man who had it in his power to say a good or bad thing of him. The press of that day was not so powerful an institution as now, but ambitious politicians courted the favor of a newspaper man with as much zeal as the same class of men have done in later days. I remember a letter Lincoln once wrote to the editor of an obscure little country newspaper in southern Illinois in which he warms up to him in the following style.† "Friend Harding: I have been reading your paper for three or four years and have paid you nothing for it." He then encloses ten dollars and admonishes the editor with innocent complacency: "Put it into your pocket, saying nothing further about it."[18] Very soon thereafter, he prepared

---

six miles south of this, the night before, and a number of our Democrats went down the next morning and escorted him to this place. Douglas spoke first one half-hour and was answered by Lovejoy one half-hour, when Douglas talked till dark, giving no opportunity for reply.

  "Yours truly,
  "John H. Bryant."[16]

°Robert Mosely, November 11, 1855, MS.[17]
†Jacob Harding, May 25, 1855, MS.

an article on political matters and sent it to the rural journalist, requesting its publication in the editorial columns of his "valued paper," but the latter, having followed Lincoln's directions and stowed the ten dollars away in his pocket, and alive to the importance of his journal's influence, declined, "because," he said, "I long ago made it a rule to publish nothing as editorial matter not written by myself." Lincoln read the editor's answer to me. Although the laugh was on Lincoln he enjoyed the joke heartily. "That editor," he said, "has a rather lofty but proper conception of true journalism."[19]

Meanwhile the Legislature had convened and the Senatorial question came on for solution. The history of this contest is generally understood, and the world has repeatedly been told how Lincoln was led to expect the place and would have won but for the apostasy of the five anti-Nebraska men of Democratic antecedents who clung to and finally forced the election of Lyman Trumbull. The student of history in after years will be taught to revere the name of Lincoln for his exceeding magnanimity in inducing his friends to abandon him at the critical period and save Trumbull, while he himself disappeared beneath the waves of defeat.°

This frustration of Lincoln's ambition had a marked effect on his political views. It was plain to him now that the "irrepressible conflict" was not far ahead. With the strengthening of his faith in a just cause so long held in abeyance he became more defiant each day. But in the very nature of things he dared not be as bold and outspoken as I. With him every word and sentence had to be weighed and its effects calculated, before being uttered: but with me that operation had to be reversed if done at all. An incident that occurred about this time will show how his views were broadening. Some time after the election of Trumbull a young negro, the son of a colored woman in Springfield known as Polly, went from his home to St. Louis and there hired as a hand on a lower Mississippi boat,—for what special service, I do not recollect,—arriving in New Orleans without what

---

°"After a number of ballots—Judd of Cook, Cook of La Salle, Palmer of Macoupin, and Allen and Baker of Madison voting for Trumbull—I asked Mr. Lincoln what he would advise us to do. He answered, 'Go for Trumbull by all means.' We understood the case to be that Shields was to be run by the Democrats at first and then to be dropped, and Joel A. Matteson put up; and it was calculated that certain of our men who had been elected on the 'Free Soil' issue would vote for him after they had acted with us long enough to satisfy their consciences and constituents. Our object was to force an election before they got through with their programme. We were savagely opposed to Matteson, and so was Mr. Lincoln, who said that if we did not drop in and unite upon Trumbull the five men above-named would go for Matteson and elect him, which would be an everlasting disgrace to the State. We reluctantly complied; went to Trumbull and elected him. I remember that Judge S. T. Logan gave up Lincoln with great reluctance. He begged hard to try him on one or two ballots more, but Mr. Lincoln urged us not to risk it longer. I never saw the latter more earnest and decided. He congratulated Trumbull warmly, although of course greatly disappointed and mortified at his own want of success."—Joseph Gillespie, letter, September 19, 1866, MS.[20]

were known as free papers.[21] Though born free he was subjected to the tyranny
of the "black code," all the more stringent because of the recent utterances of
the Abolitionists in the North, and was kept in prison until his boat had left.
Then as no one was especially interested in him, he was forgotten. After a certain length of time established by law, he would inevitably have been sold into
slavery to defray prison expenses had not Lincoln and I interposed our aid. The
mother came to us with the story of the wrong done her son and induced us to
interfere in her behalf. We went first to see the Governor of Illinois, who, after
patient and thorough examination of the law, responded that he had no right or
power to interfere. Recourse was then had to the Governor of Louisiana, who
responded in like manner. We were sorely perplexed. A second interview with
the Governor of Illinois resulting in nothing favorable Lincoln rose from his chair,
hat in hand, and exclaimed with some emphasis: "By God, Governor, I'll make
the ground in this country too hot for the foot of a slave, whether you have the
legal power to secure the release of this boy or not." Having exhausted all legal
means to recover the negro we dropped our relation as lawyers to the case. Lincoln drew up a subscription-list, which I circulated, collecting funds enough to
purchase the young man's liberty. The money we sent to Col. A. P. Field, a friend
of ours in New Orleans, who applied it as directed, and it restored the prisoner
to his overjoyed mother.

The political history of the country, commencing in 1854 and continuing till
the outbreak of the Rebellion, furnishes the student a constant succession of
stirring and sometimes bloody scenes. No sooner had Lincoln emerged from
the Senatorial contest in February, 1855, and absorbed himself in the law, than
the outrages on the borders of Missouri and Kansas began to arrest public attention. The stories of raids, election frauds, murders, and other crimes were moving eastward with marked rapidity. These outbursts of frontier lawlessness, led
and sanctioned by the avowed pro-slavery element, were not only stirring up the
Abolitionists to fever heat, but touching the hearts of humanity in general. In
Illinois an association was formed to aid the cause of "Free-Soil" men in Kansas.
In the meetings of these bands the Abolitionists of course took the most prominent part. At Springfield we were energetic, vigilant, almost revolutionary. We
recommended the employment of any means, however desperate, to promote
and defend the cause of freedom. At one of these meetings Lincoln was called
on for a speech. He responded to the request, counselling moderation and less
bitterness in dealing with the situation before us. We were belligerent in tone,
and clearly out of patience with the Government. Lincoln opposed the notion
of coercive measures with the possibility of resulting bloodshed, advising us to

eschew resort to the bullet. "You can better succeed," he declared, "with the ballot. You can peaceably then redeem the Government and preserve the liberties of mankind through your votes and voice and moral influence. . . . . Let there be peace. Revolutionize through the ballot box, and restore the Government once more to the affections and hearts of men by making it express, as it was intended to do, the highest spirit of justice and liberty. Your attempt, if there be such, to resist the laws of Kansas by force is criminal and wicked; and all your feeble attempts will be follies and end in bringing sorrow on your heads and ruin the cause you would freely die to preserve!"[22] These judicious words of counsel, while they reduced somewhat our ardor and our desperation, only placed before us in their real colors the grave features of the situation. We raised a neat sum of money, Lincoln showing his sincerity by joining in the subscription, and forwarded it to our friends in Kansas.

The Whig party, having accomplished its mission in the political world, was now on the eve of a great break-up. Lincoln realized this and, though proverbially slow in his movements, prepared to find a firm footing when the great rush of waters should come and the maddening freshet sweep former landmarks out of sight. Of the strongest significance in this connection is a letter written by him at this juncture to an old friend in Kentucky,* who called to his attention their differences of views on the wrong of slavery. Speaking of his observation of the treatment of the slaves, he says: "I confess I hate to see the poor creatures hunted down and caught and carried back to their unrequited toils; but I bite my lips and keep quiet. In 1841 you and I had rather a tedious low-water trip on a steamboat from Louisville to St. Louis. You may remember, as I well do, that from Louisville to the mouth of the Ohio, there were on board ten or a dozen slaves shackled together with irons. That sight was a continued torment to me; and I see something like it every time I touch the Ohio or any slave border. It is not fair for you to assume that I have no interest in a thing which has, and continually exercises, the power of making me miserable. You ought rather to appreciate how much the great body of the Northern people do crucify their feelings in order to maintain their loyalty to the Constitution and the Union. I do oppose the extension of slavery because my judgment and feeling so prompt me; and I am under no obligations to the contrary. If for this you and I must differ, differ we must."[23]

Finding himself drifting about with the disorganized elements that floated together after the angry political waters had subsided, it became apparent to Lincoln that if he expected to figure as a leader he must take a stand himself. Mere

---

*Letter to Joshua F. Speed, August 24, 1855, MS.

hatred of slavery and opposition to the injustice of the Kansas-Nebraska legislation were not all that were required of him. He must be a Democrat, Know-Nothing, Abolitionist, or Republican, or forever float about in the great political sea without compass, rudder, or sail. At length he declared himself. Believing the times were ripe for more advanced movements, in the spring of 1856 I drew up a paper for the friends of freedom to sign, calling a county convention in Springfield to select delegates for the forthcoming Republican State convention in Bloomington. The paper was freely circulated and generously signed. Lincoln was absent at the time and, believing I knew what his "feeling and judgment" on the vital questions of the hour were, I took the liberty to sign his name to the call. The whole was then published in the Springfield *Journal.* No sooner had it appeared than John T. Stuart, who, with others, was endeavoring to retard Lincoln in his advanced movements, rushed into the office and excitedly asked if "Lincoln had signed that Abolition call in the *Journal?*" I answered in the negative, adding that I had signed his name myself. To the question, "Did Lincoln authorize you to sign it?" I returned an emphatic "No." "Then," exclaimed the startled and indignant Stuart, "you have ruined him." But I was by no means alarmed at what others deemed inconsiderate and hasty action. I thought I understood Lincoln thoroughly, but in order to vindicate myself if assailed I immediately sat down, after Stuart had rushed out of the office, and wrote Lincoln, who was then in Tazewell County attending court, a brief account of what I had done and how much stir it was creating in the ranks of his conservative friends. If he approved or disapproved my course I asked him to write or telegraph me at once. In a brief time came his answer: "All right; go ahead. Will meet you—radicals and all." Stuart subsided, and the conservative spirits who hovered around Springfield no longer held control of the political fortunes of Abraham Lincoln.

The Republican party came into existence in Illinois as a party at Bloomington, May 29, 1856. The State convention of all opponents of anti-Nebraska legislation, referred to in a foregoing paragraph, had been set for that day. Judd, Yates, Trumbull, Swett, and Davis were there; so also was Lovejoy, who, like Otis of colonial fame, was a flame of fire. The firm of Lincoln and Herndon was represented by both members in person. The gallant William H. Bissell, who had ridden at the head of the Second Illinois Regiment at the battle of Buena Vista in the Mexican war, was nominated as governor. The convention adopted a platform ringing with strong anti-Nebraska sentiments, and then and there gave the Republican party its official christening. The business of the convention being over, Mr. Lincoln, in response to repeated calls, came forward and delivered a speech of such earnestness and power that no one who heard it will ever forget the effect it produced. In referring to this speech some years ago I used the following rather graphic language: "I have heard or read all of Mr. Lincoln's great speeches, and I give it as my opinion that the Bloomington speech was the grand effort of his life. Heretofore he had simply argued the slavery question on grounds of policy,—the statesman's grounds,—never reaching the question of the radical and the eternal right. Now he was newly baptized and freshly born; he had the fervor of a new convert; the smothered flame broke out; enthusiasm unusual to him blazed up; his eyes were aglow with an inspiration; he felt justice; his heart was alive to the right; his sympathies, remarkably deep for him, burst forth, and he stood before the throne of the eternal Right. His speech was full of fire and energy and force; it was logic; it was pathos; it was enthusiasm; it was justice, equity, truth, and right set ablaze by the divine fires of a soul maddened by the wrong; it was hard, heavy, knotty, gnarly, backed with wrath. I attempted for about fifteen minutes as was usual with me then to take notes, but at the end of that time I threw pen and paper away and lived only in the inspiration of the hour. If Mr. Lincoln was six feet, four inches high usually, at Bloomington that day he was seven feet, and inspired at that. From that day to the day of his death he stood firm in the right. He felt his great cross, had his great idea, nursed it, kept it, taught it to others, in his fidelity bore witness of it to his death, and finally sealed it with his precious blood."[24] The foregoing paragraph, used by me in a lecture in 1866, may to the average reader seem somewhat vivid in description, besides inclining to extravagance in imagery, yet although more than twenty years have passed since it was written I have never seen the need of altering a single sentence. I still adhere to the substantial truthfulness of the scene as described. Unfortunately Lincoln's speech was never written out nor printed, and we are obliged to depend for its reproduction upon personal recollection.

The Bloomington convention and the part Lincoln took in it met no such hearty response in Springfield as we hoped would follow. It fell flat, and in Lincoln's case drove from him many persons who had heretofore been his warm political friends. A few days after our return we announced a meeting at the courthouse to ratify the action of the Bloomington convention. After the usual efforts to draw a crowd, however, only three persons had temerity enough to attend. They were Lincoln, the writer, and a courageous man named John Pain. Lincoln, in answer to the "deafening calls" for a speech, responded that the meeting was larger than he *knew* it would be, and that while he knew that he himself and his partner would attend he was not sure anyone else would, and yet another man had been found brave enough to come out. "While all seems dead," he exhorted, "the age itself is not. It liveth as sure as our Maker liveth. Under all this seeming want of life and motion, the world does move nevertheless. Be hopeful, and now let us adjourn and appeal to the people."[25]

Not only in Springfield but everywhere else the founders of the Republican party—the apostles of freedom—went out to battle for the righteousness of their cause. Lincoln, having as usual been named as one of the Presidential electors, canvassed the State, making in all about fifty speeches. He was in demand everywhere. I have before me a package of letters addressed to him, inviting him to speak at almost every county seat in the State. Yates wanted him to go to one section of the State, Washburne to another, and Trumbull still another; while every crossroads politician and legislative aspirant wanted him "down in our country, where we need your help." Joshua R. Giddings wrote him words of encouragement. "You may start," said the valiant old Abolitionist in a letter from Peoria,* "on the one great issue of restoring Kansas and Nebraska to freedom, or rather of restoring the Missouri Compromise, and in this State no power on earth can withstand you on that issue."[26] The demand for Lincoln was not confined to his own State. Indiana sent for him, Wisconsin also, while Norman B. Judd and Ebenezer Peck, who were stumping Iowa, sent for him to come there. A town committee invited him to come during "our Equestrian Fair on the 9th, 10th, and 11th," evidently anticipating a three days' siege. An enthusiastic officer in a neighboring town urges him: "Come to our place, because in you do our people place more confidence than in any other man. Men who do not read want the story told as you only can tell it. Others may make fine speeches, but it would not be 'Lincoln said so in his speech.'" A jubilant friend in Chicago writes: "Push on the column of freedom. Give the Buck Africans plenty to do in Egypt. The hour of our redemption draweth nigh. We are coming to Springfield with 10,000 majority!" A postmaster, acting under the courage of his convictions, implores him to visit his neighborhood. "The Democrats here," he insists, "are dyed in the wool. Thunder and lightning would not change their political complexion. I am postmaster here," he adds, confidentially, "for which reason I must ask you to keep this private, for if old Frank [President Pierce] were to hear of my support of Frémont I would get my walking papers sure enough." A settlement of Germans in southern Indiana asked to hear him; and the president of a college, in an invitation to address the students under his charge, characterizes him as "one providentially raised up for a time like this, and even should defeat come in the contest, it would be some consolation to remember we had Hector for a leader."[27]

And thus it was everywhere. Lincoln's importance in the conduct of the

---

*J. R. Giddings, MS. letter, Sept. 18, 1855.

campaign was apparent to all, and his canvass was characterized by his usual vigor and effectiveness. He was especially noted for his attempt to break down the strength of Fillmore, who was nominated as a third party candidate and was expected to divide the Republican vote. He tried to wean away Fillmore's adherents by an adroit and ingenious letter* sent to those suspected of the latter's support, and marked confidential, in which he strove to show that in clinging to their candidate they were really aiding the election of Buchanan. But the effort proved unavailing, for in spite of all his arguments and appeals a large number of the Fillmore men clung tenaciously to their leader, resulting in Buchanan's election. The vote in Illinois stood, Buchanan 105,344, Frémont 96,180, and Fillmore 37,451. At the same time Bissell was elected governor by a majority of 4729 over W. A. Richardson, Democrat. After the heat and burden of the day Lincoln returned home, bearing with him more and greater laurels than ever. The signs of the times indicated, and the result of the canvass demonstrated, that he and he alone was powerful enough to meet the redoubtable Little Giant in a greater conflict yet to follow.

---

*One of these letters which Lincoln wrote to counteract the Fillmore movement is still in my possession. As it is more or less characteristic I copy it entire:

"Springfield, September 8, 1856.

"Harrison Maltby, Esq.

"Dear Sir:

"I understand you are a Fillmore man. Let me prove to you that every vote withheld from Frémont and given to Fillmore in this State actually lessens Fillmore's chance of being President.

"Suppose Buchanan gets all the slave States and Pennsylvania and any other one State besides; then he is elected, no matter who gets all the rest. But suppose Fillmore gets the two slave States of Maryland and Kentucky, then Buchanan is not elected; Fillmore goes into the House of Representatives and may be made President by a compromise. But suppose again Fillmore's friends throw away a few thousand votes on him in Indiana and Illinois; it will inevitably give these States to Buchanan, which will more than compensate him for the loss of Maryland and Kentucky; it will elect him, and leave Fillmore no chance in the House of Representatives or out of it.

"This is as plain as adding up the weight of three small hogs. As Mr. Fillmore has no possible chance to carry Illinois for himself it is plainly to his interest to let Frémont take it and thus keep it out of the hands of Buchanan. Be not deceived. Buchanan is the hard horse to beat in this race. Let him have Illinois, and nothing can beat him; and he will get Illinois if men persist in throwing away votes upon Mr. Fillmore. Does some one persuade you that Mr. Fillmore can carry Illinois? Nonsense! There are over seventy newspapers in Illinois opposing Buchanan, only three or four of which support Mr. Fillmore, all the rest going for Frémont. Are not these newspapers a fair index of the proportion of the votes? If not, tell me why.

"Again, of these three or four Fillmore newspapers, two at least are supported in part by the Buchanan men, as I understand. Do not they know where the shoe pinches? They know the Fillmore movement helps them, and therefore they help it.

"Do think these things over and then act according to your judgment.

"Yours very truly,

[Confidential.] "A. Lincoln."[28]

CHAPTER XIII.

I Shall be forced to omit much that happened during the interval between the election of Buchanan and the campaign of 1858, for the reason that it would not only swell this work to undue proportions, but be a mere repetition of what has been better told by other writers. It is proper to note in passing, however, that Mr. Lincoln's reputation as a political speaker was no longer bounded by the border lines of Illinois. It had passed beyond the Wabash, the Ohio, and the Mississippi rivers, and while his pronounced stand on the slavery question had increased the circle of his admirers in the North it provoked a proportionate amount of execration in the South. He could not help the feeling that he was now the leading Republican in his State, and he was therefore more or less jealous of his prerogative. Formidable in debate, plain in speech, without pretence of literary acquirements, he was none the less self-reliant. He already envied the ascendancy and domination Douglas exercised over his followers, and felt keenly the slight given him by others of his own faith whom he conceived were disposed to prevent his attaining the leadership of his party. I remember early in 1858 of his coming into the office one morning and speaking in very dejected terms of the treatment he was receiving at the hands of Horace Greeley. "I think Greeley," he complained, "is not doing me right. His conduct, I believe, savors a little of injustice. I am a true Republican and have been tried already in the hottest part of the anti-slavery fight, and yet I find him taking up Douglas, a veritable dodger,—once a tool of the South, now its enemy,—and pushing him to the front. He forgets that when he does that he pulls me down at the same time. I fear Greeley's attitude will damage me with Sumner, Seward, Wilson, Phillips, and other friends in the East."[1] This was said with so much of mingled sadness and earnestness that I was deeply impressed.

Lincoln was gloomy and restless the entire day. Greeley's letters were driving
the enthusiasm out of him.° He seemed unwilling to attend to any business,
and finally, just before noon, left the office, going over to the United States
Court room to play a game of chess with Judge Treat, and did not return again
that day. I pondered a good deal over Lincoln's dejection, and that night, after
weighing the matter well in mind, resolved to go to the eastern States myself
and endeavor to sound some of the great men there. The next day, on apprising Lincoln of my determination, he questioned its propriety. Our relations,
he insisted, were so intimate that a wrong construction might be put upon the
movement. I listened carefully to him, but as I had never been beyond the
Alleghenies I packed my valise and went, notwithstanding his objections. I had
been in correspondence on my own account with Greeley, Seward, Sumner,
Phillips, and others for several years, had kept them informed of the feelings
of our people and the political campaigns in their various stages, but had never
met any of them save Greeley. I enjoyed heartily the journey and the varied
sights and scenes that attended it. Aside from my mission, the trip was a great
success. The magnificent buildings, the display of wealth in the large cities and
prosperous manufacturing towns, broadened the views of one whose vision had
never extended beyond the limits of the Illinois prairies. In Washington I saw
and dined with Trumbull, who went over the situation with me. Trumbull had
written to Lincoln shortly before† that he thought it "useless to speculate upon
the further course of Douglas or the effect it is to have in Illinois or other States.
He himself does not know where he is going or where he will come out."[3] At my
interview with Trumbull, however, he directed me to assure Mr. Lincoln that
Douglas did not mean to join the Republican party, however great the breach
between himself and the administration might be. "We Republicans here," he
said exultingly in another letter to Lincoln, "are in good spirits, and are standing
back to let the fight go on between Douglas and his former associates. Lincoln

---

°Greeley's letters were very pointed and sometimes savage. Here is one:

"I have not proposed to instruct the Republicans of Illinois in their political duties, and I doubt very
much that even so much as is implied in your letter can be fairly deduced from anything I have written. Now let me make one prediction. If you run a candidate [for Congress] against Harris and he is
able to canvass *he will beat you badly*. He is more of a man at heart and morally than Douglas, and
has gone into this fight with more earnestness and less calculation. Of the whole Douglas party he is
the truest and best. I never spoke a dozen words with him in my life, having met him but once, but if
I lived in his district I should vote for him. As I have never spoken of him in my paper, and suppose I
never shall, I take the liberty to say this much to you. Now paddle your own dug-out!

"Yours,

"Horace Greeley."[2]

†Letter, December 25, 1857, MS.

will lose nothing by this if he can keep the attention of our Illinois people from being diverted from the great and vital question of the day to the minor and temporary issues which are now being discussed."* In Washington I saw also Seward, Wilson, and others of equal prominence. Douglas was confined to his house by illness, but on receiving my card he directed me to be shown up to his room. We had a pleasant and interesting interview. Of course the conversation soon turned on Lincoln. In answer to an inquiry regarding the latter I remarked that Lincoln was pursuing the even tenor of his way. "He is not in anybody's way," I contended, "not even in yours, Judge Douglas." He was sitting up in a chair smoking a cigar. Between puffs he responded that neither was he in the way of Lincoln or any one else, and did not intend to invite conflict. He conceived that he had achieved what he had set out to do, and hence did not feel that his course need put him in opposition to Mr. Lincoln or his party. "Give Mr. Lincoln my regards," he said, rather warmly, "when you return, and tell him I have crossed the river and burned my boat." Leaving Washington, my next point was New York, where I met the editor of the *Anti-Slavery Standard,* Horace Greeley, Henry Ward Beecher, and others. I had a long talk with Greeley, whom I noticed leaned towards Douglas. I found, however, he was not at all hostile to Lincoln. I presented the latter's case in the best phase I knew how, but while I drew but little from him, I left feeling that he hadn't been entirely won over. He introduced me to Beecher, who, as everybody else did, inquired after Lincoln and through me sent him words of encouragement and praise.† From New York I went to Boston, and from the latter place I wrote Lincoln a letter which happily I found not long since in a bundle of Lincoln's letters, and which I insert here, believing it affords a better reflex of the situation at the time than anything I might see fit to say now. Here it is:

"Revere House,
"Boston, Mass., March 24, 1858.

"Friend Lincoln.

"I am in this city of notions, and am well—very well indeed. I wrote you a hasty letter from Washington some days ago, since which time I have been in Philadelphia, Baltimore, New York, and now here. I saw Greeley, and so far as

---

*Letter, December 27, 1857, MS.[4]
†Lincoln's greatest fear was that Douglas might be taken up by the Republicans. Senator Seward, when I met him in Washington, assured me there was no danger of it, insisting that the Republicans nor any one else could place any reliance on a man so slippery as Douglas.

any of our conversation is interesting to you I will relate. And we talked, say twenty minutes. He evidently wants Douglas sustained and sent back to the Senate. He did not say so in so many words, yet his *feelings* are with Douglas. I *know* it from the spirit and drift of his conversation. He talked bitterly— somewhat so—against the papers in Illinois, and said they were fools. I asked him this question, 'Greeley, do you want to see a third party organized, or do you want Douglas to ride to power through the North, which he has so much abused and betrayed?,' and to which he replied, 'Let the future alone; it will all come right. Douglas is a brave man. Forget the past and sustain the *righteous.*' Good God, *righteous,* eh!

"Since I have landed in Boston I have seen much that was entertaining and interesting. This morning I was introduced to Governor Banks. He and I had a conversation about Republicanism and especially about Douglas. He asked me this question, 'You will sustain Douglas in Illinois, won't you?' and to which I said '*No, never!*' He affected to be much surprised, and so the matter dropped and turned on Republicanism, or in general—Lincoln. Greeley's and other sheets that laud Douglas, Harris, *et al.,* want them sustained, and will *try* to do it. Several persons have asked me the same question which Banks asked, and evidently they get their cue, ideas, or what not from Greeley, Seward, *et al.* By-the-bye, Greeley remarked to me this, 'The Republican standard is too high; we want something practical.'

"This may not be interesting to you, but, however it may be, it is my duty to state what is going on, so that you may head it off—counteract it in some way. I hope it can be done. The Northern men are cold to me—somewhat repellent.

"Your friend,
"W. H. Herndon."[5]

On my return home I had encouraging news to relate. I told Lincoln of the favorable mention I had heard of him by Phillips, Sumner, Seward, Garrison, Beecher, and Greeley. I brought with me additional sermons and lectures by Theodore Parker, who was warm in his commendation of Lincoln. One of these was a lecture on "The Effect of Slavery on the American People," which was delivered in the Music Hall in Boston, and which I gave to Lincoln, who read and returned it. He liked especially the following expression, which he marked with a pencil, and which he in substance afterwards used in his Gettysburg address: "Democracy is direct self-government, over all the people, for all the people, by all the people."[6]

Meanwhile, passing by other events which have become interwoven in the history of the land, we reach April, 1858, at which time the Democratic State convention met and, besides nominating candidates for State offices, endorsed Mr. Douglas' services in the Senate, thereby virtually renominating him for that exalted office. In the very nature of things Lincoln was the man already chosen in the hearts of the Republicans of Illinois for the same office, and therefore with singular appropriateness they passed, with great unanimity, at their convention in Springfield on the 16th of June, the characteristic resolution: "That Hon. Abraham Lincoln is our first and only choice for United States Senator to fill the vacancy about to be created by the expiration of Mr. Douglas' term of office."[7] There was of course no surprise in this for Mr. Lincoln. He had been all along led to expect it, and with that in view had been earnestly and quietly at work preparing a speech in acknowledgment of the honor about to be conferred on him. This speech he wrote on stray envelopes and scraps of paper, as ideas suggested themselves, putting them into that miscellaneous and convenient receptacle, his hat. As the convention drew near he copied the whole on connected sheets, carefully revising every line and sentence, and fastened them together, for reference during the delivery of the speech, and for publication. The former precaution, however, was unnecessary, for he had studied and read over what he had written so long and carefully that he was able to deliver it without the least hesitation or difficulty. A few days before the convention, when he was at work on the speech, I remember that Jesse K. Dubois,° who was Auditor of State, came into the office and, seeing Lincoln busily writing, inquired what he was doing or what he was writing. Lincoln answered gruffly, "It's something you may see or hear some time, but I'll not let you see it now."[9] I myself knew what he was writing, but having asked neither my opinion nor that of anyone else, I did not venture to offer any suggestions. After he had finished the final draft of the speech, he locked the office door, drew the curtain across the glass panel in the door, and read it to me. At the end of each paragraph he would halt and wait for my comments. I remember what I said after hearing the first paragraph, wherein occurs the celebrated figure of the house divided against itself: "It is true, but is it wise or politic to say so?" He responded: "That expression is a truth of all human experience, 'a house divided against itself cannot

---

°"After the convention Lincoln met me on the street and said, 'Dubois, I can tell you now what I was doing the other day when you came into my office. I was writing that speech, and I knew if I read the passage about the "house divided against itself" to you, you would ask me to change or modify it, and that I was determined not to do. I had willed it so, and was willing if necessary to perish with it.'"—Statement of Jesse K. Dubois, MS.[8]

stand,' and 'he that runs may read.' The proposition also is true, and has been for six thousand years. I want to use some universally known figure expressed in simple language as universally well-known, that may strike home to the minds of men in order to raise them up to the peril of the times. I do not believe I would be right in changing or omitting it. I would rather be defeated with this expression in the speech, and uphold and discuss it before the people, than be victorious without it."[10] This was not the first time Lincoln had endorsed the dogma that our Government could not long endure part slave and part free. He had incorporated it in a speech at Bloomington in 1856, but in obedience to the emphatic protest of Judge T. Lyle Dickey and others, who conceived the idea that its "delivery would make Abolitionists of all the North and slavery propagandists of all the South, and thereby precipitate a struggle which might end in disunion,"[11] he consented to suspend its repetition, but only for that campaign.°
Now, however, the situation had changed somewhat. There had been a shifting of scenes, so to speak. The Republican party had gained some in strength and more in moral effectiveness and force. Nothing could keep back in Lincoln any longer, sentiments of right and truth, and he prepared to give the fullest expression to both in all future contests.

Before delivering his speech he invited a dozen or so of his friends over to the library of the State House, where he read and submitted it to them. After the reading he asked each man for his opinion. Some condemned and not one endorsed it. One man, more forcible than elegant, characterized it as a "d——d fool utterance;" another said the doctrine was "ahead of its time;" and still another contended that it would drive away a good many voters fresh from the Democratic ranks. Each man attacked it in his criticism. I was the last to respond. Although the doctrine announced was rather rank, yet it suited my views, and I said, "Lincoln, deliver that speech as read and it will make you President." At the time I hardly realized the force of my prophecy. Having patiently listened to these various criticisms from his friends—all of which with a single exception were adverse—he rose from his chair, and after allud-

---

°"After the meeting was over Mr. Lincoln and I returned to the Pike House, where we occupied the same room. Immediately on reaching the room I said to him, 'What in God's name could induce you to promulgate such an opinion?' He replied familiarly, 'Upon my soul, Dickey, I think it is true.' I reasoned to show it was not a correct opinion. He argued strenuously that the opinion was a sound one. At length I said, 'Suppose you are right, that our Government cannot last part free and part slave, what good is to be accomplished by inculcating that opinion (or truth, if you please) in the minds of the people?' After some minutes reflection he rose and approached me, extending his right hand to take mine, and said, 'From respect for your judgment, Dickey, I'll promise you I won't teach the doctrine again during this campaign.'"—Letter, T. Lyle Dickey, MS., December 8, 1866.[12]

ing to the careful study and intense thought he had given the question, he answered all their objections substantially as follows: "Friends, this thing has been retarded long enough. The time has come when these sentiments should be uttered; and if it is decreed that I should go down because of this speech, then let me go down linked to the truth—let me die in the advocacy of what is just and right."[13] The next day, the 17th, the speech was delivered just as we had heard it read. Up to this time Seward had held sway over the North by his "higher-law" sentiments, but the "house-divided-against-itself" speech by Lincoln in my opinion drove the nail into Seward's political coffin.°

Lincoln had now created in reality a more profound impression than he or his friends anticipated. Many Republicans deprecated the advanced ground he had taken, the more so as the Democrats rejoiced that it afforded them an issue clear and well-defined. Numbers of his friends distant from Springfield, on reading his speech, wrote him censorious letters; and one well-informed co-worker† predicted his defeat, charging it to the first ten lines of the speech.[14] These complaints, coming apparently from every quarter, Lincoln bore with great patience. To one complainant who followed him into his office he said proudly, "If I had to draw a pen across my record, and erase my whole life from sight, and I had one poor gift or choice left as to what I should save from the wreck, I should choose that speech and leave it to the world unerased."[15]

Meanwhile Douglas had returned from Washington to his home in Chicago. Here he rested for a few days until his friends and co-workers had arranged the details of a public reception on the 9th of July, when he delivered from the balcony of the Tremont House a speech intended as an answer to the one made by Lincoln in Springfield. Lincoln was present at this reception, but took no part in it. The next day, however, he replied. Both speeches were delivered at the same place. Leaving Chicago, Douglas passed on down to Bloomington and Springfield, where he spoke on the 16th and 17th of July respectively. On the evening of the latter day Lincoln responded again in a most effective and convincing effort. The contest now took on a different phase. Lincoln's Republican friends urged him to draw Douglas into a joint debate, and he accordingly sent him a challenge on the 24th of July. It is not necessary, I suppose, to reproduce here the correspondence that passed between these great leaders. On the 30th Douglas finally

---

°If any student of oratorical history, after reading Lincoln's speech on this occasion, will refer to Webster's reply to Hayne in the Senate, he will be struck with the similarity in figure and thought in the opening lines of both speeches. In fact, it may not be amiss to note that, in this instance, Webster's effort was carefully read by Lincoln and served in part as his model.

†Leonard Swett.

accepted the proposition to "divide time, and address the same audiences," naming seven different places, one in each Congressional district, outside of Chicago and Springfield, for joint meetings.° The places and dates were, Ottawa, August 21; Freeport, August 27; Jonesboro, September 15; Charleston, September 18; Galesburg, October 7; Quincy, October 13; and Alton, October 15. "I agree to your suggestion," wrote Douglas, "that we shall alternately open and close the discussion. I will speak at Ottawa one hour, you can reply, occupying an hour and a half, and I will then follow for half an hour. At Freeport you shall open the discussion and speak one hour, I will follow for an hour and a half, and you can then reply for half an hour. We will alternate in like manner in each successive place."[18] To this arrangement Lincoln on the 31st gave his consent, "although," he wrote, "by the terms as you propose you take four openings and closes to my three."[19]

History furnishes few characters whose lives and careers were so nearly parallel as those of Lincoln and Douglas. They met for the first time at the Legislature in Vandalia in 1834, where Lincoln was a member of the House of Representatives and Douglas was in the lobby. The next year Douglas was also a member. In 1839 both were admitted to practice in the Supreme Court of Illinois on the same day.† In 1841 both courted the same young lady. In 1846

°Among the items of preparation on Lincoln's part hitherto withheld is the following letter, which explains itself:

"Springfield, June 28, 1858.

"A. Campbell, Esq.

"My Dear Sir:—In 1856 you gave me authority to draw on you for any sum not exceeding five hundred dollars. I see clearly that such a privilege would be more available now than it was then. I am aware that times are tighter now than they were then. Please write me at all events, and whether you can now do anything or not I shall continue grateful for the past.

"Yours very truly,
"A. Lincoln."[16]

The following recent letter from Mr. Campbell is not without interest:

La Salle, Ill., Dec. 12th, 1888.

"Jesse W. Weik, Esq.

"My Dear Sir:—I gave Mr. Lincoln some money in the office of Lincoln & Herndon in Springfield in 1856, but I do not remember the exact amount. It was, however, between two and three hundred dollars. I never had Mr. Lincoln's obligation for the payment of any money. I never kept any account of nor charged my memory with any money I gave him. It was given to defray his personal expenses and otherwise promote the interest of a cause which I sincerely believed to be for the public good, and without the thought or expectation of a dollar of it ever being returned. From what I knew and learned of his careful habits in money matters in the campaign of 1856 I am entirely confident that every dollar and dime I ever gave was carefully and faithfully applied to the uses and purposes for which it was given.

"Sincerely yours,
"A. Campbell."[17]

†December 3d.

both represented Illinois in Congress at Washington, the one in the upper and the other in the lower House. In 1858 they were opposing candidates for United States Senator; and finally, to complete the remarkable counterpart, both were candidates for the Presidency in 1860. While it is true that their ambitions ran in parallel lines, yet they were exceedingly unlike in all other particulars. Douglas was short,—something over five feet high,—heavy set, with a large head, broad shoulders, deep chest, and striking features. He was polite and affable, but fearless. He had that unique trait, magnetism, fully developed in his nature, and that attracted a host of friends and readily made him a popular idol. He had had extensive experience in debate, and had been trained by contact for years with the great minds and orators in Congress. He was full of political history, well informed on general topics, eloquent almost to the point of brilliancy, self-confident to the point of arrogance, and a dangerous competitor in every respect. What he lacked in ingenuity he made up in strategy, and if in debate he could not tear down the structure of his opponent's argument by a direct and violent attack, he was by no means reluctant to resort to a strained restatement of the latter's position or to the extravagance of ridicule. Lincoln knew his man thoroughly and well.° He had often met Douglas on the stump; was familiar with his tactics, and though fully aware of his "want of fixed political morals," was not averse to measuring swords with the elastic and flexible "Little Giant."

Lincoln himself was constructed on an entirely different foundation. His base was plain common-sense, direct statement, and the inflexibility of logic. In physical make-up he was cold—at least not magnetic—and made no effort to dazzle people by his bearing. He cared nothing for a following, and though he had often before struggled for a political prize, yet in his efforts he never had strained his well-known spirit of fairness or open love of the truth. He analyzed everything, laid every statement bare, and by dint of his broad reasoning powers and manliness of admission inspired his hearers with deep conviction of his earnestness and honesty. Douglas may have electrified the crowds with his eloquence or charmed them with his majestic bearing and dexterity in debate, but as each man, after the meetings were over and the applause had died away, went to his home, his head rang with Lincoln's logic and appeal to manhood.

° An erroneous impression has grown up in recent years concerning Douglas's ability and standing as a lawyer. One of the latest biographies of Lincoln credits him with many of the artifices of the "shyster." This is not only unfair, but decidedly untrue. I always found Douglas at the bar to be a broad, fair, and liberal-minded man. Although not a thorough student of the law his large fund of good common-sense kept him in the front rank. He was equally generous and courteous, and he never stooped to gain a case. I know that Lincoln entertained the same view of him. It was only in politics that Douglas demonstrated any want of inflexibility and rectitude, and then only did Lincoln manifest a lack of faith in his morals.

A brief description of Mr. Lincoln's appearance on the stump and of his manner when speaking may not be without interest. When standing erect he was six feet four inches high. He was lean in flesh and ungainly in figure. Aside from the sad, pained look due to habitual melancholy, his face had no characteristic or fixed expression. He was thin through the chest, and hence slightly stoop-shouldered. When he arose to address courts, juries, or crowds of people, his body inclined forward to a slight degree. At first he was very awkward, and it seemed a real labor to adjust himself to his surroundings. He struggled for a time under a feeling of apparent diffidence and sensitiveness, and these only added to his awkwardness. I have often seen and sympathized with Mr. Lincoln during these moments. When he began speaking, his voice was shrill, piping, and unpleasant. His manner, his attitude, his dark, yellow face, wrinkled and dry, his oddity of pose, his diffident movements—everything seemed to be against him, but only for a short time. After having arisen, he generally placed his hands behind him, the back of his left hand in the palm of his right, the thumb and fingers of his right hand clasped around the left arm at the wrist. For a few moments he played the combination of awkwardness, sensitiveness, and diffidence. As he proceeded he became somewhat animated, and to keep in harmony with his growing warmth his hands relaxed their grasp and fell to his side. Presently he clasped them in front of him, interlocking his fingers, one thumb meanwhile chasing another. His speech now requiring more emphatic utterance, his fingers unlocked and his hands fell apart. His left arm was thrown behind, the back of his hand resting against his body, his right hand seeking his side. By this time he had gained sufficient composure, and his real speech began. He did not gesticulate as much with his hands as with his head. He used the latter frequently, throwing it with vim this way and that. This movement was a significant one when he sought to enforce his statement. It sometimes came with a quick jerk, as if throwing off electric sparks into combustible material. He never sawed the air nor rent space into tatters and rags as some orators do. He never acted for stage effect. He was cool, considerate, reflective—in time self-possessed and self-reliant. His style was clear, terse, and compact. In argument he was logical, demonstrative, and fair. He was careless of his dress, and his clothes, instead of fitting neatly as did the garments of Douglas on the latter's well-rounded form, hung loosely on his giant frame. As he moved along in his speech he became freer and less uneasy in his movements; to that extent he was graceful. He had a perfect naturalness, a strong individuality; and to that extent he was dignified. He despised glitter, show, set forms, and shams. He spoke with effectiveness and to move the judgment as well as the emotions of men. There was a world of meaning and emphasis in the long, bony finger of his right hand as he dotted the ideas on the minds of his hearers. Sometimes, to express joy or pleasure, he would raise both hands at an angle of about fifty degrees, the palms upward, as if desirous of embracing the spirit of that which he loved. If the sentiment was one of detestation—denunciation of slavery, for example—both arms, thrown upward and fists clenched, swept through the air, and he expressed an execration that was truly sublime. This was one of his most effective gestures, and signified most vividly a fixed determination to drag down the object of his hatred and trample it in the dust. He always stood squarely on his feet, toe even with toe; that is, he never put one foot before the other. He neither touched nor leaned on anything for support. He made but few changes in his positions and attitudes. He never ranted, never walked backward and forward on the platform. To ease his arms he frequently caught hold, with his left hand, of the lapel of his coat, keeping his thumb upright and leaving his right hand free to gesticulate. The designer of the monument recently erected in Chicago has happily caught him in just this attitude. As he proceeded with his speech the exercise of his vocal organs altered somewhat the tone of his voice. It lost in a measure its former acute and shrilling pitch, and mellowed into a more harmonious and pleasant sound. His form expanded, and, notwithstanding the sunken breast, he rose up a splendid and imposing figure. In his defence of the Declaration of Independence—his greatest inspiration—he was "tremendous in the directness of his utterances; he rose to impassioned eloquence, unsurpassed by Patrick Henry, Mirabeau, or Vergniaud, as his soul was inspired with the thought of human right and Divine justice."° His little gray eyes flashed in a face aglow with the fire of his profound thoughts; and his uneasy movements and diffident manner sunk themselves beneath the wave of righteous indignation that came sweeping over him. Such was Lincoln the orator.[21]

We can somewhat appreciate the feeling with which Douglas, aggressive and fearless though he was, welcomed a contest with such a man as Lincoln. Four years before, in a joint debate with him, he had asked for a cessation of forensic hostilities, conceding that his opponent of rail-splitting fame had given him "more trouble than all the United States Senate together."[22] Now he was brought face to face with him again.†

It is unnecessary and not in keeping with the purpose of this work to reproduce here the speeches made by either Lincoln or Douglas in their justly renowned

---

°Horace White, who was present and reported the speech for his paper, the Chicago *Tribune.* Letter, June 9, 1865, MS.[20]
†"Douglas and I, for the first time this canvass, crossed swords here yesterday. The fire flew some, and I am glad to know I am yet alive."—Lincoln to J. O. Cunningham, Ottawa, Ill., August 22, 1858, MS.[23]

debate. Briefly stated, Lincoln's position was announced in his opening speech at Springfield: "'A house divided against itself cannot stand.' I believe this Government cannot endure permanently half slave and half free. I do not expect the Union to be dissolved, I do not expect the house to fall—but I do expect it will cease to be divided. It will become all the one thing or the other. Either the opponents of slavery will arrest the further spread of it and place it where the public mind shall rest in the belief that it is in the course of ultimate extinction; or its advocates will push it forward till it becomes alike lawful in all the states, old as well as new, North as well as South."[24] The position of Douglas on the question of slavery was one of indifference. He advocated with all his power the doctrine of "Popular Sovereignty," a proposition, as quaintly put by Lincoln, which meant that, "if one man chooses to enslave another, no third man has a right to object."[25] At the last joint discussion in Alton, Lincoln, after reflecting on the patriotism of any man who was so indifferent to the wrong of slavery that he cared not whether it was voted up or down, closed his speech with this stirring summary: "That [slavery] is the real issue. That is the issue that will continue in this country when these poor tongues of Judge Douglas and myself shall be silent. It is the eternal struggle between these two principles—right and wrong—throughout the world. They are the two principles that have stood face to face from the beginning of time, and will ever continue to struggle. The one is the common right of humanity, and the other the divine right of kings. It is the same principle, in whatever shape it develops itself. It is the same spirit that says: 'You work and toil and earn bread, and I eat it.' No matter in what shape it comes, whether from the mouth of a king who seeks to bestride the people of his own nation and live by the fruit of their labor, or from one race of men as an apology for enslaving another race, it is the same tyrannical principle."[26]

It is unnecessary, I presume, to insert here the seven questions which Douglas propounded to Lincoln at their first meeting at Ottawa, nor the historic four which Lincoln asked at Freeport. It only remains to say that in answering Lincoln at Freeport, Douglas accomplished his own political downfall. He was swept entirely away from his former foundation, and even the glory of a subsequent election to the Senate never restored him to it.

During the canvass Mr. Lincoln, in addition to the seven meetings with Douglas, filled thirty-one appointments made by the State Central Committee, besides speaking at many other times and places not previously advertised. In his trips to and fro over the State, between meetings, he would stop at Springfield sometimes, to consult with his friends or to post himself up on questions that occurred during the canvass. He kept me busy hunting up old speeches and gathering facts and statistics at the State library. I made liberal clippings bearing in any way on the questions of the hour from every newspaper I happened to see, and kept him supplied with them; and on one or two occasions, in answer to letters and telegrams, I sent books forward to him. He had a little leather bound book, fastened in front with a clasp, in which he and I both kept inserting newspaper slips and newspaper comments until the canvass opened.[27] In arranging for the joint meetings and managing the crowds Douglas enjoyed one great advantage. He had been United States Senator for several years, and had influential friends holding comfortable government offices all over the State. These men were on hand at every meeting, losing no opportunity to applaud lustily all the points Douglas made and to lionize him in every conceivable way. The ingeniously contrived display of their enthusiasm had a marked effect on certain crowds—a fact of which Lincoln frequently complained to his friends. One who accompanied him during the canvass° relates this: "Lincoln and I were at the Centralia agricultural fair the day after the debate at Jonesboro. Night came on and we were tired, having been on the fair grounds all day. We were to go north on the Illinois Central railroad. The train was due at midnight, and the depot was full of people. I managed to get a chair for Lincoln in the office of the superintendent of the railroad, but small politicians would intrude so that he could scarcely get a moment's sleep. The train came and was filled instantly. I got a seat near the door for Lincoln and myself. He was worn out, and had to meet Douglas the next day at Charleston. An empty car, called a saloon car, was hitched on to the rear of the train and locked up. I asked the conductor, who knew Lincoln and myself well,—we were both attorneys of the road,—if Lincoln could not ride in that car; that he was exhausted and needed rest; but the conductor refused. I afterwards got him in by a stratagem. At the same time George B. McClellan in person was taking Douglas around in a special car and special train; and that was the unjust treatment Lincoln got from the Illinois Central railroad. Every interest of that road and every employee was against Lincoln and for Douglas."[28]

The heat and dust and bonfires of the campaign at last came to an end. The election took place on the second of November, and while Lincoln received of the popular vote a majority of over four thousand, yet the returns from the legislative districts foreshadowed his defeat. In fact, when the Senatorial election took place in the Legislature, Douglas received fifty-four and Lincoln forty-six

---

°Henry C. Whitney, MS., July 21, 1865.

votes—one of the results of the lamentable apportionment law then in operation.°

The letters of Lincoln at this period are the best evidence of his feelings now
obtainable, and of how he accepted his defeat. To Henry Asbury, a friend who
had written him a cheerful letter admonishing him not to give up the battle, he
responded:

"Springfield, November 19, 1858.
"Mr. Henry Asbury,
"My Dear Sir:—Yours of the 13th was received some days ago. The fight
must go on. The cause of civil liberty must not be surrendered at the end of
one or even one hundred defeats. Douglas had the ingenuity to be supported
in the late contest both as the best means to break down and to uphold the
slave interest. No ingenuity can keep these antagonistic elements in harmony
long. Another explosion will soon come.
    "Yours truly,
        "A. Lincoln."[30]

To another friend† on the same day he writes: "I am glad I made the late
race. It gave me a hearing on the great and durable questions of the age which
I could have had in no other way; and though I now sink out of view and shall
be forgotten, I believe I have made some marks which will tell for the cause of
liberty long after I am gone."[31]

Before passing to later events in Mr. Lincoln's life it is proper to include in this
chapter, as a specimen of his oratory at this time, his eloquent reference to the

---

°Horace Greeley was one of the most vigilant men during the debate. He wrote to Lincoln and me many
letters which I still retain. In a letter to me during the campaign, October 6, he says with reference to
Douglas: "In his present position I could not of course support him, but he need not have been in this
position had the Republicans of Illinois been as wise and far-seeing as they are earnest and true. . . . but
seeing things are as they are, I do not wish to be quoted as authority for making trouble and division among
our friends." Soon after hearing of the result of November election he again writes: "I advise you privately
that Mr. Douglas would be the strongest candidate that the Democratic party could present for President;
but they will not present him. The old leaders wouldn't endorse it. As he is doomed to be slaughtered at
Charleston it is good policy to fatten him meantime. He will cut up the better at killing time." An inquiry
for his preference as to Presidential timber elicited this response, December 4th, "As to President, my
present judgment is Edward Bates, with John M. Read for Vice; but I am willing to go anything that looks
strong. I don't wish to load the team heavier than it will pull through. As to Douglas, he is like the man's
boy who (he said) 'didn't weigh so much as he expected, and he always knew he wouldn't.' I never thought
him very sound coin; but I didn't think it best to beat him on the back of his anti-Lecompton fight and I
am still of that opinion."[29]
†Dr. Henry.

Declaration of Independence found in a speech delivered at Beardstown, August 12, and not at Lewiston five days later, as many biographers have it. Aside from its concise reasoning, the sublime thought it suggests entitles it to rank beside that great masterpiece, his Gettysburg address. After alluding to the suppression by the Fathers of the Republic of the slave trade, he says: "These by their representatives in old Independence Hall said to the whole race of men: 'We hold these truths to be self-evident: that all men are created equal; that they are endowed by their Creator with certain inalienable rights; that among these are life, liberty, and the pursuit of happiness.' This was their majestic interpretation of the economy of the universe. This was their lofty, and wise, and noble understanding of the justice of the Creator to his creatures—yes, gentlemen, to all his creatures, to the whole great family of man. In their enlightened belief, nothing stamped with the divine image and likeness was sent into the world to be trodden on and degraded and imbruted by its fellows. They grasped not only the whole race of man then living, but they reached forward and seized upon the farthest posterity. They erected a beacon to guide their children, and their children's children, and the countless myriads who should inhabit the earth in other ages. Wise statesmen as they were, they knew the tendency of prosperity to breed tyrants, and so they established these great self-evident truths, that when in the distant future some man, some faction, some interest, should set up the doctrine that none but rich men, none but white men, or none but Anglo-Saxon white men were entitled to life, liberty, and the pursuit of happiness, their posterity might look up again to the Declaration of Independence and take courage to renew the battle which their fathers began, so that truth and justice and mercy and all the humane and Christian virtues might not be extinguished from the land; so that no man would hereafter dare to limit and circumscribe the great principles on which the temple of liberty was being built.

"Now, my countrymen, if you have been taught doctrines conflicting with the great landmarks of the Declaration of Independence; if you have listened to suggestions which would take away from its grandeur and mutilate the fair symmetry of its proportions; if you have been inclined to believe that all men are not created equal in those inalienable rights enumerated by our chart of liberty: let me entreat you to come back. Return to the fountain whose waters spring close by the blood of the Revolution. Think nothing of me; take no thought for the political fate of any man whomsoever, but come back to the truths that are in the Declaration of Independence. You may do anything with me you choose, if you will but heed these sacred principles. You may not only defeat me for the

Lincoln as He Appeared
during the Debate with
Douglas (after an ambro-
type taken by C. Jackson,
at Pittsfield, Illinois, Oct.
1, 1858)

Senate, but you may take me and put me to death. While pretending no indifference to earthly honors, I do claim to be actuated in this contest by something
higher than an anxiety for office. I charge you to drop every paltry and insignificant thought for any man's success. It is nothing; I am nothing; Judge Douglas is
nothing. But do not destroy that immortal emblem of humanity—the Declaration of American Independence."[32]

One of the newspaper men* who heard this majestic oration wrote me as follows: "The apostrophe to the Declaration of Independence to which you refer was
written by myself from a vivid recollection of Mr. Lincoln's speech at Beardstown,
August 12, 1858. On the day following the delivery of the speech, as Mr. Lincoln
and I were proceeding by steamer from Beardstown to Havana, I said to him that
I had been greatly impressed by his concluding remarks of the day previous, and
that if he would write them out for me I felt confident their publication would be
highly beneficial to our cause as well as honorable to his own fame. He replied
that he had but a faint recollection of any portion of the speech; that, like all his
campaign speeches, it was necessarily extemporaneous; and that its good or bad

*Horace White, MS., May 17, 1865.

effect depended upon the inspiration of the moment. He added that I had probably over-estimated the value of the remarks referred to. In reply to my question whether he had any objection to my writing them out from memory and putting them in the form of a verbatim report, he said, 'None at all.' I accordingly did so. I felt confident then and I feel equally assured now that I transcribed the peroration with absolute fidelity as to ideas and commendable fidelity as to language. I certainly aimed to reproduce his exact words, and my recollection of the passage as spoken was very clear. After I had finished writing I read it to Mr. Lincoln. When I had finished the reading he said, 'Well, those are my views, and if I said anything on the subject I must have said substantially that, but not nearly so well as that is said.' I remember this remark quite distinctly, and if the old steamer *Editor* is still in existence I could show the place where we were sitting. Having secured his assent to the publication I forwarded it to our paper, but inasmuch as my report of the Beardstown meeting had been already mailed I incorporated the remarks on the Declaration of Independence in my letter from Lewiston two or three days subsequently. . . . I do not remember ever having related these facts before, although they have often recurred to me as I have seen the peroration resuscitated again and again, and published (with good effect, I trust) in the newspapers of this country and England."[33]

CHAPTER XIV.

Before Mr. Lincoln surrenders himself completely to the public—for it is apparent he is fast approaching the great crisis of his career—it may not be entirely inappropriate to take a nearer and more personal view of him. A knowledge of his personal views and actions, a glimpse through the doorway of his home, and a more thorough acquaintance with his marked and strong points as they developed, will aid us greatly in forming our general estimate of the man. When Mr. Lincoln entered the domain of investigation he was a severe and persistent thinker, and had wonderful endurance; hence he was abstracted, and for that reason at times was somewhat unsocial, reticent, and uncommunicative. After his marriage it cannot be said that he liked the society of ladies; in fact, it was just what he did not like, though one of his biographers says otherwise. Lincoln had none of the tender ways that please a woman, and he could not, it seemed, by any positive act of his own make her happy. If his wife was happy, she was naturally happy, or made herself so in spite of countless drawbacks. He was, however, a good husband in his own peculiar way, and in his own way only.

If exhausted from severe and long-continued thought, he had to touch the earth again to renew his strength. When this weariness set in he would stop thought, and get down and play with a little dog or kitten to recover; and when the recovery came he would push it aside to play with its own tail. He treated men and women in much the same way. For fashionable society he had a marked dislike, although he appreciated its value in promoting the welfare of a man ambitious to succeed in politics. If he was invited out to dine or to mingle in some social gathering, and came in contact with the ladies, he treated them with becoming politeness; but the consciousness of his shortcomings as a society man rendered him unusually diffident, and at the very first opportunity he would have the men separated from their ladies and crowded close around him in one corner of the parlor, listening to one of his characteristic stories. That a lady° as proud and as ambitious to exercise the rights of supremacy in society as Mary Todd should repent of her marriage to the man I have just described surely need occasion no surprise in the mind of anyone. Both she and the man whose hand she accepted acted along the lines of human conduct, and both reaped the bitter harvest of conjugal infelicity. In dealing with Mr. Lincoln's home life perhaps I am revealing an element of his character that has heretofore been kept from the world; but in doing so I feel sure I am treading on no person's toes, for all the actors in this domestic drama are dead, and the world seems ready to hear the facts. As his married life, in the opinion of all his friends, exerted a peculiar influence over Mr. Lincoln's political career there can be no impropriety, I apprehend, in throwing the light on it now. Mrs. Lincoln's disposition and nature have been dwelt upon in another chapter, and enough has been told to show that one of her greatest misfortunes was her inability to control her temper. Admit that, and everything can be explained. However cold and abstracted her husband may have appeared to others, however impressive, when aroused, may have seemed his indignation in public, he never gave vent to his feelings at home. He always meekly accepted as final the authority of his wife in all matters of domestic concern.† This may explain somewhat the statement of Judge Davis that, "as a general rule, when all the lawyers of a Saturday evening would go home and see their families and friends, Lincoln would find some excuse and refuse to go. We said nothing, but it seemed to us all he was not domestically happy."[3] He exercised no government of any kind over his household. His children did much as they pleased. Many of their antics he approved, and he restrained them in nothing. He never reproved them or gave them a fatherly frown. He was the most indulgent parent I have ever known. He was in the habit, when at home on Sunday, of bringing his two boys, Willie and Thomas—or "Tad"—down to the office to remain while his wife attended church. He seldom accompanied her there. The boys were absolutely unrestrained in their amusement. If they pulled down all the books from the shelves, bent the points of all the pens, overturned inkstands, scattered law-

---

°Mrs. Lincoln was decidedly pro-slavery in her views. One day she was invited to take a ride with a neighboring family, some of whose members still reside in Springfield. "If ever my husband dies," she ejaculated during the ride, "his spirit will never find me living outside the limits of a slave State."[1]

†One day a man making some improvements in Lincoln's yard suggested to Mrs. Lincoln the propriety of cutting down one of the trees, to which she willingly assented. Before doing so, however, the man came down to our office and consulted Lincoln himself about it. "What did Mrs. Lincoln say?" enquired the latter. "She consented to have it taken away." "Then, in God's name," exclaimed Lincoln, "cut it down to the roots!"[2]

papers over the floor, or threw the pencils into the spittoon, it never disturbed the serenity of their father's good-nature. Frequently absorbed in thought, he never observed their mischievous but destructive pranks—as his unfortunate partner did, who thought much, but said nothing—and, even if brought to his attention, he virtually encouraged their repetition by declining to show any substantial evidence of parental disapproval.[4] After church was over the boys and their father, climbing down the office stairs, ruefully turned their steps homeward. They mingled with the throngs of well-dressed people returning from church, the majority of whom might well have wondered if the trio they passed were going to a fireside where love and white-winged peace reigned supreme. A near relative of Mrs. Lincoln,[5] in explanation of the unhappy condition of things in that lady's household, offered this suggestion: "Mrs. Lincoln came of the best stock, and was raised like a lady. Her husband was her opposite, in origin, in education, in breeding, in everything; and it is therefore quite natural that she should complain if he answered the door-bell himself instead of sending the servant to do so; neither is she to be condemned if, as you say, she raised 'merry war' because he persisted in using his own knife in the butter, instead of the silver-handled one intended for that purpose."* Such want of social polish on the part of her husband of course gave Mrs. Lincoln great offense, and therefore in commenting on it she cared neither for time nor place. Her frequent outbursts of temper precipitated many an embarrassment from which Lincoln with great difficulty extricated himself.

Mrs. Lincoln, on account of her peculiar nature, could not long retain a servant in her employ. The sea was never so placid but that a breeze would ruffle its waters. She loved show and attention, and if, when she glorified her family descent or indulged in one of her strange outbreaks, the servant could simulate absolute obsequiousness or had tact enough to encourage her social pretensions, Mrs. Lincoln was for the time her firmest friend. One servant, who adjusted herself to suit the lady's capricious ways, lived with the family for several years. She told me that at the time of the debate between Douglas and Lincoln she often heard the latter's wife boast that she would yet be mistress of the White House.

---

*A lady relative who lived for two years with the Lincolns told me that Mr. Lincoln was in the habit of lying on the floor with the back of a chair for a pillow when he read. One evening, when in this position in the hall, a knock was heard at the front door and although in his shirt-sleeves he answered the call. Two ladies were at the door whom he invited into the parlor, notifying them in his open familiar way, that he would "trot the women folks out." Mrs. Lincoln from an adjoining room witnessed the ladies' entrance and overheard her husband's jocose expression. Her indignation was so instantaneous she made the situation exceedingly interesting for him, and he was glad to retreat from the mansion. He did not return till very late at night and then slipped quietly in at a rear door.[6]

Springfield—Lincoln's Residence, 1878 (after photograph by J. A. W. Pittman)

The secret of her ability to endure the eccentricities of her mistress came out in the admission that Mr. Lincoln gave her an extra dollar each week on condition that she would brave whatever storms might arise, and suffer whatever might befall her, without complaint. It was a rather severe condition, but she lived rigidly up to her part of the contract. The money was paid secretly and without the knowledge of Mrs. Lincoln. Frequently, after tempestuous scenes between the mistress and her servant, Lincoln at the first opportunity would place his hand encouragingly on the latter's shoulder with the admonition, "Mary, keep up your courage." It may not be without interest to add that the servant afterwards married a man who enlisted in the army. In the spring of 1865 his wife managed to reach Washington to secure her husband's release from the service. After some effort she succeeded in obtaining an interview with the President. He was glad to see her, gave her a basket of fruit, and directed her to call the next day and obtain a pass though the lines and money to buy clothes for herself and children. That night he was assassinated.[7]

The following letter to the editor of a newspaper in Springfield will serve as a specimen of the perplexities which frequently beset Mr. Lincoln when his wife came in contact with others. What in this instance she said to the paper carrier we do not know; we can only intelligently infer. I have no personal recollection of the incident, although I knew the man to whom it was addressed quite well. The letter only recently came to light. I insert it without further comment.

[Private.]

"Springfield, Ill., February 20, 1857.
"John E. Rosette, Esq.
"*Dear Sir:*—Your note about the little paragraph in the *Republican* was received yesterday, since which time I have been too unwell to notice it. I had not supposed you wrote or approved it. The whole originated in mistake. You know by the conversation with me that I thought the establishment of the paper unfortunate, but I always expected to throw no obstacle in its way, and to patronize it to the extent of taking and paying for one copy. When the paper was brought to my house, my wife said to me, 'Now are you going to take another worthless little paper?' I said to her *evasively,* 'I have not directed the paper to be left.' From this, in my absence, she sent the message to the carrier. This is the whole story.
"Yours truly,
"A. LINCOLN."[8]

A man once called at the house to learn why Mrs. Lincoln had so unceremoniously discharged his niece from her employ. Mrs. Lincoln met him at the door, and being somewhat wrought up, gave vent to her feelings, resorting to such violent gestures and emphatic language that the man was glad to beat a hasty retreat. He at once started out to find Lincoln, determined to exact from him proper satisfaction for his wife's action. Lincoln was entertaining a crowd in a store at the time. The man, still laboring under some agitation, called him to the door and made the demand. Lincoln listened for a moment to his story. "My friend," he interrupted, "I regret to hear this, but let me ask you in all candor, can't you endure for a few moments what I have had as my daily portion for the last fifteen years?" These words were spoken so mournfully and with such a look of distress that the man was completely disarmed. It was a case that appealed to his feelings. Grasping the unfortunate husband's hand, he expressed in no uncertain terms his sympathy, and even apologized for having approached him. He said no more about the infuriated wife, and Lincoln afterward had no better friend in Springfield.[9]

Mr. Lincoln never had a confidant, and therefore never unbosomed himself to others. He never spoke of his trials to me or, so far as I knew, to any of his friends. It was a great burden to carry, but he bore it sadly enough and without a murmur. I could always realize when he was in distress, without being told. He was not exactly an early riser, that is, he never usually appeared at the office till about nine o'clock in the morning. I usually preceded him an hour. Sometimes, however, he would come down as early as seven o'clock—in fact, on one occasion I remember he came down before daylight. If, on arriving at the office, I found him in, I knew instantly that a breeze had sprung up over the domestic sea, and that the waters were troubled. He would either be lying on the lounge looking skyward, or doubled up in a chair with his feet resting on the sill of a back window. He would not look up on my entering, and only answered my "Good morning" with a grunt. I at once busied myself with pen and paper, or ran through the leaves of some book; but the evidence of his melancholy and distress was so plain, and his silence so significant, that I would grow restless myself, and finding some excuse to go to the court-house or elsewhere, would leave the room.

The door of the office opening into a narrow hallway was half glass, with a curtain on it working on brass rings strung on wire. As I passed out on these occasions I would draw the curtain across the glass, and before I reached the bottom of the stairs I could hear the key turn in the lock, and Lincoln was alone in his gloom. An hour in the clerk's office at the court-house, an hour longer in a neighboring store having passed, I would return. By that time either a client had dropped in and Lincoln was propounding the law, or else the cloud of despondency had passed away, and he was busy in the recital of an Indiana story to whistle off the recollections of the morning's gloom. Noon having arrived I would depart homeward for my dinner. Returning within an hour, I would find him still in the office,—although his house stood but a few squares away,—lunching on a slice of cheese and a handful of crackers which, in my absence, he had brought up from a store below. Separating for the day at five or six o'clock in the evening, I would still leave him behind, either sitting on a box at the foot of the stairway, entertaining a few loungers, or killing time in the same way on the court-house steps. A light in the office after dark attested his presence there till late along in the night, when, after all the world had gone to sleep, the tall form of the man destined to be the nation's President could have been seen strolling along in the shadows of trees and buildings, and quietly slipping in through the door of a modest frame house, which it pleased the world, in a conventional way, to call his home.[10]

Some persons may insist that this picture is too highly colored. If so, I can only answer, they do not know the facts. The majority of those who have a personal knowledge of them are persistent in their silence. If their lips could be opened and all could be known, my conclusions and statements, to say the least of them, would be found to be fair, reasonable, and true. A few words more as to Lincoln's domestic history, and I pass to a different phase of his life. One of his warmest and closest friends, who still survives, maintains the theory that, after all, Lincoln's political ascendancy and final elevation to the Presidency were due more to the influence of his wife than to any other person or cause. "The fact," insists this friend, "that Mary Todd, by her turbulent nature and unfortunate manner, prevented her husband from becoming a domestic man, operated largely in his favor; for he was thereby kept out in the world of business and politics. Instead of spending his evenings at home, reading the papers and warming his toes at his own fireside, he was constantly out with the common people, was mingling with the politicians, discussing public questions with the farmers who thronged the offices in the court-house and state house, and exchanging views with the loungers who surrounded the stove of winter evenings in the village store. The result of this continuous contact with the world was, that he was more thoroughly known than any other man in his community. His wife, therefore, was one of the unintentional means of his promotion. If, on the other hand, he had married some less ambitious but more domestic woman, some honest farmer's quiet daughter,—one who would have looked up to and worshipped him because he uplifted her,—the result might have been different. For, although it doubtless would have been her pride to see that he had clean clothes whenever he needed them; that his slippers were always in their place; that he was warmly clad and had plenty to eat; and, although the privilege of ministering to his every wish and whim might have been to her a pleasure rather than a duty; yet I fear he would have been buried in the pleasures of a loving home, and the country would never have had Abraham Lincoln for its President."[11]

In her domestic troubles I have always sympathized with Mrs. Lincoln. The world does not know what she bore, or how ill-adapted she was to bear it. Her fearless, witty, and austere nature shrank instinctively from association with the calm, imperturbable, and simple ways of her thoughtful and absent-minded husband. Besides, who knows but she may have acted out in her conduct toward her husband the laws of human revenge? The picture of that eventful evening in 1841, when she stood at the Edwards mansion clad in her bridal robes, the feast prepared and the guests gathered, and when the bridegroom came not, may have been constantly before her, and prompted her to a course of action which kept in the background the better elements of her nature. In marrying Lincoln she did not look so far into the future as Mary Owens,[12] who declined his proposal because "he was deficient in those little links which make up the chain of woman's happiness."°

By reason of his practical turn of mind Mr. Lincoln never speculated any more in the scientific and philosophical than he did in the financial world. He never undertook to fathom the intricacies of psychology and metaphysics.† Investigation into first causes, abstruse mental phenomena, the science of being, he brushed aside as trash—mere scientific absurdities. He discovered through experience that his mind, like the minds of other men, had its limitations, and hence he economized his forces and his time by applying his powers in the field of the

---

°Mrs. Lincoln died at the residence of her sister Mrs. Ninian W. Edwards, in Springfield, July 16, 1882. Her physician during her last illness says this of her: "In the late years of her life certain mental peculiarities were developed which finally culminated in a slight apoplexy, producing paralysis, of which she died. Among the peculiarities alluded to, one of the most singular was the habit she had during the last year or so of her life of immuring herself in a perfectly dark room and, for light, using a small candle-light, even when the sun was shining bright out-of-doors. No urging would induce her to go out into the fresh air. Another peculiarity was the accumulation of large quantities of silks and dress goods in trunks and by the cart-load, which she never used and which accumulated until it was really feared that the floor of the store-room would give way. She was bright and sparkling in conversation, and her memory remained singularly good up to the very close of her life. Her face was animated and pleasing; and to me she was always an interesting woman; and while the whole world was finding fault with her temper and disposition, it was clear to me that the trouble was really a cerebral disease."—Dr. Thomas W. Dresser, letter, January 3, 1889, MS.[13]

†"He was contemplative rather than speculative. He wanted something solid to rest upon, and hence his bias for mathematics and the physical sciences. He bestowed more attention on them than upon metaphysical speculations. I have heard him descant upon the problem whether a ball discharged from a gun in a horizontal position would be longer in reaching the ground than one dropped at the instant of discharge from the muzzle. He said it always appeared to him that they would both reach the ground at the same time, even before he had read the philosophical explanation."—Joseph Gillespie, letter, December 8, 1866, MS.[14]

practical. Scientifically regarded he was a realist as opposed to an idealist, a sensationist as opposed to an intuitionist, a materialist as opposed to a spiritualist.

There was more or less superstition in his nature, and, although he may not have believed implicitly in the signs of his many dreams, he was constantly endeavoring to unravel them. His mind was readily impressed with some of the most absurd superstitions.[15] His visit to the Voodoo fortune-teller in New Orleans in 1831; his faith in the virtues of the mad-stone, when he took his son Robert to Terre Haute, Indiana, to be cured of the bite of a rabid dog; and the strange double image of himself which he told his secretary, John Hay, he saw reflected in a mirror just after his election in 1860, strongly attest his inclination to superstition. He held most firmly to the doctrine of fatalism all his life. His wife, after his death, told me what I already knew, that "his only philosophy was, what is to be will be, and no prayers of ours can reverse the decree."[16] He always contended that he was doomed to a sad fate, and he repeatedly said to me when we were alone in our office: "I am sure I shall meet with some terrible end." In proof of his strong leaning towards fatalism he once quoted the case of Brutus and Caesar, arguing that the former was forced by laws and conditions over which he had no control to kill the latter, and, *vice versâ*, that the latter was specially created to be disposed of by the former. This superstitious view of life ran through his being like the thin blue vein through the whitest marble, giving the eye rest from the weariness of continued unvarying color.°

For many years I subscribed for and kept on our office table the *Westminster* and *Edinburgh Review* and a number of other English periodicals. Besides them I purchased the works of Spencer, Darwin, and the utterances of other English scientists, all of which I devoured with great relish. I endeavored, but had little success in inducing Lincoln to read them. Occasionally he would snatch one up and peruse it for a little while, but he soon threw it down with the suggestion that it was entirely too heavy for an ordinary mind to digest.† A gentleman in Springfield gave him a book called, I believe, "Vestiges of Creation," which interested him so much that he read it through. The volume was published in Edinburgh,

---

°I have heard him frequently quote the couplet,

"There's a divinity that shapes our ends,
Rough-hew them how we will."[17]

†In 1856 I purchased in New York a life of Edmund Burke. I have forgotten now who the author was, but I remember I read it through in a short time. One morning Lincoln came into the office and, seeing the book in my hands, enquired what I was reading. I told him, at the same time observing that it was an excellent work and handing the book over to him. Taking it in his hand he threw himself down on the office sofa and hastily ran over its pages, reading a little here and there. At last he closed and threw it on the table with the exclamation, "No, I've read enough of it. It's like all the others. Biographies as generally written

and undertook to demonstrate the doctrine of development or evolution. The treatise interested him greatly, and he was deeply impressed with the notion of the so-called "universal law"—evolution; he did not extend greatly his researches, but by continued thinking in a single channel seemed to grow into a warm advocate of the new doctrine. Beyond what I have stated he made no further investigation into the realm of philosophy. "There are no accidents," he said one day, "in my philosophy. Every effect must have its cause. The past is the cause of the present, and the present will be the cause of the future. All these are links in the endless chain stretching from the finite to the infinite." From what has been said it would follow logically that he did not believe, except in a very restricted sense, in the freedom of the will. We often argued the question, I taking the opposite view; he changed the expression, calling it the freedom of the mind, and insisted that man always acted from a motive. I once contended that man was free and could act without a motive. He smiled at my philosophy, and answered that it was impossible, because "the motive was born before the man."[19]

The foregoing thoughts are prefatory to the much-mooted question of Mr. Lincoln's religious belief. For what I have heretofore said on this subject, both in public lectures and in letters which have frequently found their way into the newspapers, I have been freely and sometimes bitterly assailed, but I do not intend now to reopen the discussion or to answer the many persons who have risen up and asked to measure swords with me. I merely purpose to state the bare facts, expressing no opinion of my own, and allowing each and every one to put his or her construction on them.

Inasmuch as he was so often a candidate for public office Mr. Lincoln said as little about his religious opinions as possible, especially if he failed to coincide with the Orthodox world. In illustration of his religious code I once heard him say that it was like that of an old man named Glenn, in Indiana, whom he heard speak at a church meeting, and who said: "When I do good I feel good, when I do bad I feel bad, and that's my religion."[20] In 1834, while still living in New Salem and before

are not only misleading, but false. The author of this life of Burke makes a wonderful hero out of his subject. He magnifies his perfections—if he had any—and suppresses his imperfections. He is so faithful in his zeal and so lavish in praise of his every act that one is almost driven to believe that Burke never made a mistake or a failure in his life." He lapsed into a brown study, but presently broke out again, "Billy, I've wondered why book-publishers and merchants don't have blank biographies on their shelves, always ready for an emergency; so that, if a man happens to die, his heirs or his friends, if they wish to perpetuate his memory, can purchase one already written, but with blanks. These blanks they can at their pleasure fill up with rosy sentences full of high-sounding praise. In most instances they commemorate a lie, and cheat posterity out of the truth. History," he concluded, "is not history unless it is the truth." This emphatic avowal of sentiment from Mr. Lincoln not only fixes his estimate of ordinary biography, but is my vindication in advance if assailed for telling the truth.[18]

he became a lawyer, he was surrounded by a class of people exceedingly liberal in matters of religion. Volney's "Ruins" and Paine's "Age of Reason" passed from hand to hand, and furnished food for the evening's discussion in the tavern and village store. Lincoln read both these books and thus assimilated them into his own being. He prepared an extended essay—called by many, a book—in which he made an argument against Christianity, striving to prove that the Bible was not inspired, and therefore not God's revelation, and that Jesus Christ was not the son of God. The manuscript containing these audacious and comprehensive propositions he intended to have published or given a wide circulation in some other way. He carried it to the store, where it was read and freely discussed. His friend and employer, Samuel Hill, was among the listeners, and, seriously questioning the propriety of a promising young man like Lincoln fathering such unpopular notions, he snatched the manuscript from his hands and thrust it into the stove.[21] The book went up in flames, and Lincoln's political future was secure. But his infidelity and his sceptical views were not diminished. He soon removed to Springfield, where he attracted considerable notice by his rank doctrine. Much of what he then said may properly be credited to the impetuosity and exuberance of youth. One of his closest friends, whose name is withheld, narrating scenes and reviewing discussions that in 1838 took place in the office of the county clerk, says: "Sometimes Lincoln bordered on atheism. He went far that way, and shocked me. I was then a young man, and believed what my good mother told me. . . . He would come into the clerk's office where I and some young men were writing and staying, and would bring the Bible with him; would read a chapter and argue against it. . . . Lincoln was enthusiastic in his infidelity. As he grew older he grew more discreet; didn't talk much before strangers about his religion; but to friends, close and bosom ones, he was always open and avowed, fair and honest; to strangers, he held them off from policy."[22] John T. Stuart, who was Lincoln's first partner, substantially endorses the above. "He was an avowed and open infidel," declares Stuart, "and sometimes bordered on atheism; . . . . went further against Christian beliefs and doctrines and principles than any man I ever heard; he shocked me. I don't remember the exact line of his argument; suppose it was against the inherent defects, so-called, of the Bible, and on grounds of reason. Lincoln always denied that Jesus was the Christ of God—denied that Jesus was the son of God as understood and maintained by the Christian Church."[23] David Davis tells us this: "The idea that Lincoln talked to a stranger about his religion or religious views, or made such speeches and remarks about it as are published, is to me absurd. I knew the man so well; he was the most reticent, secretive man I ever saw or expect to see. He had no faith, in the Christian sense of the term—had faith in laws, principles, causes and effects."[24] Another man° testifies as follows: "Mr. Lincoln told me that he was a kind of immortalist; that he never could bring himself to believe in eternal punishment; that man lived but a little while here; and that if eternal punishment were man's doom, he should spend that little life in vigilant and ceaseless preparation by never-ending prayer."²⁵ Another intimate friend† furnishes this: "In my intercourse with Mr. Lincoln I learned that he believed in a Creator of all things, who had neither beginning nor end, possessing all power and wisdom, established a principle in obedience to which worlds move and are upheld, and animal and vegetable life come into existence. A reason he gave for his belief was that in view of the order and harmony of all nature which we behold, it would have been more miraculous to have come about by chance than to have been created and arranged by some great thinking power. As to the Christian theory that Christ is God or equal to the Creator, he said that it had better be taken for granted; for by the test of reason we might become infidels on that subject, for evidence of Christ's divinity came to us in a somewhat doubtful shape; but that the system of Christianity was an ingenious one at least, and perhaps was calculated to do good."²⁶ Jesse W. Fell, to whom Lincoln first confided the details of his biography, furnishes a more elaborate account of the latter's religious views than anyone else. In a statement made September 22, 1870, Fell says: "If there were any traits of character that stood out in bold relief in the person of Mr. Lincoln they were those of truth and candor. He was utterly incapable of insincerity or professing views on this or any other subject he did not entertain. Knowing such to be his true character, that insincerity, much more duplicity, were traits wholly foreign to his nature, many of his old friends were not a little surprised at finding in some of the biographies of this great man statements concerning his religious opinions so utterly at variance with his known sentiments. True, he may have changed or modified these sentiments‡ after his removal from among us, though this is hardly reconcilable with the history of the man, and his entire devotion to public matters during his four years' residence at the national capital. It is possible, however, that this may be the proper solution of this conflict of opinions; or it may be that, with no intention on the part of any one to mislead

---

°William H. Hannah.
†I. W. Keys.

‡   Executive Mansion, Washington, May 27, 1865.
   "Friend Herndon:
    "Mr. Lincoln did not to my knowledge in any way change his religious ideas, opinions, or beliefs from the time he left Springfield to the day of his death. I do not know just what they were, never having heard him explain them in detail; but I am very sure he gave no outward indication of his mind having undergone any change in that regard while here.
    "Yours truly,
    "Jno. G. Nicolay."²⁷

the public mind, those who have represented him as believing in the popular theological views of the times may have misapprehended him, as experience shows to be quite common where no special effort has been made to attain critical accuracy on a subject of this nature. This is the more probable from the well-known fact, that Mr. Lincoln seldom communicated to any one his views on this subject; but be this as it may, I have no hesitation whatever in saying that whilst he held many opinions in common with the great mass of Christian believers, he did not believe in what are regarded as the orthodox or evangelical views of Christianity.

"On the innate depravity of man, the character and office of the great Head of the Church, the atonement, the infallibility of the written revelation, the performance of miracles, the nature and design of present and future rewards and punishments (as they are popularly called), and many other subjects he held opinions utterly at variance with what are usually taught in the Church. I should say that his expressed views on these and kindred topics were such as, in the estimation of most believers, would place him outside the Christian pale. Yet, to my mind, such was not the true position, since his principles and practices and the spirit of his whole life were of the very kind we universally agree to call Christian; and I think this conclusion is in no wise affected by the circumstance that he never attached himself to any religious society whatever.

"His religious views were eminently practical, and are summed up, as I think, in these two propositions: the Fatherhood of God, and the brotherhood of man. He fully believed in a superintending and overruling Providence that guides and controls the operations of the world, but maintained that law and order, and not their violation or suspension, are the appointed means by which this Providence is exercised.°

"I will not attempt any specification of either his belief or disbelief on various religious topics, as derived from conversations with him at different times during a considerable period; but as conveying a general view of his religious or theological opinions, will state the following facts. Some eight or ten years prior to his death, in conversing with him upon this subject, the writer took occasion to refer, in terms of approbation, to the sermons and writings generally of Dr. W. E. Channing; and, finding he was considerably interested in the statement I made of the opinions held by that author, I proposed to present him (Lincoln) a copy

---

°"A convention of preachers held, I think, at Philadelphia, passed a resolution asking him to recommend to Congress an amendment to the Constitution directly recognizing the existence of God. The first draft of his message prepared after this resolution was sent him did contain a paragraph calling the attention of Congress to the subject. When I assisted him in reading the proof he struck it out, remarking that he had not made up his mind as to its propriety."—MS. letter, John D. Defrees, December 4, 1866.[28]

of Channing's entire works, which I soon after did. Subsequently the contents of these volumes, together with the writings of Theodore Parker, furnished him, as he informed me, by his friend and law partner, William H. Herndon, became naturally the topics of conversation with us; and, though far from believing there was an entire harmony of views on his part with either of those authors, yet they were generally much admired and approved by him.

"No religious views with him seemed to find any favor except of the practical and rationalistic order; and if, from my recollections on this subject, I was called upon to designate an author whose views most nearly represented Mr. Lincoln's on this subject, I would say that author was Theodore Parker."[29]

The last witness to testify before this case is submitted to the reader is no less a person than Mrs. Lincoln herself. In a statement made at a time and under circumstances detailed in a subsequent chapter she said this: "Mr. Lincoln had no faith and no hope in the usual acceptation of those words. He never joined a Church; but still, as I believe, he was a religious man by nature. He first seemed to think about the subject when our boy Willie died, and then more than ever about the time he went to Gettysburg; but it was a kind of poetry in his nature, and he was never a technical Christian."[30]

No man had a stronger or firmer faith in Providence—God—than Mr. Lincoln, but the continued use by him late in life of the word God must not be interpreted to mean that he believed in a personal God. In 1854 he asked me to erase the word God from a speech which I had written and read to him for criticism because my language indicated a personal God, whereas he insisted no such personality ever existed.

My own testimony, however, in regard to Mr. Lincoln's religious views may perhaps invite discussion. The world has always insisted on making an orthodox Christian of him, and to analyze his sayings or sound his beliefs is but to break the idol. It only remains to say that, whether orthodox or not, he believed in God and immortality; and even if he questioned the existence of future eternal punishment he hoped to find a rest from trouble and a heaven beyond the grave. If at any time in his life he was sceptical of the divine origin of the Bible he ought not for that reason to be condemned; for he accepted the practical precepts of that great book as binding alike upon his head and his conscience. The benevolence of his impulses, the seriousness of his convictions, and the nobility of his character are evidences unimpeachable that his soul was ever filled with the exalted purity and sublime faith of natural religion.

CHAPTER XV.

The result of the campaign of 1858 wrought more disaster to Lincoln's finances than to his political prospects. The loss of over six months from his business, and the expenses of the canvass, made a severe drain on his personal income. He was anxious to get back to the law once more and earn a little ready money. A letter written about this time to his friend Norman B. Judd, Chairman of the Republican State Committee, will serve to throw some light on the situation he found himself in. "I have been on expenses so long, without earning anything," he says, "that I am absolutely without money now for even household expenses. Still, if you can put in $250 for me towards discharging the debt of the committee, I will allow it when you and I settle the private matter between us. This, with what I have already paid, with an outstanding note of mine, will exceed my subscription of $500. This, too, is exclusive of my ordinary expenses during the campaign, all of which, being added to my loss of time and business, bears prettily heavily upon one no better off than I am. But as I had the post of honor, it is not for me to be over-nice."[1] At the time this letter was written his property consisted of the house and lot on which he lived, a few law books and some household furniture. He owned a small tract of land in Iowa which yielded him nothing, and the annual income from his law practice did not exceed $3,000; yet the party's committee in Chicago were dunning their late standard-bearer, who, besides the chagrin of his defeat, his own expenses, and the sacrifice of his time, was asked to aid in meeting the general expenses of the campaign. At this day one is a little surprised that some of the generous and wealthy members of the party in Chicago or elsewhere did not come forward and volunteer their aid. But they did not, and whether Lincoln felt in his heart the injustice of this treatment or not, he went straight ahead in his own path and said nothing about it.

Political business being off his hands, he now conceived the idea of entering the lecture field. He began preparations in the usual way by noting down ideas on stray pieces of paper, which found a lodgment inside his hat, and finally brought forth in connected form a lecture on "Inventions."[2] He recounted the wonderful improvements in machinery, the arts, and sciences. Now and then he indulged in a humorous paragraph, and witticisms were freely sprinkled throughout the lecture. During the winter he delivered it at several towns in the central part of the State, but it was so commonplace, and met with such indifferent success, that he soon dropped it altogether.* The effort met with the disapproval of his friends, and he himself was filled with disgust. If his address in 1852, over the death of Clay, proved that he was no eulogist, then this last effort demonstrated that he was no lecturer. Invitations to deliver the lecture—prompted no doubt by the advertisement given him in the contest with Douglas—came in very freely; but beyond the three attempts named, he declined them all. "Press of business in the courts" afforded him a convenient excuse, and he retired from the field.†

During the fall of 1859 invitations to take part in the canvass came from over half-a-dozen States where elections were to be held. Douglas, fresh from the Senate, had gone to Ohio, and thither in September Lincoln, in response to the demands of party friends everywhere, followed.‡ He delivered telling and impres-

---

*"As we were going to Danville court I read to Lincoln a lecture by Bancroft on the wonderful progress of man, delivered in the preceding November. Sometime later he told us—Swett and me—that he had been thinking much on the subject and believed he would write a lecture on 'Man and His Progress.' Afterwards I read in a paper that he had come to either Bloomington or Clinton to lecture and no one turned out. The paper added, 'That doesn't look much like his being President.' I once joked him about it; he said good-naturedly, 'Don't, that plagues me.'"—Henry C. Whitney, letter, Aug. 27, 1867, MS.[3]

†   "Springfield, March 28, 1859.
"W. M. Morris, Esq.,
    "Dear Sir:—Your kind note inviting me to deliver a lecture at Galesburg is received. I regret to say I cannot do so now; I must stick to the courts awhile. I read a sort of lecture to three different audiences during the last month and this; but I did so under circumstances which made it a waste of no time whatever.
    "Yours very truly,
        "A. Lincoln."[4]

‡"He returned to the city two years after with a fame as wide as the continent, with the laurels of the Douglas contest on his brow, and the Presidency in his grasp. He returned, greeted with the thunder of cannon, the strains of martial music, and the joyous plaudits of thousands of citizens thronging the streets. He addressed a vast concourse on Fifth Street Market; was entertained in princely style at the Burnet House, and there received with courtesy the foremost citizens come to greet this rising star. With high hope and happy heart he left Cincinnati after a three days' sojourn. But a perverse fortune attended him and Cincinnati in their intercourse. Nine months after Mr. Lincoln left us, after he had been nominated for the Presidency, when he was tranquilly waiting in his cottage home at Springfield the verdict of the people, his last visit to Cincinnati and the good things he had had at the Burnet House were rudely brought to his memory by a bill presented to him from its proprietors. Before leaving the hotel he had applied to

sive speeches at Cincinnati and Columbus,° following Douglas at both places. He made such a favorable impression among his Ohio friends that, after a glorious Republican victory, the State committee asked the privilege of publishing his speeches, along with those of Douglas, to be used and distributed as a campaign document. This request he especially appreciated, because after some effort he had failed to induce any publisher in Springfield to undertake the enterprise,† thus proving anew that "a prophet is not without honor, save in his own country." In December he visited Kansas, speaking at Atchison, Troy, Leavenworth, and other towns near the border. His speeches there served to extend his reputation still further westward. Though his arguments were repetitions of the doctrine laid down in the contest with Douglas, yet they were new to the majority of his Kansas‡ hearers and were enthusiastically approved. By the close of the year he was back again in the dingy law office in Springfield.

---

the clerk for his bill; was told that it was paid, or words to that effect. This the committee had directed, but afterwards neglected its payment. The proprietors shrewdly surmised that a letter to the nominee for the Presidency would bring the money. The only significance in this incident is in the letter it brought from Mr. Lincoln, revealing his indignation at the seeming imputation against his honor, and his greater indignation at one item of the bill. 'As to wines, liquors, and cigars, we had none, absolutely none. These last may have been in Room 15 by order of committee, but I do not recollect them at all.'"—W. M. Dickson, "Harper's Magazine," June, 1884.[5]

° Douglas had written a long and carefully prepared article on "Popular Sovereignty in the Territories," which appeared for the first time in the September (1859) number of "Harper's Magazine."[6] It went back some distance into the history of the government, recounting the proceedings of the earliest Congresses, and sought to mark out more clearly than had heretofore been done "the dividing line between Federal and Local authority." In a speech at Columbus, O. Lincoln answered the "copy-right essay" categorically. After alluding to the difference of position between himself and Judge Douglas on the doctrine of Popular Sovereignty, he said: "Judge Douglas has had a good deal of trouble with Popular Sovereignty. His explanations, explanatory of explanations explained, are interminable. The most lengthy and, as I suppose, the most maturely considered of his long series of explanations is his great essay in 'Harper's Magazine.'"[7]

† A gentleman is still living, who at the time of the debate between Lincoln and Douglas, was a book publisher in Springfield. Lincoln had collected newspaper slips of all the speeches made during the debate, and proposed to him their publication in book form; but the man declined, fearing there would be no demand for such a book. Subsequently, when the speeches were gotten out in book form in Ohio, Mr. Lincoln procured a copy and gave it to his Springfield friend, writing on the fly-leaf, "Compliments of A. Lincoln."[8]

‡ How Mr. Lincoln stood on the questions of the hour, after his defeat by Douglas, is clearly shown in a letter written on the 14th of May, 1859, to a friend in Kansas, who had forwarded him an invitation to attend a Republican convention there. "You will probably adopt resolutions," he writes, "in the nature of a platform. I think the only danger will be the temptation to lower the Republican standard in order to gather recruits. In my judgment such a step would be a serious mistake, and open a gap through which more would pass out than pass in. And this would be the same whether the letting down should be in deference to Douglasism or to the Southern opposition element; either would surrender the object of the Republican organization—the preventing of the spread and nationalization of slavery. This object surrendered, the organization would go to pieces. I do not mean by this that no Southern man must be placed upon our national ticket for 1860. There are many men in the slave states for any one of whom I could cheerfully vote, to be either President or Vice-president, provided he would enable me to do so with safety to the Republican cause, without lowering the Republican standard. This is the indispensable condition of a union with us; it is idle to talk of any other. Any other would be as fruitless to the South as distasteful to the North, the whole ending

The opening of the year 1860 found Mr. Lincoln's name freely mentioned in connection with the Republican nomination for the Presidency. To be classed with Seward, Chase, McLean, and other celebrities was enough to stimulate any Illinois lawyer's pride; but in Mr. Lincoln's case, if it had any such effect, he was most artful in concealing it. Now and then some ardent friend, an editor, for example, would run his name up to the mast-head, but in all cases he discouraged the attempt. "In regard to the matter you spoke of," he answered one man who proposed his name, "I beg that you will not give it a further mention. Seriously, I do not think I am fit for the Presidency."[°]

The first effort in his behalf as a Presidential aspirant was the action taken by his friends at a meeting held in the State House early in 1860, in the rooms of O. M. Hatch, then Secretary of State. Besides Hatch there were present Norman B. Judd, chairman of the Republican State Committee, Ebenezer Peck, Jackson Grimshaw, and others of equal prominence in the party. "We all expressed a personal preference for Mr. Lincoln," relates one who was a participant in the meeting,[†] "as the Illinois candidate for the Presidency, and asked him if his name might be used at once in connection with the nomination and election. With his characteristic modesty he doubted whether he could get the nomination even if he wished it, and asked until the next morning to answer us whether his name might be announced. Late the next day he authorized us, if we thought proper to do so, to place him in the field."[11] To the question from Mr. Grimshaw whether, if the nomination for President could not be obtained, he would accept the post of Vice-president, he answered that he would not; that his name having been used for the office of President, he would not permit it to be used for any other office, however honorable it might be. This meeting was preliminary to the Decatur convention, and was also the first concerted action in his behalf on the part of his friends.

In the preceding October he came rushing into the office one morning, with the letter from New York City, inviting him to deliver a lecture there, and asked my advice and that of other friends as to the subject and character of his address. We all recommended a speech on the political situation. Remembering his poor success as a lecturer himself, he adopted our suggestions. He accepted the invitation of the New York committee, at the same time notifying them that his speech

---

in common defeat. Let a union be attempted on the basis of ignoring the slavery question, and magnifying other questions which the people are just now caring about, and it will result in gaining no single electoral vote in the South, and losing every one in the North."—MS. letter to M. W. Delahay.[9]
[°]Letter, March 5, 1859, to Thomas J. Pickett.[10]
[†]Jackson Grimshaw. Letter, Quincy, Ill., April 28, 1866, MS.

would deal entirely with political questions, and fixing a day late in February as the most convenient time. Meanwhile he spent the intervening time in careful preparation. He searched through the dusty volumes of congressional proceedings in the State library, and dug deeply into political history. He was painstaking and thorough in the study of his subject, but when at last he left for New York we had many misgivings—and he not a few himself—of his success in the great metropolis. What effect the unpretentious Western lawyer would have on the wealthy and fashionable society of the great city could only be conjectured. A description of the meeting at Cooper Institute, a list of the names of the prominent men and women present, or an account of Lincoln in the delivery of the address would be needless repetitions of well-known history.° It only remains to say that his speech was devoid of all rhetorical imagery, with a marked suppression of the pyrotechnics of stump oratory. It was constructed with a view to accuracy of statement, simplicity of language, and unity of thought. In some respects like a lawyer's brief, it was logical, temperate in tone, powerful—irresistibly driving conviction home to men's reasons and their souls. No former effort in the line of speech-making had cost Lincoln so much time and thought as this one. It is said by one of his biographers, that those afterwards engaged in getting out the speech as a campaign document were three weeks in verifying the statements and finding the historical records referred to and consulted by him.[12] This is probably a little over-stated as to time, but unquestionably the work of verification and reference, was in any event a labored and extended one.† The day following the Cooper Institute meeting, the leading New York dailies published the speech in full, and made favorable editorial mention of it and of the speaker as well. It was plain now that Lincoln had captured the metropolis. From New York he travelled to New England to visit his son Robert, who was attending college.[14] In answer to the many calls and invitations which showered on him, he spoke at various places in Connecticut, Rhode Island, and New Hampshire. In all these places he not only left deep impressions of his ability, but he convinced New

---

°On his return home Lincoln told me that for once in his life he was greatly abashed over his personal appearance. The new suit of clothes which he donned on his arrival in New York were ill-fitting garments, and showed the creases made while packed in the valise; and for a long time after he began his speech and before he became "warmed up" he imagined that the audience noticed the contrast between his Western clothes and the neat-fitting suits of Mr. Bryant and others who sat on the platform. The collar of his coat on the right side had an unpleasant way of flying up whenever he raised his arm to gesticulate. He imagined the audience noticed that also. After the meeting closed, the newspaper reporters called for slips of his speech. This amused him, because he had no idea what slips were, and besides, didn't suppose the newspapers cared to print his speech verbatim.

†Mr. Lincoln obtained most of the facts of his Cooper Institute speech from Eliott's "Debates on the Federal Constitution." There were six volumes, which he gave to me when he went to Washington in 1861.[13]

England of his intense earnestness in the great cause. The newspapers treated him with no little consideration. One paper° characterized his speech as one of "great fairness," delivered with "great apparent candor and wonderful interest. For the first half hour his opponents would agree with every word he uttered; and from that point he would lead them off little by little until it seemed as if he had got them all into his fold. He is far from prepossessing in personal appearance, and his voice is disagreeable; and yet he wins your attention from the start. He indulges in no flowers of rhetoric, no eloquent passages. . . . He displays more shrewdness, more knowledge of the masses of mankind than any public speaker we have heard since Long Jim Wilson left for California."[15]

Lincoln's return to Springfield after his dazzling success in the East was the signal for earnest congratulations on the part of his friends. Seward was the great man of the day, but Lincoln had demonstrated to the satisfaction of his friends that he was tall enough and strong enough to measure swords with the Auburn statesman. His triumph in New York and New England had shown that the idea of a house divided against itself induced as strong coöperation and hearty support in prevention of a great wrong in the East as the famous "irrepressible conflict" attracted warriors to Seward's standard in the Mississippi valley. It was apparent now to Lincoln that the Presidential nomination was within his reach. He began gradually to lose his interest in the law and to trim his political sails at the same time. His recent success had stimulated his self-confidence to unwonted proportions. He wrote to influential party workers everywhere. I know the idea prevails that Lincoln sat still in his chair in Springfield, and that one of those unlooked-for tides in human affairs came along and cast the nomination into his lap; but any man who has had experience in such things knows that great political prizes are not obtained in that way. The truth is, Lincoln was as vigilant as he was ambitious, and there is no denying the fact that he understood the situation perfectly from the start. In the management of his own interests he was obliged to rely almost entirely on his own resources. He had no money with which to maintain a political bureau, and he lacked any kind of personal organization whatever. Seward had all these things, and, behind them all, a brilliant record in the United States Senate with which to dazzle his followers. But with all his prestige and experience the latter was no more adroit and no more untiring in pursuit of his ambition than the man who had just delivered the Cooper Institute speech. A letter written by Lincoln about this time to a friend in Kansas serves to illustrate his methods, and measures the extent of his ambition. The letter is dated March 10, and is now in

---

°Manchester *Mirror*.

my possession. For obvious reasons I withhold the friend's name: "As to your kind wishes for myself," writes Lincoln, "allow me to say I cannot enter the ring on the money basis—first, because in the main it is wrong; and secondly, I have not and cannot get the money. I say in the main the use of money is wrong; but for certain objects in a political contest the use of some is both right and indispensable. With me, as with yourself, this long struggle has been one of great pecuniary loss. I now distinctly say this: If you shall be appointed a delegate to Chicago I will furnish one hundred dollars to bear the expenses of the trip."[16] There is enough in this letter to show that Lincoln was not only determined in his political ambition, but intensely practical as well. His eye was constantly fastened on Seward, who had already freely exercised the rights of leadership in the party. All other competitors he dropped out of the problem. In the middle of April he again writes his Kansas friend: "Reaching home last night I found yours of the 7th. You know I was recently in New England. Some of the acquaintances while there write me since the election that the close vote in Connecticut and the quasi-defeat in Rhode Island are a drawback upon the prospects of Governor Seward; and Trumbull writes Dubois to the same effect. Do not mention this as coming from me. Both these States are safe enough in the fall."[17] But, while Seward may have lost ground near his home, he was acquiring strength in the West. He had invaded the very territory Lincoln was intending to retain by virtue of his course in the contest with Douglas. Lincoln's friend in Kansas, instead of securing that delegation for him, had suffered the Seward men to outgeneral him, and the prospects were by no means flattering. "I see by the dispatches," writes Lincoln, in a burst of surprise, "that, since you wrote, Kansas has appointed delegates and instructed for Seward. Don't stir them up to anger, but come along to the convention and I will do as I said about expenses."[18] Whether the friend ever accepted Lincoln's generous offer I do not know,* but it may not be without interest to state that within ten days after the latter's inauguration he appointed him to a Federal office with comfortable salary attached, and even asked for his preferences as to other contemplated appointments in his own State.† In

---

*This case illustrates quite forcibly Lincoln's weakness in dealing with individuals. This man[19] I know had written Lincoln, promising to bring the Kansas delegation to Chicago for him if he would only pay his expenses. Lincoln was weak enough to make the promise, and yet such was his faith in the man that he appointed him to an important judicial position and gave him great prominence in other ways. What President or candidate for President would dare do such a thing now?
†The following is in my possession:

"Executive Mansion, March 13, 1861.

"——————, Esq.
"My Dear Sir:
    "You will start for Kansas before I see you again; and when I saw you a moment this morning I forgot

the rapid, stirring scenes that crowd upon each other from this time forward the individuality of Lincoln is easily lost sight of. He was so thoroughly interwoven in the issues before the people of Illinois that he had become a part of them. Among his colleagues at the bar he was no longer looked upon as the Circuit-Court lawyer of earlier days. To them it seemed as if the nation were about to lay its claim upon him. His tall form enlarged, until, to use a figurative expression, he could no longer pass through the door of our dingy office. Reference has already been made to the envy of his rivals at the bar, and the jealousy of his political contemporaries. Very few indeed were free from the degrading passion; but it made no difference in Lincoln's treatment of them. He was as generous and deferred to them as much as ever. The first public movement by the Illinois people in his interest was the action of the State convention, which met at Decatur on the 9th and 10th of May. It was at this convention that Lincoln's friend and cousin, John Hanks, brought in the two historic rails which both had made in the Sangamon bottom in 1830, and which served the double purpose of electrifying the Illinois people and kindling the fire of enthusiasm that was destined to sweep over the nation. In the words of an ardent Lincoln delegate, "These rails were to represent the issue in the coming contest between labor free and labor slave; between democracy and aristocracy. Little did I think," continues our jubilant and effusive friend, "of the mighty consequences of this little incident; little did I think that the tall, and angular, and bony rail-splitter who stood in girlish diffidence bowing with awkward grace would fill the chair once filled by Washington, and that his name would echo in chants of praise along the corridor of all coming time."[21] A week later the hosts were gathered for the great convention in Chicago. David Davis had rented rooms in the Tremont House and opened up "Lincoln's headquarters." I was not a delegate, but belonged to the contingent which had Lincoln's interests in charge. Judge Logan was the Springfield delegate, and to him Lincoln had given a letter authorizing the withdrawal of his name whenever his friends deemed such action necessary or proper. Davis was the active man, and had the business management in charge. If any negotiations were made, he made them. The convention was held in a monster building called the Wigwam. No one who has ever attempted a description of it has overdrawn its enthusiasm and exciting scenes. Amid all the din and confusion, the curbstone contentions, the promiscuous wrangling of delegates, the deafening roar of the assembled hosts, the contest narrowed down to a neck-and-neck race

to ask you about some of the Kansas appointments, which I intended to do. If you care much about them you can write, as I think I shall not make the appointments just yet.

    "Yours in haste,
      "A. Lincoln."[20]

between the brilliant statesman of Auburn and the less pretentious, but manly rail-splitter from the Sangamon bottoms. With the proceedings of the convention the world is already well familiar. On the first ballot Seward led, but was closely followed by Lincoln; on the second Lincoln gained amazingly; on the third the race was an even one until the dramatic change by Carter, of Ohio, when Lincoln, swinging loose, swept grandly to the front. The cannon planted on the roof of the Wigwam belched forth a boom across the Illinois prairies. The sound was taken up and reverberated from Maine to California. With the nomination of Hannibal Hamlin, of Maine, the convention adjourned. The delegates—victorious and vanquished alike—turned their steps homeward, and the great campaign of 1860 had begun. The day before the nomination the editor of the Springfield *Journal* arrived in Chicago with a copy of the Missouri *Democrat,* in which Lincoln had marked three passages referring to Seward's position on the slavery question. On the margin of the paper he had written in pencil, "I agree with Seward in his 'Irrepressible Conflict,' but I do not endorse his 'Higher Law' doctrine." Then he added in words underscored, "Make no contracts that will bind me."[22] This paper was brought into the room where Davis, Judd, Logan, and I were gathered, and was read to us. But Lincoln was down in Springfield, some distance away from Chicago, and could therefore not appreciate the gravity of the situation; at least so Davis argued, and, viewing it in that light, the latter went ahead with his negotiations. What the consequences of these deals were will appear later on. The news of his nomination found Lincoln at Springfield in the office of the *Journal.* Naturally enough he was nervous, restless, and laboring under more or less suppressed excitement. He had been tossing ball—a pastime frequently indulged in by the lawyers of that day, and had played a few games of billiards to keep down, as another has expressed it, "the unnatural excitement that threatened to possess him."[23] When the telegram containing the result of the last ballot came in, although apparently calm and undisturbed, a close observer could have detected in the compressed lip and serious countenance evidences of deep and unusual emotion. As the balloting progressed he had gone to the office of the *Journal,* and was sitting in a large arm-chair there when the news of his nomination came. What a line of scenes, stretching from the barren glade in Kentucky to the jubilant and enthusiastic throng in the Wigwam at Chicago, must have broken in upon his vision as he hastened from the newspaper office to "tell a little woman down the street the news!"[24] In the evening his friends and neighbors called to congratulate him. He thanked them feelingly and shook them each by the hand. A day later the committee from the convention, with George Ashmun, of Massachusetts, at its head, called, and delivered formal notice of his nomination. This meeting took place at his house. His response was couched in polite and dignified language, and many of the committee, who now met him for the first time, departed with an improved impression of the new standard-bearer. A few days later he wrote his official letter of acceptance, in which he warmly endorsed the resolutions of the convention. His actions and utterances so far had begun to dissipate the erroneous notion prevalent in some of the more remote Eastern States, that he was more of a backwoods boor than a gentleman; but with the arrival of the campaign in dead earnest, people paid less attention to the candidates and more to the great issues at stake. Briefly stated, the Republican platform was a declaration that "the new dogma, that the Constitution carries slavery into all the Territories, is a dangerous political heresy, revolutionary in tendency and subversive of the peace and harmony of the country; that the normal condition of all the Territories is that of freedom; that neither Congress, the territorial legislature, nor any individual can give legal existence to slavery in any territory; that the opening of the slave trade would be a crime against humanity."[25] Resolutions favoring a homestead law, river and harbor improvements, and the Pacific railroad were also included in the platform. With these the Republicans, as a lawyer would say, went to the country. The campaign which followed was one with few parallels in American history. There was not only the customary exultation and enthusiasm over candidates, but there was patient listening and hard thinking among the masses. The slavery question, it was felt, must soon be decided. Threats of disunion were the texts of many a campaign speech in the South: in fact, as has since been shown, a deep laid conspiracy to overthrow the Union was then forming, and was only awaiting the election of a Republican President to show its hideous head. The Democratic party was struggling under the demoralizing effects of a split, in which even the Buchanan administration had taken sides. Douglas, the nominee of one wing, in his desperation had entered into the canvass himself, making speeches with all the power and eloquence at his command. The Republicans, cheered over the prospect, had joined hands with the Abolitionists, and both were marching to victory under the inspiration of Lincoln's sentiment, that "the further spread of slavery should be arrested, and it should be placed where the public mind shall rest in the belief of its ultimate extinction."[26]

As the canvass advanced and waxed warm I tendered my services and made a number of speeches in the central part of the State. I remember, in the midst of a speech at Petersburg, and just as I was approaching an oratorical climax, a man out of breath came rushing up to me and thrust a message into my hand. I was somewhat frustrated and greatly alarmed, fearing it might contain news of some accident in my family; but great was my relief when I read it, which I did aloud. It was a message from Lincoln, telling me to be of good cheer, that Ohio, Pennsylvania, and Indiana had gone Republican.°

These were then October States, and this was the first gun for the great cause. It created so much demonstration, such a burst of enthusiasm and confusion, that the crowd forgot they had any speaker; they ran yelling and hurrahing out of the hall, and I never succeeded in finishing the speech.

As soon as officially notified of his nomination† Mr. Lincoln moved his head-quarters from our office to a room in the State House building, and there, with his secretary, John G. Nicolay, he spent the busy and exciting days of his campaign. Of course he attended to no law business, but still he loved to come to our office of evenings, and spend an hour with a few choice friends in a friendly privacy which was denied him at his public quarters. These were among the last meetings we had with Lincoln as our friend and fellow at the bar; and they are also the most delightful recollections any of us have retained of him.‡ At last the

---

°The handwriting of the note was a little tremulous, showing that Lincoln was excited and nervous when he wrote it. Following is a copy of the original MS.:

"Springfield, Ill., October 10, 1860.
"Dear William: I cannot give you details, but it is entirely certain that Pennsylvania and Indiana have gone Republican very largely. Pennsylvania 25,000, and Indiana 5000 to 10,000. Ohio of course is safe.
"Yours as ever,
"A. Lincoln."[27]

†Following is Lincoln's letter of acceptance:

"Springfield, Ill., June 23, 1860.
"Sir: I accept the nomination tendered me by the convention over which you presided, of which I am formally apprised in a letter of yourself and others, acting as a committee of the convention for that purpose. The declaration of principles which accompanies your letter meets my approval, and it shall be my care not to violate it or disregard it in any part. Imploring the assistance of Divine Providence, and with due regard to the views and feelings of all who were represented in the convention, to the rights of all the states and territories and people of the nation, to the inviolability of the Constitution, and the perpetual union, prosperity, and harmony of all, I am most happy to coöperate for the practical success of the principles declared by the convention.
"Your obliged friend and fellow-citizen,
"Hon. George Ashmun."   "Abraham Lincoln."[28]

‡One of what Lincoln regarded as the remarkable features of his canvass for President was the attitude of some of his neighbors in Springfield. A poll of the voters had been made in a little book and given to him. On running over the names he found that the greater part of the clergy of the city—in fact all but three—were against him. This depressed him somewhat, and he called in Dr. Newton Bateman, who as Superintendent of Public Instruction occupied the room adjoining his own in the State House, and whom he habitually addressed as "Mr. Schoolmaster." He commented bitterly on the attitude of the preachers and many of their followers, who, pretending to be believers in the Bible and God-fearing Christians, yet by their votes demonstrated that they cared not whether slavery was voted up or down. "God cares and humanity cares," he reflected, "and if they do not they surely have not read their Bible aright."[29]

turmoil and excitement and fatigue of the campaign were over: the enthusiastic political workers threw aside their campaign uniforms, the boys blew out their torches, and the voter approached the polls with his ballot. On the morning of election day I stepped in to see Mr. Lincoln, and was surprised to learn that he did not intend to cast his vote. I knew of course that he did so because of a feeling that the candidate for a Presidential office ought not to vote for his own electors; but when I suggested the plan of cutting off the Presidential electors and voting for the State officers, he was struck with the idea, and at last consented. His appearance at the polls, accompanied by Ward Lamon, the lamented young Ellsworth, and myself, was the occasion of no little surprise because of the general impression which prevailed that he did not intend to vote. The crowd around the polls opened a gap as the distinguished voter approached, and some even removed their hats as he deposited his ticket and announced in a subdued voice his name, "Abraham Lincoln."[30]

The election was held on the 6th of November. The result showed a popular vote of 1,857,610 for Lincoln; 1,291,574 for Douglas; 850,022 for Breckenridge; and 646,124 for Bell. In the electoral college Lincoln received 180 votes, Breckenridge 72, Bell 39, and Douglas 12.° Mr. Lincoln having now been elected, there remained, before taking up the reins of government, the details of his departure from Springfield, and the selection of a cabinet.

°Lincoln electors were chosen in seventeen of the free States, as follows: Maine, New Hampshire, Massachusetts, Rhode Island, Connecticut, Vermont, New York, Pennsylvania, Ohio, Indiana, Illinois, Michigan, Wisconsin, Minnesota, Iowa, California, Oregon; and in one State,—New Jersey,—owing to a fusion between Democrats, Lincoln secured four and Douglas three of the electors. Alabama, Arkansas, Delaware, Florida, Georgia, Louisiana, Maryland, Mississippi, North, and South Carolina, and Texas went for Breckenridge; Kentucky, Tennessee, and Virginia for Bell; while Douglas secured only one entire State—Missouri.

CHAPTER XVI.

The election over, Mr. Lincoln scarcely had time enough to take a breath until another campaign and one equally trying, so far as a test of his constitution and nerves was concerned, as the one through which he had just passed, opened up before him. I refer to the siege of the cabinet-makers and office-seekers. It proved to be a severe and protracted strain and one from which there seemed to be no relief, as the President-elect of this renowned democratic Government is by custom and precedent expected to meet and listen to everybody who calls to see him. "Individuals, deputations, and delegations," says one of Mr. Lincoln's biographers, "from all quarters pressed in upon him in a manner that might have killed a man of less robust constitution. The hotels of Springfield were filled with gentlemen who came with light baggage and heavy schemes. The party had never been in office. A clean sweep of the 'ins' was expected, and all the 'outs' were patriotically anxious to take the vacant places. It was a party that had never fed; and it was voraciously hungry. Mr. Lincoln and Artemus Ward saw a great deal of fun in it; and in all human probability it was the fun alone that enabled Mr. Lincoln to bear it."[1]

His own election of course disposed of any claims Illinois might have had to any further representation in the cabinet, but it afforded Mr. Lincoln no relief from the argumentative interviews and pressing claims of the endless list of ambitious statesmen in the thirty-two other states, who swarmed into Springfield from every point of the compass. He told each one of them a story, and even if he failed to put their names on his slate they went away without knowing that fact, and never forgot the visit.° He had a way of pretending to assure his visitor that in

---

° A newspaper correspondent who had been sent down from Chicago to "write up" Mr. Lincoln soon after his nomination, was kind enough several years ago to furnish me with an account of his visit. As some of

the choice of his advisers he was "free to act as his judgment dictated," although David Davis, acting as his manager at the Chicago convention, had negotiated with the Indiana and Pennsylvania delegations, and assigned places in the cabinet to Simon Cameron and Caleb Smith, besides making other "arrangements" which Mr. Lincoln was expected to ratify. Of this he was undoubtedly aware, although in answer to a letter from Joshua R. Giddings, of Ohio, congratulating him on his nomination, he said,° "It is indeed most grateful to my feelings that the responsible position assigned me comes without conditions."[3] Out of regard to the dignity of the exalted station he was about to occupy, he was not as free in discussing the matter of his probable appointments with some of his personal friends as they had believed he would be. In one or two instances, I remember, the latter were offended at his seeming disregard of the claims of old friendship. My advice was not asked for on such grave subjects, nor had I any right or reason to believe it would be; hence I never felt slighted or offended. On some occasions in our office, when Mr. Lincoln had come across from the State House for a rest or

---

his reminiscences are more or less interesting, I take the liberty of inserting a portion of his letter. "A what-not in the corner of the room," he relates, "was laden with various kinds of shells. Taking one in my hand, I said, 'This, I suppose, is called a Trocus by the geologist or naturalist.' Mr. Lincoln paused a moment as if reflecting and then replied, 'I do not know, for I never studied either geology or natural history.' I then took to examining the few pictures that hung on the walls, and was paying more than ordinary attention to one that hung above the sofa. He was immediately at my left and pointing to it said, 'That picture gives a very fair representation of my homely face.' . . . The time for my departure nearing, I made the usual apologies and started to go. 'You cannot get out of the town before a quarter past eleven,' remonstrated Mr. Lincoln, 'and you may as well stay a little longer.' Under pretence of some unfinished matters down town, however, I very reluctantly withdrew from the mansion. 'Well,' said Mr. Lincoln, as we passed into the hall, 'suppose you come over to the State House before you start for Chicago.' After a moment's deliberation I promised to do so. Mr. Lincoln, following without his hat, and continuing the conversation, shook hands across the gate, saying, 'Now, come over.' I wended my way to my hotel, and after a brief period was in his office at the State House. Resuming conversation, he said, 'If the man comes with the key before you go, I want to give you a book.' I certainly hoped the man *would* come with the key. Some conversation had taken place at the house on which his book treated,—but I had forgotten this,—and soon Mr. Lincoln absented himself for perhaps two minutes and returned with a copy of the debates between himself and Judge Douglas. He placed the book on his knee, as he sat back on two legs of his chair, and wrote on the fly-leaf, 'J. S. Bliss, from A. Lincoln.' Besides this he marked a complete paragraph near the middle of the book. While sitting in the position described little Willie, his son, came in and begged his father for twenty-five cents. 'My son,' said the father, 'what do you want with twenty-five cents?' 'I want it to buy candy with,' cried the boy. 'I cannot give you twenty-five cents, my son, but will give you five cents,' at the same time putting his thumb and finger into his vest pocket and taking therefrom five cents in silver, which he placed upon the desk before the boy. But this did not reach Willie's expectations; he scorned the pile, and turning away clambered down-stairs and through the spacious halls of the Capitol, leaving behind him his five cents and a distinct reverberation of sound. Mr. Lincoln turned to me and said, 'He will be back after that in a few minutes.' 'Why do you think so?' said I. 'Because, as soon as he finds I will give him no more he will come and get it.' After the matter had been nearly forgotten and conversation had turned in an entirely different channel, Willie came cautiously in behind my chair and that of his father, picked up the specie, and went away without saying a word."—J. S. Bliss, letter, Jan. 29, 1867, MS.[2]

°Letter, May 21st, 1860, MS.

a chat with me, he would relate now and then some circumstance—generally an amusing one—connected with the settlement of the cabinet problem, but it was said in such a way that one would not have felt free to interrogate him about his plans. Soon after his election I received from my friend Joseph Medill, of Chicago, a letter which argued strongly against the appointment of Simon Cameron to a place in the cabinet, and which the writer desired I should bring to Mr. Lincoln's attention. I awaited a favorable opportunity, and one evening when we were alone in our office I gave it to him. It was an eloquent protest against the appointment of a corrupt and debased man, and coming from the source it did—the writer being one of Lincoln's best newspaper supporters—made a deep impression on him. Lincoln read it over several times, but refrained from expressing any opinion. He did say however that he felt himself under no promise or obligation to appoint anyone; that if his friends made any agreements for him they did so over his expressed direction and without his knowledge. At another time he said that he wanted to give the South, by way of placation, a place in his cabinet; that a fair division of the country entitled the Southern States to a reasonable representation there, and if not interfered with he would make such a distribution as would satisfy all persons interested. He named three persons who would be acceptable to him. They were Botts, of Virginia; Stephens, of Georgia; and Maynard, of Tennessee. He apprehended no such grave danger to the Union as the mass of people supposed would result from Southern threats, and said he could not in his heart believe that the South designed the overthrow of the Government. This is the extent of my conversation about the cabinet. Thurlow Weed, the veteran in journalism and politics, came out from New York and spent several days with Lincoln. He was not only the representative of Senator Seward, but rendered the President-elect signal service in the formation of his cabinet. In his autobiography Mr. Weed relates numerous incidents of this visit. He was one day opposing the claims of Montgomery Blair, who aspired to a cabinet appointment, when Mr. Lincoln inquired of Weed whom he would recommend. "Henry Winter Davis," was the response. "David Davis, I see, has been posting you up on this question," retorted Lincoln. "He has Davis on the brain. I think Maryland must be a good State to move from." The President then told a story of a witness in court in a neighboring county, who on being asked his age replied, "Sixty." Being satisfied he was much older the question was repeated, and on receiving the same answer, the court admonished the witness, saying, "The court knows you to be much older than sixty." "Oh, I understand now," was the rejoinder; "you're thinking of those ten years I spent on the eastern shore of Maryland; that was so much time lost and don't count."[4]

Before Mr. Lincoln's departure from Springfield, people who knew him personally were frequently asked what sort of man he was. I received many letters, generally from the Eastern States, showing that much doubt still existed in the minds of the people whether he would prove equal to the great task that lay in store for him. Among others who wrote me on the subject was the Hon. Henry Wilson, late Vice-president of the United States, whom I had met during my visit to Washington in the spring of 1858. Two years after Mr. Lincoln's death, Mr. Wilson wrote me as follows: "I have just finished reading your letter dated December 21, 1860, in answer to a letter of mine asking you to give me your opinion of the President just elected. In this letter to me you say of Mr. Lincoln what more than four years of observation confirmed. After stating that you had been his law partner for over eighteen years and his most intimate and bosom friend all that time you say, 'I know him better than he does himself. I know this seems a little strong, but I risk the assertion. Lincoln is a man of heart—aye, as gentle as a woman's and as tender—but he has a will strong as iron. He therefore loves all mankind, hates slavery and every form of despotism. Put these together—love for the slave, and a determination, a will, that justice, strong and unyielding, shall be done when he has the right to act, and you can form your own conclusion. Lincoln will fail here, namely, if a question of political economy—if any question comes up which is doubtful, questionable, which no man can demonstrate, then his friends can rule him; but when on justice, right, liberty, the Government, the Constitution, and the Union, then you may all stand aside: he will rule then, and no man can move him—no set of men can do it. There is no fail here. This is Lincoln, and you mark my prediction. You and I must keep the people right; God will keep Lincoln right.' These words of yours made a deep impression upon my mind, and I came to love and trust him even before I saw him. After an acquaintance of more than four years I found that your idea of him was in all respects correct—that he was the loving, tender, firm, and just man you represented him to be; while upon some questions in which moral elements did not so clearly enter he was perhaps too easily influenced by others. Mr. Lincoln was a genuine democrat in feelings, sentiments, and actions. How patiently and considerately he listened amid the terrible pressure of public affairs to the people who thronged his ante-room! I remember calling upon him one day during the war on pressing business. The ante-room was crowded with men and women seeking admission. He seemed oppressed, careworn, and weary. I said to him, 'Mr. President, you are too exhausted to see this throng waiting to see you; you will wear yourself out and ought not see these people to-day.' He replied, with one of those smiles in which sadness seemed to mingle, 'They don't want much; they get but little, and I must see them.' During the war his heart was oppressed and his life burdened with the conflict between the tenderness of his nature and what seemed to be the imperative demands of duty. In the darkest hours of the conflict desertions from the army were frequent, and army officers urgently pressed the execution of the sentences of the law; but it was with the greatest effort that he would bring himself to consent to the execution of the judgment of the military tribunals. I remember calling early one sabbath morning with a wounded Irish officer, who came to Washington to say that a soldier who had been sentenced to be shot in a day or two for desertion had fought gallantly by his side in battle. I told Mr. Lincoln we had come to ask him to pardon the poor soldier. After a few moments' reflection he said, 'My officers tell me the good of the service demands the enforcement of the law; but it makes my heart ache to have the poor fellows shot. I will pardon this soldier, and then you will all join in blaming me for it. You censure me for granting pardons, and yet you all ask me to do so.' I say again, no man had a more loving and tender nature than Mr. Lincoln."[5]

Before departing for Washington Mr. Lincoln went to Chicago° for a few days' stay, and there by previous arrangement met his old friend, Joshua F. Speed. Both were accompanied by their wives, and while the latter were out shopping the two husbands repaired to Speed's room at the hotel. "For an hour or more," relates Speed, "we lived over again the scenes of other days. Finally Lincoln threw himself on the bed, and fixing his eyes on a spot in the ceiling asked me this question, 'Speed, what is your pecuniary condition? are you rich or poor?' I answered, addressing him by his new title, 'Mr. President, I think I can anticipate what you are going to say. I'll speak candidly to you on the subject. My pecuniary condition is satisfactory to me now; you would perhaps call it good. I do not think you have within your gift any office I could afford to take.' Mr. Lincoln then proposed to make Guthrie, of Kentucky, Secretary of War, but did not want to write to him—asked me to feel of him. I did as requested, but the Kentucky statesman declined on the ground of his advanced age, and consequent physical inability to fill the position. He gave substantial assurance of his loyal sentiments, however, and insisted that the Union should be preserved at all hazards."[6]

Late in January Mr. Lincoln informed me that he was ready to begin the preparation of his inaugural address. He had, aside from his law books and the few gilded volumes that ornamented the centre-table in his parlor at home, com-

---

°A lady called one day at the hotel where the Lincolns were stopping in Chicago to take Mrs. Lincoln out for a promenade or a drive. She was met in the parlor by Mr. Lincoln, who, after a hurried trip upstairs to ascertain the cause of the delay in his wife's appearance, returned with the report that "She will be down as soon as she has all her trotting harness on."

paratively no library. He never seemed to care to own or collect books. On the other hand I had a very respectable collection, and was adding to it every day. To my library Lincoln very frequently had access. When, therefore, he began on his inaugural speech he told me what works he intended to consult. I looked for a long list, but when he went over it I was greatly surprised. He asked me to furnish him with Henry Clay's great speech delivered in 1850; Andrew Jackson's proclamation against Nullification; and a copy of the Constitution. He afterwards called for Webster's reply to Hayne, a speech which he read when he lived at New Salem, and which he always regarded as the grandest specimen of American oratory.[7] With these few "volumes," and no further sources of reference, he locked himself up in a room upstairs over a store across the street from the State House, and there, cut off from all communication and intrusion, he prepared the address. Though composed amid the unromantic surroundings of a dingy, dusty, and neglected back room, the speech has become a memorable document. Posterity will assign to it a high rank among historical utterances; and it will ever bear comparison with the efforts of Washington, Jefferson, Adams, or any that preceded its delivery from the steps of the national Capitol.

After Mr. Lincoln's rise to national prominence, and especially since his death, I have often been asked if I did not write this or that paper for him; if I did not prepare or help prepare some of his speeches. I know that other and abler friends of Lincoln have been asked the same question.° To people who made such enquiries I always responded, "You don't understand Mr. Lincoln. No man ever asked less aid than he; his confidence in his own ability to meet the requirements of every hour was so marked that his friends never thought of tendering their aid, and therefore no one could share his responsibilities. I never wrote a line for him; he never asked me to. I was never conscious of having exerted any influence over him. He often called out my views on some philosophical question, simply because I was a fond student of philosophy, and conceding that I had given the subject more attention than he; he often asked as to the use of a word or the turn of a sentence, but if I volunteered to recommend or even suggest a change of language which involved a change of sentiment I found him the most inflexible man I have ever seen."

One more duty—an act of filial devotion—remained to be done before Abraham Lincoln could announce his readiness to depart for the city of Washington— a place from which it was unfortunately decreed he should never return. In the

---

° "I know it was the general impression in Washington that I knew all about Lincoln's plans and ideas, but the truth is, I knew nothing. He never confided to me anything of his purposes."—David Davis, statement, September 20, 1866.[8]

first week of February he slipped quietly away from Springfield and rode to Farmington in Coles County, where his aged step-mother was still living. Here, in the little country village, he met also the surviving members of the Hanks and Johnston families. He visited the grave of his father, old Thomas Lincoln, which had been unmarked and neglected for almost a decade, and left directions that a suitable stone should be placed there to mark the spot. Retracing his steps in the direction of Springfield he stopped over-night in the town of Charleston, where he made a brief address, recalling many of his boyhood exploits, in the public hall. In the audience were many persons who had known him first as the stalwart young ox-driver when his father's family drove into Illinois from southern Indiana. One man had brought with him a horse which the President-elect, in the earlier days of his law practice, had recovered for him in a replevin suit; another one was able to recite from personal recollection the thrilling details of the famous wrestling match between Lincoln the flatboatman in 1830 and Daniel Needham; and all had some reminiscence of his early manhood to relate. The separation from his step-mother was particularly touching.° The parting, when the good old woman, with tears streaming down her cheeks, gave him a mother's benediction, expressing the fear that his life might be taken by his enemies, will never be forgotten by those who witnessed it. Deeply impressed by this farewell scene Mr. Lincoln reluctantly withdrew from the circle of warm friends who crowded around him, and, filled with gloomy forebodings of the future, returned to Springfield.[11] The great questions of state having been pretty well settled in his own mind, and a few days yet remaining before his final departure, his neighbors and old friends called to take leave of him and pay their "best respects." Many of these callers were from New Salem, where he had made his start in life, and each one had some pleasant or amusing incident of earlier days to call up when they met. Hannah Armstrong, who had "foxed" his trowsers with buckskin in the days when he served as surveyor

---

°Lincoln's love for his second mother was a most filial and affectionate one. His letters show that he regarded the relation truly as that of mother and son. November 4, 1851, he writes her after the death of his father:

"Dear Mother:

"Chapman tells me he wants you to go and live with him. If I were you I would try it awhile. If you get tired of it (as I think you will not) you can return to your own home. Chapman feels very kindly to you; and I have no doubt he will make your situation very pleasant.

"Sincerely your son,

"A. Lincoln."[9]

On the 9th of the same month he writes his step-brother John D. Johnston: "If the land can be sold so that I can get three hundred dollars to put to interest for mother I will not object if she does not. But before I will make a deed the money must be had, or secured beyond all doubt at ten per cent."[10]

under John Calhoun, and whose son Lincoln had afterwards acquitted in the trial for murder at Beardstown, gave positive evidence of the interest she took in his continued rise in the world. She bade him good-bye, but was filled with a presentiment that she would never see him alive again. "Hannah," he said, jovially, "if they do kill me I shall never die again."[12] Isaac Cogsdale, another New Salem pioneer, came, and to him Lincoln again admitted his love for the unfortunate Anne Rutledge. Cogsdale afterwards told me of this interview. It occurred late in the afternoon. Mr. Nicolay, the secretary, had gone home, and the throng of visitors had ceased for the day. Lincoln asked about all the early families of New Salem, calling up the peculiarities of each as he went over the list. Of the Rutledges he said: "I have loved the name of Rutledge to this day. I have kept my mind on their movements ever since." Of Anne he spoke with some feeling: "I loved her dearly. She was a handsome girl, would have made a good, loving wife; she was natural, and quite intellectual, though not highly educated. I did honestly and truly love the girl, and think often of her now."[13]

Early in February the last item of preparation for the journey to Washington had been made. Mr. Lincoln had disposed of his household goods and furniture to a neighbor, had rented his house; and as these constituted all the property he owned in Illinois there was no further occasion for concern on that score. In the afternoon of his last day in Springfield he came down to our office to examine some papers and confer with me about certain legal matters in which he still felt some interest. On several previous occasions he had told me he was coming over to the office "to have a long talk with me," as he expressed it. We ran over the books and arranged for the completion of all unsettled and unfinished matters. In some cases he had certain requests to make—certain lines of procedure he wished me to observe. After these things were all disposed of he crossed to the opposite side of the room and threw himself down on the old office sofa, which, after many years of service, had been moved against the wall for support. He lay for some moments, his face towards the ceiling, without either of us speaking. Presently he inquired, "Billy,"—he always called me by that name,—"how long have we been together?" "Over sixteen years," I answered. "We've never had a cross word during all that time, have we?" to which I returned a vehement, "No, indeed we have not." He then recalled some incidents of his early practice and took great pleasure in delineating the ludicrous features of many a lawsuit on the circuit. It was at this last interview in Springfield that he told me of the efforts that had been made by other lawyers to supplant me in the partnership with him. He insisted that such men were weak creatures, who, to use his own language, "hoped to secure a law practice by hanging to his coat-tail." I never saw him in a

290 I HERNDON'S LINCOLN

more cheerful mood. He gathered a bundle of books and papers he wished to take with him and started to go; but before leaving he made the strange request that the sign-board which swung on its rusty hinges at the foot of the stairway should remain. "Let it hang there undisturbed,"* he said, with a significant lowering of his voice. "Give our clients to understand that the election of a President makes no change in the firm of Lincoln and Herndon. If I live I'm coming back some time, and then we'll go right on practising law as if nothing had ever happened." He lingered for a moment as if to take a last look at the old quarters, and then passed through the door into the narrow hallway. I accompanied him downstairs. On the way he spoke of the unpleasant features surrounding the Presidential office. "I am sick of office-holding already," he complained, "and I shudder when I think of the tasks that are still ahead." He said the sorrow of parting from his old associations was deeper than most persons would imagine, but it was more marked in his case because of the feeling which had become irrepressible that he would never return alive. I argued against the thought, characterizing it as an illusory notion not in harmony or keeping with the popular ideal of a President. "But it is in keeping with my philosophy," was his quick retort. Our conversation was frequently broken in upon by the interruptions of passers-by, who, each in succession, seemed desirous of claiming his attention. At length he broke away from them all. Grasping my hand warmly and with a fervent "Good-bye," he disappeared down the street, and never came back to the office again. On the morning following this last interview, the 11th day of February, the Presidential party repaired to the railway station, where the train which was to convey them to Washington awaited the ceremony of departure. The intention was to stop at many of the principal cities along the route, and plenty of time had been allotted for the purpose. Mr. Lincoln had told me that a man named Wood had been recommended to him by Mr. Seward, and he had been placed in charge of the party as a sort of general manager. The party, besides the President, his wife, and three sons, Robert, William, and Thomas, consisted of his brother-in-law, Dr. W. S. Wallace, David Davis, Norman B. Judd, Elmer E. Ellsworth, Ward H. Lamon, and the President's two secretaries, John

---

*In answer to the many inquiries made of me, I will say here that during this last interview Mr. Lincoln, for the first time, brought up the subject of an office under his administration. He asked me if I desired an appointment at his hands, and, if so, what I wanted. I answered that I had no desire for a Federal office, that I was then holding the office of Bank Commissioner of Illinois under appointment of Governor Bissell, and that if he would request my retention in office by Yates, the incoming Governor, I should be satisfied. He made the necessary recommendation, and Governor Yates complied. I was present at the meeting between Yates and Lincoln, and I remember that the former, when Lincoln urged my claims for retention in office, asked Lincoln to appoint their mutual friend A. Y. Ellis postmaster at Springfield. I do not remember whether Lincoln promised to do so or not, but Ellis was never appointed.[14]

G. Nicolay and John Hay. Colonel E. V. Sumner and other army gentlemen were also in the car, and some friends of Mr. Lincoln—among them O. H. Browning, Governor Yates, and ex-Governor Moore—started with the party from Springfield, but dropped out at points along the way. The day was a stormy one, with dense clouds hanging heavily overhead. A goodly throng of Springfield people had gathered to see the distinguished party safely off. After the latter had entered the car the people closed about it until the President appeared on the rear platform. He stood for a moment as if to suppress evidences of his emotion, and removing his hat made the following brief but dignified and touching address:° "Friends: No one who has never been placed in a like position can understand my feelings at this hour, nor the oppressive sadness I feel at this parting. For more than a quarter of a century I have lived among you, and during all that time I have received nothing but kindness at your hands. Here I have lived from my youth until now I am an old man. Here the most sacred ties of earth were assumed. Here all my children were born; and here one of them lies buried. To you, dear friends, I owe all that I have, all that I am. All the strange, checkered past seems to crowd now upon my mind. To-day I leave you. I go to assume a task more difficult than that which devolved upon Washington. Unless the great God who assisted him shall be with and aid me, I must fail; but if the same omniscient mind and almighty arm that directed and protected him shall guide and support me I shall not fail—I shall succeed. Let us all pray that the God of our fathers may not forsake us now. To him I commend you all. Permit me to ask that with equal sincerity and faith you will invoke his wisdom and guidance for me. With these words I must leave you, for how long I know not. Friends, one and all, I must now bid you an affectionate farewell."[15]

At the conclusion of this neat and appropriate farewell the train rolled slowly out, and Mr. Lincoln, still standing in the doorway of the rear car, took his last view of Springfield. The journey had been as well advertised as it had been carefully planned, and therefore, at every town along the route, and at every stop, great crowds were gathered to catch a glimpse of the President-elect.† Mr. Lincoln usually gratified the wishes of the crowds, who called him out for a speech

---

°I was not present when Mr. Lincoln delivered his farewell at the depot in Springfield, and never heard what he said. I have adopted the version of his speech as published in our papers. There has been some controversy over the exact language he used on that occasion, and Mr. Nicolay has recently published the speech from what he says is the original MS., partly in his own and partly in the handwriting of Mr. Lincoln. Substantially, however, it is like the speech as reproduced here from the Springfield paper.

†"Before Mr. Lincoln's election in 1860 I, then a child of eleven years, was presented with his lithograph. Admiring him with my whole heart, I thought still his appearance would be much improved should he cultivate his whiskers. Childish thoughts must have utterance. So I proposed the idea to him, expressing

Springfield—Passenger Station Great Western Railway. Where Mr. Lincoln Delivered his Farewell Speech, Feb. 11th, 1861.

whether it was down on the regular programme of movements or not. In all cases his remarks were well-timed and sensibly uttered. At Indianapolis, where the Legislature was in session, he halted for a day and delivered a speech the burden of which was an answer to the Southern charges of coercion and invasion. From Indianapolis he moved on to Cincinnati and Columbus, at the last-named place meeting the Legislature of Ohio. The remainder of the journey convinced Mr. Lincoln of his strength in the affections of the people. Many, no doubt, were full of curiosity to see the now famous rail-splitter, but all were outspoken

as well as I was able the esteem in which he was held among honest men. A few days after I received this kind and friendly letter:

"'Springfield, Ill., October 19, 1860.

"'Miss Grace Bedell.

"'*My Dear Little Miss:*—Your very agreeable letter of the 15th is received. I regret the necessity of saying I have no daughter. I have three sons—one seventeen, one nine, and one seven. They with their mother constitute my whole family. As to the whiskers, as I have never worn any, do you not think that people would call it a piece of silly affectation were I to begin wearing them now?

"'I am your true friend and sincere well-wisher,

"'A. LINCOLN.'

"It appears I was not forgotten, for after his election to the Presidency, while on his journey to Washington, the train stopped at Westfield, Chautauqua County, at which place I then resided. Mr. Lincoln said, 'I have a correspondent in this place, a little girl whose name is Grace Bedell, and I would like to see her.' I was conveyed to him; he stepped from the cars, extending his hand and saying, 'You see I have let these whiskers grow for you, Grace,' kissed me, shook me cordially by the hand, and was gone. I was frequently afterward assured of his remembrance.'"—Grace G. Bedell, MS. letter, Dec. 14, 1866.[16]

and earnest in their assurances of support. At Steubenville, Pittsburg, Cleveland, Buffalo, Albany, New York, and Philadelphia he made manly and patriotic speeches. These speeches, plain in language and simple in illustration, made every man who heard them a stronger friend than ever of the Government. He was skilful enough to warn the people of the danger ahead and to impress them with his ability to deal properly with the situation, without in any case outlining his intended policy or revealing the forces he held in reserve.° At Pittsburg he advised deliberation and begged the American people to keep their temper on both sides of the line. At Cleveland he insisted that "the crisis, as it is called, is an artificial crisis and has no foundation in fact;" and at Philadelphia he assured his listeners that under his administration there would be "no bloodshed unless it was forced upon the Government, and then it would be compelled to act in self-defence."[20] This last utterance was made in front of Independence Hall, where, a few moments before, he had unfurled to the breeze a magnificent new flag, an impressive ceremony performed amid the cheers swelling from the vast sea of upturned faces before him. From Philadelphia his journey took him to Harrisburg, where he visited both branches of the Legislature then in session. For an account of the remainder of this now famous trip I beg to quote from the admirable narrative of Dr. Holland. Describing the welcome tendered him by the Legislature at Harrisburg, the latter says: "At the conclusion of the exercises of the day Mr. Lincoln, who was known to be very weary, was permitted to pass undisturbed to his apartments in the Jones House. It was popularly understood

---

°The following are extracts from Mr. Lincoln's letters written during the campaign in answer to his position with reference to the anticipated uprisings in the Southern States. They are here published for the first time:

[From a letter to L. Montgomery Bond, Esq., Oct. 15, 1860.]
"I certainly am in no temper and have no purpose to embitter the feelings of the South, but whether I am inclined to such a course as would in fact embitter their feelings you can better judge by my published speeches than by anything I would say in a short letter if I were inclined now, as I am not, to define my position anew."[17]

[From a letter to Samuel Haycraft, dated, Springfield, Ill., June 4, 1860.]
"Like yourself I belonged to the old Whig party from its origin to its close. I never belonged to the American party organization, nor ever to a party called a Union party; though I hope I neither am or ever have been less devoted to the Union than yourself or any other patriotic man."[18]

[Private and Confidential.]

Springfield, Ill., Nov. 13, 1860.

"Hon. Samuel Haycraft.
"MY DEAR SIR:—Yours of the 9th is just received. I can only answer briefly. Rest fully assured that the good people of the South who will put themselves in the same temper and mood towards me which you do will find no cause to complain of me.
"Yours very truly,
"A. Lincoln."[19]

that he was to start for Washington the next morning, and the people of Harrisburg supposed they had only taken a temporary leave of him. He remained in his rooms until nearly six o'clock, when he passed into the street, entered a carriage unobserved in company with Colonel Lamon, and was driven to a special train on the Pennsylvania railroad in waiting for him. As a matter of precaution the telegraph wires were cut the moment he left Harrisburg, so that if his departure should be discovered intelligence of it could not be communicated at a distance. At half-past ten the train arrived at Philadelphia, and here Mr. Lincoln was met by a detective, who had a carriage in readiness in which the party were driven to the depot of the Philadelphia, Wilmington, and Baltimore railroad. At a quarter past eleven they arrived and very fortunately found the regular train, which should have left at eleven, delayed. The party took berths in the sleeping-car, and without change of cars passed directly through Baltimore to Washington, where Mr. Lincoln arrived at half-past six o'clock in the morning and found Mr. Washburne anxiously awaiting him. He was taken into a carriage and in a few minutes he was talking over his adventures with Senator Seward at Willard's Hotel."[21] The remaining members of the Presidential party from whom Mr. Lincoln separated at Harrisburg left that place on the special train intended for him; and as news of his safe arrival in Washington had been already telegraphed over the country no attempt was made to interrupt their safe passage through Baltimore. As is now generally well known many threats had up to that time been made that Mr. Lincoln, on his way to Washington, should never pass through Baltimore alive. It was reported and believed that conspiracies had been formed to attack the train, blow it up with explosives or in some equally effective way dispose of the President-elect. Mr. Seward and others were so deeply impressed with the grave features of the reports afloat that Allan Pinkerton, the noted detective of Chicago, was employed to investigate the matter and ferret out the conspiracy, if any existed. This shrewd operator went to Baltimore, opened an office as a stock-broker, and through his assistants—the most adroit and serviceable of whom was a woman—was soon in possession of inside information. The change of plans and trains at Harrisburg was due to his management and advice. Some years before his death Mr. Pinkerton furnished me with a large volume of the written reports of his subordinates and an elaborate account by himself of the conspiracy and the means he employed to ferret it out. The narrative, thrilling enough in some particulars, is too extended for insertion here. It is enough for us to know that the tragedy was successfully averted and that Mr. Lincoln was safely landed in Washington.

In January preceding his departure from Springfield Mr. Lincoln, becoming somewhat annoyed, not to say alarmed, at the threats emanating from Baltimore and other portions of the country adjacent to Washington, that he should not reach the latter place alive, and that even if successful in reaching the Capitol his inauguration should in some way be prevented, determined to ascertain for himself what protection would be given him in case an effort should be made by an individual or a mob to do him violence. He sent a young military officer in the person of Thomas Mather, then Adjutant-General of Illinois, to Washington with a letter to General Scott, in which he recounted the threats he had heard and ventured to inquire as to the probability of any attempt at his life being made on the occasion of his inauguration. General Mather, on his arrival in Washington, found General Scott confined to his room by illness and unable to see visitors. On Mather calling a second time and sending in his letter he was invited up to the sick man's chamber. "Entering the room," related Mather in later years, "I found the old warrior, grizzly and wrinkled, propped up in the bed by an embankment of pillows behind his back. His hair and beard were considerably disordered, the flesh seemed to lay in rolls across his warty face and neck, and his breathing was not without great labor. In his hand he still held Lincoln's letter. He was weak from long-continued illness, and trembled very perceptibly. It was evident that the message from Lincoln had wrought up the old veteran's feelings. 'General Mather,' he said to me, in great agitation, 'present my compliments to Mr. Lincoln when you return to Springfield, and tell him I expect him to come on to Washington as soon as he is ready. Say to him that I'll look after those Maryland and Virginia rangers myself; I'll plant cannon at both ends of Pennsylvania avenue, and if any of them show their heads or raise a finger I'll blow them to hell.' On my return to Springfield," concludes Mather, "I hastened to assure Mr. Lincoln that, if Scott were alive on the day of the inauguration, there need be no alarm lest the performance be interrupted by any one. I felt certain the hero of Lundy's Lane would give the matter the care and attention it deserved."[22]

Having at last reached his destination in safety, Mr. Lincoln spent the few days preceding his inauguration at Willard's Hotel, receiving an uninterrupted stream of visitors and friends. In the few unoccupied moments allotted him, he was carefully revising his inaugural address. On the morning of the 4th of March he rode from his hotel with Mr. Buchanan in an open barouche to the Capitol. There, slightly pale and nervous, he was introduced to the assembled multitude by his old friend Edward D. Baker, and in a fervid and impressive manner delivered his address. At its conclusion the customary oath was administered by the venerable Chief Justice Taney, and he was now clothed with all the powers and privileges of Chief Magistrate of the nation. He accompanied Mr. Buchanan to the White House, and here the historic bachelor of Lancaster bade him farewell, bespeaking for him a peaceful, prosperous, and successful administration.

One who witnessed the impressive scene left the following graphic description of the inauguration and its principal incidents: "Near noon I found myself a member of the motley crowd gathered about the side entrance to Willard's Hotel. Soon an open barouche drove up, and the only occupant stepped out. A large, heavy, awkward-moving man, far advanced in years, short and thin gray hair, full face, plentifully seamed and wrinkled, head curiously inclined to the left shoulder, a low-crowned, broad-brimmed silk hat, an immense white cravat like a poultice, thrusting the old-fashioned standing collar up to the ears, dressed in black throughout, with swallow-tail coat not of the newest style. It was President Buchanan, calling to take his successor to the Capitol. In a few minutes he reappeared, with Mr. Lincoln on his arm; the two took seats side-by-side, and the carriage rolled away, followed by a rather disorderly and certainly not very imposing procession. I had ample time to walk to the Capitol, and no difficulty in securing a place where everything could be seen and heard to the best advantage. The attendance at the inauguration was, they told me, unusually small, many being kept away by anticipated disturbance, as it had been rumored—truly, too—that General Scott himself was fearful of an outbreak, and had made all possible military preparations to meet the emergency. A square platform had been built out from the steps to the eastern portico, with benches for distinguished spectators on three sides. Douglas, the only one I recognized, sat at the extreme end of the seat on the right of the narrow passage leading from the steps. There was no delay, and the gaunt form of the President-elect was soon visible, slowly making his way to the front. To me, at least, he was completely metamorphosed—partly by his own fault, and partly through the efforts of injudicious friends and ambitious tailors. He was raising (to gratify a very young lady, it is said) a crop of whiskers, of the blacking-brush variety, coarse, stiff, and ungraceful; and in so doing spoiled, or at least seriously impaired, a face which, though never handsome, had in its original state a peculiar power and pathos. On the present occasion the whiskers were reinforced by brand-new clothes from top to toe; black dress-coat, instead of the usual frock, black cloth or satin vest, black pantaloons, and a glossy hat evidently just out of the box. To cap the climax of novelty, he carried a huge ebony cane, with a gold head the size of an egg. In these, to him, strange habiliments, he looked so miserably uncomfortable that I could not help pitying him. Reaching the platform, his discomfort was visibly increased by not knowing what to do with hat and cane; and so he stood there, the target for ten thousand eyes, holding cane in one hand and hat in the other, the very picture of helpless embarrassment. After some hesitation he pushed the cane into a corner of the railing, but could not find a place for the hat except on the floor, where I could see he did not like to risk it. Douglas, who fully took in the situation, came to the rescue of his old friend and rival, and held the precious hat until the owner needed it again; a service which, if predicted two years before, would probably have astonished him. The oath of office was administered by Chief Justice Taney, whose black robes, attenuated figure, and cadaverous countenance reminded me of a galvanized corpse. Then the President came forward, and read his inaugural address in a clear and distinct voice. It was attentively listened to by all, but the closest listener was Douglas, who leaned forward as if to catch every word, nodding his head emphatically at those passages which most pleased him. There was some applause, not very much nor very enthusiastic. I must not forget to mention the presence of a Mephistopheles in the person of Senator Wigfall, of Texas, who stood with folded arms leaning against the doorway of the Capitol, looking down upon the crowd and the ceremony with a contemptuous air, which sufficiently indicated his opinion of the whole performance. To him the Southern Confederacy was already an accomplished fact. He lived to see it the saddest of fictions."[23]

CHAPTER XVII.

Lincoln, the President, did not differ greatly from Lincoln the lawyer and politician. In the latter capacity only had his old friends in Illinois known him. For a long time after taking his seat they were curious to know what change, if any, his exalted station had made in him. He was no longer amid people who had seen him grow from the village lawyer to the highest rank in the land, and whose hands he could grasp in the confidence of a time-tried friendship; but now he was surrounded by wealth, power, fashion, influence, by adroit politicians and artful schemers of every sort. In the past his Illinois and particularly his Springfield friends° had shared the anxiety and responsibility of every step he had made; but now they were no longer to continue in the partnership. Many of them wanted

---

°Lincoln, even after his elevation to the Presidency, always had an eye out for his friends, as the following letters will abundantly prove:

"Executive Mansion, Washington, April 20, 1864.

"Calvin Truesdale, Esq.

"Postmaster, Rock Island, Ill.:

"Thomas J. Pickett, late agent of the Quartermaster's Department for the Island of Rock Island, has been removed or suspended from that position on a charge of having sold timber and stone from the island for his private benefit. Mr. Pickett is an old acquaintance and friend of mine, and I will thank you, if you will, to set a day or days and place on and at which to take testimony on the point. Notify Mr. Pickett and one J. B. Danforth (who as I understand makes the charge) to be present with their witnesses. Take the testimony in writing offered by both sides, and report it in full to me. Please do this for me.

"Yours truly,

"A. Lincoln."[1]

The man Pickett was formerly the editor of a newspaper in northern Illinois, and had, to use an expression of later days, inaugurated in the columns of his paper Lincoln's boom for the Presidency. When he afterwards fell under suspicion, no one came to his rescue sooner than the President himself.

The following letter needs no explanation:

no office, but all of them felt great interest as well as pride in his future. A few attempted to keep up a correspondence with him, but his answers were tardy and irregular. Because he did not appoint a goodly portion of his early associates to comfortable offices, and did not interest himself in the welfare of everyone whom he had known in Illinois, or met while on the circuit, the erroneous impression grew that his elevation had turned his head. There was no foundation for such an unwarranted conclusion. Lincoln had not changed a particle. He was overrun with duties and weighted down with cares; his surroundings were different and his friends were new, but he himself was the same calm, just, and devoted friend as of yore. His letters were few and brief, but they showed no lack of gratitude or appreciation, as the following one to me will testify:[4]

"Executive Mansion, February 3, 1862.

"Dear William:

"Yours of January 30th is just received. Do just as you say about the money matters. As you well know, I have not time enough to write a letter of respectable length. God bless you, says

"Your friend,

"A. Lincoln."*

His letters to others were of the same warm and generous tenor, but yet the foolish notion prevailed that he had learned to disregard the condition and claims of his Springfield friends. One of the latter who visited Washington returned somewhat displeased because Mr. Lincoln failed to inquire after the health and welfare of each one of his old neighbors. The report spread that

---

"Executive Mansion, Washington, August 27, 1862.

"Hon. Wash. Talcott.

"*My Dear Sir:*—I have determined to appoint you collector. I now have a very special request to make of you, which is, that you will make no war upon Mr. Washburne, who is also my friend, and of longer standing than yourself. I will even be obliged if you can do something for him if occasion presents.

"Yours truly"

"A. Lincoln."[2]

Mr. Talcott, to whom it was addressed, was furnished a letter of introduction by the President, as follows:

"The Secretary of the Treasury and the Commissioner of Internal Revenue will please see Mr. Talcott, one of the best men there is, and, if any difference, one they would like better than they do me.

"A. Lincoln."[3]

August 18, 1862.

*On February 19, 1863, I received this despatch from Mr. Lincoln:

"Would you accept a job of about a month's duration, at St. Louis, $5 a day and mileage. Answer.

"A. Lincoln."[5]

he cared nothing for his home or the friends who had made him what he was. Those who entertained this opinion of the man forgot that he was not exactly the property of Springfield and Illinois, but the President of all the States in the Union.°

In this connection it may not be out of order to refer briefly to the settlement by Mr. Lincoln of the claims his leading Illinois friends had on him. As before observed his own election to the Presidency cancelled Illinois as a factor in the cabinet problem, but in no wise disposed of the friends whom the public expected and whom he himself intended should be provided for. Of these latter the oldest and most zealous and effective was David Davis.† It is not extravagance, taking their long association together in mind, to say that Davis had done more for Lincoln than any dozen other friends he had. Of course, after Lincoln was securely installed in office, the people, especially in Illinois, awaited his recognition of Davis. What was finally done is minutely told in a letter by Leonard Swett, which it is proper here to insert:

"Chicago, Ill., August 29, 1887.

"William H. Herndon.

"*My Dear Sir:*—Your inquiry in reference to the circumstances of the appointment of David Davis as one of the Justices of the Supreme Court reached me last evening. In reply I beg leave to recall the fact, that in 1860 the politicians of Illinois were divided into three divisions, which were represented in the Decatur convention by the votes on the nomination for Governor. The largest vote was for Norman B. Judd, of Chicago, his strength in the main being the northern part of the State. I was next in order of strength, and Richard Yates the third, but the divisions were not materially unequal. The result was Yates was nominated, his strength being about Springfield and Jacksonville, extending to Quincy on the west, and mine was at Bloomington and vicinity and south and southeast.

"These divisions were kept up awhile after Mr. Lincoln's election, and were considered in the distribution of Federal patronage. A vacancy in the United

---

°The following letter from a disappointed Illinois friend will serve to illustrate the perplexities that beset Lincoln in disposing of the claims of personal friendship. It was written by a man of no inconsiderable reputation in Illinois, where he at one time filled a State office: "Lincoln is a singular man, and I must confess I never knew him. He has for twenty years past used me as a plaything to accomplish his own ends; but the moment he was elevated to his proud position he seems all at once to have entirely changed his whole nature and become altogether a new being. He knows no one, and the road to his favor is always open to his enemies, while the door is hermetically sealed to his old friends."[6]
†"I had done Lincoln many, many favors, had electioneered for him, spent my money for him, worked and toiled for him."—David Davis, statement, September 20, 1866.[7]

States Senate occurred early in 1861 by the death of Stephen A. Douglas, and Governor Yates appointed Oliver H. Browning, of Quincy, to fill the vacancy. There was also a vacancy upon the Supreme Bench of the United States to be filled from this general vicinity by Mr. Lincoln in the early part of his adminis- tration, and Judge Davis, of Bloomington, and Mr. Browning, of Quincy, were aspirants for the position. Mr. Browning had the advantage that Lincoln was new in his seat, and Senators were August personages; and, being in the Sen- ate and a most courteous and able gentleman, Mr. Browning succeeded in securing nearly all the senatorial strength, and Mr. Lincoln was nearly swept off his feet by the current of influence. Davis' supporters were the circuit law- yers mainly in the eastern and central part of the State. These lawyers were at home, and their presence was not a living force felt constantly by the Presi- dent at Washington.

"I was then living at Bloomington, and met Judge Davis every day. As months elapsed we used to get word from Washington in reference to the condition of things; finally, one day the word came that Lincoln had said, 'I do not know what I may do when the time comes, but there has never been a day when if I had to act I should not have appointed Browning.' Judge Davis, General Orme, and myself held a consultation in my law-office at Blooming- ton. We decided that the remark was too Lincolnian to be mistaken and no man but he could have put the situation so quaintly. We decided also that the appointment was gone, and sat there glum over the situation. I finally broke the silence, saying in substance, 'The appointment is gone and I am going to pack my carpet-sack for Washington.' 'No, you are not,' said Davis. 'Yes, I am,' was my reply. 'Lincoln is being swept off his feet by the influence of these Sen- ators, and I will have the luxury of one more talk with him before he acts.'

"I did go home, and two days thereafter, in the morning about seven o'clock—for I knew Mr. Lincoln's habits well—was at the White House and spent most of the forenoon with him. I tried to impress upon him that he had been brought into prominence by the Circuit Court lawyers of the old eighth Circuit, headed by Judge Davis. 'If,' I said, 'Judge Davis, with his tact and force, had not lived, and all other things had been as they were, I believe you would not now be sitting where you are.' He replied gravely, 'Yes, that is so.' 'Now it is a common law of mankind,' said I, 'that one raised into prominence is expected to recognize the force that lifts him, or, if from a pinch, the force that lets him out. The Czar Nicholas was once attacked by an assassin; a kindly hand warded off the blow and saved his life. The Czar hunted out the owner of that hand and strewed his pathway with flowers through life. The Emperor

Napoleon III. has hunted out everybody who even tossed him a biscuit in his prison at Ham and has made him rich. Here is Judge Davis, whom you know to be in every respect qualified for this position, and you ought in justice to yourself and public expectation to give him this place.' We had an earnest pleasant forenoon, and I thought I had the best of the argument, and I think he thought so too.

"I left him and went to Willard's Hotel to think over the interview, and there a new thought struck me. I therefore wrote a letter to Mr. Lincoln and returned to the White House. Getting in, I read it to him and left it with him. It was, in substance, that he might think if he gave Davis this place the latter when he got to Washington would not give him any peace until he gave me a place equally as good; that I recognized the fact that he could not give this place to Davis, which would be charged to the Bloomington faction in our State politics, and then give me anything I would have and be just to the party there; that this appointment, if made, should kill 'two birds with one stone;' that I would accept it as one-half for me and one-half for the Judge; and that thereafter, if I or any of my friends ever troubled him, he could draw that letter as a plea in bar on that subject. As I read it Lincoln said, 'If you mean that among friends as it reads I will take it and make the appointment.' He at once did as he said.

"He then made a request of the Judge after his appointment in reference to a clerk in his circuit, and wrote him a notice of the appointment, which Davis received the same afternoon I returned to Bloomington.

"Judge Davis was about fifteen years my senior. I had come to his circuit at the age of twenty-four, and between him and Lincoln I had grown up leaning in hours of weakness on their own great arms for support. I was glad of the opportunity to put in the mite of my claims upon Lincoln and give it to Davis, and have been glad I did it every day since.

"An unknown number of people have almost every week since, speaking perhaps extravagantly, asked me in a quasi-confidential manner, 'How was it that you and Lincoln were so intimate and he never gave you anything?' I have generally said, 'It seems to me that is my question, and so long as I don't complain I do not see why you should.' I may be pardoned also for saying that I have not considered every man not holding an office out of place in life. I got my eyes open on this subject before I got an office, and as in Washington I saw the Congressman in decline I prayed that my latter end might not be like his.

"Yours truly,

"Leonard Swett."[8]

Before his departure for Washington, Mr. Lincoln had on several occasions referred in my presence to the gravity of the national questions that stared him in the face; yet from what he said I caught no definite idea of what his intentions were. He told me he would rely upon me to keep him informed of the situation about home, what his friends were saying of him, and whether his course was meeting with their approval. He suggested that I should write him frequently, and that arrangements would be made with his private secretary, Mr. Nicolay, that my letters should pass through the latter's hands unopened. This plan was adhered to, and I have every reason now to believe that all my letters to Lincoln, although they contained no great secrets of state, passed unread into his hands. I was what the newspaper men would call a "frequent contributor." I wrote oftener than he answered, sometimes remitting him his share of old fees, sometimes dilating on national affairs, but generally confining myself to local politics and news in and around Springfield. I remember of writing him two copious letters, one on the necessity of keeping up the draft, the other admonishing him to hasten his Proclamation of Emancipation. In the latter I was especially fervid, assuring him if he emancipated the slaves, he could "go down the other side of life filled with the consciousness of duty well done, and along a pathway blazing with eternal glory."[9] How my rhetoric or sentiments struck him I never learned, for in the rush of executive business he never responded to either of the letters. Late in the summer of 1861, as elsewhere mentioned in these chapters, I made my first and only visit to Washington while he was President. My mission was intended to promote the prospects of a brother-in-law, Charles W. Chatterton, who desired to lay claim to an office in the Bureau of Indian Affairs. Mr. Lincoln accompanied me to the office of the Commissioner of Indian Affairs,—William P. Dole of Paris, Illinois,—told a good story, and made the request which secured the coveted office—an Indian agency—in an amazingly short time. This was one of the few favors I asked of Mr. Lincoln, and he granted it "speedily—without delay; freely—without purchase; and fully—without denial."[10] I remained in Washington for several days after this, and, notwithstanding the pressure of business, he made me spend a good portion of the time at the White House. One thing he could scarcely cease from referring to was the persistence of the office-seekers. They slipped in, he said, through the half-opened doors of the Executive Mansion; they dogged his steps if he walked; they edged their way through the crowds and thrust their papers in his hands when he rode;* and, taking it all in all, they well-nigh worried him to death. He said that,

---

*He said that one day, as he was passing down Pennsylvania avenue, a man came running after him, hailed him, and thrust a bundle of papers in his hands. It angered him not a little, and he pitched the papers back, saying, "I'm not going to open shop here."

if the Government passed through the Rebellion without dismemberment, there was the strongest danger of its falling a prey to the rapacity of the office-seeking class. "This human struggle and scramble for office," were his words, "for a way to live without work, will finally test the strength of our institutions."[11] A good part of the day during my stay I would spend with him in his office or waiting-room. I saw the endless line of callers, and met the scores of dignitaries one usually meets at the White House, even now; but nothing took place worthy of special mention here. One day Horace Maynard and Andrew Johnson, both senators from Tennessee, came in arm-in-arm. They declined to sit down, but at once set to work to discuss with the President his recent action in some case in which they were interested. Maynard seemed very earnest in what he said. "Beware, Mr. President," he said, "and do not go too fast. There is danger ahead." "I know that," responded Lincoln, good-naturedly, "but I shall go just so fast and only so fast as I think I'm right and the people are ready for the step." Hardly half-a-dozen words followed, when the pair wheeled around and walked away. The day following I left Washington for home. I separated from Mr. Lincoln at the White House. He followed me to the rear portico, where I entered the carriage to ride to the railroad depot. He grasped me warmly by the hand and bade me a fervent "Good-bye." It was the last time I ever saw him alive.

Mrs. Ninian Edwards, who, it will be remembered, was the sister of Mrs. Lincoln, some time before her death furnished me an account of her visit to Washington, some of the incidents of which are so characteristic that I cannot refrain from giving them room here.[12] This lady, without endeavoring to suppress mention of her sister's many caprices and eccentricities while mistress of the White House, remarked that, having been often solicited by the Lincolns to visit them, she and her husband, in answer to the cordial invitation, at last made the journey to Washington. "One day while there," she relates, "in order to calm his mind, to turn his attention away from business and cheer him up, I took Mr. Lincoln down through the conservatory belonging to the Executive Mansion, and showed him the world of flowers represented there. He followed me patiently through. 'How beautiful these flowers are! how gorgeous these roses! Here are exotics,' I exclaimed, in admiration, 'gathered from the remotest corners of the earth, and grand beyond description.' A moody silence followed, broken finally by Mr. Lincoln with this observation: 'Yes, this whole thing looks like spring; but do you know I have never been in here before. I don't know why it is so, but I never cared for flowers; I seem to have no taste, natural or acquired, for such things.' I induced him one day," continued Mrs. Edwards, "to walk to the Park north of the White House. He hadn't been there, he said, for a year. On such occasions, when alone or in the company of a close friend, and released from the restraint of his official surroundings, he was wont to throw from his shoulders many a burden. He was a man I loved and respected. He was a good man, an honest and true one. Much of his seeming disregard, which has been tortured into ingratitude, was due to his peculiar construction. His habits, like himself, were odd and wholly irregular. He would move around in a vague, abstracted way, as if unconscious of his own or any one else's existence. He had no expressed fondness for anything, and ate mechanically. I have seen him sit down at the table absorbed in thought, and never, unless recalled to his senses, would he think of food. But, however peculiar and secretive he may have seemed, he was anything but cold. Beneath what the world saw lurked a nature as tender and poetic as any I ever knew. The death of his son Willie, which occurred in Washington, made a deep impression on him. It was the first death in his family, save an infant who died a few days after its birth in Springfield.[13] On the evening we strolled through the Park he spoke of it with deep feeling, and he frequently afterward referred to it. When I announced my intention of leaving Washington he was much affected at the news of my departure. We were strolling through the White House ground, when he begged me with tears in his eyes to remain longer. 'You have such strong control and such an influence over Mary,' he contended, 'that when troubles come you can console me.' The picture of the man's despair never faded from my vision. Long after my return to Springfield, on reverting to the sad separation, my heart ached because I was unable in my feeble way to lighten his burden."

In the summer of 1866 I wrote to Mrs. Lincoln, then in Chicago, asking for a brief account of her own and her husband's life or mode of living while at the White House. She responded as follows:[*]

"375 West Washington Street,
"Chicago, Ill., August 28, 1866.

"Hon. Wm. H. Herndon.

"*My Dear Sir:*—Owing to Robert's absence from Chicago your last letter to him was only shown me last evening. The recollection of my beloved husband's truly affectionate regard for you, and the knowledge of your great love and reverence for the best man that ever lived, would of itself cause you to be cherished with the sincerest regard by my sons and myself. In my overwhelming bereavement those who loved my idolized husband aside from disinterested motives are very precious to me and mine. My grief has been so uncon-

---

[*]From MSS. in Author's possession.

trollable that, in consequence, I have been obliged to bury myself in solitude, knowing that many whom I would see could not fully enter into the state of my feelings. I have been thinking for some time past I would like to see you and have a long conversation. I wish to know if you will be in Springfield next Wednesday week, September 4; if so, at ten o'clock in the morning you will find me at the St. Nicholas Hotel. Please mention this visit to Springfield to no one. It is a most sacred one, as you may suppose, to visit the tomb which contains my all in life—my husband. . . . If it will not be convenient, or if business at the time specified should require your absence, should you visit Chicago any day this week I will be pleased to see you. I remain,

> "Very truly,
> "Mary Lincoln."[14]

I met Mrs. Lincoln at the hotel in Springfield according to appointment. Our interview was somewhat extended in range, but none the less interesting. Her statement made at the time now lies before me. "My husband intended," she said, "when he was through with his Presidential term, to take me and our boys with him to Europe. After his return from Europe he intended to cross the Rocky Mountains and go to California, where the soldiers were to be digging out gold to pay the national debt. During his last days he and Senator Sumner became great friends, and were closely attached to each other. They were down the river after Richmond was taken—were full of joy and gladness at the thought of the war being over. Up to 1864 Mr. Lincoln wanted to live in Springfield, and if he died be buried there also; but after that and only a short time before his death he changed his mind slightly, but never really settled on any particular place. The last time I remember of his referring to the matter he said he thought it would be good for himself and me to spend a year or more travelling. As to his nature, he was the kindest man, most tender husband, and loving father in the world. He gave us all unbounded liberty, saying to me always when I asked for anything, 'You know what you want, go and get it,' and never asking if it were necessary. He was very indulgent to his children. He never neglected to praise them for any of their good acts. He often said, 'It is my pleasure that my children are free and happy, and unrestrained by parental tyranny. Love is the chain whereby to bind a child to its parents.'

"My husband placed great reliance on my knowledge of human nature, often telling me, when about to make some important appointment, that he had no knowledge of men and their motives. It was his intention to remove Seward as soon as peace with the South was declared. He greatly disliked Andrew Johnson.

Once the latter, when we were in company, followed us around not a little. It displeased Mr. Lincoln so much he turned abruptly and asked, loud enough to be heard by others, 'Why is this man forever following me?' At another time, when we were down at City Point, Johnson, still following us, was drunk. Mr. Lincoln in desperation exclaimed, 'For God's sake don't ask Johnson to dine with us.' Sumner, who was along, joined in the request. Mr. Lincoln was mild in his manners, but he was a terribly firm man when he set his foot down. None of us, no man or woman, could rule him after he had once fully made up his mind. I could always tell when in deciding anything he had reached the ultimatum. At first he was very cheerful, then he lapsed into thoughtfulness, bringing his lips together in a firm compression. When these symptoms developed I fashioned myself accordingly, and so did all others have to do sooner or later. When we first went to Washington many thought Mr. Lincoln was weak, but he rose grandly with the circumstances. I told him once of the assertion I had heard coming from the friends of Seward, that the latter was the power behind the throne; that he could rule him. He replied, 'I may not rule myself, but certainly Seward shall not. The only ruler I have is my conscience—following God in it—and these men will have to learn that yet.'

"Some of the newspaper attacks on him gave him great pain. I sometimes read them to him, but he would beg me to desist, saying, 'I have enough to bear now, but yet I care nothing for them. If I'm right I'll live, and if wrong I'll die anyhow; so let them fight at me unrestrained.' My playful response would be, 'The way to learn is to hear both sides.' I once assured him Chase and certain others who were scheming to supplant him ought to be restrained in their evil designs. 'Do good to them who hate you,' was his generous answer, 'and turn their ill-will into friendship.'

"I often told Mr. Lincoln that God would not let any harm come of him. We had passed through four long years—terrible and bloody years—unscathed, and I believed we would be released from all danger. He gradually grew into that belief himself, and the old gloomy notion of his unavoidable taking-off was becoming dimmer as time passed away. Cheerfulness merged into joyfulness. The skies cleared, the end of the war rose dimly into view when the great blow came and shut him out forever."[15]

For a glimpse of Lincoln's habits while a resident of Washington and an executive officer, there is no better authority than John Hay, who served as one of his secretaries. In 1866, Mr. Hay, then a member of the United States Legation in Paris, wrote me an interesting account, which so faithfully delineates Lincoln in his public home that I cannot refrain from quoting it entire. Although the letter

Mrs. Lincoln in the
White House (after a
photograph by Brady,
1861)

was written in answer to a list of questions I asked, and was prepared without any
attempt at arrangement, still it is none the less interesting. "Lincoln went to bed
ordinarily," it begins, "from ten to eleven o'clock, unless he happened to be kept up
by important news, in which case he would frequently remain at the War Department till one or two. He rose early. When he lived in the country at the Soldiers'
Home he would be up and dressed, eat his breakfast (which was extremely frugal,
an egg, a piece of toast, coffee, etc.), and ride into Washington, all before eight
o'clock. In the winter, at the White House, he was not quite so early. He did not
sleep well, but spent a good while in bed. 'Tad' usually slept with him. He would
lie around the office until he fell asleep, and Lincoln would shoulder him and
take him off to bed. He pretended to begin business at ten o'clock in the morning,
but in reality the ante-rooms and halls were full long before that hour—people

anxious to get the first axe ground. He was extremely unmethodical; it was a four years' struggle on Nicolay's part and mine to get him to adopt some systematic rules. He would break through every regulation as fast as it was made. Anything that kept the people themselves away from him he disapproved, although they nearly annoyed the life out of him by unreasonable complaints and requests. He wrote very few letters, and did not read one in fifty that he received. At first we tried to bring them to his notice, but at last he gave the whole thing over to me, and signed, without reading them, the letters I wrote in his name.[16] He wrote perhaps half-a-dozen a week himself—not more. Nicolay received members of Congress and other visitors who had business with the Executive office, communicated to the Senate and House the messages of the President, and exercised a general supervision over the business. I opened and read the letters, answered them, looked over the newspapers, supervised the clerks who kept the records, and in Nicolay's absence did his work also. When the President had any rather delicate matter to manage at a distance from Washington he rarely wrote, but sent Nicolay or me. The House remained full of people nearly all day. At noon the President took a little lunch—a biscuit, a glass of milk in winter, some fruit or grapes in summer. He dined between five and six, and we went off to our dinner also. Before dinner was over, members and Senators would come back and take up the whole evening. Sometimes, though rarely, he shut himself up and would see no one. Sometimes he would run away to a lecture, or concert, or theatre for the sake of a little rest. He was very abstemious—ate less than any man I know. He drank nothing but water, not from principle but because he did not like wine or spirits. Once, in rather dark days early in the war, a temperance committee came to him and said the reason we did not win was because our army drank so much whiskey as to bring the curse of the Lord upon them. He said it was rather unfair on the part of the aforesaid curse, as the other side drank more and worse whiskey than ours did. He read very little. He scarcely ever looked into a newspaper unless I called his attention to an article on some special subject. He frequently said, 'I know more about it than any of them.' It is absurd to call him a modest man. No great man was ever modest. It was his intellectual arrogance and unconscious assumption of superiority that men like Chase and Sumner never could forgive. I believe that Lincoln is well understood by the people; but there is a patent-leather, kid-glove set who know no more of him than an owl does of a comet blazing into his blinking eyes.* Their estimates of him are in many cases

---

*Bancroft's eulogy on Lincoln never pleased the latter's lifelong friends—those who knew him so thoroughly and well. February 16, 1866, David Davis, who had heard it, wrote me: "You will see Mr. Bancroft's oration before this reaches you. It is able, but Mr. Lincoln is in the background. His analysis of Mr. Lincoln's

310 | HERNDON'S LINCOLN

disgraceful exhibitions of ignorance and prejudice. Their effeminate natures shrink instinctively from the contact of a great reality like Lincoln's character. I consider Lincoln's republicanism incarnate—with all its faults and all its virtues. As, in spite of some rudeness, republicanism is the sole hope of a sick world, so Lincoln, with all his foibles, is the greatest character since Christ."[18]

In 1863 Mr. Lincoln was informed one morning that among the visitors in the ante-room of the White House was a man who claimed to be his relative. He walked out and was surprised to find his boyhood friend and cousin, Dennis Hanks. The latter had come to see his distinguished relative on a rather strange mission. A number of persons living in Coles County, in Illinois, offended at the presence and conduct of a few soldiers who were at home from the war on furlough at the town of Charleston, had brought about a riot, in which encounter several of the latter had been killed. Several of the civilian participants who had acted as leaders in the strife had been arrested and sent to Fort McHenry or some other place of confinement equally as far from their homes. The leading lawyers and politicians of central Illinois were appealed to, but they and all others who had tried their hands had been signally unsuccessful in their efforts to secure the release of the prisoners. Meanwhile some one of a sentimental turn had conceived the idea of sending garrulous old Dennis Hanks to Washington, fondly believing that his relationship to the President might in this last extremity be of some avail. The novelty of the project secured its adoption by the prisoners' friends, and Dennis, arrayed in a suit of new clothes, set out for the national capital. I have heard him describe this visit very minutely. How his appearance in Washington and his mission struck Mr. Lincoln can only be imagined. The President, after listening to him and learning the purpose of his visit, retired to an adjoining room and returned with an extremely large roll of papers labelled, "The Charleston Riot Case," which he carefully untied and gravely directed his now diplomatic cousin to read. Subsequently, and as if to continue the joke, he sent him down to confer with the Secretary of War. He soon returned from the latter's office with the report that the head of the War Department could not be found; and it was well enough that he did not meet that abrupt and oftentimes demonstrative official.

---

character is superficial. It did not please me. How did it satisfy you?" On the 22d he again wrote: "Mr. Bancroft totally misconceived Mr. Lincoln's character in applying 'unsteadiness' and confusion to it. Mr. Lincoln grew more steady and resolute, and his ideas were never confused. If there were any changes in him after he got here they were for the better. I thought him always master of his subject. He was a much more self-possessed man than I thought. He *thought* for himself, which is a rare quality nowadays. How could Bancroft know anything about Lincoln except as he judged of him as the public do? He never saw him, and is himself as cold as an icicle. I should never have selected an old Democratic politician, and that one from Massachusetts, to deliver an eulogy on Lincoln."[17]

In the course of time, however, the latter happened in at the Executive Mansion, and there, in the presence of Dennis, the President sought to reopen the now noted Charleston case. Adopting Mr. Hanks' version, the Secretary, with his characteristic plainness of speech, referring to the prisoners, declared that "every d——d one of them should be hung." Even the humane and kindly enquiry of the President, "If these men should return home and become good citizens, who would be hurt?"[19] failed to convince the distinguished Secretary that the public good could be promoted by so doing. The President not feeling willing to override the Judgment of his War Secretary in this instance, further consideration of the case ceased, and his cousin returned to his home in Illinois with his mission unaccomplished.°

Dennis retained a rather unfavorable impression of Mr. Stanton, whom he described as a "frisky little Yankee with a short coat-tail." "I asked Abe," he said to me once, "why he didn't kick him out. I told him he was too fresh altogether." Lincoln's answer was, "If I did, Dennis, it would be difficult to find another man to fill his place."[20] The President's cousin† sat in the office during the endless interviews that take place between the head of the nation and the latter's loyal subjects. He saw modesty and obscurity mingling with the arrogance of pride and distinction. One day an attractive and handsomely dressed woman called to procure the release from prison of a relative in whom she professed the deepest interest. She was a good talker, and her winning ways seemed to be making a deep impression on the President. After listening to her story he wrote a few lines on a card, enclosing it in an envelope and directing her to take it to the Secretary of War. Before sealing it he showed it to Dennis. It read: "This woman, dear Stanton, is a little smarter than she looks to be." She had, woman-like, evidently overstated her case. Before night another woman called, more humble in appearance, more plainly clad. It was the old story. Father and son both in the army, the former in prison. Could not the latter be discharged from the army and sent home to help his mother? A few strokes of the pen, a gentle nod of the head, and the little woman, her eyes filling with tears and expressing a grateful acknowledgment her tongue could not utter, passed out.[21]

°The subsequent history of these riot cases I believe is that the prisoners were returned to Illinois to be tried in the State courts there; and that by successive changes of venue and continuances the cases were finally worn out.

†During this visit Mr. Lincoln presented Dennis with a silver watch, which the latter still retains as a memento alike of the donor and his trip to Washington.

CHAPTER XVIII.

Before passing to a brief and condensed view of the great panorama of the war it will interest the reader and no doubt aid him greatly in drawing the portrait of Lincoln to call up for the purpose two friends of his, whose testimony is not only vivid and minute, but for certain reasons unusually appropriate and essential. The two were devoted and trusted friends of Lincoln; and while neither held office under him, both were offered and both declined the same. That of itself ought not to be considered as affecting or strengthening their statements, and yet we sometimes think that friends who are strong enough to aid us, and yet, declining our aid, take care of themselves, are brave enough to tell us the truth. The two friends of Lincoln here referred to are Joshua F. Speed and Leonard Swett. In quoting them I adhere strictly to their written statements now in my possession.[1] The former, under date of December 6, 1866, says: "Mr. Lincoln was so unlike all the men I had ever known before or seen or known since that there is no one to whom I can compare him. In all his habits of eating, sleeping, reading, conversation, and study he was, if I may so express it, regularly irregular; that is, he had no stated time for eating, no fixed time for going to bed, none for getting up. No course of reading was chalked out. He read law, history, philosophy, or poetry; Burns, Byron, Milton, or Shakespeare and the newspapers, retaining them all about as well as an ordinary man would any one of them who made only one at a time his study. I once remarked to him that his mind was a wonder to me; that impressions were easily made upon it and never effaced. 'No,' said he, 'you are mistaken; I am slow to learn, and slow to forget that which I have learned. My mind is like a piece of steel—very hard to scratch anything on it, and almost impossible after you get it there to rub it out.' I give this as his own illustration of the character of his mental faculties; it is as good as any I have seen from anyone.

"The beauty of his character was its entire simplicity. He had no affectation in anything. True to nature, true to himself, he was true to everybody and everything around him. When he was ignorant on any subject, no matter how simple it might make him appear, he was always willing to acknowledge it. His whole aim in life was to be true to himself, and being true to himself he could be false to no one.

"He had no vices, even as a young man. Intense thought with him was the rule and not, as with most of us, the exception. He often said that he could think better after breakfast, and better walking than sitting, lying, or standing. His world-wide reputation for telling anecdotes and telling them so well was in my judgment necessary to his very existence. Most men who have been great students, such as he was, in their hours of idleness have taken to the bottle, to cards or dice. He had no fondness for any of these. Hence he sought relaxation in anecdotes. So far as I now remember of his study for composition, it was to make short sentences and a compact style. Illustrative of this it might be well to state that he was a great admirer of the style of John C. Calhoun. I remember reading to him one of Mr. Calhoun's speeches in reply to Mr. Clay in the Senate, in which Mr. Clay had quoted precedent. Mr. Calhoun replied (I quote from memory) that 'to legislate upon precedent is but to make the error of yesterday the law of to-day.' Lincoln thought that was a great truth and grandly uttered.

"Unlike all other men, there was entire harmony between his public and private life. He must believe he was right, and that he had truth and justice with him, or he was a weak man; but no man could be stronger if he thought he was right.

"His familiar conversations were like his speeches and letters in this: that while no set speech of his (save the Gettysburg address) will be considered as entirely artistic and complete, yet, when the gems of American literature come to be selected, as many will be culled from Lincoln's speeches as from any American orator. So of his conversation, and so of his private correspondence; all abound in gems.[2]

"My own connection or relation with Mr. Lincoln during the war has so often been commented on, and its extent so often enlarged upon, I feel impelled to state that during his whole administration he never requested me to do anything, except in my own State, and never much in that except to advise him as to what measures and policy would be most conducive to the growth of a healthy Union sentiment.

"My own opinion of the history of the Emancipation Proclamation is that Mr. Lincoln foresaw the necessity for it long before he issued it. He was anxious to avoid it, and came to it only when he saw that the measure would subtract from its labor, and add to our army quite a number of good fighting men. I have heard of the charge of duplicity against him by certain Western members of Congress. I never believed the charge, because he has told me from his own lips that the charge was false. I, who knew him so well, could never after that credit the report. At first I was opposed to the Proclamation, and so told him. I remember well our conversation on the subject. He seemed to treat it as certain that I would recognize the wisdom of the act when I should see the harvest of good which we would ere long glean from it. In that conversation he alluded to an incident in his life, long passed, when he was so much depressed that he almost contemplated suicide. At the time of his deep depression he said to me that he had 'done nothing to make any human being remember that he had lived,' and that to connect his name with the events transpiring in his day and generation, and so impress himself upon them as to link his name with something that would redound to the interest of his fellow man, was what he desired to live for. He reminded me of that conversation, and said with earnest emphasis, 'I believe that in this measure [meaning his Proclamation], my fondest hope will be realized.' Over twenty years had passed between the two conversations.[3]

"The last interview but one I had with him was about ten days prior to his last inauguration. Congress was drawing to a close; it had been an important session; much attention had to be given to the important bills he was signing; a great war was upon him and the country; visitors were coming and going to the President with their varying complaints and grievances from morning till night with almost as much regularity as the ebb and flow of the tide; and he was worn down in health and spirits. On this occasion I was sent for, to come and see him. Instructions were given that when I came I should be admitted. When I entered his office it was quite full, and many more—among them not a few Senators and members of Congress—still waiting. As soon as I was fairly inside, the President remarked that he desired to see me as soon as he was through giving audiences, and that if I had nothing to do I could take the papers and amuse myself in that or any other way I saw fit till he was ready. In the room, when I entered, I observed sitting near the fireplace, dressed in humble attire, two ladies modestly waiting their turn. One after another of the visitors came and went, each bent on his own particular errand, some satisfied and others evidently displeased at the result of their mission. The hour had arrived to close the door against all further callers. No one was left in the room now except the President, the two ladies, and me. With a rather peevish and fretful air he turned to them and said, 'Well, ladies, what can I do for you?' They both commenced to speak at once. From what they said he soon learned that one was the wife and the other the mother of two men imprisoned for resisting the draft in western Pennsylvania. 'Stop,' said he, 'don't say any more. Give me your petition.' The old lady responded, 'Mr. Lincoln, we've got no petition; we couldn't write one and had no money to pay for writing one, and I thought best to come and see you.' 'Oh,' said he, 'I understand your cases.' He rang his bell and ordered one of the messengers to tell General Dana to bring him the names of all the men in prison for resisting the draft in western Pennsylvania. The General soon came with the list. He enquired if there was any difference in the charges or degrees of guilt. The General replied that he knew of none. 'Well, then,' said he, 'these fellows have suffered long enough, and I have thought so for some time, and now that my mind is on the subject I believe I will turn out the whole flock. So, draw up the order, General, and I will sign it.' It was done and the General left the room. Turning to the women he said, 'Now, ladies, you can go.' The younger of the two ran forward and was in the act of kneeling in thankfulness. 'Get up,' he said; 'don't kneel to me, but thank God and go.' The old lady now came forward with tears in her eyes to express her gratitude. 'Good-bye, Mr. Lincoln,' said she; 'I shall probably never see you again till we meet in heaven.' These were her exact words. She had the President's hand in hers, and he was deeply moved. He instantly took her right hand in both of his and, following her to the door, said, 'I am afraid with all my troubles I shall never get to the resting-place you speak of; but if I do I am sure I shall find you. That you wish me to get there is, I believe, the best wish you could make for me. Good-bye.'

"We were now alone. I said to him, 'Lincoln, with my knowledge of your nervous sensibility, it is a wonder that such scenes as this don't kill you.' He thought for a moment and then answered in a languid voice, 'Yes, you are to a certain degree right. I ought not to undergo what I so often do. I am very unwell now; my feet and hands of late seem to be always cold, and I ought perhaps to be in bed; but things of the sort you have just seen don't hurt me, for, to tell you the truth, that scene is the only thing to-day that has made me forget my condition or given me any pleasure. I have, in that order, made two people happy and alleviated the distress of many a poor soul whom I never expect to see. That old lady,' he continued, 'was no counterfeit. The mother spoke out in all the features of her face. It is more than one can often say that in doing right one has made two people happy in one day. Speed, die when I may, I want it said of me by those who know me best, that I always plucked a thistle and planted a flower when I thought a flower would grow.' What a fitting sentiment! What a glorious recollection!"[4]

The recollections of Lincoln by Mr. Swett are in the form of a letter dated January 17, 1866. There is so much of what I know to be true in it, and it is so graphically told, that although there may be some repetition of what has already been touched upon in the preceding chapters, still I believe that the portrait of Lincoln will be made all the more life-like by inserting the letter without abridgment.[5]

"Chicago, Ill., Jan. 17, 1866.
"Wm. H. Herndon, Esq.
"Springfield, Ill.

"*Dear Sir:* I received your letter to day, asking me to write you Friday. Fearing if I delay, you will not get it in time, I will give you such hasty thoughts as may occur to me to-night. I have mislaid your second lecture, so that I have not read it at all, and have not read your first one since about the time it was published. What I shall say, therefore, will be based upon my own ideas rather than a review of the lecture.

"Lincoln's whole life was a calculation of the law of forces and ultimate results. The whole world to him was a question of cause and effect. He believed the results to which certain causes tended; he did not believe that those results could be materially hastened or impeded. His whole political history, especially since the agitation of the slavery question, has been based upon this theory. He believed from the first, I think, that the agitation of slavery would produce its overthrow, and he acted upon the result as though it was present from the beginning. His tactics were to get himself in the right place and remain there still, until events would find him in that place. This course of action led him to say and do things which could not be understood when considered in reference to the immediate surroundings in which they were done or said. You will remember, in his campaign against Douglas in 1858, the first ten lines of the first speech he made defeated him. The sentiment of the 'house divided against itself' seemed wholly inappropriate. It was a speech made at the commencement of a campaign, and apparently made for the campaign. Viewing it in this light alone, nothing could have been more unfortunate or inappropriate. It was saying just the wrong thing; yet he saw it was an abstract truth, and standing by the speech would ultimately find him in the right place. I was inclined at the time to believe these words were hastily and inconsiderately uttered, but subsequent facts have convinced me they were deliberate and had been matured. Judge T. L. Dickey says, that at Bloomington, at the first Republican Convention in 1856, he uttered the same sentences in a speech delivered there, and that after the meeting was over, he (Dickey) called his attention to these remarks.

"Lincoln justified himself in making them by stating they were true; but finally, at Dickey's urgent request, he promised that for his sake, or upon his advice, he would not repeat them. In the summer of 1859, when he was dining with a party of his intimate friends at Bloomington, the subject of his Springfield speech was discussed. We all insisted it was a great mistake, but he justified himself, and finally said, 'Well, gentlemen, you may think that speech was a mistake, but I never have believed it was, and you will see the day when you will consider it was the wisest thing I ever said.'

"He never believed in political combinations, and consequently, whether an individual man or class of men supported or opposed him, never made any difference in his feelings, or his opinions of his own success. If he was elected, he seemed to believe that no person or class of persons could ever have defeated him, and if defeated, he believed nothing could ever have elected him. Hence, when he was a candidate, he never wanted anything done for him in the line of political combination or management. He seemed to want to let the whole subject alone, and for everybody else to do the same. I remember, after the Chicago Convention, when a great portion of the East were known to be dissatisfied at his nomination, when fierce conflicts were going on in New York and Pennsylvania, and when great exertions seemed requisite to harmonize and mould in concert the action of our friends, Lincoln always seemed to oppose all efforts made in the direction of uniting the party. I arranged with Mr. Thurlow Weed after the Chicago Convention to meet him at Springfield. I was present at the interview, but Lincoln said nothing. It was proposed that Judge Davis should go to New York and Pennsylvania to survey the field and see what was necessary to be done. Lincoln consented, but it was always my opinion that he consented reluctantly.

"He saw that the pressure of a campaign was the external force coercing the party into unity. If it failed to produce that result, he believed any individual effort would also fail. If the desired result followed, he considered it attributable to the great cause, and not aided by the lesser ones. He sat down in his chair in Springfield and made himself the Mecca to which all politicians made pilgrimages. He told them all a story, said nothing, and sent them away. All his efforts to procure a second nomination were in the same direction. I believe he earnestly desired that nomination. He was much more eager for it than he was for the first, and yet from the beginning he discouraged all efforts on the part of his friends to obtain it. From the middle of his first term all his adversaries were busily at work for themselves. Chase had three or four secret societies and an immense patronage extending all over the country. Frémont was constantly at work, yet Lincoln would never do anything either to hinder them or to help himself.

"He was considered too conservative, and his adversaries were trying to outstrip him in satisfying the radical element. I had a conversation with him upon this subject in October, 1863, and tried to induce him to recommend in his annual message a constitutional amendment abolishing slavery. I told him I was not very radical, but I believed the result of the war would be the extermination of slavery; that Congress would pass the amendment making the slave free, and that it was proper at that time to be done. I told him also, if he took that stand, it was an outside position, and no one could maintain himself upon any measure more radical, and if he failed to take the position, his rivals would. Turning to me suddenly he said, 'Is not the question of emancipation doing well enough now?' I replied it was. 'Well,' said he, 'I have never done an official act with a view to promote my own personal aggrandizement, and I don't like to begin now. I can see that emancipation is coming; whoever can wait for it will see it; whoever stands in its way will be run over by it.'

"His rivals were using money profusely; journals and influences were being subsidized against him. I accidentally learned that a Washington newspaper, through a purchase of the establishment, was to be turned against him, and consulted him about taking steps to prevent it. The only thing I could get him to say was that he would regret to see the paper turned against him. Whatever was done had to be done without his knowledge. Mr. Bennett of the *Herald,* with his paper, you know, is a power. The old gentleman wanted to be noticed by Lincoln, and he wanted to support him. A friend of his, who was certainly in his secrets, came to Washington and intimated if Lincoln would invite Bennett to come over and chat with him, his paper would be all right. Mr. Bennett wanted nothing, he simply wanted to be noticed. Lincoln in talking about it said, 'I understand it; Bennett has made a great deal of money, some say not very properly, now he wants me to make him respectable. I have never invited Mr. Bryant or Mr. Greeley here; I shall not, therefore, especially invite Mr. Bennett.' All Lincoln would say was, that he was receiving everybody, and he should receive Mr. Bennett if he came.

"Notwithstanding his entire inaction, he never for a moment doubted his second nomination. One time in his room discussing with him who his real friends were, he told me, if I would not show it, he would make a list of how the Senate stood. When he got through, I pointed out some five or six, and I told him I knew he was mistaken about them. Said he, 'You may think so, but you keep that until the convention and tell me then whether I was right.' He was right to a man. He kept a kind of account book of how things were progressing, for three or four months, and whenever I would get nervous and think things were going wrong, he would get out his estimates and show how everything on the great scale of action, such as the resolutions of legislatures, the instructions of delegates, and things of that character, were going exactly as he expected. These facts with many others of a kindred nature, have convinced me that he managed his politics upon a plan entirely different from any other man the country has ever produced.

"He managed his campaigns by ignoring men and by ignoring all small causes, but by closely calculating the tendencies of events and the great forces which were producing logical results.

"In his conduct of the war he acted upon the theory that but one thing was necessary, and that was a united North. He had all shades of sentiments and opinions to deal with, and the consideration was always presented to his mind, how can I hold these discordant elements together?

"It was here that he located his own greatness as a President. One time, about the middle of the war, I left his house about eleven o'clock at night, at the Soldiers' Home. We had been discussing the discords in the country, and particularly the States of Missouri and Kentucky. As we separated at the door he said, 'I may not have made as great a President as some other men, but I believe I have kept these discordant elements together as well as anyone could.'[6] Hence, in dealing with men he was a trimmer, and such a trimmer the world has never seen. Halifax, who was great in his day as a trimmer, would blush by the side of Lincoln; yet Lincoln never trimmed in principles, it was only in his conduct with men. He used the patronage of his office to feed the hunger of these various factions. Weed always declared that he kept a regular account-book of his appointments in New York, dividing his various favors so as to give each faction more than it could get from any other source, yet never enough to satisfy its appetite.

"They all had access to him, they all received favors from him, and they all complained of ill treatment; but while unsatisfied, they all had 'large expectations,' and saw in him the chance of obtaining more than from anyone else whom they could be sure of getting in his place. He used every force to the best possible advantage. He never wasted anything, and would always give more to his enemies than he would to his friends; and the reason was, because he never had anything to spare, and in the close calculation of attaching the factions to him, he counted upon the abstract affection of his friends as an element to be offset against some gift with which he must appease his enemies. Hence, there was always some truth in the charge of his friends that he failed to reciprocate their devotion with his favors. The reason was, that he had only just so much to give away—'He always had more horses than oats.'

"An adhesion of all forces was indispensable to his success and the success of the country; hence he husbanded his means with the greatest nicety of calculation. Adhesion was what he wanted; if he got it gratuitously he never wasted his substance paying for it.

"His love of the ludicrous was not the least peculiar of his characteristics. His love of fun made him overlook everything else but the point of the joke sought after. If he told a good story that was refined and had a sharp point, he did not like it any the better because it was refined. If it was outrageously vulgar,[7] he never seemed to see that part of it, if it had the sharp ring of wit; nothing ever reached him but the wit. Almost any man that will tell a very vulgar story, has, in a degree, a vulgar mind; but it was not so with him; with all his purity of character and exalted morality and sensibility, which no man can doubt, when hunting for wit he had no ability to discriminate between the vulgar and the refined substances from which he extracted it. It was the wit he was after, the pure jewel, and he would pick it up out of the mud or dirt just as readily as he would from a parlor table.

"He had great kindness of heart. His mind was full of tender sensibilities, and he was extremely humane, yet while these attributes were fully developed in his character, and, unless intercepted by his judgment, controlled him, they never did control him contrary to his judgment. He would strain a point to be kind, but he never strained it to breaking. Most men of much kindly feeling are controlled by this sentiment against their judgment, or rather that sentiment beclouds their judgment. It was never so with him; he would be just as kind and generous as his judgment would let him be—no more. If he ever deviated from this rule, it was to save life. He would sometimes, I think, do things he knew to be impolitic and wrong to save some poor fellow's neck. I remember one day being in his room when he was sitting at his table with a large pile of papers before him, and after a pleasant talk he turned quite abruptly and said, 'Get out of the way, Swett; to-morrow is butcher-day, and I must go through these papers and see if I cannot find some excuse to let these poor fellows off.' The pile of papers he had were the records of courts martial of men who on the following day were to be shot. He was not examining the records to see whether the evidence sustained the findings; he was purposely in search of occasions to evade the law, in favor of life.[8]

"Some of Lincoln's friends have insisted that he lacked the strong attributes of personal affection which he ought to have exhibited; but I think this is a mistake. Lincoln had too much justice to run a great government for a few favors;[9] and the complaints against him in this regard, when properly digested, seem to amount to this and no more, that he would not abuse the privileges of his situation.

"He was certainly a very poor hater. He never judged men by his like or dislike for them. If any given act was to be performed, he could understand that his enemy could do it just as well as anyone. If a man had maligned him or been guilty of personal ill-treatment, and was the fittest man for the place, he would give him that place just as soon as he would give it to a friend.

"I do not think he ever removed a man because he was his enemy or because he disliked him.

"The great secret of his power as an orator, in my judgment, lay in the clearness and perspicuity of his statements. When Mr. Lincoln had stated a case it was always more than half argued and the point more than half won. It is said that some one of the crowned heads of Europe proposed to marry when he had a wife living. A gentleman, hearing of this proposition, replied, how could he? 'Oh,' replied his friend, 'he could marry and then he could get Mr. Gladstone to make an explanation about it.' This was said to illustrate the convincing power of Mr. Gladstone's statement.[10]

"Mr. Lincoln had this power greater than any man I have ever known. The first impression he generally conveyed was, that he had stated the case of his adversary better and more forcibly than his opponent could state it himself. He then answered that statement of facts fairly and fully, never passing by or skipping over a bad point.

"When this was done he presented his own case. There was a feeling, when he argued a case, in the mind of any man who listened to it, that nothing had been passed over; yet if he could not answer the objections he argued, in his own mind, and himself arrive at the conclusion to which he was leading others, he had very little power of argumentation. The force of his logic was in conveying to the minds of others the same clear and thorough analysis he had in his own, and if his own mind failed to be satisfied, he had little power to satisfy anybody else.[11] He never made a sophistical argument in his life, and never could make one. I think he was of less real aid in trying a thoroughly bad case than any man I was ever associated with. If he could not grasp the whole case and believe in it, he was never inclined to touch it.

"From the commencement of his life to its close, I have sometimes doubted whether he ever asked anybody's advice about anything. He would listen to everybody; he would hear everybody; but he rarely, if ever, asked for opinions. I never knew him in trying a case to ask the advice of any lawyer he was associated with.

"As a politician and as President, he arrived at all his conclusions from his own reflections, and when his opinion was once formed, he never doubted but what it was right.

"One great public mistake of his character, as generally received and acquiesced in, is that he is considered by the people of this country as a frank, guileless, and unsophisticated man. There never was a greater mistake. Beneath a smooth surface of candor and apparent declaration of all his thoughts and feelings, he exercised the most exalted tact and the wisest discrimination. He handled and moved men remotely as we do pieces upon a chess-board. He retained through life all the friends he ever had, and he made the wrath of his enemies to praise him. This was not by cunning or intrigue, in the low acceptation of the term, but by far-seeing reason and discernment. He always told enough only of his plans and purposes to induce the belief that he had communicated all, yet he reserved enough to have communicated nothing. He told all that was unimportant with a gushing frankness, yet no man ever kept his real purposes closer, or penetrated the future further with his deep designs.[12]

"You ask me whether he changed his religious opinions towards the close of his life. I think not. As he became involved in matters of the greatest importance, full of great responsibility and great doubt, a feeling of religious reverence, a belief in God and his justice and overruling power increased with him. He was always full of natural religion; he believed in God as much as the most approved Church member, yet he judged of Him by the same system of generalization as he judged everything else. He had very little faith in ceremonials or forms. In fact he cared nothing for the form of anything.[13] But his heart was full of natural and cultivated religion. He believed in the great laws of truth, and the rigid discharge of duty, his accountability to God, the ultimate triumph of the right and the overthrow of wrong. If his religion were to be judged by the lines and rules of Church creeds he would fall far short of the standard; but if by the higher rule of purity of conduct, of honesty of motive, of unyielding fidelity to the right, and acknowledging God as the supreme ruler, then he filled all the requirements of true devotion, and his whole life was a life of love to God, and love of his neighbor as of himself.

"Yours truly,
"Leonard Swett."

CHAPTER XIX.

The outlines of Mr. Lincoln's Presidential career are alone sufficient to fill a volume, and his history after he had been sworn into office by Chief Justice Taney is so much a history of the entire country, and has been so admirably and thoroughly told by others, that I apprehend I can omit many of the details and still not impair the portrait I have been endeavoring to draw in the mind of the reader. The rapid shifting of scenes in the drama of secession, the disclosure of rebellious plots and conspiracies, the threats of Southern orators and newspapers, all culminating in the attack on Fort Sumter, brought the newly installed President face to face with the stern and grave realities of a civil war.° Mr. Lincoln's military knowledge had been acquired in the famous campaign against the Indian Chief Black Hawk on the frontier in 1832, the thrilling details of which he had already given the country in a Congressional stump-speech; and to this store of experience he had made little if any addition. It was therefore generally conceded that in grappling with the realities of the problem which now confronted both himself and the country he would be wholly dependent on those who had made the profession of arms a life-work. Those who held such hastily conceived notions of Mr. Lincoln were evidently misled by his well-known and freely advertised Democratic manners. Anybody had a right, it was supposed, to advise him of his duty; and he was so conscious of his shortcomings as a military President that the army officers and Cabinet would run the Government and

---

° "Lincoln then told me of his last interview with Douglas. 'One day Douglas came rushing in,' he related, 'and said he had just got a telegraph despatch from some friends in Illinois urging him to come out and help set things right in Egypt, and that he would go, or stay in Washington, just where I thought he could do the most good. I told him to do as he chose, but that he could probably do best in Illinois. Upon that he shook hands with me and hurried away to catch the next train. I never saw him again.'"—Henry C. Whitney, MS. letter, November 13, 1866.[1]

conduct the war. That was the popular idea. Little did the press, or people, or politicians then know that the country lawyer who occupied the executive chair was the most self-reliant man who ever sat in it, and that when the crisis came his rivals in the Cabinet, and the people everywhere, would learn that he and he alone would be master of the situation.

It is doubtless true that for a long time after his entry into office he did not assert himself; that is, not realizing the gigantic scale upon which the war was destined to be fought, he may have permitted the idea to go forth that being unused to the command of armies he would place himself entirely in the hands of those who were.° The Secretary of State, whose ten years in the Senate had acquainted him with our relations to foreign powers, may have been lulled into the innocent belief that the Executive would have no fixed or definite views on international questions. So also of the other Cabinet officers; but alas for their fancied security! It was the old story of the sleeping lion. Old politicians, eyeing him with some distrust and want of confidence, prepared themselves to control his administration, not only as a matter of right, but believing that he would be compelled to rely upon them for support. A brief experience taught them he was not the man they bargained for.

Next in importance to the attack on Fort Sumter, from a military standpoint, was the battle of Bull Run. How the President viewed it is best illustrated by an incident furnished by an old friend† who was an associate of his in the Legislature of Illinois, and who was in Washington when the engagement took place. "The night after the battle," he relates, "accompanied by two Wisconsin Congressmen, I called at the White House to get the news from Manassas, as it was then called, having failed in obtaining any information at Seward's office and elsewhere. Stragglers were coming with all sorts of wild rumors, but nothing more definite than that there had been a great engagement; and the bearer of each report had barely escaped with his life. Messengers bearing despatches to the President and Secretary of War were constantly arriving, but outsiders could gather nothing worthy of belief. Having learned that Mr. Lincoln was at the War Department we started thither, but found the building surrounded by a great crowd, all as much in the dark as we. Removing a short distance away we sat down to rest. Presently Mr. Lincoln and Mr. Nicolay, his private secretary, came along, headed for the

---

°"I was in Washington in the Indian service for a few days before August, 1861, and I merely said to Lincoln one day, 'Everything is drifting into the war, and I guess you will have to put me in the army.' He looked up from his work and said, good-humoredly, 'I'm making generals now. In a few days I will be making quartermasters, and then I'll fix you.'"—H. C. Whitney, MS. letter, June 13, 1866.[2]
†Robert L. Wilson, MS., Feb. 10, 1866.

White House. It was proposed by my companions that as I was acquainted with the President I should join him and ask for the news. I did so, but he said that he had already told more than under the rules of the War Department he had any right to, and that, although he could see no harm in it, the Secretary of War had forbidden his imparting information to persons not in the military service. 'These war fellows,' he said, complainingly, 'are very strict with me, and I regret that I am prevented from telling you anything; but I must obey them, I suppose, until I get the hang of things.' 'But, Mr. President,' I insisted, 'if you cannot tell me the news, you can at least indicate its nature, that is, whether good or bad.' The suggestion struck him favorably. Grasping my arm he leaned over, and placing his face near my ear, said, in a shrill but subdued voice, 'It's d——d bad.' It was the first time I had ever heard him use profane language, if indeed it was profane in that connection; but later, when the painful details of the fight came in, I realized that, taking into consideration the time and the circumstances, no other term would have contained a truer qualification of the word 'bad.'"[3]

"About one week after the battle of Bull Run," relates another old friend—Whitney—from Illinois, "I made a call on Mr. Lincoln, having no business except to give him some presents which the nuns at the Osage Mission school in Kansas had sent to him through me. A Cabinet meeting had just adjourned, and I was directed to go at once to his room. He was keeping at bay a throng of callers, but, noticing me enter, arose and greeted me with his old-time cordiality. After the room had been partially cleared of visitors Secretary Seward came in and called up a case which related to the territory of New Mexico. 'Oh, I see,' said Lincoln; 'they have neither Governor nor Government. Well, you see Jim Lane; the secretary is his man, and he must hunt him up.' Seward then left, under the impression, as I then thought, that Lincoln wanted to get rid of him and diplomacy at the same time. Several other persons were announced, but Lincoln notified them all that he was busy and could not see them. He was playful and sportive as a child, told me all sorts of anecdotes, dealing largely in stories about Charles James Fox, and enquired after several odd characters whom we both knew in Illinois. While thus engaged General James was announced. This officer had sent in word that he would leave town that evening, and must confer with the President before going. 'Well, as he is one of the fellows who make cannons,' observed Lincoln, 'I suppose I must see him. Tell him when I get through with Whitney I'll see him.' No more cards came up, and James left about five o'clock, declaring that the President was closeted with 'an old Hoosier from Illinois, and was telling dirty yarns while the country was quietly going to hell.' But, however indignant General James may have felt, and whatever the people may have thought, still the President was full of the war. He got down his maps of the seat of war," continues Whitney, "and gave me a full history of the preliminary discussions and steps leading to the battle of Bull Run. He was opposed to the battle, and explained to General Scott by those very maps how the enemy could by the aid of the railroad reinforce their army at Manassas Gap until they had brought every man there, keeping us meanwhile successfully at bay. 'I showed to General Scott our paucity of railroad advantages at that point,' said Lincoln, 'and their plenitude, but Scott was obdurate and would not listen to the possibility of defeat. Now you see I was right, and Scott knows it, I reckon. My plan was, and still is, to make a strong feint against Richmond and distract their forces before attacking Manassas. That problem General McClellan is now trying to work out.' Mr. Lincoln then told me of the plan he had recommended to McClellan, which was to send gunboats up one of the rivers—not the James—in the direction of Richmond, and divert the enemy there while the main attack was made at Manassas. I took occasion to say that McClellan was ambitious to be his successor. 'I am perfectly willing,' he answered, 'if he will only put an end to this war.'"*

The interview of Mr. Whitney with the President on this occasion is especially noteworthy because the latter unfolded to him his idea of the general plan formed in his mind to suppress the rebellion movement and defeat the Southern army. "The President," continues Mr. Whitney, "now explained to me his theory of the Rebellion by the aid of the maps before him. Running his long forefinger down the map he stopped at Virginia. 'We must drive them away from here (Manassas Gap),' he said, 'and clear them out of this part of the State so that they cannot threaten us here (Washington) and get into Maryland. We must keep up a good and thorough blockade of their ports. We must march an army into east Tennessee and liberate the Union sentiment there. Finally we must rely on the people growing tired and saying to their leaders: "We have had enough of this thing, we will bear it no longer."'"[5]

Such was Mr. Lincoln's plan for heading off the Rebellion in the summer of 1861. How it enlarged as the war progressed, from a call for seventy-five thousand volunteers to one for five hundred thousand men and five hundred millions of dollars, is a matter now of well-known history. The war once inaugurated, it was plain the North had three things to do. These were: the opening of the Mississippi River; the blockade of the Southern ports; and the capture of Richmond. To accomplish these great and vital ends the deadly machinery of war was set in motion. The long-expected upheaval had come, and as the torrent of fire broke forth the people in

---

*This interview with Lincoln was written out during the war, and contains many of his peculiarities of expression.[4]

the agony of despair looking aloft cried out, "Is our leader equal to the task?" That he was the man for the hour is now the calm, unbiased judgment of all mankind.

The splendid victories early in 1862 in the southwest, which gave the Union cause great advance toward the entire redemption of Kentucky, Tennessee, and Missouri from the presence of rebel armies and the prevalence of rebel influence, were counterbalanced by the dilatory movements and inactive policy of McClellan, who had been appointed in November of the preceding year to succeed the venerable Scott. The forbearance of Lincoln in dealing with McClellan was only in keeping with his well-known spirit of kindness; but, when the time came and circumstances warranted it, the soldier-statesman found that the President not only comprehended the scope of the war, but was determined to be commander-in-chief of the army and navy himself. When it pleased him to place McClellan again at the head of affairs, over the protest of such a wilful and indomitable spirit as Stanton, he displayed elements of rare leadership and evidence of uncommon capacity. His confidence in the ability and power of Grant, when the press and many of the people had turned against the hero of Vicksburg, was but another proof of his sagacity and sound judgment.

As the bloody drama of war moves along we come now to the crowning act in Mr. Lincoln's career—that sublime stroke with which his name will be forever and indissolubly united—the emancipation of the slaves. In the minds of many people there had been a crying need for the liberation of the slaves. Laborious efforts had been made to hasten the issuance by the President of the Emancipation Proclamation, but he was determined not to be forced into premature and inoperative measures. Wendell Phillips abused and held him up to public ridicule from the stump in New England. Horace Greeley turned the batteries of the New York *Tribune* against him; and, in a word, he encountered all the rancor and hostility of his old friends the Abolitionists. General Frémont having in the fall of 1861 undertaken by virtue of his authority as a military commander to emancipate the slaves in his department, the President annulled the order, which he characterized as unauthorized and premature. This precipitated an avalanche of fanatical opposition. Individuals and delegations, many claiming to have been sent by the Lord, visited him day after day, and urged immediate emancipation. In August, 1862, Horace Greeley repeated the "prayer of twenty millions of people" protesting against any further delay. Such was the pressure from the outside. All his life Mr. Lincoln had been a believer in the doctrine of gradual emancipation. He advocated it while in Congress in 1848; yet even now, as a military necessity, he could not believe the time was ripe for the general liberation of the slaves. All the coercion from without, and all the blandishments from within, his political household failed to move him.

An heroic figure, indifferent alike to praise and blame, he stood at the helm and waited. In the shadow of his lofty form the smaller men could keep up their petty conflicts. Towering thus, he overlooked them all, and fearlessly abided his time. At last the great moment came. He called his Cabinet together and read the decree. The deed was done, unalterably, unhesitatingly, irrevocably, and triumphantly. The people, at first profoundly impressed, stood aloof, but, seeing the builder beside the great structure he had so long been rearing, their confidence was abundantly renewed. It was a glorious work, "sincerely believed to be an act of justice warranted by the constitution upon military necessity," and upon it its author "invoked the considerate judgment of mankind and the gracious favor of Almighty God."[6] I believe Mr. Lincoln wished to go down in history as the liberator of the black man. He realized to its fullest extent the responsibility and magnitude of the act, and declared it was "the central act of his administration and the great event of the nineteenth century."[7] Always a friend of the negro, he had from boyhood waged a bitter unrelenting warfare against his enslavement. He had advocated his cause in the courts, on the stump, in the Legislature of his State and that of the nation, and, as if to crown it with a sacrifice, he sealed his devotion to the great cause of freedom with his blood. As the years roll slowly by, and the participants in the late war drop gradually out of the ranks of men, let us pray that we may never forget their deeds of patriotic valor; but even if the details of that bloody struggle grow dim, as they will with the lapse of time, let us hope that so long as a friend of free man and free labor lives the dust of forgetfulness may never settle on the historic form of Abraham Lincoln.

As the war progressed, there was of course much criticism of Mr. Lincoln's policy, and some of his political rivals lost no opportunity to encourage opposition to his methods. He bore everything meekly and with sublime patience, but as the discontent appeared to spread he felt called upon to indicate his course. On more than one occasion he pointed out the blessings of the Emancipation Proclamation or throttled the clamorer for immediate peace. In the following letter to James C. Conkling° of Springfield, Ill., in reply to an invitation to attend a mass meeting of "Unconditional Union" men to be held at his old home, he not only disposed of the advocates of compromise, but he evinced the most admirable skill in dealing with the questions of the day;

°   "Springfield, Ill., January 11, 1889.
"Jesse W. Weik, Esq.
"*Dear Sir:*
    "I enclose you a copy of the letter dated August 26, 1863, by Mr. Lincoln to me. It has been carefully compared with the original and is a correct copy, except that the words commencing 'I know as fully as one can know' to the words 'You say you will fight to free negroes' were not included in the

"Executive Mansion,
"Washington, August 26, 1863.

"Hon. James C. Conkling.

"*My Dear Sir:*

"Your letter inviting me to attend a mass meeting of Unconditional Union men, to be held at the Capitol of Illinois, on the 3d day of September, has been received.

"It would be very agreeable to me to thus meet my old friends at my own home; but I cannot, just now, be absent from here so long as a visit there would require.

"The meeting is to be of all those who maintain unconditional devotion to the Union; and I am sure my old political friends will thank me for tendering, as I do, the nation's gratitude to those other noble men, whom no partisan malice, or partisan's hope, can make false to the nation's life.

"There are those who are dissatisfied with me. To such I would say: You desire peace; and you blame me that we do not have it. But how can we attain it? There are but three conceivable ways.

"First, to suppress the rebellion by force of arms. This I am trying to do. Are you for it? If you are, so far we are agreed. If you are not for it, a second way is, to give up the Union. I am against this. Are you for it? If you are, you should say so plainly. If you are not for *force*, nor yet for *dissolution*, there only remains some imaginable *compromise*. I do not believe any compromise, embracing the maintenance of the Union, is now possible. All I learn leads to a directly opposite belief. The strength of the rebellion is its military—its army. That army dominates all the country and all the people within its range. Any offer of terms made by any man or men within that range in opposition

---

original, but were telegraphed the next day with instructions to insert. The following short note in Mr. Lincoln's own handwriting accompanied the letter:

[Private.]   "'War Department,
                                                                              "'Washington City, D.C., August 27, 1862.

"'*My Dear Conkling:*

"'I cannot leave here now. Herewith is a letter instead. You are one of the best public readers. I have but one suggestion—read it very slowly. And now God bless you, and all good Union men.

"'Yours as ever,

"'A. Lincoln.'

"Mr. Bancroft, the historian, in commenting on this letter, considers it addressed to me as one who was criticising Mr. Lincoln's policy. On the contrary, I was directed by a meeting of 'Unconditional Union' men to invite Mr. Lincoln to attend a mass meeting composed of such men, and he simply took occasion to address his opponents through the medium of the letter.

"Yours truly,

"James C. Conkling."[8]

to that army is simply nothing for the present, because such man or men have no power whatever to enforce their side of a compromise, if one were made with them. To illustrate: suppose refugees from the South, and peace men of the North, get together in convention and frame and proclaim a compromise embracing a restoration of the Union; in what way can that compromise be used to keep Lee's army out of Pennsylvania? Meade's army can keep Lee's army out of Pennsylvania, and I think can ultimately drive it out of existence.

"But no paper compromise, to which the controllers of Lee's army are not agreed, can at all affect that army. In an effort at such compromise we should waste time, which the enemy would improve to our disadvantage; and that would be all. A compromise, to be effective, must be made either with those who control the rebel army, or with the people first liberated from the domination of that army by the success of our own army. Now allow me to assure you that no word or intimation from that rebel army or from any of the men controlling it, in relation to any peace compromise, has ever come to my knowledge or belief.

"All changes and insinuations to the contrary are deceptive and groundless. And I promise you that, if any such proposition shall hereafter come, it shall not be rejected and kept a secret from you. I freely acknowledge myself the servant of the people, according to the bond of service—the United States Constitution, and that, as such, I am responsible to them.

"But to be plain, you are dissatisfied with me about the negro. Quite likely there is a difference of opinion between you and myself upon that subject.

"I certainly wish that all men could be free, while I suppose you do not. Yet I have neither adopted nor proposed any measure which is not consistent with even your view, provided you are for the Union. I suggested compensated emancipation; to which you replied you wished not to be taxed to buy negroes. But I had not asked you to be taxed to buy negroes, except in such way as to save you from greater taxation to save the Union exclusively by other means.

"You dislike the Emancipation Proclamation, and, perhaps, would have it retracted. You say it is unconstitutional—I think differently. I think the Constitution invests its Commander-in-chief with the law of war in time of war. The most that can be said, if so much, is that slaves are property. Is there—has there ever been—any question that by the law of war, property, both of enemies and friends, may be taken when needed?

"And is it not needed wherever taking it helps us or hurts the enemy? Armies the world over destroy enemies' property when they cannot use it; and even destroy their own to keep it from the enemy. Civilized belligerents do all in their power to help themselves or hurt the enemy, except a few things regarded as barbarous or cruel.

"Among the exceptions are the massacre of vanquished foes and non-combatants, male and female.

"But the proclamation, as law, either is valid or is not valid.

"If it is not valid, it needs no retraction. If it is valid, it cannot be retracted any more than the dead can be brought to life. Some of you profess to think its retraction would operate favorably for the Union.

"Why *better* after the retraction than *before* the issue?

"There was more than a year and a half of trial to suppress the rebellion before the proclamation issued, the last one hundred days of which passed under an explicit notice that it was coming, unless averted by those in revolt returning to their allegiance.

"The war has certainly progressed as favorably for us since the issue of the proclamation as before.

"°I know as fully as one can know the opinion of others that some of the commanders of our armies in the field who have given us our most important successes believe the emancipation policy and the use of the colored troops constituted the heaviest blow yet dealt to the Rebellion, and that at least one of these important successes could not have been achieved when it was but for the aid of black soldiers. Among the commanders holding these views are some who have never had any affinity with what is called abolitionism or with Republican party policies, but who held them purely as military opinions. I submit these opinions as being entitled to some weight against the objections often urged that emancipation and arming the blacks are unwise as military measures, and were not adopted as such in good faith.°,9

"You say you will not fight to free negroes. Some of them seem willing to fight for you; but no matter.

"Fight you, then, exclusively to save the Union. I issued the proclamation on purpose to aid you in saving the Union. Whenever you shall have conquered all resistance to the Union, if I shall urge you to continue fighting, it will be an apt time then for you to declare you will not fight to free negroes.

"I thought that in your struggle for the Union, to whatever extent the negroes should cease helping the enemy, to that extent it weakened the enemy in his resistance to you. Do you think differently? I thought that whatever

---

°See note p. 328–29.

negroes can be got to do as soldiers leaves just so much less for white soldiers to do, in saving the Union. Does it appear otherwise to you?

"But negroes, like other people, act upon motives. Why should they do anything for us, if we will do nothing for them? If they stake their lives for us, they must be prompted by the strongest motive—even the promise of freedom. And the promise being made, must be kept.

"The signs look better. The Father of Waters again goes unvexed to the sea. Thanks to the great North-west for it. Nor yet wholly to them. Three hundred miles up they met New England, Empire, Keystone, and Jersey, hewing their way right and left. The Sunny South too, in more colors than one, also lent a hand.

"On the spot, their part of the history was jotted down in black and white. The job was a great national one; and let none be barred who bore an honorable part in it. And while those who have cleared the great river may well be proud, even that is not all. It is hard to say that anything has been more bravely and well done than at Antietam, Murfreesboro, Gettysburg, and on many fields of lesser note. Nor must Uncle Sam's web-feet be forgotten. At all the watery margins they have been present. Not only on the deep sea, the broad bay, and the rapid river, but also up the narrow, muddy bayou, and wherever the ground was a little damp, they have been, and made their tracks, thanks to all. For the great republic—for the principle it lives by and keeps alive—for man's vast future—thanks to all.

"Peace does not appear so distant as it did. I hope it will come soon and come to stay, and so come as to be worth the keeping in all future time. It will then have been proved that, among free men, there can be no successful appeal from the ballot to the bullet; and that they who take such appeal are sure to lose their case and pay the cost. And then there will be some black men who can remember that, with silent tongue, and clenched teeth, and steady eye, and well-poised bayonet, they have helped mankind on to this great consummation; while I fear there will be some white ones, unable to forget that, with malignant heart and deceitful speech, they have strove to hinder it.

"Still, let us not be over-sanguine of a speedy final triumph. Let us be quite sober. Let us diligently apply the means, never doubting that a just God, in his own good time, will give us the rightful result.

"Yours very truly,

"A. LINCOLN."[10]

The summer and fall of 1864 were marked by Lincoln's second Presidential campaign, he, and Andrew Johnson, of Tennessee, for Vice-President, having been nominated at Baltimore on the 8th of June. Frémont, who had been placed in the field by a convention of malcontents at Cleveland, Ohio, had withdrawn in September, and the contest was left to Lincoln and General George B. McClellan, the nominee of the Democratic convention at Chicago. The canvass was a heated and bitter one. Dissatisfied elements appeared everywhere. The Judge Advocate-General of the army (Holt) created a sensation by the publication of a report giving conclusive proof of the existence of an organized secret association at the North, controlled by prominent men in the Democratic party, whose objects were the overthrow by revolution of the administration in the interest of the rebellion.° Threats were rife of a revolution at the North, especially in New York City, if Mr. Lincoln were elected. Mr. Lincoln went steadily on in his own peculiar way. In a preceding chapter Mr. Swett has told us how indifferent he appeared to be regarding any efforts to be made in his behalf. He did his duty as President, and rested secure in the belief that he would be re-elected whatever might be done for or against him. The importance of retaining Indiana in the column of Republican States was not to be overlooked. How the President

---

°"Mr. Lincoln was advised, and I also so advised him, that the various military trials in the Northern and Border States, where the courts were free and untrammelled, were unconstitutional and wrong; that they would not and ought not to be sustained by the Supreme Court; that such proceedings were dangerous to liberty. He said he was opposed to hanging; that he did not like to kill his fellow-man; that if the world had no butchers but himself it would go bloodless. When Joseph E. McDonald went to Lincoln about these military trials and asked him not to execute the men who had been convicted by the military commission in Indiana he answered that he would not hang them, but added, 'I'll keep them in prison awhile to keep them from killing the Government.' I am fully satisfied therefore that Lincoln was opposed to these military commissions, especially in the Northern States, where everything was open and free."— David Davis, statement, September 10, 1866, to W. H. H.[11]

"I was counsel for Bowles, Milligan, *et al.*, who had been convicted of conspiracy by military tribunal in Indiana. Early in 1865 I went to Washington to confer with the President, whom I had known, and with whom in earlier days I had practised law on the circuit in Illinois. My clients had been sentenced, and unless the President interfered were to have been executed. Mr. Hendricks, who was then in the Senate, and who seemed to have little faith in the probability of executive clemency, accompanied me to the White House. It was early in the evening, and so many callers and visitors had preceded us we anticipated a very brief interview. Much to our surprise we found Mr. Lincoln in a singularly cheerful and reminiscent mood. He kept us with him till almost eleven o'clock. He went over the history of my clients' crime as shown by the papers in the case, and suggested certain errors and imperfections in the record. The papers, he explained, would have to be returned for correction, and that would consume no little time. 'You may go home, Mr. McDonald,' he said, with a pleased expression, 'and I'll send for you when the papers get back; but I apprehend and hope there will be such a jubilee over yonder,' he added, pointing to the hills of Virginia just across the river, 'we shall none of us want any more killing done.' The papers started on their long and circuitous journey, and sure enough, before they reached Washington again Mr. Lincoln's prediction of the return of peace had proved true."—Hon. Joseph E. McDonald, statement, August 28, 1888, to J. W. W.[12]

viewed it, and how he proposed to secure the vote of the State, is shown in the following letter written to General Sherman:

> "Executive Mansion,
> "Washington, September 19, 1864.
>
> "Major General Sherman:
> "The State election of Indiana occurs on the 11th of October, and the loss of it to the friends of the Government would go far towards losing the whole Union cause. The bad effect upon the November election, and especially the giving the State government to those who will oppose the war in every possible way, are too much to risk if it can be avoided. The draft proceeds, notwith-standing its strong tendency to lose us the State. Indiana is the only important State voting in October whose soldiers cannot vote in the field. Anything you can safely do to let her soldiers or any part of them go home and vote at the State election will be greatly in point. They need not remain for the Presidential election, but may return to you at once. This is in no sense an order, but is merely intended to impress you with the importance to the army itself of your doing all you safely can, yourself being the judge of what you can safely do.
> "Yours truly,
> "A. Lincoln."°

The election resulted in an overwhelming victory for Lincoln. He received a majority of over four hundred thousand in the popular vote—a larger majority than had ever been received by any other President up to that time. He carried not only Indiana, but all the New England States, New York, Pennsylvania, all the Western States, West Virginia, Tennessee, Louisiana, Arkansas, and the newly admitted State of Nevada. McClellan carried but three states: New Jersey, Delaware, and Kentucky. The result, as Grant so aptly expressed it in his telegram of congratulation, was "a victory worth more to the country than a battle won."[14] A second time Lincoln stood in front of the great Capitol to take the oath of office administered by his former rival, Salmon P. Chase, whom he himself had appointed to succeed the deceased Roger B. Taney. The problem of the war was now fast working its own solution. The cruel stain of slavery had been effaced from the national escutcheon, and the rosy morn of peace began to dawn behind the breaking clouds of the great storm.† Lincoln, firm but kind,

---

°Unpublished MS.[13]
†Bearing on the mission of the celebrated Peace Commission the following bit of inside history is not without interest:

in his inaugural address bade his misguided brethren of the South come back. With a fraternal affection characteristic of the man, and strictly in keeping with his former utterances, he asked for the return of peace. "With malice towards none, with charity for all," he implored his fellow-countrymen, "with firmness in the right as God gives us to see the right, let us finish the work we are in, to bind up the nation's wounds, to care for him who shall have borne the battle and for his widow and his orphans, to do all which may achieve and cherish a just and a lasting peace among ourselves and with all nations."[16] With the coming of spring the great armies, awakening from their long winter's sleep, began preparations for the closing campaign. Sherman had already made that grandest march of modern times, from the mountains of Tennessee through Georgia to the sea, while Grant, with stolid indifference to public criticism and newspaper abuse, was creeping steadily on through swamp and ravine to Richmond. Thomas had defeated Hood in Tennessee, sending the latter back with his army demoralized, cut in pieces, and ruined. The young and daring Sheridan had driven Early out of the Shenandoah Valley after a series of brilliant engagements. The "Kearsarge" had sunk the "Alabama" in foreign waters. Farragut had captured Mobile, and the Union forces held undisputed possession of the West and the Mississippi Valley

---

"I had given notice that at one o'clock on the 31st of January I would call a vote on the proposed constitutional amendment abolishing slavery in the United States. The opposition caught up a report that morning that Peace Commissioners were on the way to the city or were in the city. Had this been true I think the proposed amendment would have failed, as a number who voted for it could easily have been prevailed upon to vote against it on the ground that the passage of such a proposition would be offensive to the commissioners. Accordingly I wrote the President this note:

"'House of Representatives,
"'January 31, 1865.

"'*Dear Sir:*
"'The report is in circulation in the House that Peace Commissioners are on their way or in the city, and is being used against us. If it is true, I fear we shall lose the bill. Please authorize me to contradict it, if it is not true.
"'Respectfully,
"'J. M. Ashley.'

To the President.
"Almost immediately came the reply, written on the back of my note:
"'So far as I know there are no Peace Commissioners in the city or likely to be in it.
"'A. Lincoln.'
January 31, 1865.

"Mr. Lincoln knew that the commissioners were then on their way to Fortress Monroe, where he expected to meet them, and afterwards did meet them. You see how he answered my note for my purposes, and yet how truly. You know how he afterwards met the so-called commission, whom he determined at the time he wrote this note should not come to the city. One or two gentlemen were present when he wrote the note, to whom he read it before sending it to me."—J. M. Ashley, M. C., letter, November 23, 1866, MS.[15]

Five Views of Abraham Lincoln

from the lakes to the gulf. Meanwhile Sherman, undaunted by the perils of a further march through the enemy's country, returning from the sea, was aiming for Richmond, where Grant, with bull-dog tenacity, held Lee firmly in his grasp. Ere long, the latter, with his shattered army reduced to half its original numbers, evacuated Richmond, with Grant in close pursuit. A few days later the boys in blue overtook those in gray at Appomattox Court-house, and there, under the warm rays of an April sun, the life was at last squeezed out of the once proud but now prostrate Confederacy. "The sun of peace had fairly risen. The incubus of war that had pressed upon the nation's heart for four long, weary years was lifted; and the nation sprang to its feet with all possible demonstrations of joyous exultation."[17]

Mr. Lincoln himself had gone to the scene of hostilities in Virginia. He watched the various military manœuvres and operations, which involved momentous consequences to the country; he witnessed some of the bloody engagements participated in by the army of the Potomac. Within a day after its surrender he followed the victorious Union army into the city of Richmond. In this unfortunate city—once the proud capital of Virginia—now smoking and in ruins, he beheld the real horrors of grim war. Here too he realized in a bountiful measure the earnest gratitude of the colored people, who everywhere crowded around him and with cries of intense exultation greeted him as their deliverer. He now returned to Washington, not like Napoleon fleeing sorrowfully from Waterloo bearing the tidings of his own defeat, but with joy proclaiming the era of Union victory and peace among men. "The war was over. The great rebellion which for four long years had been assailing the nation's life was quelled. Richmond, the rebel capital, was taken; Lee's army had surrendered; and the flag of the Union was floating in reassured supremacy over the whole of the National domain. Friday, the 14th of April, the anniversary of the surrender of Fort Sumter in 1861 by Major Anderson to the rebel forces, had been designated by the Government as the day on which the same officer should again raise the American flag upon the fort in the presence of an assembled multitude, and with ceremonies befitting so auspicious an occasion. The whole land rejoiced at the return of peace and the prospect of renewed prosperity to the country. President Lincoln shared this common joy, but with a deep intensity of feeling which no other man in the whole land could ever know. He saw the full fruition of the great work which had rested so heavily on his hands and heart for four years past. He saw the great task—as momentous as had ever fallen to the lot of man—which he had approached with such unfeigned diffidence, nearly at an end. The agonies of war had passed away; he had won the imperishable renown which is the reward of those who save their country; and he could devote himself now to the welcome task of healing the wounds which war had made, and consolidating by a wise and magnanimous policy the severed sections of our common Union. His heart was full of the generous sentiments which these circumstances were so well calculated to inspire. He was cheerful and hopeful of the success of his broad plans for the treatment of the conquered people of the South. With all the warmth of his loving nature, after the four years of storm through which he had been compelled to pass, he viewed the peaceful sky on which the opening of his second term had dawned. His mind was free from forebodings and filled only with thoughts of kindness and of future peace." But alas for the vanity of human confidence! The demon of assassination lurked near. In the midst of the general rejoicing at the return of peace Mr. Lincoln was stricken down by the assassin, John Wilkes Booth, in Ford's Theatre at Washington. The story of his death, though oft repeated, is the saddest and most impressive page in American history. I cannot well forbear reproducing its painful and tragic details here.°

"Mr. Lincoln for years had a presentiment that he would reach a high place and then be stricken down in some tragic way. He took no precautions to keep out of the way of danger. So many threats had been made against him that his friends were alarmed, and frequently urged him not to go out unattended. To all their entreaties he had the same answer: 'If they kill me the next man will be just as bad for them. In a country like this, where our habits are simple, and must be, assassination is always possible, and will come if they are determined upon it.'

"Whatever premonition of his tragic fate he may have had, there is nothing to prove that he felt the nearness of the awful hour. Doomed men rise and go about their daily duties as unoppressed, often, as those whose paths know no shadow. On that never-to-be-forgotten 14th of April President Lincoln passed the day in the usual manner. In the morning his son, Captain Robert Lincoln, breakfasted with him. The young man had just returned from the capitulation of Lee, and he described in detail all the circumstances of that momentous episode of the close of the war, to which the President listened with the closest interest. After breakfast the President spent an hour with Speaker Colfax, talking about his future policy, about to be submitted to his Cabinet. At eleven o'clock he met the Cabinet. General Grant was present. He spent the afternoon with Governor Oglesby, Senator Yates, and other friends from Illinois. He was invited by the manager of Ford's theatre, in Washington, to attend in the evening a performance of the play,

---

°For the details of the assassination and the capture and subsequent history of the conspirators, I am indebted to Mrs. Gertrude Garrison, of New York, who has given the subject no little study and investigation. J. W. W.[18]

'Our American Cousin,' with Laura Keene as the leading lady. This play, now so well known to all play-goers, in which the late Sothern afterward made fortune and fame, was then comparatively unheralded. Lincoln was fond of the drama. Brought up in a provincial way, in the days when theatres were unknown outside of the larger cities, the beautiful art of the actor was fresh and delightful to him. He loved Shakespeare, and never lost an opportunity of seeing his characters rendered by the masters of dramatic art. But on that evening, it is said, he was not eager to go. The play was new, consequently not alluring to him; but he yielded to the wishes of Mrs. Lincoln and went. They took with them Miss Harris and Major Rathbone, daughter and stepson of Senator Harris, of New York.

"The theatre was crowded. At 9:20 the President and his party entered. The audience rose and cheered enthusiastically as they passed to the 'state box' reserved for them. Little did anyone present dream that within the hour enthusiasm would give place to shrieks of horror. It was ten o'clock when Booth came upon the scene to enact the last and greatest tragedy of the war. He had planned carefully, but not correctly. A good horse awaited him at the rear of the theatre, on which he intended to ride into friendly shelter among the hills of Maryland. He made his way to the President's box—a double one in the second tier, at the left of the stage. The separating partition had been removed, and both boxes thrown into one.

"Booth entered the theatre nonchalantly, glanced at the stage with apparent interest, then slowly worked his way around into the outer passage leading toward the box occupied by the President. At the end of an inner passage leading to the box door, one of the President's "messengers" was stationed to prevent unwelcome intrusions. Booth presented a card to him, stating that Mr. Lincoln had sent for him, and was permitted to pass. After gaining an entrance and closing the hall door, he took a piece of board prepared for the occasion, and placed one end of it in an indentation in the wall, about four feet from the floor, and the other against the molding of the door panel a few inches higher, making it impossible for any one to enter from without. The box had two doors. He bored a gimlet hole in the panel of one, reaming it out with his knife, so as to leave it a little larger than a buckshot on the inside, while on the other side it was big enough to give his eye a wide range. Both doors had spring locks. To secure against their being locked he had loosened the screws with which the bolts were fastened.

"So deliberately had he planned that the very seats in the box had been arranged to suit his purpose by an accomplice, one Spangler, an attaché of the theatre. The President sat in the left-hand corner of the box, nearest the audience, in an easy arm-chair. Next him, on the right, sat Mrs. Lincoln. A little distance to the right of both, Miss Harris was seated, with Major Rathbone at her left, and a little in the rear of Mrs. Lincoln, who, intent on the play, was leaning forward, with one hand resting on her husband's knee. The President was leaning upon one hand, and with the other was toying with a portion of the drapery. His face was partially turned to the audience, and wore a pleasant smile.

"The assassin swiftly entered the box through the door at the right, and the next instant fired. The ball entered just behind the President's left ear, and, though not producing instantaneous death, completely obliterated all consciousness.

"Major Rathbone heard the report, and an instant later saw the murderer, about six feet from the President, and grappled with him, but his grasp was shaken off. Booth dropped his pistol and drew a long, thin, deadly-looking knife, with which he wounded the major. Then, touching his left hand to the railing of the box, he vaulted over to the stage, eight or nine feet below. In that descent an unlooked-for and curious thing happened, which foiled all the plans of the assassin and was the means of bringing him to bay at last. Lincoln's box was draped with the American flag, and Booth, in jumping, caught his spur in its folds, tearing it down and spraining his ankle. He crouched as he fell, falling upon one knee, but soon straightened himself and stalked theatrically across the stage, brandishing his knife and shouting the State motto of Virginia, 'Sic semper tyrannis!' afterward adding, 'The South is avenged!' He made his exit on the opposite side of the stage, passing Miss Keene as he went out. A man named Stewart, a tall lawyer of Washington, was the only person with presence of mind enough to spring upon the stage and follow him, and he was too late.

"It had all been done so quickly and dramatically that many in the audience were dazed, and could not understand that anything not a part of the play had happened. When, at last, the awful truth was known to them there ensued a scene, the like of which was never known in a theatre before. Women shrieked, sobbed, and fainted. Men cursed and raved, or were dumb with horror and amazement. Miss Keene stepped to the front and begged the frightened and dismayed audience to be calm. Then she entered the President's box with water and stimulants. Medical aid was summoned and came with flying feet, but came too late. The murderer's bullet had done its wicked work well. The President hardly stirred in his chair, and never spoke or showed any signs of consciousness again.

"They carried him immediately to the house of Mr. Petersen, opposite the theatre, and there, at 7:22 the next morning, the 15th of April, he died.

"The night of Lincoln's assassination was a memorable one in Washington. Secretary Seward was attacked and wounded while lying in bed with a broken arm.

"The murder of the President put the authorities on their guard against a wide-reaching conspiracy, and threw the public into a state of terror. The awful event was felt even by those who knew not of it. Horsemen clattered through the silent streets of Washington, spreading the sad tidings, and the telegraph wires carried the terrible story everywhere. The nation awakened from its dream of peace on the 15th of April, 1865, to learn that its protector, leader, friend, and restorer had been laid low by a stage-mad 'avenger.' W. O. Stoddard, in his 'Life of Lincoln,' says: 'It was as if there had been a death in every house throughout the land. By both North and South alike the awful news was received with a shudder and a momentary spasm of unbelief. Then followed one of the most remarkable spectacles in the history of the human race, for there is nothing else at all like it on record. Bells had tolled before at the death of a loved ruler, but never did all bells toll so mournfully as they did that day. Business ceased. Men came together in public meetings as if by a common impulse, and party lines and sectional hatreds seemed to be obliterated.'[19]

"The assassination took place on Friday evening, and on the following Sunday funeral services were held in all the churches in the land, and every church was draped in mourning."[20]

The death of Mr. Lincoln was an indescribable shock to his fellow countrymen. The exultation of victory over the final and successful triumph of Union arms was suddenly changed to the lamentations of grief. In every household throughout the length and breadth of the land there was a dull and bitter agony as the telegraph bore tidings of the awful deed. The public heart, filled with joy over the news from Appomattox, now sank low with a sacred terror as the sad tidings from the Capitol came in. In the great cities of the land all business instantly ceased. Flags drooped half-mast from every winged messenger of the sea, from every church spire, and from every public building. Thousands upon thousands, drawn by a common feeling, crowded around every place of public resort and listened eagerly to whatever any public speaker chose to say. Men met in the streets and pressed each other's hands in silence, and burst into tears. The whole nation, which the previous day had been jubilant and hopeful, was precipitated into the depths of a profound and tender woe. It was a memorable spectacle to the world—a whole nation plunged into heartfelt grief and the deepest sorrow.

The body of the dead President, having been embalmed, was removed from the house in which the death occurred to the White House, and there appropriate funeral services were held. After the transfer of the remains to the Capitol, where the body was exposed to view in the Rotunda for a day, preparations were made for the journey to the home of the deceased in Illinois. On the following day (April 21) the funeral train left Washington amid the silent grief of the thousands who had gathered to witness its departure. At all the great cities along the route stops were made, and an opportunity was given the people to look on the face of the illustrious dead. The passage of this funeral train westward through country, village, and city, winding across the territory of vast States, along a track of more than fifteen hundred miles, was a pageant without a parallel in the history of the continent or the world. At every halt in the sombre march vast crowds, such as never before had collected together, filed past the catafalque for a glimpse of the dead chieftain's face. Farmers left their farms, workmen left their shops, societies and soldiers marched in solid columns, and the great cities poured forth their population in countless masses. From Washington the funeral train moved to Baltimore, thence to Harrisburg, Philadelphia, New York, Albany, Buffalo, Cleveland, Columbus, Indianapolis, Chicago, and at last to Springfield.

As the funeral cortège passed through New York it was reverently gazed upon by a mass of humanity impossible to enumerate. No ovation could be so eloquent as the spectacle of the vast population, hushed and bareheaded under the bright spring sky, gazing upon his coffin. Lincoln's own words over the dead at Gettysburg came to many as the stately car went by: "The world will little note nor long remember what we say here, but it can never forget what they did here."[21]

It was remembered, too, that on the 22d of February, 1861, as he raised the American flag over Independence Hall, in Philadelphia, he spoke of the sentiment in the Declaration of Independence which gave liberty not only to this country, but, "I hope," he said, "to the world for all future time. But if this country cannot be saved without giving up that principle, I was about to say I would rather be assassinated upon this spot than surrender it."[22]

When he died the veil that hid his greatness was torn aside, and the country then knew what it had possessed and lost in him. A New York paper, of April 29, 1865, said: "No one who personally knew him but will now feel that the deep, furrowed sadness of his face seemed to forecast his fate. The genial gentleness of his manner, his homely simplicity, the cheerful humor that never failed, are now seen to have been but the tender light that played around the rugged heights of his strong and noble nature. It is small consolation that he died at the moment of the war when he could best be spared, for no nation is ever ready for the loss of such a friend. But it is something to remember that he lived to see the slow day breaking. Like Moses, he had marched with us through the wilderness. From the height of patriotic vision he beheld the golden fields of the future waving in peace and plenty. He beheld, and blessed God, but was not to enter in."[23]

In a discourse delivered on Lincoln on the 23d of that month, Henry Ward Beecher said:

"And now the martyr is moving in triumphal march, mightier than when alive. The nation rises up at every stage of his coming. Cities and states are his pall-bearers, and the cannon speaks the hours with solemn progression. Dead, dead, dead, he yet speaketh. Is Washington dead? Is Hampden dead? Is any man that was ever fit to live dead? Disenthralled of flesh, risen to the unobstructed sphere where passion never comes, he begins his illimitable work. His life is now grafted upon the infinite, and will be fruitful as no earthly life can be. Pass on, thou that hast overcome. Ye people, behold the martyr whose blood, as so many articulate words, pleads for fidelity, for law, for liberty."[24]

The funeral train reached Springfield on the 3d of May. The casket was borne to the State House and placed in Representative Hall—the very chamber in which in 1854 the deceased had pronounced that fearful invective against the sin of human slavery. The doors were thrown open, the coffin lid was removed, and we who had known the illustrious dead in other days, and before the nation lay its claim upon him, moved sadly through and looked for the last time on the silent, upturned face of our departed friend. All day long and through the night a stream of people filed reverently by the catafalque. Some of them were his colleagues at the bar; some his old friends from New Salem; some crippled soldiers fresh from the battle-fields of the war; and some were little children who, scarce realizing the impressiveness of the scene, were destined to live and tell their children yet to be born the sad story of Lincoln's death.

At ten o'clock in the morning of the second day, as a choir of two-hundred-and-fifty voices sang "Peace, Troubled Soul," the lid of the casket was shut down forever. The remains were borne outside and placed in a hearse, which moved at the head of a procession in charge of General Joseph Hooker to Oak Ridge cemetery. There Bishop Matthew Simpson delivered an eloquent and impressive funeral oration, and Rev. Dr. Gurley, of Washington, offered up the closing prayer. While the choir chanted "Unveil Thy Bosom, Faithful Tomb," the vault door opened and received to its final rest all that was mortal of Abraham Lincoln.

"It was soon known that the murder of Lincoln was one result of a conspiracy which had for its victims Secretary Seward and probably Vice-President Johnson, Secretary Stanton, General Grant, and perhaps others.[25] Booth had left a card for Mr. Johnson the day before, possibly with the intention of killing him. Mr. Seward received wounds, from which he soon recovered. Grant, who was to have accompanied Lincoln to the theatre on the night of the assassination, and did not, escaped unassailed. The general conspiracy was poorly planned and lamely executed. It involved about twenty-five persons. Mrs. Surratt, David C. Harold, Lewis Payne, Edward Spangler, Michael O'Loughlin, J. W. Atzerodt, Samuel

Arnold, and Dr. Samuel Mudd, who set Booth's leg, which was dislocated by the fall from the stage-box, were among the number captured and tried.

"After the assassination Booth escaped unmolested from the theatre, mounted his horse, and rode away, accompanied by Harold, into Maryland. Cavalrymen scoured the country, and eleven days after the shooting discovered them in a barn on Garrett's farm, near Port Royal on the Rappahannock. The soldiers surrounded the barn and demanded a surrender. After the second demand Harold surrendered, under a shower of curses from Booth, but Booth refused, declaring that he would never be taken alive. The captain of the squad then fired the barn. A correspondent thus describes the scene:

"'The blaze lit up the recesses of the great barn till every wasp's nest and cobweb in the roof were luminous, flinging streaks of red and violet across the tumbled farm gear in the corner. They tinged the beams, the upright columns, the barricades, where clover and timothy piled high held toward the hot incendiary their separate straws for the funeral pile. They bathed the murderer's retreat in a beautiful illumination, and, while in bold outlines his figure stood revealed, they rose like an impenetrable wall to guard from sight the hated enemy who lit them. Behind the blaze, with his eye to a crack, Colonel Conger saw Wilkes Booth standing upright upon a crutch. At the gleam of fire Booth dropped his crutch and carbine, and on both hands crept up to the spot to espy the incendiary and shoot him dead. His eyes were lustrous with fever, and swelled and rolled in terrible beauty, while his teeth were fixed, and he wore the expression of one in the calmness before frenzy. In vain he peered, with vengeance in his look; the blaze that made him visible concealed his enemy. A second he turned glaring at the fire, as if to leap upon it and extinguish it, but it had made such headway that he dismissed the thought. As calmly as upon the battle-field a veteran stands amidst the hail of ball and shell and plunging iron, Booth turned and pushed for the door, carbine in poise, and the last resolve of death, which we name despair, set on his high, bloodless forehead.

"'Just then Sergeant Boston Corbett fired through a crevice and shot Booth in the neck. He was carried out of the barn and laid upon the grass, and there died about four hours afterward. Before his misguided soul passed into the silence of death he whispered something which Lieutenant Baker bent down to hear. "Tell mother I die for my country," he said, faintly. Reviving a moment later he repeated the words, and added, "I thought I did for the best."

"'His days of hiding and fleeing from his pursuers had left him pale, haggard, dirty, and unkempt. He had cut off his mustache and cropped his hair close to his head, and he and Harold both wore the Confederate gray uniform.'

"Booth's body was taken to Washington, and a post mortem examination of it held on board the monitor 'Montauk,'and on the night of the 27th of April it was given in charge of two men in a rowboat, who, it is claimed, disposed of it in secrecy—how, none but themselves know. Numerous stories have been told of the final resting-place of that hated dead man. Whoever knows the truth of it tells it not.

"Sergeant Corbett, who shot Booth, fired without orders. The last instructions given by Colonel Baker to Colonel Conger and Lieutenant Baker were: 'Don't shoot Booth, but take him alive.' Corbett was something of a fanatic, and for a breach of discipline had once been court-martialled and sentenced to be shot. The order, however, was not executed, but he had been drummed out of the regiment. He belonged to Company L of the Sixteenth New York Cavalry. He was English by birth, but was brought up in this country, and learned the trade of hat finisher. While living in Boston he joined the Methodist Episcopal Church. Never having been baptized, he was at a loss to know what name to adopt, but after making it a subject of prayer he took the name of Boston, in honor of the place of his conversion. He was ever undisciplined and erratic. He is said to be living in Kansas, and draws a pension from the Government.

"Five of the conspirators were tried, and three, Payne, Harold, and Mrs. Surratt, were hanged.[26] Dr. Mudd was sent to the Dry Tortugas for a period of years, and there did such good work among the yellow-fever sufferers during an epidemic that he was pardoned and returned to this country. He died only about two years ago at his home in Maryland, near Washington. Atzerodt was sent to the Dry Tortugas also, and died there years ago. John Surratt fled to Italy, and there entered the Papal guards. He was discovered by Archbishop Hughes, and by the courtesy of the Italian government, though the extradition laws did not cover his case, was delivered over to the United States for trial. At his first trial the jury hung; at the second, in which Edwards Pierrepont was the Government counsel, Surratt got off on the plea of limitations. He undertook to lecture, and began at Rockville, Md. The *Evening Star,* of Washington, reported the lecture, which was widely copied, and was of such a feeble character that it killed him as a lecturer. He went to Baltimore, where, it is said, he still lives. Spangler, the scene-shifter, who was an accomplice of Booth, was sent to the Dry Tortugas, served out his term and died about ten years ago. McLoughlin, who was arrested because of his acquaintance with the conspirators, was sent to the Dry Tortugas and there died.

"Ford's Theatre was never played in after that memorable night. Ten or twelve days after the assassination Ford attempted to open it, but Stanton prevented it, and the Government bought the theatre for $100,000, and converted it into a medical museum. Ford was a Southern sympathizer. He ran two theatres until four years ago, one in Washington and one in Baltimore. Alison Naylor, the livery man who let Booth have his horse, still lives in Washington. Major Rathbone, who was in the box with Lincoln when he was shot, died within the last four years. Stewart, the man who jumped on the stage to follow Booth, and announced to the audience that he had escaped through the alley, died lately. Strange, but very few persons can now be found who were at the theatre that night. Laura Keene died a few years ago.

"Booth the assassin was the third son of the eminent English tragedian Junius Brutus Booth, and the brother of the equally renowned Edwin Booth. He was only twenty-six years old when he figured as the chief actor in this horrible drama. He began his dramatic career as John Wilkes, and as a stock actor gained a fair reputation, but had not achieved any special success. He had played chiefly in the South and West, and but a few times in New York. Some time before the assassination of Lincoln he had abandoned his profession on account of a bronchial affection. Those who knew him and saw him on that fatal Friday say that he was restless, like one who, consciously or unconsciously, was overshadowed by some awful fate. He knew that the President and his party intended to be present at Ford's theatre in the evening, and he asked an acquaintance if he should attend the performance, remarking that if he did he would see some unusually fine acting. He was a handsome man. His eyes were large and dark, his hair dark and inclined to curl, his features finely moulded, his form tall, and his address pleasing."[27]

Frederick Stone, counsel for Harold after Booth's death, is authority for the statement that the occasion for Lincoln's assassination was the sentiment expressed by the President in a speech delivered from the steps of the White House on the night of April 11, when he said: "If universal amnesty is granted to the insurgents I cannot see how I can avoid exacting in return universal suffrage, or at least suffrage on the basis of intelligence and military service."[28] Booth was standing before Mr. Lincoln on the outskirts of the crowd. "That means nigger citizenship," he said to Harold by his side. "Now, by God! I'll put him through." But whatever may have been the incentive, Booth seemed to crave the reprehensible fame that attaches to a bold and dramatically wicked deed. He may, it is true, have been mentally unhinged, but, whether sane or senseless, he made for himself an infamous and endless notoriety when he murdered the patient, forbearing man who had directed our ship of state through the most tempestuous waters it ever encountered.

In the death of Lincoln the South, prostrate and bleeding, lost a friend; and his unholy taking-off at the very hour of the assured supremacy of the Union cause ran the iron into the heart of the North. His sun went down suddenly, and whelmed the country in a darkness which was felt by every heart; but far up the clouds sprang apart, and soon the golden light, flooding the heavens with radiance, illuminated every uncovered brow with the hope of a fair to-morrow. His name will ever be the watchword of liberty. His work is finished, and sealed forever with the veneration given to the blood of martyrs. Yesterday a man reviled and abused, a target for the shafts of malice and hatred: to-day an apostle. Yesterday a power: to-day a prestige, sacred, irresistible. The life and the tragic death of Mr. Lincoln mark an epoch in history from which dates the unqualified annunciation by the American people of the greatest truth in the bible of republicanism—the very keystone of that arch of human rights which is destined to overshadow and remodel every government upon the earth. The glorious brightness of that upper world, as it welcomed his faint and bleeding spirit, broke through upon the earth at his exit—it was the dawn of a day growing brighter as the grand army of freedom follows in the march of time.

Lincoln's place in history will be fixed—aside from his personal characteristics—by the events and results of the war. As a great political leader who quelled a rebellion of eight millions of people, liberated four millions of slaves, and demonstrated to the world the ability of the people to maintain a government of themselves, by themselves, for themselves, he will assuredly occupy no insignificant place.

To accomplish the great work of preserving the Union cost the land a great price. Generations of Americans yet unborn, and humanity everywhere, for years to come will mourn the horrors and sacrifices of the first civil war in the United States; but above the blood of its victims, above the bones of its dead, above the ashes of desolate hearths, will arise the colossal figure of Abraham Lincoln as the most acceptable sacrifice offered by the nineteenth century in expiation of the great crime of the seventeenth. Above all the anguish and tears of that immense hecatomb will appear the shade of Lincoln as the symbol of hope and of pardon.

This is the true lesson of Lincoln's life: real and enduring greatness, that will survive the corrosion and abrasion of time, of change, and of progress, must rest upon character. In certain brilliant and what is understood to be most desirable endowments how many Americans have surpassed him. Yet how he looms above them all! Not eloquence, nor logic, nor grasp of thought; not statesmanship, nor power of command, nor courage; not any nor all of these have made him what he is, but these, in the degree in which he possessed them, conjoined to those qualities comprised in the term character, have given him his fame—have made him for all time to come the great American, the grand, central figure in American—perhaps the world's—history.

CHAPTER XX.*

Soon after the death of Mr. Lincoln Dr. J. G. Holland came out to Illinois from his home in Massachusetts to gather up materials for a life of the dead President.[1] The gentleman spent several days with me, and I gave him all the assistance that lay in my power. I was much pleased with him, and awaited with not a little interest the appearance of his book. I felt sure that even after my long and intimate acquaintance with Mr. Lincoln I never fully knew and understood him, and I therefore wondered what sort of a description Dr. Holland, after interviewing Lincoln's old-time friends, would make of his individual characteristics. When the book appeared he said this:[2] "The writer has conversed with multitudes of men who claimed to know Mr. Lincoln intimately: yet there are not two of the whole number who agree in their estimate of him. The fact was that he rarely showed more than one aspect of himself to one man. He opened himself to men in different directions. To illustrate the effect of the peculiarity of Mr. Lincoln's intercourse with men it may be said that men who knew him through all his professional and political life offered opinions as diametrically opposite as these, viz.: that he was a very ambitious man, and that he was without a particle of ambition; that he was one of the saddest men that ever lived, and that he was one of the jolliest men that ever lived; that he was very religious, but that he was not a Christian; that he was a Christian, but did not know it; that he was so far from being a religious man or a Christian that 'the less said upon that subject the better;' that he was the most cunning man in America, and that he had not a particle of cunning in him; that he had the strongest personal attachments, and

---

*The substance of this chapter, I delivered in the form of a lecture to a Springfield audience in 1866. W. H. H.

that he had no personal attachments at all—only a general good feeling towards everybody; that he was a man of indomitable will, and that he was a man almost without a will; that he was a tyrant, and that he was the softest-hearted, most brotherly man that ever lived; that he was remarkable for his pure-mindedness, and that he was the foulest in his jests and stories of any man in the country; that he was a witty man, and that he was only a retailer of the wit of others; that his apparent candor and fairness were only apparent, and that they were as real as his head and his hands; that he was a boor, and that he was in all respects a gentleman; that he was a leader of the people, and that he was always led by the people; that he was cool and impassive, and that he was susceptible of the strongest passions. It is only by tracing these separate streams of impression back to their fountain that we are able to arrive at anything like a competent comprehension of the man, or to learn why he came to be held in such various estimation. Men caught only separate aspects of his character—only the fragments that were called into exhibition by their own qualities."°

Dr. Holland had only found what Lincoln's friends had always experienced in their relations with him—that he was a man of many moods and many sides. He never revealed himself entirely to any one man, and therefore he will always to a certain extent remain enveloped in doubt. Even those who were with him through long years of hard study and under constantly varying circumstances can hardly say they knew him through and through. I always believed I could read him as thoroughly as any man, and yet he was so different in many respects from any other one I ever met before or since his time that I cannot say I com-

---

°I beg to note here in passing the estimate of Lincoln's mind and character by one of his colleagues at the bar in Springfield who still survives, but whose name, for certain reasons, I am constrained to withhold. I still retain the original MS. written by him twenty years ago. "I am particularly requested," he said, "to write out my opinion of the mind of Abraham Lincoln, late President of the United States, and I consent to do so without any other motive than to comply with the request of a brother lawyer, for, if I know myself, no other motive would induce me to do it, because, while Mr. Lincoln and I were always good friends, I believe myself wholly indifferent to the future of his memory. The opinion I now have was formed by a personal and professional acquaintance of over ten years, and has not been altered or influenced by any of his promotions in public life. The adulation by base multitudes of a living, and the pageantry surrounding a dead, President do not shake my well-settled convictions of the man's mental calibre. Physiologically and phrenologically the man was a sort of monstrosity. His frame was large, long, bony, and muscular; his head, small and disproportionately shaped. He had large, square jaws; large, heavy nose; small, lascivious mouth; and soft, tender, bluish eyes. I would say he was a cross between Venus and Hercules. I believe it to be inconsistent with the laws of human organization for any such creature to possess a mind capable of anything called great. The man's mind partook of the incongruities of his body. He had no mind not possessed by the most ordinary of men. It was simply the peculiarity of his mental and the oddity of his physical structure, as well as the qualities of his heart that singled him out from the mass of men. His native love of justice, truth and humanity led his mind a great way in the accomplishment of his objects in life. That passion or sentiment steadied and determined an otherwise indecisive mind."[3]

prehended him. In this chapter I give my recollection of his individual characteristics as they occur to me, and allow the world to form its own opinion. If my recollection of the man destroys any other person's ideal, I cannot help it. By a faithful and lifelike description of Lincoln the man, and a study of his peculiar and personal traits, perhaps some of the apparent contradictions met with by Dr. Holland will have melted from sight.

Mr. Lincoln was six feet four inches high, and when he left the city of his home for Washington was fifty-one years old, having good health and no gray hairs, or but few, on his head. He was thin, wiry, sinewy, raw-boned; thin through the breast to the back, and narrow across the shoulders; standing he leaned forward—was what may be called stoop-shouldered, inclining to the consumptive by build. His usual weight was one hundred and eighty pounds. His organization—rather his structure and functions—worked slowly. His blood had to run a long distance from his heart to the extremities of his frame, and his nerve force had to travel through dry ground a long distance before his muscles were obedient to his will. His structure was loose and leathery; his body was shrunk and shrivelled; he had dark skin, dark hair, and looked woe-struck. The whole man, body and mind, worked slowly, as if it needed oiling. Physically he was a very powerful man, lifting with ease four hundred, and in one case six hundred, pounds. His mind was like his body, and worked slowly but strongly. Hence there was very little bodily or mental wear and tear in him. This peculiarity in his construction gave him great advantage over other men in public life. No man in America—scarcely a man in the world—could have stood what Lincoln did in Washington and survived through more than one term of the Presidency.[4]

When he walked he moved cautiously but firmly; his long arms and giant hands swung down by his side. He walked with even tread, the inner sides of his feet being parallel. He put the whole foot flat down on the ground at once, not landing on the heel; he likewise lifted his foot all at once, not rising from the toe, and hence he had no spring to his walk. His walk was undulatory—catching and pocketing time, weariness, and pain, all up and down his person, and thus preventing them from locating. The first impression of a stranger, or a man who did not observe closely, was that his walk implied shrewdness and cunning—that he was a tricky man; but in reality, it was the walk of caution and firmness. In sitting down on a common chair he was no taller than ordinary men. His legs and arms were abnormally, unnaturally long, and in undue proportion to the remainder of his body. It was only when he stood up that he loomed above other men.

Mr. Lincoln's head was long, and tall from the base of the brain and from the eyebrows. His head ran backwards, his forehead rising as it ran back at a low angle, like Clay's, and unlike Webster's, which was almost perpendicular. The size of his hat measured at the hatter's block was seven and one-eighth, his head being, from ear to ear, six and one-half inches, and from the front to the back of the brain eight inches. Thus measured it was not below the medium size. His forehead was narrow but high; his hair was dark, almost black, and lay floating where his fingers or the winds left it, piled up at random. His cheek-bones were high, sharp, and prominent; his jaws were long and upcurved; his nose was large, long, blunt, and a little awry towards the right eye; his chin was sharp and upcurved; his eyebrows cropped out like a huge rock on the brow of a hill; his long, sallow face was wrinkled and dry, with a hair here and there on the surface; his cheeks were leathery; his ears were large, and ran out almost at right angles from his head, caused partly by heavy hats and partly by nature; his lower lip was thick, hanging, and undercurved, while his chin reached for the lip upcurved; his neck was neat and trim, his head being well balanced on it; there was the lone mole on the right cheek, and Adam's apple on his throat.

Thus stood, walked, acted and looked Abraham Lincoln. He was not a pretty man by any means, nor was he an ugly one; he was a homely man, careless of his looks, plain-looking and plain-acting. He had no pomp, display, or dignity, so-called. He appeared simple in his carriage and bearing. He was a sad-looking man; his melancholy dripped from him as he walked. His apparent gloom impressed his friends,* and created sympathy for him—one means of his great success. He was gloomy, abstracted, and joyous—rather humorous—by turns; but I do not think he knew what real joy was for many years.

Mr. Lincoln sometimes walked our streets cheerily, he was not always gloomy,

---

*Lincoln's melancholy never failed to impress any man who ever saw or knew him. The perpetual look of sadness was his most prominent feature. The cause of this peculiar condition was a matter of frequent discussion among his friends. John T. Stuart said it was due to his abnormal digestion. His liver failed to work properly—did not secrete bile—and his bowels were equally as inactive. "I used to advise him to take blue-mass pills," related Stuart, "and he did take them before he went to Washington, and for five months while he was President, but when I came on to Congress he told me he had ceased using them because they made him cross."[5] The reader can hardly realize the extent of this peculiar tendency to gloom. One of Lincoln's colleagues in the Legislature of Illinois is authority for the statement coming from Lincoln himself that this "mental depression became so intense at times he never dared carry a pocket knife."[6] Two things greatly intensified his characteristic sadness: one was the endless succession of troubles in his domestic life, which he had to bear in silence; and the other was unquestionably the knowledge of his own obscure and lowly origin. The recollection of these things burned a deep impress on his sensitive soul.

As to the cause of this morbid condition my idea has always been that it was occult, and could not be explained by any course of observation and reasoning. It was ingrained, and being ingrained, could not be reduced to rule, or the cause arrayed. It was necessarily hereditary, but whether it came down from a long line of ancestors and far back, or was simply the reproduction of the saddened life of Nancy Hanks, cannot well be determined. At any rate it was part of his nature, and could no more be shaken off than he could part with his brains.

and then it was that on meeting a friend he greeted him with plain "Howd'y?" clasping his hand in both of his own, and gave him a hearty soul-welcome. On a winter's morning he might be seen stalking towards the market-house, basket on arm, his old gray shawl wrapped around his neck, his little boy Willie or Tad running along at his heels asking a thousand boyish questions, which his father, in deep abstraction, neither heeded nor heard.° If a friend met or passed him, and he awoke from his reverie, something would remind him of a story he had heard in Indiana, and tell it he would, and there was no alternative but to listen.

Thus, I repeat, stood and walked and talked this singular man. He was odd, but when that gray eye and that face and those features were lit up by the inward soul in fires of emotion, then it was that all those apparently ugly features sprang into organs of beauty or disappeared in the sea of inspiration that often flooded his face. Sometimes it appeared as if Lincoln's soul was fresh from its Creator.

I have asked the friends and foes of Mr. Lincoln alike what they thought of his perceptions. One gentleman of unquestioned ability and free from all partiality or prejudice said, "Mr. Lincoln's perceptions were slow, a little perverted, if not somewhat distorted and diseased."[8] If the meaning of this is that Mr. Lincoln saw things from a peculiar angle of his being, and from this was susceptible to nature's impulses, and that he so expressed himself, then I have no objection to what is said. Otherwise I dissent. Mr. Lincoln's perceptions were slow, cold, clear, and exact. Everything came to him in its precise shape and color. To some men the world of matter and of man comes ornamented with beauty, life, and action; and hence more or less false and inexact. No lurking illusion or other

---

°"I lived next door to the Lincolns for many years, knew the family well. Mr. Lincoln used to come to our house, his feet encased in a pair of loose slippers, and with an old, faded pair of trousers fastened with one suspender. He frequently came to our house for milk. Our rooms were low, and he said one day, 'Jim, you'll have to lift your loft a little higher; I can't straighten out under it very well.' To my wife, who was short of stature, he used to say that little people had some advantages: they required less 'wood and wool to make them comfortable.' In his yard Lincoln had but little shrubbery. He once planted some rose bushes, to which he called my attention, but soon neglected them altogether. He never planted any vines or fruit trees, seemed to have no fondness for such things. At one time, yielding to my suggestion, he undertook to keep a garden in the rear part of his yard, but one season's experience sufficed to cure him of all desire for another. He kept his own horse, fed and curried it when at home; he also fed and milked his own cow, and sawed his own wood. Mr. Lincoln and his wife agreed moderately well. Frequently Mrs. Lincoln's temper would get the better of her. If she became furious, as she often did, her husband tried to pay no attention to her. He would sometimes laugh at her, but generally he would pick up one of the children and walk off. I have heard her say that if Mr. Lincoln had remained at home more she could have loved him better. One day while Mr. Lincoln was absent—he had gone to Chicago to try a suit in the United States Court—his wife and I formed a conspiracy to take off the roof and raise his house. It was originally a frame structure one story and a half high. When Lincoln returned he met a gentleman on the sidewalk and looking at his own house and manifesting great surprise, inquired: 'Stranger, can you tell me where Lincoln lives?' The gentleman gave him the necessary information, and Lincoln gravely entered his own premises."—Statement, James Gourly, February 9, 1866.[7]

error, false in itself and clad for the moment in robes of splendor, ever passed undetected or unchallenged over the threshold of his mind—that point which divides vision from the realm and home of thought. Names to him were nothing, and titles naught—assumption always standing back abashed at his cold, intellectual glare. Neither his perceptions nor intellectual vision were perverted, distorted, or diseased. He saw all things through a perfect mental lens. There was no diffraction or refraction there. He was not impulsive, fanciful, or imaginative; but cold, calm, and precise. He threw his whole mental light around the object, and after a time, substance and quality stood apart, form and color took their appropriate places, and all was clear and exact in his mind. His fault, if any, was that he saw things less than they really were; less beautiful and more frigid. He crushed the unreal, the inexact, the hollow, and the sham. He saw things in rigidity rather than in vital action. He saw what no man could dispute, but he failed to see what might have been seen.

To some minds the world is all life, a soul beneath the material; but to Mr. Lincoln no life was individual that did not manifest itself to him. His mind was his standard. His mental action was deliberate, and he was pitiless and persistent in pursuit of the truth. No error went undetected, no falsehood unexposed, if he once was aroused in search of the truth. The true peculiarity of Mr. Lincoln has not been seen by his various biographers; or, if seen, they have failed wofully to give it that importance which it deserves. Newton beheld the law of the universe in the fall of an apple from a tree to the ground; Owen saw the animal in its claw; Spencer saw evolution in the growth of a seed; and Shakespeare saw human nature in the laugh of a man. Nature was suggestive to all these men. Mr. Lincoln no less saw philosophy in a story and an object lesson[9] in a joke. His was a new and original position, one which was always suggesting something to him. The world and man, principles and facts, all were full of suggestions to his susceptible soul. They continually put him in mind of something. His ideas were odd and original for the reason that he was a peculiar and original creation himself.

His power in the association of ideas was as great as his memory was tenacious and strong. His language indicated oddity and originality of vision as well as expression. Words and language are but the counterparts of the idea—the other half of the idea; they are but the stinging, hot, leaden bullets that drop from the mould; in a rifle, with powder stuffed behind them and fire applied, they are an embodied force resistlessly pursuing their object. In the search for words Mr. Lincoln was often at a loss. He was often perplexed to give proper expression to his ideas; first, because he was not master of the English language; and secondly, because there were, in the vast store of words, so few that contained the exact coloring, power, and shape of his ideas. This will account for the frequent resort by him to the use of stories, maxims, and jokes in which to clothe his ideas, that they might be comprehended. So true was this peculiar mental vision of his that, though mankind has been gathering, arranging, and classifying facts for thousands of years, Lincoln's peculiar standpoint could give him no advantage over other men's labor. Hence he tore down to their deepest foundations all arrangements of facts, and constructed new ones to govern himself. He was compelled from his peculiar mental organization to do this. His labor was great and continuous.

The truth about Mr. Lincoln is that he read less and thought more than any man in his sphere in America. No man can put his finger on any great book written in the last or present century that he read thoroughly. When young he read the Bible, and when of age he read Shakespeare; but, though he often quoted from both, he never read either one through. He is acknowledged now to have been a great man, but the question is what made him great. I repeat, that he read less and thought more than any man of his standing in America, if not in the world. He possessed originality and power of thought in an eminent degree. Besides his well established reputation for caution, he was concentrated in his thoughts and had great continuity of reflection. In everything he was patient and enduring. These are some of the grounds of his wonderful success.

Not only were nature, man, and principle suggestive to Mr. Lincoln, not only had he accurate and exact perceptions, but he was causative; his mind, apparently with an automatic movement, ran back behind facts, principles, and all things to their origin and first cause—to that point where forces act at once as effect and cause. He would stop in the street and analyze a machine. He would whittle a thing to a point, and then count the numberless inclined planes and their pitch making the point. Mastering and defining this, he would then cut that point back and get a broad transverse section of his pine-stick, and peel and define that. Clocks, omnibuses, language, paddle-wheels, and idioms never escaped his observation and analysis. Before he could form an idea of anything, before he would express his opinion on a subject, he must know its origin and history in substance and quality, in magnitude and gravity. He must know it inside and outside, upside and downside. He searched and comprehended his own mind and nature thoroughly, as I have often heard him say. He must analyze a sensation, an idea, and run back in its history to its origin, and purpose. He was remorseless in his analysis of facts and principles. When all these exhaustive processes had been gone through with he could form an idea and express it; but no sooner. He had no faith, and no respect for "say so's," come though they might from tradition or authority. Thus everything had to run through the crucible, and be tested by the fires of his analytic mind; and when at last he did speak, his utterances rang out with the clear and keen ring of gold upon the counters of the understanding. He reasoned logically through analogy and comparison. All opponents dreaded his originality of idea, his condensation, definition, and force of expression; and woe be to the man who hugged to his bosom a secret error if Lincoln got on the chase of it. I repeat, woe to him! Time could hide the error in no nook or corner of space in which he would not detect and expose it.

Though gifted with accurate and acute perception, though a profound thinker as well as analyzer, still Lincoln's judgment on many and minor matters was oftentimes childish. By the word judgment I do not mean what mental philosophers would call the exercise of reason, will—understanding; but I use the term in its popular sense. I refer to that capacity or power which decides on the fitness, the harmony, or, if you will, the beauty and appropriateness of things. I have always thought, and sometimes said, Lincoln lacked this quality in his mental structure. He was on the alert if a principle was involved or a man's rights at stake in a transaction; but he never could see the harm in wearing a sack-coat instead of a swallowtail to an evening party, nor could he realize the offense of telling a vulgar yarn if a preacher happened to be present.°

As already expressed, Mr. Lincoln had no faith. In order to believe, he must see and feel, and thrust his hand into the place. He must taste, smell, and handle before he had faith or even belief. Such a mind manifestly must have its time. His forte and power lay in digging out for himself and securing for his mind its own food, to be assimilated unto itself. Thus, in time he would form opinions and conclusions that no human power could overthrow. They were as irresistible as the rush of a flood; as convincing as logic embodied in mathematics. And yet the question arises: "Had Mr. Lincoln great, good common-sense?" A variety of opinions suggest themselves in answer to this. If the true test is that a man shall judge the rush and whirl of human actions and transactions as wisely and accu-

---

°Sometime in 1857 a lady reader or elocutionist came to Springfield and gave a public reading in a hall immediately north of the State House. As lady lecturers were then rare birds, a very large crowd greeted her. Among other things she recited "Nothing to Wear," a piece in which is described the perplexities that beset "Miss Flora McFlimsey" in her efforts to appear fashionable. In the midst of one stanza, in which no effort is made to say anything particularly amusing, and during the reading of which the audience manifested the most respectful silence and attention, some one in the rear seats burst out into a loud, coarse laugh—a sudden and explosive guffaw. It startled the speaker and audience, and kindled a storm of unsuppressed laughter and applause. Everyone looked back to ascertain the cause of the demonstration, and was greatly surprised to find that it was Mr. Lincoln. He blushed and squirmed with the awkward diffidence of a schoolboy. What prompted him to laugh no one was able to explain. He was doubtless wrapped up in a brown study, and, recalling some amusing episode, indulged in laughter without realizing his surroundings. The experience mortified him greatly.[10]

rately as though indefinite time and proper conditions were at his disposal, then I am compelled to follow the logic of things and admit that he had no great stock of common-sense; but if, on the other hand, the time and conditions were ripe, his common-sense was in every case equal to the emergency. He knew himself, and never trusted his dollar or his fame in casual opinions—never acted hastily or prematurely on great matters.

Mr. Lincoln believed that the great leading law of human nature is motive. He reasoned all ideas of a disinterested action out of my mind. I used to hold that an action could be pure, disinterested, and wholly free from selfishness; but he divested me of that delusion. His idea was that all human actions were caused by motives, and that at the bottom of these motives was self. He defied me to act without motive and unselfishly; and when I did the act and told him of it, he analyzed and sifted it to the last grain. After he had concluded, I could not avoid the admission that he had demonstrated the absolute selfishness of the entire act. Although a profound analyzer of the laws of human nature he could form no just construction of the motives of the particular individual. He knew but little of the play of the features as seen in the "human face divine." He could not distinguish between the paleness of anger and the crimson tint of modesty. In determining what each play of the features indicated he was pitiably weak.

The great predominating elements of Mr. Lincoln's peculiar character were: first, his great capacity and power of reason; second, his conscience and his excellent understanding; third, an exalted idea of the sense of right and equity; fourth, his intense veneration of the true and the good. His conscience, his heart and all the faculties and qualities of his mind bowed submissively to the despotism of his reason. He lived and acted from the standard of reason—that throne of logic, home of principle—the realm of Deity in man. It is from this point Mr. Lincoln must be viewed. Not only was he cautious, patient, and enduring; not only had he concentration and great continuity of thought; but he had profound analytical power. His vision was clear, and he was emphatically the master of statement. His pursuit of the truth, as before mentioned, was indefatigable. He reasoned from well-chosen principles with such clearness, force, and directness that the tallest intellects in the land bowed to him. He was the strongest man I ever saw, looking at him from the elevated standpoint of reason and logic. He came down from that height with irresistible and crashing force. His Cooper Institute and other printed speeches will prove this; but his speeches before the courts—especially the Supreme Court of Illinois—if they had been preserved, would demonstrate it still more plainly. Here he demanded time to think and prepare. The office of reason is to determine the truth. Truth is the power of reason, and Lincoln loved truth for its own sake. It was to him reason's food.

Conscience, the second great quality of Mr. Lincoln's character, is that faculty which induces in us love of the just. Its real office is justice; right and equity are its correlatives. As a court, it is in session continuously; it decides all acts at all times. Mr. Lincoln had a deep, broad, living conscience. His reason, however, was the real judge; it told him what was true or false, and therefore good or bad, right or wrong, just or unjust, and his conscience echoed back the decision. His conscience ruled his heart; he was always just before he was generous. It cannot be said of any mortal that he was always absolutely just. Neither was Lincoln always just; but his general life was. It follows that if Mr. Lincoln had great reason and great conscience he must have been an honest man; and so he was. He was rightfully entitled to the appellation "Honest Abe." Honesty was his polar star.

Mr. Lincoln also had a good understanding; that is, the faculty that comprehends the exact state of things and determines their relations, near or remote. The understanding does not necessarily enquire for the reason of things. While Lincoln was odd and original, while he lived out of himself and by himself, and while he could absorb but little from others, yet a reading of his speeches, messages, and letters satisfies us that he had good understanding. But the strongest point in his make-up was the knowledge he had of himself; he comprehended and understood his own capacity—what he did and why he did it—better perhaps than any man of his day. He had a wider and deeper comprehension of his environments, of the political conditions especially, than men who were more learned or had had the benefits of a more thorough training.

He was a very sensitive man,—modest to the point of diffidence,—and often hid himself in the masses to prevent the discovery of his identity. He was not indifferent, however, to approbation and public opinion. He had no disgusting egotism and no pompous pride, no aristocracy, no haughtiness, no vanity. Merging together the qualities of his nature he was a meek, quiet, unobtrusive gentleman.

As many contradictory opinions prevail in reference to Mr. Lincoln's heart and humanity as on the question of his judgment. As many persons perhaps contend that he was cold and obdurate as that he was warm and affectionate. The first thing the world met in contact with him was his head and conscience; after that he exposed the tender side of his nature—his heart, subject at all times to his exalted sense of right and equity, namely his conscience. In proportion as he held his conscience subject to his head, he held his heart subject to his head and conscience. His humanity had to defer to his sense of justice and the eternal right.

His heart was the lowest of these organs, if we may call them such—the weakest of the three. Some men have reversed this order and characterized his heart as his ruling organ. This estimate of Mr. Lincoln endows him with love regardless of truth, justice, and right. The question still is, was Lincoln cold and heartless, or warm and affectionate? Can a man be all heart, all head, and all conscience? Some of these are masters over the others, some will be dominant, ruling with imperial sway, and thus giving character to the man. What, in the first place, do we mean by a warm-hearted man? Is it one who goes out of himself and reaches for others spontaneously, seeking to correct some abuse to mankind because of a deep love for humanity, apart from equity and truth, and who does what he does for love's sake? If so, Mr. Lincoln was a cold man. If a man, woman, or child approached him, and the prayer of such an one was granted, that itself was not evidence of his love. The African was enslaved and deprived of his rights; a principle was violated in doing so. Rights imply obligations as well as duties. Mr. Lincoln was President; he was in a position that made it his duty, through his sense of right, his love of principle, the constitutional obligations imposed upon him by the oath of office, to strike the blow against slavery. But did he do it for love? He has himself answered the question: "I would not free the slaves if I could preserve the Union without it."[11] When he freed the slaves there was no heart in the act. This argument can be used against his too enthusiastic friends.

In general terms his life was cold—at least characterized by what many persons would deem great indifference. He had, however, a strong latent capacity to love: but the object must first come in the guise of a principle, next it must be right and true—then it was lovely in his sight. He loved humanity when it was oppressed—an abstract love as against the concrete love centered in an individual. He rarely used terms of endearment, and yet he was proverbially tender and gentle. He gave the key-note to his own character when he said: "With malice towards none, with charity for all." In proportion to his want of deep, intense love he had no hate and bore no malice. His charity for an imperfect man was as broad as his devotion to principle was enduring.

"But was not Mr. Lincoln a man of great humanity?" asks a friend at my elbow; to which I reply, "Has not that question been answered already?" Let us suppose it has not. We must understand each other. What is meant by his humanity? Is it meant that he had much of human nature in him? If so, I grant that he was a man of humanity. If, in the event of the above definition being unsatisfactory or untrue, it is meant that he was tender and kind, then I again agree. But if the inference is that he would sacrifice truth or right in the slightest degree for the love of a friend, then he was neither tender nor kind; nor did he have any humanity. The law of human nature is such that it cannot be all head, all conscience, and all heart in one person at the same time. Our Maker so constituted things that, where God through reason blazed the way, we might boldly walk therein. The glory of Mr. Lincoln's power lay in the just and magnificent equipoise of head, conscience, and heart; and here his fame must rest or not at all.

Not only were Mr. Lincoln's perceptions good; not only was nature suggestive to him; not only was he original and strong; not only had he great reason, good understanding; not only did he love the true and the good—the eternal right; not only was he tender and sympathetic and kind;—but, in due proportion and in legitimate subordination, he had a glorious combination of them all. Through his perceptions—the suggestiveness of nature, his originality and strength; through his magnificent reason, his understanding, his conscience, his tenderness, quick sympathy, his heart; he approximated as nearly as human nature and the imperfections of man would permit to an embodiment of the great moral principle, "Do unto others as ye would they should do unto you."

Of Mr. Lincoln's will-power there are two opinions also: one that he lacked any will; the other that he was all will. Both these contradictory views have their vehement and honest champions. For the great underlying principles of mind in man he had great respect. He loved the true first, the right second, and the good last. His mind struggled for truth, and his soul reached out for substances. He cared not for forms, ways, methods—the non-substantial things of this world. He could not, by reason of his structure and mental organization, care anything about them. He did not have an intense care for any particular or individual man—the dollar, property, rank, orders, manners, or similar things; neither did he have any avarice or other like vice in his nature. He detested somewhat all technical rules in law, philosophy, and other sciences—mere forms everywhere—because they were, as a general thing, founded on arbitrary thoughts and ideas, and not on reason, truth, and the right. These things seemed to him lacking in substance, and he disregarded them because they cramped the originality of his genius. What suited a little narrow, critical mind did not suit Mr. Lincoln any more than a child's clothes would fit his father's body. Generally he took no interest in town affairs or local elections; he attended no meetings that pertained to local interests. He did not care—because by reason of his nature he could not—who succeeded to the presidency of this or that society or railroad company; who made the most money; who was going to Philadelphia, and what were the costs of such a trip; who was going to be married; who among his friends got this office or that—who was elected street commissioner or health inspector. No principle of truth, right, or justice being involved in any of these things he could not be moved by them.° He could not understand why men struggled so desperately for the little glory or lesser salary the small offices afforded. He made this remark to me one day in Washington: "If ever this free people—this Government—is utterly demoralized, it will come from this human struggle for office—a way to live without work."[13] It puzzled him a good deal, he said, to get at the root of this dreaded disease, which spread like contagion during the nation's death struggle.

Because he could not feel a deep interest in the things referred to, nor manifest the same interest in those who were engaged in the popular scramble, he was called indifferent—nay, ungrateful—to his friends. This estimate of the man was a very unjust as well as unfair one. Mr. Lincoln loved his friends with commendable loyalty; in many cases he clung to them tenaciously, like iron to iron welded; and yet, because he could not be actively aroused, nor enter into the spirit of their anxiety for office, he was called ungrateful. But he was not so. He may have seemed passive and lacking in interest; he may not have measured his friendly duties by the applicant's hot desire; but yet he was never ungrateful. Neither was he a selfish man. He would never have performed an act, even to promote himself to the Presidency, if by that act any human being was wronged. If it is said that he preferred Abraham Lincoln to anyone else in the pursuit of his ambition, and that because of this he was a selfish man, then I can see no impropriety in the charge. Under the same conditions we should all be equally guilty.

Remembering that Mr. Lincoln's mind moved logically, slowly, and cautiously, the question of his will and its power is easily solved. Although he cared but little for simple facts, rules, and methods, he did care for the truth and right of principle. In debate he courteously granted all the forms and non-essential things to his opponent. Sometimes he yielded nine points out of ten. The nine he brushed aside as husks or rubbish; but the tenth, being a question of substance, he clung to with all his might. On the underlying principles of truth and justice his will was as firm as steel and as tenacious as iron. It was as solid, real, and vital as an idea on which the world turns. He scorned to support or adopt an untrue position, in proportion as his conscience prevented him from doing an unjust thing. Ask him to sacrifice in the slightest degree his convictions of

---

°A bitter, malignant fool who always had opposed Lincoln and his friends, and had lost no opportunity to abuse them, induced Lincoln to go to the Governor of Illinois and recommend him for an important office in the State Militia. There being no principle at stake Lincoln could not refuse the request. When his friends heard of it they were furious in their denunciation of his action. It mortified him greatly to learn that he had displeased them. "And yet," he said, a few days later, dwelling on the matter to me in the office, "I couldn't well refuse the little the fellow asked of me. Sometimes I feel," he added, dryly, "that it's a good thing I wasn't born a woman."[12]

truth°—as he was asked to do when he made his "house-divided-against-itself speech"—and his soul would have exclaimed with indignant scorn, "The world perish first!"

Such was Lincoln's will. Because on one line of questions—the non-essential—he was pliable, and on the other he was as immovable as the rocks, have arisen the contradictory notions prevalent regarding him. It only remains to say that he was inflexible and unbending in human transactions when it was necessary to be so, and not otherwise. At one moment he was pliable and expansive as gentle air; at the next as tenacious and unyielding as gravity itself.

Thus I have traced Mr. Lincoln through his perceptions, his suggestiveness, his judgment, and his four predominant qualities: powers of reason, understanding, conscience, and heart. In the grand review of his peculiar characteristics, nothing creates such an impressive effect as his love of the truth. It looms up over everything else. His life is proof of the assertion that he never yielded in his fundamental conception of truth to any man for any end.

All the follies and wrong Mr. Lincoln ever fell into or committed sprang out of these weak points: the want of intuitive judgment; the lack of quick, sagacious knowledge of the play and meaning of men's features as written on the face; the want of the sense of propriety of things; his tenderness and mercy; and lastly, his unsuspecting nature. He was deeply and sincerely honest himself, and assumed that others were so. He never suspected men; and hence in dealing with them he was easily imposed upon.

All the wise and good things Mr. Lincoln ever did sprang out of his great reason, his conscience, his understanding, his heart, his love of the truth, the right, and the good. I am speaking now of his particular and individual faculties and qualities, not of their combination or the result of any combinations. Run out these qualities and faculties abstractly, and see what they produce. For instance, a tender heart, a strong reason, a broad understanding, an exalted conscience, a love of the true and the good must, proportioned reasonably and applied practically, produce a man of great power and great humanity.

As illustrative of a combination in Mr. Lincoln's organization, it may be said that his eloquence lay in the strength of his logical faculty, his supreme power of reasoning, his great understanding, and his love of principle; in his clear and

---

°"Again, Mr. Lincoln seems to me too true and honest a man to have his eulogy written, and I have no taste for writing eulogies. I am sure that, if he were alive, he would feel that the exact truth regarding himself was far more worthy of himself and of his biographer than any flattering picture. I loved the man as he was, with his rugged features, his coarse, rebellious hair, his sad, dreamy eyes; and I love to see him, and I hope to describe him, as he was, and not otherwise."—Robert Dale Owen, January 22, 1867, MS.[14]

accurate vision; in his cool and masterly statement of principles around which the issues gather; and in the statement of those issues and the grouping of the facts that are to carry conviction to the minds of men of every grade of intelligence. He was so clear that he could not be misunderstood or long misrepresented. He stood square and bolt upright to his convictions, and anyone who listened to him would be convinced that he formed his thoughts and utterances by them. His mind was not exactly a wide, broad, generalizing, and comprehensive mind, nor yet a versatile, quick, and subtle one, bounding here and there as emergencies demanded; but it was deep, enduring, strong, like a majestic machine running in deep iron grooves with heavy flanges on its wheels.

Mr. Lincoln himself was a very sensitive man, and hence, in dealing with others, he avoided wounding their hearts or puncturing their sensibility. He was unusually considerate of the feelings of other men, regardless of their rank, condition, or station. At first sight he struck one with his plainness, simplicity of manner, sincerity, candor, and truthfulness. He had no double interests and no overwhelming dignity with which to chill the air around his visitor. He was always easy of approach and thoroughly democratic. He seemed to throw a charm around every man who ever met him. To be in his presence was a pleasure, and no man ever left his company with injured feelings unless most richly deserved.

The universal testimony, "He is an honest man," gave him a firm hold on the masses, and they trusted him with a blind religious faith. His sad, melancholy face excited their sympathy, and when the dark days came it was their heart-strings that entwined and sustained him. Sympathy, we are told, is one of the strongest and noblest incentives to human action. With the sympathy and love of the people to sustain him, Lincoln had unlimited power over them; he threw an invisible and weightless harness over them, and drove them through disaster and desperation to final victory. The trust and worship by the people of Lincoln were the result of his simple character. He held himself not aloof from the masses. He became one of them. They feared together, they struggled together, they hoped together; thus melted and moulded into one, they became one in thought, one in will, one in action. If Lincoln cautiously awaited the full development of the last fact in the great drama before he acted, when longer waiting would be a crime, he knew that the people were determinedly at his back. Thus, when a blow was struck, it came with the unerring aim and power of a bolt from heaven. A natural king—not ruling men, but leading them along the drifts and trends of their own tendencies, always keeping in mind the consent of the governed, he developed what the future historian will call the sublimest order of conservative statesmanship.

Whatever of life, vigor, force, and power of eloquence his peculiar qualities gave him; whatever there was in a fair, manly, honest, and impartial administration of justice under law to all men at all times; whatever there was in a strong will in the right governed by tenderness and mercy; whatever there was in toil and sublime patience; whatever there was in these things or a wise combination of them, Lincoln is justly entitled to in making up the impartial verdict of history. These limit and define him as a statesman, as an orator, as an executive of the nation, and as a man. They developed in all the walks of his life; they were his law; they were his nature, they were Abraham Lincoln.

This long, bony, sad man floated down the Sangamon river in a frail canoe in the spring of 1831. Like a piece of driftwood he lodged at last, without a history, strange, penniless, and alone. In sight of the capital of Illinois, in the fatigue of daily toil he struggled for the necessaries of life. Thirty years later this same peculiar man left the Sangamon river, backed by friends, by power, by the patriotic prayers of millions of people, to be the ruler of the greatest nation in the world.

As the leader of a brave people in their desperate struggle for national existence, Abraham Lincoln will always be an interesting historical character. His strong, honest, sagacious, and noble life will always possess a peculiar charm. Had it not been for his conservative statesmanship, his supreme confidence in the wisdom of the people, his extreme care in groping his way among facts and before ideas, this nation might have been two governments to-day. The low and feeble circulation of his blood; his healthful irritability, which responded so slowly to the effects of stimuli; the strength of his herculean frame; his peculiar organism, conserving its force; his sublime patience; his wonderful endurance; his great hand and heart, saved this country from division, when division meant its irreparable ruin.

The central figure of our national history, the sublime type of our civilization, posterity, with the record of his career and actions before it, will decree that, whether Providence so ordained it or not, Abraham Lincoln was the man for the hour.

The End.

APPENDIX

The following letters by Mr. Lincoln to his relatives were at one time placed in my hands. As they have never before been published entire I have thought proper to append them here. They are only interesting as showing Mr. Lincoln's affection for his father and step-mother, and as specimens of the good, sound sense with which he approached every undertaking. The list opens with a letter to his father written from Washington while a member of Congress:

"Washington, Dec. 24, 1848.
"My Dear Father:
"Your letter of the 7th was received night before last. I very cheerfully send you the twenty dollars, which sum you say is necessary to save your land from sale. It is singular that you should have forgotten a judgment against you—and it is more singular that the plaintiff should have let you forget it so long, particularly as I suppose you have always had property enough to satisfy a judgment of that amount. Before you pay it, it would be well to be sure you have not paid, or at least that you cannot prove you have paid it.
"Give my love to Mother and all the Connections.
"Affectionately, your son,
"A. LINCOLN."[1]

His step-brother, John D. Johnston, for whom Mr. Lincoln always exhibited the affection of a real brother, was the recipient of many letters. Some of them were commonplace, but between the lines of each much good, homely philosophy may be read. Johnston, whom I knew, was exactly what his distinguished step-brother charged—an idler. In every emergency he seemed to fall back on Lincoln for assistance. The aid generally came, but with it always some plain but sensible suggestion. The series opens as follows:

"Springfield, Feb. 23, 1850.

"*Dear Brother:*

"Your letter about a mail contract was received yesterday. I have made out a bid for you at $120, guaranteed it myself, got our P. M. here to certify it, and send it on. Your former letter, concerning some man's claim for a pension, was also received. I had the claim examined by those who are practised in such matters, and they decide he cannot get a pension.

"As you make no mention of it, I suppose you had not learned that we lost our little boy. He was sick fifteen days, and died in the morning of the first day of this month. It was not our *first*, but our second child. We miss him very much.

"Your Brother, in haste,

"A. Lincoln."

"To John D. Johnston."[2]

Following is another, which, however, bears no date:

"*Dear Johnston:*

"Your request for eighty dollars I do not think it best to comply with now. At the various times when I have helped you a little you have said to me, 'We can get along very well now,' but in a very short time I find you in the same difficulty again. Now this can only happen by some defect in your conduct. What that defect is, I think I know. You are not *lazy*, and still you are an *idler*. I doubt whether, since I saw you, you have done a good whole day's work in any one day. You do not very much dislike to work, and still you do not work much, merely because it does not seem to you that you could get much for it. This habit of uselessly wasting time is the whole difficulty; and it is vastly important to you, and still more so to your children, that you should break the habit. It is more important to them because they have longer to live, and can keep out of an idle habit, before they are in it, easier than they can get out after they are in.

"You are in need of some ready money, and what I propose is that you shall go to work 'tooth and nail' for somebody who will give you money for it. Let father and your boys take charge of things at home, prepare for a crop, and make the crop, and you go to work for the best money wages, or in discharge of any debt you owe, that you can get,—and to secure you a fair reward for your labor, I now promise you that for every dollar you will, between this and the first of next May, get for your own labor, either in money or as your own indebtedness, I will then give you one other dollar. By this, if you hire yourself at ten dollars a month, from me you will get ten more, making twenty dollars a month for your work. In this I do not mean you shall go off to St. Louis, or the lead mines, or the gold mines in California, but I mean for you to go at it for the best wages you can get close to home in Coles County. Now if you will do this, you will be soon out of debt, and, what is better, you will have a habit that will keep you from getting in debt again. But if I should now clear you out, next year you would be just as deep in as ever. You say you would give your place in heaven for $70 or $80. Then you value your place in heaven very cheap, for I am sure you can, with the offer I make, get the seventy or eighty dollars for four or five months' work.

"You say, if I will furnish you the money, you will deed me the land, and if you don't pay the money back you will deliver possession. Nonsense! If you can't now live with the land, how will you then live without it? You have always been kind to me, and I do not mean to be unkind to you. On the contrary, if you will but follow my advice, you will find it worth more than eight times eighty dollars to you.

"Affectionately,
"Your brother,
"A. Lincoln."[3]

The following, written when the limit of Thomas Lincoln's life seemed rapidly approaching, shows in what esteem his son held the relation that existed between them:

"Springfield, Jan'y 12, 1851.

"*Dear Brother:*

"On the day before yesterday I received a letter from Harriett, written at Greenup. She says she has just returned from your house; and that Father is very low, and will hardly recover. She also says that you have written me two letters; and that although you do not expect me to come now, you wonder that I do not write. I received both your letters, and although I have not answered them, it is not because I have forgotten them, or [not] been interested about them, but because it appeared to me I could write nothing which could do any good. You already know I desire that neither Father or Mother shall be in want of any comfort either in health or sickness while they live; and I feel sure you have not failed to use my name, if necessary, to procure a doctor, or any-thing else for Father in his present sickness. My business is such that I could hardly leave home now, if it were not, as it is, that my own wife is sick-a-bed (it is a case of baby-sickness, and I suppose is not dangerous). I sincerely hope Father may yet recover his health; but at all events tell him to remember to call upon and confide in our great, and good, and merciful Maker, who will not turn away from him in any extremity. He notes the fall of a sparrow, and num-bers the hairs of our heads; and He will not forget the dying man who puts his trust in Him. Say to him that if we could meet now it is doubtful whether it would not be more painful than pleasant; but that if it be his lot to go now he will soon have a joyous meeting with many loved ones gone before, and where the rest of us, through the help of God, hope ere long to join them.

"Write me again when you receive this.

"Affectionately,

"A. Lincoln."[4]

Lincoln's mentor-like interest in his step-mother and his shiftless and almost unfortunate step-brother was in no wise diminished by the death of his father. He writes:

"Springfield, Aug. 31, 1851.

"Dear Brother:

"Inclosed is the deed for the land. We are all well, and have nothing in the way of news. We have had no cholera here for about two weeks.

"Give my love to all, and especially to Mother.

"Yours as ever,

"A. Lincoln."[5]

No more practical or kindly-earnest advice could have been given than this:

"Shelbyville, Nov. 4, 1851.

"Dear Brother:

"When I came into Charleston day before yesterday I learned that you are anxious to sell the land where you live, and move to Missouri. I have been thinking of this ever since, and cannot but think such a notion is utterly foolish. What can you do in Missouri better than here? Is the land richer? Can you there, any more than here, raise corn and wheat and oats without work? Will anybody there, any more than here, do your work for you? If you intend to go to work, there is no better place than right where you are; if you do not intend to go to work you cannot get along anywhere. Squirming and crawling about from place to place can do no good. You have raised no crop this year, and what you really want is to sell the land, get the money and spend it. Part with the land you have, and, my life upon it, you will never after own a spot big enough to bury you in. Half you will get for the land you spend in moving to Missouri, and the other half you will eat and drink and wear out, and no foot of land will be bought. Now I feel it is my duty to have no hand in such a piece of foolery. I feel that it is so even on your own account, and particularly on *Mother's* account. The eastern forty acres I intend to keep for Mother while she lives; if you *will not cultivate it,* it will rent for enough to support her; at least it will rent for something. Her dower in the other two forties she can let you have, and no thanks to me.

"Now do not misunderstand this letter. I do not write it in any unkindness. I write it in order, if possible, to get you to *face* the truth, which truth is, you are destitute because you have idled away all your time. Your thousand pretences for not getting along better are all nonsense; they deceive nobody but yourself. *Go to work* is the only cure for your case.

"A word for Mother: Chapman tells me he wants you to go and live with him. If I were you I would try it awhile. If you get tired of it (as I think you will not) you can return to your own home. Chapman feels very kindly to you; and I have no doubt he will make your situation very pleasant.

"Sincerely your son,
"A. Lincoln."[6]

The list closes with this one written by Lincoln while on the circuit:

"Shelbyville, Nov. 9, 1851.
"*Dear Brother:*
"When I wrote you before, I had not received your letter. I still think as I did; but if the land can be sold so that I get three hundred dollars to put to interest for Mother, I will not object if she does not. But before I will make a deed, the money must be had, or secured beyond all doubt at ten percent.

"As to Abraham, I do not want him *on my own account;* but I understand he wants to live with me so that he can go to school and get a fair start in the world, which I very much wish him to have. When I reach home, if I can make it convenient to take, I will take him, provided there is no mistake between us as to the object and terms of my taking him.

"In haste, as ever,
"A. Lincoln."[7]

AN INCIDENT ON THE CIRCUIT.

"In the spring term of the Tazewell County Court in 1847, which at that time was held in the village of Tremont, I was detained as a witness an entire week. Lincoln was employed in several suits, and among them was one of Case vs. Snow Bros. The Snow Bros., as appeared in evidence (who were both minors), had purchased from an old Mr. Case what was then called a 'prairie team,' consisting of two or three yoke of oxen and prairie plow, giving therefor their joint note for some two hundred dollars; but when pay-day came refused to pay, pleading the minor act. The note was placed in Lincoln's hands for collection. The suit was called and a jury impanelled. The Snow Bros. did not deny the note, but pleaded through their counsel that they were minors, and that Mr. Case knew they were at the time of the contract and conveyance. All this was admitted by Mr. Lincoln, with his peculiar phrase, 'Yes, gentlemen, I reckon that's so.' The minor act was read and its validity admitted in the same manner. The counsel of the defendants were permitted without question to state all these things to the jury, and to show by the statute that these minors could not be held responsible for their contract. By this time you may well suppose that I began to be uneasy. 'What!' thought I, 'this good old man, who confided in these boys, to be wronged in this way, and even his counsel, Mr. Lincoln, to submit in silence!' I looked at the court, Judge Treat, but could read nothing in his calm and dignified demeanor. Just then, Mr. Lincoln slowly got up, and in his strange, half-erect attitude and clear, quiet accent began: '*Gentlemen of the Jury,* are you willing to allow these boys to begin life with this shame and disgrace attached to their character? If you are, *I* am not. The best judge of human character that ever wrote has left these immortal words for all of us to ponder:

"Good name in man or woman, dear my lord,
Is the immediate jewel of their souls:
Who steals my purse steals trash; 'tis something, nothing;
'Twas mine, 'tis his, and has been slave to thousands;

But he that filches from me my good name
Robs me of that which not enriches him
And makes me poor indeed.'"[8]

"Then rising to his full height, and looking upon the defendants with the compassion of a brother, his long right arm extended toward the opposing counsel, he continued: 'Gentlemen of the jury, these poor innocent boys would never have attempted this low villainy had it not been for the advice of these lawyers.' Then for a few minutes he showed how even the noble science of law may be prostituted. With a scathing rebuke to those who thus belittle their profession, he concluded: 'And now, gentlemen, you have it in *your* power to set these boys right before the world.' He plead for the young men only; I think he did not mention his client's name. The jury, without leaving their seats, decided that the defendants must pay the debt; and the latter, after hearing Lincoln, were as willing to pay it as the jury were determined they should. I think the entire argument lasted not above five minutes."—George W. Minier, statement, Apr. 10, 1882.[9]

LINCOLN'S FELLOW LAWYERS.

Among Lincoln's colleagues at the Springfield bar, after his re-entry into politics in 1854, and until his elevation to the Presidency, were, John T. Stuart, Stephen T. Logan, John A. McClernand, Benjamin S. Edwards, David Logan, E. B. Herndon, W. J. Ferguson, James H. Matheney, C. C. Brown, N. M. Broadwell, Charles W. Keyes, John E. Rosette, S. T. Zane, J. C. Conkling, Shelby M. Cullom, and G. M. Shutt.[10] There were others, notably John M. Palmer and Richard J. Oglesby, who came in occasionally from other counties and tried suits with and against us, but they never became members of our bar, strictly speaking, till after the war had closed.—W. H. H.

THE TRUCE WITH DOUGLAS.—TESTIMONY OF IRWIN.

"The conversation took place in the office of Lincoln & Herndon, in the presence of P. L. Harrison, William H. Herndon, Pascal Enos, and myself. It originated in this way: After the debate at Springfield on the 4th and 5th of October, 1854, William Jayne, John Cassiday, Pascal Enos, the writer, and others whose names I do not now remember, filled out and signed a written request to Lincoln to follow Douglas until he 'ran him into his hole' or made him halloo 'Enough,' and that day Lincoln was giving in his report. He said that the next morning after the Peoria debate Douglas came to him and flattered him that he knew more on the question of Territorial organization in this government than all the Senate of the United States, and called his mind to the trouble the latter had given him. He added that Lincoln had already given him more trouble than all the opposition in the Senate, and then proposed to Lincoln that if he (Lincoln) would go home and not follow him, he (Douglas) would go to no more of his appointments, would make no more speeches, and would go home and remain silent during the rest of the campaign. Lincoln did not make another speech till after the election."—B. F. Irwin, statement, Feb. 8, 1866, unpublished MS.[11]

See *ante*, pp. 230–31.

THE BLOOMINGTON CONVENTION.

Following is a copy of the call to select delegates to the Bloomington Convention held May 29, 1856, when the Republican party in Illinois came into existence. It will be remembered that I signed Lincoln's name under instructions from him by telegraph. The original document I gave several years ago to a friend in Boston, Mass.:

> "We, the undersigned, citizens of Sangamon County, who are opposed to the repeal of the Missouri Compromise, and the present administration, and who are in favor of restoring to the general government the policy of Washington and Jefferson, would suggest the propriety of a County Convention, to be held in the city of Springfield on Saturday, the 24th day of May, at 2 o'clock, P. M., to appoint delegates to the Bloomington Convention.
> "A. Lincoln,
> "W. H. Herndon and others."[12]

The decided stand Lincoln took in this instance, and his speech in the Convention, undoubtedly paved the way for his leadership in the Republican party.—W. H. H.

AN OFFICE DISCUSSION—LINCOLN'S IDEA OF WAR.

One morning in 1859, Lincoln and I, impressed with the probability of war between the two sections of the country, were discussing the subject in the office. "The position taken by the advocates of State Sovereignty," remarked Lincoln, "always reminds me of the fellow who contended that the proper place for the big kettle was inside of the little one." To me, war seemed inevitable, but

when I came to view the matter squarely, I feared a difficulty the North would
have in controlling the various classes of people and shades of sentiment, so as
to make them an effective force in case of war: I feared the lack of some great
head and heart to lead us onward. Lincoln had great confidence in the masses,
believing that, when they were brought face to face with the reality of the conflict, all differences would disappear, and that they would be merged into one.
To illustrate his idea he made use of this figure: "Go to the river bank with a
coarse sieve and fill it with gravel. After a vigorous shaking you will observe that
the small pebbles and sand have sunk from view and fallen to the ground. The
next larger in size, unable to slip between the wires, will still be found within
the sieve. By thorough and repeated shakings you will find that, of the pebbles
still left in the sieve, the largest ones will have risen to the top. Now," he continued, "if, as you say, war is inevitable and will shake this country from centre to
circumference, you will find that the little men will fall out of view in the shaking. The masses will rest on some solid foundation, and the big men will have
climbed to the top. Of these latter, one greater than all the rest will leap forth
armed and equipped—the people's leader in the conflict." Little did I realize
the strength of the masses when united and fighting for a common purpose;
and much less did I dream that the great leader soon to be tried was at that very
moment touching my elbow!—W. H. H.

LINCOLN AND THE KNOW-NOTHINGS.

Among other things used against Lincoln in the campaign of 1860 was the charge
that he had been a member of a Know-Nothing lodge. When the charge was
laid at his door he wrote the following letter to one of his confidential political
friends. I copy from the original MS.:

[Confidential.]

"Springfield, Ills., July 21, 1860.
"Hon. A. Jonas.
"*My Dear Sir:*
"Yours of the 20th is received. I suppose as good, or even better, men than
I may have been in American or Know-Nothing lodges; but, in point of fact, I
never was in one, at Quincy or elsewhere. I was never in Quincy but one day
and two nights while Know-Nothing lodges were in existence, and you were

with me that day and both those nights. I had never been there before in my life; and never afterwards, till the joint debate with Douglas in 1858. It was in 1854, when I spoke in some hall there, and after the speaking you, with others, took me to an oyster saloon, passed an hour there, and you walked with me to, and parted with me at, the Quincy House quite late at night. I left by stage for Naples before daylight in the morning, having come in by the same route after dark the evening previous to the speaking, when I found you waiting at the Quincy House to meet me. A few days after I was there, Richardson, as I understood, started the same story about my having been in a Know-Nothing lodge. When I heard of the charge, as I did soon after, I taxed my recollection for some incident which could have suggested it; and I remembered that, on parting with you the last night, I went to the office of the Hotel to take my stage passage for the morning, was told that no stage office for that line was kept there, and that I must see the driver before retiring, to insure his calling for me in the morning; and a servant was sent with me to find the driver, who, after taking me a square or two, stopped me, and stepped perhaps a dozen steps farther, and in my hearing called to some one, who answered him, apparently from the upper part of a building, and promised to call with the stage for me at the Quincy House. I returned and went to bed, and before day the stage called and took me. This is all.

"That I never was in a Know-Nothing lodge in Quincy I should expect could be easily proved by respectable men who were always in the lodges, and never saw me there. An affidavit of one or two such would put the matter at rest.

"And now, a word of caution. Our adversaries think they can gain a point if they could force me to openly deny the charge, by which some degree of offence would be given to the Americans. For this reason it must not publicly appear that I am paying any attention to the charge.

"Yours truly,

"A. Lincoln."[13]

LINCOLN'S VIEWS ON THE RIGHTS OF SUFFRAGE.

At one time, while holding the office of attorney for the city of Springfield, I had a case in the Supreme Court, which involved the validity or constitutionality of a law regulating the matter of voting. Although a city case, it really abridged the right of suffrage. Being Lincoln's partner I wanted him to assist me in arguing the questions involved. He declined to do so, saying: "I am opposed to the limitation or lessening of the right of suffrage; if anything, I am in favor of its extension or enlargement. I want to lift men up—to broaden rather than contract their privileges."—W.H.H.

THE BURIAL OF THE ASSASSIN BOOTH.

Upon reaching Washington with the body of Booth—having come up the Potomac—it was at once removed from the tug-boat to a gun-boat that lay at the dock at the Navy Yard, where it remained about thirty-six hours. It was there examined by the Surgeon-General and staff and other officers, and identified by half a score of persons who had known him well. Toward evening of the second day Gen. L. C. Baker, then chief of the 'Detective Bureau of the War Department,' received orders from Secretary of War Stanton to dispose of the body. Stanton said, 'Put it where it will not be disturbed until Gabriel blows his last trumpet.' I was ordered to assist him. The body was placed in a row-boat, and, taking with us one trusty man to manage the boat, we quietly floated down the river. Crowds of people all along the shore were watching us. For a blind we took with us a heavy ball and chain, and it was soon going from lip to lip that we were about to sink the body in the Potomac. Darkness soon came on, completely concealing our movements, and under its cover we pulled slowly back to the old Penitentiary, which during the war was used as an arsenal. The body was then lifted from the boat and carried through a door opening on the river front. Under the stone floor of what had been a prison cell a shallow grave was dug, and the body, with the United States blanket for a 'winding-sheet,' was there interred. There also it remained till Booth's accomplices were hanged. It was then taken up and buried with his companions in crime. I have since learned that the remains were again disinterred and given to his friends, and that they now rest in the family burial-place in Baltimore, Md."—*From MS. of L. B. Baker, late Lieut. and A.Q.M. lst D. C. Cav.*[14]

A TRIBUTE TO LINCOLN BY A COLLEAGUE AT THE BAR.

"The weird and melancholy association of eloquence and poetry had a strong fascination for Mr. Lincoln's mind. Tasteful composition, either of prose or poetry, which faithfully contrasted the realities of eternity with the unstable and fickle fortunes of time, made a strong impression on his mind. In the indulgence of this melancholy taste it is related of him that the poem, '*Immortality*,' he knew by rote and appreciated very highly. He had a strange liking for the verses, and they bear a just resemblance to his fortune. Mr. Lincoln, at the time of his assassination, was encircled by a halo of immortal glory such as had never before graced the brow of mortal man. He had driven treason from its capital city, had slept in the palace of its once proud and defiant, but now vanquished leader, and had saved his country and its accrued glories of three-quarters of a century from destruction. He rode, not with the haughty and imperious brow of an ancient conqueror, but with the placid complacency of a pure patriot, through the streets of the political Babylon of modern times. He had ridden over battlefields immortal in history, when, in power at least, he was the leader. Having assured the misguided citizens of the South that he meant them no harm beyond a determination to maintain the government, he returned buoyant with hope to the Executive Mansion where for four long years he had been held, as it were, a prisoner.

"Weary with the stories of state, he goes to seek the relaxation of amusement at the theatre; sees the gay crowd as he passes in; is cheered and graciously smiled upon by fair women and brave men; beholds the gorgeous paraphernalia of the stage, the brilliantly lighted scene, the arched ceiling, with its grotesque and inimitable figuring to heighten the effect and make the occasion one of unalloyed pleasure. The hearts of the people beat in unison with his over a redeemed and ransomed land. A pause in the play—a faint pistol shot is heard. No one knows its significance save the hellish few who are in the plot. A wild shriek, such as murder wrings from the heart of woman, follows: the proud form of Mr. Lincoln has sunk in death. The scene is changed to a wild confusion such as no poet can describe, no painter delineate. Well might the murdered have said and oft repeated:

> "'Tis the wink of an eye, 'tis the draught of a breath,
> From the blossom of health to the paleness of death,
> From the gilded saloon to the bier and the shroud,—
> Oh, why should the spirit of mortal be proud?'"

[*From a speech by Hon. Lawrence Weldon, at a bar-meeting held in the United States Court at Springfield, Ills., in June,* 1865.][15]

{*The following item was added to the original Appendix in the 1892 edition.*}

LINCOLN AT FORT MONROE.

An interesting recollection of Lincoln comes from the pen of Colonel LeGrand B. Cannon, of New York. One cannot fail to be impressed with the strength of the side-light thrown by these reminiscences on a life as peculiar, in some respects, as it was grand and unique in others:

"It was my great good fortune," relates Colonel Cannon, "to know something of Mr. Lincoln distinct from his official life. Intensely in earnest I entered the service at the opening of the Rebellion as a staff officer in the regular army and was assigned to the Department of Virginia, with Headquarters at Fort Monroe. Major-General Wool was in command of the Department, and I was honored by him as his chief-of-staff, and enjoyed his entire confidence. It was the only gate open for communication with the rebel government, and General Wool was the agent for such intercourse.

"In the early stages of the war there was a want of harmony between the army and navy about us which seriously embarrassed military operations, resulting in the President and Secretaries Chase and Stanton coming to Fort Monroe to adjust matters. Domestic comforts were limited at headquarters, and the President occupied my room. I was (in accordance with military etiquette) assigned to him as 'Aide-in-Waiting' and Secretary. Although I had frequently met the President as 'Bearer of Dispatches,' I was not a little prejudiced, and a good deal irritated, at the levity which he was charged with indulging in. In grave matters, jesting and frolicking seemed to me shocking, with such vital matters at stake, and I confess to thinking of Nero.

"But this all changed when I came to know him; and I very soon discerned that he had a sad nature; but that, although a terrible burden, his sadness did not originate in his great official responsibilities. I had heard that his home was not pleasant, but did not know that there was more beyond it.

"The day after Mr. Lincoln came to us he said to me: 'I suppose you have neither a Bible nor a copy of Shakespeare here?' I replied that I had a Bible, and the General had Shakespeare, and that the latter never missed a night without reading it. 'Won't he lend it to me?' inquired the President. I answered, 'Yes,' and, of course, obtained it for him.

"The day following he read by himself in one of my offices, two hours or more, entirely alone, I being engaged in a connecting room on duty. He finally interrupted me, inviting me to rest while he would read to me. He read from *Macbeth, Lear,* and finally, *King John.* In reading the passage where Constance bewails to the King the loss of her child, I noticed that his voice trembled and he was deeply moved. Laying the book on the table he said:

"'Did you ever dream of a lost friend and feel that you were having a sweet communion with that friend, and yet a consciousness that it was not a reality?'

"'Yes,' I replied, 'I think almost any one may have had such an experience.'

"'So do I,' he mused; 'I dream of my dead boy, Willie, again and again.'[16]

"I shall never forget the sigh nor the look of sorrow that accompanied this expression.[17] He was utterly overcome; his great frame shook, and, bowing down on the table he wept as only such a man in the breaking down of a great sorrow could weep. It is needless to say that I wept in sympathy, and quietly left the room that he might recover without restraint.

"Lincoln never again referred to his boy, but he made me feel that he had given me a sacred confidence, and he ever after treated me with a tenderness and regard that won my love.

"Again, some days later, I had been absent on a reconnaissance, and returned late in the afternoon. I was in my room dressing for dinner (which was a very formal affair, as, besides the Administration, we had, almost daily, distinguished foreigners to dine) when the President came in. Seeing me in full uniform he said:

"'Why, Colonel, you're fixing up mighty fine. Suppose you lend me your comb and brush, and I'll put on a few touches, too.'

"I handed the desired articles to him and he toyed with the comb awhile and then laid it down, exclaiming:

"'This thing will never get through my hair. Now, if you have such a thing as they comb a horse's tail with, I believe I can use it.' After a merry laugh, he continued: 'By the way, I can tell you a good story about my hair. When I was nominated, at Chicago, an enterprising fellow thought that a great many people would like to see how Abe Lincoln looked, and, as I had not long before sat for a photograph, this fellow having seen it, rushed over and bought the negative. He at once got out no end of wood-cuts, and, so active was their circulation, they were selling in all parts of the country. Soon after they reached Springfield I heard a boy crying them for sale on the streets. "Here's your likeness of Abe Lincoln!" he shouted. "Buy one; price only two shillings! Will look a good deal better when he gets his hair combed!"'"[18]

CHAPTERS ADDED IN THE
1892 EDITION

{*The original edition of 1889 had twenty consecutively numbered chapters plus an appendix. In the 1892 edition, the text was revised and two new chapters were included. The first of the new chapters, on Lincoln's 1848 campaign visit to Massachusetts, was composed mainly of materials written or supplied by Edward L. Pierce and placed between original chapters 13 and 14.*}

NEW CHAPTER ON LINCOLN IN MASSACHUSETTS

Immediately following the adjournment of Congress in August, 1848, Mr. Lincoln set out for Massachusetts to take part in the presidential campaign. Being the only Whig in the delegation in Congress from Illinois, he was expected to do gallant work for his chief, General Taylor. As this chapter in his career seems to have escaped the notice of former biographers, the writers have thought best to insert here extracts from the various descriptions which they have been able to obtain of the tour and its incidents.

One of the most interesting accounts is from the pen of Hon. Edward L. Pierce, of Milton, Mass., whose memory is not less tenacious than is his style happy and entertaining.[1] He says:

"It is not known at whose instance Mr. Lincoln made his visits to Massachusetts in 1848. The Whigs of the State were hard pressed at the time by a formidable secession growing out of General Taylor's nomination, and led by Henry Wilson, Charles Francis Adams, Charles Allen, Charles Sumner, Stephen C. Phillips, John G. Palfrey, E. Rockwood Hoar, Richard H. Dana, Jr., Anson Burlingame, John A. Andrew, and other leaders who had great weight with the people and were all effective public speakers. Generally the State had had a sufficient supply of orators of its own, but in that emergency some outside aid was sought. Gen. Leslie Coombs was invited from Kentucky, and Mr. Lincoln was induced to come also, on his way home from Washington at the end of the session.

"The Whig State Convention met at Worcester, September 13th. The Free-Soil secession was greater here than in any part of the State. It was led by Judge Charles Allen, who was elected to Congress from the district. There was a meeting of the Whigs at the City Hall on the evening before the convention. Ensign Kellogg presided and except his introductory remarks, Mr. Lincoln's speech, which lasted one and a half or two hours, was the only one. The Boston *Advertiser's* report was nearly a column in length. It said: 'Mr. Lincoln has a very tall and thin figure, with an intellectual face, showing a searching mind and a cool judgment. He spoke in a clear and cool and very eloquent manner, carrying the audience with him in his able arguments and brilliant illustrations, only interrupted by warm and frequent applause. He began by expressing a real feeling of modesty in addressing an audience "this side of the mountains," a part of the country where, in the opinion of the people of his section, everybody was supposed to be instructed and wise. But he had devoted his attention to the question of the coming presidential election, and was not unwilling to exchange with all whom he might meet the ideas to which he had arrived.' This passage gives some reason to suppose that, conscious of his powers, he was disposed to try them before audiences somewhat different from those to which he had been accustomed, and therefore he had come to New England. The first part of his speech was a reply, at some length, to the charge that General Taylor had no political principles; and he maintained that the General stood on the true Whig principle, that the will of the people should prevail against executive influence or the veto power of the President. He justified the Whigs for omitting to put a national platform before the people, and, according to a Free-Soil report, said that a political platform should be frowned down whenever and wherever presented. But the stress of his speech was against the Free-Soilers, whose position as to the exclusion of slavery from the territories, he claimed, to be that of the Whigs; while the former were subject to the further criticism that they had but one principle, reminding him of the Yankee peddler, who, in offering for sale a pair of pantaloons, described them as 'large enough for any man, and small enough for any boy.' He condemned the Free-Soilers as helping to elect Cass, who was less likely to promote freedom in the territories than Taylor and passed judgment on them as having less principle than any party. To their defence of their right and duty to act independently, 'leaving consequences to God,' he replied, that 'when divine or human law does not clearly point out what is our duty, it must be found out by an intelligent judgment, which takes in the results of action.' The Free-Soilers were much offended by a passage which does not appear in the Whig report. Referring to the anti-slavery men, he said they were better treated in Massachusetts than in the West, and turning to William S. Lincoln, of Worcester, who had lived in Illinois, he remarked that in that State they had recently killed one of them. This allusion to Lovejoy's murder at Alton, was thought by the Free-Soilers to be heartless, and it was noted that Mr. Lincoln did not repeat it in other speeches. It was probably a casual remark, which came into his mind at the moment, and meant but little, if anything. Cheers were given at the end of the speech for the eloquent Whig member from Illinois. The Whig reports spoke of the speech as 'masterly and convincing' and 'one of the best ever made in Worcester;' while the Free-Soil report describes it as 'a pretty tedious affair.' The next morning he spoke at an open-air meeting, following Benjamin F. Thomas and Ex-Governor Levi Lincoln, but his speech was cut short by the arrival by train of the delegates from Boston, who, with the speakers, proceeded at once to the hall. The convention listened to a long address to the people, reported by a committee, and then to a brilliant speech from Rufus Choate, followed by others from Robert C. Winthrop, the Whig Speaker of the House of Representatives, Charles Hudson, M. C. and Benjamin F. Thomas. Mr. Lincoln listened to these, but was not himself called out.

"Mr. Lincoln spoke at Washingtonian Hall, Bromfield street, Boston, on the 15th, his address lasting an hour and a half, and, according to the report, 'seldom equaled for sound reasoning, cogent argument and keen satire.' Three cheers were given for 'the Lone Star of Illinois,' on account of his being the only Whig member from the State. He spoke at Lowell the 16th, and at the Lower Mills, Dorchester, now a part of Boston, on Monday, the 18th. At this last place the meeting was held in Richmond Hall, and the chairman was N. F. Safford, living till 1891, who introduced him as one of the Lincolns of Hingham, and a descendant of Gen. Benjamin Lincoln. Mr. Lincoln, as he began, disclaimed descent from the Revolutionary officer, but said, playfully, that he had endeavored in Illinois to introduce the principles of the Lincolns of Massachusetts. A few of his audience are still living. They were struck with his height, as he arose in the low-studded hall. He spoke at Chelsea on the 19th, and a report states that his speech 'for aptness of illustration, solidity of argument, and genuine eloquence, was hard to beat.' Charles Sumner had defended the Free-Soil cause at the same place the evening before. Mr. Lincoln spoke at Dedham, in Temperance Hall, on the 20th, in the daytime. Two Whig nominating conventions met there the same day, at one of which Horace Mann was nominated for a second term in Congress. A report states that he 'spoke in an agreeable and entertaining way.' He left abruptly to take a train in order to meet another engagement, and was escorted to the station by the Dorchester band. The same evening he spoke at Cambridge. The report describes him as 'a capital specimen of a Sucker Whig, six feet at least in his stockings.' Of his speech, it was said that 'it was plain, direct and to the point, powerful and convincing, and telling with capital effect upon the immense audience. It was a model speech for the campaign.' His last speech was on the 22d, at Tremont Temple, with George Lunt presiding, in company with William H. Seward, whom he followed, ending at 10.30 P.M. The Whig newspaper, the *Atlas,* the next morning gave more than a column to Mr. Seward's speech, but stated that it had no room for the notes which had been taken of Mr. Lincoln's, describing it, however, as 'powerful and convincing, and cheered to the echo.' The Free-Soil paper (Henry Wilson's) refers to the meeting, mentioning Mr. Seward, but not Mr. Lincoln. The next day Mr. Lincoln left Boston for Illinois. The *Atlas* on Monday contained this paragraph: 'In answer to the many applications which we daily receive from different parts of the State for this gentleman to speak, we have to say that he left Boston on Saturday morning on his way home to Illinois.'

"It is evident from all the contemporaneous reports, that Mr. Lincoln made a marked impression on all his audiences. Their attention was drawn at once to his striking figure; they enjoyed his quaintness and humor; and they recognized his logical power and his novel way of putting things. Still, so far as his points are given in the public journals, he did not rise at any time above partisanship, and he gave no sign of the great future which awaited him as a political antagonist, a master of language, and a leader of men. But it should be noted, in connection with this estimate, that the Whig case, as put in that campaign, was chiefly one of personalities, and was limited to the qualities and career of Taylor as a soldier, and to ridicule of his opponent, General Cass. Mr. Lincoln, like the other Whig speakers, labored to prove that Taylor was a Whig.

"Seward's speech at Tremont Temple, to which Lincoln listened, seems to have started a more serious vein of thought on slavery in the mind of the future President. That evening, when they were together as fellow-lodgers at a hotel, Lincoln said: 'Governor Seward, I have been thinking about what you said in your speech. I reckon you are right. We have got to deal with this slavery question, and got to give much more attention to it hereafter than we have been doing.'*

"It is curious now to recall how little support, in the grave moments of his

---

*Seward's Life, vol. ii, p. 80.[2]

national career which came twelve years later, Mr. Lincoln received from the Whigs of Massachusetts, then conspicuous in public life, whom he met on his visit. Mr. Lunt, who presided at Faneuil Hall, was to the end of his life a pro-slavery conservative. Judge Thomas, in Congress, during the early part of the civil war, was obstructive to the President's policy. Mr. Winthrop voted against Lincoln in 1860 and 1864. Mr. Choate died in 1859, but, judged by his latest utterances, his marvelous eloquence would have been no patriotic inspiration if he had outlived the national struggle. On the other hand, the Free-Soilers of Massachusetts, whom Mr. Lincoln came here to discredit, became, to a man, his supporters; and on many of their leaders he relied as his support in the great conflict. Sumner was chairman of the Senate Committee on Foreign Affairs during the war; Wilson was chairman of the Committee on Military Affairs; Adams was Minister to England; and Andrew War-Governor of the State. These, as well as Palfrey, Burlingame and Dana, who, in 1848, almost every evening addressed audiences against both Taylor and Cass, while Mr. Lincoln was here, were earnest and steadfast in their devotion to the Government during the civil war; and the last three received important appointments from him. How the press treated Mr. Lincoln may be learned from the following editorial in the Lowell *Journal and Courier,* in its issue of September 18, 1848:

Whig Meeting.

The sterling Whigs of Lowell came together last Saturday evening, at the City Hall. The meeting was called to order by the Chairman of the Whig Central Committee, Hon. Linus Child. Homer Bartlett, Esq., was chosen chairman, and A. Gilman, secretary. After a few animating remarks from the Chairman, he introduced George Woodman, Esq., of Boston, who made a very pertinent and witty offhand speech, which was frequently interrupted by the spontaneous plaudits of the audience. At the close of his speech Mr. Woodman introduced the Hon. Abraham Lincoln, of Illinois. It would be doing injustice to his speech to endeavor to give a sketch of it. It was replete with good sense, sound reasoning, and irresistible argument, and spoken with that perfect command of manner and matter which so eminently distinguishes the Western orators. He disabused the public of the erroneous suppositions that Taylor was not a Whig; that Van Buren was anything more than a thorough Loco-foco on all subjects other than Free Territory, and hardly safe on that; and showed up, in a masterly manner, the inconsistency and folly of those Whigs, who, being drawn off from the true and oldest free-soil organization known among the parties of the Union, would now lend their influence and votes to help Mr. Van Buren into the presidential chair. His speech was interrupted by frequent cheers of the audience. At the close the secretary, by request, read the letter of General Taylor to Captain Alison, which had just been received, in which he says: "From the beginning till now, I have declared myself to be a Whig, on all proper occasions."[3]

"Ex-Governor Gardner, after a brief history of the Whig Convention at Worcester, Mass., contributes this pleasing reminiscence:

"'Gov. Levi Lincoln, the oldest living Ex-Governor of Massachusetts, resided in Worcester. He was a man of culture and wealth; lived in one of the finest houses in that town, and was a fine specimen of a gentleman of the old school. It was his custom to give a dinner party when any distinguished assemblage took in Worcester, and to invite its prominent participants. He invited to dine, on this occasion, a company of gentlemen, among them myself, who was a delegate from Boston. The dining-room and table arrangements were superb, the dinner exquisite, the wines abundant, rare, and of the first quality.

"'I well remember the jokes between Governor Lincoln and Abraham Lincoln as to their presumed relationship. At last the latter said: "I *hope* we both belong, as the Scotch say, to the same clan; but I *know* one thing, and that is, that we are both good Whigs."

"'That evening there was held in Mechanics' Hall (an immense building) a mass-meeting of delegates and others, and Lincoln was announced to speak. No one there had ever heard him on the stump, and in fact knew anything about him. When he was announced, his tall, angular, bent form, and his manifest awkwardness and low tone of voice, promised nothing interesting. But he soon warmed to his work. His style and manner of speaking were novelties in the East. He repeated anecdotes, told stories admirable in humor and in point, interspersed with bursts of true eloquence, which constantly brought down the house. His sarcasm of Cass, Van Buren and the Democratic party was inimitable, and whenever he attempted to stop, the shouts of "Go on! go on!" were deafening. He probably spoke over an hour, but so great was the enthusiasm time could not be measured. It was doubtless one of the best efforts of his life. He spoke a day or two afterward in Faneuil Hall, with William H. Seward, but I did not hear him.

"'In 1861 business called me to Washington, and I paid my respects to the President at the White House. He came forward smiling and with extended hand, saying: "You and I are no strangers; we dined together at Governor Lincoln's in 1848." When one remembers the increased burden on the President's mind at this trying time, the anxieties of the war, the army, the currency, and the rehabilitating the civil officers of the country, it seemed astonishing to me to hear him continue: "Sit down. Yes, I had been chosen to Congress then from the wild West, and with hayseed in my hair I went to Massachusetts, the most cultured State in the Union, to take a few lessons in deportment. That was a grand dinner—a superb dinner; by far the finest I ever saw in my life. And the great men who were there, too! Why, I can tell you just how they were arranged at table." He began at one end, and mentioned the names in order, and, I verily believe, without the omission of a single one.'[4]

"This chapter would be incomplete without the account of Mr. George H. Monroe, a young man living in Dedham, Mass., in 1848, who, forty years later, wrote out his recollections of Mr. Lincoln's visit to that town. Mr. Monroe has a vivid and retentive memory, and has since been identified with the public life and journalism of Massachusetts: 'Massachusetts, on account of the great defection of Whigs to the Free-Soilers, and Daniel Webster's sudden and damaging attitude toward General Taylor's nomination to the presidency, began to be considered rather doubtful ground for the Whigs. The national committee sent Mr. Lincoln to the State, after Congress had adjourned, to make some speeches. Our people knew very little about him then. I lived in Dedham, the shire town of Norfolk county, and was secretary of a Whig club there. One of the county courts was in session, and it was determined to have a meeting in the daytime, before it adjourned. I was commissioned to go to Boston to engage the speaker. I went at once to see my friend, Colonel Schouler, of the Boston *Atlas*. He told me that a new man had just come into the State from Washington, who, he thought, would answer our purpose exactly, and said he would get him for me if possible. That man was Abraham Lincoln. When the day for the meeting came I went to the Tremont House and found Mr. Lincoln there. I remember well how tall, awkward and ungainly he was in appearance. I remember how reticent he was, too, but I attributed this to my own youth, for I was only just past twenty-one years of age. He was as sober a man in point of expression as ever I saw. There were others in the party later, but in the journey out in the cars he scarcely said a word to one of us. I did not see him smile on any part of the journey. He seemed uneasy and out of sympathy with his surroundings, as it were. I should say that the atmosphere of Boston was not congenial to him. We took him to one of the most elegant houses in the town of Dedham, and here he seemed still less, if possible, at home. The thing began to look rather blue for us. When we went over to the hall it was not much better. It was a small hall, and it was only about half full; for Mr. Lincoln had not spoken in Boston yet, and there was nothing in his name particularly to attract. But at last he arose to speak, and almost instantly there was a change. His indifferent manner vanished as soon as he opened his mouth. He went right to his work. He wore a black alpaca sack, and he turned up the sleeves of this, and then the cuffs of his shirt. Next he loosened his necktie, and soon after he took it off altogether. All the time he was gaining upon his audience. He soon had it as by a spell. I never saw men more delighted. His style was the most familiar and off-hand possible. His eye had lighted up and changed the whole expression of his countenance. He began to bubble out with humor. But the chief charm of the address lay in the homely way he made his points. There was no attempt at eloquence or finish of style. But, for plain pungency of humor, it would have been difficult to surpass his speech. In this making of points which come home to the general mind, I don't think Lincoln was ever surpassed by any American orator. I often thought of it afterward, when he was exhibiting this faculty in a more ambitious way on a broader field. The speech which I am trying to describe was not a long one. It abruptly ended in a half-hour's time. The bell that called to the steam cars sounded. Mr. Lincoln instantly stopped. "I am engaged to speak at Cambridge to-night," said he, "and I must leave." The whole audience seemed to rise in protest. "Oh, no! go on! finish it!" was heard on every hand. One gentleman arose and pledged himself to take his horse and carry him across the country. But Mr. Lincoln was inexorable. "I can't take any risks," said he. "I have engaged to go to Cambridge, and I must be there. I came here as I agreed, and I am going there in the same way." A more disappointed audience was never seen; but Mr. Lincoln had fairly wakened it up, and it stayed through the afternoon and into the evening to listen to other speakers. We tried to get him to come again, but it was impossible. I heard the speech finished afterward in Tremont Temple, Boston; and it is a notable fact that on the same evening, and from the same platform, William H. Seward also spoke, and made the only political speech he ever delivered in Boston. Who could have dreamed then that in Lincoln we were listening to the man who was to be the future president of the United States, and to leave a reputation second only to that of Washington! Mr. Lincoln moved his Boston audience in much the same way I have described, but Mr. Seward made the first speech, and was looked upon as the chief star, of course. Seward's speech was much more ambitious and comprehensive than that of Lincoln. The latter had not begun to treat broad principles in the 1848 campaign. Mr. Seward's argument was a triumph of intellect, after the most careful preparation. I don't think Mr. Lincoln had ever written his speech at all. He aimed at not much more than to be bright, effective and taking with his audience, and his success was perfect here.'"[5]

{Also added to the 1892 edition was a chapter on the Lincoln-Douglas debates written by Horace White and made to follow the third chapter of the 1889 edition.}

NEW CHAPTER ON LINCOLN-DOUGLAS DEBATES

The importance of a more accurate and elaborate history of the debate between Lincoln and Douglas has induced Mr. Weik and me to secure, for publication in these pages, the account by Horace White, of this world-renowned forensic contest. Mr. White's means of knowledge, as fully set forth in the article, are exceptional, and his treatment of the subject is not less entertaining than truthful. It is certainly a great contribution to history and we insert it without further comment:

"It was my good fortune to accompany Mr. Lincoln during his political campaign against Senator Douglas in 1858, not only at the joint debates but also at most of the smaller meetings where his competitor was not present. We travelled together many thousands of miles. I was in the employ of the Chicago *Tribune*, then called the *Press and Tribune*. Senator Douglas had entered upon his campaign with two short-hand reporters, James B. Sheridan and Henry Binmore, whose duty it was to 'write it up' in the columns of the Chicago *Times*. The necessity of counteracting or matching that force became apparent very soon, and I was chosen to write up Mr. Lincoln's campaign.

"I was not a short-hand reporter. The verbatim reporting for the Chicago *Tribune* in the joint debates was done by Mr. Robert R. Hitt, late Assistant Secretary of State, and the present Representative in Congress from the 6th District of Illinois. Verbatim reporting was a new feature in journalism in Chicago, and Mr. Hitt was the pioneer thereof. The publication of Senator Douglas's opening speech in that campaign, delivered on the evening of July 9th, by the *Tribune* the next morning, was a feat hitherto unexampled in the West, and most mortifying to the Democratic newspaper, the *Times,* and to Sheridan and Binmore, who, after taking down the speech as carefully as Mr. Hitt had done, had gone to bed intending to write it out next day, as was then customary.

"All of the seven joint debates were reported by Mr. Hitt for the *Tribune,* the manuscript passing through my hands before going to the printers, but no changes were made by me except in a few cases where confusion on the platform, or the blowing of the wind, had caused some slight hiatus or evident mistake in catching the speaker's words. I could not resist the temptation to *italicise* a few passages in Mr. Lincoln's speeches, where his manner of delivery had been especially emphatic.

"The volume containing the debates, published in 1860 by Follett, Foster & Co., of Columbus, Ohio, presents Mr. Lincoln's speeches as they appeared in the Chicago *Tribune*, and Mr. Douglas's as they appeared in the Chicago *Times*.[1]

Of course, the speeches of both were published simultaneously in both papers. The Chicago *Times'* reports of Mr. Lincoln's speeches were not at all satisfactory to Mr. Lincoln's friends, and this led to a charge that they were purposely mutilated in order to give his competitor a more scholarly appearance before the public—a charge indignantly denied by Sheridan and Binmore. There was really no foundation for this charge. Of course, Sheridan and Binmore took more pains with Mr. Douglas's speeches than with those of his opponent. That was their business. It was what they were paid for, and what they were expected to do. The debates were all held in the open air, on rude platforms hastily put together, shaky, and overcrowded with people. The reporters' tables were liable to be jostled and their manuscript agitated by the wind. Some gaps were certain to occur in the reporters' notes and these, when occurring in Mr. Douglas's speeches, would certainly be straightened out by his own reporters, who would feel no such responsibility for the rough places in Mr. Lincoln's. Then it must be added that there were fewer involved sentences in Mr. Douglas's *extempore* speeches than in Mr. Lincoln's. Douglas was the more practiced and more polished speaker of the two, and it was easier for a reporter to follow him. All his sentences were round and perfect in his mind before he opened his lips. This was not always the case with Mr. Lincoln's.

"My acquaintance with Mr. Lincoln began four years before the campaign of which I am writing, in October, 1854. I was then in the employ of the Chicago *Evening Journal.* I had been sent to Springfield to report the political doings of State Fair week for that newspaper. Thus it came about that I occupied a front seat in the Representatives' Hall, in the old State House, when Mr. Lincoln delivered the speech already described in this volume. The impression made upon me by the orator was quite overpowering. I had not heard much political speaking up to that time. I have heard a great deal since. I have never heard anything since, either by Mr. Lincoln, or by anybody, that I would put on a higher plane of oratory. All the strings that play upon the human heart and understanding were touched with masterly skill and force, while beyond and above all skill was the overwhelming conviction pressed upon the audience that the speaker himself was charged with an irresistible and inspiring duty to his fellow men. This conscientious impulse drove his arguments through the heads of his hearers down into their bosoms, where they made everlasting lodgment. I had been nurtured in the Abolitionist faith, and was much more radical than Mr. Lincoln himself on any point where slavery was concerned, yet it seemed to me, when this speech was finished, as though I had had a very feeble conception of the wickedness of the Kansas-Nebraska Bill. I was filled, as never before, with the sense of my own duty and responsibility as a citizen toward the aggressions of the slave power.

"Having, since then, heard all the great public speakers of this country subsequent to the period of Clay and Webster, I award the palm to Mr. Lincoln as the one who, although not first in all respects, would bring more men, of doubtful or hostile leanings, around to his way of thinking by talking to them on a platform, than any other.

"Although I heard him many times afterward I shall longest remember him as I then saw the tall, angular form with the long, angular arms, at times bent nearly double with excitement, like a large flail animating two smaller ones, the mobile face wet with perspiration which he discharged in drops as he threw his head this way and that like a projectile—not a graceful figure, yet not an ungraceful one. After listening to him a few minutes, when he had got well warmed with his subject, nobody would mind whether he was graceful or not. All thought of grace or form would be lost in the exceeding attractiveness of what he was saying.

"Returning to the campaign of 1858—I was sent by my employers to Springfield to attend the Republican State Convention of that year. Again I sat at a short distance from Mr. Lincoln when he delivered the 'house-divided-against-itself' speech, on the 17th of June. This was delivered from manuscript, and was the only one I ever heard him deliver in that way. When it was concluded he put the manuscript in my hands and asked me to go to the *State Journal* office and read the proof of it. I think it had already been set in type. Before I had finished this task Mr. Lincoln himself came into the composing room of the *State Journal* and looked over the revised proofs. He said to me that he had taken a great deal of pains with this speech, and that he wanted it to go before the people just as he had prepared it. He added that some of his friends had scolded him a good deal about the opening paragraph and 'the house divided against itself,' and wanted him to change it or leave it out altogether, but that he believed he had studied this subject more deeply than they had, and that he was going to stick to that text whatever happened.

"On the 9th of July, Senator Douglas returned to Chicago from Washington City. He had stopped a few days at Cleveland, Ohio, to allow his friends to arrange a grand *entrée* for him. It was arranged that he should arrive about eight o'clock in the evening by the Michigan Central Railway, whose station was at the foot of Lake street, in which street the principal hotel, the Tremont House, was situated, and that he should be driven in a carriage drawn by six horses to the hotel, where he should make his first speech of the campaign. To carry out this arrangement it was necessary that he should leave the Michigan Southern Railway at Laporte and go to Michigan City, at which place the Chicago committee of reception took him in charge. It was noted by the Chicago *Times* that some malicious person at Michigan City had secretly spiked the only cannon in the town, so that the Douglas men were obliged to use an anvil on the occasion.

"When Mr. Douglas and his train arrived at the Lake street station, the crowd along the street to the hotel, four or five blocks distant, was dense, and, for the Chicago of that day, tremendous. It was with great difficulty that the six-horse team got through it at all. Banners, bands of music, cannon and fireworks added their various inspiration to the scene. About nine o'clock Mr. Douglas made his appearance on a balcony on the Lake street side of the hotel and made his speech. Mr. Lincoln sat in a chair just inside the house, very near the speaker, and was an attentive listener.

"Mr. Douglas's manner on this occasion was courtly and conciliatory. His argument was plausible but worthless—being, for the most part, a rehash of his 'popular sovereignty' dogma; nevertheless, he made a good impression. He could make more out of a bad case, I think, than any other man this country has ever produced, and I hope the country will never produce his like again in this particular. If his fate had been cast in the French Revolution, he would have out-demagogued the whole lot of them. I consider the use he made of this chip called popular sovereignty, riding upon it safely through some of the stormiest years in our history, and having nothing else to ride upon, a feat of dexterity akin to genius. But mere dexterity would not alone have borne him along his pathway in life. He had dauntless courage, unwearied energy, engaging manners, boundless ambition, unsurpassed powers of debate, and strong personal magnetism. Among the Democrats of the North his ascendency was unquestioned and his power almost absolute. He was exactly fitted to hew his way to the Presidency, and he would have done so infallibly if he had not made the mistake of coquetting with slavery. This was a mistake due to the absence of moral principle. If he had been as true to freedom as Lincoln was he would have distanced Lincoln in the race. It was, in fact, no easy task to prevent the Republicans from flocking after him in 1858, when he had, for once only, sided with them, in reference to the Lecompton Constitution. There are some reasons for believing that Douglas would have separated himself from the slave-holders entirely after the Lecompton fight, if he had thought that the Republicans would join in re-electing him to the Senate. Yet the position taken by the party in Illinois was perfectly sound. Douglas was too slippery to make a bargain with. He afterwards redeemed himself in the eyes of his opponents by an immense service to the Union, which no other man could have rendered; but, up to this time, there was nothing for anti-slavery men to do but to beat him if they could.

"I will add here that I had no personal acquaintance with Mr. Douglas, although my opportunities for meeting him were frequent. I regarded him as the most dangerous enemy of liberty, and, therefore, as my enemy. I did not want to know him. Accordingly, one day when Mr. Sheridan courteously offered to present me to his chief, I declined without giving any reason. Of course, this was a mistake; but, at the age of twenty-four, I took my politics very seriously. I thought that all the work of saving the country had to be done then and there. I have since learned to leave something to time and Providence.

"Mr. Lincoln's individual campaign began at Beardstown, Cass county, August 12th. Douglas had been there the previous day, and I had heard him. His speech had consisted mainly of tedious repetitions of 'popular sovereignty,' but he had taken occasion to notice Lincoln's conspiracy charge, and had called it 'an infamous lie.' He had also alluded to Senator Trumbull's charge that he (Douglas) had, two years earlier, been engaged in a plot to force a bogus constitution on the people of Kansas without giving them an opportunity to vote upon it. 'The miserable, craven-hearted wretch,' said Douglas, 'he would rather have both ears cut off than to use that language in my presence, where I could call him to account.' Before entering upon this subject, Douglas turned to his reporters and said 'Take this down.' They did so and it was published a few days later in the St. Louis *Republican*. This incident furnished the text of the Charleston joint debate on the 18th of September.[2]

"Mr. Douglas's meeting at Beardstown was large and enthusiastic, but was composed of a lower social stratum than the Republican meeting of the following day. Mr. Lincoln came up the Illinois River from the town of Naples in the steamer *Sam Gaty*. Cass county and the surrounding region was by no means hopeful Republican ground. Yet Mr. Lincoln's friends mustered forty horsemen and two bands of music, beside a long procession on foot to meet him at the landing. Schuyler county sent a delegation of three hundred, and Morgan county was well represented. These were mostly Old Line Whigs who had followed Lincoln in earlier days. Mr. Lincoln's speech at Beardstown was one of the best he ever made in my hearing, and was not a repetition of any other. In fact, he never repeated himself except when some remark or question from the audience led him back upon a subject that he had already discussed. Many times did I marvel to see him get on a platform at some out-of-the-way place and begin an entirely new speech, equal, in all respects, to any of the joint debates, and continue for two hours in a high strain of argumentative power and eloquence, without saying anything that I had heard before. After the Edwardsville meeting I said to him that it was wonderful to me that he could find new things to say everywhere, while Douglas was parroting his popular sovereignty speech at every place. He replied that Douglas was not lacking in versatility, but that he had a theory that the popular sovereignty speech was the one to win on, and that the audiences whom he addressed would hear it only once and would never know whether he made the same speech elsewhere or not, and would never care. Most likely, if their attention were called to the subject, they would think that was the proper thing to do. As for himself, he said that he could not repeat to-day what he had said yesterday. The subject kept enlarging and widening in his mind as he went on, and it was much easier to make a new speech than to repeat an old one.

"It was at Beardstown that Mr. Lincoln uttered the glowing words that have come to be known as the apostrophe to the Declaration of Independence, the circumstances attending which are narrated in another part of this book.[3] Probably the apostrophe, as printed, is a trifle more florid than as delivered, and, therefore, less forcible.

"The following passage, from the Beardstown speech, was taken down by me on the platform by long-hand notes and written out immediately afterward:

The Conspiracy Charge.

"'I made a speech in June last in which I pointed out, briefly and consecutively, a series of public measures leading directly to the nationalization of slavery—the spreading of that institution over all the Territories and all the States, old as well as new, North as well as South. I enumerated the repeal of the Missouri Compromise, which, every candid man must acknowledge, conferred upon emigrants to Kansas and Nebraska the right to carry slaves there and hold them in bondage, whereas formerly they had no such right; I alluded to the events which followed that repeal, events in which Judge Douglas's name figures quite prominently; I referred to the Dred Scott decision and the extraordinary means taken to prepare the public mind for that decision; the efforts put forth by President Pierce to make the people believe that, in the election of James Buchanan, they had endorsed the doctrine that slavery may exist in the free Territories of the Union—the earnest exhortation put forth by President Buchanan to the people to stick to that decision whatever it might be—the close-fitting niche in the Nebraska bill, wherein the right of the people to govern themselves is made "subject to the constitution of the United States"—the extraordinary haste made by Judge Douglas to give this decision an endorsement at the capitol of Illinois. I alluded to other concurring circumstances, which I need not repeat now, and I said that, though I could not open the bosoms of men and find out their secret motives, yet, when I found the framework of a barn, or a bridge, or any other structure, built by a number of carpenters—Stephen and Franklin and Roger and James—and so built that each tenon had its proper mortice, and the whole forming a symmetrical piece of workmanship, I should say that those carpenters all worked on an intelligible plan, and understood each other from the beginning. This embraced the main argument in my speech before the Republican State Convention in June. Judge Douglas received a copy of my speech some two weeks before his return to Illinois. He had ample time to examine and reply to it if he chose to do so. He did examine and he did reply to it, but he wholly overlooked the body of my argument, and said nothing about the "conspiracy charge," as he terms it. He made his speech up of complaints against our tendencies to negro equality and amalgamation. Well, seeing that Douglas had had the process served on him, that he had taken notice of the process, that he had come into court and pleaded to a part of the complaint, but had ignored the main issue, I took a default on him. I held that he had no plea to make to the general charge. So when I was called on to reply to him, twenty-four hours afterward, I renewed the charge as explicitly as I could. My speech was reported and published on the following morning, and, of course, Judge Douglas saw it. He went from Chicago to Bloomington and there made another and longer speech, and yet took no notice of the "conspiracy charge." He then went to Springfield and made another elaborate argument, but was not prevailed upon to know anything about the outstanding indictment. I made another speech at Springfield, this time taking it for granted that Judge Douglas was satisfied to take his chances in the campaign with the imputation of the conspiracy hanging over him. It was not until he went into a small town, Clinton, in De Witt county, where he delivered his fourth or fifth regular speech, that he found it convenient to notice this matter at all. At that place (I was standing in the crowd when he made his speech), he bethought himself that he was charged with something, and his reply was that his "self-respect alone prevented him from calling it a falsehood." Well, my friends, perhaps he so far lost his self-respect in Beardstown as to actually call it a falsehood.

"'But now I have this reply to make: that while the Nebraska bill was pending, Judge Douglas helped to vote down a clause giving the people of the Territories the right to exclude slavery if they chose; that neither while the bill was pending, nor at any other time, would he give his opinion whether the people had the right to exclude slavery, though respectfully asked; that he made a report, which I hold in my hand, from the Committee on Territories, in which he said the rights of the people of the Territories, in this regard, are "held in abeyance," and cannot be immediately exercised; that the Dred Scott decision expressly denies any such right, but declares that neither Congress nor the Territorial Legislature can keep slavery out of Kansas and that Judge Douglas endorses that decision. All these charges are new; that is, I did not make them in my original speech. They are additional and cumulative testimony. I bring them forward now and dare Judge Douglas to deny one of them. Let him do so and I will prove them by such testimony as shall confound him forever. I say to you, that it would be more to the purpose for Judge Douglas to say that he did not repeal the Missouri Compromise; that he did not make slavery possible where it was impossible before; that he did not leave a niche in the Nebraska bill for the Dred Scott decision to rest in; that he did not vote down a clause giving the people the right to exclude slavery if they wanted to; that he did not refuse to give his individual opinion whether a Territorial Legislature could exclude slavery; that he did not make a report to the Senate, in which he said that the rights of the people, in this regard, were held in abeyance and could not be immediately excercised; that he did not make a hasty endorsement of the Dred Scott decision over at Springfield;* that he does not now endorse that decision; that that decision does not take away from the Territorial Legislature the right to exclude slavery; and that he did not, in the original Nebraska bill, so couple the words State and Territory together that what the Supreme Court has done in forcing open all the Territories to slavery it may yet do in forcing open all the States. I say it would be vastly more to the point for Judge Douglas to say that he did not do some of these things; that he did not forge some of these links of testimony, than to go vociferating about the country that possibly he may hint that somebody is a liar.'[4]

"The next morning, August 13th, we boarded the steamer *Editor* and went to Havana, Mason county. Mr. Lincoln was in excellent spirits. Several of his old Whig friends were on board, and the journey was filled up with politics and story-telling. In the latter branch of human affairs, Mr. Lincoln was most highly gifted. From the beginning to the end of our travels the fund of anecdotes never failed, and, wherever we happened to be, all the people within ear-shot would begin to work their way up to this inimitable story-teller. His stories were always *apropos* of something going on, and oftenest related to things that had happened in his own neighborhood. He was constantly being reminded of one, and, when he told it, his facial expression was so irresistibly comic that the bystanders generally exploded in laughter before he reached what he called the 'nub' of it. Although the intervals between the meetings were filled up brimful with mirth in this way,

---

*This refers to Douglas's speech of June 12, 1857.

Mr. Lincoln indulged very sparingly in humor in his speeches. I asked him one day why he did not oftener turn the laugh on Douglas. He replied that he was too much in earnest, and that it was doubtful whether turning the laugh on any-body really gained any votes.

"We arrived at Havana while Douglas was still speaking. The deputation that met Mr. Lincoln at the landing suggested that he should go up to the grove where the Democratic meeting was going on and hear what Douglas was saying. But he declined to do so, saying: 'the Judge was so put out by my listening to him at Bloomington and Clinton that I promised to leave him alone at his own meetings for the rest of the campaign. I understand that he is calling Trumbull and myself liars, and if he should see me in the crowd he might be so ashamed of himself as to omit the most telling part of his argument.' I strolled up to the Douglas meeting just before its conclusion, and there met a friend who had heard the whole. He was in a state of high indignation. He said that Douglas must certainly have been drinking before he came on the platform, because he had called Lincoln 'a liar, a coward, a wretch and a sneak.'

"When Mr. Lincoln replied, on the following day, he took notice of Douglas's hard words in this way:

"'I am informed that my distinguished friend yesterday became a little excited, nervous (?) perhaps, and that he said something about fighting, as though looking to a personal encounter between himself and me. Did anybody in this audience hear him use such language? (Yes, Yes.) I am informed, further, that somebody in his audience, rather more excited or nervous than himself, took off his coat and offered to take the job off Judge Douglas's hands and fight Lincoln himself. Did anybody here witness that warlike proceeding? (Laughter and cries of "yes.") Well, I merely desire to say that I shall fight neither Judge Douglas nor his second. I shall not do this for two reasons, which I will explain. In the first place a fight would prove nothing which is in issue in this election. It might establish that Judge Douglas is a more muscular man than myself, or it might show that I am a more muscular man than Judge Douglas. But this subject is not referred to in the Cincinnati platform, nor in either of the Springfield platforms. Neither result would prove him right or me wrong. And so of the gentleman who offered to do his fighting for him. If my fighting Judge Douglas would not prove any thing, it would certainly prove nothing for me to fight his bottle-holder. My second reason for not having a personal encounter with Judge Douglas is that I don't believe he wants it himself. He and I are about the best friends in the world, and when we get together he would no more think of fighting me than of fighting his wife. Therefore, when the Judge talked about fighting he was not giving vent to any ill-feeling of his own, but was merely trying to excite—well, let us say enthusiasm against me on the part of his audience. And, as I find he was tolerably successful in this, we will call it quits."[5]

"At Havana I saw Mrs. Douglas (*née* Cutts) standing with a group of ladies a short distance from the platform on which her husband was speaking, and I thought I had never seen a more queenly face and figure. I saw her frequently afterward in this campaign, but never personally met her till many years later, when she had become the wife of General Williams of the regular army, and the mother of children who promised to be as beautiful as herself. There is no doubt in my mind that this attractive presence was very helpful to Judge Douglas in the campaign. It is certain that the Republicans considered her a dangerous element.

"From Havana we went to Lewistown and thence to Peoria, still following on the heels of the Little Giant, but nothing of special interest happened at either place. As we came northward Mr. Lincoln's meetings grew in size, but at Lewistown the Douglas gathering was much the larger of the two and was the most considerable in point of numbers I had yet seen.

"The next stage brought us to Ottawa, the first joint debate, August 21st. Here the crowd was enormous. The weather had been very dry and the town was shrouded in dust raised by the moving populace. Crowds were pouring into town from sunrise till noon in all sorts of conveyances, teams, railroad trains, canal boats, cavalcades, and processions on foot, with banners and inscriptions, stirring up such clouds of dust that it was hard to make out what was underneath them. The town was covered with bunting, and bands of music were tooting around every corner, drowned now and then by the roar of cannon. Mr. Lincoln came by railroad and Mr. Douglas by carriage from La Salle. A train of seventeen passenger cars from Chicago attested the interest felt in that city in the first meeting of the champions. Two great processions escorted them to the platform in the public square. But the eagerness to hear the speaking was so great that the crowd had taken possession of the square and the platform, and had climbed on the wooden awning overhead, to such an extent that the speakers and the committees and reporters could not get to their places. Half an hour was consumed in a rough-and-tumble skirmish to make way for them, and, when finally this was accomplished, a section of the awning gave way with its load of men and boys, and came down on the heads of the Douglas committee of reception. But, fortunately, nobody was hurt.

"Here I was joined by Mr. Hitt and also by Mr. Chester P. Dewey of the New York *Evening Post*, who remained with us until the end of the campaign. Hither, also, came quite an army of young newspaper men, among whom was Henry Villard, in behalf of Forney's Philadelphia *Press*. I have preserved Mr. Dewey's sketch of the two orators as they appeared on the Ottawa platform, and I introduce it here as a graphic description by a new hand:

"'Two men presenting wider contrasts could hardly be found, as the representatives of the two great parties. Everybody knows Douglas, a short, thick-set, burly man, with large, round head, heavy hair, dark complexion, and fierce, bull-dog look. Strong in his own real power, and skilled by a thousand conflicts in all the strategy of a hand-to-hand or a general fight; of towering ambition, restless in his determined desire for notoriety, proud, defiant, arrogant, audacious, unscrupulous, "Little Dug" ascended the platform and looked out impudently and carelessly on the immense throng which surged and struggled before him. A native of Vermont, reared on a soil where no slave stood, he came to Illinois a teacher, and from one post to another had risen to his present eminence. Forgetful of the ancestral hatred of slavery to which he was the heir, he had come to be a holder of slaves, and to owe much of his fame to continued subservience to Southern influence.

"'The other—Lincoln—is a native of Kentucky, of poor white parentage, and, from his cradle, has felt the blighting influence of the dark and cruel shadow which rendered labor dishonorable and kept the poor in poverty, while it advanced the rich in their possessions. Reared in poverty, and to the humblest aspirations, he left his native State, crossed the line into Illinois, and began his career of honorable toil. At first a laborer, splitting rails for a living—deficient in education, and applying himself even to the rudiments of knowledge—he, too, felt the expanding power of his American manhood, and began to achieve the greatness to which he has succeeded. With great difficulty, struggling through the tedious formularies of legal lore, he was admitted to the bar, and rapidly made his way to the front ranks of his profession. Honored by the people with office, he is still the same honest and reliable man. He volunteers in the Black Hawk war, and does the State good service in its sorest need. In every relation of life, socially and to the State, Mr. Lincoln has been always the pure and honest man. In physique he is the opposite to Douglas. Built on the Kentucky type, he is very tall, slender and angular, awkward even in gait and attitude. His face is sharp, large-featured and unprepossessing. His eyes are deep-set under heavy brows, his forehead is high and retreating, and his hair is dark and heavy. In repose, I must confess that "Long Abe's" appearance is *not* comely. But stir him up and the fire of his genius plays on every feature. His eye glows and sparkles; every lineament, now so ill-formed, grows brilliant and expressive, and you have before you a man of rare power and of strong magnetic influence. He *takes* the people every time, and there is no getting away from his sturdy good sense, his unaffected sincerity and the unceasing play of his good humor, which accompanies his close logic and smoothes the way to conviction. Listening to him on Saturday, calmly and unprejudiced, I was convinced that he had no superior as a stump-speaker. He is clear, concise and logical, his language is eloquent and at perfect command. He is altogether a more fluent speaker than Douglas, and in all the arts of debate fully his equal. The Republicans of Illinois have chosen a champion worthy of their heartiest support, and fully equipped for the conflict with the great Squatter Sovereign.'[6]

"One trifling error of fact will be noticed by the readers of these volumes in Mr. Dewey's sketch. It relates to Douglas, and it is proper to correct it here. Mr. Douglas was never a slave-holder. As a trustee or guardian, he held a plantation in Louisiana with the slaves thereon, which had belonged to Col. Robert Martin, of North Carolina, the maternal grandfather of his two sons by his first marriage. It is a fact that Douglas refused to accept this plantation and its belongings as a gift to himself from Colonel Martin in the life-time of the latter. It was characteristic of him that he declined to be an owner of slaves, not because he sympathized with the Abolitionists, but because, as he said once in a debate with Senator Wade, 'being a Northern man by birth, by education and residence, and intending always to remain such, it was impossible for me to know, understand, and provide for the happiness of those people.'[7]

"At the conclusion of the Ottawa debate, a circumstance occurred which, Mr. Lincoln said to me afterwards, was extremely mortifying to him. Half a dozen Republicans, roused to a high pitch of enthusiasm for their leader, seized him as he came down from the platform, hoisted him upon their shoulders and marched off with him, singing the 'Star-Spangled Banner,' or 'Hail Columbia,' until they reached the place where he was to spend the night. What use Douglas made of this incident, is known to the readers of the joint debates. He said a few days later, at Joliet, that Lincoln was so used up in the discussion that his knees trembled, and he had to be carried from the platform, and he caused this to be printed in the newspapers of his own party. Mr. Lincoln called him to account for this fable at Jonesboro.

"The Ottawa debate gave great satisfaction to our side. Mr. Lincoln, we thought, had the better of the argument, and we all came away encouraged. But the Douglas men were encouraged also. In his concluding half hour, Douglas spoke with great rapidity and animation, and yet with perfect distinctness, and his supporters cheered him wildly.

"The next joint debate was to take place at Freeport, six days later. In the interval, Mr. Lincoln addressed meetings at Henry, Marshall county; Augusta, Hancock county, and Macomb, McDonough county. During this interval he prepared the answers to the seven questions put to him by Douglas at Ottawa, and wrote the four questions which he propounded to Douglas at Freeport. The second of these, viz.:'Can the people of a United States Territory, in any lawful way, against the wish of any citizen of the United States, exclude slavery from its limits prior to the formation of a State Constitution?' was made the subject of a conference between Mr. Lincoln and a number of his friends from Chicago, among whom were Norman B. Judd and Dr. C. H. Ray, the latter the chief editor of the *Tribune*. This conference took place at the town of Dixon. I was not present, but Doctor Ray told me that all who were there counselled Mr. Lincoln not to put that question to Douglas, because he would answer it in the affirmative and thus probably secure his re-election. It was their opinion that Lincoln should argue strongly from the Dred Scott decision, which Douglas endorsed, that the people of the Territories could not lawfully exclude slavery prior to the formation of a State Constitution, but that he should not force Douglas to say yes or no. They believed that the latter would let that subject alone as much as possible in order not to offend the South, unless he should be driven into a corner. Mr. Lincoln replied that to draw an affirmative answer from Douglas on this question was exactly what he wanted, and that his object was to make it impossible for Douglas to get the vote of the Southern States in the next Presidential election. He considered that fight much more important than the present one and he would be willing to lose this in order to win that.°

"The result justified Mr. Lincoln's prevision. Douglas did answer in the affirmative. If he had answered in the negative he would have lost the Senatorial election, and that would have ended his political career. He took the chance of being able to make satisfactory explanations to the slaveholders, but they would have nothing to do with him afterward.

"The crowd that assembled at Freeport on the 27th of August was even larger than that at Ottawa. Hundreds of people came from Chicago and many from the neighboring State of Wisconsin. Douglas came from Galena the night before the debate, and was greeted with a great torch-light procession. Lincoln came the following morning from Dixon, and was received at the railway station by a dense crowd, filling up all the adjacent streets, who shouted themselves hoarse

---

°Mr. Lincoln's words are given in Mr. Arnold's biography thus: "I am after larger game; the battle of 1860 is worth a hundred of this."⁸ Mr. Arnold's authority is not mentioned, but these are exactly the words that Doctor Ray repeated to me.

when his tall form was seen emerging from the train. Here, again, the people had seized upon the platform, and all the approaches to it, an hour before the speaking began, and a hand-to-hand fight took place to secure possession.

"After the debate was finished, we Republicans did not feel very happy. We held the same opinion that Mr. Judd and Doctor Ray had—that Douglas's answer had probably saved him from defeat. We did not look forward, and we did not look South, and even if we had done so, we were too much enlisted in this campaign to swap it for another one which was two years distant. Mr. Lincoln's wisdom was soon vindicated by his antagonist, one of whose earliest acts, after he returned to Washington City, was to make a speech (February 23, 1859) defending himself against attacks upon the 'Freeport heresy,' as the Southerners called it. In that debate Jefferson Davis was particularly aggravating, and Douglas did not reply to him with his usual spirit.

"It would draw this chapter out to unreasonable length, if I were to give details of all the small meetings of this campaign. After the Freeport joint debate, we went to Carlinville, Macoupin county, where John M. Palmer divided the time with Mr. Lincoln. From this place we went to Clinton, De Witt county, via Springfield and Decatur. During this journey an incident occurred which gave unbounded mirth to Mr. Lincoln at my expense.

"We left Springfield about nine o'clock in the evening for Decatur, where we were to change cars and take the north-bound train on the Illinois Central Railway. I was very tired and I curled myself up as best I could on the seat to take a nap, asking Mr. Lincoln to wake me up at Decatur, which he promised to do. I went to sleep, and when I did awake I had the sensation of having been asleep a long time. It was daylight and I knew that we should have reached Decatur before midnight. Mr. Lincoln's seat was vacant. While I was pulling myself together, the conductor opened the door of the car and shouted 'State Line.' This was the name of a shabby little town on the border of Indiana. There was nothing to do but to get out and wait for the next train going back to Decatur. About six o'clock in the evening I found my way to Clinton. The meeting was over, of course, and the Chicago *Tribune* had lost its expected report, and I was out of pocket for railroad fares. I wended my way to the house of Mr. C. H. Moore, where Mr. Lincoln was staying, and where I, too, had been an expected guest. When Mr. Lincoln saw me coming up the garden path, his lungs began to crow like a chanticleer, and I thought he would laugh, *sans* intermission, an hour by his dial. He paused long enough to say that he had fallen asleep, also, and did not wake up till the train was starting *from* Decatur. He had very nearly been carried past the station himself, and, in his haste to get out, had forgotten all about his promise to waken me. Then he began to laugh again. The affair was so irresistibly funny, in his view, that he told the incident several times in Washington City when I chanced to meet him, after he became President, to any company who might be present, and with such contagious drollery that all who heard it would shake with laughter.

"Our course took us next to Bloomington, McLean county; Monticello, Piatt county, and Paris, Edgar county. At the last-mentioned place (September 8th) we were joined by Owen Lovejoy, who had never been in that part of the State before. The fame of Lovejoy as an Abolitionist had preceded him, however, and the people gathered around him in a curious and hesitating way, as though he were a witch who might suddenly give them lock-jaw or bring murrain on their cattle, if he were much provoked. Lovejoy saw this and was greatly amused by it, and when he made a speech in the evening, Mr. Lincoln having made his in the day-time, he invited the timid ones to come up and feel of his horns and examine his cloven foot and his forked tail. Lovejoy was one of the most effective orators of his time. After putting his audience in good humor in this way, he made one of his impassioned speeches which never failed to gain votes where human hearts were responsive to the wrongs of slavery. Edgar county was in the Democratic list, but this year it gave a Republican majority on the legislative and congressional tickets, and I think Lovejoy's speech was largely accountable for the result.

"My notes of the Paris meeting embrace the following passage from Mr. Lincoln's speech:

What Is Popular Sovereignty?

"'Let us inquire what Judge Douglas really invented when he introduced the Nebraska Bill? He called it Popular Sovereignty. What does that mean? It means the sovereignty of the people over their own affairs—in other words, the right of the people to govern themselves. Did Judge Douglas invent this? Not quite. The idea of Popular Sovereignty was floating about several ages before the author of the Nebraska Bill was born—indeed, before Columbus set foot on this continent. In the year 1776 it took form in the noble words which you are all familiar with: "We hold these truths to be self-evident, that all men are created equal," etc. Was not this the origin of Popular Sovereignty as applied to the American people? Here we are told that governments are instituted among men deriving their just powers from the consent of the governed. If that is not Popular Sovereignty, then I have no conception of the meaning of words. If Judge Douglas did not invent this kind of Popular Sovereignty, let us pursue the inquiry and find out what kind he did invent. Was it the right of emigrants to Kansas and Nebraska to govern themselves, and a lot of "niggers," too, if they wanted them? Clearly this was no invention of his, because General Cass put forth the same doctrine in 1848 in his so-called Nicholson letter, six years before Douglas thought of such a thing. Then what was it that the "Little Giant" invented? It never occurred to General Cass to call his discovery by the odd name of Popular Sovereignty. He had not the face to say that the right of the people to govern "niggers" was the right of the people to govern themselves. His notions of the fitness of things were not moulded to the brazenness of calling the right to put a hundred "niggers" through under the lash in Nebraska a "sacred right of self-government." And here, I submit to you, was Judge Douglas's discovery, and the whole of it. He discovered that the right to breed and flog negroes in Nebraska was Popular Sovereignty."[9]

"The next meetings in their order were Hillsboro, Montgomery county; Greenville, Bond county, and Edwardsville, Madison county. At Edwardsville (September 13th) I was greatly impressed with Mr. Lincoln's speech, so much so, that I took down the following passages, which, as I read them now, after the lapse of thirty-one years, bring back the whole scene with vividness before me—the quiet autumn day in the quaint old town; the serious people clustered around the platform; Joseph Gillespie officiating as chairman, and the tall, gaunt, earnest man, whose high destiny and tragic death were veiled from our eyes, appealing to his old Whig friends, and seeking to lift them up to his own level:

"'I have been requested,' he said, 'to give a concise statement of the difference, as I understand it, between the Democratic and the Republican parties on the leading issues of the campaign. This question has been put to me by a gentleman whom I do not know. I do not even know whether he is a friend of mine or a supporter of Judge Douglas in this contest, nor does that make any difference. His question is a proper one. Lest I should forget it, I will give you my answer before proceeding with the line of argument I have marked out for this discussion.

"'The difference between the Republican and the Democratic parties on the leading issues of this contest, as I understand it, is that the former consider slavery a moral, social and political wrong, while the latter do not consider it either a moral, a social or a political wrong; and the action of each, as respects the growth of the country and the expansion of our population, is squared to meet these views. I will not affirm that the Democratic party consider slavery morally, socially and politically right, though their tendency to that view has, in my opinion, been constant and unmistakable for the past five years. I prefer to take, as the accepted maxim of the party, the idea put forth by Judge Douglas, that he "don't care whether slavery is voted down or voted up." I am quite willing to believe that many Democrats would prefer that slavery should be always voted down, and I know that some prefer that it be always "voted up;" but I have a right to insist that their action, especially if it be their constant action, shall determine their ideas and preferences on this subject. Every measure of the Democratic party of late years, bearing directly or indirectly on the slavery question, has corresponded with this notion of utter indifference, whether slavery or freedom shall outrun in the race of empire across to the Pacific—every measure, I say, up to the Dred Scott decision, where, it seems to me, the idea is boldly suggested that slavery is better than freedom. The Republican party, on the contrary, hold that this government was instituted to secure the blessings of freedom, and that slavery is an unqualified evil to the negro, to the white man, to the soil, and to the State. Regarding it as an evil, they will not molest it in the States where it exists, they will not overlook the constitutional guards which our fathers placed around it; they will do nothing that can give proper offense to those who hold slaves by legal sanction; but they will use every constitutional method to prevent the evil from becoming larger and involving more negroes, more white men, more soil, and more States in its deplorable consequences. They will, if possible, place it where the public mind shall rest in the belief that it is in course of ultimate peaceable extinction in God's own good time. And to this end they will, if possible, restore the government to the policy of the fathers—the policy of preserving the new Territories from the baneful influence of human bondage, as the northwestern Territories were sought to be preserved by the ordinance of 1787, and the Compromise Act of 1820. They will oppose, in all its length and breadth, the modern Democratic idea, that slavery is as good as freedom, and ought to have room for expansion all over the continent, if people can be found to carry it. All, or nearly all, of Judge Douglas's arguments are logical, if you admit that slavery is as good and as right as freedom, and not one of them is worth a rush if you deny it. This is the difference, as I understand it, between the Republican and Democratic parties.[10]

o o o o o o o o o o o o

"'My friends, I have endeavored to show you the logical consequences of the Dred Scott decision, which holds that the people of a Territory cannot prevent the establishment of slavery in their midst. I have stated what cannot be gainsaid, that the grounds upon which this decision is made are equally applicable to the free States as to the free Territories, and that the peculiar reasons put forth by Judge Douglas for endorsing this decision, commit him, in advance, to the next decision and to all other decisions coming from the same source. And when, by all these means, you have succeeded in dehumanizing the negro; when you have put him down and made it impossible for him to be but as the beasts of the field; when you have extinguished his soul in this world and placed him where the ray of hope is blown out as in the darkness of the damned, are you quite sure that the demon you have roused will not turn and rend you? What constitutes the bulwark of our own liberty and independence? It is not our frowning battlements, our bristling sea coasts, our army and our navy. These are not our reliance against tyranny. All of those may be turned against us without making us weaker for the struggle. Our reliance is in the love of liberty which God has planted in us. Our defense is in the spirit which prizes liberty as the heritage of all men, in all lands everywhere. Destroy this spirit and you have planted the seeds of despotism at your own doors. Familiarize yourselves with the chains of bondage and you prepare your own limbs to wear them. Accustomed to trample on the rights of others, you have lost the genius of your own independence and become the fit subjects of the first cunning tyrant who rises among you. And let me tell you, that all these things are prepared for you by the teachings of history, if the elections shall promise that the next Dred Scott decision and all future decisions will be quietly acquiesced in by the people.'[11]

"From Edwardsville we went to the Jonesboro joint debate. The audience here was small, not more than 1,000 or 1,500, and nearly all Democrats. This was in the heart of Egypt. The country people came into the little town with ox teams mostly, and a very stunted breed of oxen, too. Their wagons were old-fashioned, and looked as though they were ready to fall in pieces. A train with three or four carloads of Douglas men came up, with Douglas himself, from Cairo. All who were present listened to the debate with very close attention, and there was scarcely any cheering on either side. Of course we did not expect any in that place. The reason why Douglas did not get much, was that Union county was a stronghold of the 'Danites,' or Buchanan Democrats. These were a pitiful minority everywhere except in the two counties of Union and Bureau. The reason for this peculiarity in the two counties named, must lie in the fact that Union county was the home of the United States Marshal for the Southern District, W. L. Dougherty; and Bureau, that of the Marshal for the Northern District, Charles N. Pine. Evidently both these men worked their offices for all they were worth, and the result would seem to show that Marshalships are peculiarly well fitted to the purpose of turning voters from their natural leanings. In Bureau county the 'Danites' polled more votes than the Douglas Democrats. In Union, they divided the party into two nearly equal parts. In no other county did they muster a corporal's guard; James W. Sheahan, the editor of the *Times*, told me, with great glee, after the election, that at one of the voting places in Chicago, where the two Democratic judges of election were Irish, a few 'Danite' votes were offered, but that the judges refused to receive them, saying gravely, 'We don't take that kind.' They thought it was illegal voting.

"The only thing noteworthy that I recall at Jonesboro was not political and not even terrestrial. It was the splendid appearance of Donati's comet in the sky, the evening before the debate. Mr. Lincoln greatly admired this strange visitor, and he and I sat for an hour or more in front of the hotel looking at it.

"From Jonesboro we went to Centralia, where a great State Fair was sprawling over the prairie, but there was no speaking there. It was not good form to have political bouts at State Fairs, and I believe that the managers had prohibited them. After one day at this place, where great crowds clustered around both Lincoln and Douglas whenever they appeared on the grounds, we went to Charleston, Coles county, September 18th, where the fourth joint debate took place.

"This was a very remarkable gathering, the like of which we had not seen elsewhere. It consisted of a great outpouring (or rather inpouring) of the rural population, in their own conveyances. There was only one line of railroad here, and only one special train on it. Yet, to my eye, the crowd seemed larger than at either Ottawa or Freeport, in fact the largest of the series, except the one at Galesburg, which came later. The campaign was now at its height, the previous debates having stirred the people into a real fever. 'It is astonishing,' said Mr. Dewey, in his letter from Charleston to the *Evening Post*, 'how deep an interest in politics this people take. Over long weary miles of hot, dusty prairie, the processions of eager partisans come on foot, on horseback, in wagons drawn by horses or mules; men, women and children, old and young; the half-sick just out of the last "shake," children in arms, infants at the maternal fount; pushing on in clouds of dust under a blazing sun, settling down at the town where the meeting is, with hardly a chance for sitting, and even less opportunity for eating, waiting in anxious groups for hours at the places of speaking; talking, discussing, litigious, vociferous, while the roar of artillery, the music of bands, the waving of banners, the huzzas of the crowds, as delegation after delegation appears; the cry of peddlers vending all sorts of wares, from an infallible cure for "agur" to a monster water-melon in slices to suit purchasers—combined to render the occasion one scene of confusion and commotion. The hour of one arrives, and a perfect rush is made for the grounds; a column of dust rising to the heavens, and fairly deluging those who are hurrying on through it. Then the speakers come, with flags and banners and music, surrounded by cheering partisans. Their arrival at the grounds and immediate approach to the stand, is the signal for shouts that rend the heavens. They are introduced to the audience amid prolonged and enthusiastic cheers, they are interrupted by frequent applause and they sit down finally among the same uproarious demonstrations. The audience sit or stand patiently, throughout, and, as the last word is spoken, make a break for their homes, first hunting up lost members of their families, gathering their scattered wagon loads together, and, as the daylight fades away, entering again upon the broad prairies and slowly picking their way back to the place of beginning.'[12]

"Both Lincoln and Douglas left the train at Mattoon, distant some ten miles from Charleston, to accept the escort of their respective partisans. Mattoon was then a comparatively new place, a station on the Illinois Central Railway peopled by Northern men. Nearly the whole population of this town turned out to escort Mr. Lincoln along the dusty highway to Charleston. In his procession was a chariot containing thirty-two young ladies, representing the thirty-two States of the Union, and carrying banners to designate the same. Following this, was one young lady on horseback holding aloft a banner inscribed, 'Kansas—I will be free.' As she was very good looking, we thought that she would not remain free always. The muses had been wide awake also, for, on the side of the chariot, was the stirring legend:

'Westward the star of empire takes its way;
The girls link-on to Lincoln, as their mothers did to Clay.'

"The Douglas procession was likewise a formidable one. He, too, had his chariot of young ladies, and, in addition, a mounted escort. The two processions stretched an almost interminable distance along the road, and were marked by a moving cloud of dust.

"Before the Charleston debate, Mr. Lincoln had received (from Senator Trumbull, I suppose) certain official documents to prove that Douglas had attempted, in 1856, to bring Kansas into the Union without allowing the people to vote upon her constitution, and with these he put the Little Giant on the defensive, and pressed him so hard that we all considered that our side had won a substantial victory.

"The Democrats seemed to be uneasy and dissatisfied, both during the debate and afterward. Mr. Isaac N. Arnold, in his biography of Lincoln, page 148, relates an incident in the Charleston debate on the authority of 'a spectator' (not named), to this effect: that near the end of Mr. Lincoln's closing speech, Douglas became very much excited and walked rapidly up and down the platform behind Lincoln, holding a watch in his hand; that the instant the watch showed the half hour, he called out 'Sit down! Lincoln, sit down! Your time is up.'[13]

"This must be a pure invention. My notes show nothing of the kind. I sat on the platform within ten feet of Douglas all the time that Lincoln was speaking. If any such dramatic incident had occurred, I should certainly have made a note of it, and even without notes I think I should have remembered it. Douglas was too old a campaigner to betray himself in this manner, whatever his feelings might have been.

"After the debate was ended and the country people had mostly dispersed, the demand for speeches was still far from being satisfied. Two meetings were started in the evening, with blazing bonfires in the street to mark the places. Richard J. Oglesby, the Republican nominee for Congress (afterward General, Governor and Senator), addressed one of them. At the Douglas meeting, Richard T. Merrick and U. F. Linder were the speakers. Merrick was a young lawyer from Maryland, who had lately settled in Chicago, and a fluent and rather captivating orator. Linder was an Old Line Whig, of much natural ability, who had sided with the Democrats on the break-up of his own party. Later in the campaign Douglas wrote him a letter saying: 'For God's sake, Linder, come up here and help me.'[14] This letter got into the newspapers, and, as a consequence, the receiver of it was immediately dubbed, 'For-God's-Sake Linder,' by which name he was popularly known all the rest of his days.

"There was nothing of special interest between the Charleston debate and that which took place at Galesburg, October 7th. Here we had the largest audience of the whole series and the worst day, the weather being very cold and raw, notwithstanding which, the people flocked from far and near. One feature of the Republican procession was a division of one hundred ladies and an equal number of gentlemen on horseback as a special escort to the carriage containing Mr. Lincoln. The whole country seemed to be swarming and the crowd stood three hours in the college grounds, in a cutting wind, listening to the debate. Mr. Lincoln's speech at Galesburg was, in my judgment, the best of the series.

"At Quincy, October 13th, we had a fine day and a very large crowd, although not so large as at Galesburg. The usual processions and paraphernalia were on hand. Old Whiggery was largely represented here, and, in front of the Lincoln procession, was a live raccoon on a pole, emblematic of a by-gone day and a by-gone party. When this touching reminder of the past drew near the hotel where we were staying, an old weather-beaten follower of Henry Clay, who was standing near me, was moved to tears. After mopping his face he made his way up to Mr. Lincoln, wrung his hand and burst into tears again. The wicked Democrats carried at the head of their procession a dead 'coon, suspended by its tail. This was more in accord with existing facts than the other specimen, but our prejudices ran in favor of live 'coons in that part of Illinois. Farther north we did not set much store by them. Here I saw Carl Schurz for the first time. He was hotly in the fray, and was an eager listener to the Quincy debate. Another rising star, Frank P. Blair, Jr., was battling for Lincoln in the southern part of the State.

"The next day both Lincoln and Douglas, and their retainers, went on board the steamer *City of Louisiana,* bound for Alton. Here the last of the joint debates took place, October 15th. The day was pleasant but the audience was the smallest of the series, except the one at Jonesboro. The debate passed off quietly and without any incident worthy of note.

"The campaign was now drawing to a close. Everybody who had borne an active part in it was pretty well fagged out, except Mr. Lincoln. He showed no signs of fatigue. Douglas's voice was worn down to extreme huskiness. He took great pains to save what was left of his throat, but to listen to him moved one's pity. Nevertheless, he went on doggedly, bravely, and with a jaunty air of confidence. Mr. Lincoln's voice was as clear and far-reaching as it was the day he spoke at Beardstown, two months before—a high-pitched tenor, almost a falsetto, that could be heard at a greater distance than Douglas's heavy basso. The battle continued till the election (November 2d), which took place in a cold, pelting rainstorm, one of the most uncomfortable in the whole year. But nobody minded the weather. The excitement was intense all day in all parts of the State. The Republican State ticket was elected by a small plurality, the vote being as follows:

For State Treasurer.
    Miller (Republican),————————125,430
    Fondey (Douglas Democrat),————————121,609
    Dougherty (Buchanan Democrat),————5,079

"The Legislature consisted of twenty-five Senators and seventy-five Representatives. Thirteen Senators held over from the preceding election. Of these, eight were Democrats and five Republicans. Of the twelve Senators elected this year, the Democrats elected six and the Republicans six. So the new Senate was composed of fourteen Democrats and eleven Republicans.

"Of the seventy-five members of the House of Representatives, the Democrats elected forty and the Republicans thirty-five.

"On joint ballot, therefore, the Democrats had fifty-four and the Republicans forty-six. And by this vote was Mr. Douglas re-elected Senator.

"Mr. Isaac N. Arnold, in his biography, says that Mr. Lincoln lost the election because a number of the holding-over Senators, representing districts that actually gave Republican majorities in this election, were Democrats.[15] This is an error, and an inexcusable one for a person who is writing history. The apportionment of the State into Legislative districts had become, by the growth and movement of population, unduly favorable to the Democrats; that is, it required fewer votes on the average to elect a member in a Democratic district than in a Republican district. But ideal perfection is never attained in such matters. By the rules of the game Douglas had fairly won. The Republicans claimed that the Lincoln members of the Lower House of the Legislature received more votes, all told, than the Douglas members. These figures are not, at this writing, accessible to me, but my recollection is that, even on this basis, Douglas scored a small majority. There were five thousand Democratic votes to be accounted for, which had been cast for Dougherty for State Treasurer, and of these, the Douglas candidates for the Legislature would naturally get more than the Lincoln candidates.

"What is more to the purpose, is that the Republicans gained 29,241 votes, as against a Democratic gain of 21,332 (counting the Douglas and Buchanan vote together), over the presidential election of 1856. There were 37,444 votes for Fillmore in that year, and there was also an increase of the total vote of 13,129. These 50,573 votes, or their equivalents, were divided between Lincoln and Douglas in the ratio of 29 to 21.

"Mr. Lincoln, as he said at the Dixon Conference, had gone after 'larger game,' and he had bagged it to a greater extent than he, or anybody, then, imagined. But the immediate prize was taken by his great rival.

"I say great rival, with a full sense of the meaning of the words. I heard Mr. Douglas deliver his speech to the members of the Illinois Legislature, April 25, 1861, in the gathering tumult of arms. It was like a blast of thunder. I do not think that it is possible for a human being to produce a more prodigious effect with spoken words, than he produced on those who were within the sound of his voice. He was standing in the same place where I had first heard Mr. Lincoln. The veins of his neck and forehead were swollen with passion, and the perspiration ran down his face in streams. His voice had recovered its clearness from the strain of the previous year, and was frequently broken with emotion. The amazing force that he threw into the words: 'When hostile armies are marching under new and odious banners against the government of our country, the shortest way to peace is the most stupendous and unanimous preparation for war,'[16] seemed to shake the whole building. That speech hushed the breath of treason in every corner of the State. Two months later he was in his grave. He was only forty-eight years old.

"The next time I saw Mr. Lincoln, after the election, I said to him that I hoped he was not so much disappointed as I had been. This, of course, 'reminded him of a little story.' I have forgotten the story, but it was about an over-grown boy who had, met with some mishap, 'stumped' his toe, perhaps, and who said that 'it hurt too much to laugh, and he was too big to cry.'

"Mention has been made of the 'Danites' in the campaign. They were the Buchanan office-holders and their underlings, and, generally, a contemptible lot. The chief dispenser of patronage for Illinois was John Slidell, Senator from Louisiana. He took so much interest in his vocation that he came to Chicago as early as the month of July, to see how the postmasters were doing their work. He hated Douglas intensely, and slandered him vilely, telling stories about the cruel treatment and dreadful condition of the negroes on the Douglas plantation in Louisiana. These stories were told to Dr. Daniel Brainard, the surgeon of the U. S. Marine Hospital. Brainard was a Buchanan Democrat, like all the other federal office-holders, but was a very distinguished surgeon; in fact, at the head of his profession, and a man of wealth and social standing. He became convinced that Slidell's story about the Douglas negroes was true, and he communicated it to Doctor Ray, and urged him to publish it in the *Tribune*. Doctor Ray did so, without, however, giving any names. It made no little commotion. Presently, the New Orleans *Picayune* denied the truth of the statement, concerning the condition and treatment of the negroes, and called it 'an election canard.' Then the Chicago *Times* called for the authority, and the *Tribune* gave the names of Brainard and Slidell. The latter at once published a card in the Washington *Union*, denying that he had ever made the statements attributed to him by Brainard. The latter was immediately in distress. He first denied that he had made the statements imputed to him, but afterward admitted that he had had conversations with a Republican editor about the hardships of the Douglas negroes, but denied that he had given Slidell as authority. Nobody doubted that the authorship of the story was correctly stated in the first publication. It was much too circumstantial to have been invented, and Doctor Ray was not the man to publish lies knowingly.

"The 'Danites' held a State convention at Springfield, September 8th, or, rather, they had called one for that date, but the attendance was so small that they organized it as a convention of the Sixth Congressional District. John C. Breckinridge and Daniel S. Dickinson had been announced as speakers for the occasion, but neither of them appeared. Breckinridge took no notice of this meeting, or of his invitation to be present. A telegram was read from Dickinson, sending 'a thousand greetings,' and this, the Douglas men said, was liberal, being about ten to each delegate. Ex-Gov. John Reynolds was the principal speaker. Douglas was in Springfield the same day. He met his enemies by chance at the railway station, and glared defiance at them.

"Mention should be made of the services of Senator Trumbull in the campaign. Mr. Trumbull was a political debator, scarcely, if at all, inferior to either Lincoln or Douglas. He had given Douglas more trouble in the Senate, during the three years he had been there, than anybody else in that body. He had known Douglas from his youth, and he knew all the joints in his armor. He possessed a courage equal to any occasion, and he wielded a blade of tempered steel. He was not present at any of the joint debates, or at any of Mr. Lincoln's separate meetings, but addressed meetings wherever the State Central Committee sent him. Mr. Lincoln often spoke of him to me, and always in terms of admiration. That Mr. Lincoln was sorely disappointed at losing the Senatorship in 1855, when Trumbull was elected, is quite true, but he knew, as well as anybody, that in the then condition of parties, such a result could not be avoided. Judd, Palmer and Cook had been elected to the Legislature as Democrats. The Republican party was not yet born. The political elements were in the boiling stage. These men could not tell what kind of crystallization would take place. The only safe course for them, looking to their constituencies, was to vote for a Democrat who was opposed to the extension of slavery. Such a man they found in Lyman Trumbull, and they knew that no mistake would be made in choosing him. I say that Mr. Lincoln knew all this as fully as anybody could. I do not remember having any talk with him on that subject, for it was then somewhat stale. But I do remember the hearty good feeling that he cherished toward Trumbull and the three men here mentioned, who were chiefly instrumental in securing Trumbull's election.

"Douglas scented danger when Trumbull took the field, and, with his usual adroitness, sought to gain sympathy by making it appear that it was no fair game. At Havana, in the speech already alluded to, he made a rather moving remonstrance against this 'playing of two upon one,' as he called it. Mr. Lincoln, in his speech at the same place, thought it worth while to reply:

"'I understand,' he said, 'that Judge Douglas, yesterday, referred to the fact that both Judge Trumbull and myself are making speeches throughout the State to beat him for the Senate, and that he tried to create sympathy by the suggestion that this was playing *two upon one* against him. It is true that Judge Trumbull has made a speech in Chicago, and I believe he intends to co-operate with the Republican Central Committee in their arrangements for the campaign, to the extent of making other speeches in different parts of the State. Judge Trumbull is a Republican like myself, and he naturally feels a lively interest in the success of his party. Is there anything wrong about that? But I will show you how little Judge Douglas's appeal to your sympathies amounts to. At the next general election, two years from now, a Legislature will be elected, which will have to choose a successor to Judge Trumbull. Of course, there will be an effort to fill his place with a Democrat. This person, whoever he may be, is probably out making stump-speeches against me, just as Judge Douglas is. He may be one of the present Democratic members of the Lower House of Congress—but, whoever he is, I can tell you that he has got to make some stump-speeches now, or his party will not nominate him for the seat occupied by Judge Trumbull. Well, are not Judge Douglas and this man playing *two upon one* against me, just as much as Judge Trumbull and I are playing *two upon one* against Judge Douglas? And, if it happens that there are two Democratic aspirants for Judge Trumbull's place, are they not playing *three upon one* against me, just as we are playing *two upon one* against Judge Douglas?"[17]

"Douglas had as many helpers as Lincoln had. His complaint implied that there was nobody on the Democratic side who was anywhere near being a match for Trumbull, and this was the fact.

"I think that this was the most important intellectual wrestle that has ever taken place in this country, and that it will bear comparison with any which history mentions. Its consequences we all know. It gave Mr. Lincoln such prominence in the public eye that his nomination to the Presidency became possible and almost inevitable. It put an apple of discord in the Democratic party which hopelessly divided it at Charleston, thus making Republican success in 1860 morally certain. This was one of Mr. Lincoln's designs, as has been already shown. Perhaps the Charleston schism would have taken place, even if Douglas had not been driven into a corner at Freeport, and compelled to proclaim the doctrine of 'unfriendly legislation,' but it is more likely that the break would have been postponed a few years longer.

"Everything stated in this chapter is taken from memoranda made at the time of occurrence. I need not say that I conceived an ardent attachment to Mr. Lincoln. Nobody could be much in his society without being strongly drawn to him.

"Horace White."

New York, *February 27, 1890.*

Editors' Annotations

EDITORS' INTRODUCTION

1. *Atlantic Monthly* 64 (1889): 711–12.

2. Don E. and Virginia Fehrenbacher, eds., *Recollected Words of Abraham Lincoln* (Stanford, Calif.: Stanford University Press, 1996), 238.

3. J. G. Holland, *The Life of Abraham Lincoln* (Springfield, Mass.: Gurdon Bill, 1866); Ward H. Lamon, *The Life of Abraham Lincoln; from His Birth to His Inauguration as President* (Boston: James R. Osgood, 1872) (hereafter cited as Lamon, *Life of Abraham Lincoln*); Isaac Newton Arnold, *The Life of Abraham Lincoln* (Chicago: A. C. McClurg, 1884). The Nicolay and Hay biography began publication serially in the *Century Magazine* in 1886 and was published in its final and complete form in John G. Nicolay and John Hay, *Abraham Lincoln: A History*, 10 vols. (New York: Century, 1890).

4. Paul M. Angle, ed., "Editor's Preface," in *Herndon's Life of Lincoln*, by William H. Herndon and Jesse W. Weik (1930; reprint, Cleveland: World Publishing, 1949), xxxvii (hereafter cited as Angle Edition).

5. See Douglas L. Wilson, "William H. Herndon and the 'Necessary Truth,'" in *Lincoln Before Washington: New Perspectives on the Illinois Years* (Urbana: University of Illinois Press, 1997), 37–52.

6. See Paul M. Angle, "Lincoln's First Love?" *Lincoln Centennial Association Bulletin* 9 (Dec. 1, 1927): 1–7; J. G. Randall, "Sifting the Ann Rutledge Evidence," *Lincoln the President: Springfield to Gettysburg* (New York: Dodd, Mead, 1945), 2:321–42.

7. David Donald, *Lincoln's Herndon* (New York: Alfred A. Knopf, 1948), passim. See, for example, 194–96, 348–59.

8. For example, Ruth Painter Randall, *Mary Lincoln: Biography of a Marriage* (Boston: Little, Brown, 1953), 36ff; John J. Duff, *A. Lincoln: Prairie Lawyer* (New York: Rinehart, 1960), 109, 169.

9. Jean Baker, "Commentary on 'Lincoln's Quest for Union,'" in *The Historian's Lincoln: Pseudohistory, Psychohistory, and History*, ed. Gabor S. Boritt (Urbana: University of Illinois Press, 1988), 244.

10. John Y. Simon, "Abraham Lincoln and Ann Rutledge," *Journal of the Abraham Lincoln Association* 11 (1990): 28. For other reevaluations of Herndon and his informants, see Michael Burlingame, *The Inner World of Abraham Lincoln* (Urbana: University of Illinois Press, 1994); Douglas L. Wilson, *Lincoln Before Washington: New Perspectives on*

the Illinois Years; and Douglas L. Wilson, *Honor's Voice: The Transformation of Abraham Lincoln* (New York: Alfred A. Knopf, 1998).

11. See David Herbert Donald's authoritative assessment of this problem in his *Lincoln* (New York: Simon and Schuster, 1995), 609.

12. Paul M. Angle first laid out problems presented by the evidence on which the Ann Rutledge story rested in 1927 in the essay cited in note 6. By far the most influential critique of the historical basis for the story is found in J. G. Randall's essay, "Sifting the Ann Rutledge Evidence," also cited in note 6. The case for reinstating the Ann Rutledge story as a legitimate part of Lincoln biography is laid out in Simon, "Abraham Lincoln and Ann Rutledge," 13–33; Douglas L. Wilson, "Abraham Lincoln, Ann Rutledge, and the Evidence of Herndon's Informants," in Wilson, *Lincoln Before Washington*, 74–98; and John Evangelist Walsh, *The Shadows Rise: Abraham Lincoln and the Ann Rutledge Legend* (Urbana: University of Illinois Press, 1993).

13. Douglas L. Wilson and Rodney O. Davis, eds., *Herndon's Informants: Letters, Interviews, and Statements About Abraham Lincoln* (Urbana: University of Illinois Press, 1998) (hereafter cited as *Herndon's Informants*).

14. Benjamin P. Thomas, *Abraham Lincoln: A Biography* (New York: Alfred A. Knopf, 1952), 526.

15. All accounts of the life and career of William H. Herndon are indebted, as this one is, to the resourceful scholarship that informs David Herbert Donald's 1948 biography, *Lincoln's Herndon*, cited above. A corrected edition, with a new introduction by the author, appeared in 1989: David Herbert Donald, *Lincoln's Herndon: A Biography* (New York: Da Capo Press). Unless otherwise specified, all biographical information is drawn from this source. For a second look at Herndon by his biographer, see David Herbert Donald, *"We Are Lincoln Men": Abraham Lincoln and His Friends* (New York: Simon and Schuster, 2003), chap. 3, "'I Could Read His Secrets': Lincoln and William H. Herndon."

16. William H. Herndon (hereafter cited as WHH) to Wendell Phillips, May 12, 1857, Wendell Phillips Papers, Houghton Library, Harvard University.

17. Duff, *A. Lincoln*, 271.

18. William D. Beard, "Dalby Revisited: A New Look at Lincoln's 'Most Far-Reaching Case' in the Illinois Supreme Court," *Journal of the Abraham Lincoln Association* 20 (1999): 1–16.

19. WHH to Charles Gunther, Feb. 5, 1887, Lincoln Collection, Chicago Historical Society.

20. John L. Scripps to WHH, May 9, 1865, *Herndon's Informants*, 3.

21. See *Herndon's Informants*, xiii–xvii.

22. WHH to Josiah G. Holland, May 26, 1865, Josiah G. Holland Papers, New York Public Library.

23. WHH to Lamon, Feb. 24, 1869 [1870], Ward Hill Lamon Papers, Huntington Library, San Marino, Calif. (hereafter cited as Lamon Papers).

24. These reports came to Herndon in letters and interviews, all of which are collected in *Herndon's Informants* and can be located through the index.

25. Simon, "Abraham Lincoln and Ann Rutledge," 15.

26. WHH to Charles H. Hart, Jan. 12, 1867, Hart Papers, Huntington Library, San Marino, Calif. (hereafter cited as Hart Papers).

27. WHH to Charles H. Hart, June 29, 1866, Hart Papers.

28. WHH to Charles H. Hart, Apr. 13, 1866, Hart Papers.

29. See note 3 above. For an account of how this book got written, see Albert V. House Jr., "The Trials of a Ghost-Writer of Lincoln Biography: Chauncey F. Black's Authorship of Lamon's *Lincoln,*" *Journal of the Illinois State Historical Society* 31 (1938): 262–96.

30. For the story of the Lamon-Black biography and its reception, see Rodney O. Davis, ed., "Introduction to the Bison Books Edition," Ward H. Lamon, *The Life of Abraham Lincoln from His Birth to His Inauguration as President* (Lincoln: University of Nebraska Press, 1999), v–xv.

31. WHH to Jesse W. Weik (hereafter cited as JWW), Oct. 1, 1881, Herndon-Weik Collection, Library of Congress (hereafter cited as H-W).

32. WHH to JWW, Oct. 1 and Oct. 8, 1881, H-W. Biographical information on Weik is taken from Donald, *Lincoln's Herndon.*

33. The account Weik gives in the early pages of his book *The Real Lincoln* of a four-year association with Herndon in Springfield begun soon after his graduation from college (1875) is not borne out by the documentary record and seems to be a faulty recollection. There is no indication that they met before November 25, 1882, when Weik's diary reads: "At noon called at Fleury's drugstore and met Mr. W. H. Herndon with whom I corresponded before." (From notes on Weik's diary supplied courtesy of David H. Donald.)

34. WHH to JWW, May 6, 1885, H-W.

35. WHH to JWW, Aug. 5, 1885, H-W.

36. Ibid.

37. Donald, *Lincoln's Herndon,* 299.

38. WHH to JWW, Jan. 15, 1886, H-W.

39. WHH to JWW, Jan. 19, 1886, H-W.

40. WHH to JWW, Jan. 26, 1886, H-W.

41. See WHH to JWW, Aug. 5, 1886, H-W.

42. Charles L. Webster & Co. to JWW, Nov. 4, 1886, cited in Donald, *Lincoln's Herndon,* 312.

43. WHH to JWW, Sept. 23, 1886, H-W.

44. For the meeting and the contract, see Donald, *Lincoln's Herndon,* 313. For the transfer of the Lincoln Record to Weik, see WHH to JWW, Nov. 15, 1886, H-W.

45. "Letters, 1847–1869," Folder 1, William Henry Herndon Papers, Abraham Lincoln Presidential Library, Springfield (hereafter cited as Herndon Papers).

46. WHH to JWW, Dec. 13, 1886, H-W.

47. WHH to JWW, Jan. 14, 1887, H-W.

48. WHH to Truman H. Bartlett, Aug. 4, 1887, Bartlett Papers, Massachusetts Historical Society (hereafter cited as Bartlett Papers).

49. Weik Diary, Aug. 29, 1887. For producing scanned images of entries in Weik's diary from 1887 and 1888 and generously making them available for use in this edition, the editors are grateful to his granddaughter, Ann Grifalconi.

50. These draft chapters and monographs are all in H-W.

51. "Preface," undated document in WHH's hand, H-W. This ten-page document is on Pension Office stationery of the kind used in the Greencastle session in August 1887 and seems to be the one Herndon is described as writing on August 2 (Weik Diary). Weik's substantially rewritten version of this preface is an untitled carbon typescript dated "Springfield, Ills. September 1st, 1887" (Jesse William Weik Papers, Abraham Lincoln

Presidential Library, Springfield) (hereafter cited as Weik Papers). The date seems to be an approximation, for Weik's diary reveals that Herndon remained in Greencastle until September 5 and could not have been in Springfield.

52. "Preface," undated document in WHH's hand, H-W.

53. "Finished the last chapter of the book in afternoon and at night began to rewrite the first one" (Weik Diary, Sept. 20, 1887).

54. WHH to JWW, Sept. 20, 1888, H-W.

55. Donald, Lincoln's Herndon, 318.

56. Ibid.

57. This sixteen-page manuscript (H-W 5454–72) contains a descriptive passage in Weik's hand that is based on Herndon's description of the landscape at New Salem in his Ann Rutledge lecture. Strikeouts show Weik's attempts to reign in Herndon's exuberant outpouring of language. What was finally printed in the book was a single sentence that was a fraction of the length of the original passage.

58. Microfilm Edition: Group 4, Reel 11, Exposure 2901, H-W.

59. Donald, Lincoln's Herndon, 318. Donald notes that these are "Chapters VI (the Lincoln-Rutledge romance), IX (the Lincoln-Todd wedding), XI (Lincoln as a lawyer), XIV (Lincoln's domestic difficulties), and XX (analysis of Lincoln's character)."

60. WHH to JWW, Dec. 24, 1887, H-W.

61. WHH to Bartlett, Nov. 16, 1888, Bartlett Papers.

62. WHH to JWW, Dec. 22, 1888, H-W.

63. Herndon's Lincoln (1889 edition), 181; current edition, 120n. Like many of the dates assigned by Weik to the interviews, this one does not appear on the source document and seems to be fictitious.

64. Herndon's Informants, 518.

65. Herndon's Lincoln (1889 edition), 25; current edition, 29.

66. "The content and interpretation in the Herndon-Weik biography was Herndon's; the composition was largely Weik's" (Donald, Lincoln's Herndon, 318). As noted above and elsewhere, the editors of the present edition, while in basic agreement, would qualify somewhat both parts of Donald's conclusion.

67. See WHH to JWW, Sept. 20, 1888, HW.

68. When Weik's literary agent, Gertrude Garrison, advised Weik to have the manuscript copyrighted before making a contract, Weik conferred with Ridpath, who helped him prepare a title page to accompany his application. The book was copyrighted in Weik's name only (entries for Aug. 3 and 4, Weik Diary).

69. For example, "Received a letter and contract from Belford Clark & Co of New York relative to the publication of my book"; "completing my MS"; "my book." Entries for Aug. 13, 26, and 28, 1888, Weik Diary.

70. Carbon copy of typescript, dated "Springfield, Ills. September 1st, 1887," Weik Papers. The word "obligated," or its intended equivalent, has been inadvertently omitted in the typescript.

71. Ridpath's role in the flap over the preface, which apparently included authoring some of the language that offended Herndon, is indicated in Weik's diary entry for October 23 ("In evening went up to Ridpath's and talked about new preface to our book") and by Herndon's letter to Weik of November 13, 1888: "Jesse, I am sorry that you let that closet critic—that severe judge of mechanical literature write any part of your preface." H-W.

72. WHH to JWW, Nov. 7, 1888, H-W.

73. Ibid.

74. Ibid.

75. This language also appears in a two-page handwritten document that seems to have been a draft of compromise language, written sometime after Herndon's demurrer. Donald (*Lincoln's Herndon*, 328n) believes it is not in Herndon's handwriting, which may be the case, though it bears a strong resemblance to his hand. It begins, "In a work produced under joint authorship . . ." Herndon Papers.

76. WHH to Bartlett, Dec. 20, 1889, Bartlett Papers.

77. *Nation* 49 (Aug. 29, 1889): 173–74, as quoted in Donald, *Lincoln's Herndon*, 333.

78. Quoted in Angle Edition, xxxiv.

79. WHH to JWW, Nov. 4, 1889, H-W.

80. *New York Times*, July 21, 1889.

81. *Atlantic Monthly* 64 (Nov. 1889): 712.

82. Horace White to WHH, Jan. 18, 1890, H-W.

83. The progress of this negotiation is shown in Charles Scribner's Sons to JWW, Oct. 1, 1891, Weik Papers; White to JWW, Oct. 6, Nov. 10, 1891, H-W.

84. White and Scribner's agreed that such portions of the biography as the "Chronicles of Reuben" (about the inadvertent bed-switching of two bridal couples during a frontier Indiana infare) or any suggestions of Lincoln's questionable ancestry or legitimacy, should be deleted, to which Herndon and Weik reluctantly assented. See White to JWW, Sept. 22, 30, Oct. 16, 1890, Feb. 11, 1891; WHH to JWW, Nov. 5, 1890, both H-W; JWW to White, Sept. 9, 1890, Horace White Papers, Abraham Lincoln Presidential Library, Springfield; and Belford, Clarke and Co. to Weik, June 30, Nov. 1, 1890, Weik Papers.

85. For an account of Weik's activities after Herndon's death and transcriptions of his own informant materials, see Michael Burlingame, ed., *The Real Lincoln* (Lincoln: University of Nebraska Press, 2002).

86. Emanuel Hertz, ed., *The Hidden Lincoln: From the Letters and Papers of William H. Herndon* (New York: Viking Press, 1938).

87. A small portion of the materials in Weik's possession came to the Abraham Lincoln Presidential Library in Springfield, where they are now part of the Weik Papers.

88. See note 13 above.

89. Quoted anonymously in Angle Edition, xxxvi; identified in Donald, *Lincoln's Herndon*, 333.

PREFACE

1. Herndon's preface went through several revisions and became a source of controversy between the authors (see the Editors' Introduction). It was omitted in the second (1892) edition and replaced by an introduction by Horace White. See William H. Herndon and Jesse W. Weik, *Abraham Lincoln: The True Story of a Great Life*, 2 vols. (New York: D. Appleton, 1892).

2. Leonard Swett to WHH, Feb. 14, 1866, *Herndon's Informants*, 213–14. Swett's text has been substantially altered so as to suppress his principal admonition, namely, that "you must not let your Efforts run in the line of developing his [Lincoln's] weaknesses."

3. Although JWW visited Kentucky in researching this biography, WHH never did:

"I never was in KY . . . since the assassination of Mr. Lincoln," (WHH to JWW, Feb. 9, 1887, H-W). This error probably reflects a misunderstanding on the part of JWW, who composed the text.

CHAPTER I

1. John L. Scripps to WHH, June 24, 1865, *Herndon's Informants,* 57. The quotations from Scripps that follow belong to the same letter.

2. See *Herndon's Informants* for the testimony on this: Dennis F. Hanks to WHH, Feb. 10, 22, 28, 1866 (198–99, 220–22); WHH interview with John Hanks, [1865–66?] (454); John Hanks to JWW, June 12, 1887 (615). For AL's claiming that his mother was a Hanks, see Abraham Lincoln to Jesse W. Fell, Dec. 20, 1859, and "Autobiography Written for John L. Scripps," c. June 1860, Roy P. Basler et al., eds. *The Collected Works of Abraham Lincoln,* 9 vols. (New Brunswick, N.J.: Rutgers University Press, 1953), 3:511, 4:61 (hereafter cited as *Collected Works*).

3. In the 1892 edition, the word "illegitimate" was removed from this sentence and the remainder of the paragraph following this sentence was eliminated.

4. AL to Jesse W. Fell, Enclosing Autobiography, Dec. 20, 1859, *Collected Works* 3:511.

5. See WHH, Notes from Lincoln Family Bible, Sept. 9, 1865, *Herndon's Informants,* 110–11.

6. This footnote, which was eliminated in the 1892 edition, is largely based on Michael Marion Cassidy, statement to JWW, Mar. 28, 1887, *Herndon's Informants,* 613–15. The quotation about the source of AL's name derives from an anonymous letter to WHH, *Herndon's Informants,* 571.

7. The first ten sentences of this paragraph were purged from the 1892 edition so as to make it begin, "Abraham Lincoln, the grandfather of the President . . ."

8. This footnote, eliminated in the 1892 edition, refers to JWW interview with Robert L. Wintersmith, Mar. 23, 1887, *Herndon's Informants,* 613.

9. AL to Samuel Haycraft, May 28, 1860, *Collected Works,* 4:56. AL's remark is only partially quoted. The complete sentence reads: "You are mistaken about my mother—her maiden name was Nancy Hanks."

10. This footnote was eliminated in the 1892 edition.

11. AL to Samuel Haycraft, June 4, 1860, *Collected Works* 4:69–70.

12. See Thomas Speed, "The Wilderness Road: A Description of the Routes of Travel by Which the Pioneers and Early Settlers First Came to Kentucky," *Filson Club Publications* 2 (1886): 34–38, and *Mississippi Valley Historical Review* 7, no. 4 (Mar. 1921): 365–68. While the 1886 version is the likely source, the journal was for a time kept by a Calk descendant in Mt. Sterling, Kentucky, and JWW, who visited that locality in March 1887, may have adapted this passage from the original.

13. Charles Friend to WHH, Mar. 19, 1866, *Herndon's Informants,* 234–35.

14. AL to Jesse W. Fell, Enclosing Autobiography, Dec. 20, 1859, *Collected Works* 3:511.

15. According to AL, Mordecai moved to Illinois, and his brother Josiah, mentioned later, moved to Indiana. "Autobiography Written for John L. Scripps," 61.

16. This is a regularized extract from William Clagett, statement to Charles Friend, Feb. [1866?], *Herndon's Informants,* 220.

17. A somewhat embellished extract from Henry Pirtle to WHH, June 27, 1865, *Herndon's Informants*, 65.

18. The sketch of Thomas Lincoln that follows is based mainly on Erastus Wright's interview with Dennis F. Hanks, June 8, 1865; WHH's interview with Dennis F. Hanks, June 13, 1865; and A. H. Chapman, statement to WHH, [ante Sept. 8, 1865], *Herndon's Informants*, 27–28, 35–43, 95–97.

19. AL to John D. Johnston, Jan. 12, 1851, *Collected Works* 2:96–97.

20. The following sketch of Nancy Hanks Lincoln seems to be drawn mainly from A. H. Chapman, statement to WHH, [ante Sept. 8, 1865]; WHH's interview with Nathaniel Grigsby, Sept. 12, 1865; and WHH's interview with John Hanks, [1865–66], *Herndon's Informants*, 96, 111, 113, 454. Judged by these and other sources in *Herndon's Informants*, this sketch overstates Nancy Lincoln's disposition to melancholy.

21. Dennis F. Hanks to WHH, Feb. 22, 1866, *Herndon's Informants*, 221. This footnote was altered in the 1892 edition to remove references to Hanks's illegitimacy.

22. This quotation is drawn from John B. Helm to WHH, Aug. 1, 1865, *Herndon's Informants*, 83. The letter clearly dates this meeting as occurring in 1816, not 1806.

CHAPTER II

1. The sketch of AL's sister that follows draws from Erastus Wright's interview with Dennis Hanks, June 8, 1865; WHH's interview with Dennis F. Hanks, June 13, 1865; WHH's interview with John Hanks, [1865–66]; and John Hanks to JWW, June 12, 1887, *Herndon's Informants*, 28, 38, 456, 615.

2. AL himself is the authority for his and his sister's early schooling. "Autobiography Written for John L. Scripps," [c. June 1860], *Collected Works* 4:61.

3. John B. Helm to WHH, June 20, 1865, *Herndon's Informants*, 48. It is doubtful that Helm knew AL.

4. This quotation is stitched together from two different letters: Samuel Haycraft to WHH, [June 1865], Dec. 7, 1866, *Herndon's Informants*, 67, 502. Haycraft was never a schoolmate of AL.

5. John Duncan to WHH, Feb. 21, 1867, *Herndon's Informants*, 557.

6. Gollaher's testimony is reported in Charles Friend to WHH, Mar. 19, 1866, *Herndon's Informants*, 235.

7. The idea that Thomas Lincoln left Kentucky partly because of slavery did not originate with AL's biographers but with AL himself. See "Autobiography Written for John L. Scripps," 61. For testimony that slavery was not an issue, see WHH's interview with Dennis F. Hanks, June 13, 1865; and E. R. Burba to WHH, Mar. 31, 1866, *Herndon's Informants*, 36, 240.

8. The whiskey story is in WHH's interview with Dennis F. Hanks, June 13, 1865, *Herndon's Informants*, 38.

9. The account of the move to Indiana derives mainly from WHH's interview with Dennis F. Hanks, June 13, 1865; and A. H. Chapman, statement to WHH, [ante Sept. 8, 1865], *Herndon's Informants*, 38, 98.

10. Sources for the plants and animals of early Indiana: WHH's interview with Dennis F. Hanks, Sept. 8, 1865; Dennis F. Hanks to WHH, Jan. 6, May 4, 1866; and J. W. Wartmann to WHH, June 19, 1866, *Herndon's Informants*, 104, 154, 252, 260–61.

11. Dennis F. Hanks to WHH, Jan. 6, 1866, *Herndon's Informants*, 154.

12. WHH's interview with Dennis F. Hanks, June 13, 1865, *Herndon's Informants*, 39. The story of AL shooting a turkey on the wing is an exaggeration of what Hanks told WHH. More details on turkeys are in WHH's interview with Dennis F. Hanks, June 13, 1865, *Herndon's Informants*, 39.

13. David Turnham to WHH, Feb. 21, 1866, *Herndon's Informants*, 217.

14. J. Rowan Herndon to WHH, June 21, 1865, *Herndon's Informants*, 51. The version given here is much changed from the original.

15. This description of the Lincoln home seems to be based on that in Lamon, *Life of Abraham Lincoln*, 26. Lamon's principal sources were WHH's interview with Dennis F. Hanks, June 13, 1865; and A. H. Chapman, written statement, [ante Sept. 8, 1865], *Herndon's Informants*, 40, 99.

16. Harriet A. Chapman to WHH, Dec. 10, 1866, *Herndon's Informants*, 513.

17. WHH's interview with Dennis F. Hanks, June 13, 1865; and JWW's interview with Dennis F. Hanks, [1886?], *Herndon's Informants*, 37, 598. The footnote ascribing this story to Harriet Chapman is in error.

18. David Turnham to WHH, Feb. 21, 1866, *Herndon's Informants*, 216–17.

19. David Turnham to WHH, Dec. 17, 1866, *Herndon's Informants*, 518. JWW's rewriting of Turnham's testimony here results in a reversal of his meaning. Turnham had written: "So far as his being accustomed to deep thoughtfulness and lost in reflection. He never was but on the Contrary was always quickwitted and ready for an answer."

20. This description of symptoms is taken from a letter from an Illinois physician, Dr. Theo. Lemon, to Ward Hill Lamon and printed in Lamon, *Life of Abraham Lincoln*, 27. The source of "milk-sick" was milk from cows that had eaten poison snake-root, a common weed.

21. Dennis F. Hanks to WHH, Mar. 7, 1866, *Herndon's Informants*, 226.

22. WHH's interview with Dennis F. Hanks, June 13, 1865, *Herndon's Informants*, 40.

23. There is scant warrant in WHH's informant evidence for this view of Nancy Hanks Lincoln as a miserable and defeated woman. Instead, most informants comment on her amiability, kindness, and intelligence. See John Miles's interview with John Hanks, May 25, 1865; Erastus Wright's interview with Dennis F. Hanks, June 8, 1865; WHH's interview with Dennis F. Hanks, June 13, 1865; Nathaniel Grigsby to WHH, Sept. 4, 1865; and WHH's interview with Nathaniel Grigsby, Sept. 12, 1865, *Herndon's Informants*, 5, 27, 37, 93, 113. For mention of her sadness, see WHH's interview with John Hanks, [1865–66], *Herndon's Informants*, 454. This sketch may owe more to Lamon, *Life of Abraham Lincoln*, 11.

24. This account is stitched together from two letters: Samuel Haycraft to John B. Helm, July 5, 1865; and Samuel Haycraft to WHH, Dec. 7, 1866, *Herndon's Informants*, 85, 503.

25. John B. Helm to WHH, Aug. 1, 1865, *Herndon's Informants*, 82. Though included here, the Lincolns do not appear on Helm's list of uncouth Kentuckians: "The Bushes were rough, uncouth, uneducated beyond any thing that would seem credible now to speak of but the Hanks—Enlows &c—were along way below the Bushes again."

26. This view of Sarah Bush Lincoln and the effect of her arrival owes much to A. H. Chapman, statement to WHH, [ante Sept. 8, 1865], *Herndon's Informants*, 99. A similar version is in Lamon, *Life of Abraham Lincoln*, 30–32.

27. Harriet A. Chapman to WHH, Dec. 17, 1865, *Herndon's Informants*, 145.

28. Recast from WHH's interview with Sarah Bush Lincoln, Sept. 8, 1865, *Herndon's Informants*, 108.

29. WHH's interview with Matilda Johnston Moore, Sept. 8, 1865, *Herndon's Informants*, 110.

30. David Turnham to WHH, Sept. 15, 1865, *Herndon's Informants*, 121; Nathaniel Grigsby to WHH, Sept. 4, 1865, *Herndon's Informants*, 93. Grigsby said that Andrew Crawford was Lincoln's first teacher.

31. E. R. Burba to WHH, Mar. 31, 1866, *Herndon's Informants*, 241. Burba is here reporting on what was remembered by others of AL in Kentucky, not Indiana.

32. Nathaniel Grigsby to WHH, Sept. 4, 1865, *Herndon's Informants*, 94.

33. WHH's interview with Nathaniel Grigsby, Sept. 12, 1865, *Herndon's Informants*, 113.

34. This is quite different from what WHH recorded at his interview with Sarah Bush Lincoln on September 8, 1865, which reads: "As a usual thing Mr Lincoln never made Abe quit reading to do anything if he could avoid it. He would do it himself first. Mr. Lincoln could read a little & could scarcely write his name: hence he wanted, as he himself felt the uses & necessities of Education his boy Abraham to learn & he Encouraged him to do it in all ways he could" (*Herndon's Informants*, 107–8).

35. WHH's interview with Nathaniel Grigsby, Sept. 12, 1865, *Herndon's Informants*, 112.

36. On AL's early writings, see Nathaniel Grigsby to WHH, Sept. 4, 1865; WHH's interview with Nathaniel Grigsby, Sept. 12, 1865; WHH's interview with William Wood, Sept. 15, 1865; and David Turnham to WHH, Sept. 5, 1866, *Herndon's Informants*, 94, 112, 123–24, 334.

37. Physical description of AL drawn from WHH's interview with Nathaniel Grigsby, Sept. 12, 1865; and WHH's interview with Anna Caroline (not Kate) Roby Gentry, Sept. 17, 1865, *Herndon's Informants*, 112, 131. That Lincoln's skin was yellow is not in the testimony.

38. This description of AL's Indiana schoolboy attire is drawn from WHH's interview with Nathaniel Grigsby, Sept. 12, 1865; WHH's interview with John Romine, Sept. 14, 1865; and WHH's interview with David Turnham, Sept. 15, 1865, *Herndon's Informants*, 113, 118, 121.

39. Recast from WHH's interview with Anna Caroline Gentry, Sept. 17, 1865, *Herndon's Informants*, 131.

40. The testimony of Anna Caroline Gentry (WHH's interview, Sept. 17, 1865, *Herndon's Informants*, 132) is here imaginatively reconstructed.

41. WHH's interview with Absalom Roby, Sept. 17, 1865, *Herndon's Informants*, 132.

42. For AL's early reading, see WHH's interviews with the following in *Herndon's Informants*: Dennis F. Hanks, June 13, Sept. 8, 1865 (37, 41, 106), Matilda Johnston Moore, Sept. 12, 1865 (109), Nathaniel Grigsby, Sept. 12, 1865 (112), David Turnham, Sept. 15, 1865 (121), and John Hanks, [1865–66] (455).

43. Differing accounts of the Crawford affair are WHH's interview with Elizabeth Crawford, Sept. 16, 1865; and Judge John Pitcher's testimony in Oliver C. Terry to JWW, July 1888, *Herndon's Informants*, 125, 662.

44. AL Sum Book, [1824–26], *Collected Works* 1:1.

45. These lines did not originate with Lincoln but are from the first two stanzas of Isaac Watts's hymn "The Shortness of Life, and the Goodness of God." See *Herndon's Informants*, 135n.

46. Joseph C. Richardson, statement to WHH, [1865–66], *Herndon's Informants*, 473.

47. WHH's interview with John Romine, Sept. 14, 1865, *Herndon's Informants*, 118.

48. WHH's interviews with Sarah Bush Lincoln on September 8, 1865, and Elizabeth Crawford on September 16, 1865 (*Herndon's Informants*, 107, 126), depict AL's studious habits as a boy. That AL wrote and ciphered on every flat surface in the cabin is an exaggeration.

49. WHH's interview with Sarah Bush Lincoln, Sept. 8, 1865, *Herndon's Informants*, 107. In this recasting of her testimony, Mrs. Lincoln's role in AL's youthful practice of writing has been exaggerated.

50. WHH's interview with John Hanks, [1865–66], *Herndon's Informants*, 455.

CHAPTER III

1. David Turnham to WHH, Sept. 16, Oct. 12, 1865, *Herndon's Informants*, 129, 138. Dennis Hanks also claims to have introduced AL to this book: Dennis Hanks to WHH, Dec. 27, 1865, *Herndon's Informants*, 147.

2. Lamar's letter is here misdated (see next note).

3. Recast from John W. Lamar to WHH, May 18, 1867, *Herndon's Informants*, 560. In Lamar's original, Larkins's horse ran five miles in four minutes.

4. Based on WHH's interview with Green B. Taylor, Sept. 16, 1865, *Herndon's Informants*, 130. AL's waving a bottle over his head came not from Taylor but from another Indiana informant, John Oskins. The last sentence, in which AL supposedly taunts the crowd, is not in the testimony and seems to be a fabrication.

5. WHH's interview with Elizabeth Crawford, Sept. 16, 1865, and Elizabeth Crawford to WHH, Apr. 19, 1866, *Herndon's Informants*, 126, 245.

6. Elizabeth Crawford to WHH, May 3, 1866, *Herndon's Informants*, 249–50. AL's authorship of these lines is doubtful.

7. John W. Lamar to J. W. Wartmann, Jan. 3, 1887, *Herndon's Informants*, 599.

8. The entire story of the Grigsby weddings, including AL's mischievous efforts and "The Chronicles of Reuben," was eliminated from the 1892 edition. WHH, who died in 1891, had resisted this removal: "The Episode is a part of his history—explains the *germs of his wit & his humor*" (WHH to JWW, Mar. 7, 1890, H-W).

9. This "chapter" is somewhat rewritten from the report of Elizabeth Crawford to WHH, Jan. 4, 1866, *Herndon's Informants*, 151–52.

10. Elizabeth Crawford to WHH, Jan. 4, 1866, *Herndon's Informants*, 151–52. Somewhat cleaned up from the original, in which the next to last line is: "besids your low Croch proclaimes you a botch." These lines, and the apology for them that follows in the next paragraph, were eliminated in the 1892 edition.

11. WHH's interview with Nathaniel Grigsby, Sept. 12, 1865; and WHH's interview with Joseph C. Richardson, Sept. [14?], 1865, *Herndon's Informants*, 113, 120.

12. A reference to AL's withering attack on Jesse B. Thomas in the 1840 campaign, described at page 130.

13. David Turnham to WHH, Dec. 30, 1865, *Herndon's Informants*, 148.

14. Dennis F. Hanks to WHH, Dec. 24, 1865, *Herndon's Informants*, 146. "Drunk" has been substituted for Hanks's "broke." The song beginning "The turbaned Turk . . ." is titled "None Can Love Like an Irishman."

15. Elizabeth Crawford to WHH, Feb. 21, 1865, *Herndon's Informants*, 215–16. The second song is "John Adkin's Farewell."

16. WHH's interview with Dennis F. Hanks, Sept. 8, 1865, *Herndon's Informants*, 105. This is a creative rewriting of Hanks's testimony, which barely mentions political speeches.

17. WHH's interview with S. T. Johnson, Sept. 14, 1865, *Herndon's Informants*, 115.

18. AL included this incident in some biographical notes he prepared for campaign biographers. See *Collected Works* 4:62. WHH's description of the incident is in Microfilm Edition: Group 4, Reel 11, Exposures 2821–22, H-W.

19. Oliver C. Terry to JWW, July 1, 1888, *Herndon's Informants*, 662, quoting John Pitcher.

20. WHH's interview with William Wood, Sept. 15, 1865, *Herndon's Informants*, 124.

21. WHH's interview with Joseph C. Richardson, Sept. [14?], 1865, *Herndon's Informants*, 120.

22. WHH's interview with William Wood, Sept. 15, 1865, *Herndon's Informants*, 125.

23. Ibid., 124.

24. Sources for AL's first flatboat trip are in *Herndon's Informants:* J. W. Wartmann to WHH, June 19, 1865 (47); Nathaniel Grigsby to WHH, Sept. 4, 1865 (94); WHH's interview with Nathaniel Grigsby, Sept. 12, 1865 (114); WHH's interview with John Romine, Sept. 14, 1865 (118); and WHH's interview with Anna Caroline Gentry, Sept. 17, 1865 (131).

25. Elizabeth Crawford to WHH, Apr. 19, 1866, *Herndon's Informants*, 245.

26. Ibid., 246.

27. Dennis F. Hanks to WHH, Dec. 24, 1865, *Herndon's Informants*, 146. As above, "drunk" has been substituted for Hanks's "broke."

28. Drawn from George U. Miles, statement to WHH, [1866], *Herndon's Informants*, 536. Though these superstitions are identified with early Indiana settlers, Miles was one of WHH's Illinois informants. This paragraph and the next owe much to similar ones in Lamon, *Life of Abraham Lincoln*, 44–45.

29. See Dennis F. Hanks to WHH, Mar. 7, 1866, *Herndon's Informants*, 226.

30. A version of this story is told in WHH's interview with Jesse K. Dubois, Dec. 1, 1888, *Herndon's Informants*, 718–19.

CHAPTER IV

1. WHH's interview with John Hanks, [1865–66], *Herndon's Informants*, 456.

2. "Family Record Written by Abraham Lincoln," *Collected Works* 2:95.

3. WHH's interview with John Hanks, [1865–66], *Herndon's Informants*, 456. Hanks gives credit to himself and AL for only one thousand rails.

4. Ibid.

5. The correct spelling is "Offutt."

6. WHH's interview with John Hanks, [1865–66], *Herndon's Informants*, 456.

7. The Buckhorn Inn is described in WHH's interview with Wesley Elliott, [1865–66], *Herndon's Informants,* 447.

8. WHH's interview with Caleb Carman, Oct. 12, 1866, *Herndon's Informants,* 373.

9. WHH's interview with John Hanks, [1865–66], *Herndon's Informants,* 457.

10. Coleman Smoot to WHH, May 7, 1866, *Herndon's Informants,* 254. This account of the flatboat adventure seems to follow in the wake of that in Lamon, *Life of Abraham Lincoln,* 80–82.

11. WHH's interview with John Hanks, [1865–66], *Herndon's Informants,* 457. See also WHH's interview with John Hanks, June 13, 1865; and Coleman Smoot to WHH, May 7, 1866, *Herndon's Informants,* 44, 254.

12. WHH's interview with John Hanks, [1865–66], *Herndon's Informants,* 457.

13. Ibid.

14. Ibid. AL's own autobiographical statement asserts that Hanks did not go farther than St. Louis on this trip. AL may have made this remark to his stepbrother, John D. Johnston. See John Hanks to JWW, June 12, 1887, *Herndon's Informants,* 615.

15. The wrestle with Needham is described in WHH's interview with Augustus H. Chapman, [1865–66], *Herndon's Informants,* 439.

16. This description is based on WHH's lecture, "Abraham Lincoln. Miss Ann Rutledge. New Salem. Pioneering and the Poem," delivered in Springfield, November 16, 1865, and printed in advance as a broadside. The description is also indebted to that in Lamon, *Life of Abraham Lincoln,* 85–86.

17. Ibid., 86.

18. AL's "floating driftwood" remark was recalled in William G. Greene to WHH, May 29, 1865, *Herndon's Informants,* 12.

19. WHH's interview with Mentor Graham, May 29, 1865, *Herndon's Informants,* 8–9. The poll books from this election survive, and while they show that AL voted in New Salem on August 1, 1831, the clerks of record were Mentor Graham and Abram Bergen.

20. J. Rowan Herndon to WHH, July 3, 1865, *Herndon's Informants,* 69. Rowan Herndon's version, which has been rewritten here, does not specify that this story was one told on AL's first election day in New Salem.

21. AL's role in Dr. Nelson's move is depicted in James Short to WHH, July 7, 1865; and John McNamar to WHH, June 4, 1866, *Herndon's Informants,* 73, 259.

22. WHH's interview with William G. Greene, May 30, 1865, *Herndon's Informants,* 17–18.

23. Testimony that Offutt was "a clear-headed, brisk man of affairs" is lacking. For the "others," see WHH's interviews with Mentor Graham, May 29, 1865; Hardin Bale, May 29, 1865; and William G. Greene, May 30, 1865, *Herndon's Informants,* 9, 13, 18.

24. Lamon, *Life of Abraham Lincoln,* 91.

25. WHH objected, while reading proofs, to JWW's descriptive phrase (borrowed from Lamon) for the Clary's Grove boys, "generous parcel of ruffians": "The children, grand & great grand children of these people are some of the best people in Menard and it would not do to say *Ruffians*" (Nov. 10, 1888, H-W). JWW changed the word to "rowdies."

26. WHH's interview with William G. Greene, May 30, 1865, *Herndon's Informants,* 17.

27. This description of the outcome of the Armstrong wrestle, which has an enraged AL shaking Armstrong by the throat, had become standard in nineteenth-century Lincoln

biography, but it is based on only one highly questionable account: Robert B. Rutledge to WHH, [c. Nov. 1, 1866], *Herndon's Informants*, 386. Other accounts indicate that Armstrong took advantage of AL and threw him unfairly or that the bout ended in a tie. For an analysis of the conflicting testimony and its treatment in Lincoln biography, see Douglas L. Wilson, *Honor's Voice: The Transformation of Abraham Lincoln* (New York: Alfred A. Knopf, 1998), 19–43.

28. The reference is to AL's defense of the Armstrongs' son, William ("Duff") Armstrong, in a murder trial in 1858, recounted on 221–22.

29. "Vaner" was actually John Vance. See WHH's interview with Mentor Graham, May 29, 1865, *Herndon's Informants*, 10. WHH's copyist, John G. Springer, mistakenly transcribed Mentor Graham's testimony about Lincoln's acquisition of a grammar "at one Vances" as "at one Vaner's." Lamon's account, the source followed here, was based on the copyist's transcriptions, not the originals. See Lamon, *Life of Abraham Lincoln*, 95.

30. James Hall to WHH, Sept. 17, 1873, *Herndon's Informants*, 580–81. Hall had read of Offutt's disappearance in Lamon's biography (Lamon, *Life of Abraham Lincoln*, 145). In fact, Offutt had been in touch with AL in 1861 and before: Denton Offutt to AL, Sept. 7, 1859, Feb. 11, 1861 (ff. 1865, 7287), Abraham Lincoln Papers, Library of Congress (hereafter cited as Abraham Lincoln Papers).

31. Such an advertisement began to appear in the Springfield newspaper, the *Sangamo Journal*, on March 29, 1832.

32. When WHH read this sentence in galley proof, he was uncertain that he had actually seen Lincoln on this occasion. He wrote his collaborator, JWW, who had written the sentence, to make sure from WHH's records (which were in JWW's possession) that Lincoln had gone with the *Talisman* all the way to Bogue's mill. "Try and get me right— If L came up to Bogues mill I saw Lincoln, & if he did not then I did not see him at Bogues mill" (WHH to JWW, Nov. 10, 1888, H-W).

33. Bogue to Edward Mitchell, *Sangamo Journal*, Jan. 26, 1832.

34. For the ball after the *Talisman*'s arrival, see WHH interview with H. E. Dummer, [1865–66]; and WHH interview with John Lightfoot, Sept. 13, 1887, *Herndon's Informants*, 442, 639.

35. Verses supplied to WHH by James H. Matheny, n.d., *Herndon's Informants*, 704.

36. J. Rowan Herndon to WHH, June 11, 1865, *Herndon's Informants*, 34.

37. Ibid.

CHAPTER V

1. See "Articles of Agreement and Capitulation Between the United States and the Sauk and Fox," [June 30, 1831], in *The Black Hawk War, 1831–32, Collections of the Illinois State Historical Library*, comp. and ed. Ellen M. Whitney (Springfield: Illinois State Historical Library, 1970–78), 2:86.

2. See Donald Jackson, ed., *Black Hawk: An Autobiography* (Urbana: University of Illinois Press, 1955), 120.

3. "Speech in the U.S. House of Representatives on the Presidential Question," July 27, 1848, *Collected Works* 1:509–10.

4. Identical versions of this story are Ben: Perley Poore in Allen Thorndike Rice, ed.,

Reminiscences of Abraham Lincoln by Distinguished Men of His Time (New York: North American Publishing, 1886), 218–19, and Francis Fisher Browne, *The Every-Day Life of Abraham Lincoln* (New York: N. D. Thompson, 1886), 107.

5. See AL to Jesse W. Fell, Enclosing Autobiography, Dec. 20, 1859; and "Autobiography Written for John L. Scripps," [c. June 1860], *Collected Works* 3:512, 4:64.

6. On the conflict between federal and state authority, see WHH's interview with William G. Greene, May 30, 1865, *Herndon's Informants,* 19–20.

7. David Pantier to WHH, July 21, 1865, *Herndon's Informants,* 78.

8. Ibid.

9. WHH's interview with William G. Greene, May 30, 1865, *Herndon's Informants,* 18. See also WHH's interview with Royal Clary, Oct. [1866?], *Herndon's Informants,* 372.

10. WHH's interview with William G. Greene, May 30, 1865, *Herndon's Informants,* 19.

11. The original of this letter has not been located.

12. A cured hog jowl.

13. George M. Harrison to WHH, Jan. 29, 1867, *Herndon's Informants,* 554–55. AL was no longer a captain when he served with the author of this account but had reenlisted as a private in Capt. Jacob Early's Independent Spy Company.

14. George H. Harrison to WHH, Jan. 29, 1867, *Herndon's Informants,* 555. Harrison's testimony says nothing about AL's being a "standard-bearer." He wrote: "The mess unanimously pitched upon him as our water bearer and he accepted the office."

15. AL had three terms of service in the Black Hawk War: April 21–May 27, 1832, when he commanded a company raised in the New Salem area; May 28–June 16, when he reenlisted as a private in a company led by Capt. Elijah Iles; and June 16–July 10, when he again reenlisted as a private in Captain Early's Independent Spy Company. See *The Black Hawk War, 1831–32,* 1:176–78, 1:227–30, 1:549–46.

16. Joseph S. Wilson to James Harlan, June 27, 1865, *Herndon's Informants,* 62–63. According to the original, the first land warrant was located in Range 15 West, not Range 39 West.

17. "Communication to the People of Sangamo County," Mar. 9, 1832, *Collected Works* 1:5–9.

18. Not identified. This may be an elaboration of the testimony of James Gourley, who told WHH ([1865–66], *Herndon's Informants,* 451) that AL ran on "whig principles" four years later in the 1836 political campaign.

19. McNamar's first name was John. See John McNamar to G. U. Miles, May 5, 1866, *Herndon's Informants,* 253.

20. "Communication to the People of Sangamon County," Mar. 9, 1832, *Collected Works* 1:8–9.

21. Abner Y. Ellis, statement to WHH, enclosed in Ellis to WHH, Jan. 23, 1866, *Herndon's Informants,* 171. Ellis is here referring to the 1834 campaign, not that of 1832.

22. WHH interview with James A. Herndon, [1865–66], *Herndon's Informants,* 460. See also J. Rowan Herndon to WHH, May 28, 1865, June 21, 1865, *Herndon's Informants,* 7, 51.

23. Abner Y. Ellis, statement to WHH, enclosed in Ellis to WHH, Jan. 23, 1866, *Herndon's Informants,* 171. Ellis probably copied the speech, which he erroneously dates as 1834, from the *Illinois State Journal* (Springfield), Nov. 5, 1864, where it had been placed by WHH.

24. When reading proof, WHH explained the history of this item by way of correcting JWW's account: "James Herndon first got and wrote out for me Lincoln's first speech in the summer of '65 & I had it published in the Sangamon Journal and then I suppose Ellis got it out of the Journal & sent it to me probably at my request" (Nov. 22, 1888, H-W). See James A. Herndon to WHH, May 29, 1865, *Herndon's Informants*, 16.

25. Abner Y. Ellis, statement to WHH, enclosed in Ellis to WHH, Jan. 23, 1866, *Herndon's Informants*, 171. Here Ellis is referring to the election of 1834, not 1832.

26. This reckoning came not from the poll book but from William G. Greene (Greene to WHH, May 29, 1865; and WHH's interview with Greene, May 30, 1865, *Herndon's Informants*, 12, 20). Lincoln once claimed to have garnered 277 out of 284 votes ("Autobiography Written for John L. Scripps," 64), whereas Ida Tarbell, who saw the now-missing poll book, says Lincoln's total was 277 out of 300. See Benjamin F. Thomas, "Lincoln: Voter and Candidate, 1831–49," *Bulletin of the Abraham Lincoln Association* 36 (Sept. 1934): 5.

27. Sources for this story are WHH's interview with William G. Greene, May 30, 1865; James Short to WHH, July 7, 1865; and WHH's interview with James Davis, [1865], *Herndon's Informants*, 20, 74, 529. This version contains echoes of that given in Lamon, *Life of Abraham Lincoln*, 136–37. Berry and Lincoln never had a mercantile monopoly in New Salem; Samuel Hill remained in business throughout this time.

28. For the career of Berry and Lincoln in New Salem, see *Herndon's Informants*: J. Rowan Herndon to WHH, May 28, 1865 (7), WHH's interview with Hardin Bale, May 29, 1865 (13), WHH's interview with William G. Greene, May 30, 1865 (20), Abner Y. Ellis, statement to WHH, enclosed with Ellis to WHH, Jan. 23, 1866 (170–71), WHH's interview with Royal Clary, Oct. [1866?] (371), WHH's interview with Caleb Carman, Oct. 12, 1866 (373), J. Rowan Herndon to WHH, Oct. 28, 1866 (379), and WHH's interview with James A. Herndon, [1865–66] (460).

29. James Rutledge, Henry Onstot, and Nelson Alley.

30. WHH's sources for AL's law study at New Salem include the following interviews in *Herndon's Informants*: Mentor Graham, May 29, 1865 (9), Henry McHenry, May 29, 1865 (14), H. E. Dummer, [1865–66] (442), Russell Godbey, [1865–66] (450), James Gourley, [1865–66] (451), Henry McHenry, [1866] (534), Robert B. Rutledge to WHH, Nov. 30, 1866 (426), and Robert B. Rutledge to WHH, Dec. 4, 1866 (497). The remark about "shorter extremities" is from Lamon, *Life of Abraham Lincoln*, 140.

31. Somewhat embellished from WHH's interviews with Russell Godbey, [1865–66], *Herndon's Informants*, 449–50. When reading proof, WHH protested to JWW: "Godby never hired L to work on a farm." See WHH to JWW, Nov. 22, 1888, H-W.

32. WHH's interview with James A. Herndon, [1865–66], *Herndon's Informants*, 460–61.

33. This passage given as a single quotation combines, with embellishments, portions of two letters of Robert B. Rutledge to WHH: Nov. 30, Dec. 4, 1866, *Herndon's Informants*, 426, 498.

34. WHH's interview with John McNamar, Oct. 16, 1866, *Herndon's Informants*, 375.

35. WHH's interview with William G. Greene, May 30, 1865, *Herndon's Informants*, 21.

36. Abner Y. Ellis, statement to WHH, enclosed in Ellis to WHH, Jan. 23, 1866, *Herndon's Informants*, 172. Hentz's novels were all published well after AL had left New Salem.

37. Abner Y. Ellis to WHH, c. Jan. 1866, *Herndon's Informants*, 161.

38. Abner Y. Ellis to WHH, Feb. 1, 1866, *Herndon's Informants*, 190–91.

39. Abner Y. Ellis, statement to WHH, enclosed in Ellis to WHH, Jan. 23, 1866, *Herndon's Informants*, 170.

40. Ibid.

41. James Short, as cited in N. W. Branson to WHH, Aug. 3, 1865, *Herndon's Informants*, 91.

42. Abner Y. Ellis, statement to WHH, enclosed in Ellis to WHH, Jan. 23, 1866, *Herndon's Informants*, 170.

43. Abner Y. Ellis to WHH, Feb. 1, 1866, *Herndon's Informants*, 189–90. In the original Ellis version, the story of Bap McNabb's rooster is represented as one AL told, not something in which he was a participant. Thus Lincoln's role as referee is unauthorized by Ellis's testimony and appears to be an embellishment added by JWW. Ellis places the cockfight in "old Sangamon Town," a community on the Sangamon River between Springfield and New Salem. See Thomas F. Schwartz, "Lincoln Never Said That: Abraham Lincoln, Cockfighting, and Animal Rights," *For the People: A Newsletter of the Abraham Lincoln Association* 5, no. 1 (Spring 2003): 1, 6–7.

44. Lamon, *Life of Abraham Lincoln*, 146.

45. WHH's interview with John Moore Fisk, Feb. 18, 1887, *Herndon's Informants*, 715. Fisk remembered that AL was recommended to Calhoun by Simmons.

46. AL to Henry Asbury, Nov. 19, 1858, *Collected Works* 3:339. The quotation is not exact.

47. WHH's interview with Elizabeth Herndon Bell, [Mar. 1887?], *Herndon's Informants*, 606.

48. Graham as quoted in WHH to JWW, Jan. 9, 1886, H-W.

49. WHH's interview with Henry McHenry, May 29, 1865, *Herndon's Informants*, 14.

50. Not identified. A similar quotation is cited in David Herbert Donald, *Lincoln's Herndon: A Biography* (New York: Da Capo Press, 1989), 153.

51. WHH's interview with Henry McHenry, May 29, 1865, *Herndon's Informants*, 14–15.

52. Russell Godbey to WHH, Aug. 17, 1887, *Herndon's Informants*, 624. See also WHH's interviews with Russell Godbey, [1865–66], *Herndon's Informants*, 449, 450.

53. James Short to WHH, July 7, 1865, *Herndon's Informants*, 74. See also in *Herndon's Informants* WHH's interviews with Hardin Bale, May 29, 1865 (13), William G. Greene, May 30, 1865 (20), clipping from *Menard Axis*, [Feb. 16, 1862], enclosed in John Hill to WHH, June 6, 1865 (24–25), John McNamar to WHH, Dec. 1, 1866 (493), and JWW's interview with Travis Elmore, [1883?] (593).

54. Derived from WHH's interview with Charles Chandler, [1885–89], *Herndon's Informants*, 720–21.

55. Sources for AL's reading and religious skepticism in *Herndon's Informants*: clipping from *Menard Axis*, [Feb. 6, 1862], enclosed in John Hill to WHH, June 6, 1865 (24), John Hill to WHH, June 27, 1865 (61–62), Abner Y. Ellis, statement to WHH, enclosed in Ellis to WHH, Jan. 23, 1866 (172), Abner Y. Ellis to WHH, Jan. 30, 1866 (179), Abner Y. Ellis to WHH, Feb. 14, 1866 (210), and Abner Y. Ellis to WHH, Dec. 11, 1866 (513).

56. J. Rowan Herndon to WHH, May 28, 1865; WHH's interview with Hardin Bale,

May 29, 1865; WHH's interview with William G. Greene, May 30, 1865; and WHH's interview with Hardin Bale, 1866, *Herndon's Informants*, 7, 13, 19, 528.

57. The whiskey barrel story appears in William Makepeace Thayer, *The Pioneer Boy and How He Became President* (Boston: Walker, Wise, 1863), 249–53, and is reported in William G. Greene to WHH, June 11, 1865; and Robert B. Rutledge to WHH, c. Nov. 1, 1866, *Herndon's Informants*, 33, 387. Skepticism about this feat is expressed in Lamon, *Life of Abraham Lincoln*, 154.

58. J. Rowan Herndon to WHH, May 28, 1865, *Herndon's Informants*, 8.

59. WHH's interview with John T. Stuart, [1865–66], *Herndon's Informants*, 480.

60. Coleman Smoot to WHH, May 7, 1866, *Herndon's Informants*, 254.

CHAPTER VI

1. This chapter relies heavily on a monograph WHH prepared for the use of his collaborator: "Miss Rutlege and Lincoln," Microfilm Edition: Group 4, Roll 11, Exposures 3488–3511, H-W. Rutledge's family spelled her first name "Ann."

2. Isaac Newton Arnold, *The Life of Abraham Lincoln* (Chicago: A. C. McClurg, 1884), 42.

3. Robert B. Rutledge to WHH, Dec. 4, 1866, *Herndon's Informants*, 497. Rutledge's letter does not imply that AL's characteristically sunny disposition changed with Ann Rutledge's death but pleads ignorance of AL's state of mind after that event, "as I saw little of him after the time."

4. JWW interview with Elizabeth Herndon Bell, Aug. 24, 1883, *Herndon's Informants*, 591.

5. WHH's interview with William G. Greene, May 30, 1865, *Herndon's Informants*, 21. William G. Greene is here misidentified as his brother L. M. Greene.

6. WHH's interview with Esther Summers Bale, 1866, *Herndon's Informants*, 527. The evocative last sentence given here appears in WHH's monograph "Miss Rutlege & Lincoln" (Microfilm Edition: Group 4, Reel 11, Exposure 3490, H-W) in such a way as to suggest that it came from Bale, but it is not found in WHH's interview. In his Springfield lecture on AL and Ann Rutledge, WHH attributes this remark to William G. Greene, though it is not found in any known interview with Greene, either. See WHH, "Abraham Lincoln. Miss Ann Rutledge. New Salem. Pioneering and the Poem," lecture delivered in Springfield, Nov. 16, 1866, and published as a broadside; WHH interview with William G. Greene, May 30, 1865, *Herndon's Informants*, 21.

7. John McNeil's real name was John McNamar. McNamar had lived in New Salem at least two years before AL's arrival and departed for New York about a year later in 1832. See John McNamar to G. U. Miles, May 5, 1866; and John McNamar to WHH, June 4, 1866, *Herndon's Informants*, 252, 259.

8. This sentence is liberally adapted from a passage in WHH's monograph "Miss Rutlege & Lincoln," cited above.

9. This quotation was fabricated from information given in John McNamar to G. U. Miles, May 5, 1866; and Robert B. Rutledge to WHH, [c. Nov. 1, 1866], *Herndon's Informants*, 252, 383.

10. For McNamar's trip east, see John McNamar to G. U. Miles, May 5, 1866; and Robert B. Rutledge to WHH, [c. Nov. 1, 1866], *Herndon's Informants*, 252, 383. The latter source, and John McNamar to WHH (Jan. 20, 1867, *Herndon's Informants*, 546),

indicate that McNamar was delayed by the illness of his parents' family rather than by his own.

11. On McNamar and his name change, see newspaper clipping based on "Gath" in the *New York Tribune,* Feb. 15, 1867, enclosed in Robert B. Rutledge to WHH, Mar. 6, 1867; WHH's interview with Parthena Nance Hill, [Mar. 1887?]; and WHH's interview with Jasper Rutledge, Mar. 9, 1887, *Herndon's Informants,* 559, 604–5, 606. The speculation given here about why McNamar called himself McNeil does not appear in the testimony.

12. There is little evidence in the testimony that the absent McNamar wrote a series of letters to Ann Rutledge, but see George U. Miles to WHH, Mar. 23, 1866; WHH's interview with Parthena Nance Hill, [Mar. 1887?]; and WHH's interview with Jasper Rutledge, Mar. 9, 1887, *Herndon's Informants,* 237, 604–5, 606.

13. None of the surviving testimony by A. Y. Ellis bears on this point, so that it is difficult to discern whether this testimony is based on a confession by Lincoln or represents Ellis's speculation.

14. Lamon, *Life of Abraham Lincoln,* 162.

15. This quotation combines portions of John McNamar to G. U. Miles, May 5, 1866; and John McNamar to WHH, Jan. 20, 1867, *Herndon's Informants,* 253, 545–46.

16. Edited from John McNamar to G. U. Miles, May 5, 1866, *Herndon's Informants,* 252–53.

17. There is no surviving testimony that "all New Salem encouraged his suit" but much to suggest that very few residents were aware of the courtship. Nor is there testimony that Ann Rutledge sent such a letter to McNamar, while one knowledgeable informant, Ann's brother, doubted it. See Robert B. Rutledge to WHH, Nov. 21, 1866, *Herndon's Informants,* 409.

18. Ann's remark, paraphrased here, was reportedly made to her cousin, James McGrady Rutledge, not her brother. Robert B. Rutledge to WHH, Nov. 21, 1866, *Herndon's Informants,* 409.

19. AL's visit to the dying Ann is reported in WHH's interview with William G. Greene, May 30, 1865; John Jones, statement, Oct. 22, 1866, enclosed in Robert B. Rutledge to WHH, [c. Nov. 1, 1866]; and WHH's interview with James McGrady Rutledge, Mar. 1887, *Herndon's Informants,* 21, 387, 608.

20. Adapted from John M. Rutledge to WHH, Nov. 25, 1866, *Herndon's Informants,* 423. Rutledge indeed attests to Ann's singing this hymn, but not that she sang it for AL during her last illness.

21. John Jones, statement, Oct. 22, 1866, enclosed in Robert B. Rutledge to WHH, [c. Nov. 1, 1866], *Herndon's Informants,* 387.

22. Robert B. Rutledge to WHH, [c. Nov. 1, 1866], *Herndon's Informants,* 383.

23. Testimony about AL's grief after Rutledge's death is abundant. See *Herndon's Informants:* WHH's interview with Hardin Bale, May 29, 1865 (13), WHH's interview with William G. Greene, May 30, 1865 (21), clipping from *Menard Axis,* [Feb. 15, 1862], enclosed in John Hill to WHH, June 6, 1865 (25), James Short to WHH, July 7, 1865 (73), Lynn NcNulty Greene to WHH, July 30, 1865 (80), Henry McHenry to WHH, Jan. 8, 1866 (155–56), George U. Miles to WHH, Mar. 23, 1866 (236), WHH's interview with Mentor Graham, Apr. 2, 1866 (243), Benjamin F. Irwin to WHH, Aug. 27, 1866 (325), Benjamin F. Irwin to WHH, Sept. 22, 1866 (353), Robert B. Rutledge to WHH, [c. Nov.

1, 1866] (383), John Jones, statement, Oct. 22, 1866, enclosed in Robert B. Rutledge to WHH, [c. Nov. 1, 1866] (387), Thompson Ware McNeely to WHH, Nov. 12, 1866 (397), Thompson Ware McNeely to WHH, Nov. 28, 1866 (424), Caleb Carman to WHH, Nov. 30, 1866 (430), WHH's interview with Isaac Cogdal, [1865–66] (440), WHH's interview with Isaac Cogdal, [1865–66] (441), and Elizabeth Abell to WHH, Feb. 15, 1867 (557).

24. Recast from WHH's interview with William G. Greene, May 30, 1865, *Herndon's Informants*, 21.

25. Elaborated version of Abner Y. Ellis, statement for WHH, enclosed in Abner Y. Ellis to WHH, Jan. 23, 1866, *Herndon's Informants*, 173. Other accounts in *Herndon's Informants* make much less of AL's emotions at Green's Masonic service: George U. Miles to WHH, Mar. 23, 1866 (237), John Bennett to WHH, Aug. 3, 1866 (263), and WHH's interview with Johnson Gaines Greene, Oct. 5, 1866 (366). Bowling Green's home was north, not south, of town.

26. Lamon, *Life of Abraham Lincoln*, 165.

27. Joshua F. Speed to WHH, Nov. 30, 1866, *Herndon's Informants*, 431.

28. Adapted from Robert L. Wilson to WHH, Feb. 10, 1866, *Herndon's Informants*, 205.

29. McNamar's return and AL's state of mind are described in John McNamar to G. U. Miles, May 5, 1866, *Herndon's Informants*, 253, but not in these words. This passage is based on one in WHH's monograph "Miss Rutlege and Lincoln": "McNamar says that Lincoln looked desolate—distressed—crushed—like one consumed with some consuming agony."

CHAPTER VII

1. Benjamin R. Vineyard to JWW, Jan. 13, 1887; Nancy G. Vineyard to JWW, Feb. 4, 1887; and Benjamin R. Vineyard to JWW, Mar. 14, 1887, *Herndon's Informants*, 599–600, 601, 609–11.

2. For sketches of Mary Owens, see *Herndon's Informants:* WHH's interview with Mentor Graham, Apr. 2, 1866 (243), L. M. Greene to WHH, May 3, 1866 (250), Mary Owens Vineyard to WHH, Aug. 6, 1866 (265), WHH's interview with Caleb Carman, Oct. 12, 1866 (374), WHH's interview with Esther Summers Bale, [1866] (527), and WHH's interview with Johnson Gaines Greene, [1866] (530).

3. Mary Owens Vineyard to WHH, Aug. 6, 1866, *Herndon's Informants*, 265.

4. L. M. Greene to WHH, May 3, 1866, *Herndon's Informants*, 250. Greene's estimate of Mary Owens's weight (180 pounds) has been deleted.

5. WHH's interview with Esther Summers Bale, [1866], *Herndon's Informants*, 527.

6. Edited from WHH's interview with Johnson Gaines Greene, [1866], *Herndon's Informants*, 530.

7. Benjamin R. Vineyard to JWW, Mar. 14, 1887, *Herndon's Informants*, 610.

8. Mary Owens Vineyard's letters given here were not copied from the originals, which WHH presumably returned, but from Lamon, *Life of Abraham Lincoln*, 176–77. Lamon employed not the originals but the copies of this and other documents he purchased from Herndon. Mary Owens Vineyard to WHH, May 1, 1866, Lamon, *Life of Abraham Lincoln*, 176; *Herndon's Informants*, 248.

9. Mary Owens Vineyard to WHH, May 22, 1866, Lamon, *Life of Abraham Lincoln*,

176; *Herndon's Informants*, 255–56. The date of this letter, as shown by the Springer copy, is May 23.

10. Mary Owens Vineyard to WHH, July 22, 1866, Lamon, *Life of Abraham Lincoln*, 177; *Herndon's Informants*, 262–63.

11. AL to Mary S. Owens, Dec. 13, 1836, *Collected Works* 1:54–55.

12. AL to Mary S. Owens, May 7, 1837, *Collected Works* 1:78–79.

13. AL to Mary S. Owens, Aug. 16, 1837, *Collected Works* 1:94–95.

14. Apparently a reference to the caption of the frontispiece to David Ramsay's *Life of George Washington*, a work Lincoln was said to have read in Indiana. The engraving shows a large rock labeled "Washington," against which a huge wave is breaking. See David Ramsay, *Life of George Washington*, 5th ed. (Baltimore: Cushing and Jewell, 1818).

15. AL to Mrs. Orville H. Browning, Apr. 1, 1838, Lamon, *Life of Abraham Lincoln*, 181–83; *Collected Works* 1:117–19.

16. Benjamin R. Vineyard to JWW, Mar. 14, 1877, *Herndon's Informants*, 611.

CHAPTER VIII

1. The "lobby" was the unofficial "Third House" of the Illinois legislature. Composed of legislators, lawyers, officeholders, and office seekers around the capitol, it met at night to deliberate current issues, sometimes facetiously but also to influence legislation.

2. Lamon, *Life of Abraham Lincoln*, 185.

3. AL mainly concerned himself with legislation benefiting northern Sangamon County in his first session—with roads, a bridge, and Sangamon River improvement by way of the Beardstown and Sangamon Canal.

4. AL to the Editor of the *Sangamo Journal*, June 13, 1836, Lamon, *Life of Abraham Lincoln*, 186–87; *Collected Works* 1:48.

5. For the Edwards-Morris confrontation, see WHH's interview with James Gourley, [1865–66], *Herndon's Informants*, 451.

6. AL to Robert Allen, June 21, 1836, *Collected Works* 1:48–49. This letter was published in the *Illinois State Journal*, May 10, 1865.

7. Robert L. Wilson to WHH, Feb. 10, 1866, *Herndon's Informants*, 202.

8. Ibid., 203.

9. Joshua F. Speed, statement to WHH, [1865–66], *Herndon's Informants*, 477–78.

10. Ibid., 478.

11. Robert L. Wilson to WHH, Feb. 10, 1866, *Herndon's Informants*, 204.

12. This probably derives from a speech given in the "lobby" of the general assembly during the 1840–41 session in which Douglas accused Lyman Trumbull of advocating repudiation of the state's internal improvement debt. See James W. Sheahan, *The Life of Stephen A. Douglas* (New York: Harper and Brothers, 1860), 48.

13. Lamon, *Life of Abraham Lincoln*, 195. For AL as the "DeWitt Clinton of Illinois," see WHH's interview with Joshua F. Speed, [1865–66], *Herndon's Informants*, 476.

14. The phrase "commensurate with the wants of the people" is taken from Lamon, *Life of Abraham Lincoln*, 196, who in turn was quoting Thomas Ford, *A History of Illinois*, ed. Rodney O. Davis (Urbana: University of Illinois Press, 1995), 124.

15. Robert L. Wilson to WHH, Feb. 10, 1866, *Herndon's Informants*, 204.

16. Illinois *House Journal*, 1836–37, 1st sess., 243–44.

17. *Collected Works* 1:74–75.

18. Recast from WHH's interview with H. E. Dummer, [1865–66], *Herndon's Informants*, 442. For a text of the interview on which this is based, see the Editors' Introduction, this volume.

19. WHH's interview with Christopher C. Brown, [1865–66], *Herndon's Informants*, 438.

20. WHH's interview with John T. Stuart, [1865–66], *Herndon's Informants*, 479.

21. Joshua F. Speed, statement for WHH, [by 1882], *Herndon's Informants*, 589–90.

22. The poem that follows is from WHH's interview with James H. Matheny, [1865–66], *Herndon's Informants*, 470. (The spelling "Matheney," used throughout the biography, is incorrect.) The verse has here been altered from the version given in the interview:

> Whatever Spiteful fools may Say—,
> Each jealous, ranting yelper—
> No woman ever *played* the *whore*
> Unless She had a man to help her.

In the 1892 edition, the verse was eliminated, and the resulting breach in the narrative, following the words "her frailty, perhaps," was patched in this way: "Unfortunately, the manuscript has not been preserved. Matheney was able, several years ago, to repeat a single stanza, but claimed that after the lapse of so many years it was all he could recall. Perhaps in the end it is best his memory was no more retentive. Reproduced here exactly as in the original, it might suggest more than one construction or offend against the canons of approved taste; in either event I shall omit it" (1:180).

23. Greatly expanded from JWW's interview with James H. Matheny, Sept. 12, 1888, *Herndon's Informants*, 667.

24. "Address Before the Young Men's Lyceum of Springfield, Illinois," Jan. 27, 1838, *Collected Works* 1:108–15. The Lyceum address was delivered while the memory of the killing of Elijah P. Lovejoy on Nov. 7, 1837, at Alton was still fresh. The burning of Francis Macintosh, a free black man in St. Louis, actually took place in April 1836.

25. *Sangamo Journal*, Feb. 3, 1838; *Collected Works* 1:115.

26. Printed in the *Sangamo Journal*, Mar. 6, 1840, and as a pamphlet. See "Speech on the Sub-Treasury," Dec. 26, 1839, *Collected Works* 1:159–79.

27. For AL's regret for his role in Illinois's financial crisis, see "Remarks in Illinois Legislature: Amending a Bill Providing Interest on State Debt," Dec. 4, 1840, *Collected Works* 1:216.

28. WHH's interview with James H. Matheny, [1865–66], *Herndon's Informants*, 472.

29. WHH's interview with Ninian W. Edwards, [1865–66], *Herndon's Informants*, 447.

30. This account reflects WHH's interview with "the brother of the editor," John B. Weber, [c. Nov. 1, 1866], *Herndon's Informants*, 389, and Josiah Holland's notes on a conversation with Usher F. Linder in Josiah G. Holland to WHH, Aug. 19, 1867, *Herndon's Informants*, 569.

31. The "skinning of Thomas" was well remembered. See *Herndon's Informants*: Abner Y. Ellis to WHH, c. Jan. 1866 (161), Jan. 30, 1866 (179), Feb. 14, 1866 (210); Samuel C. Parks to WHH, Mar. 25, 1866 (239); and WHH's interview with David Davis, Sept. 20,

1866 (350). See also Albert T. Bledsoe's review of Ward Hill Lamon's biography in the *Southern Review* (1873), reprinted in Rufus Rockwell Wilson, ed., *Lincoln Among His Friends* (Caldwell, Idaho: Caxton Printers, 1942), 467–68.

32. Joseph Gillespie to WHH, Jan. 31, 1866, *Herndon's Informants*, 181.

CHAPTER IX

1. AL to Mrs. Orville H. Browning, Apr. 1, 1838, *Collected Works* 1:119.

2. Mary Owens Vineyard to WHH, May 23, 1866, *Herndon's Informants*, 256.

3. Drawn from WHH's interview with Mary Todd Lincoln, [Sept. 1866], *Herndon's Informants*, 357, 359. The year of the interview was actually 1866; the name of MTL's French teacher was Victorie Charlotte Leclere Mentelle.

4. This account of MTL's genealogy derives from her sister Emilie T. Helm, statements for WHH, [post-July 1871–89] and [post-1866–89], *Herndon's Informants*, 693–94, 695–96.

5. A documentary source for this remark has not been located.

6. Much rewritten and with interpolations, this passage derives from WHH's interviews with Elizabeth Todd Edwards, [1865–66], and with Elizabeth Todd and Ninian W. Edwards, July 27, 1887, *Herndon's Informants*, 443–44, 623.

7. JWW's notes on his interview with Harriet A. Chapman (*Herndon's Informants*, 646) suggests that MTL told her a somewhat different, if highly improbable, story: "Mrs L. was engaged to Sen Douglas but she broke off engagement—she became sick—Douglas did not want to release her but her bro in law Dr Wallace who was treating her told Douglas he must give her up. Ms L. told Ms C. that she was engaged to D." His notes are undated.

8. Derived from WHH's interview with Joshua F. Speed, [1865–66], *Herndon's Informants*, 475–77.

9. Derived from WHH's interview with Joshua F. Speed, [1865–66], *Herndon's Informants*, 477. Most of the dialogue does not appear in the text of the interview.

10. There is no testimony to support the existence of an aborted wedding on January 1, 1841. For reason to doubt that any significant event in AL's life took place on that date, see Douglas L. Wilson, *Honor's Voice: The Transformation of Abraham Lincoln* (New York: Alfred A. Knopf, 1998), 221–31.

11. WHH has been charged with fabricating this aborted wedding ceremony, and while its date and incidental details (such as the bridal gown and flowers) appear to be no more than conjectures, the incident itself comes directly from the testimony of the sister with whom MTL was then living, Elizabeth Todd Edwards, who told the story to both WHH and JWW (see WHH's interview with Elizabeth Todd Edwards, [1865–66]; and JWW's interview with Elizabeth and Ninian W. Edwards, Dec. 20, 1883, *Herndon's Informants*, 443, 592). Ida M. Tarbell interviewed members of MTL's family in the 1890s, and they all protested strongly that no such aborted ceremony, with assembled guests and defaulting bridegroom, ever took place (see Tarbell, *The Life of Abraham Lincoln*, 2 vols. [New York: McClure, Phillips, 1902], 1:174–79). No wedding license having been registered, and no other confirming evidence having come to light, it seems likely that Elizabeth Todd Edwards was confused about the occasion at which AL failed to appear, which may have been a dinner to announce an engagement. Martinette Hardin McKee, who was a young girl at the time and related to MTL, remembered a similar occasion at which MTL was humiliated by the non-appearance of AL. She, too, represents this as a wedding sup-

WEATHER ADVISORY INFORMATION

Today we are experiencing weather conditions which may prevent your flight from landing at your planned destination. If the weather causes airport conditions or visibility to be below standard FAA and Company safety requirements we may not be able to operate your flight or may have to fly to an alternate airport. This information is being provided so that you are aware of what options you have for your travel. Should you have any questions please see an Allegiant Air Representative.

BEFORE DEPARTURE:

You may elect not to fly on the flight you are currently scheduled for and have the option to rebook yourself for a flight on a later date, within seven (7) days of original departure date. We will be happy to confirm you on another Allegiant Air flight at no additional cost. Please keep in mind; due to our limited flight schedule in certain cities, seats may be limited on upcoming flights. Any meal or overnight expense will not be provided by Allegiant Air. Please contact our Customer Care Department at 1-702-505-8888, (option 2) for all requests.

AFTER DEPARTURE:

If you elect to remain on your scheduled flight and we are unable to land at your destination airport, the flight may proceed to an alternate airport. While the flight is at the alternate airport, the destination weather will be re-evaluated and the decision to continue, or not, will be made by Allegiant Air. If it is determined the flight cannot proceed to the destination city, the flight may, at Allegiant Air's option, return to your origin city. If possible, you will have the option to deplane at the diversion city and obtain alternate transportation to your destination. If you decide to deplane at the alternate city, Allegiant Air will not be liable for any cost for alternate transportations, meals, hotel or any other overnight expenses incurred. Depending on the alternate city's ground capabilities, it may not always be possible to off load checked luggage. If you chose to deplane and we cannot off load your checked luggage, your luggage will be sent to your destination on a later Allegiant Air flight. All luggage will be kept at your destination city for Customer pick up at your convenience.

If Allegiant Air decides to return your flight to your origin city and you stay on that flight, Allegiant Air will not be liable for any meals or any other overnight expenses incurred. We will assist in finding discounted or "Distressed Passenger" rates at local hotels to help minimize the cost and inconvenience. Please check with an Allegiant Air representative once back in your origin city and they will assist you.

In the event your flight is prevented from landing at your planned destination and we fly to an alternate airport, Allegiant Air, at its discretion, may elect not to return to its point of origin. Instead, the decision may be made to reschedule the flight to operate on a future date from the alternate airport to the original planned destination. Allegiant Air will not be liable for any meals or any other overnight expenses incurred. We will assist in finding discounted or "Distressed Passenger" rates at local hotels to help minimize the cost and inconvenience.

UNACCOMPANIED MINORS AND TRAVELERS (14 to 17 years of age):

When there is a Weather Advisory issued for either the departure or arrival city, and/or the potential for a flight to be diverted enroute, Allegiant Air will not permit anyone under the age of 18 traveling alone to travel on the affected flight. When minors are denied travel, please see an agent or contact our Customer Care Department at 1-702-505-8888 (option 2) for all options.

We apologize for the inconvenience today's weather conditions have created. While we have no control over the weather, we are committed to doing everything we can to assist you and get you to your final destination.

allegiant

per, but she may have been influenced by the accounts of the defaulting bridegroom in either Lamon's *Life of Abraham Lincoln* or *Herndon's Lincoln*. See Marietta Holdstock Brown, "A Romance of Lincoln" (newspaper clipping, n.d., but late nineteenth century), reprinted in "Martinette Hardin McKee Recalls Lincoln and Mary Todd," ed. Michael Burlingame, *Lincoln Herald* 97, no. 2 (Summer 1995): 72.

12. WHH's interview with Joshua F. Speed, [1865–66], *Herndon's Informants*, 475.

13. AL to John T. Stuart, Jan. 20, 1841, *Collected Works* 1:229–30. This letter, like many others in the book from Lincoln's hand, may have been copied from the serialized version of Nicolay and Hay's biography. See John G. Nicolay and John Hay, "Abraham Lincoln: A History: Lincoln in Springfield," *Century Illustrated Monthly Magazine* 33, no. 3 (Jan. 1887): 378.

14. AL was incapacitated for only one week. For details, see Wilson, *Honor's Voice*, 234–35.

15. Speed left Springfield in the late spring of 1841; AL did not follow him to Kentucky until early August.

16. WHH was alerted to the existence of this poem in his interview with Joshua F. Speed, [c. June 10, 1865] (see *Herndon's Informants,* 30), where the date of publication was given as "about 1840." Subsequently, WHH said Speed told him it was published in 1838 (WHH to Ward Hill Lamon, Feb. 25, 1870, Lamon Papers). Richard Lawrence Miller has identified what appears to be the poem in question, "The Suicide's Soliloquy," published in the *Sangamo Journal*, Aug. 25, 1838. See his articles "Lincoln's 'Suicide' Poem: Has It Been Found?" *For the People: A Newsletter of the Abraham Lincoln Association* 6, no. 1 (Spring 2004): 1, 6, and "What Is Hell to One Like Me . . . ?" *American Heritage* 55, no. 4 (Aug./Sept. 2004).

17. Joshua F. Speed to WHH, Feb. 7, 1866, *Herndon's Informants*, 197.

18. From a toast before the Society of the Loyal Legion at Cincinnati, May 4, 1887; cited in Albert J. Beveridge, *Abraham Lincoln, 1809–1858*, 2 vols. (Boston: Houghton Mifflin Company, 1928), 1:320n.

19. Joshua F. Speed to WHH, Nov. 30, 1866, *Herndon's Informants*, 430–31. The quotation in the footnote appears later in the same letter.

20. AL to Joshua F. Speed, Jan. [3?] 1842, *Collected Works* 1:265–66; Lamon, *Life of Abraham Lincoln*, 244–46. The copies of AL's letters that Speed sent to WHH are not in the Herndon-Weik Collection and may have been returned to Speed. The text of AL's letters to Speed as reproduced in this biography derives from those printed in Lamon, which were based on the transcriptions of these letters made by John G. Springer for WHH and subsequently purchased by Lamon.

21. AL to Joshua F. Speed, Jan. [3?], 1842, Lamon, *Life of Abraham Lincoln*, 246; *Collected Works* 1:266.

22. AL to Joshua F. Speed, Feb. 3, 1842, Lamon, *Life of Abraham Lincoln*, 246; *Collected Works* 1:267–68.

23. AL to Joshua F. Speed, Feb. 13, 1842, Lamon, *Life of Abraham Lincoln*, 247; *Collected Works* 1:269–70.

24. AL to Joshua F. Speed, Feb. 25, 1842, Lamon, *Life of Abraham Lincoln*, 247–48; *Collected Works* 1:281.

25. AL to Joshua F. Speed, Feb. 25, 1842, Lamon, *Life of Abraham Lincoln*, 249; *Collected Works* 1:280.

26. AL to Joshua F. Speed, Mar. 27, 1842, Lamon, *Life of Abraham Lincoln*, 249–50; *Collected Works* 1:282–83.

27. AL to Joshua F. Speed, Mar. 27, 1842, Lamon, *Life of Abraham Lincoln*, 249–50; *Collected Works* 1:283. The copy of this letter sent to WHH by Speed has not been located. The copy made by WHH's copyist, John G. Springer, betrays no sign of Speed's marginal notation.

28. AL to Joshua F. Speed, July 4, 1842, Lamon, *Life of Abraham Lincoln*, 251; *Collected Works* 1:289. In the original manuscript, printed in *Collected Works*, the last word of the quotation is "rowing." The word "sowing," given here, comes by way of Lamon.

29. AL to Joshua F. Speed, Oct. 5, 1842, Lamon, *Life of Abraham Lincoln*, 252; *Collected Works* 1:302.

30. AL to Joshua F. Speed, Oct. 5, 1842, Lamon, *Life of Abraham Lincoln*, 252; *Collected Works* 1:303.

31. WHH's interview with Elizabeth Todd Edwards, [1865–66], *Herndon's Informants*, 444. The clause "if misfortune befell the engagement all knowledge of it would be hidden from the world" is an interpolation.

32. The details of the Shields affair are actually given further on in this chapter.

33. James H. Matheny to JWW, Aug. 21, 1888, *Herndon's Informants*, 665. The account given here has been completely rewritten and much embroidered.

34. Thomas W. Dresser to JWW, Jan. 3, 1889, *Herndon's Informants*, 671. According to the original, Dresser graduated from Brown University in 1823.

35. WHH's interview with James H. Matheny, May 3, 1866, *Herndon's Informants*, 251. That AL was "pale and trembling" is not in the testimony.

36. "Junius" was a Whig correspondent of the *London Public Advertiser*, 1769–71. The quotation appears in a letter to the Duke of Grafton, Feb. 17, 1770. *The Letters of Junius from the Latest London Edition* (New York: Leavitt, 1850), 2:8.

37. Sarah Rickard Barret to WHH, Aug. 3, 1888, *Herndon's Informants*, 663–64. In rewriting Barret's testimony, JWW changed the time of the proposal: "Mr. Lincoln did Propose marriage to me in the winter of 1840 and 41."

38. On December 5, 1840, in order to prevent a quorum and an undesired vote, AL and two Whig colleagues jumped out a window of the Springfield church in which the Illinois House of Representatives was temporarily meeting.

39. AL to Joshua F. Speed, Oct. 5, 1842, Lamon, *Life of Abraham Lincoln*, 252; *Collected Works* 1:302.

40. Dr. Addison S. Goddard, a Methodist minister. See *Collected Works* 1:294n.

41. According to the editors of *Collected Works* (1:294n), this refers to Milton Wash, a clerk in Shields's office who had embezzled state funds.

42. The word "baby," which appears at this point in the newspaper original, was apparently unreadable in the source followed by Lamon (*Life of Abraham Lincoln*, 256), which is the source being followed here.

43. Lamon, *Life of Abraham Lincoln*, 253–57; *Collected Works* 1:291–97; originally published in *Sangamo Journal*, Sept. 2, 1842.

44. Lamon, *Life of Abraham Lincoln*, 257–59; originally published in *Sangamo Journal*, Sept. 9, 1842.

45. Lamon, *Life of Abraham Lincoln*, 259; originally published in *Sangamo Journal*, Sept. 16, 1842. In the original, and in Lamon, "Auditor's" is rendered "A——s."

46. John D. Whiteside to Editor, Oct. 3, 1842, Lamon, *Life of Abraham Lincoln*, 260–62; originally published in *Sangamo Journal*, Oct. 7, 1842.

47. James Shields to AL, Sept. 17, 1842, *Collected Works* 1:299–300n.

48. AL to James Shields, Sept. 17, 1842, *Collected Works* 1:299.

49. James Shields to AL, Sept. 17, 1842, *Collected Works* 1:300n.

50. "Memorandum of Duel Instructions to Elias H. Merryman," [Sept. 19, 1842], *Collected Works* 1:300–301.

51. Elias H. Merryman to Editor, Oct. 8, 1842, Lamon, *Life of Abraham Lincoln*, 262–69; originally published in *Sangamo Journal*, Oct. 14, 1842.

52. AL to Joshua F. Speed, Oct. 5, 1842, Lamon, *Life of Abraham Lincoln*, 252; *Collected Works* 1:302–3.

53. "Temperance Address," Feb. 22, 1842, *Collected Works* 1:277–78; originally published in *Sangamo Journal*, Mar. 25, 1842.

54. Much elaborated from its source, Joseph Gillespie to WHH, Jan. 31, 1866, *Herndon's Informants*, 180, which says only "He was once pressed into service to entertain Mr Van Buren at rochester in your County & succeeded to admiration."

55. AL to Rowland, Smith & Company, Apr. 24, 1844, *Collected Works* 1:335. The sentence "We are not real estate agents, we are lawyers" is not in the original text.

56. AL to Joshua F. Speed, Mar. 24, 1843, Lamon, *Life of Abraham Lincoln*, 270; *Collected Works* 1:319.

57. AL to Richard S. Thomas, Feb. 14, 1843, *Collected Works* 1:307.

58. AL to Martin S. Morris, Mar. 26, 1843, Lamon, *Life of Abraham Lincoln*, 270–72; *Collected Works* 1:319–20.

59. Abner Y. Ellis to WHH, Feb. 14, 1866, *Herndon's Informants*, 211. The date of this letter given in the footnote is in error.

60. WHH's interview with James H. Matheny, May 3, 1866, *Herndon's Informants*, 251; Lamon, *Life of Abraham Lincoln*, 273.

61. See Nicolay and Hay, "Abraham Lincoln," 396.

62. This footnote closely follows a passage on the same topic in Lamon, *Life of Abraham Lincoln*, 275.

63. The date for this meeting seems to be a mistake. Such a meeting, at which Lincoln spoke in favor of prosecuting the Mexican War, took place in Springfield on May 30, 1846, shortly after Congress declared war on Mexico on May 11 (*Sangamo Journal*, June 4, 1846). Lincoln was elected in August of that year but was not entitled to be sworn in as a member of the House of Representatives until December 1847, by which time he was opposing the war.

64. AL to WHH, Dec. 13, 1847, Lamon, *Life of Abraham Lincoln*, 280; *Collected Works* 1:420.

65. AL to WHH, Jan. 8, 1848, Lamon, *Life of Abraham Lincoln*, 280–81; *Collected Works* 1:430–31.

66. "Speech in the United States House of Representatives: The War with Mexico," Jan. 12, 1848, Lamon, *Life of Abraham Lincoln*, 282; *Collected Works* 1:432.

67. "'Spot' Resolutions in the United States House of Representatives," Dec. 22, 1847, Lamon, *Life of Abraham Lincoln*, 282; *Collected Works* 1:421.

68. "Speech in the United States House of Representatives," Lamon, *Life of Abraham Lincoln*, 288–89, 291; *Collected Works* 1:439, 439–40, 441–42.

69. AL to WHH, Jan. 19, 1848, Lamon, *Life of Abraham Lincoln*, 291; *Collected Works* 1:445.

70. AL to Albert G. Hodges, Apr. 4, 1864, *Collected Works* 7:281.

71. AL to WHH, Feb. 1, 1848, Lamon, *Life of Abraham Lincoln*, 291; *Collected Works* 1:446–48.

72. AL to WHH, Feb. 1, 1848, Lamon, *Life of Abraham Lincoln*, 291–92; *Collected Works* 1:446–47, 448.

73. AL to WHH, Feb. 2, 1848, *Collected Works* 1:448.

74. AL to WHH, Feb. 15, 1848, Lamon, *Life of Abraham Lincoln*, 293; *Collected Works* 1:451–52.

75. AL to WHH, June 12, 1848, Lamon, *Life of Abraham Lincoln*, 294; *Collected Works* 1:477. In Lamon, this letter's recipient is listed as Archibald Williams.

76. AL to WHH, June 22, 1848, Lamon, *Life of Abraham Lincoln*, 295; *Collected Works* 1:490–91.

77. On June 30, 1848, the *Illinois State Register* alleged that WHH had been forbidden to speak at a Taylor ratification meeting by "Messrs. Logan, Stuart, Edwards, etc." because of his independence and lack of enthusiasm for Judge Logan's candidacy for the U.S. House of Representatives.

78. AL to WHH, July 10, 1848, Lamon, *Life of Abraham Lincoln*, 296–97; *Collected Works* 1:497–98.

79. AL to WHH, June 22, 1848, Lamon, *Life of Abraham Lincoln*, 296; *Collected Works* 1:492.

80. "Speech in U.S. House of Representatives on the Presidential Question," July 27, 1848, Lamon, *Life of Abraham Lincoln*, 306–8n; *Collected Works* 1:508–10. The point about this portion of the speech having been omitted from previous biographies echoes Lamon, *Life of Abraham Lincoln*, 306n.

81. In fact, AL never introduced the bill he prepared for this purpose. See text and notes, "Remarks and Resolution Introduced in United States House of Representatives Concerning Abolition of Slavery in the District of Columbia," Jan. 10, 1849, *Collected Works* 2:20–22.

82. AL to Philo H. Thompson, Apr. 26, 1849, Lamon, *Life of Abraham Lincoln*, 309; *Collected Works* 2:44.

83. AL to WHH, Jan. 5, 1849, Lamon, *Life of Abraham Lincoln*, 309–10; *Collected Works* 2:18–19.

84. George W. Rives.

85. AL to George W. Rives, Dec. 15, 1849, *Collected Works* 2:69.

CHAPTER X

1. AL to Joshua F. Speed, May 18, 1843, in Lamon, *Life of Abraham Lincoln*, 272; *Collected Works* 1:325.

2. AL to Joshua F. Speed, July 4, 1842, in Lamon, *Life of Abraham Lincoln*, 251; *Collected Works* 1:289. For an explanation of "sowing" for "rowing," see Chapter IX, note 27.

3. "Application for Patent on an Improved Method of Lifting Vessels over Shoals," Mar. 10, 1849, *Collected Works* 2:36. This account of Lincoln's invention given in the text derives from one of WHH's brief monographs, "Lincoln's Boat," Microfilm Edition: Group 4, Reel 11, Exposures 3541–44, H-W.

4. Joshua F. Speed to WHH, Feb. 14, 1866, *Herndon's Informants*, 213.

5. AL to Joshua F. Speed, Feb. 20, 1849, *Collected Works* 2:28–29. James Lowery Donaldson ("Don:") Morrison was a St. Clair County Whig politician.

6. Elizabeth Sawyer to JWW, Oct. 12, 1888, *Herndon's Informants*, 712.

7. WHH to JWW, Jan. 8, 1886, H-W.

8. Clipping from the *Terre Haute Express*, n.d., enclosed in Thomas H. Nelson to JWW, Sept. 16, 1887, *Herndon's Informants*, 640–42.

9. On AL and the governorship of Oregon Territory, see WHH's interview with John T. Stuart, [1865–66], *Herndon's Informants*, 479–80.

10. Lamon, *Life of Abraham Lincoln*, 327; WHH's interview with David Davis, Sept. 20, 1866, *Herndon's Informants*, 349.

11. Rewritten from WHH's interview with David Davis, Sept. 20, 1866, *Herndon's Informants*, 349.

12. This passage is based on a fuller and more colorful account in WHH to JWW, Nov. 13, 1885, H-W. See also WHH's interview with H. H. Hoagland, [Mar. 7, 1887], *Herndon's Informants*, 603.

13. Lamon, *Life of Abraham Lincoln*, 316; Henry C. Whitney, statement to WHH, Nov. [1866?], *Herndon's Informants*, 407. As in Lamon, Whitney's original wording after the word "order"—"but that you would not make much of a lawyer"—is here deleted.

14. AL to Joshua F. Speed, Mar. 27, 1842, Lamon, *Life of Abraham Lincoln*, 250; *Collected Works* 1:283.

15. AL to John T. Stuart, Dec. 23, 1839, Lamon, *Life of Abraham Lincoln*, 316n; *Collected Works* 1:158.

16. AL to Andrew McCallen, July 4, 1851, *Collected Works* 2:106.

17. AL to John McLean, Dec. 6, 1854, *Collected Works* 2:291.

18. AL to Richard S. Thomas, June 27, 1850, *Collected Works* 2:80.

19. Some of John H. Littlefield's recollections of AL given here were not included in the interview appearing in October 16, 1887 issue of the *Brooklyn Eagle* cited, indicating that another source has been employed.

20. Lawrence Weldon (draft for speech), Aug. 1, 1865, *Herndon's Informants*, 88–89. In the original, Weldon gives the correct title of the poem, "Mortality."

21. "The Enquiry" was originally published in Charles Mackay, *Songs* (London: Bradbury and Evans, 1855).

22. Judge Samuel Treat, statement to WHH, [1865–66], *Herndon's Informants*, 483.

23. J. Henry Shaw to WHH, Sept. 5, 1866, *Herndon's Informants*, 333.

24. AL to John M. Brockman, Sept. 25, 1860, *Collected Works* 4:121.

25. Adapted from WHH to JWW, Jan. 9, 1886, H-W.

26. AL to Hayden Keeling, Mar. 3, 1859, *Collected Works* 3:371.

27. Adapted from WHH to JWW, Mar. 5, 1886, H-W. Lincoln's expedient justification for withdrawing the plea does not appear in WHH's letter.

28. WHH elsewhere identifies this as the Peachy Quinn Harrison case and Judge Edward Young Rice as the presiding judge in question. See WHH to JWW, Nov. 20, 1885, Jan. 4, 1889, H-W. The surviving transcript of this case does not confirm WHH's recollection. See transcript, *People v. Peachy Quinn Harrison*, Sangamon County Circuit Court, 1859, in *The Law Practice of Abraham Lincoln: Complete Documentary Edition*, ed. Martha Benner and Cullom Davis (Urbana: University of Illinois, 2000). See also

Robert Bray, "The P. Quinn Harrison Murder Trial," *Lincoln Herald*, 99, no. 2 (Summer 1997): 59–79.

29. Grant Goodrich to WHH, Dec. 9, 1866, *Herndon's Informants*, 510.

CHAPTER XI

1. Leonard Swett, statement to Henry C. Whitney, in Henry C. Whitney to WHH, Aug. 29, 1887, *Herndon's Informants*, 635–36.

2. Quoted from Lamon, *Life of Abraham Lincoln*, 313. This is from an address by Judge David Davis at Indianapolis, Indiana, May 19, 1865, reprinted in Rufus Rockwell Wilson, comp., *Intimate Memories of Lincoln* (Elmira, N.Y.: Primavera Press, 1945), 69.

3. Somewhat rearranged from WHH's interview with David Davis, Sept. 20, 1866, *Herndon's Informants*, 351.

4. WHH's interview with David Davis, [1866], *Herndon's Informants*, 529. The final sentence in the quotation does not appear in the original interview.

5. The assessment of AL as a lawyer draws from WHH to JWW, Oct. 22, 1885, Dec. 9, 1886, Feb. 18, 1887, H-W; and WHH's monograph, "Lincoln as Lawyer Politician & Statesman," Microfilm Edition, Group 4, Reel 11, Exposures 3565–95, H-W.

6. The source for the text of this legal argument is a copy made by WHH and incorporated into "Lincoln as Lawyer Politician & Statesman," Exposures 3578–81, H-W; "Notes of Argument in a Law Case," June 15, [1858?], *Collected Works* 2:459–60.

7. WHH's interview with David Davis, Sept. 20, 1866, *Herndon's Informants*, 350. WHH related the story that follows in letters to JWW of November 12 and 13, 1885 (H-W), but neither included the notes for Lincoln's argument, which appear nowhere else in WHH's papers. This case has been identified as having been brought to trial in 1846 in behalf of an elderly New Salem acquaintance of AL, Rebecca Thomas. The factual details revealed by pension and court records show the selectiveness of WHH's recollection and raise serious doubts about the heroic character of AL's defense. See Paul H. Verduin, "A New Lincoln Discovery: Rebecca Thomas, His 'Revolutionary War Widow,'" *Lincoln Herald* 98, no. 1 (Spring 1996): 3–11.

8. Andrew H. Goodpasture, statement to WHH, Mar. 31, 1869, *Herndon's Informants*, 572–73, citing the account of an eyewitness, Rev. R. D. Taylor.

9. JWW's interview with Joseph E. McDonald, Aug. 28, 1888, *Herndon's Informants*, 667, much elaborated from very sketchy notes.

10. Joseph Gillespie to WHH, Jan. 31, 1866, *Herndon's Informants*, 182, 184. The sentences in this quotation are far apart in the original. The case in question was Buckmaster for the use of *Denhom v. Beames and Arthur.*

11. WHH's interview with A. F. Lord, [1865–66], *Herndon's Informants*, 469; not a letter, as represented.

12. This sartorial description owes much to Henry C. Whitney to WHH, June 23, 1887, *Herndon's Informants*, 617.

13. JWW's interview with Leonard Swett, [c. 1887–89], *Herndon's Informants*, 732.

14. WHH's interview with David Davis, Sept. 20, 1866, *Herndon's Informants*, 350. The second sentence does not appear in the interview.

15. Leonard Swett to WHH, Jan. 15, 1866, *Herndon's Informants*, 160.

16. Pieced together from Henry C. Whitney to WHH, Nov. 13, 1866; Whitney to WHH, Dec. 30, 1866; and Whitney to WHH, Aug. 27, 1887, *Herndon's Informants*, 398, 525, 634.

17. Henry C. Whitney to WHH, Aug. 27, 1887, *Herndon's Informants*, 634.

18. Mark W. Delahay, "The Life and Character of Abraham Lincoln," a lecture, set in type but not published, Huntington Library, San Marino, Calif.

19. Drawn from Henry C. Whitney to WHH, Aug. 27, 1887; and Henry C. Whitney, statement to WHH, [1887?], *Herndon's Informants*, 630–31, 647–49. The two sentences beginning "In court" and ending with the word "guess" do not appear in these sources.

20. McClellan could not have been the official involved.

21. W. M. Dickson, "Abraham Lincoln at Cincinnati," *Harper's New Monthly Magazine* 69 (June 1884): 62. Stanton's description of AL is not present in this source. It was apparently inserted from Donn Piatt, *Memories of the Men Who Saved the Union* (New York: Belford, Clark., 1887), 56. See William M. Dickson to JWW, Apr. 17, 1888, *Herndon's Informants*, 655, expressing disbelief that "Stanton used unseemly language towards Mr. L."

22. Henry C. Whitney to WHH, Sept. 17, 1887, *Herndon's Informants*, 643–44.

23. Embellished from Abner Y. Ellis to WHH, Jan. 30, 1866, *Herndon's Informants*, 179–80.

24. Edward Eggleston, "The Graysons," *Century Illustrated Monthly Magazine* 35 (1887–88): 40–49, 298–308, 368–78, 562–74, 681–92, 834–45; 36 (1888): 78–90, 265–75, 341–52, 528–35.

25. Drawn from two letters: J. Henry Shaw to WHH, Aug. 22, 1866; and J. Henry Shaw to WHH, Sept. 5, 1866, *Herndon's Informants*, 316, 333. The rewriting of the testimony results here in a change of meaning. In Shaw's original, it was Jack Armstrong, the father, who is said to have befriended AL and the father, not the advocate, that the jury admired: "He told the jury of his once being a poor, friendless boy; that Armstrong's father took him into his house, fed and clothed him & gave him a home &c. the particulars of which were told so pathetically that the jury forgot the guilt of the boy in their admiration of the father."

26. WHH's interview with Hannah Armstrong, [1866], *Herndon's Informants*, 526.

27. Isaac Newton Arnold, *The Life of Abraham Lincoln* (Chicago: A. C. McClurg, 1884), 90.

CHAPTER XII

1. "Autobiography Written for John L. Scripps," [c. June 1860], *Collected Works* 4:67.

2. Lamon, *Life of Abraham Lincoln,* 340–42; "Speech to the Springfield Scott Club," Aug. 14, 26, 1852, *Collected Works* 2:150–51. Lamon correctly makes the point that AL sought permission to make this speech rather than having been invited to make it.

3. WHH recorded three versions of this story: WHH's interview with John T. Stuart, [late June 1865]; WHH's interview with John T. Stuart, [1865–66]; and WHH's interview with John T. Stuart, Dec. 20, 1866, *Herndon's Informants*, 64, 482, 519.

4. The following list of books and newspapers at the Lincoln and Herndon office is mainly delineated in WHH to JWW, Oct. 28, 1885, H-W.

5. "Second Inaugural Address," Mar. 4, 1865, *Collected Works* 8:333.

6. Lamon, *Life of Abraham Lincoln,* 342–43; for Benton's charge, see *Appendix to the Congressional Globe,* 33rd Cong.,1st sess., 31:559.

7. "'A House Divided': Speech at Springfield, Illinois," June 16, 1858, *Collected Works* 2:462.

8. Joseph Gillespie to WHH, Jan. 31, 1866, Lamon, *Life of Abraham Lincoln,* 347; *Herndon's Informants,* 183. Unlike the fuller citation of this source in Lamon, the passage

given here is misleading. The first two sentences are not those of AL but of "a Kentuckian" he quoted to Gillespie, and only the final sentence represents AL's own views. Following Lamon, this text gives "mercenary possession" for Gillespie's "mercenary passion."

9. Joseph Gillespie to WHH, Jan. 31, 1866, Lamon, *Life of Abraham Lincoln,* 347; *Herndon's Informants,* 183–84.

10. Lamon, *Life of Abraham Lincoln,* 349–50. The text given here is virtually identical, but Lamon's has ellipses in several places to show omitted material. Originally published in the *Illinois Daily Journal,* Oct. 10, 1854.

11. Stephen Whitehurst was editor of the *Conservative.*

12. For the proslavery inclinations of such backers of the *Conservative* as John T. Stuart, James H. Matheny, and John E. Rosette, as well as AL's reaction, see WHH's letters to JWW of Sept. 22, 1887 and Jan. 8, 1889, H-W.

13. This account relies on that in Lamon, *Life of Abraham Lincoln,* 353–59, and on WHH to JWW, Feb. 8, 1888, H-W. In his letter, WHH not only summarizes the incident but also refers JWW to this passage in Lamon, *Life of Abraham Lincoln.*

14. "First Debate with Stephen A. Douglas at Ottawa, Illinois," Aug. 21, 1858, *Collected Works* 3:13.

15. "Speech at Peoria, Illinois," Oct. 16, 1854, *Collected Works* 2:247–81; originally published in *Illinois Journal,* Oct. 21, 23–28, 1854. For the supposed truce with Douglas, mentioned below, see Paul M. Angle, "The Peoria Truce," *Journal of the Illinois State Historical Society* 21 (1929): 500–505.

16. John H. Bryant to Robert Boal, Mar. 15, 1866, enclosed in Robert Boal to WHH, Mar. 17, 1866, *Herndon's Informants,* 232.

17. AL to Jacob Harding, Nov. 11, 1854, enclosed in Jacob Harding to WHH, Jan. 7, 1867, *Herndon's Informants,* 542–44; *Collected Works* 2:286. Both the date and the name of the recipient are wrong. "Nix cum arous" is probably an approximation of the German expression *Nicht kommt daraus* ("Nothing comes of it").

18. AL to Jacob Harding, May 25, 1855, enclosed in Jacob Harding to WHH, Jan. 7, 1867, *Herndon's Informants,* 543; *Collected Works* 2:312. The original shows that, rather than ten dollars, AL sent Harding a receipt of Sylvanus Sandford to claims amounting to ten dollars, which Harding might be able to collect from Sandford.

19. Jacob Harding to WHH, Jan. 7, 1867, *Herndon's Informants,* 542. The date of Harding's refusal seems to have been 1858, not, as suggested here, 1855. See Robert Mosely to WHH, Jan. [1866?], and enclosure (AL to Mosely, July 2, 1858), *Herndon's Informants,* 188–89.

20. Joseph Gillespie to WHH, Sept. 19, 1866, *Herndon's Informants,* 344.

21. John Shelly was the unfortunate young Springfield black man. See B. F. Jonas to AL, June 4, 1857, Abraham Lincoln Papers, Library of Congress.

22. Quoted from Lamon, *Life of Abraham Lincoln,* 373, whose source is WHH's third Springfield lecture on AL, "Facts Illustrative of Mr. Lincoln's Patriotism and Statesmanship," delivered in Springfield, Illinois, Jan. 24, 1866. For a text of this lecture, see *Abraham Lincoln Quarterly* 3, no. 4 (Dec. 1944): 190.

23. AL to Joshua F. Speed, Aug. 24, 1855, Lamon, *Life of Abraham Lincoln,* 369; *Herndon's Informants,* 52–53; *Collected Works* 2:320.

24. Quoted from Lamon, *Life of Abraham Lincoln,* 375–76, whose source is WHH's second Springfield lecture, "Analysis of the Characteristics of Abraham Lincoln," deliv-

ered in Springfield, Illinois, Dec. 26, 1865. See *Abraham Lincoln Quarterly* 1, no. 8 (Dec. 1941): 424–25.

25. Quoted from Lamon, *Life of Abraham Lincoln*, 378, whose source was WHH to Ward Hill Lamon, Mar. 1, 1870, Lamon Papers, Huntington Library. Given the existence of newspaper accounts of an enthusiastic Springfield meeting, at which AL spoke, to ratify the nominations made at the Bloomington convention on June 10, either the meagerness of the turnout given here is exaggerated or WHH confused this with another occasion. *Illinois State Journal*, June 11, 1856; *Illinois State Register*, June 12, 1856.

26. Joshua R. Giddings to AL, Sept. 18, 1856, H-W.

27. N. B. Judd and E. Peck to AL, July 7, 1856; W. S. Gale et al. to AL, Aug. 12, 1856; John S. Wilson to AL, Sept. 11, 1856; John Hawes to AL, Sept. 19, 1856; William T. Page to AL, June 30, 1856; and J. M. Sturtevant to AL, Sept. 16, 1856. These invitations are in Microfilm Edition: Group 2, Reel 2, Exposures 305–47, H-W.

28. Apparently a printed form letter. See "Form Letter to Fillmore Men," Sept. 8, 1856, *Collected Works* 2:374. The editors note: "Copies of this letter were lithographed and mailed out by Lincoln with date line and salutation added to suit."

CHAPTER XIII

1. Based on WHH to JWW, Dec. 23, 1885, H-W.

2. Horace Greeley to WHH, May 30, 1858, H-W.

3. A copy of this letter, Lyman Trumbull to AL, Dec. 25, 1857, is in the Trumbull Family Collection, Abraham Lincoln Presidential Library, Springfield (hereafter cited as Trumbull Collection).

4. A copy of this letter, Lyman Trumbull to AL, Dec. 25, 1857 (not Dec. 27), is in the Trumbull Collection.

5. WHH to AL, Mar. 24, 1858, H-W.

6. Theodore Parker, "The Effect of Slavery on the American People," *Additional Speeches, Addresses, and Occasional Sermons* (Boston: Rufus Leighton Jr., 1855), 191.

7. Quoted from Lamon, *Life of Abraham Lincoln*, 397.

8. Rewritten from WHH's interview with Jesse Dubois, [1865–66], *Herndon's Informants*, 442.

9. Paraphrased from ibid.

10. From Lamon, *Life of Abraham Lincoln*, 397, whose source was WHH's third Springfield lecture, "Facts Illustrative of Mr. Lincoln's Patriotism and Statesmanship." See *Abraham Lincoln Quarterly* 3, no. 4 (Dec. 1944): 184.

11. T. Lyle Dickey to WHH, Dec. 8, 1866, *Herndon's Informants*, 505.

12. Quoted and paraphrased from T. Lyle Dickey to WHH, Dec. 8, 1866, *Herndon's Informants*, 505.

13. This account of AL's conference before giving the "House Divided" speech closely follows Lamon, *Life of Abraham Lincoln*, 398–99, which in turn follows WHH's interview with John Armstrong, Feb. 1870, *Herndon's Informants*, 575.

14. Leonard Swett to WHH, Jan. 17, 1866, Lamon, *Life of Abraham Lincoln*, 407; *Herndon's Informants*, 163.

15. Lamon, *Life of Abraham Lincoln*, 407, deriving from WHH's interview with John Armstrong, Feb. 1870, *Herndon's Informants*, 505.

16. AL to Alexander Campbell, June 25, 1858, *Collected Works* 2:473.

17. Drawn from two different letters from Alexander Campbell to JWW, both Dec. 12, 1888, *Herndon's Informants*, 669–70.

18. Stephen A. Douglas to AL, July 30, 1858, *Collected Works* 2:531–32n.

19. AL to Stephen A. Douglas, July 31, 1858, *Collected Works* 2:531.

20. Horace White to WHH, May 17, 1865, *Herndon's Informants*, 4.

21. This description of AL on the stump is based on WHH's fragmentary essay "Lincoln's Ways," Microfilm Edition: Group 4, Reel 11, Exposures 3517–26, H-W.

22. Benjamin F. Irwin to WHH, Feb. 14, 1866, *Herndon's Informants*, 211.

23. AL to J. O. Cunningham, Aug. 22, 1858, *Collected Works* 3:37.

24. Lamon, *Life of Abraham Lincoln*, 400; "'A House Divided': Speech at Springfield, Illinois," June 16, 1858, *Collected Works* 2:461–62.

25. Lamon, *Life of Abraham Lincoln*, 400; *Collected Works* 2:462.

26. "'Mr. Lincoln's Reply,' Seventh and Last Debate with Stephen A. Douglas at Alton, Illinois," Oct. 15, 1858, *Collected Works* 3:315.

27. This scrapbook is in H-W.

28. Henry C. Whitney, statement to WHH, Nov. 1866, *Herndon's Informants*, 406. The date given in the footnote appears to be fictitious.

29. Horace Greeley to WHH, Oct. 6, 1858; and Horace Greeley to WHH, Nov. 14, 1858, H-W. The December 4 letter from Greeley is not in H-W.

30. AL to Henry Asbury, Nov. 19, 1858, probably quoted from the serialization of Nicolay and Hay's biography: John G. Nicolay and John Hay, "Abraham Lincoln: A History: The Lincoln Douglas Debates," *Century Illustrated Monthly Magazine* 34, no. 3 (July 1887): 396; *Collected Works* 3:339.

31. AL to Anson G. Henry, Nov. 19, 1858; as with the preceding letter to Asbury, this is probably quoted from Nicolay and Hay, "Abraham Lincoln," 396; *Collected Works* 3:339.

32. "Speech at Lewistown, Illinois," Aug. 17, 1858, *Collected Works* 2:546–47.

33. Horace White to WHH, May 17, 1865, *Herndon's Informants*, 4–5. The original account of the speech in White's paper, the *Chicago Press and Tribune* (Aug. 21, 1858), has a Lewistown dateline and is signed "G. P." See *Collected Works* 2:544n.

CHAPTER XIV

1. JWW interview with John S. Bradford, [1883–89], *Herndon's Informants*, 729.

2. WHH interview with P. P. Enos, [1865–66], *Herndon's Informants*, 448–49.

3. WHH's interview with David Davis, Sept. 20, 1866, *Herndon's Informants*, 349.

4. WHH described the boys' behavior at the law office, sometimes more pungently than is rendered here, in three letters to JWW: Nov. 19, 1885; Jan. 9, 1886; and Feb. 18, 1887, H-W.

5. Expanded from JWW's interview with Emilie T. Helm, Mar. 22, 1887, *Herndon's Informants*, 612.

6. JWW's interview with Harriet A. Chapman, [1886–87], *Herndon's Informants*, 646.

7. Drawn from JWW's interview with Margaret Ryan, Oct. 27, 1886, *Herndon's Informants*, 596–97. Some of the details have been changed.

8. *Collected Works* 2:389–90. The location of the original is not known; the text in *Collected Works* is taken from this biography.

9. WHH's interview with James H. Matheny, Jan. 1887; and JWW's interview with James H. Matheny, Sept. 12, 1888, *Herndon's Informants*, 713–14, 667, 667n. The offended man was Jacob Taggart of Springfield, the pronunciation of whose name was probably something nearly like "tiger," which is the way it is recorded in WHH's interview.

10. The picture of Lincoln's sad presence at the law office is adapted from WHH to JWW, Jan. 16, 1886, H-W.

11. This may well be a fabricated statement giving voice to the common sentiment of several people close to AL. In *Herndon's Informants*, see WHH's interview with John T. Stuart, [late June 1865], quoting Joshua F. Speed (63), Edgar Conkling to WHH, Aug. 3, 1867 (565), Henry C. Whitney to WHH, June 23, 1887 (617), WHH's interview with Elizabeth and Ninian Edwards, July 27, 1887 (623), and JWW's interview with Milton Hay, [c. 1883–88] (729).

12. Mary Owens Vineyard to WHH, May 23, 1866, *Herndon's Informants*, 256.

13. Thomas W. Dresser to JWW, Jan. 3, 1889, *Herndon's Informants*, 671.

14. Joseph Gillespie to WHH, Dec. 8, 1866, *Herndon's Informants*, 505–6.

15. Sources for what follows on AL's superstition: on the voodoo fortune teller, Isaac N. Arnold mentions a "tradition," the origin of which neither he nor WHH could ascertain, in Isaac Newton Arnold, *The Life of Abraham Lincoln* (Chicago: A. C. McClurg, 1884), 31 and 31n; on the madstone, see Joseph Gillespie to WHH, Jan. 31, 1866, and WHH's interview with Frances Todd Wallace, [1865–66], *Herndon's Informants*, 182, 485; the mirror image story was first told by Noah Brooks in "Personal Recollections of Abraham Lincoln," *Harper's New Monthly Magazine* 31, no. 182 (July 1865): 224–25, then repeated but erroneously attributed to Hay in Lamon, *Life of Abraham Lincoln*, 476–77, which seems to be the source employed here; on AL's "only philosophy," see note 16 below; on AL's certainty of a terrible end, see WHH to JWW, Nov. 14, 1885, Feb. 6, 1887; and on Brutus and Caesar, see WHH to JWW, Feb. 25, 1887, all in H-W.

16. WHH's interview with Mary Todd Lincoln, Sept. 1866, *Herndon's Informants*, 358, 360. WHH's interview notes suggest that MTL remembered this saying as "no cares of ours" and that WHH remembered the same maxim being worded "no prayers of ours."

17. *Hamlet*, 5.2.10–11.

18. WHH told this story twice in his letters to JWW: Dec. 21, 1885, and Feb. 1887, H-W. JWW first drafted this version of the story for inclusion in the preface as part of the justification for telling unpalatable or unwelcome truths. When the preface was revised, the anecdote was omitted, but WHH noticed its omission and pleaded with his collaborator to find a place for it (WHH to JWW, Feb. 5, 1889, H-W). AL's reported remarks about history and the truth, so often quoted afterward, do not appear in WHH's letters.

19. This brief sketch of AL's views on evolution and free will derives from two of WHH's monographs, "*Notes* that I wish to write out more particularly & more fully sometime" and "Lincoln's Philosophy & Religion" (Microfilm Edition: Group 4, Reel 11, Exposures 2815–20 and 3368–88, H-W) and also draws from WHH to JWW, Feb. 6, 1887, H-W.

20. JWW's interview with Dillard C. Donnohue, Feb. 13, 1887, *Herndon's Informants*, 602.

21. On AL's work on infidelity, see *Herndon's Informants*: clipping from *Menard Axis*, [Feb. 15, 1862], enclosed in John Hill to WHH, June 6, 1865 (24), John Hill to WHH, June 27, 1865 (61–62), WHH's interview with James H. Matheny, Nov. 1866 (432), WHH's inter-

view with Isaac Cogdal, [1865–66] (441), and WHH's interview with James H. Matheny, [by Mar. 2, 1870] (577).

22. Quoted from Lamon, *Life of Abraham Lincoln*, 488; WHH's interview with James H. Matheny, [by Mar. 2, 1870], *Herndon's Informants*, 576.

23. Quoted from Lamon, *Life of Abraham Lincoln*, 488; WHH's interview with John T. Stuart, [by Mar. 2, 1870], *Herndon's Informants*, 576.

24. Quoted from Lamon, *Life of Abraham Lincoln*, 489; WHH interviews with David Davis, Sept. 20, 1866, and [1866], *Herndon's Informants*, 348, 529.

25. Quoted from Lamon, *Life of Abraham Lincoln*, 489; WHH's interview with William H. Hannah, [1865–66], *Herndon's Informants*, 458. The original notes of WHH's interview show that Hannah quoted AL as calling himself "a Kind of universalist," referring to the Protestant denomination that believes in universal salvation. The source being used here is Lamon, which attempts to correct an error in the transcription made by John G. Springer. Springer misread the word "universalist" for "immoralist," which Lamon changed to "immortalist."

26. Quoted from Lamon, *Life of Abraham Lincoln*, 490; James W. Keyes, statement to WHH, [1865–66], *Herndon's Informants*, 464.

27. John G. Nicolay to WHH, May 27, 1865, *Herndon's Informants*, 6.

28. John D. DeFrees to WHH, Dec. 4, 1866, *Herndon's Informants*, 497.

29. Quoted from Lamon, *Life of Abraham Lincoln*, 490–92; Jesse W. Fell to Ward Hill Lamon, Sept. 22, 1870, enclosed in Jesse W. Fell to WHH, Sept. 20, 1870, *Herndon's Informants*, 578–80.

30. WHH's interview with Mary Todd Lincoln, [Sept. 1866], *Herndon's Informants*, 360.

CHAPTER XV

1. AL to Norman B. Judd, Nov. 16, 1858, probably copied from John Nicolay and John Hay, "Abraham Lincoln: A History: The Lincoln-Douglas Debates," *Century Illustrated Monthly Magazine* 34, no. 3 (July 1887): 396; *Collected Works* 3:337.

2. Although the editors of *Collected Works* believed AL had delivered two versions of the same lecture, "Discoveries and Inventions" (2:437–42, 3:356–63), AL himself declared, "{I} have never got up but one lecture; and that, I think, a rather poor one" (4:40). That there was, indeed, only one lecture, of which the two "versions" are constituent parts, has been demonstrated by Wayne C. Temple in a two-part article, "Lincoln the Lecturer," *Lincoln Herald*, pt. 1, 101, no. 3 (Fall 1999): 94–110; pt. 2, 101, no. 4 (Winter 1999): 146–63. Temple also shows that AL delivered his lecture at least six times.

3. Henry C. Whitney to WHH, Aug. 27, 1887, *Herndon's Informants*, 633.

4. AL to William M. Morris, Mar. 28, 1859, *Collected Works* 3:374.

5. W. M. Dickson, "Abraham Lincoln at Cincinnati," *Harper's New Monthly Magazine* 69 (June 1884): 65–66.

6. Stephen A. Douglas, "The Dividing Line Between Federal and Local Authority: Popular Sovereignty in the Territories," *Harper's Magazine* 19, no. 112 (Sept. 1859): 519–37.

7. "Speech at Columbus, Ohio," Sept. 16, 1859, *Collected Works* 3:405.

8. See Johnson and Bradford to AL, Mar. 21, 1859, Abraham Lincoln Papers, Library of Congress.

9. AL to Mark W. Delahay, May 14, 1859, *Collected Works* 3:379.

10. AL to Thomas J. Pickett, Apr. 16, 1859, quoted from Lamon, *Life of Abraham Lincoln*, 422; *Collected Works* 3:377. The date of the letter here, as in Lamon, is in error.

11. Jackson Grimshaw to WHH, Apr. 28, 1866, *Herndon's Informants*, 247.

12. Lamon, *Life of Abraham Lincoln*, 425.

13. Jonathan Elliot, comp., *The Debates in the Several State Conventions on the Adoption of the Federal Constitution as Recommended by the General Convention at Philadelphia, in 1787* (Washington, D.C.: By and for the Editor, 1836–45).

14. Robert Todd Lincoln was attending Phillips Exeter Academy in preparation for entering Harvard.

15. Quoted from Lamon, *Life of Abraham Lincoln*, 442; *Manchester* (New Hampshire) *Mirror*, Mar. 2, 1860.

16. AL to Mark W. Delahay, Mar. 16, 1860, *Collected Works* 4:32.

17. AL to Mark W. Delahay, Apr. 14, 1860, *Collected Works* 4:44.

18. Ibid.

19. Mark W. Delahay, a somewhat dissolute attorney, politician, and newspaper editor, was a longtime friend who was married to a distant relative of AL. After moving to Kansas, he kept AL informed of political developments, championed Republican party interests, and promoted AL's presidential prospects. AL appointed him to a federal judgeship in 1861.

20. AL to Mark W. Delahay, Mar. 13, 1861, *Collected Works* 4:283.

21. —— Johnson to WHH, [1865–66], *Herndon's Informants*, 463–64.

22. *Collected Works* 4:50, citing this biography as the source.

23. Lamon, *Life of Abraham Lincoln*, 451. The next sentence is also heavily indebted to Lamon's text, which says of AL's reaction to the news of his nomination: "Mr. Lincoln seemed to be calm, but a close observer could detect in his countenance the indications of deep emotion."

24. Probably based on Charles S. Zane, statement for WHH, [1865–66], and WHH's interview with Zane, [1865–66], *Herndon's Informants*, 491, 492.

25. The Republican platform was first published in the *Chicago Press and Tribune*, May 18, 1860. The passage given here is drawn from Resolutions 7, 8, and 9.

26. "'A House Divided': Speech at Springfield, Illinois," June 16, 1858, *Collected Works* 2:461.

27. WHH sent JWW an account of this incident and a copy of the text of AL's letter in an undated letter (Microfilm Edition: Group 7, Roll 4, Exposures 27–28, H-W); AL to WHH, Oct. 10, 1860, *Collected Works* 4:126, citing WHH's copy. The original letter, which WHH says he gave to a Mr. Parker in 1881, has not been located.

28. AL to George Ashmun, May 23, 1860, Lamon, *Life of Abraham Lincoln*, 453–54; *Collected Works* 4:52–53.

29. J. G. Holland, *The Life of Abraham Lincoln* (Springfield, Mass.: Gurdon Bill, 1866), 236–37.

30. AL's decision to vote is reported in WHH to JWW, Nov. 14, 1885, H-W, where the idea of cutting off the top of the ticket originates with AL.

CHAPTER XVI

1. Lamon, *Life of Abraham Lincoln*, 457.

2. J. S. Bliss to WHH, Jan. 29, 1867, *Herndon's Informants*, 551–53.

3. AL to Joshua R. Giddings, May 21, 1860, *Collected Works* 4:51.

4. See Henry C. Whitney, statement for WHH, [1887?], *Herndon's Informants*, 647. Whitney's source is Thurlow Weed's autobiography, *Life of Thurlow Weed, Including His Autobiography and a Memoir* (Boston: Houghton, Mifflin, 1883–84), 1:607.

5. Henry Wilson to WHH, May 30, 1867, *Herndon's Informants*, 561–62. Wilson's original has WHH the law partner of AL for sixteen years, not eighteen.

6. WHH's interview with Joshua F. Speed, [1865–66], *Herndon's Informants*, 475.

7. WHH described AL requesting reference materials for his inaugural address on at least two occasions, and on neither did he say that Lincoln asked for a copy of Webster's reply to Hayne. Rather, he indicated on both occasions that Lincoln knew and admired Webster's reply, with the implication that he didn't need to consult a copy of it. See WHH to JWW, Jan. 1, 1886, H-W, and WHH's third Springfield lecture on AL, "Facts Illustrative of Mr. Lincoln's Patriotism and Statesmanship," *Abraham Lincoln Quarterly*, 3:4 (December 1944), 194.

8. WHH's interview with David Davis, Sept. 19, 1866, *Herndon's Informants*, 346–47.

9. AL to John D. Johnston, Nov. 4, 1851, Lamon, *Life of Abraham Lincoln*, 338; *Collected Works* 2:112.

10. AL to John D. Johnson, Nov. 9, 1851, Lamon, *Life of Abraham Lincoln*, 338; *Collected Works* 2:112.

11. This account of AL's 1861 visit to his stepmother is based on the following sources in *Herndon's Informants:* Augustus H. Chapman to WHH, Oct. 8, 1865 (135–37), WHH's interview with Augustus H. Chapman, [1865–66] (439); George B. Balch, statement to JWW, Apr. 10, 1885 (593–94), and George B. Balch, statement to JWW, [1885?] (596).

12. WHH's interview with Hannah Armstrong, 1866, Lamon, *Life of Abraham Lincoln*, 465; *Herndon's Informants*, 527.

13. WHH's interview with Isaac Cogdal, [1865–66], Lamon, *Life of Abraham Lincoln*, 168; *Herndon's Informants*, 440.

14. For WHH's account of Lincoln's offer of an appointment, see his monograph in Microfilm Edition: Group 4, Reel 11, Exposures 3450–59, H-W.

15. "Farewell Address at Springfield, Illinois," Feb. 11, 1861, Lamon, *Life of Abraham Lincoln*, 506. This version of the speech was originally published in the *Illinois State Journal*, Feb. 12, 1861. For the different published versions of this address, see *Collected Works* 4:190–91.

16. Grace Bedell to WHH, Dec. 14, 1866, *Herndon's Informants*, 517; AL to Grace Bedell, Oct. 19, 1860, *Collected Works* 4:129.

17. AL to L. Montgomery Bond, Oct. 15, 1860, *Collected Works* 4:128.

18. AL to Samuel Haycraft, June 4, 1860, *Collected Works* 4:70.

19. AL to Samuel Haycraft, Nov. 13, 1860, *Collected Works* 4:139.

20. For AL's Pittsburgh speech, see Lamon, *Life of Abraham Lincoln*, 509; *Collected Works* 4:210–15; for Cleveland, Lamon, *Life of Abraham Lincoln*, 509; *Collected Works* 4:215; for Philadelphia, Lamon, *Life of Abraham Lincoln*, 511; *Collected Works* 4:241.

21. J. G. Holland, *The Life of Abraham Lincoln* (Springfield, Mass.: Gurdon Bill, 1866), 273–74.

22. These remarks presumably were made to Weik, who claimed to have interviewed Mather in Springfield. See Jesse W. Weik, *The Real Lincoln*, ed. Michael Burlingame (1922; reprint, Lincoln: University of Nebraska Press, 2002), 304–6.

23. Apparently quoted from Francis Fisher Browne, *The Every-Day Life of Abraham Lincoln* (New York: N. D. Thompson, 1886), 402–4.

CHAPTER XVII

1. AL to Calvin Truesdale, Apr. 20, 1863, *Collected Works* 6:182.
2. AL to Wait Talcott, Aug. 27, 1862, *Collected Works* 5:397.
3. AL to Salmon P. Chase, Aug. 18, 1862, *Collected Works* 5:379.
4. AL to WHH, Feb. 3, 1862, *Collected Works* 5:118.
5. AL to WHH, Feb. 19, 1863, *Collected Works* 6:111.
6. Jesse K. Dubois to Henry C. Whitney, Apr. 6, 1865, *Herndon's Informants*, 620. In the original, Dubois claims that AL used him for a plaything "for 30 years past."
7. WHH's interview with David Davis, Sept. 20, 1866, *Herndon's Informants*, 349.
8. No original for this letter has been found. The text given here is reprinted in *Herndon's Informants*, 709–11. Browning's first name is Orville, not Oliver.
9. Only one letter from WHH to AL survives in the Abraham Lincoln Papers: WHH to AL, Aug. 29, 1863. It relates to legal business and the forthcoming Union meeting to be held in Springfield on September 3.
10. This legal terminology originates in Sir Edward Coke's commentary on the Magna Carta.
11. The remark about office seekers looking for a way to "live without work," which appears two other places in this book (p. 184 and p. 360), comes from WHH's second Springfield lecture, "Analysis of the Character of Abraham Lincoln," delivered in Springfield on December 26, 1865, which is the basis for Chapter XX. For a text of the lecture, see *Abraham Lincoln Quarterly* 1, no. 8 (Dec. 1941): 406–7.
12. The account given here is based on WHH's interview with Elizabeth Todd Edwards, [1865–66], *Herndon's Informants*, 444–45, greatly embellished and rearranged.
13. AL's second son, Edward Baker Lincoln, whose death in 1850 was the first in the AL family, lived to be almost four years of age. The error does not appear in the original interview.
14. Mary Todd Lincoln to WHH, Aug. 28, [1866], *Herndon's Informants*, 326–27.
15. WHH's interview with Mary Todd Lincoln, [Sept. 1866], *Herndon's Informants*, 359–61, greatly rewritten and elaborated, with many interpretive renderings and much left out.
16. For Hay and AL's wartime correspondence, see Michael Burlingame, "The Authorship of the Bixby Letter," in *At Lincoln's Side: John Hay's Civil War Correspondence and Selected Writings*, ed. Michael Burlingame (Carbondale: Southern Illinois University Press, 2000), 169–84.
17. David Davis to WHH, Feb. 22, [1866], *Herndon's Informants*, 218. George Bancroft, an eminent historian and orator, delivered a eulogy on Lincoln before Congress on February 12, 1866. Davis's first letter on Bancroft's eulogy (Feb. 16, 1866) has not been located.
18. John Hay to WHH, Sept. 5, 1866, *Herndon's Informants*, 331–32. Hay's original text refers to "Miss Nancy Bancroft & the rest of that patent leather kid glove set" and names Bancroft's eulogy specifically as the "disgraceful exhibition." Hays letter reads: "I consider Lincoln Republicanism incarnate" (*Herndon's Informants*, 332).
19. JWW's interview with Dennis Hanks, Mar. 26, 1888, *Herndon's Informants*, 654.
20. Ibid.
21. Ibid.

CHAPTER XVIII

1. The quotations that follow "adhere strictly" to the written statements of Joshua F. Speed and Leonard Swett in the sense that they are drawn from specific written sources. As usual, they contain editorial changes and interpolations, some of which have been noted.

2. The portion of the quotation up to this point is from Joshua F. Speed to WHH, Dec. 6, 1866, *Herndon's Informants*, 498–500.

3. Joshua F. Speed to WHH, Feb. 7, 1866, *Herndon's Informants*, 197. The last sentence is an interpolation.

4. Joshua F. Speed to WHH, Jan. 12, 1866, *Herndon's Informants*, 156–58. The two exclamatory sentences at the end of the quotation are not in Speed's original letters and probably were not intended to be included in the quotation.

5. Although written in 1866, WHH allowed Swett to revise this letter in 1887, which is the version given here. For a transcription of the original 1866 version, with significant differences noted, see Leonard Swett to WHH, Jan. 17, 1866, *Herndon's Informants*, 162–68.

6. The passage "It was here . . . as anyone could'" was added in 1887. See note 5 above.

7. The word "vulgar" was substituted in 1887 for "low and dirty." See note 5 above.

8. Following this sentence, Swett's original 1866 version contained a personal anecdote about pleading for the life of a condemned soldier. See *Herndon's Informants*, 166.

9. In the 1866 version, this word is "favorites." See note 5 above.

10. The Gladstone anecdote was added in 1887. See note 5 above.

11. A sentence from the 1866 version is here omitted. See note 5 above and *Herndon's Informants*, 167.

12. The characterization of AL in the 1866 version of the letter ended here. The paragraph on AL's religion that follows originally preceded this one. See note 5 above.

13. This sentence was substituted in 1887 for "Whether he went to Church once a month or once a year troubled him but very little. He failed to observe the Sabbath very scrupulously. I think he read 'Petroleum V. Nasby' as much as he did the Bible. He would ridicule the Puritans, or swear in a moment of vexation." See note 5 above.

CHAPTER XIX

1. Henry C. Whitney, statement for WHH, [Nov. 1866?], *Herndon's Informants*, 405–6. The final sentence does not appear in the original text.

2. Henry C. Whitney to WHH, June 23, 1887, *Herndon's Informants*, 619.

3. Robert L. Wilson to WHH, Feb. 10, 1866, *Herndon's Informants*, 207.

4. Henry C. Whitney, statement for WHH, [Nov. 1866?], *Herndon's Informants*, 404–5. The basis for Whitney's statement being, as the footnote declares, "written out during the war," does not appear in the original statement.

5. Henry C. Whitney, statement for WHH, [Nov. 1866?], *Herndon's Informants*, 405.

6. "Emancipation Proclamation," Jan. 1, 1863, *Collected Works* 6:30.

7. AL is reported as saying to Francis P. Carpenter that the Emancipation Proclamation was "the central act of my administration and the great event of the nineteenth century." Francis P. Carpenter, *Six Months at the White House* (New York: Hurd and Houghton, 1866), 90.

8. James C. Conkling to JWW, Jan. 11, 1889, *Herndon's Informants*, 672. The original does not include the sentence "The following short note in Mr. Lincoln's own handwriting accompanied the letter" nor the short message from AL that follows it. The text of AL's letter, dated 1863, not 1862, is in *Collected Works* 6:414.

9. The asterisks at the beginning and end of this paragraph mark the insertion Conkling said was telegraphed to him later. See his letter to JWW in the footnote. For the text of this letter, see AL to Conkling, Aug. 31, 1863, *Collected Works* 6:423.

10. AL to James C. Conkling, Aug. 26, 1863, *Collected Works* 6:406–10.

11. WHH's interview with David Davis, Sept. 20, 1866, *Herndon's Informants*, 348–49.

12. JWW's interview with Joseph E. McDonald, Aug. 28, 1888, *Herndon's Informants*, 667, greatly expanded from the original notebook entry.

13. AL to William T. Sherman, Sept. 19, 1864, *Collected Works* 8:11.

14. The congratulatory telegram was from Grant to Secretary of War Edwin M. Stanton. See Grant to Stanton, Nov. 10, 1864, John Y. Simon, ed. *The Papers of Ulysses S. Grant* (Carbondale: Southern Illinois University Press, 1984), 12:398.

15. James M. Ashley to WHH, Nov. 23, 1866, enclosing copy of James M. Ashley to AL, Jan. 31, [1865], with endorsement by AL, *Herndon's Informants*, 413–14.

16. "Second Inaugural Address," Mar. 4, 1865, *Collected Works* 8:333. This transcription is not exact.

17. J. G. Holland, *The Life of Abraham Lincoln* (Springfield, Mass.: Gurdon Bill, 1866), 508–9.

18. Gertrude Garrison was the literary agent who helped JWW find a publisher for the manuscript that became *Herndon's Lincoln*. She also seems to have authored the account that follows of AL's assassination. See the letters between Garrison and JWW, Weik Papers, Abraham Lincoln Presidential Library.

19. William O. Stoddard, *Abraham Lincoln: The True Story of a Great Life* (New York: Fords, Howard & Hulbert, 1884), 461–62.

20. Garrison contribution stops here, but continues on p. 343. See note 18 above.

21. "Address Delivered at the Dedication of the Cemetery at Gettysburg," Nov. 19, 1863, *Collected Works* 7:18–23.

22. "Speech in Independence Hall, Philadelphia, Pennsylvania," Feb. 22, 1861, *Collected Works* 4:240.

23. *Harper's Weekly* 9, no. 435 (Apr. 29, 1865): 258.

24. Henry Ward Beecher, "Sermon at Plymouth Church, Brooklyn, New York, Sunday Morning, April 23, 1865," in *Patriotic Addresses in America and England, from 1850 to 1885* (Boston: Pilgrim Press, 1887), 712.

25. The account of Booth's conspiracy given here in quotation marks on pp. 343–46 is presumably by Gertrude Garrison. See note 18 above.

26. George Atzerodt was hanged along with Payne, Herold, and Mrs. Surratt and was not, as related below, sent to the Dry Tortugas. This error was corrected in the second printing (1890) of the first edition.

27. This presumably marks the end of Gertrude Garrison's contribution. See notes 18 and 25 above.

28. The source followed here is unknown, but it is in error. AL's "Last Public Address" on April 11, 1865, concerned issues of reconstruction, including black suffrage, but it nowhere spoke, as the text given here does, of either "universal amnesty" or "universal suffrage." See

Collected Works 8:403. For Stone's report to George Alfred Townsend, see William Hanchett, *The Lincoln Murder Conspiracies* (Urbana: University of Illinois Press, 1983), 254n, citing Townsend's *Katy of Catoctin* (New York: D. Appleton, 1886), 490, 490n.

CHAPTER XX

1. This chapter draws from one of the draft chapters WHH wrote out for JWW's use, "Lincoln Individually" (H-W), and from published excerpts of his first and second Springfield lectures on the mind and character of Abraham Lincoln, delivered December 12 and December 26, 1865. WHH had given the manuscripts of these lectures to Ward Hill Lamon and had not retained copies, but abridged versions and summaries were widely circulated in contemporary newspapers. The most convenient access to these excerpts at the time this biography was written was Francis B. Carpenter's popular book, *Six Months at the White House* (New York: Hurd and Houghton, 1866), 323–50. WHH refers JWW to Carpenter's book in some of his letters and memoranda, including "Lincoln Individually." Here, the substance of the lectures as given in the Carpenter excerpts has been paraphrased.

2. J. G. Holland, *The Life of Abraham Lincoln* (Springfield, Mass.: Gurdon Bill, 1866), 241–42. A portion of Holland's text has been silently deleted. Following the sentence "He opened himself to men in different directions," Holland's text reads: "It was rare that he exhibited what was religious in him; and he never did this at all, except when he found just the nature and character that were sympathetic with that aspect and element of his character. A great deal of his best, deepest, largest life he kept almost constantly from view, because he would not expose it to the eyes and apprehension of the careless multitude."

3. Elliott B. Herndon, statement to WHH, [1865–66], *Herndon's Informants*, 459–60.

4. This description is based on a passage in "Lincoln Individually" (see note 1 above).

5. Henry C. Whitney to WHH, June 23 and Aug. 27, 1887, *Herndon's Informants*, 617, 631–32, in both instances citing John T. Stuart.

6. Robert L. Wilson to WHH, Feb. 10, 1866, *Herndon's Informants*, 205.

7. A somewhat reorganized version of WHH's interview with James Gourley, [1865–66], *Herndon's Informants*, 451–53.

8. This impartial witness has not been identified. His testimony is recorded, possibly from memory, in "Lincoln Individually" (H-W). See note 1 above.

9. Instead of "object lesson," both WHH's manuscript of "Lincoln Individually" and Carpenter's excerpt in *Six Months at the White House* (329) have "schoolmaster." The passage that follows seems to represent a recasting of Carpenter's text.

10. WHH's interview with Richard M. Lawrence, June 23, 1888, *Herndon's Informants*, 715–16. The emphasis in the original interview is not on the incongruity of AL's laughter but on his "heavenly feeling at the turn of something in the piece. Lincoln felt glorious and forgot for the moment in his deep feeling where he was and what he was doing."

11. AL's exact words were "If I could save the Union without freeing *any* slave I would do it." AL to Horace Greeley, Aug. 22, 1862, *Collected Works* 5:388.

12. The "malignant fool" has not been identified. The last remark attributed to AL appears previously on p. 203 and p. 230. It was omitted in the 1892 edition.

13. This remark appears twice previously in the book at p. 184 and p. 304.

14. Robert Dale Owen to WHH, Jan. 22, 1867, Microfilm Edition, Group 4, Roll 9, Exposure 1398, H-W.

APPENDIX

1. AL to Thomas Lincoln and John D. Johnston, Dec. 24, 1848, *Collected Works* 2:15.

2. AL to John D. Johnston, Feb. 23, 1850, *Collected Works* 2:76–77. In *Collected Works*, the dead child (Edward Baker Lincoln) is said to have been ill "fiftytwo days."

3. AL to Thomas Lincoln and John D. Johnston, Dec. 24, 1848, *Collected Works* 2:15–16.

4. AL to John D. Johnston, Jan. 12, 1851, *Collected Works* 2:96–97.

5. AL to John D. Johnston, Aug. 31, 1851, *Collected Works* 2:110.

6. AL to John D. Johnston, Nov. 5, 1851, *Collected Works* 2:111–12.

7. AL to John D. Johnston, Nov. 14, 1851, *Collected Works* 2:112.

8. *Othello*, 3.3.156–61.

9. This statement may have been borrowed from Osborn H. Oldroyd, *The Lincoln Memorial: Album-Immortelles* (New York, 1882), where it appears in much the same form.

10. Errors in the initials of AL's colleagues at the bar were corrected in the 1892 edition: W. I. Ferguson, C. S. Zane, and G. W. Shutt.

11. Benjamin F. Irwin to WHH, Feb. 8, 1866, *Herndon's Informants*, 197–98. The contents have been reordered.

12. "Call for Republican Convention," May 10, 1856, *Collected Works* 2:340. This originally appeared in the *Illinois State Journal*, May 10, 1856.

13. AL to Abraham Jonas, July 21, 1860, *Collected Works* 4:85–86.

14. Luther B. Baker, statement, [1887–88], *Herndon's Informants*, 670–71.

15. Abridged version of Lawrence Weldon (drafts for speech), Aug. 1, 1865, *Herndon's Informants*, 88–90. In the original, Weldon gives the correct title of the poem, "Mortality."

16. The phrase "again and again" is not in Cannon's original letter.

17. This sentence is not in Cannon's letter.

18. LeGrand B. Cannon to WHH, Oct. 7, [1889], *Herndon's Informants*, 679–80, except as noted above.

1892 CHAPTER ON LINCOLN IN MASSACHUSETTS

1. JWW pieced this chapter together from a number of statements contributed by Edward L. Pierce, most of which are printed in *Herndon's Informants*.

2. Frederick W. Seward, *Seward at Washington as Senator and Secretary of State*, 2 vols. (New York: Derby and Miller, 1891), 2:80.

3. Up to this point, virtually all of the material in this chapter is drawn from Edward L. Pierce, statement for WHH, [1887?], *Herndon's Informants*, 688–92.

4. This reminiscence of Gov. Levi Lincoln by Gov. Henry J. Gardner was supplied by Edward L. Pierce on May 27, 1890, and is printed in *Herndon's Informants*, 698–99.

5. This account by George Harris Monroe appeared in the *Boston Sunday Herald* on April 26, 1885, and presumably was supplied by Edward L. Pierce.

1892 CHAPTER ON LINCOLN-DOUGLAS DEBATES

1. *Political Debates Between Hon. Abraham Lincoln and Hon. Stephen A. Douglas in the Celebrated Campaign of 1858, in Illinois* (Columbus, Ohio: Follett and Foster, 1860).

2. Article signed "B. B." in the St. Louis *Missouri Republican,* Aug. 16, 1858.

3. See pp. 254–55. The account of the speech containing AL's apostrophe to the Declaration of Independence in the *Chicago Press and Tribune* (Aug. 21, 1858) has a Lewistown (rather than Beardstown) dateline and is signed "G. P." The editors of Lincoln's *Collected Works,* being unable to identify "G. P.," concluded that White's claim, as stated here, "deserves to be considered." See *Collected Works* 2:544n, 546–47.

4. "Speech at Beardstown, Illinois," Aug. 12, 1858, *Collected Works* 2:538–41.

5. "Speech at Havana, Illinois," Aug. 14, 1858, *Collected Works* 2:541–42.

6. Article signed "Bayou," *New York Evening Post,* Aug. 23, 1858.

7. "Execution of the United States Laws," Speech of Hon. S. A. Douglas of Illinois, Delivered in the Senate of the United States, Feb. 23, 1855 (Washington, D.C.: Office of the *Congressional Globe,* 1855), 5.

8. Isaac Newton Arnold, *The Life of Abraham Lincoln* (Chicago: A. C. McClurg, 1884), 151.

9. The version of the speech given here is somewhat abbreviated from that appearing in White's newspaper at the time, the *Chicago Press and Tribune* (Sept. 11, 1858). "Speech at Paris, Illinois," Sept. 7, 1858, *Collected Works* 3:90–91.

10. "Speech at Edwardsville, Illinois," Sept. 11, 1858, *Collected Works* 3:91–93.

11. Ibid., 95–96.

12. Article signed "Bayou," *New York Evening Post,* Sept. 25, 1858.

13. Arnold, *Life of Abraham Lincoln,* 148.

14. Telegram to Usher F. Linder of Charleston, Illinois, Aug. 1858, *The Letters of Stephen A. Douglas,* ed. Robert W. Johannsen (Urbana: University of Illinois Press, 1961), 427.

15. Arnold, *Life of Abraham Lincoln,* 153.

16. *Speech of Senator Douglas Before the Legislature of Illinois, April 25, 1861,* [Springfield, 1861], 6.

17. "Speech at Havana, Illinois," 542–43.

Acknowledgments

This volume is the first to appear in the Lincoln Studies Center Publication Series. As indicated in the Editors' Preface, a member of the center's Board of Advisors, the late Prof. William E. Gienapp of Harvard University, first suggested the creation of a publication series dedicated to Lincoln source material under the sponsorship of the Lincoln Studies Center. For their assistance and encouragement in the development of the series, the editors wish to thank the other members of the Board of Advisors, past and present. As this volume goes to press, the members are Michael Burlingame, Jennifer Fleischner, William Lee Miller, Lucas E. Morel, Phillip S. Paludan, Gerald J. Prokopowicz, John R. Sellers, and Kenneth J. Winkle.

Our involvement with William H. Herndon and Jesse W. Weik has extended through the better part of two decades and into our retirement from full-time teaching and administration, as the Lincoln Studies Center at Knox College has become the entity within which we work. Over that time, we have become indebted to literally dozens of librarians, scholars, and researchers from all over the country. What follows can be only a partial accounting of those to whom we are obliged.

Since this edition of the Herndon-Weik biography derives directly from our work with the material contained in our previous volume, *Herndon's Informants: Letters, Interviews and Statements about Abraham Lincoln* (1998), we are pleased to acknowledge once again the courtesy and helpful assistance we received at the three repositories where the pertinent original material is located. Most of the letters and interviews gathered by William H. Herndon, as well as his many reminiscent letters to his collaborator, Jesse W. Weik, are in the Herndon-Weik Collection at the Library of Congress. Over the years, the assistance of Manuscript Division staff, particularly that of John R. Sellers, Mary Wolfskill, and Jeffrey Flanery, has been truly invaluable. We are equally indebted to the staff at the Huntington Library, which holds the Ward Hill Lamon Papers and where we were handsomely aided and assisted in our many visits by Virginia Renner, John Rhodehamel, Martin Ridge, Robert Skotheim, and Paul M. Zall. Not the least of the Huntington's assistance came in the form of research fellowships, which greatly expedited our efforts. At the Illinois State Historical Library, recently incorporated into the Abraham Lincoln Presidential Library and Museum, which holds important collections of both Herndon and Weik papers, we enjoyed the assistance of Janice Petterchak, Katherine Harris, Kim Bauer, and Cheryl Schnirring. Thomas Schwartz, State Historian of Illinois and co-ordinator of the Abraham Lincoln Symposium, assisted us in a great many ways and gave us early opportunities to speak on aspects of our research. The Massachusetts Historical Society, the Houghton Library at Harvard University, and the New York Public Library have also shared important resources, for which we remain grateful.

We are pleased to acknowledge a special debt of gratitude to Ann Grifalconi, the granddaughter of Jesse W. Weik, who generously shared digital scans of parts of the diary her grandfather kept while working on this biography. These were critical in helping to clarify his role in the composition of the book.

Two great-granddaughters of William H. Herndon, Helen Louise Herndon and Beverly Beebe, kindly furnished us with genealogical information about their ancestor. David Herbert Donald, whose pioneering research on Herndon and his biography laid the foundation for all subsequent scholarship on the subject, has been kind enough to offer advice and share important source materials. Jane Davis helped us by doing research at the New York Public Library.

At Knox College, Dean Lawrence Breitbrode has been a stalwart supporter of the Lincoln Studies Center and its projects, providing both financial and moral support that made the enterprise possible. We are fortunate to have had the benefit of the efforts of committed and enthusiastic Knox College students as research assistants; James Williams, Suellen Riley, Todd Trainor, and Joel Ward all performed important tasks of transcription, proofreading, and research. The staff at the Knox College Library, especially Jeffrey Douglas, Anne Giffey, Sharon Clayton, Laurie Sauer, Carley Robison, and Kay VanderMeulen, have given us every needed assistance. And we are happy to acknowledge the help of Anne Taylor, who gave us needed advice at a crucial time.

To Dr. Willis Regier, Director of the University of Illinois Press, we extend thanks for enthusiastic support for the Lincoln Studies Center Publication Series.

We are greatly indebted to Michael F. Bishop, Executive Director of the U.S. Abraham Lincoln Bicentennial Commission, to Harold Holzer, Hon. Richard Durbin, and Hon. Ray LaHood, the commission's co-chairs, and to the members of the commission for substantial assistance in helping to underwrite the publication of this volume.

And to our wives, Sharon E. Wilson and Norma G. Davis, for transcription and proofreading assistance and for steadfastness and forbearance throughout, we owe more than we can properly express.

Corrigenda

The following is a list of typographical and proofing errors in the original text that have been corrected in this edition.

1889 EDITION

Page No.	Correction
11	canvass of 1858] canvas of 1858
16n	autobiography] antobiography
19	creek;"] creek";
42	country'] country'"
42	'I ran] "'I ran
42	long breath.'] long breath.'"
45n	°The original] †The original
46n	†April] °April
46	table.] table
50	heard."] heard.
52	Wood] Woods
52	Wood] Woods
52n	'You see] "You see
52n	sweep.'"] sweep."
52	pounds.] pounds
62n	"I am] 'I am
62n	today."] today.'
62n	"If you] 'If you
62n	Bible."'"] Bible.'"
65	'Denton Offut'] "Denton Offut"
67	down-stream.] down-stream,
79	reading.] reading."

88	canvass] canvas
88	returned,"] returned,
88	"according] according
93	scholar as Mr. Lincoln] scholar as Mr Lincoln
103	"Friend] Friend
112	'Many Voters'] "Many Voters"
118n	R. L. Wilson] R. S. Wilson
119n	foregoing report] foregeing report
120n	"Lincoln used to] Lincoln used to
124	two or three] two or there
126	unshaded,] unshaded.
139n	"Lincoln wrote] Lincoln wrote
142	Whiteside] Whitesides
144n	'old timer'] "old timer"
148	honester woman] honester women
165	E. H. Merryman.°] E. H. Merryman.
165n	anticipated./°°°] anticipated./°°
165n	LINCOLN.] LINCOLN."
185	succeeded] suceeeded
196n	H. C. Whitney] W. C. Whitney
197n	underneath] uuderneath
199	critter."'] critter."
202	case.'"] case."
205	peeled] pealed
208	scars] scares
212	so decide."] so decide."
214n	'I acted,' he said, 'on the theory that he was "possuming"] "I acted," he said, "on the theory that he was 'possuming'
215	venturesome] ventursome
216	colleagues,°] colleagues,
216	'the court'] "the court"
220	continent.'] continent.
220	Stanton;"] Stanton";
221n	has been] has heen
223	canvass] canvas
223n	this one."] this one.
224	"Billy . . . spontaneous."] 'Billy . . . spontaneous.'
230	he cried, "enough,"] he cried, "enough,'

233	Field] Fields
237	Presidential] Presidental
240	Alleghenies] Alleghanies
242	won't] wont
243n	with it.'"] with it."
244n	strenuously] strenously
252	A. Lincoln."] A. Lincoln.'
260	"Mary] " Mary
265	"the motive] the motive
271	held.] held,
272n	Columbus, O.] Columbus, O,
272n	'Harper's Magazine.'"] "Harper's Magazine."
289	had been moved] had been mveod
290	harmony] harmory
290n	Bissell] Bissel
293	every man] évery man
297	to the rescue] to rescue
300	CHICAGO, ILL.,] CHICAGO, ILL..,
310	Lincoln republicanism incarnate] Lincoln's republicanism incarnate
324	eyeing] eying
326	We . . . longer."""] 'We . . . longer.'"
327	unbiased] unbiassed
329	"Washington] Washington
330	All charges] All changes
330	Constitution] constitution
341	obliterated.'] obliterated.
344	"'His days] "His days
345	'Montauk,'] "Montauk,"
347	American] Amercan
369	'prairie team'] "prairie team"
370	villainy] villany

1892 EDITION

Page No.	Correction
381	"Mr. Lincoln] Mr. Lincoln
382	"It is evident] It is evident

382	"Seward's speech] Seward's speech
382	'Governor Seward] "Governor Seward
382	have been doing.'] have been doing."
382	"It is curious] It is curious
384	"Ex-Governor Gardner] Ex-Governor Gardner
384	"'Gov. Levi Lincoln] "Gov. Levi Lincoln
384	"'I well remember] "I well remember
384	"I *hope*] 'I hope
384	good Whigs."] good Whigs.'
384	"'That evening] "That evening
384	"Go on! go on!"] 'Go on! go on!'
384	"'In 1861] "In 1861
384	"You and I] 'You and I
384	in 1848."] in 1848.'
384	"Sit down.] 'Sit down.
385	at table."] at table.'
385	single one.'] single one."
385	"This chapter] This chapter
385	'Massachusetts, on account] "Massachusetts, on account
386	"I am engaged] 'I am engaged
386	to-night," said he, "and] to-night,' said he, 'and
386	must leave."] must leave.'
386	"Oh, no! go on! finish it!"] 'Oh, no! go on! finish it!'
386	"I can't take any risks,"] 'I can't take any risks,'
386	"I have engaged] 'I have engaged
386	the same way."] the same way.'
386	perfect here.'"] perfect here."
392	"subject . . . States"] 'subject . . . States'
393	"conspiracy charge,"] 'conspiracy charge,'
393	"conspiracy charge."] 'conspiracy charge.'
393	"self-respect . . . falsehood."] 'self-respect . . . falsehood.'
395	"yes."] 'yes.'
397	"Long Abe's"] 'Long Abe's'
401	"We . . . equal,"] 'We . . . equal,'
402	"niggers"] 'niggers'
402	govern "niggers"] govern 'niggers'
402	hundred "niggers"] hundred 'niggers'
402	"sacred . . . government."] 'sacred . . . government.'

403   "don't . . . voted up."] 'don't . . . voted up.'
403   "voted up;"] 'voted up;'
405   "shake,"] 'shake,'
405   "agur"] 'agur'
407   "After] 'After
407   popularly known] popularly know

Index

ship with William Berry, 77–78; studying law, 78–80, 427n; as a reader, 79–80; storytelling, 80–81; shyness around women, 82, 218, 256; abstemiousness, 82, 309; as a surveyor, 83–85; postmaster at New Salem, 85; reads Paine, Volney, Voltaire, 87; religious skepticism, 87, 265–66, 428–29n; love affair with Ann Rutledge, 89–96; grief and depression at Ann Rutledge's death, 95–96, 429n, 430n; courtship of Mary Owens, 97–109; letters to Mary Owens, 102–5; letter to Mrs. Browning, 105–9; weak on financial matters, 117

LIFE IN SPRINGFIELD, ILLINOIS
—Roommate of Joshua Speed and WHH, xviii, 123; composes verse for literary society, 126, 433n; punishes wife beater, 126n; gives address before Young Men's Lyceum, 126–27; meets and courts Mary Todd, 134–35, 246; seeks to end courtship, 136; proposes to Sarah Rickard, 145n; fails to appear at wedding, 137, 434n; feared suicidal, 137; depression, 137–39; poem on suicide, 138, 435n; consults Daniel Drake, 139n; retires from practice with Stuart, 167; accompanies Speed to Kentucky, 138–39; letters to Joshua Speed, 139–43; reassured by Speed's marriage, 141, 143; delivers temperance address, 165–66; caricatures Shields in second "Lost Townships" letter, 147–52; dueling affair with Shields, 142, 154–66; acts as "friend" to Merryman, 142; marriage to Mary Todd, 144; initiates practice with Herndon, 168; secures patent for invention, 188–89, 189n, 438n; domestic life, 256–63; good husband "in his own peculiar way" only, 256; meekly accepted wife's authority, 257; indulgent treatment of his children, 257; lack of social refinement, 258; difficulties with his wife, 257–63; admits to being "evasive" with MTL, 260; censure for domestic troubles divided equally between AL and MTL, 132; wife as "unintentional means" of AL's promotion, 262–63; writes to dying father, 21; religious belief, 265–69, 267–68n, 322; not an orthodox Christian, 269; susceptibility to women, 203; aids Springfield negro imprisoned in New Orleans, 233; financial sacrifice in Senate campaign, 270; annual income, 270; trip to see stepmother, 288, 448n; recalls Ann Rutledge, 289; last visit with WHH in Springfield, 289–90, 290n; fears he will not return alive, 290; farewell address, 291, 291n;

speeches en route to Washington, 292–93; Baltimore assassination conspiracy, 293–95
THE PRESIDENCY
—Inauguration, 295–97; appoints David Davis to Supreme Court, 300–302; hounded by office seekers, 303–4; as indulgent parent, 306; domestic habits in White House, 308; unmethodical character, 309; "unconscious assumption of authority," 309; last interview with Douglas, 323n; response to Bull Run, 325, 326; death of his second son, 365; issues Emancipation Proclamation, 327–28, 313–14; public letter to James C. Conkling, 328–32; election of 1864, 333–34; on military trials, 333n; theory of a united North, 319; never wasted political favors, 319; letter to Sherman on Indiana soldier vote, 334; re-elected, 334; Second Inaugural message, 335; visit to Richmond, 337; assassination, 339–40; funeral train to Illinois, 341–43; buried at Springfield, 343; on war and leadership during wartime, 371–72
POLITICAL CAREER
—First campaign for Illinois legislature, 74–76; second campaign for Illinois legislature, 87–88; first term in Illinois legislature, 110–11; meets Stephen A. Douglas, 110–11, 246; 1836 campaign announcement, 112; responds to George Forquer, 115–16; second term in legislature, 116–20; role in internal improvements promotion, 116–18, 127; role in removing state capital to Springfield, 118; protest against proslavery resolutions, 119–20; in Springfield political debate, 127; defends Edward D. Baker, 129–30; "skinning" of Jesse B. Thomas, 49, 130, 433n; campaign of 1840, 130–31; debates Douglas, 131; loses congressional nomination to Baker, 169–70; accused of being part of the aristocracy, 170; speaks in former Indiana neighborhood, 171; candidate for Congress in 1846, 172; charged with religious infidelity, 172; urges prosecution of Mexican War, 173, 437n; elected to Congress, 172; opposes Mexican War in Congress, 175–77; letters from Washington to WHH, 177–80, 184; favors Taylor in 1848 presidential campaign, 178; speech in Congress satirizing Lewis Cass, 181–83; speeches in Massachusetts, 1848, 379–86; drafts bill to emancipate slaves in the District of Columbia, 183, 438n; seeks appointment as commissioner of the General Land Office, 189–90; considers and rejects

clothe his ideas, 354; read less and thought more, 354; analytical mind, 354; lacked judgment in certain things, 355; believed the law of human nature was motive, 356; willing to acknowledge his ignorance, 313; WHH's appraisal of AL's perceptions, intellect, and character, 352–63; clarity of statement, 321; stated adversary's case better than his opponent, 321; not effective if he did not believe in his argument, 321; contradictory appraisals of, 348–49; "physiologically and phrenologically," a monstrosity, 349n

Lincoln, Benjamin, 381

Lincoln, Edward Baker (AL's second son), 449n; death of, 365, 449n

Lincoln, Josiah (uncle of AL), 19, 20, 20n; moved to Indiana, 418n

Lincoln, Levi: entertains AL at Worcester, Massachusetts, 384

Lincoln, Mary Todd: WHH's reporting on, xvii, xxvii; mortification over WHH's Ann Rutledge lecture, xxii; description and characteristics, 132–34; meets AL, 134; courted by Douglas, 135, 140, 434n; aborted wedding ceremony, xxii, 137, 434n; marriage to AL, 144; role in writing "Lost Townships" letters, 147, 152–54; ambition for AL, 186–87; proslavery sentiments of, 257n; AL defers to, 257n; inability to control temper, 257–58, 258n; bothered by AL's lack of social refinement, 258; trouble with servants, 258–60; "unintentional means" of AL's promotion, 262–63; WHH's sympathy with MTL in her domestic troubles, 263; censure for domestic troubles attributed equally to AL and MTL, 132; last illness and death, 263n; on AL's religious belief, 269; told by AL of nomination, 278; on train to Washington, 290; letter to WHH, 305–6; WHH's interview of, 306–7; assessment of AL, 306–7; dislike for Seward, 306–7; portrait, 308; at assassination scene, 339–40

Lincoln, Mordecai (uncle of AL), 19, 20n; Indian hater, 20; moved to Illinois, 418n

Lincoln, Nancy Hanks (mother of AL), 16, 133; illegitimacy revealed by AL, xxi, 16; AL's debt to her, 16; marriage to Thomas Lincoln, 17; description and characteristics, 21–22, 31, 420n; victim of the "milk-sick," 30–31; death, 31

Lincoln, Robert Todd (AL's oldest son): and WHH's Ann Rutledge lecture, xxii; and projected Scribner's edition of WHH biography, xxxiv; treated by madstone, 264; visited by AL

in New England, 274; on train to Washington, 290; breakfast with AL on April 14, 1865, 338

Lincoln, Sarah (AL's sister), 17; confusion over given name, 17n; description and characteristics, 24; attends school with AL, 35; "quick-minded" and "intelligent," 35; praised by Elizabeth Crawford, 43; marriage and death, 24, 44–45

Lincoln, Sarah Bush (AL's stepmother), 31; portrait, 32; brief courtship and marriage to Thomas Lincoln, 32; reorganizes Lincoln household, 32–33; description and characteristics, 32; affection for AL, 33n; anxiety for AL after election, 33n, 288; encouraged AL's reading, 35n, 40, 421n; AL's concern for, 288n, 368–69; AL visits before leaving for Washington, 288

Lincoln, Thomas (AL's father), xxi, 17, 19, 51; as fatherless boy, 20; marriage to Nancy Hanks, 17, 20; religion of, 20; description and characteristics, 20–21; move to Indiana, 25–27; incensed at treatment of coon dog, 28n; coffin builder, 30–31; carpenter and cabinetmaker, 36, 36n; resistance to AL's reading, 35n; move to Illinois, 55–57; letter from AL, 364; impending death of, 366; death of, 21, 57; AL visits grave of, 288

Lincoln, Thomas (infant brother of AL), 17

Lincoln, Thomas "Tad" (AL's youngest son), 197, 352; behavior at AL's law office, 257–58; on train to Washington, 290; sleeps with father in White House, 308

Lincoln, William Wallace "Willie" (AL's son), 352; behavior at AL's law office, 257–58; requests money for candy, 283n; on train to Washington, 290; impression made on AL by death of, 305; AL's dreaming of, 376

Lincoln-Douglas Debates, 245–55, 258; Horace White's chapter on, 387–412; published volume of, 387; dispute over newspaper reporting of, 388; Chester Dewey's coverage of, 396–97, 405–6; first debate at Ottawa, 396–98; Freeport Debate, 399–400; Jonesboro Debate, 404–5; Charleston Debate, 405–7; Galesburg Debate, 407; Quincy Debate, 407–8; Alton Debate, 408

Linder, Usher F.: called upon for help by Douglas, 407

Littlefield, John H.: describes law office of AL and WHH, 197n, 197–99, 439n

Lobby, The, 110, 432n

Logan, David, 370

Logan, Stephen T., 194, 198, 138, 171, 175, 231,

WILLIAM H. HERNDON (1818–91) was Abraham Lincoln's law partner from 1844 until Lincoln became president in 1861. After Lincoln's assassination, Herndon collected an extensive archive of letters and interviews about his law partner, which, along with his own recollections, are the major sources for *Herndon's Lincoln*.

JESSE W. WEIK (1857–1930) was a native of Greencastle, Indiana, and a graduate of what is now DePauw University. In their collaboration on this biography, William H. Herndon provided almost all of the source material, and Weik composed almost all of the text.

DOUGLAS L. WILSON is a codirector of the Lincoln Studies Center at Knox College in Galesburg, Illinois. He is the author of *Lincoln before Washington: New Perspectives on the Illinois Years* and a coeditor (with Rodney O. Davis) of *Herndon's Informants*.

RODNEY O. DAVIS is a codirector of the Lincoln Studies Center at Knox College in Galesburg, Illinois. He is the editor of Thomas Ford's *History of Illinois* and a coeditor (with Douglas L. Wilson) of *Herndon's Informants*.

The Knox College Lincoln Studies Center Series

Herndon's Lincoln   *William H. Herndon and Jesse W. Weik; edited by Douglas L. Wilson and Rodney O. Davis*

The University of Illinois Press
is a founding member of the
Association of American University Presses.

Composed in 10/13.5 New Caledonia
with New Caledonia, Copperplate display
by Celia Shapland
for the University of Illinois Press
Designed by Paula Newcomb
Manufactured by Thomson-Shore, Inc.

University of Illinois Press
1325 South Oak Street
Champaign, IL 61820-6903
www.press.uillinois.edu